INTRODUCTION TO COMPUTER ENGINEERING

INTRODUCTION TO COMPUTER ENGINEERING

Logic Design and the 8086 Microprocessor

Richard E. Haskell

Oakland University
Rochester, Michigan

PRENTICE HALL   Englewood Cliffs, New Jersey 07632

Library of Congress Cataloging-in-Publication Data

Haskell, Richard E.
    Introduction to computer engineering : logic design and the 8086
microprocessor / Richard E. Haskell.
        p.   cm.
    Includes bibliographical references and index.
    ISBN 0-13-489436-7
    1. Logic design. 2. Intel 8086 (Microprocessor)   I. Title.
TK7868.L6H35 1993
621.39'16--dc20   92-30702
                                                        CIP

Editorial/production supervision: *Nancy Menges*
Cover design: *Patricia McGowan*
Manufacturing buyer: *David Dickey*
Prepress buyer: *Linda Behrens*
Acquisitions editor: *Peter Janzow*

The author and publisher of this book have used their best efforts in preparing
this book. These efforts include the development, research, and testing of the
theories and programs to determine their effectiveness. The author and
publisher make no warranty of any kind, expressed or implied, with regard to
these programs or the documentation contained in this book. The author and
publisher shall not be liable in any event for incidental or consequential
damages in connection with, or arising out of, the furnishing, performance, or
use of these programs.

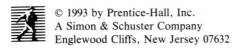
Printed in the United States of America

10 9 8 7 6 5 4 3 2 1

ISBN 0-13-489436-7

Prentice-Hall International (UK) Limited, *London*
Prentice-Hall of Australia Pty. Limited, *Sydney*
Prentice-Hall Canada Inc., *Toronto*
Prentice-Hall Hispanoamericana, S.A., *Mexico*
Prentice-Hall of India Private Limited, *New Delhi*
Prentice-Hall of Japan, Inc., *Tokyo*
Simon & Schuster Asia Pte. Ltd., *Singapore*
Editora Prentice-Hall do Brasil, Ltda., *Rio de Janeiro*

Contents

PART II DIGITAL LOGIC

Preface

A core engineering course in microprocessors and digital logic has been taught to all freshmen engineering majors at Oakland University for the past decade. The prerequisites for the course are a calculus course and an introductory programming course in Pascal. For the first several years, the first half of the course included 6502 assembly language programming on an Apple II, and during the second half of the course the students conducted a series of digital logic experiments in which the Apple II served as a logic analyzer for TTL circuits built on a protoboard.

Recently, this course has been upgraded to reflect advances in computer technology. The first change is the use of IBM PCs and/or PC compatibles as the computer in the laboratory. This has the considerable advantage of exposing students to the details of a computer that has become a de facto standard in both the office and the laboratory. The second change is to reverse the order of presentation and cover digital logic before the assembly language. The third change is the use of programmable logic devices (PLDs) in the laboratory instead of the old 7400 TTL chips. This has several advantages. First, PLDs are quickly replacing TTL chips in most new designs, and an early introduction to this technology is therefore relevant. Second, the basic concepts of PLDs are easily understood by beginning students. Although a relatively new technology, it is not an advanced subject that requires a lot of prior knowledge. It really represents another level of integration, just as TTL chips integrated many discrete transistors on a single chip. Third, the students can do more realistic experiments in the lab (for example, a 4-bit adder/subtractor rather than a 2-bit adder) because all the "wiring" of gates is done by the computer inside the chip. Finally, the students are exposed to a real example of computer-aided design early in their program. This leads to good design practice, which is beneficial in later courses.

While the use of PLDs in a freshman course taken by all engineering majors may seem unusual and even radical, it actually has a very positive effect. Just as the PLD is a real productivity enhancer from the point of view of the digital design engineer, it can be a learning productivity enhancer for the student. By being able to explore alternate designs easily and actually realize them in the lab using erasable PLDs, the student is able to grasp design concepts quickly and easily.

The goal of this book is to provide the beginning student with a broad look at both the hardware and software aspects of computer engineering, but in enough depth so that the student will gain real understanding and skills that can be used in later courses. Some introductory books take a global view of computer engineering by describing a generic computer. Our experience has been that it is better to use a real computer so that students can see how things are really done. It is much easier for students to learn bottom up by discovering things for themselves. Only when they have this experience can we help them generalize the basic concepts by putting their learning experience into a broader context. An important part of the course that uses this book is the accompanying laboratory in which students do weekly assignments in a structured laboratory environment. In a typical course the students will do six or seven lab assignments in digital logic and five or six assembly language labs. The laboratory assignments are included as an integral part of the book. Indeed, to a large extent the contents of the book are built around the laboratory experiments that the students are doing. This is the only way that the breadth of topics can be covered in a freshman course.

This book is used in a core engineering course taken by all engineering and computer science students. For most mechanical engineering students, this will probably be their last look at digital logic and microprocessors. On the other hand, electrical and computer engineering majors will follow this course with a junior course on computer hardware design and a senior course on microprocessor interfacing and design. Computer science and computer engineering students will also take a sophomore course on assembly language programming.

This book is divided into three parts. The first part, made up of the first two chapters, contains an overview of digital logic and microprocessors and a discussion of number systems. Part II consists of Chapters 3 through 8 and covers digital logic, with an emphasis on the use of PLDs as a tool for learning digital logic design. Chapters 9 through 17 make up Part III and are an introduction to microprocessors using the 8086 of the IBM PC or PC compatibles as the example. PCs containing an 80286, 80386, or 80486 can just as easily be used with this book (we use 80286 PC compatibles in our lab) since, when these computers are turned on, they come up in the real mode, which means they look like a fast 8086. When taught at Oakland University, the chapters are covered in the order presented. Some of the more advanced topics, including all of Chapter 8 and some of the later chapters, are not always covered in a single course. It is possible to cover the microprocessor material in Part III before the digital logic material in Part II.

In fact, when we used the 6502 microprocessor and the Apple II in this course, we taught it in that order. It is easier to study the somewhat more complex nature of the 8086 microprocessor if the students are exposed to the digital logic material first. This is also the order in which the material is covered in most other engineering programs.

Part III describes the use of a powerful software monitor program called TUTOR that comes with the book. This monitor enhances the understanding of the 8086 microprocessor by allowing the student to easily see what is going on inside the computer. The TUTOR monitor displays the contents of all registers and any region of memory within both the code segment and the data segment simultaneously. It allows the student to single-step through programs, set breakpoints, disassemble any program code, load and inspect any disk file, and much more. It can be used as a powerful debugging tool for .EXE files created with a macro assembler. Such .EXE files can be loaded directly into TUTOR, in which they can be inspected, debugged, and executed. The resulting debugged program can then be executed from DOS without change. This disk containing TUTOR also contains most of the examples discussed in the book. This means that the student can load these examples into TUTOR and execute them and/or single-step through the program to see exactly what the program does in detail.

Another unique feature of this book is the use of a PC signal generator and logic analyzer that runs on the PC to analyze the digital circuits designed in Part II of the book. This program, which is also included on the TUTOR disk, allows the student to set individual bits in an 8-bit output port by pressing keys 0 and 1 on the keyboard and displays, in real time, the individual bits of an input port. Pressing function key *F1* will display on the screen the truth table generated by outputing the 16 combinations of four different output lines and reading the corresponding inputs (up to five) from the student's digital circuit. The discussion of digital logic in Chapters 3 through 8 is based around a series of experiments in which the students program a single erasable PLD that can be used in all the experiments. In each experiment the PLD is exercised using the logic analyzer. The logic analyzer is used in conjunction with a standard parallel printer port. The source listing of the logic analyzer program is included on the TUTOR disk. Complete laboratory assignments are included throughout the book that can be used in the laboratory part of the course.

Many colleagues and students have influenced the development of this book. Their stimulating discussions, probing questions, and critical comments are greatly appreciated.

Richard E. Haskell
CSE Department
Oakland University
Rochester, Michigan 48309

1

Computers and Digital Logic

1.1 HISTORY OF COMPUTERS AND MICROPROCESSORS

The computer as we know it today dates only from the time of World War II. In fact, the impetus for building the ENIAC in 1944 at the Moore School of Electrical Engineering at the University of Pennsylvania was the need to compute ballistic firing tables for artillery shells. However, the history of computers goes back a long way, as can be seen from the summary in Table 1.1.

Although the abacus has been used for thousands of years as an aid to calculation, it is really that, an aid in which the person doing the calculating has to actually move the beads on the wires in the appropriate way. The idea of having a machine actually *do* the calculation originated in the early 1600s. The most famous of these machines was the Pascaline, designed by Blaise Pascal at the age of 19 to help his father, who was tax commissioner for upper Normandy, figure tax levies. Pascal built 5- to 8-digit versions of the Pascaline in which a dial, axle, and gears were associated with each digit. The calculator could add, subtract by forming the 9's complement of the subtrahend and adding, and multiply and divide by repeated addition and subtraction. The Pascaline tended to malfunction due to mechanical failures, had limited computing capability, and was a commercial failure.

Charles Babbage (1792–1871) is considered to be the father of computing. In an effort to produce a machine that could compute mathematical tables (such as logarithms), he built a working model of his *difference engine* in 1822. This model could compute 6-digit numbers in a table by a *method of differences*. Babbage made detailed plans for a full-scale difference engine that could calculate

TABLE 1.1   SOME IMPORTANT EVENTS IN THE HISTORY OF COMPUTERS

Date	Event
3000 B.C.	The abacus is developed in Babylonia. This device, which uses columns of beads on wires or rods to represent digits, is still used in some places in the Far East today to perform calculations.
1614–1617	John Napier, a Scottish mathematician, invents logarithms, which allows one to multiply by adding and to divide by subtracting. He invented rods, or numbered sticks, which allowed one to multiply or divide large numbers by moving the rods in a particular way.
1623	Wilhelm Schickard, German professor, invents the first mechanical calculator called the *calculating clock*.
1630	William Oughtred, English mathematician and clergyman, invents the slide rule.
1642–1644	Blaise Pascal, French mathematician, physicist, and religious philosopher, invents the Pascaline, the first mechanical calculator that became widely known.
1672–1674	Gottfried Wilhelm von Leibniz, German mathematician, diplomat, historian, jurist, and inventor of differential calculus, invents a mechanical calculator called the stepped reckoner. The calculator had a unique gear, the *Leibniz wheel*, that served as a mechanical multiplier. Although the calculator never worked, its design had a major influence on future mechanical calculators.
1823–1839	Charles Babbage, English mathematician and inventor, begins work on his *difference engine*, which was designed to automate the process of calculating logarithms. With much work and funding from the government, the difference engine was never finished. In 1834, Babbage starts work on a more powerful machine, called the *analytical engine*, which is recognized as the first general-purpose computer. It was about 100 years ahead of its time, required precision mechanical gears that could not be accurately produced at the time, and never worked. Babbage is considered to be the father of computing.
1854	George Boole, English logician and mathematician, publishes *Investigation of the Laws of Thought*, which gave a mathematical basis for logic.
1890	Herman Hollerith, American inventor, uses his punched cards for tabulating the 1890 census. He founded the Tabulating Machine Company in 1896, which eventually became IBM in 1924.
1906	Lee De Forest, American physicist, invents the triode, a three-electrode vacuum tube. These tubes would not be used in computers until the 1940s.
1936	Alan M. Turing, English logician, publishes a paper, *On Computable Numbers*, which demonstrates that arbitrary computations can be made with a finite state machine (an automaton). Turing plays a significant role in the development of the early computers in England after World War II.
1937	George Stibitz, a physicist at Bell Telephone Laboratories, builds binary circuits using relays that can add, subtract, multiply, and divide.
1938	Konrad Zuse, German engineer, constructs the Z1, the first binary calculating machine. In 1941, he completed the Z3, a general-purpose electromechanical calculating machine.
1938	Claude Shannon, based on his master's thesis at MIT, publishes *A Symbolic Analysis of Relay and Switching Circuits* in which he showed how symbolic logic and binary mathematics could be applied to relay circuits.
1942	John V. Atanasoff, Iowa State University professor, completes a simple electronic computing machine.
1943	The IBM–Harvard Mark I, a large electromechanical calculator, is operational.

TABLE 1.1   SOME IMPORTANT EVENTS IN THE HISTORY OF COMPUTERS

Date	Event
1944–1945	J. Presper Eckert and John W. Mauchly design and build the ENIAC at the Moore School of Electrical Engineering at the University of Pennsylvania. This was the first fully functional electronic calculator.
1946	John von Neumann, who had been a consultant on the ENIAC project and had written an influential report on the follow-on EDVAC project, begins his own computer project at the Institute for Advanced Study at Princeton.
1947	Walter Brattain, John Bardeen, and William Schockley invent the transistor at Bell Laboratories.
1948	The first stored program is run on the Manchester Mark I electronic computer in England.
1951	The first commercially manufactured computers, the Ferranti Mark I and the UNIVAC, are delivered.
1953	IBM's first electronic computer, the 701, is delivered.
1958	Jack Kilby, an engineer at Texas Instruments, builds a phase-shift oscillator as the first integrated circuit (IC).
1959	Robert Noyce, co-founder of Fairchild Semiconductor in 1958, produces the first planar process integrated circuit. This would lead to the practical mass production of reliable integrated circuits. In 1968, Noyce will establish Intel.
1963	The first minicomputer is introduced by the Digital Equipment Corporation (DEC).
1964	IBM introduces the System/360 family of mainframe computers.
1969	IBM researchers develop the first on-chip programmable logic array (PLA).
1971	Marcian E. Hoff, Jr., an engineer at Intel, invents the first microprocessor.
1975	Intersil introduces the first field programmable logic array (FPLA).
1977	Stephen Wozniak and Steven Jobs introduce the Apple II personal computer.
1978	Monolithic Memories introduces the programmable array logic (PAL) device.
1981	The IBM PC is introduced.
1983	Lattice Semiconductor is founded and produces a family of electrically erasable programmable logic devices (PLDs) called *generic array logic* (GAL) devices.

numbers to 20 places and produce a metal plate for printing the tables. The machine was to be run with steam and would be 10 feet high, 10 feet wide, and 5 feet deep. With funds from the British government, Babbage and his chief mechanical engineer, Joseph Clement, worked for the next dozen years in an attempt to build the difference engine. There were many technical and personal problems (current machine tools could not meet the precision required by Babbage, and Babbage's wife died and he had serious disagreements with Clement) that kept the difference engine from being completed. In 1834, Babbage conceived of a more powerful *analytical engine* that could solve any mathematical problem, not just those based on the method of differences. This new engine would make his difference engine obsolete, so he turned his attention to the analytical engine. The government eventually got fed up and cancelled the project in 1842. Babbage continued to work on the design of his analytical engine for the rest of his life, even though he knew that it could not be built at that time. He produced thousands of pages of notes on the analytical engine, which would contain hundreds of axles and thousands of gears and wheels of all kinds. It had many of the components of present-day computers, including a store (memory) and a mill (CPU). Punched cards were used for external programming of the machine.

The use of punched cards for programming was inspired by the automatic loom, invented by Joseph-Marie Jacquard in 1801, which was controlled by punched cards. In 1880, Herman Hollerith was working as a special agent for the U.S. Census. The data from the 1880 census would take years to tabulate. In the meantime, Hollerith, who became an instructor in mechanical engineering at MIT in 1882, invented an electromechanical system that could count and sort punched cards containing statistical data. Hollerith's tabulating machine was used to tabulate the 1890 census data in six weeks. In 1896, Hollerith formed the Tabulating Machine Company, which was later to become IBM.

The next major thrust in the development of computers came during World War II with the development of the ENIAC (Electronic Numerical Integrator and Calculator) at the Moore School of Electrical Engineering at the University of Pennsylvania. J. Presper Eckert and John W. Mauchly were the chief designers of this large electronic calculator. In 1944, under a contract from the Ordnance Department, they began work on a follow-on computer, EDVAC (Electronic Discrete Variable Computer), that was to be the first stored program computer. However, disagreements over patent rights caused Eckert and Mauchly to resign from the Moore School in 1946 and to start their own company, the Electronic Control Company, with the goal of producing a Universal Automatic Computer, the UNIVAC. Financial problems caused them to reorganize as the Eckert–Mauchly Computer Corporation in 1948 and to finally sell out to Remington Rand in 1950. The first UNIVAC was delivered to the Census in 1951.

IBM quickly got into the act and delivered their first electronic computer in 1953 and, as they say, the rest is history! Six years earlier the invention of the transistor at Bell Laboratories was to have a major impact on the development of computers. The idea that electrons inside a *semiconductor* could control electric currents and voltages the way that large, power-hungry vacuum tubes did was to transform the electronics industry in a fundamental and far-reaching way. The advances in solid-state technology led to the development of the integrated circuit in the 1960s and the microprocessor and programmable logic devices in the 1970s and 1980s.

Lattice Semiconductor, the last entry in Table 1.1, is not the first company to produce PLDs, nor is it the largest. Rather, it is representative of the hundreds of small companies that have been created as a result of the major technological advances associated with the development of computers. It also produces the GAL 16V8, which is the programmable logic device that we will describe in detail and use in the experiments in this book.

A major revolution in the computer industry has taken place in the past 20 years, starting with the invention of the microprocessor at Intel. A few of the major milestones during this period are shown in Table 1.2.

The making of the first microprocessor was made possible by the remarkable development of integrated circuits during the 1960s. This technology allowed hundreds and then thousands of transistors to be etched onto a single piece of silicon. This led to the design of integrated circuits in which more and more logic elements were incorporated into a single chip. In 1969, Intel undertook a contract to develop a set of integrated circuits that could be used to make a programmable electronic calculator. Instead of developing yet another special-purpose integrated

TABLE 1.2   HISTORY OF MICROPROCESSORS

Date	Microprocessor	Comment
1971	Intel 4004	First microprocessor (4 bits)
1972	Intel 8008	First 8-bit microprocessor
1974	Intel 8080	
1975	Motorola 6800	5 Volts only (1 MHz)
1976	MOS Technology 6502	Used in Apple II, PET, Atari
1977	Motorola 6802	128-Byte internal RAM
1978	Motorola 6801	Single-chip microcomputer
1978	Intel 8086/8088	40,000 Transistors (16-bit data)
1979	Motorola 68000	68,000 Transistors
1979	Motorola 68701	MCU–EPROM–I/O
1979	Motorola 6805	Low-cost microcontroller
1979	Motorola 6809	Used in TRS-80 color computer
1981	**IBM PC,** uses Intel 8088	
1982	Motorola 68010	
1982	Motorola 68008	
1984	Intel 80286	10 MHz, 130,000 transistors
1984	Motorola 68020	32-Bit address and data busses
1985	Motorola 68020 (20 MHz)	
1986	Motorola 68020 (25 MHz)	
1986	Intel 80386	16 MHz, 275,000 transistors
1987	Motorola 68030	
1988	Motorola 68030 (33 MHz)	
1989	Intel 80486	25 MHz, 1,000,000 transistors
1990	Intel 80486	50 MHz
1992	Intel 80586	4,000,000 Transistors
1995	Intel 80686	22,000,000 Transistors
2000	Intel 80786	100,000,000 Transistors (250 MHz)

circuit with only a limited function, Intel chose to produce a more general purpose device, the 4004 microprocessor, that could be programmed to perform many different functions. This first microprocessor had only four data lines over which both address information and data had to be sent to memory devices. Intel put this chip on the market in 1971 as part of a four-chip set that formed a micro-programmable computer. The 4004 had many limitations, and the following year Intel introduced the 8008 and 2 years later the 8080, which became widely used in numerous different applications.

The Intel 8080 was an 8-bit microprocessor, which means that it had eight data lines going to memory. It also had 16 address lines, which meant that it could address a total of $2^{16} = 65,536$ different memory locations. The Motorola 6800, 6802, 6801, 68701, 6805, and 6809, as well as the MOS Technology 6502, all have this basic 8-bit structure, as shown in Figure 1.1.

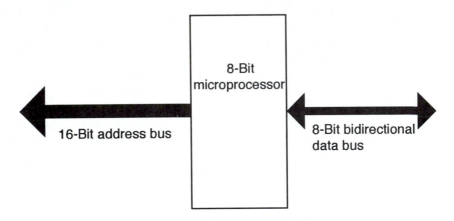

Figure 1.1 An 8-bit microprocessor has an 8-bit data bus and a 16-bit address bus.

In Figure 1.1, eight separate lines form the 8-bit bidirectional *data bus*. All data move between the microprocessor chip and the memory chips over this data bus in groups of 8 bits called *bytes*. A high voltage (5 volts) is considered to be a binary digit (bit) 1, and a low voltage (0 volts) is considered to be a binary digit 0. Thus, at some instant of time, the data bus might contain the 8 bits, or byte, 01101010. The rightmost bit is bit 0, the least significant bit (LSB), and the leftmost bit is bit 7, the most significant bit (MSB) (see Fig. 1.2). In Chapter 2 we will see how this 8-bit byte can represent a binary number in a base 2 number system.

Intel introduced the 8086/8088 microprocessors in 1978. The 8088 still had an 8-bit data bus, while the 8086 provided a 16-bit data bus so that 2 bytes of data could be moved to and from memory at the same time. The 8086/8088 also increased the number of address lines to 20. This means that these microprocessors can address $2^{20} = 1,048,576$ possible memory locations. This number is equal to

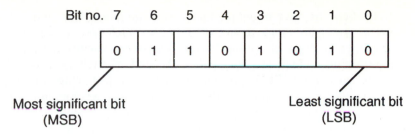

Figure 1.2   A byte (8 bits) of data on the data bus.

1,024K where 1K = 1,024. It is also called 1 Mbyte (megabyte) of memory. We will study the 8086 microprocessor in some detail in Part III of this book.

In 1979, Motorola introduced its first 16-bit microprocessor, the 68000. This is the microprocessor that Apple chose to use in its Macintosh computers. The 68000 has a 16-bit data bus and a 24-bit address bus. This means that a 68000 can address a total of 2^{24} = 16 Mbytes of memory. The Motorola 68020, introduced in 1984, increased the size of both the data bus and the address bus to 32 bits. This means that 4 bytes at a time can be moved to and from memory, and the microprocessor can, in principle, address directly 2^{32} = 4 Gbytes (gigabytes) of memory, where a Gbyte is equal to 1,024 Mbytes.

Intel's 80386, introduced in 1986, also provides complete 32-bit operation. However, the register structure of the 8086 does not lend itself to an easy extension to 32-bit addresses. This is not the case with the Motorola 68000 family of microprocessors in which all registers are 32 bits wide. This made their migration from 8- to 32-bit processors an easier transition than in the Intel family of microprocessors.

As you can see from Table 1.2, both the speed at which the microprocessor can run and the number of transistors that can be packed into the chip have increased dramatically in recent years. The predictions, shown at the bottom of the table, indicate that this trend will continue over the next few years. The revolution isn't over yet!

1.2 DIGITAL LOGIC

Digital logic is the basis of all digital computers. We deal with logical variables that have only two values: 0 or 1, *true* or *false*, HI or LO. In Chapter 3 we will see that there are three fundamental operators for these logical variables: AND, OR, and NOT. What is remarkable is that *any* computer of *any* complexity can be made from elements that perform only these three basic operations. Much of what we do in this book is to see how we can build more and more complex digital circuits from these three fundamental operations.

There are several unique features of this book. The first is that we will use the programmable logic device (PLD) as a vehicle for learning about digital logic. In particular, we will use the GAL 16V8, an electrically erasable PLD, in all the experiments, which are included at the end of each chapter. This has several advantages. First, PLDs are quickly replacing TTL chips in most new designs, and an early introduction to this technology is therefore relevant. Second, the basic concepts of PLDs are easily understood. Although a relatively new technology, it is not an advanced subject that requires a lot of prior knowledge. It really represents another level of integration, just as TTL chips integrated many discrete transistors on a single chip. Third, you can do more realistic experiments in the lab (for example, a 4-bit adder/subtractor rather than a 2-bit adder) because all the "wiring" of gates is done by the computer inside the chip. Finally, you will be exposed to a real example of computer-aided design. This should lead to good design practice, which will be beneficial in later courses. Being able to explore alternate designs easily and actually realize them in the lab using erasable PLDs should give you a better understanding of the basic design concepts.

Another unique feature of this book is the use of a PLD signal generator and logic analyzer that runs on the PC to analyze the digital circuits designed in the book. This program, which is included on the disk with the book, allows you to set individual bits in an 8-bit output port by pressing keys 0 and 1 on the keyboard and displays, in real time, the individual bits of an input port. Pressing function key *F1* will display on the screen the truth table generated by outputting the 16 combinations of four different output lines and reading the corresponding inputs (up to five) from your digital circuit. The discussion of digital logic in Chapters 3 through 8 is based around a series of experiments in which you will program a single erasable PLD, the GAL 16V8, that can be used in all the experiments. In each experiment the PLD is exercised using the logic analyzer.

We will begin our discussion of digital logic by studying number systems in Chapter 2. Our main interest is going to be with the binary (base 2) number system. We will see that hexadecimal (base 16) and octal (base 8) are useful shorthand notations for representing binary numbers. In Chapter 3 we will look at basic logic gates and, in the process, discover the basic structure of a programmable logic device (PLD). In Chapter 4 we will learn how to program the GAL 16V8 using the CUPL design language. We will show how to program all the basic gates into this single chip. In Chapter 5 you will learn the basic theorems of Boolean algebra and learn to reduce Boolean functions using Karnaugh maps. You will also see how computers use tabular methods to reduce logical expressions. Chapter 6 covers the design of combinational logic circuits, including examples of comparators, adders and subtractors, decoders and encoders, multiplexers and demultiplexers, and code converters. The design of sequential circuits is covered in Chapter 7. You will learn how to use the GAL 16V8 to design various counters and shift registers. How data are stored in computer memories is discussed in Chapter 8.

1.3 MICROPROCESSORS

In Part III we will study microprocessors by taking a close look at the microprocessor used in IBM PCs and PC compatibles. These computers have become an industry standard for a small, desktop computer used in the office and the lab. The first IBM PC introduced in 1981 used the Intel 8088 microprocessor. Newer versions of the PC introduced since that time have used newer Intel microprocessors, including the 8086, the 80286, the 80386, and the 80486. The assembly language for the 8086 is identical to that of the 8088. The main difference between these two chips is the fact that the 8088 uses only 8 data lines to address memory, while the 8086 uses 16 data lines. While the newer 80x86 microprocessors have introduced some new instructions, they are upward compatible with the 8086. The assembly language studied in Part III of this book forms the basis for programming with any of these chips. PCs based on the 80386 are popular today. When they are turned on, they come up in the *real* mode, which means that they look like a fast 8086. These 80x86 microprocessors can also be programmed in the *protected* mode. Programs written in the protected mode cannot be run on the older 8086. All the programs written in this book will run on PCs that contain any of these microprocessors running in the real mode. Throughout this book we will refer to 8086 assembly language programming with the understanding that these programs will also run on an 8088 machine and on an 80x86 machine running in the real mode.

What is the 8086 microprocessor and how does it work? That is the question we seek to answer in Part III of this book. This book is unique in that it uses a special monitor program called TUTOR that runs on any IBM PC or PC compatible to help you learn about microprocessors. The TUTOR monitor shows you what is going on inside the computer at any instant. It has been specially designed to be easy to use and to make it easier for you to learn about microprocessors.

When writing assembly language programs, you will need to use an assembler that automatically converts instruction mnemonics to machine language code. We describe the operation of the IBM PC Macro Assembler (MASM) and related macro assemblers in Chapter 11. However, you will gain considerable insight into the operation of microprocessors if you initially use the TUTOR monitor to load some short programs we have already written in Chapters 9 and 10. The TUTOR monitor will make it easy for you to enter these programs into the computer, run them, and watch them execute by single stepping through each instruction. The TUTOR monitor can also be used as a powerful debugging aid for programs that you later write using an assembler.

A summary of the TUTOR monitor and a description of how to run it are given in Appendix B. It will be a helpful guide to you until you become familiar with its use. Most of the commands will be introduced in the book, with examples, as the need arises. You will find the TUTOR monitor very easy to use. We will start using the TUTOR monitor in Chapter 9.

Later chapters in this book cover various parts of a PC computer system from both a hardware and software point of view. The video screen is covered in Chapter 13. Hardware interrupts, sound, and the printer interface are discussed in Chapter 14. A collection of DOS subroutines for reading and writing data to a disk is developed in Chapter 15. A detailed discussion of graphics in Chapter 16, including the development of Hercules graphics routines, will give you a good idea of how graphics on a PC works. Finally, in Chapter 17 we develop a complete interrupt-driven terminal program that will allow you to communicate over a serial line to other computers.

Assembly Language Programming

With all the high-level languages around, why should you be interested in learning assembly language? There are several reasons. First, assembly language programs are fast. It is not uncommon for an assembly language program to execute orders of magnitude faster than a corresponding program written in BASIC. This can be important if you want to fill the screen instantaneously with information or if you need to control some time-critical process.

Second, assembly language programming lets you access the lowest levels of the computer hardware. This is essential when interfacing the computer to external devices or when trying to get the most performance from the computer hardware. Third, most applications of microprocessors are in dedicated systems in which a single program is always executed. This program is normally stored as machine code in a read-only memory (ROM) or in a programmable read-only memory (PROM). Most such programs are written in assembly language.

Finally, learning assembly language will give you a much better understanding of how a computer works. There has traditionally been considerable mystery surrounding computers. Such mystery has inevitably led to suspicion and fear. Large computer facilities have not contributed to a better understanding of what computers are and how they work. Small personal computers, such as the PC, have made it possible for you to become the master of your own computer. This book will open up the PC and show you what makes it tick. You will be able to make it do anything you want. This feeling of control, power, and understanding is something you must experience to fully appreciate. Therefore, let's begin.

2

Number Systems

Data inside a computer are represented by *binary digits* or *bits*. The logical values of these binary digits are denoted by 0 and 1, while the corresponding physical values can be any two-state property such as a high (5 volts) or low (0 volts) voltage or two different directions of magnetization. It is therefore convenient to represent numbers inside the computer in a binary number system. Hexadecimal and octal numbers are often used as a shorthand for representing binary numbers.

In this chapter you will learn:

- How to count in binary and hexadecimal
- How integers and fractional numbers are represented in any base
- How to convert numbers from one base to another
- How negative numbers are represented in the computer

By the end of this chapter you should be able to

- Convert any binary, hexadecimal, or octal number to the corresponding decimal number
- Convert any decimal number to the corresponding binary, hexadecimal, or octal number
- Take the two's complement of any binary or hexadecimal integer.

2.1 COUNTING IN BINARY AND HEXADECIMAL

Consider a box containing one marble. If the marble is in the box, we will say that the box is *full* and associate the digit 1 with the box. If we take the marble out of the box, the box will be *empty*, and we will then associate the digit 0 with the box. The two binary digits 0 and 1 are called *bits*, and with 1 bit we can count from zero (box empty) to one (box full), as shown in Fig. 2.1.

0 = empty box   1 = full box   **Figure 2.1** You can count from 0 to 1
no. of marbles = 0   no. of marbles = 1   with 1 bit.

Consider now a second box that can also be full (1) or empty (0). However, when this box is full, it will contain *two* marbles as shown in Fig. 2.2. With these two boxes (2 bits) we can count from zero to three, as shown in Fig. 2.3. Note that the value of each 2-bit binary number shown in Fig. 2.3 is equal to the total number of marbles in the two boxes.

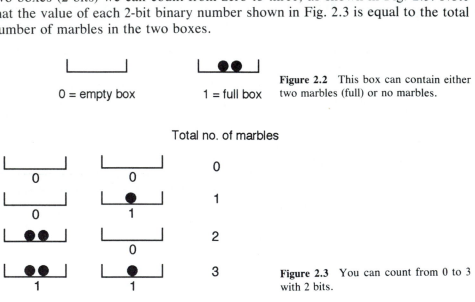

0 = empty box   1 = full box

Figure 2.2 This box can contain either two marbles (full) or no marbles.

Total no. of marbles

Figure 2.3 You can count from 0 to 3 with 2 bits.

We can add a third bit to the binary number by adding a third box that is full (bit = 1) when it contains four marbles and is empty (bit = 0) when it contains no marbles. It must be either full (bit = 1) or empty (bit = 0). With this third box (3 bits), we can count from 0 to 7, as shown in Fig. 2.4.

If you want to count beyond 7, you must add another box. How many marbles should this fourth box contain when it is full (bit = 1)? It should be clear that this box must contain eight marbles. The binary number 8 would then be written as 1000. Remember that a 1 in a binary number means that the corresponding box is full of marbles, and the number of marbles that constitutes a full

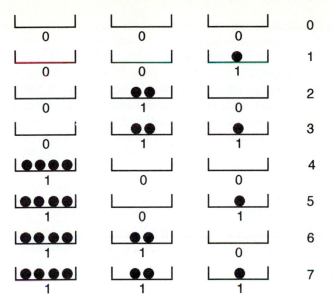

Figure 2.4 columns and values:

0	0	0	0
0	0	1	1
0	1	0	2
0	1	1	3
1	0	0	4
1	0	1	5
1	1	0	6
1	1	1	7

Figure 2.4 You can count from 0 to 7 with 3 bits.

box varies as 1, 2, 4, 8, starting at the right. This means that with 4 bits we can count from 0 to 15, as shown in Fig. 2.5.

It is convenient to represent the total number of marbles in the four boxes, represented by the 4-bit binary numbers shown in Fig. 2.5, by a single digit. We call this a *hexadecimal* digit, and the 16 hexadecimal digits are shown in the right

No. of marbles in each full box (bit = 1)				Total no. of marbles	Hex digit
8	4	2	1		
0	0	0	0	0	0
0	0	0	1	1	1
0	0	1	0	2	2
0	0	1	1	3	3
0	1	0	0	4	4
0	1	0	1	5	5
0	1	1	0	6	6
0	1	1	1	7	7
1	0	0	0	8	8
1	0	0	1	9	9
1	0	1	0	10	A
1	0	1	1	11	B
1	1	0	0	12	C
1	1	0	1	13	D
1	1	1	0	14	E
1	1	1	1	15	F

Figure 2.5 You can count from 0 to 15 with 4 bits.

column in Fig. 2.5. The hexadecimal digits 0 to 9 are the same as the decimal digits 0 to 9. However, the decimal numbers 10 to 15 are represented by the hexadecimal digits A to F. Thus, for example, the hexadecimal digit D is equivalent to the decimal number 13.

To count beyond 15 in binary, you must add more boxes. Each full box you add must contain twice as many marbles as the previous full box. With 8 bits you can count from 0 to 255. A few examples are shown in Fig. 2.6. The decimal number that corresponds to a given binary number is equal to the total number of marbles in all the boxes. To find this number, just add up all the marbles in the full boxes (the ones with binary digits equal to 1).

No. of marbles in each full box (bit = 1)								Total no. of marbles
128	64	32	16	8	4	2	1	
0	0	1	1	0	1	0	0	52
1	0	1	0	0	0	1	1	163
1	1	1	1	1	1	1	1	255

Figure 2.6   You can count from 0 to 255 with 8 bits.

As the length of a binary number increases, it becomes more cumbersome to work with. We then use the corresponding *hexadecimal number* as a shorthand method of representing the binary number. This is very easy to do. You just divide the binary number into groups of 4 bits starting at the right and then represent each 4-bit group by its corresponding hexadecimal digit given in Fig. 2.5. For example, the binary number

is equivalent to the hexadecimal number 9AH. We will often use the letter H following a number to indicate a hexadecimal number. You should verify that the total number of marbles represented by this binary number is 154. However, instead of counting the marbles in the *binary boxes*, you can count the marbles in *hexadecimal boxes*, where the first box contains A × 1 = 10 marbles and the second box contains 9 × 16 = 144 marbles. Therefore, the total number of marbles is equal to 144 + 10 = 154.

A third hexadecimal box would contain a multiple of $16^2 = 256$ marbles, and a fourth hexadecimal number would contain a multiple of $16^3 = 4,096$ marbles. As an example, the 16-bit binary number

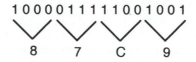

TABLE 2.1 HEXADECIMAL AND DECIMAL CONVERSION

15		Byte		8	7		Byte		0
15	Char	12	11	Char	8	7	Char	4	3	Char	0
Hex	Dec	Hex	Dec	Hex	Dec	Hex	Dec
0	0	0	0	0	0	0	0
1	4,096	1	256	1	16	1	1
2	8,192	2	512	2	32	2	2
3	12,288	3	768	3	48	3	3
4	16,384	4	1,024	4	64	4	4
5	20,480	5	1,280	5	80	5	5
6	24,576	6	1,536	6	96	6	6
7	28,672	7	1,792	7	112	7	7
8	32,768	8	2,048	8	128	8	8
9	36,864	9	2,304	9	144	9	9
A	40,960	A	2,560	A	160	A	10
B	45,056	B	2,816	B	176	B	11
C	49,152	C	3,072	C	192	C	12
D	53,248	D	3,328	D	208	D	13
E	57,344	E	3,584	E	224	E	14
F	61,440	F	3,840	F	240	F	15

is equivalent to the decimal number 34,761 (that is, it represents 34,761 marbles). This can be seen by expanding the hexadecimal number as follows:

$$
\begin{aligned}
8 \times 16^3 &= 8 \times 4{,}096 = 32{,}768 \\
7 \times 16^2 &= 7 \times 256 = 1{,}792 \\
C \times 16^1 &= 12 \times 16 = 192 \\
9 \times 16^0 &= 9 \times 1 = \underline{\quad 9} \\
&\qquad\qquad\qquad\quad 34{,}761
\end{aligned}
$$

You can see that by working with hexadecimal numbers you can reduce by a factor of 4 the number of digits that you have to work with.

Table 2.1 will allow you to conveniently convert hexadecimal numbers of up to four digits to their decimal equivalent. Note, for example, how the four terms in the conversion of 87C9H can be read directly from the table.

2.2 POSITIONAL NOTATION

Binary numbers are numbers to the base 2 and hexadecimal numbers are numbers to the base 16. An integer number N can be written in any base b using the following positional notation:

$$N = P_4P_3P_2P_1P_0 = P_4b^4 + P_3b^3 + P_2b^2 + P_1b^1 + P_0b^0$$

where the number always starts with the least significant digit on the right.

For example, the decimal number 584 is a base 10 number and can be expressed as

$$584_{10} = (5 \times 10^2) + (8 \times 10^1) + (4 \times 10^0)$$

$$= 500 + 80 + 4$$

$$= 584_{10}$$

A number to the base b must have b different digits. Thus, decimal numbers (base 10) use the 10 digits 0 to 9.

A binary number is a base 2 number and therefore uses only the two digits 0 and 1. For example, the binary number 110100 is the base 2 number

$$110100_2 = (1 \times 2^5) + (1 \times 2^4) + (0 \times 2^3) + (1 \times 2^2) + (0 \times 2^1) + (0 \times 2^0)$$

$$= 32 + 16 + 0 + 4 + 0 + 0$$

$$= 52_{10}$$

This is the same as the first example in Fig. 2.6, where the total number of marbles is 52 (32 + 16 + 4).

A hexadecimal number is a base 16 number and therefore needs 16 different digits to represent the number. We use the ten digits 0 to 9 plus the six letters A to F as shown in Fig. 2.5. For example, the hexadecimal number 3AF can be written as the base 16 number

$$3AF_{16} = (3 \times 16^2) + (A \times 16^1) + (F \times 16^0)$$

$$= (3 \times 256) + (10 \times 16) + (15 \times 1)$$

$$= 768 + 160 + 15$$

$$= 943_{10}$$

Microcomputers move data around in groups of 8-bit binary bytes. Therefore, it is natural to describe the data in the computer as binary, or base 2, numbers. As we have seen, this is simplified by using hexadecimal numbers where each hex digit represents 4 binary digits. Some larger computers represent binary numbers in groups of 3 bits rather than 4. The resulting number is an *octal*, or base 8, number. Octal numbers use only the 8 digits 0 to 7. For example, the octal number 457 can be written as the base 8 number

$$457_8 = (4 \times 8^2) + (5 \times 8^1) + (7 \times 8^0)$$

$$= 256 + 40 + 7$$

$$= 303_{10}$$

Fractional Numbers

The positional notation given above for integer numbers can be generalized for numbers involving fractions as follows:

$$N = \dots P_2P_1P_0.P_{-1}P_{-2}P_{-3} \dots = \dots + P_2b^2 + P_1b^1 + P_0b^0$$
$$+ P_{-1}b^{-1} + P_{-2}b^{-2} + P_{-3}b^{-3} + \cdots$$

As an example, consider the base 10 number 375.17. Using the above definition, this is equal to

$$N = (3 \times 10^2) + (7 \times 10^1) + (5 \times 10^0) + (1 \times 10^{-1}) + (7 \times 10^{-2})$$
$$= 300 + 70 + 5 + 0.1 + 0.07$$
$$= 375.17$$

In this case the *radix*, or base, is 10 and the *radix point* (decimal point) separates the integer part of the number from the fractional part.

Consider now the binary number 1101.11. This is equivalent to what decimal number? Using the above definition, we can write

$$1101.11_2 = (1 \times 2^3) + (1 \times 2^2) + (0 \times 2^1) + (1 \times 2^0)$$
$$+ (1 \times 2^{-1}) + (1 \times 2^{-2})$$
$$= 8 + 4 + 0 + 1 + \frac{1}{2} + \frac{1}{4}$$
$$= 13.75_{10}$$

Following the same technique, we can write the hexadecimal number 1AB.6 as

$$1AB.6_{16} = (1 \times 16^2) + (10 + 16^1) + (11 \times 16^0) + (6 \times 16^{-1})$$
$$= 256 + 160 + 11 + \frac{6}{16}$$
$$= 427.375_{10}$$

As a final example, consider the octal number 173.25. We can find the equivalent decimal number by expanding the octal number as follows:

$$173.25_8 = (1 \times 8^2) + (7 \times 8^1) + (3 \times 8^0) + (2 \times 8^{-1}) + (5 \times 8^{-2})$$
$$= 64 + 56 + 3 + \frac{2}{8} + \frac{5}{64}$$
$$= 123.328125_{10}$$

The examples in this section show how you can convert a number in any base to a decimal number. In the following section we will look at how to convert a decimal number to any other base and how to convert among binary, hexadecimal, and octal.

2.3 NUMBER SYSTEM CONVERSIONS

In the previous section you saw how you can convert a number in any base to its decimal equivalent by expanding the number using the definition of the positional notation of the number. For a hexadecimal number containing a maximum of four hex digits, it is easy to use Table 2.1 to find the conversion by simply adding the corresponding decimal values from each of the four columns. Note that the entries in the four columns of Table 2.1 are simply the hex digits multiplied by 16^3, 16^2, 16^1, and 16^0, respectively.

   If you don't have Table 2.1 (or a calculator that converts hex numbers to decimal), you can use the following shortcut to convert a hex integer to decimal. To convert the hexadecimal number $A7_{16}$ to decimal, multiply $A \times 16$ and add 7. For longer hexadecimal numbers, start with the leftmost digit (the most significant), multiply it by 16, and add the next hex digit. Multiply this result by 16 and add the next hex digit. Continue this process until you have added the rightmost digit. For example, to convert $87C9_{16}$ to decimal, you can do this:

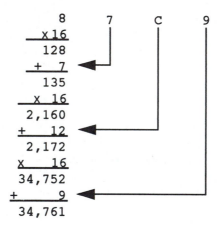

Therefore, $87C9_{16} = 34{,}761_{10}$. This technique will work for any base. You just multiply by the current base, rather than 16, in each step of the process.

Binary ↔ Hex

Converting a binary number to hex is trivial. You simply partition the binary number in groups of 4 bits, starting at the radix point, and read the hex digits by inspection using the hex digit definitions in Fig. 2.5. For example, the binary number 11010101000.1111010111 can be partitioned as follows:

0110	1010	1000	.	1111	0101	1100
6	A	8	.	F	5	C

Therefore, $11010101000.1111010111_2 = 6A8.F5C_{16}$. Note that leading zeros can be added to the integer part of the binary number, and trailing zeros can be added to the fractional part to produce a 4-bit hex digit.

Going from hex to binary is just as easy. You just write down the 4 binary digits corresponding to each hex digit by inspection (using the table in Fig. 2.5).

Binary ↔ Octal

Converting a binary number to octal is just as easy as converting it to hex. In this case you just partition the binary number in groups of 3 bits rather than 4 and read the octal digits (0 to 7) by inspection. Again the grouping is done starting at the radix point. Using as an example, the same binary number 11010101000.1111010111 that we just converted to hex we would convert it to octal as follows:

011	010	101	000	.	111	101	011	100
3	2	5	0	.	7	5	3	4

Therefore, $11010101000.1111010111_2 = 3250.7534_8$. Note again that leading zeros must be added to the integer part of the binary number, and trailing zeros must be added to the fractional part to produce 3-bit octal digits.

You reverse the process to go from octal to binary. Just write down the 3 binary digits corresponding to each octal digit by inspection.

Hex ↔ Octal

When converting from hex to octal or from octal to hex, it is easiest to go through binary. Thus, for example, to convert $6A8.F5C_{16}$ to octal, you would first convert it to the binary number 11010101000.1111010111_2 by inspection, as shown in the example above. Then you would convert this binary number to 3250.7534_8, as we just did in the previous example.

Decimal to Hex

Suppose you want to convert a decimal integer 167 to its hexadecimal equivalent. The easiest way to figure this out is to look at Table 2.1. The closest decimal value in this table that does not exceed 167 is 160 in the second column from the right. This corresponds to the hexadecimal digit A as the second digit from the right ($A \times 16^1 = 10 \times 16 = 160$). To find the hexadecimal digit to use in the rightmost position, subtract 160 from 167. Thus the decimal number 167_{10} is equivalent to the hexadecimal number $A7_{16}$. What binary number is this?

How can you convert a decimal integer to hexadecimal if you don't have Table 2.1 around? Here's a shortcut. Divide the decimal number by 16 and keep track of the remainder. Keep dividing the results by 16 and writing down the remainders at each step until the result is zero. The equivalent hexadecimal number is all the remainders read backward. For example, this is how to convert the decimal number 167_{10} to hexadecimal:

$$167/16 = 10 \quad \text{with remainder} \quad 7$$
$$10/16 = 0 \quad \text{with remainder} \quad 10 = A$$

read backward

$$\therefore \quad 167_{10} = A7_{16}$$

Here's the example we gave at the beginning of this section.

$$34{,}761_{10} = ?_{16}$$

$$34{,}761/16 = 2{,}172 \quad \text{with remainder} \quad 9$$
$$2{,}172/16 = 135 \quad \text{with remainder} \quad 12 = C$$
$$135/16 = 8 \quad \text{with remainder} \quad 7$$
$$8/16 = 0 \quad \text{with remainder} \quad 8$$

read up

Therefore, $34{,}761_{10} = 87C9_{16}$. Again, this technique will work for converting a decimal integer to any base. You just divide by the base, keep track of the remainders, and read up.

When converting a decimal number containing a fractional part, you divide the problem into two parts. First, convert the integer part using the technique just described. Then you can use the following rule to convert the fractional part: Multiply the fractional part by the base, keep track of the integer part, and read down. As an example, suppose you want to convert the decimal number 3901.78125_{10} to its hexadecimal equivalent. You would first convert the integer part by dividing by the base, keeping track of the remainder, and reading up:

$$3901/16 = 243 \quad \text{with remainder} \quad 13 = D$$
$$243/16 = 15 \quad \text{with remainder} \quad 3$$
$$15/16 = 0 \quad \text{with remainder} \quad 15 = F$$

read up

Therefore, $3901_{10} = F3D_{16}$. To convert the fractional part, multiply by the base, keep track of the integer part, and read down:

read down ⟶

$$0.78125 \times 16 = 12.5 \qquad \text{integer part} = 12 = C$$
$$0.5 \times 16 = 8.0 \qquad \text{integer part} = 8$$

Therefore, $0.78125_{10} = 0.C8_{16}$. Combining the integer and fractional parts, we have found that $3901.78125_{10} = F3D.C8_{16}$.

This rule for converting the fractional part of a decimal number will work for any base. Sometimes the remainder may never become zero and you will have a continuing fraction. This means that there is no exact conversion of the decimal fraction. For example, suppose you want to represent the decimal value 0.1_{10} as a binary number. Following our rule, we would write

read down ⟶

$$0.1 \times 2 = 0.2 \qquad \text{integer part} = 0$$
$$0.2 \times 2 = 0.4 \qquad \text{integer part} = 0$$
$$0.4 \times 2 = 0.8 \qquad \text{integer part} = 0$$
$$0.8 \times 2 = 1.6 \qquad \text{integer part} = 1$$
$$0.6 \times 2 = 1.2 \qquad \text{integer part} = 1$$
$$0.2 \times 2 = 0.4 \qquad \text{integer part} = 0$$
$$0.4 \times 2 = 0.8 \qquad \text{integer part} = 0$$
$$0.8 \times 2 = 1.6 \qquad \text{integer part} = 1$$
$$0.6 \times 2 = 1.2 \qquad \text{integer part} = 1$$

It is clear that the remainder will never go to zero and that the pattern 0011 will go on forever. Thus, 0.1_{10} can only be approximated as

$$0.1_{10} \approx 0.000110011..._2$$

This means that 0.1_{10} cannot be represented exactly in a computer as a binary number of any size!

2.4 NEGATIVE NUMBERS

An 8-bit binary number can represent one of 256 (2^8) possible values between 0 and 255. However, we also need to represent negative numbers. The leftmost bit in a binary number is the *sign bit*. If this bit is zero, the number is positive; if this bit is one, the number is negative. However, in the 8086 (and in most computers today), when the most significant bit is one, the magnitude of the negative number is *not* given by the binary value of the remaining bits in the number.

Rather a *two's complement* representation of negative numbers is used. The reason for this is that the same circuitry, an adder, can be used for both addition and subtraction.

The idea of being able to subtract by adding can be seen by an example using decimal (base 10) numbers. Suppose you want to subtract 35 from 73. The answer is 38. You can obtain this result by taking the 10's complement of 35 (this is what you have to add to 35 to get 100; that is, 65) and adding it to 73. The result is 138, as shown in Fig. 2.7. If you ignore the leading 1 (the carry), then the remaining value, 38, is the correct answer.

$$
\begin{array}{ccc}
73 & & 73 \\
-35 & \text{10's complement} & +65 \\
\hline
38 & & 138
\end{array}
$$

Ignore carry ⟶

Figure 2.7   Decimal subtraction can be done by taking the 10's complement of the subtrahend and adding.

In binary arithmetic, negative numbers are stored in their *two's complement* form. You can find the two's complement of a binary number in several ways. Note that the 10's complement of 35 can be found by subtracting 35 from 99 (this gives the 9's complement) and then adding 1. That is,

$$
\begin{array}{r}
99 \\
-35 \\
\hline
64 \\
+\ 1 \\
\hline
65
\end{array}
$$

The two's complement of the 8-bit binary number 01001101 is the 8-bit binary number you must add to this number to obtain 100000000. You can find it by subtracting the number from 11111111 and adding 1. Note that subtracting an 8-bit binary number from 11111111 (called the one's complement) is equivalent to complementing each bit in the byte; that is, each 1 is changed to a 0, and each 0 is changed to a 1. Therefore, the one's complement of 01001101 is 10110010 and the two's complement of 01001101 is

$$
\begin{array}{rl}
& 01001101 \\
\text{one's complement} = & 10110010 \\
\text{add} & \underline{\qquad 1} \\
\text{two's complement} = & 10110011
\end{array}
$$

There is an easier way to take the two's complement of a binary number. You just start at the rightmost bit and copy down all bits until you have copied down the first 1. Then complement (that is, change from 1 to 0 or 0 to 1) all the remaining bits. For example,

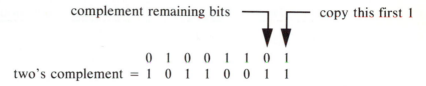

$$\begin{array}{l} 0\ \ 1\ \ 0\ \ 0\ \ 1\ \ 1\ \ 0\ \ 1 \\ \text{two's complement} = 1\ \ 0\ \ 1\ \ 1\ \ 0\ \ 0\ \ 1\ \ 1 \end{array}$$

As a second example,

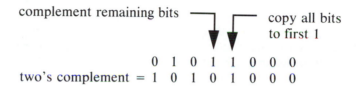

$$\begin{array}{l} 0\ \ 1\ \ 0\ \ 1\ \ 1\ \ 0\ \ 0\ \ 0 \\ \text{two's complement} = 1\ \ 0\ \ 1\ \ 0\ \ 1\ \ 0\ \ 0\ \ 0 \end{array}$$

Verify that if you add the 8-bit binary numbers given in the examples above to their two's complement value you obtain 100000000.

An 8-bit byte can contain positive values between 00000000 and 01111111, that is, between 00H and 7FH. This corresponds to decimal values between 0 and 127. A byte in which bit 7 is a 1 is interpreted as a negative number whose magnitude can be found by taking the two's complement. For example, how is -75_{10} stored in the computer? First, write down the binary or hex value of the number, 4BH, as shown in Fig. 2.8. Then take its two's complement. The value -75_{10} is therefore stored in the computer as B5H. Note that if you take the two's complement of a positive number between 0 and 7FH the result will always have bit 7 (the most significant bit) set to 1.

$$\begin{array}{rcl} 75_{10} &=& 4BH = 01001011 \\ \text{Two's complement} = -75_{10} &=& B5H = 10110101 \\ \text{Two's complement of} \quad B5H &=& 4BH = 01001011 \end{array}$$

Figure 2.8 The negative of a binary number is found by taking the two's complement.

Given a negative number (with bit 7 set), you can always find the magnitude of this number by taking the two's complement. For example, the two's complement of B5H (-75_{10}) is 4BH ($+75_{10}$), as shown in Fig. 2.8.

Note that the two's complement of 01H is FFH and the two's complement of 80H is 80H, as shown in Fig. 2.9. This last example shows that signed 8-bit binary numbers "wrap around" at 80H. That is, the largest positive number is 7FH $= 127_{10}$, and the smallest negative number (largest magnitude) is 80H $= -128_{10}$. This is shown in Table 2.2.

$$
\begin{array}{rcccl}
& & 1_{10} & = 01\text{H} & = 00000001 \\
\text{Two's complement} = & & -1_{10} & = \text{FFH} & = 11111111 \\
& & 128_{10} & = 80\text{H} & = 10000000 \\
\text{Two's complement} = & & -128_{10} & = 80\text{H} & = 10000000
\end{array}
$$

Figure 2.9 Negative 8-bit numbers can range between FFH (-1) and 80H (-128).

Table 2.2 also shows that the hex values between 80H and FFH can be interpreted *either* as negative numbers between -128 and -1 *or* as positive numbers between 128 and 255. Sometimes you will treat them as negative numbers and sometimes you will treat them as positive values. It is up to you as the programmer to make sure you know whether a particular byte is being treated as a signed or as an unsigned number.

Whereas bit 7 is the sign in an 8-bit byte, bit 15 is the sign in a 16-bit word. A 16-bit signed word can have values ranging from 8000H $= -32,768_{10}$ to 7FFFH $= +32,767_{10}$. Similarly, bit 31 is the sign bit in a 32-bit double word. Such a double word can have values ranging from 80000000H $= -2,147,483,648_{10}$ to 7FFFFFFFH $= +2,147,483,647_{10}$.

TABLE 2.2 POSITIVE AND NEGATIVE BINARY NUMBERS

Signed decimal	Hex	Binary	Unsigned decimal
-128	80	10000000	128
-127	81	10000001	129
-126	82	10000010	130
—	—	—	—
—	—	—	—
—	—	—	—
-3	FD	11111101	253
-2	FE	11111110	254
-1	FF	11111111	255
0	00	00000000	0
1	01	00000001	1
2	02	00000010	2
3	03	00000011	3
—	—	—	—
—	—	—	—
—	—	—	—
125	7D	01111101	125
126	7E	01111110	126
127	7F	01111111	127

EXERCISES

2.1. Convert the following decimal numbers to their hexadecimal equivalent.

   a. 42

   b. 31729

   c. 2173

   d. 249

   e. 125

   f. 62433

2.2. Convert the following hexadecimal numbers to their decimal equivalent.

   a. EF

   b. 7134

   c. 5AC

   d. AA

   e. 5C

   f. F21C

2.3. Convert the following numbers:

   a. $110101001011_2 = ?_{16}$

   b. $10101101010_2 = ?_8$

   c. $533.25_{10} = ?_2$

   d. $1010.101_2 = ?_{10}$

   e. $42.36_8 = ?_{10}$

2.4. Convert the following numbers:

   a. $3B4.C_{16} = ?_{10}$

   b. $8000_{16} = ?_{10}$

   c. $241.1_{10} = ?_8$

   d. $241.1_{10} = ?_{16}$

   e. $1AE7.B_{16} = ?_{10}$

2.5. Find the hex values for the following decimal numbers.

   a. -7

   b. -101

   c. -68

   d. -25

   e. -120

   f. -5

2.6. The following hex values correspond to what negative decimal numbers?

   a. CDH

   b. F3H

   c. E2H

   d. 85H

   e. 99H

   f. ABH

3

Basic Logic Gates

All digital systems are made from a few basic digital circuits that we call *logic gates*. These circuits perform the basic logic functions that we will describe in this chapter. The physical realization of these logic gates has changed over the years from mechanical relays to electronic vacuum tubes to transistors to integrated circuits containing thousands of transistors.

In this chapter you will learn:

- Definitions of the basic gates in terms of truth tables and logic equations
- De Morgan's theorem
- How gates defined in terms of positive and negative logic are related
- To use multiple-input gates
- How to perform a sum of products and a product of sums design from a truth table specification
- How to use standard TTL chips to make a simple programmable logic device.

3.1 TRUTH TABLES AND LOGIC EQUATIONS

All data in a computer are stored as binary digits. These bits can be thought of as the logical values 0 and 1, where a 1 is considered to be *true* and a 0 is considered to be *false*. The actual physical quantities associated with a 0 and a 1 might be a low (0 volts) or high (5 volts) voltage.

A truth table will define the logical outputs (0 or 1) of the gate for all possible logical inputs. In this section we will define the three basic gates, NOT, AND,

26

and OR, by means of their truth tables. We will then use these basic gates to
define some additional gates. Using truth tables, we will discover the important
De Morgan's theorem. We will then consider the possibility of considering 0 to
be *true* and 1 to be *false*. This will give us a better insight into the various gates.
Finally, we will look at the definitions of multiple-input gates.

The Three Basic Gates

NOT gate.   The definition of the NOT gate, or inverter, is shown in Fig.
3.1. The logic symbol for the inverter has a single input X and a single output Y.
The value of Y is the complement of the input. Thus, as shown in the truth table
in Fig. 3.1, if X is 0, then Y is 1, whereas if X is 1, then Y is 0. The NOT gate
simply inverts the logic state of the input.

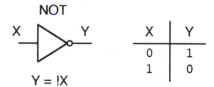

X	Y
0	1
1	0

Figure 3.1   The NOT gate or inverter.

$$Y = !X$$

The equation for the inverter in Fig. 3.1 is given as $Y = !X$. We read this
as "Y equals *NOT X*." In this book we will use the exclamation point $!$ as the
negation operator. The prime, bar, slash, and $\neg$ are sometimes used to indicate
the NOT operation, as in

$$Y = X' \qquad Y = \overline{X} \qquad Y = /X \qquad Y = \neg X$$

The reason we will use $Y = !X$ is that this is the notation used by the CUPL
software we will use to compile our logic equations to program a programmable
logic device (PLD). Inasmuch as all the equations you will write to program these
devices will use the $!$ as the negation operator, you might as well get used to it
from the beginning.

AND gate.   The definition of the AND gate is shown in Fig. 3.2. The AND
gate logic symbol has two inputs, X and Y, and the single output Z. From the
truth table in Fig. 3.2, we see that the output Z of an AND gate is 1 (true or high)

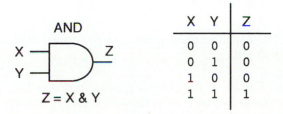

X	Y	Z
0	0	0
0	1	0
1	0	0
1	1	1

$$Z = X \, \& \, Y$$

Figure 3.2   The AND gate.

only if *both* inputs, *X and Y*, are 1 (true or high). The output *Z* will be zero if either *X* or *Y* or both are zero.

The equation for the AND gate in Fig. 3.2 is given as $Z = X \& Y$. We read this as "*Z* equals *X AND Y*." In this book we will use the ampersand & as the *and* operator. Other common ways to indicate the AND operation are

$$X \cdot Y \quad X \wedge Y \quad X * Y \quad XY$$

The last form involving the juxtaposition of *X* and *Y* limits you to logic variables containing a single letter. We will be using names for our logic variables in which case *XY* could represent a *single* logic variable. The reason we will use $Z = X \& Y$ for the AND operation is that this is the notation used by the CUPL software to program a PLD.

OR gate. The definition of the OR gate is shown in Fig. 3.3. The OR gate logic symbol has two inputs, *X* and *Y*, and the single output *Z*. From the truth table in Fig. 3.3, we see that the output *Z* of an OR gate is 1 (true or high) if *either* input, *X or Y*, or both are 1 (true or high). The output *Z* will be zero only if both *X* and *Y* are zero.

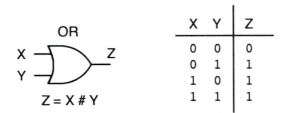

X	Y	Z
0	0	0
0	1	1
1	0	1
1	1	1

Figure 3.3 The OR gate.

The equation for the OR gate in Fig. 3.3 is given as $Z = X \# Y$. We read this as "*Z* equals *X OR Y*." In this book we will use the pound sign # as the OR operator. Other common ways to indicate the OR operation are

$$X + Y \quad X \vee Y$$

Again, the reason we will use $Z = X \# Y$ for the OR operation is that this is the notation used by the CUPL software to program a PLD.

As surprising as it may seem, all digital systems, including all computers, can be built from only the three basic gates: NOT, AND, and OR. We will begin by showing that three other common gates can be built from our basic three.

Three New Gates

Three new gates, NAND, NOR, and Exclusive-OR, can be formed from our three basic gates: NOT, AND, and OR.

NAND gate. The definition of the NAND gate is shown in Fig. 3.4. The logic symbol for a NAND gate is like an AND gate with a small circle (or bubble) on the output. From the truth table in Fig. 3.4, we see that the output of a NAND gate is 0 (low) only if both inputs are 1 (high). The NAND gate is equivalent to an AND gate followed by an inverter (NOT-AND), as shown by the two truth tables in Fig. 3.4.

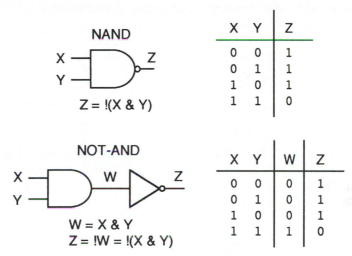

X	Y	Z
0	0	1
0	1	1
1	0	1
1	1	0

X	Y	W	Z
0	0	0	1
0	1	0	1
1	0	0	1
1	1	1	0

Figure 3.4   The NAND gate.

NOR gate.   The definition of the NOR gate is shown in Fig. 3.5. The logic symbol for a NOR gate is like an OR gate with a small circle (or bubble) on the output. From the truth table in Fig. 3.5, we see that the output of a NOR gate is 1 (high) only if both inputs are 0 (low). The NOR gate is equivalent to an OR gate followed by an inverter (NOT-OR), as shown by the two truth tables in Fig. 3.5.

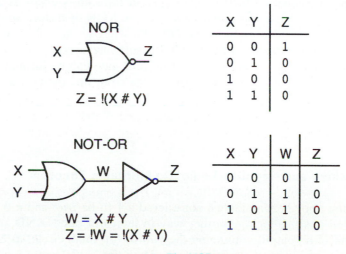

X	Y	Z
0	0	1
0	1	0
1	0	0
1	1	0

X	Y	W	Z
0	0	0	1
0	1	1	0
1	0	1	0
1	1	1	0

Figure 3.5   The NOR gate.

Exclusive-OR gate. The definition of the Exclusive-OR, or XOR, gate is shown in Fig. 3.6. The XOR gate logic symbol is like an OR gate symbol with an extra curved vertical line on the input. From the truth table in Fig. 3.6, we see that the output Z of an XOR gate is 1 (true or high) if *either* input, X *or* Y, is 1 (true or high), but *not* both. The output Z will be zero if both X and Y are the same (either both 1 or both 0).

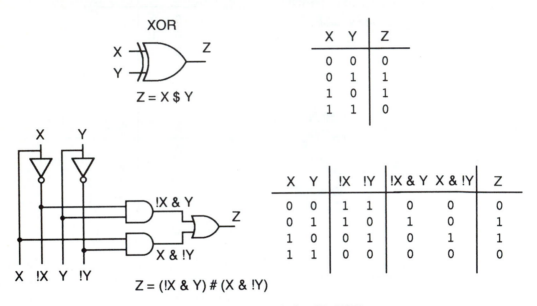

Figure 3.6 The Exclusive-OR (XOR) gate.

The equation for the XOR gate in Fig. 3.6 is given as $Z = X \$ Y$. In this book we will use the dollar sign $\$$ as the XOR operator. Sometimes the symbol $\oplus$ is used to denote Exclusive-OR. We will use the dollar sign $\$$ because that is the symbol recognized by the CUPL software used to program a PLD.

From Fig. 3.6 we see that the XOR gate can be formed with two inverters, two AND gates, and an OR gate. Note from this figure and truth table that the Exclusive-OR can be written as

$$Z = X \$ Y$$

$$= (! X \ \& \ Y) \ \# \ (X \ \& \ ! Y)$$

Positive and Negative Logic: De Morgan's Theorem

In the above examples we considered a 1 to be *true* and a 0 to be *false*. This is called positive logic. Another way to interpret our NAND and NOR gates is to think of an output containing the bubble (or small circle) as being *true* when the output is 0. This is negative logic. Then the NAND gate is just an AND gate in which the output is *true* (0) only when both inputs are true (1). Look at the truth table for the NAND gate in Fig. 3.4 to see this.

We can even put bubbles on the input to our gates and think of them as having true values when the inputs are 0 (negative logic). Remember that the bubble is equivalent to putting an inverter (NOT gate) there. If we put two bubbles on the input to an OR gate, we get a NAND gate, as shown in Fig. 3.7. Compare the truth table in Fig. 3.7 with that in Fig. 3.4 to see that it really is a NAND gate. The OR-type symbol in Fig. 3.7 is just an alternate representation of a NAND gate.

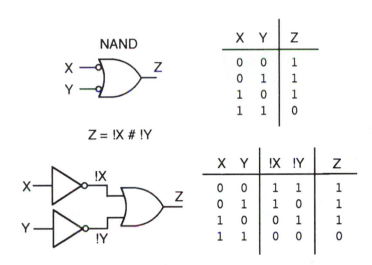

X	Y	Z
0	0	1
0	1	1
1	0	1
1	1	0

$$Z = !X \# !Y$$

X	Y	!X	!Y	Z
0	0	1	1	1
0	1	1	0	1
1	0	0	1	1
1	1	0	0	0

Figure 3.7   An alternate representation of a NAND gate.

Note in the representation shown in Fig. 3.7 that we can think of a NAND gate as an OR gate in which the output is *true* (1) if either or both inputs are *true* (0). Because the two forms of the NAND gate shown in Figs. 3.4 and 3.7 are equivalent, that is, they have the same truth table, the two equations for the NAND gate given in the figures must be equal. We can therefore write

$$Z \;=\; !X \;\#\; !Y \;=\; !(X \;\&\; Y) \tag{3.1}$$

which is one form of *De Morgan's theorem.*

Let's apply this same idea of thinking of an output containing the bubble as being *true* when the output is 0 to the NOR gate in Fig. 3.5. Then the NOR gate is just an OR gate in which the output is *true* (0) when either or both inputs are true (1).

If we put two bubbles on the input to an AND gate, we get a NOR gate, as shown in Fig. 3.8. Compare the truth table in Fig. 3.8 with that in Fig. 3.5 to see that it really is a NOR gate. The AND-type symbol in Fig. 3.8 is just an alternate representation of a NOR gate.

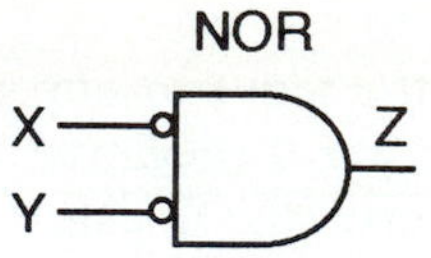

NOR

X	Y	Z
0	0	1
0	1	0
1	0	0
1	1	0

Z = !X & !Y

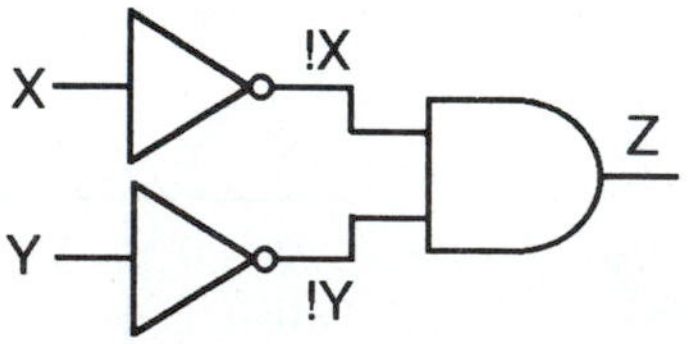

X	Y	!X	!Y	Z
0	0	1	1	1
0	1	1	0	0
1	0	0	1	0
1	1	0	0	0

Figure 3.8 An alternate representation of a NOR gate.

Note in the representation shown in Fig. 3.8 that we can think of a NOR gate as an AND gate in which the output is *true* (1) only if both inputs are *true* (0). Because the two forms of the NOR gate shown in Figs. 3.5 and 3.8 are equivalent, that is, they have the same truth table, the two equations for the NOR gate given in these figures must be equal. We can therefore write

$$Z = !X \ \& \ !Y = !(X \ \# \ Y) \qquad (3.2)$$

which is another form of *De Morgan's theorem*.

The symbol for an inverter can also have the bubble on the input, as shown in Fig. 3.9. From this figure we see that

$$!!X = X \qquad (3.3)$$

which represents two inverters forming a noninverting buffer.

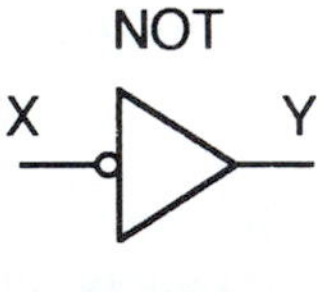

NOT

X	Y
0	1
1	0

Y = !X

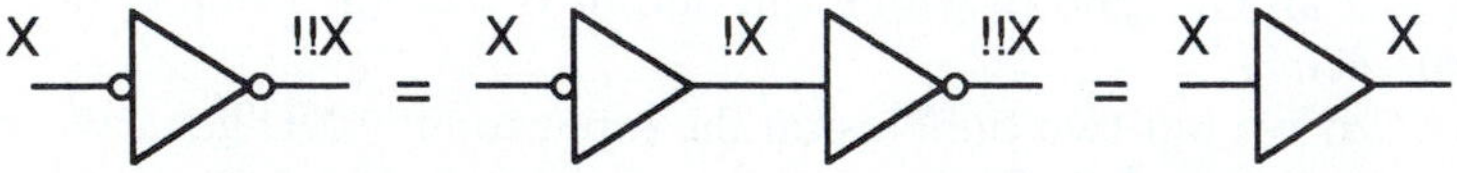

Figure 3.9 An alternate representation of an inverter.

From Eqs. (3.1) to (3.3) we see that we can state both forms of De Morgan's theorem as follows:

1. NOT all variables.
2. Change & to # or # to &.
3. NOT the result.

For example,

$$!X \# !Y = !(!!X \& !!Y) = !(X \& Y)$$

$$!(X \& Y) = !!(!X \# !Y) = !X \# !Y$$

$$!X \& !Y = !(!!X \# !!Y) = !(X \# Y) \qquad (3.4)$$

$$!(X \# Y) = !!(!X \& !Y) = !X \& !Y$$

Multiple-input Gates

The AND, OR, NAND, and NOR gates we have studied so far are not limited to having two inputs. The basic definitions hold for multiple inputs. For example, the output Z_1 of the 4-input AND gate in Fig. 3.10 will be high (1) only if all four inputs are high (1). The output Z_2 of the 8-input OR gate in Fig. 3.10 will be high (1) if any of the eight inputs are high (1). It will only be low (0) when all eight inputs are low (0). The output Z_3 of the 8-input NAND gate in Fig. 3.10 will be low (0) only if all eight inputs are high (1). The output Z_4 of the 5-input NOR gate in Fig. 3.10 will be low (0) if any of the five inputs are high (1). It will only be high (1) when all five inputs are low (0).

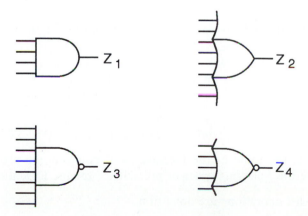

Figure 3.10   Multiple-input gates.

3.2 BASIC DIGITAL DESIGN

It is easy to design a digital circuit from its truth table definition. We will illustrate the procedure by designing the Exclusive-OR circuit shown in Fig. 3.6. There are two different methods of design that lead to two different circuits that perform the same function. We will look at each of these methods separately.

Sum of Products Design

We can form a product term, called a *minterm*, for each row of a truth table. The minterm is formed by ANDing together a value associated with each input variable. If the value of the variable in a particular row of the truth table is 1, we include the variable name, such as X. If the value of the variable in a particular row of the truth table is 0, we include the negation of the variable name, such as $!X$. Thus, the minterm in row 0 (numbering the rows from 0 to 3) will be $m0 = !X \& !Y$ because both X and Y are 0 in this row, as shown in Fig. 3.11. On the other hand, the minterm in row 2 will be $m2 = X \& !Y$. All four minterms are shown in Fig. 3.11.

X	Y	minterms
0	0	m0 = !X & !Y
0	1	m1 = !X & Y
1	0	m2 = X & !Y
1	1	m3 = X & Y

X	Y	Z	
0	0	0	
0	1	1	← m1 = !X & Y
1	0	1	← m2 = X & !Y
1	1	0	

$$Z = m1 \ \# \ m2$$
$$= (!X \& Y) \ \# \ (X \& !Y)$$

Figure 3.11 Sum of products design based on the 1's of the output.

On the right side of Fig. 3.11 we show the truth table for the Exclusive-OR function. If we focus on the rows in which the output is 1 (true), we see that the output Z will be true (1) if either the minterm $m1$ is true *or* if the minterm $m2$ is true. Note that $m1$ will be true if X is 0 and Y is 1 because then $!X \& Y$ will be 1. We can then write the equation for Z by simply ORing the minterms associated with each output that is 1. From Fig. 3.11 we see that

$$Z = m1 \ \# \ m2$$
$$= (!X \& Y) \ \# \ (X \& !Y)$$

(3.5)

which is the same as the Exclusive-OR equation we used in Fig. 3.6. We will assume the following order of precedence for the logical operators $!$, $\&$, and $\#$.

1. All ! operations are done first.
2. All & operations are done next.
3. All # operations are done last.

Equation (3.5) can then be written without the parentheses as

$$Z = !X \& Y \# X \& !Y \qquad\qquad (3.6)$$

ORing all the minterms associated with each 1 in the output column of a truth table leads to a *sum of products* design. The OR operator # is a logical sum and the AND operator & is a logical product. The logical circuit corresponding to Eq. (3.6) is the one shown in Fig. 3.6.

Product of Sums Design

Instead of focusing on the 1's in the output column of a truth table, suppose we focus on the 0's, as shown in Fig. 3.12. Note that in this case Z is NOT the minterm *m0* AND it is NOT the minterm *m3*. What does it mean to be NOT a minterm? From the definitions of minterms in Fig. 3.11 and using De Morgan's theorem from Eq. (3.4), we can write

$$NOT\ minterm\ m0 = !m0$$
$$= !(!X \& !Y)$$
$$= !!(X \# Y)$$
$$= X \# Y$$

We call this the *maxterm, M0*. The maxterms for all rows in the truth table are given in Fig. 3.13. Note that each maxterm is NOT the corresponding minterm. Use De Morgan's theorem to verify each maxterm expression.

X	Y	Z
0	0	0
0	1	1
1	0	1
1	1	0

Z is NOT minterm m0
AND it is NOT minterm m3

Z = !m0 & !m3

Figure 3.12   Focusing on the 0's will lead to a product of sums design.

X	Y	minterms	maxterms
0	0	m0 = !X & !Y	M0 = !m0 = X # Y
0	1	m1 = !X & Y	M1 = !m1 = X # !Y
1	0	m2 = X & !Y	M2 = !m2 = !X # Y
1	1	m3 = X & Y	M3 = !m3 = !X # !Y

Figure 3.13   A maxterm is NOT the corresponding minterm.

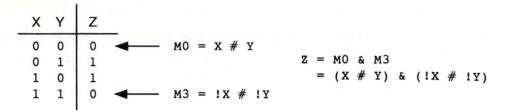

X	Y	Z
0	0	0
0	1	1
1	0	1
1	1	0

M0 = X # Y

M3 = !X # !Y

Z = M0 & M3
  = (X # Y) & (!X # !Y)

Figure 3.14 Product of sums design based on the 0's of the output.

Combining the results in Figs. 3.12 and 3.13, we see that we can write an equation for Z as the product ($\&$) of all maxterms for rows in which the output is a zero. Thus, as shown in Fig. 3.14, the equation for the Exclusive-OR is

$$Z = M0 \ \& \ M3 \qquad\qquad (3.7)$$
$$= (X \ \# \ Y) \ \& \ (!X \ \# \ !Y)$$

which is in the form of a product ($\&$) of sums ($\#$). The logic circuit corresponding to Eq. (3.7) is shown in Fig. 3.15. Compare this with the Exclusive-OR circuit shown in Fig. 3.6. Note that different logic circuits can perform the identical function.

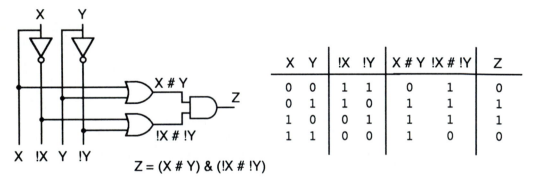

X	Y	!X	!Y	X # Y	!X # !Y	Z
0	0	1	1	0	1	0
0	1	1	0	1	1	1
1	0	0	1	1	1	1
1	1	0	0	1	0	0

Z = (X # Y) & (!X # !Y)

Figure 3.15 Logic diagram for product of sums Exclusive-OR design.

3.3 A PROGRAMMABLE LOGIC DEVICE

We have seen in this chapter that any logic circuit can be built from NOT, AND, and OR gates. Two general forms of circuits representing a sum of products and a product of sums design are shown in Figs. 3.6 and 3.15, respectively. Consider the sum of products circuit shown in Fig. 3.6. If we could change the connections between the inputs to the AND gates and the input lines X, $!X$, Y, and $!Y$, we could change the logic function of Z to be something completely different. This is what programmable logic devices, or PLDs, do. We will illustrate the process by building a simple 2-input, 1-output PLD from our three basic gates.

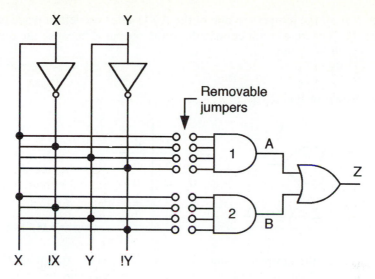

Figure 3.16 A programmable logic circuit.

A 2-Input, 1-Output PLD

Consider the logic circuit shown in Fig. 3.16, which includes two 4-input AND gates. All four inputs to each AND gate are connected to all four input lines X, $!X$, Y, and $!Y$ through eight removable jumpers. Suppose that all the jumpers are initially connected. Then the output Z can be written as

```
Z = A # B

  = (X & !X & Y & !Y) # (X & !X & Y & !Y)

  = 0 & 0 # 0 & 0

  = 0
```

where we have used the fact that

```
X & !X = 0
```

as shown in Fig. 3.17.

X	!X	Z
0	1	0
0	1	0
1	0	0
1	0	0

Figure 3.17 X & !X = 0.

If all the jumpers to one of the AND gates are left in place (connected), then that AND gate will not contribute to the output Z because the output of the AND gate will be 0 and

$$X \ \# \ 0 \ = \ X$$

as shown in Fig. 3.18.

X	0	Z
0	0	0
0	0	0
1	0	1
1	0	1

$$Z = X \ \# \ 0 = X$$

Figure 3.18 $X \ \# \ 0 = X$.

If all the jumpers to one of the AND gates are removed, then all the inputs to the AND gate will be 1. This is because an unconnected input to the AND gate is pulled high by an internal resistor in the chip. We say that the unconnected input *floats* high. The output of the AND gate will be 1, and therefore the output of the OR gate will be 1, regardless of the output of the other AND gate.

Suppose you wanted to reduce the circuit in Fig. 3.16 to a single 2-input AND gate. You would simply set the jumpers as shown in Fig. 3.19. Similarly, to produce an OR gate you would set the jumpers as shown in Fig. 3.20. Finally, to produce an Exclusive-OR gate, you would set the jumpers as shown in Fig. 3.21. Compare this figure with the logic circuit in Fig. 3.6.

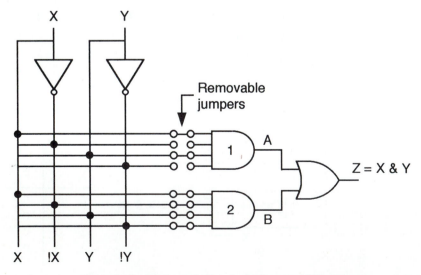

Figure 3.19   Jumper selection to produce an AND gate.

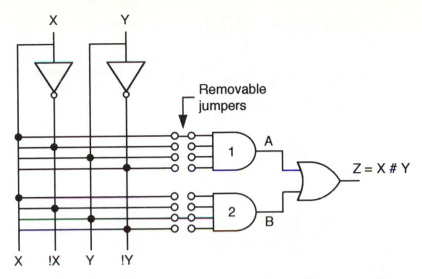

Figure 3.20   Jumper selection to produce an OR gate.

Examples of producing other logic functions with this single circuit will be left to exercises associated with Experiment 1 described later in this chapter.

TTL Chips

The 7400 series of TTL (transistor–transistor logic) chips has been in widespread use for many years. There are several different families of these chips, defined

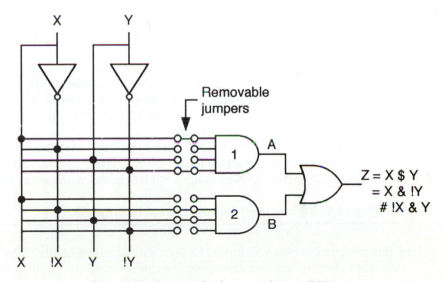

Figure 3.21   Jumper selection to produce an XOR gate.

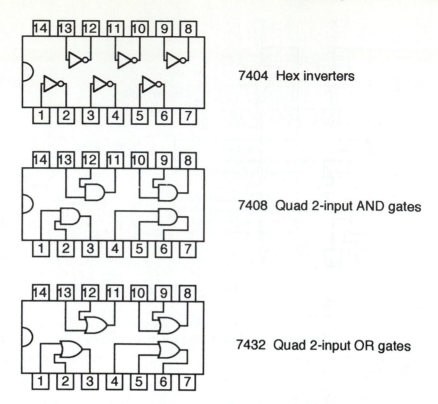

Figure 3.22 TTL chips for the three basic gates.

by speed and power consumption. Any of the families will be suitable for the experiment to be described next.

Many of the chips in this family are 14-pin chips in a dual-in-line package (DIP). Pin 14 is connected to +5 volts and pin 7 is connected to ground. Figure 3.22 shows the pin connections for the TTL chips containing the three basic gates. Note that there are six NOT gates in the 7404, four AND gates in the 7408, and four OR gates in the 7432.

The pinouts for the 7400 NAND gates, the 7402 NOR gates, and the 7486 Exclusive-OR gates are shown in Fig. 3.23. Similarly, the pinouts for the 7421 4-input AND gates and the 7430 8-input NAND gate are shown in Fig. 3.24.

Experiment 1: Structure of a Programmable Logic Device

In this experiment you will build the logic circuit given in Fig. 3.16 in order to study the behavior of a programmable logic device and the truth tables of simple gates.

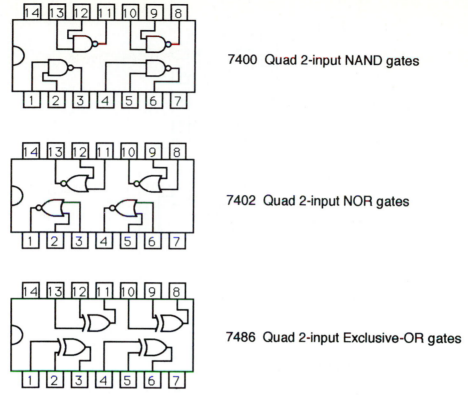

Figure 3.23   TTL chips for NAND, NOR, and XOR gates.

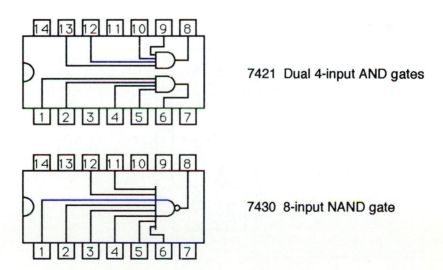

Figure 3.24   TTL chips for some multiple-input gates.

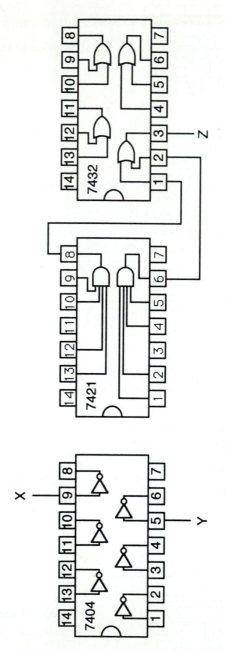

Figure 3.25 Layout of chips on protoboard for logic circuit in Fig. 3.16.

Setup.   Place a 7404, a 7421, and a 7432 on a protoboard in the order shown in Fig. 3.25. Connect the output of the two 4-input AND gates to the input of an OR gate as shown. The output of the OR gate will be the output Z shown in the logic circuit in Fig. 3.16. The two inputs X and Y will come into pins 9 and 5 of the 7404. By connecting jumper wires between pins 5, 6, 8, 9 of the 7404 and pins 1, 2, 4, 5 and 9, 10, 12, 13 of the 7421 you can make any of the jumper connections in Fig. 3.16.

Logic analyzer.   On the disk accompanying this book are two programs called *LOGIC1.EXE* and *LOGIC2.EXE*. When you execute either program by typing *logic1* (or *logic2*) from DOS, you will obtain the screen display shown in Fig. 3.26. This program controls eight output lines going out through the printer port and displays the instantaneous value of five input lines coming into the printer port. If your PC has only one printer port, you must use *logic1*, but the port cannot then be connected to a printer. If you have two printer ports with one connected to a printer, the other one can be used for your logic experiments by using the *logic2* program.

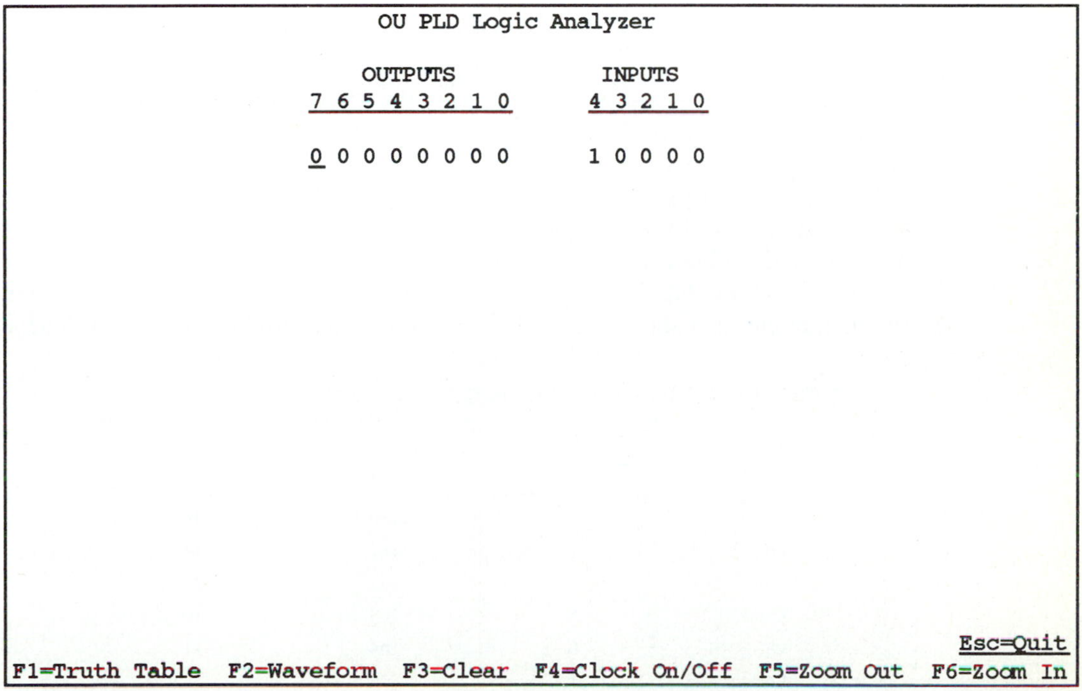

```
                        OU PLD Logic Analyzer

              OUTPUTS              INPUTS
           7 6 5 4 3 2 1 0       4 3 2 1 0

           0 0 0 0 0 0 0 0       1 0 0 0 0




                                                              Esc=Quit
 F1=Truth Table   F2=Waveform   F3=Clear   F4=Clock On/Off   F5=Zoom Out   F6=Zoom In
```

Figure 3.26   Initial screen display of *logic* program.

Pin No.	Signal	Direction
1	Strobe	Out
2	Data bit 0	Out
3	Data bit 1	Out
4	Data bit 2	Out
5	Data bit 3	Out
6	Data bit 4	Out
7	Data bit 5	Out
8	Data bit 6	Out
9	Data bit 7	Out
10	Acknowledge	In
11	Busy	In
12	Out of paper	In
13	Select	In
14	Auto feed	Out
15	I/O error	In
16	Initialize printer	Out
17	Select in	Out
18–25	Ground	

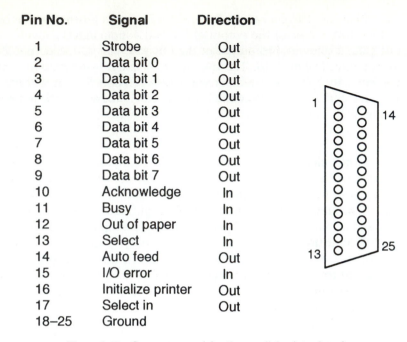

Figure 3.27   Connector used for the parallel printer interface.

The parallel printer port on the PC uses the 25-pin connector shown in Fig. 3.27. You can control the logic levels on pins 2 to 9 using the logic analyzer. These are called signals *Out0* to *Out7*, as shown in Table 3.1, and the current values on these eight pins are shown on the screen under the heading *Outputs*. You can change any of these values by moving the cursor with the right and left cursor keys and typing a 1 or a 0 at the appropriate bit position.

The five values, *In0* to *In4*, displayed under the *Inputs* heading on the screen are the instantaneous values on pins 10 to 13 and 15, as shown in Table 3.1. These

TABLE 3.1   LOGIC ANALYZER PIN CONNECTIONS

Outputs	Printer port pin no.	Inputs	Printer port pin no.
Out0	2	In0	15
Out1	3	In1	13
Out2	4	In2	12
Out3	5	In3	10
Out4	6	In4	11
Out5	7		
Out6	8		
Out7	9		

five values are "live" on the screen, which means whenever one of these values changes the value on the screen will change immediately.

The eight output lines and the five input lines should be brought out to a protoboard. The output lines, *Out0* to *Out7*, will become the inputs to your circuit, and the outputs of your circuit will be connected to the input lines *In0* to *In4*. If you connect the five lines *Out0* to *Out4* directly to the five input lines *In0* to *In4*, you will be able to see how the inputs on the screen change as you manually change the output lines.

When you press function key *F1*, the values on the four output lines, *Out0* to *Out3*, are changed in sequence from 0000 to 1111, and the corresponding inputs are displayed in subsequent rows on the screen to produce an automatic truth table, as shown in Fig. 3.28. Note that the high-order output bits, *Out4* to *Out7*, will be whatever you entered manually at the top of the screen.

Procedure.

1. Connect all jumpers and show that the output is always 0 for any input. Press function key *F1* in the logic analyzer to produce the truth table on the computer screen. Press *Shift-PrtScn* to print this screen to the printer (assuming you have a separate printer port for the printer).

```
                    OU PLD Logic Analyzer

            OUTPUTS                  INPUTS
         7 6 5 4 3 2 1 0           4 3 2 1 0


         1 0 1 0 0 0 0 0           1 0 0 0 0


         1 0 1 0 0 0 0 0           1 0 0 0 0
         1 0 1 0 0 0 0 1           1 0 0 0 0
         1 0 1 0 0 0 1 0           1 0 0 0 0
         1 0 1 0 0 0 1 1           1 0 0 0 0
         1 0 1 0 0 1 0 0           1 0 0 0 0
         1 0 1 0 0 1 0 1           1 0 0 0 0
         1 0 1 0 0 1 1 0           1 0 0 0 0
         1 0 1 0 0 1 1 1           1 0 0 0 0
         1 0 1 0 1 0 0 0           1 0 0 0 0
         1 0 1 0 1 0 0 1           1 0 0 0 0
         1 0 1 0 1 0 1 0           1 0 0 0 0
         1 0 1 0 1 0 1 1           1 0 0 0 0
         1 0 1 0 1 1 0 0           1 0 0 0 0
         1 0 1 0 1 1 0 1           1 0 0 0 0
         1 0 1 0 1 1 1 0           1 0 0 0 0
         1 0 1 0 1 1 1 1           1 0 0 0 0
                                                  Esc=Quit
 F1=Truth Table   F2=Waveform   F3=Clear   F4=Clock On/Off   F5=Zoom Out   F6=Zoom In
```

Figure 3.28   Press function key *F1* to produce a truth table.

2. Connect the proper jumpers to make the output the following gates:
   a. AND gate
   b. OR gate
   c. XOR gate
   d. NAND gate (see Exercise 3.7)
   e. NOR gate (see Exercise 3.7)
   f. XNOR gate (see Exercise 3.7)

For each of these gates, measure the truth table using the logic analyzer and print the results on the printer.

EXERCISES

3.1. a. Make a truth table for the following circuit and show that $Z = !X$.

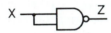

b. Make a truth table for the following circuit and show that $Z = X$ & Y.

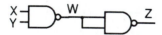

c. Make a truth table for the following circuit and show that $Z = X$ # Y.

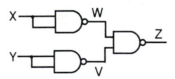

This shows that you can build NOT, AND, and OR gates from only NAND gates. A NAND gate is therefore called a *universal element*.

3.2. a. Make a truth table for the following circuit and show that $Z = !X$.

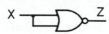

b. Make a truth table for the following circuit and show that $Z = X$ # Y.

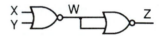

c. Make a truth table for the following circuit and show that $Z = X$ & Y.

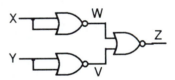

This shows that you can build NOT, AND, and OR gates from only NOR gates. A NOR gate is therefore called a *universal element*.

3.3. Make a truth table and show that the Exclusive-OR gate can be used as a controlled inverter by verifying that

$$Z = X \quad \text{if } Y = 0$$

$$Z = !X \text{ if } Y = 1$$

3.4. a. Make a truth table for the XNOR (NOT-XOR) gate that has the following symbol.

X	Y	Z
0	0	1
0	1	0
1	0	1
1	1	1

b. Write a sum-of-products equation for the output of the XNOR gate.

c. Draw a logic diagram for the XNOR gate in terms of NOT, AND, and OR gates.

3.5 a. Show that the following gate is equivalent to an OR gate. Show that this is also an AND gate in which the input and output *true* values are zero.

b. Show that the following gate is equivalent to an AND gate. Show that this is also an OR gate in which the input and output *true* values are zero.

3.6. From the form of De Morgan's theorem given in Eq. (3.4), show that

$$X \& Y = !(!X \# !Y)$$

and

$$X \# Y = !(!X \& !Y)$$

3.7. Show how to connect the jumpers in Fig. 3.16 to form the following:

a. NAND gate

b. NOR gate

c. XNOR gate (see Exercise 3.4)

3.8. a. Write an equation for Z in the given truth table using a sum-of-products design.

b. Draw a logic diagram for this design.

c. Repeat (a) using a product of sums design.

d. Draw a logic diagram for the design in (c).

3.9. a. Write an equation for Z in the given truth table using a sum-of-products design.

X	Y	Z
0	0	0
0	1	0
1	0	0
1	1	1

b. Draw a logic diagram for this design.

c. Repeat (a) using a product of sums design.

d. Draw a logic diagram for the design in (c).

3.10. a. Write an equation for Z in the given truth table using a sum-of-products design.

X	Y	Z
0	0	1
0	1	0
1	0	1
1	1	0

b. Draw a logic diagram for this design.

c. Repeat (a) using a product of sums design.

d. Draw a logic diagram for the design in (c).

3.11. In Fig. 3.17 we showed that

$$X \& !X = 0$$

By making a truth table show that

$$X \# !X = 1$$

3.12. In Fig. 3.18 we showed that

$$X \# 0 = X$$

By making a truth table show that:

a. $X \# 1 = 1$
b. $X \& 0 = 0$
c. $X \& 1 = X$

3.13. By making a truth table show that:

a. $X \# X = X$
b. $X \& X = X$

4

Programmable Logic Devices

The TTL chips described in Chapter 3 and used in Experiment 1 are called small scale integrated circuits (SSI) and were produced originally in the late 1960s. These SSI chips would typically contain the equivalent of a few dozen transistors. In digital circuits a transistor is the basic electronic component that can switch current (and therefore voltage) on and off. Advances in integrated-circuit technology have been steady and rapid over the past 25 years. SSI chips were quickly followed by MSI (medium scale integrated circuits) containing hundreds of transistors and then LSI (large scale integrated circuits) containing thousands of transistors. VLSI chips (very large scale integrated circuits) produced in the 1980s contain hundreds of thousands of transistors. Some of the most recent high-performance microprocessors contain over a million transistors on a single chip.

The idea of using all this circuit power for flexibility by which the same chip can be reconfigured to perform different functions, led to the development of the microprocessor in the early 1970s. In this case the flexibility is achieved by having the microprocessor execute different programs that are stored in memory. In the late 1970s and all through the 1980s, a wide variety of different programmable logic devices (PLDs) was produced in which the function of dozens of TTL chips could be programmed into a single PLD chip. This same chip could be programmed to perform a completely different function. Many of these PLDs are erasable and can be reused if a mistake is made in programming them. In the experiments in this book we will use a particular type of PLD called a GAL (generic array logic), which is electrically erasable. This means that the chip can be erased and reprogrammed in a matter of a few seconds.

In this chapter, you will learn:

- The basic structure of a PLD and the notation used to describe its operation
- The basic operation of the GAL 16V8 programmable logic device
- How to write a CUPL program that will produce the function of basic gates in the GAL 16V8
- How to compile a CUPL program to produce a documentation file and a download file used to program the PLD
- To understand the fuse plot given in the documentation file
- To program the PLD using the download file

4.1 BASIC PLD STRUCTURE

In Experiment 1 in Chapter 3 you found that the circuit shown in Fig. 4.1 can produce all the basic gate functions by simply changing the jumpers to the inputs of the AND gates. This is the basic structure of a type of PLD called a PAL (programmable array logic) device.[1] The particular PLD we will use in this book is called a GAL (generic array logic) device.[2] The GAL has a more complex output circuit than that shown in Fig. 4.1, which allows it to emulate the behavior of over 20 previously developed, popular PLDs. We will study the various features of the GAL 16V8 as we go through the book. The GAL 16V8 is electrically

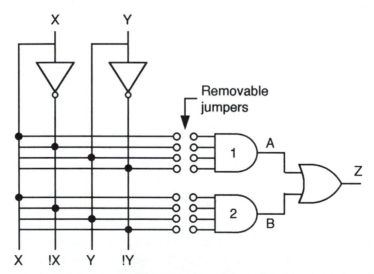

Figure 4.1 Basic PLD structure used in Experiment 1.

[1] PAL is a trademark of Advanced Micro Devices.
[2] GAL is a trademark of Lattice Semiconductor Corporation.

erasable, so you will be able to use a single GAL chip for all the experiments in this book.

Instead of containing the two AND gates shown in Fig. 4.1, the GAL 16V8 actually contains 64 AND gates with 32 inputs each, rather than 4. This makes drawing the circuits more difficult! To make it easier, we use the notation shown in Fig. 4.2 where the four input lines to each AND gate in Fig. 4.1 have been collapsed into a single line (which still represents the original four), and a connected jumper (or fuse) is shown as an × at the intersections to the various input lines. The presence of the × means that the connection is made. We break the connection by removing the ×.

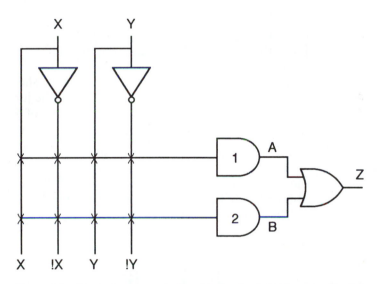

Figure 4.2 Alternate representation of logic circuit in Fig. 4.1 with all jumpers connected.

Recalling the results of Experiment 1 in Chapter 3, we can represent the connections for the Exclusive-OR function as shown in Fig. 4.3. Note that the output A of AND gate 1 is X & $!Y$, and the output B of AND gate 2 is $!X$ & Y.

The GAL 16V8

The GAL 16V8 is the 20-pin chip whose pinouts are shown in Fig. 4.4. Pins 12 to 19 are normally used for outputs, but they can also be used as an input if they are not needed for an output. Pins 2 to 9 are input pins. Pin 1 can be either a normal input or a clock input for sequential circuits. (We will cover sequential circuits in Chapters 7 and 8.) Pin 11 can be either a normal input or an *output enable* input that can enable and disable the output pins. Pin 20 must be connected to +5 volts and pin 10 must be connected to ground.

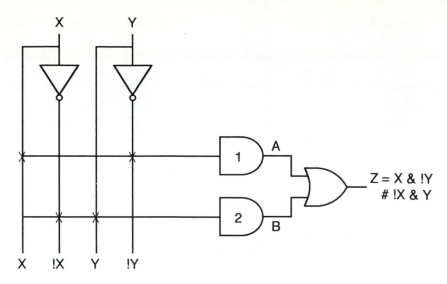

Figure 4.3   PLD connections for the Exclusive-OR.

In the simplest configuration, each output pin of the GAL 16V8 is connected to the output of an 8-input OR gate, as shown in Fig. 4.5. Each of the eight AND gates shown in Fig. 4.5 has 32 inputs, of which only 8 are shown. These are divided into two groups of four, with the inputs from pin 2 going to the first group of four vertical lines on the left and the inputs from pin 3 going to the second group of four vertical lines. Note that the inputs from pins 2 and 3 use the symbol

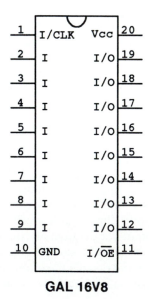

GAL 16V8

Figure 4.4   Pinouts for the GAL 16V8 PLD.

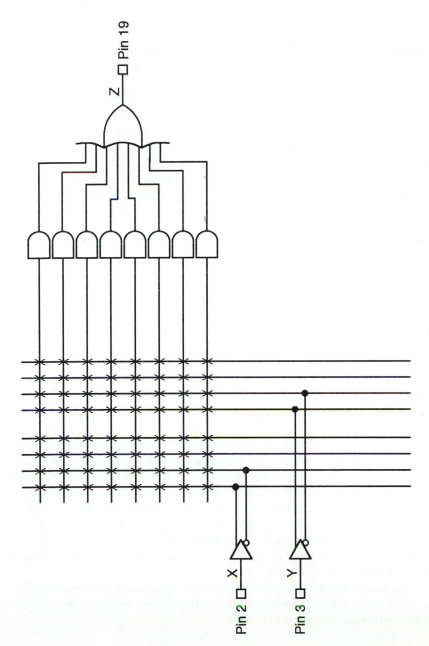

Figure 4.5 Simplified schematic of a portion of the GAL 16V8 PLD.

to generate both the function and its inverse. The two vertical lines shown not connected in each group are actually connected to a signal (and its inverse) that is fed back from the output.

The AND and OR gates shown in Fig. 4.5 are duplicated eight times for all output pins in the GAL 16V8. The vertical lines connected to the input lines are connected to *all* the AND gates in the chip. This means that every input variable may appear in any product term for any output. The complete data sheet for the GAL 16V8 is given in Appendix F.

This chip clearly gives us a lot of flexibility in producing arbitrary output functions based on many input functions. We just have to remove the proper ×'s! This will require a computer program to help us, and we will see how to do this in the next section.

4.2 DESIGNING BASIC GATES IN A PLD

We will illustrate the programming of a PLD by means of a specific example. We will program the chip to contain two inverters and single AND, NAND, OR, NOR, XOR, and XNOR gates, as shown in Fig. 4.6. The two inputs X and Y will be connected to pins 2 and 3 in the PLD, and the outputs of the gates will go to pins 12 to 19, as shown.

The CUPL Design Language

CUPL (Universal Compiler for Programmable Logic)[3] is a design tool for converting a digital design into a fuse map that a programming device uses to remove the proper ×'s in Fig. 4.5. ABEL (Advanced Boolean Expression Language)[4] is a similar universal compiler and, like CUPL, can be used to program most present-day PLDs. Both of these software packages, versions of which run on MS DOS PCs, are derivatives of PALASM, the original PAL Assembler written at Monolithic Memories (since acquired by Advanced Micro Devices) and now in the public domain. A number of PLD manufacturers also provide design tools for their own PLDs.

There are several methods for entering the design information into CUPL. The most basic is to simply write in the Boolean expressions. We will do this for the gate example shown in Fig. 4.6.

---

[3] CUPL is a trademark of Logical Devices, Incorporated.

[4] ABEL is a trademark of Data I/O Corporation.

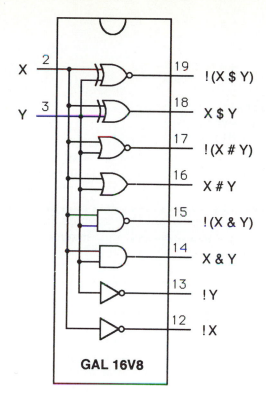

Figure 4.6 Eight different gates to be programmed into the GAL 16V8.

Source file, exp2.pld.   The first step in programming a PLD is to generate a source file containing the Boolean expressions for the design. You can use any convenient text editor, such as EMACS, to produce this file. CUPL comes with an EZ editor, but you can use any editor in a nondocument mode that produces a straight text file. Using such an editor, you should type in the text shown in Listing 4.1.

The first 10 lines in the program are header information. Do not change the words in the left column, but modify the entries on each line as follows:

Name   This should be the filename of the program. In this example the filename is EXP2.PLD. You must use the extension PLD for your filenames. By using Exp2 for the Name, all files, including the fuse map download file, will have this name with different extensions.

Partno   This can be any kind of ID number that you want.

Revision   You can update this number when you make changes.

Date   Put today's date here.

Designer   This is YOU!

Listing 4.1   *exp2.pld*

```
Name            Exp2;
Partno          OU0001;
Revision        04;
Date            7/17/91;
Designer        R. E. Haskell;
Company         Oakland University;
Location        Rochester, MI;
Assembly        CSE 171;
Device          G16V8;
Format          j;

/******************************************************************/
/*                                                                */
/*      This is an example to demonstrate how CUPL               */
/*      compiles simple gates.                                    */
/*                                                                */
/******************************************************************/
/*        Target Device:  G16V8                                   */
/******************************************************************/

/* Inputs:   define inputs to simple gates */

Pin 2 =   x;
Pin 3 =   y;

/* Outputs:   define outputs as active HI levels */

Pin 12 = invx;
Pin 13 = invy;
Pin 14 = and;
Pin 15 = nand;
Pin 16 = or;
Pin 17 = nor;
Pin 18 = xor;
Pin 19 = xnor;

/* Logic:   examples of simple gates expressed in CUPL */

invx = !x;                 /* inverters */
invy = !y;
and  = x & y;              /* and gate */
nand = !(x & y);           /* nand gate */
or   = x # y;              /* or gate */
nor  = !(x # y);           /* nor gate */
xor  = x $ y;              /* exclusive or gate */
xnor = !(x $ y);           /* exclusive nor gate */
```

Company	Put your college or university here.
Location	This is normally used to describe the location on a PC board where the PLD is to go. You can put any useful information or nothing here.
Assembly	Again this is for PC board information. Put your course number here.
Device	This is optional. By including G16V8 here, we won't have to include it in the command line every time we run CUPL.
Format	Type j here. This tells CUPL that we want to produce a JEDEC output format for our download file. This line is optional, but if we don't include it here, we would have to type -j on the command line everytime we run CUPL.

In a CUPL program, any comments can be included between /* and */. Following the header are comments that describe the purpose of the program and the target device.

We then define which pins are associated with the inputs and outputs using statements of the form

```
Pin # = variable;
```

Note that all CUPL statements must end with a semicolon. We used x and y for our input variables and made up descriptive names for the outputs. Variable names can contain up to 31 characters and can start with a numeric digit, a letter, or underscore, but must contain at least one letter. Variables distinguish between upper- and lowercase letters.

Following the pin definitions, we write our logic equations. The form of these logic equations is

$$var = exp$$

where *var* is one of our defined output variables and *exp* is a logic expression that defines the logical value to be assigned to the variable *var* by the assignment operator =. Note that we have written the logic equation for each gate in terms of its gate definition.

After typing Listing 4.1 into the file *exp2.pld*, the next step is to compile this program using CUPL. The directory containing CUPL should be in the PATH command in the AUTOEXEC.BAT file. This will mean that DOS can always find CUPL regardless of your current directory. Go to the subdirectory containing your file *exp2.pld* and type

```
cupl -fax exp2
```

```
C:\CUPL\CSE171 >cupl -fax exp2
CUPL: Universal Compiler for Programmable Logic
Version 4.0a   Serial# MD-40A-7985
Copyright (C)  1983,1990 Logical Devices, Inc.
Licensed to OAKLAND UNIVERSITY


cuplx
time: 1 secs
cupla
time: 1 secs
cuplb
time: 1 secs
cuplm
time: 1 secs
cuplc
time: 2 secs
total time: 8 secs

C:\CUPL\CSE171 >
```

Figure 4.7 Running CUPL to compile Listing 4.1.

This will cause CUPL to run and produce the screen output shown in Fig. 4.7. The term $-fax$ in the input line are three options: $-f$, $-a$, and $-x$. (You can enter these in any order, for example, $-xfa$, but $-fax$ is easier to remember!) The $-x$ option tells CUPL to produce a documentation file with the extension *.DOC*, and the $-f$ option will include a fuse map and chip diagram in the *.DOC* file. The $-a$ option will generate an absolute file with the extension *.ABS* that is used with the logic simulator CSIM. We will show how to use CSIM in Chapter 5, but we will get into the habit of generating this absolute file when we run CUPL. The last entry, *exp 2*, is the filename of our program where CUPL assumes that the extension is *.PLD*.

If we had not included the *Device* and *Format* lines in the header of our program, then we would have had to type

```
cupl -jfax G16V8 exp2
```

when running CUPL. As long as we always use the same PLD (as we will in this book), it is easier to include the same *Device* line in the header of all our programs.

Documentation file, exp2.doc. To view the documentation file *exp2.doc*, type the following command from DOS:

```
type exp2.doc |more
```

This will display the file *exp2.doc* one screenfull at a time. You can scroll a screen at a time by pressing any key. At the end of this file, you will find the chip diagram produced by CUPL as shown in Fig. 4.8.

```
===================================
            Chip Diagram
===================================

          |       Exp2      |
     x---|1              20|---x Vcc
  x  x---|2              19|---x xnor
  y  x---|3              18|---x xor
     x---|4              17|---x nor
     x---|5              16|---x or
     x---|6              15|---x nand
     x---|7              14|---x and
     x---|8              13|---x invy
     x---|9              12|---x invx
GND  x---|10             11|---x
         |_____|
```

Figure 4.8   The chip diagram is printed in the .DOC file when you include the −fx option.

Before this chip diagram in the .DOC file is a fuse plot that shows which connections in the PLD have been blown (or removed) for each output pin. For example, the fuse plots for pins 12 to 15 are shown in Fig. 4.9. Look at the fuse plot for pin 12. The rows in this plot represent the inputs to the eight AND gates shown in Fig. 4.5. The $\times$'s (and −'s) in each row represent the $\times$ connections shown in Fig. 4.5. The first four correspond to the first four vertical lines in Fig. 4.5, the first two of which are the x input from pin 2. The next four $\times$'s correspond to the next four vertical lines in Fig. 4.5, the first two of which are connected to the y input from pin 3. The remaining $\times$'s correspond (in groups of four) to the input pins 4 to 9.

From Fig. 4.5 we see that to produce !X we should connect the second vertical line to one of the AND gates and remove all other inputs to that particular AND gate. The connections to all other AND gates should remain intact so that the outputs of those AND gates will be zero and not contribute to the output of the OR gate. This is exactly what is shown for pin 12 in Fig. 4.9, where CUPL has chosen to blow the fuses in the top AND gate, but could have used any one of the eight.

Look at the pin 13 fuse map in Fig. 4.9. Do you see how this represents !Y from Fig. 4.5? The connection is made in the second vertical line of the second group of four in Fig. 4.5.

We programmed the AND gate to have its output on pin 14. Note from the pin 14 fuse map in Fig. 4.9 that two connections to the top 32-input AND gate in the PLD remain intact: one connected to X and the other connected to Y. This will therefore produce $X \& Y$ as desired.

Now look at pin 15 that is supposed to produce the NAND gate !$(X \& Y)$. It has the same two fuses connected as the AND gate at pin 14! Note, however, that at the top center of the fuse map for pin 15 is the notation *Pol x*, whereas in the fuse map for pin 14 it reads *Pol* − . This represents the output polarity control.

```
Pin #15   02052   Pol x    02124   Acl x
  01024  x---x-------------------------
  01056  xxxxxxxxxxxxxxxxxxxxxxxxxxxxxxxx
  01088  xxxxxxxxxxxxxxxxxxxxxxxxxxxxxxxx
  01120  xxxxxxxxxxxxxxxxxxxxxxxxxxxxxxxx
  01152  xxxxxxxxxxxxxxxxxxxxxxxxxxxxxxxx
  01184  xxxxxxxxxxxxxxxxxxxxxxxxxxxxxxxx
  01216  xxxxxxxxxxxxxxxxxxxxxxxxxxxxxxxx
  01248  xxxxxxxxxxxxxxxxxxxxxxxxxxxxxxxx
Pin #14   02053   Pol -    02125   Acl x
  01280  x---x-------------------------
  01312  xxxxxxxxxxxxxxxxxxxxxxxxxxxxxxxx
  01344  xxxxxxxxxxxxxxxxxxxxxxxxxxxxxxxx
  01376  xxxxxxxxxxxxxxxxxxxxxxxxxxxxxxxx
  01408  xxxxxxxxxxxxxxxxxxxxxxxxxxxxxxxx
  01440  xxxxxxxxxxxxxxxxxxxxxxxxxxxxxxxx
  01472  xxxxxxxxxxxxxxxxxxxxxxxxxxxxxxxx
  01504  xxxxxxxxxxxxxxxxxxxxxxxxxxxxxxxx
Pin #13   02054   Pol -    02126   Acl x
  01536  -----x-------------------------
  01568  xxxxxxxxxxxxxxxxxxxxxxxxxxxxxxxx
  01600  xxxxxxxxxxxxxxxxxxxxxxxxxxxxxxxx
  01632  xxxxxxxxxxxxxxxxxxxxxxxxxxxxxxxx
  01664  xxxxxxxxxxxxxxxxxxxxxxxxxxxxxxxx
  01696  xxxxxxxxxxxxxxxxxxxxxxxxxxxxxxxx
  01728  xxxxxxxxxxxxxxxxxxxxxxxxxxxxxxxx
  01760  xxxxxxxxxxxxxxxxxxxxxxxxxxxxxxxx
Pin #12   02055   Pol -    02127   Acl x
  01792  -x-------------------------
  01824  xxxxxxxxxxxxxxxxxxxxxxxxxxxxxxxx
  01856  xxxxxxxxxxxxxxxxxxxxxxxxxxxxxxxx
  01888  xxxxxxxxxxxxxxxxxxxxxxxxxxxxxxxx
  01920  xxxxxxxxxxxxxxxxxxxxxxxxxxxxxxxx
  01952  xxxxxxxxxxxxxxxxxxxxxxxxxxxxxxxx
  01984  xxxxxxxxxxxxxxxxxxxxxxxxxxxxxxxx
  02016  xxxxxxxxxxxxxxxxxxxxxxxxxxxxxxxx
  LEGEND     X : fuse not blown
             - : fuse blown
```

Figure 4.9 Fuse plot for pins 12 to 15 of Listing 4.1.

The output of the OR gate in Fig. 4.5 doesn't go directly to the output pin, but rather goes through an Exclusive-OR gate and an inverter, as shown in Fig. 4.10.

The Exclusive-OR gate serves as a programmable inverter (see Exercise 3.3), where if $B = 0$, then $C = A$, while if $B = 1$, then $C = !A$, as shown in Fig. 4.10. If the polarity fuse is closed, indicated by an $\times$, then B will be connected to ground (0) and C will be the same as the output of the OR gate A. But there is an inverter between C and the output pin, so for this case the output pin will be $!A$. This is the case for pin 15 in Fig. 4.9, where the output pin will have the value $!(X \& Y)$.

Note for pins 12 to 14 that the polarity fuse is blown, which means that $C = !A$ in Fig. 4.10 or the output pin is the same as A, the output of the OR gate.

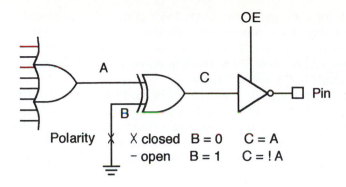

OE

A

C

B

Pin

Polarity   X   X closed   B = 0   C = A
               - open   B = 1   C = ! A

Figure 4.10   Polarity control using an XOR gate on the output pins of the GAL 16V8.

```
Pin #19   02048  Pol x   02120  Ac1 x
 00000  x----x-------------------------
 00032  -x--x-------------------------
 00064  xxxxxxxxxxxxxxxxxxxxxxxxxxxxxxxx
 00096  xxxxxxxxxxxxxxxxxxxxxxxxxxxxxxxx
 00128  xxxxxxxxxxxxxxxxxxxxxxxxxxxxxxxx
 00160  xxxxxxxxxxxxxxxxxxxxxxxxxxxxxxxx
 00192  xxxxxxxxxxxxxxxxxxxxxxxxxxxxxxxx
 00224  xxxxxxxxxxxxxxxxxxxxxxxxxxxxxxxx
Pin #18   02049  Pol -   02121  Ac1 x
 00256  x----x-------------------------
 00288  -x--x-------------------------
 00320  xxxxxxxxxxxxxxxxxxxxxxxxxxxxxxxx
 00352  xxxxxxxxxxxxxxxxxxxxxxxxxxxxxxxx
 00384  xxxxxxxxxxxxxxxxxxxxxxxxxxxxxxxx
 00416  xxxxxxxxxxxxxxxxxxxxxxxxxxxxxxxx
 00448  xxxxxxxxxxxxxxxxxxxxxxxxxxxxxxxx
 00480  xxxxxxxxxxxxxxxxxxxxxxxxxxxxxxxx
Pin #17   02050  Pol x   02122  Ac1 x
 00512  x-----------------------------
 00544  ----x-------------------------
 00576  xxxxxxxxxxxxxxxxxxxxxxxxxxxxxxxx
 00608  xxxxxxxxxxxxxxxxxxxxxxxxxxxxxxxx
 00640  xxxxxxxxxxxxxxxxxxxxxxxxxxxxxxxx
 00672  xxxxxxxxxxxxxxxxxxxxxxxxxxxxxxxx
 00704  xxxxxxxxxxxxxxxxxxxxxxxxxxxxxxxx
 00736  xxxxxxxxxxxxxxxxxxxxxxxxxxxxxxxx
Pin #16   02051  Pol -   02123  Ac1 x
 00768  x-----------------------------
 00800  ----x-------------------------
 00832  xxxxxxxxxxxxxxxxxxxxxxxxxxxxxxxx
 00864  xxxxxxxxxxxxxxxxxxxxxxxxxxxxxxxx
 00896  xxxxxxxxxxxxxxxxxxxxxxxxxxxxxxxx
 00928  xxxxxxxxxxxxxxxxxxxxxxxxxxxxxxxx
 00960  xxxxxxxxxxxxxxxxxxxxxxxxxxxxxxxx
 00992  xxxxxxxxxxxxxxxxxxxxxxxxxxxxxxxx
LEGEND       X : fuse not blown
             - : fuse blown
```

Figure 4.11   Fuse plot for pins 16 to 19 of Listing 4.1.

The output circuitry for each pin in the GAL 16V8 is actually more complicated than that shown in Fig. 4.10. Among other things, each output contains a latch that is able to store a value even if the input changes. We won't be concerned about these details yet, but will study them in detail when we look into latches and sequential circuits in Chapters 7 and 8.

Figure 4.11 shows the fuse maps for pins 16 to 19 in the PLD of Listing 4.1. The OR gate at pin 16 uses two of the PLD AND gates: one inputting X and the other Y. Note that the NOR gate uses these same two fuses but just keeps the output polarity fuse closed to produce $!(X \# Y)$. Do you see how the fuse plots for pins 18 and 19 in Fig. 4.11 produce XOR and XNOR respectively? Note that each of these gates uses two of the PLD AND gates with two inputs to each AND gate. Compare these with the example in Fig. 4.3.

The absolute file (with the extension .ABS) that we generated when we ran CUPL with the $-a$ option is used by the simulator CSIM. This simulator allows

```
CUPL          4.0a  Serial# MD-40A-7985
Device        g16v8s  Library DLIB-h-26-9
Created       Thu Jul 18 13:27:16 1991
Name          Exp2
Partno        OU0001
Revision      04
Date          7/17/91
Designer      R. E. Haskell
Company       Oakland University
Assembly      CSE 171
Location      Rochester, MI
*QP20
*QF2194
*G0
*F0
*L00000 011110111111111111111111111111111
*L00032 101101111111111111111111111111111
*L00256 011110111111111111111111111111111
*L00288 101101111111111111111111111111111
*L00512 011111111111111111111111111111111
*L00544 111101111111111111111111111111111
*L00768 011111111111111111111111111111111
*L00800 111101111111111111111111111111111
*L01024 011101111111111111111111111111111
*L01280 011101111111111111111111111111111
*L01536 111110111111111111111111111111111
*L01792 101111111111111111111111111111111
*L02048 010101111000110000001100000001100
*L02080 000011001010101011100100000000000
*L02112 000000000000000001111111111111111
*L02144 111111111111111111111111111111111
*L02176 11111111111111110
*C394C
* DB34
```

Figure 4.12 The JEDEC file for Listing 4.1.

you to test the design with some test vectors before programming the PLD. We will show you how to do this in Experiment 3 in Chapter 5. We will test Listing 4.1 in a real circuit in Experiment 2 in this chapter. First, we will take a look at the JEDEC file, *exp2.jed*, that we produced when we ran CUPL.

JEDEC file, exp2.jed.   In addition to the documentation file *exp2.doc*, CUPL produces a JEDEC (Joint Electronic Device Engineering Council) file, *exp2.jed*, for downloading the fuse data to a PLD programming device. This file contains an industry-standard fuse map format that can be understood by programming devices built by many different manufacturers.

The contents of this file for Listing 4.1 are shown in Fig. 4.12. The first part of this file (up to the first asterisk, *, character) contains some comments taken from the header information in our source file, *exp2.pld*. The line *QP20 means there are 20 pins for the chip, and the line *QF2194 means there are a total of 2,194 programmable fuses in the device. The actual fuse data start in the lines beginning with an "L" (fuse link field). In these data a 0 corresponds to a fuse left intact (the ×'s in Figs. 4.9 and 4.11), while a 1 corresponds to a blown fuse (the −'s in Figs. 4.9 and 4.11). You should be able to recognize the various gates in our program by comparing the first 12 rows in Fig. 4.12 with the fuse maps in Figs. 4.9 and 4.11. The number at the beginning of each row (following the "L") in Fig. 4.12 is an offset number indicating where in the chip the fuses in that row are located. All fuses in the chip not specifically identified are left intact. The hex number 394C following the C in the next to last line is a fuse checksum used for error checking. The hex number DB34 in the last line is a transmission checksum.

Now that you have compiled Listing 4.1 and produced a JEDEC file, you are ready to actually program the chip and test it in a real circuit.

Experiment 2: Basic Gates

1. Type in Listing 4.1 and compile it using CUPL as described in this chapter.
2. Program the GAL 16V8. This step will vary depending on your particular PLD programmer. Typically, you will insert the chip in a chip carrier socket and run some software on a PC that is connected to the PLD programming device. The software will download your file *exp2.jed* to the programming device and program the chip in a matter of a few seconds. You don't have to worry about the chip being erased. The programming process automatically erases the chip electrically before it programs it.
3. Connect the two outputs *Out0* and *Out1* from the PC logic analyzer to the two inputs *X* and *Y* on pins 2 and 3 of your PLD. Connect pins 12 to 15 of your PLD chip to the four inputs *In4* to *In1*, respectively. Run the logic analyzer program and press function key *F1* to produce the truth table for

these four gates (the two inverters, AND and NAND). Verify the results and print out the truth table by pressing *Shift-PrtScn*.

4. Connect pins 16 to 19 of your PLD chip to the four inputs *In4* to *In1*, respectively. Run the logic analyzer program and press function key *F1* to produce the truth table for these four gates (OR, NOR, XOR, and XNOR). Verify the results and print out the truth table by pressing *shift-PrtScn*.

EXERCISES

4.1. Indicate which ✕'s remain if the circuit in Fig. 4.2 is programmed to produce:

   a. $Z = !X$
   b. $Z = !Y$
   c. $Z = X \& Y$
   d. $Z = X \# Y$
   e. $Z = !(X \& Y)$
   f. $Z = !(X \# Y)$
   g. $Z = !(X \$ Y)$

4.2. Modify the source file *exp2.pld* so that

the input pins are pins 3 and 4. Compile the program using CUPL and note how the fuse map in the *.DOC* file is modified. Explain.

4.3. Modify Listing 4.1 so as to compute *xnor* using the logic equation

$$xnor = !X \& !Y \# X \& Y$$

Compile the program using CUPL and compare the fuse map for pin 19 with that shown in Fig. 4.11.

5

Boolean Algebra and Logic Equations

George Boole (1815–1864) was a self-taught English logician and mathematician who never went to college. In 1847, he published *The Mathematical Analysis of Logic—Being an Essay Towards a Calculus of Deductive Reasoning*, and in 1854 he published *An Investigation of the Laws of Thought*. These works, in which he developed an algebra of logic (now called Boolean algebra), established the relationship between mathematics and logic.

The English philosopher and mathematician Bertrand Russell (1872–1970) and Alfred North Whitehead (1862–1947) published the first of their three-volume *Principia Mathematica* in 1910. This transformed Boolean algebra into a powerful system of *symbolic logic*. In probably the most influential master's thesis ever published, Claude E. Shannon, while a student at MIT in 1938, showed that Boolean algebra, the calculus of symbolic logic, could be applied to relay circuits. He called this switching algebra and showed how these logic equations could allow you to construct circuits to do such things as add and subtract binary numbers.[1] In this book we will use the terms Boolean algebra and switching algebra interchangeably.

In this chapter you will learn:

- The basic theorems of switching algebra
- How to verify these theorems using a truth table

---

[1] Claude E. Shannon, "A Symbolic Analysis of Relay and Switching Circuits," *Trans. AIEE*, Vol. 57, pp. 713–723, 1938. After earning a Ph.D. at MIT, Shannon joined Bell Laboratories in 1941 where he became the father of modern-day information theory.

- How to verify these theorems using Venn diagrams
- How to use Boolean algebra to reduce the complexity of a logic equation
- How to use Karnaugh maps to reduce the number of terms in a logic equation
- The techniques used by computers to minimize the number of terms in a logic equation.

5.1 SWITCHING ALGEBRA THEOREMS

We have already become familiar with some logic equations in Chapter 3 and have even proved certain simple theorems related to logic equations. In this section we will study the important Boolean algebra, or switching algebra, theorems that will be useful to us in our design of digital circuits.

One-variable Theorems

Table 5.1 shows a list of switching algebra theorems involving a single logical variable. Some of these we have already seen in Chapter 3, and the others you should have proved in the exercises in Chapter 3. All these expressions are easily verified by showing that each expression holds for values of $X = 0$ and $X = 1$.

TABLE 5.1   ONE-VARIABLE SWITCHING ALGEBRA THEOREMS

	OR version	AND version	See
Identities	X # 0 = X	X & 1 = X	Exercise 3.12, Fig. 3.18
	X # 1 = 1	X & 0 = 0	
Complements	X # !X = 1	X & !X = 0	Exercise 3.11, Fig. 3.17
Indempotence	X # X = X	X & X = X	Exercise 3.13
Involution	!!X = X		Eq. (3.3)

We have already seen in Chapter 3 how some of these theorems are useful in understanding the operation of a PLD. For example, Fig. 5.1 shows the basic PLD structure discussed in Chapter 4 with all fuses intact. The theorem $X \& !X = 0$ tells us that, when any of these input pairs to a PLD AND gate are both connected (left intact), the output of that AND gate will be zero regardless of any other connection to that AND gate. This will be so because of the theorem $X \& 0 = 0$. When the output of such an AND gate is zero, it makes no contribution to the output of the following OR gate because of the theorem $X \# 0 = X$.

Note also that, if all the fuses in a single row in Fig. 5.1 are blown, all inputs to the AND gate will float high, and the output of the AND gate will be 1. Because of the theorem $X \# 1 = 1$, the output of the OR gate will then be 1, regardless of the fuses in any other row. We saw in Chapter 4 that, in general, all the fuses are left intact, except for the particular row, or rows, of interest. And in these

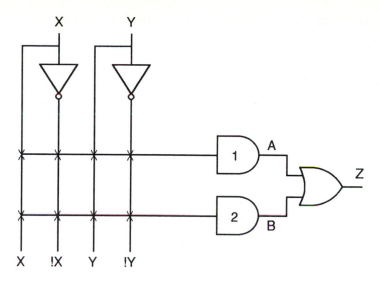

Figure 5.1   Basic PLD structure with all fuses intact.

rows all the fuses are blown except for the particular input values of interest (see the fuse maps in Figs. 4.9 and 4.11).

Principle of duality.   In Table 5.1, note that the theorems in the AND-version column differ from the theorems in the OR-version column in that the # has been replaced with a &, all 0's become 1's, and all 1's become 0's. This is a general *principle of duality*, which holds for any Boolean theorem or identity. It states that any such theorem or identity will remain true if all # and & symbols are interchanged and all 0's and 1's are interchanged. We will see this principle of duality in the two- and three-variable theorems we will look at next.

Two- and Three-variable Theorems

Table 5.2 shows a list of two- and three-variable switching algebra theorems. They are divided into five groups and we will look at each group separately. Note in each group that the (b) version is just the dual of the (a) version.

Commutative laws.   The commutative laws, (1a) and (1b) in Table 5.2, should be obvious. They are true because the output values Z in the two middle rows of the truth tables in Figs. 3.2 and 3.3 are the same. That is, the same value of Z occurs regardless of the order of X and Y.

Associative laws.   The associative laws, (2a) and (2b) in Table 5.2, state that for three (or more) input variables the order in which an OR or AND operation of all variables is carried out is immaterial. We can always prove any of these

TABLE 5.2   TWO- AND THREE-VARIABLE SWITCHING ALGEBRA THEOREMS

Commutative laws	(1a)	X # Y = Y # X
	(1b)	X & Y = Y & X
Associative laws	(2a)	X # (Y # Z) = (X # Y) # Z
	(2b)	X & (Y & Z) = (X & Y) & Z
Distributive laws	(3a)	X # (Y & Z) = (X # Y) & (X # Z)
	(3b)	X & (Y # Z) = (X & Y) # (X & Z)
Unity	(4a)	(X & Y) # (!X & Y) = Y
	(4b)	(X # Y) & (!X # Y) = Y
Absorption	(5a)	X # (X & Y) = X
	(5b)	X & (X # Y) = X
	(6a)	X # (!X & Y) = X # Y
	(6b)	X & (!X # Y) = X & Y

theorems by making a truth table and showing that the law holds for all possibilities. This is shown for the associative law, (2a), in Fig. 5.2. A useful graphical technique, called *Venn diagrams*, can be used to verify this and the other theorems in Table 5.2.

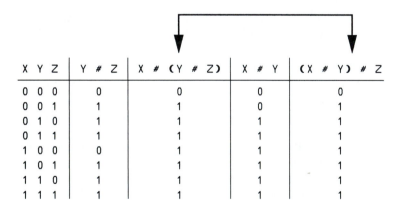

X Y Z	Y # Z	X # (Y # Z)	X # Y	(X # Y) # Z
0 0 0	0	0	0	0
0 0 1	1	1	0	1
0 1 0	1	1	1	1
0 1 1	1	1	1	1
1 0 0	0	1	1	1
1 0 1	1	1	1	1
1 1 0	1	1	1	1
1 1 1	1	1	1	1

Figure 5.2   Truth table for the associative law X # (Y # Z) = (X # Y) # Z.

Venn diagrams.   A *Venn diagram* is a graphical representation of a logical variable or Boolean function. The Venn diagram in Fig. 5.3a represents the logical variable X as a circle within a unit square. The area inside the circle is thought of as representing a *true* value of X; that is, $X = 1$. The area outside the circle represents values of $X = 0$ or $!X$.

If we have two variables, X and Y, then each is represented by a circle. The area inside X will represent true values of X, and the area inside Y will represent true values of Y. The area that is outside X but inside Y represents the Boolean function $!X$ & Y, as shown by the shaded area in Fig. 5.3b.

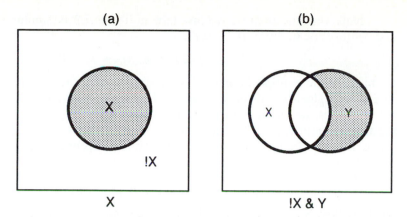

Figure 5.3   Venn diagram for logical variable X and Boolean function !X & Y.

The three logical variables X, Y, and Z would each have their own circles. The Venn diagrams for the Boolean functions $(X \& Y)$, $(X \& Z)$, $(Y \& Z)$, and $(X \& Y \& Z)$ are shown in Fig. 5.4. Note in each case that the shaded area represents that part of the diagrams in which the *true* values of the variables overlap. This means that *both* (or *all*) variables must be *true* for the AND operation to be true.

The validity of the associative law (2b) in Table 5.2 should be apparent from the Venn diagrams in Fig. 5.4. If you AND the $(Y \& Z)$ area in Figure 5.4c with X, you will get the same area (shown in Fig. 5.4d) that you get if you AND the $(X \& Y)$ area in Fig. 5.4a with Z.

The OR operation Venn diagrams are shown in Fig. 5.5. Note in this case that the shaded area covers all logical variables because the OR operation is true if either or both variables are true. The associative law (2a) in Table 5.2 that we proved with the truth table in Fig. 5.2 can also be seen from the Venn diagrams in Fig. 5.5. It doesn't matter whether we add (OR) X to $(Y \# Z)$ in Fig. 5.5c or if we add Z to $(X \# Y)$ in Fig. 5.5a. We will always get the total shaded area shown in Fig. 5.5d.

Distributive laws.   The distributive laws (3a) and (3b) in Table 5.2 can also be verified using Venn diagrams. Figure 5.6a shows that if we OR X with $(Y \& Z)$ from Fig. 5.4c we get the same shaded area as if we ANDed (found the common overlap of) $(X \# Y)$ from Fig. 5.5a with $(X \# Z)$ from Fig. 5.5b.

Similarly, the shaded area shown in Fig. 5.6b can be achieved by ANDing X with $(Y \# Z)$ from Fig. 5.5c. It can also be obtained by ORing (adding together) the areas $(X \& Y)$ from Fig. 5.4a and $(X \& Z)$ from Fig. 5.4b. This verifies the distributive law (3b) in Table 5.2.

Note that the distributive law (3b) in Table 5.2 is similar to the familiar distributive law in ordinary algebra:

$$X \cdot (Y + Z) = X \cdot Y + X \cdot Z$$

In this case the multiplication of X is distributed over the various addition terms. In Boolean algebra, not only is the AND (logical multiplication) operation distributed over the various OR (logical addition) terms as in (3b) of Table 5.2, but the OR operation also gets distributed over the various AND terms as in (3a) of Table 5.2. The analogous expression in ordinary algebra clearly is NOT true.

Unity.   The unity theorem (4a) in Table 5.2 can be verified in a number of ways. Note that if we add (OR) the shaded area of (X & Y) in Fig. 5.4a to the shaded area ($!X$ & Y) in Fig. 5.3b we just get Y.

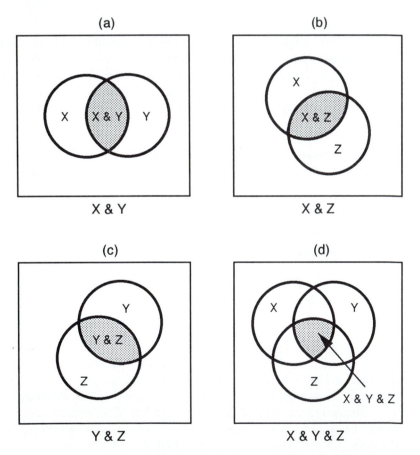

Figure 5.4   Venn diagrams for AND operations.

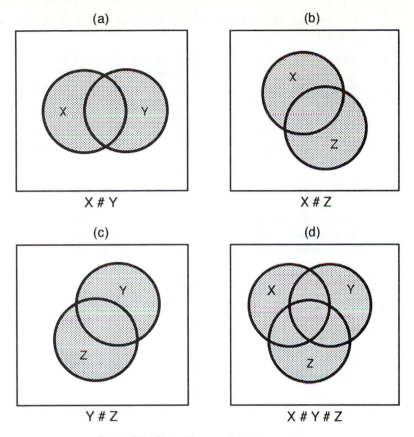

(a)

X # Y

(b)

X # Z

(c)

Y # Z

(d)

X # Y # Z

Figure 5.5   Venn diagrams for OR operations.

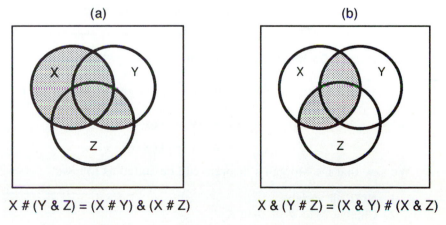

(a)

X # (Y & Z) = (X # Y) & (X # Z)

(b)

X & (Y # Z) = (X & Y) # (X & Z)

Figure 5.6   Venn diagrams illustrating distributive laws.

We can also derive (4a) in Table 5.2 from the theorems we already know. We can write

```
( X  &  Y )  #  ( !X  &  Y )  =  ( Y  &  X )  #  ( Y  &  !X )      Table 5.2 (1b)
                             =  Y  &  ( X  #  !X )               Table 5.2 (3b)
                             =  Y  &  1                          Table 5.1
                             =  Y                               Table 5.1
```

Similarly, for theorem (4b) in Table 5.2 we can write

```
( X  #  Y )  &  ( !X  #  Y )  =  ( Y  #  X )  &  ( Y  #  !X )      Table 5.2 (1b)
                             =  Y  #  ( X  &  !X )               Table 5.2 (3a)
                             =  Y  #  0                          Table 5.1
                             =  Y                               Table 5.1
```

Can you see how this last theorem can be verified using Venn diagrams? These unity theorems are sometimes called *combining* theorems.

The form of this unity theorem given in (4a) of Table 5.2 is particularly useful in reducing the number of terms in a logic equation. If you find product terms in a sum of products expression that differ only by one variable and its complement, you can "factor out" the common part, and the logical sum (#) of the variable and its complement will be 1. We will use this fact in Section 5.2 to reduce Boolean functions using a graphical method known as Karnaugh maps.

Absorption.   Two forms of the absorption theorem are shown in Table 5.2. In (5a,b) the Y gets absorbed, while in (6a,b) the $!X$ gets absorbed. The forms (5a,b) are sometimes called the *covering* theorem, where X is said to *cover* Y.

It is easy to see that, if you add the shaded area (X & Y) in Fig. 5.4a to X in Fig. 5.3a, you just get X. Similarly, if you AND X with (X # Y) in Fig. 5.5a, you still just get X.

If you add the shaded areas in Fig. 5.3a (X) and Fig. 5.3b ($!X$ & Y), you get the area (X # Y) in Fig. 5.5a, thus verifying the absorption theorem (6a) in Table 5.2. Can you see how Venn diagrams can be used to verify theorem (6b) in Table 5.2?

Generalized De Morgan's Theorem

In Chapter 3 we proved the following forms of the important De Morgan's theorem:

$$!X \# !Y = !(X \& Y)$$

$$!X \& !Y = !(X \# Y)$$

We saw that De Morgan's theorem can be stated as follows:

1. NOT all variables.
2. Change & to # or # to &.
3. NOT the result.

This result holds for any Boolean function, not just the forms shown above. For example, the Boolean function

$$F = X \& Y \# X \& Z \# Y \& Z \qquad (5.1)$$

is equivalent to the function

$$F = !((!X \# !Y) \& (!X \# !Z) \& (!Y \# !Z)) \qquad (5.2)$$

which is also equivalent to

$$F = !(!(X \& Y) \& !(X \& Z) \& !(Y \& Z)) \qquad (5.3)$$

This form of F is written entirely in terms of NAND functions and can be implemented by the circuit diagram in Fig. 5.7.

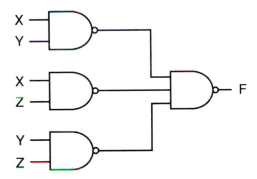

Figure 5.7   Implementation of the function F = !(!(X & Y) & !(X & Z) & !(Y & Z)) using NAND gates.

In Fig. 3.7, we saw that a NAND gate can be written as an OR symbol with active low (bubble) inputs. Thus, the circuit in Fig. 5.7 can be redrawn as the equivalent circuit in Fig. 5.8.

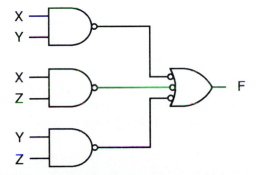

Figure 5.8   Circuit equivalent to that in Fig. 5.7 in terms of NAND gates.

Remember that a bubble on a gate is equivalent to putting an inverter there. If an output bubble is connected to an input bubble, then both bubbles can be removed because this is just like going through two inverters (*!!X* = *X*). Thus,

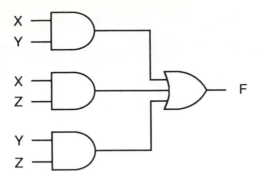

Figure 5.9 You can add or remove bubbles that are connected without changing the function of a logic circuit.

we could redraw Fig. 5.8 as shown in Fig. 5.9, which is just the logic circuit implementation of Eq. (5.1)!

5.2 KARNAUGH MAPS

In the last section we saw how switching algebra theorems can be used to reduce the number of product terms in a Boolean function. This will reduce the number of logic elements needed to realize the circuit. In a PLD it is important to reduce the number of product terms so that the Boolean functions will "fit" into the PLD. For example, the GAL 16V8 that we used in Chapter 4 has eight AND gates feeding the OR gate associated with each output pin. This means that we can't program into this PLD a Boolean function that has more than eight product terms. If we have a Boolean function represented by a truth table with many input variables, then every 1 in the output column will represent a product term in the sum of products representation. If there are more than eight of these product terms, we will have to reduce the number to fit it into the GAL 16V8. (As we will see later in this chapter, the computer will reduce the number of product terms for us, but we need to know how to do it ourselves.)

A simple graphical method will allow you to reduce the number of terms in a Boolean function that contains two, three, or four logical variables. The technique uses what are called *Karnaugh maps*, or *K-maps*. For more than four logical variables, the use of K-maps becomes cumbersome and impossible for a large number of variables. Various computer-based tabular methods can be used in these cases. We will look at these computer-based minimization methods in Section 5.3. In this section we will see how to use K-maps.

Two-variable K-maps

Consider the truth table from Exercise 3.8, which is shown in Fig. 5.10a. If you did that exercise, you found that the sum of products representation of the output function F is

$$F = !X \ \& \ !Y \ \# \ X \ \& \ !Y \ \# \ X \ \& \ Y \qquad (5.4)$$

Minterm	X	Y	F
m0	0	0	1
m1	0	1	0
m2	1	0	1
m3	1	1	1

(a)   (b)   (c)

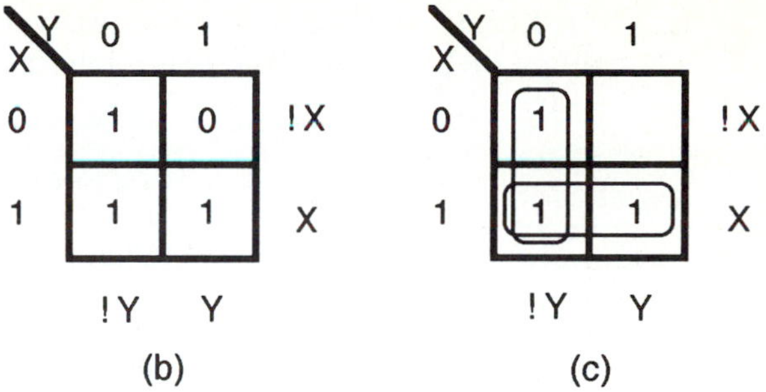

Figure 5.10   A two-variable Karnaugh map.

This equation can be written in the following *sum of minterms* notation:

$$F(X,Y) = m0 \# m2 \# m3 \tag{5.5}$$
$$= \sum(0,2,3)$$

From our switching algebra theorems, we can reduce this as follows:

```
F = !X & !Y # X & !Y # X & Y
  = (!X # X) & !Y # X & Y        distributive, Table 5.2 (3b)
  = !Y # X & Y                   complement, Table 5.1
  = !Y # X                       absorption, Table 5.2(6a)
```

Note that this is just the product of sums solution from Exercise 3.8.

   This result is easily obtained by inspection of a two-variable K-map. A K-map is an alternate representation of a truth table in the form of a box of 2×2 squares as shown in Fig. 5.10. The possible values of X (0, 1) are used as labels for the rows and the possible values of Y (0, 1) are used as labels for the columns. Thus, each square represents one of the minterms shown in the truth table in Fig. 5.10a. The logical values of the output function F are inserted in the appropriate minterm square as shown in Fig. 5.10b. Note that exactly the same information is contained in Figs. 5.10a and b.

   We will refer to the upper-left square as the minterm $m0$ square, or the 00 square. Similarly, the upper-right square is the minterm $m1$, or 01, square; the lower left is the minterm $m2$, or 10, square; and the lower-right square is the minterm $m3$, or 11, square.

   In a K-map, we normally only show the 1's of the output function and leave the squares containing a zero blank, as shown in Fig. 5.10c. Now note that if a 1 occurs in two adjacent squares then two minterms in the sum of products expression will have a variable and its complement in these two terms. We will then be able to eliminate this variable, as we have seen above.

For example, consider the two vertical 1's that we have circled in the left column of Fig. 5.10c. The two minterms associated with these 1's are

```
m0 # m2 = !X & !Y # X & !Y

        = (!X # X) & !Y

        = 1 & !Y

        = !Y
```

Therefore, these circled 1's contribute the value *!Y* to the output *F*. This is easy to see from Fig. 5.10c. Anytime the circled 1's cover both the 0 and 1 of a variable, that variable can be eliminated. In this case the circled 1's cover both *!X* and *X* and therefore *X* can be eliminated. This leaves only *!Y* because the circled 1's are in the 0 column of *Y*. Note that we have labeled this column *!Y* at the bottom of the map.

Another set of circled 1's is shown on the bottom row of the map in Fig. 5.10c. Note that this circled set covers both *Y* and *!Y*, so *Y* can be eliminated. Since it is in the 1 row of *X*, this just leaves *X*. Therefore, the Boolean function *F* can be written as

```
F = !Y # X
```

as we found above.

The rule for using a two-variable K-map is to circle all adjacent 1's and then read the result as described above. Note that the circled set of 1's can overlap. If the 1's are not adjacent, for example, if you have only minterms *m0* and *m3*, then you circle each individual 1 and no reduction is possible.

The original sum of products solution for *F* was

```
F = !X & !Y # X & !Y # X & Y
```

and includes three product terms. Therefore, this Boolean function would not fit into our two-AND gate PLD structure shown in Fig. 5.1. However, by reducing it to *!Y # X*, it fits in easily.

What would CUPL do if you programmed in this output function *F*? Try it. If you make a source file called *test.pld* and type

```
cupl -fax test
```

you will find, by looking at the *test.doc* file, that the logic equation has been reduced to

```
F = !Y # X & Y
```

This is the first intermediate result we obtained above when we reduced the equation using our switching algebra theorems. However, it is not reduced as much as possible, as we showed with the K-map. The reason is that CUPL uses a quick minimization algorithm as a default. This executes faster than three other minimization algorithms that CUPL can use. You can tell CUPL to use a better algorithm by including *m2*, *m3*, or *m4* in the option list when you run CUPL. For example, if you type

```
cupl -faxm2 test
```

CUPL will use the Quine–McCluskey algorithm, which will find the minimum form

$$F = X \# !Y$$

We will look at these computer minimization methods in Section 5.3.

Three-variable K-maps

K-maps are most useful for problems containing three or four logical variables. The basic ideas described for the two-variable case still apply. For three variables, X, Y, and Z, we draw the K-map as shown in Fig. 5.11. This map has two rows

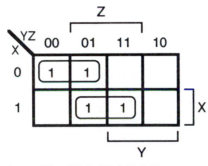

$$F = !X \& !Y \# X \& Z$$

Figure 5.11   A three-variable K-map.

and four columns, which gives us eight squares corresponding to the eight min-terms of a three-variable function. The rows correspond to the X values of 0 and 1, just as in the two-variable case. But now we need to include both variables Y and Z in the column labels. Each column is labeled with two binary values. The first is the Y value and the second is the Z value. We must include all four pos-sibilities (00 01 10 11). But note that we do *not* write them in this order. Rather we switch the order of the last two and order them (00 01 11 10). The reason we do this is that we must change only one variable at a time (from 1 to 0 or from 0 to 1) in moving from one column to the next. Note that when we do this the two middle columns correspond to $Z = 1$ *(true)*, while the last two columns correspond to $Y = 1$ *(true)*.

We circle adjacent 1's just as we did in the two-variable case to eliminate variables. For example, the function shown in Fig. 5.11 is given by the four sum of products terms

$$F = !X \& !Y \& !Z \# !X \& !Y \& Z$$

$$\# X \& !Y \& Z \# X \& Y \& Z$$

We can reduce this to two terms by circling the two adjacent sets of 1's, as shown in Fig. 5.11. The top pair will eliminate the Z because it covers both a 0 and 1 of the Z. What's left is a 0 for the X and a 0 for the Y, and therefore the remaining term is $!X \& !Y$. Similarly, the bottom pair of 1's covers a 0 and 1 of the Y and a 1 for the Z and X. Thus, the remaining term is $X \& Z$. The function F can then be reduced to

$$F = !X \& !Y \# X \& Z$$

You should always circle as many 1's at a time as possible as long as the number is a power of 2 (for example, 2, 4, or 8). For example, in Fig. 5.12 you would circle all four 1's in the bottom row. This will eliminate both Z and Y and leave only X. The other circled pair eliminates X, leaving $Y \& !Z$. This function is therefore written in reduced form as $F = X \# Y \& !Z$.

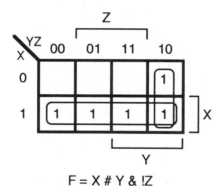

F = X # Y & !Z

Figure 5.12 The circled sets should be as large as possible.

If four 1's occur in a large square, rather than a row, you circle the large square as shown in Fig. 5.13. This large circled square will eliminate both X and Y, leaving only Z. The circled pair in the upper left eliminates Z, leaving $!X \& !Y$, while the circled pair in the lower right eliminates Z, leaving $X \& Y$. Thus, the reduced function is

$$F = Z \# !X \& !Y \# X \& Y$$

You can think of the rightmost column as wrapping around to be connected to the leftmost column. Therefore, a 1 in the leftmost column is adjacent to a 1 in the same row of the rightmost column. These should be circled as shown in Fig. 5.14. This circled pair will eliminate Y, leaving $!X \& !Z$. The lower circled pair in Fig. 5.14 contributes $X \& Z$ to the function, whose reduced form is then

$$F = !X \& !Z \# X \& Z$$

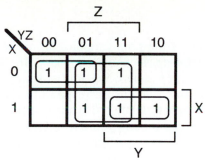

F = !X & !Y # Z # X & Y

Figure 5.13 Four 1's in a square pattern should be circled.

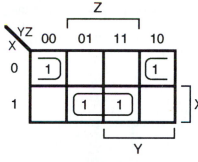

F = !X & !Z # X & Z

Figure 5.14 The leftmost column is adjacent to the rightmost column.

As a final example, note in Figure 5.15 that you should circle as many groups of 1's at a time as you can (without including any zeros), even when they overlap other groups. In this case the reduced form of the function

$$F = !Z \# Y$$

has only two terms, each containing a single variable.

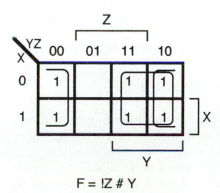

F = !Z # Y

Figure 5.15 Make the circled sets of 1's as large as possible.

Four-variable K-maps

A Boolean function made up of the four variables W, X, Y, and Z can be represented by a four-variable K-map, as shown in Fig. 5.16. This is a natural extension of the three-variable case, where the four rows correspond to the two variables W and X, and the four columns correspond to the variables Y and Z. Note that the order of the row labels (00 01 11 10) must be the same as the columns so that only one variable changes state in going from one row to the next. Again the rightmost column is adjacent to the leftmost column, and the top row is adjacent to the bottom row. You can therefore connect 1's at opposite ends of the map within the same circled set.

Figure 5.16 shows how each of the four circled sets contributes to the reduced function

$$F = !W \& Y \& !Z \# !W \& X \# X \& Y \# W \& !Y \& Z$$

Note that the original sum of products function would have contained *nine* product terms (one for each 1 in the map).

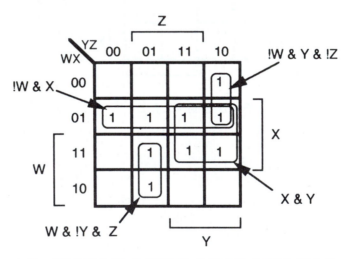

$$F = !W \& Y \& !Z \# !W \& X \# X \& Y \# W \& !Y \& Z$$

Figure 5.16   Example of a four-variable K-map.

5.3 COMPUTER MINIMIZATION TECHNIQUES

We have seen that using Karnaugh maps can make it easy to find the minimum number of product terms in a Boolean function containing no more than four logical variables. However, many real problems will have many more than four logical variables and K-maps won't help us here. Computer programs are used to simplify Boolean functions containing large numbers of variables. These computer methods use techniques based on a tabulation method. These methods are not easy for humans to do, but they can be automated for machine computation. Understanding how these methods work provides additional insight into simplifying Boolean functions.

The method we will look at is called the *Quine–McCluskey* method and is implemented in CUPL as option *m2*. Additional methods are provided in CUPL (options *m3* and *m4*) that are more efficient (execute faster than Quine–McCluskey) but may not be guaranteed to produce the optimum simplification.

Tabular Representations

Any product term in a sum of products representation of a Boolean function is called an *implicant*, because it implies that the function will have the value 1 if any product term is 1. For example, in the function

$$F = \quad X \ \& \ !Y \ \& \ Z$$
$$\# \ !X \ \& \ !Z$$
$$\# \ !X \ \& \ Y$$

all three product terms, X & $!Y$ & Z, $!X$ & $!Z$, and $!X$ & Y, are implicants. In this case the first product term is the minterm *m5*. If we write the minterm number 5 as a binary number 101, these three binary digits correspond to values of the three variables XYZ, where a 1 in the binary number means a true value of the variable and a 0 means a false value (or a true value of the complement !). Thus, 101 is an alternate way of writing X & $!Y$ & Z.

What if some variable is missing from a product term? We then insert a dash (-) in its position in the corresponding binary number. For example, $!X$ & $!Z$ would be represented as 0-0 and $!X$ & Y would be represented as 01-. We will call these *tabular representations* or the *tabular form* of each product term.

As another example, the K-map from Fig. 5.16 is redrawn in Fig. 5.17, where the tabular representations of each product term associated with the four circled sets of 1's are shown under each product term. Note from this figure that it is easy to write the tabular form for each circled set directly from the labels on the K-map. The first two digits of the tabular form are from the row labels and the last two digits are from the column labels. If the circled set covers both a 0 and a 1 of a particular bit location, that bit location becomes a dash (-). For example, in Fig. 5.17 the tabular form 0-10 ($!W$ & Y & $!Z$) is found from the circled set in the upper right of the map as follows: (1) the first two digits are 0- because the set covers 00 and 01 of the row labels, and thus X is a don't care; (2) the last two digits of the tabular form are 10 because this is the label of the last column. Study Fig. 5.17 until you see how the other tabular forms are produced.

If we produce a product term by expanding the size of the circled set of 1's in a K-map as much as possible, that is, expanding it any more would cover a 0 in the map, then the resulting product term, or implicant, is called a *prime im-*

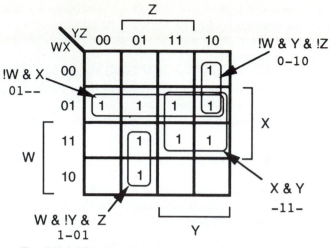

$$F = !W \& Y \& !Z \# !W \& X \# X \& Y \# W \& !Y \& Z$$

Figure 5.17 Tabular forms associated with each product term.

plicant. Such a prime implicant cannot have any of its variables removed from the product term and still imply the logic function. We will now look at a method by which a computer can find these prime implicants.

Prime Implicants

Consider the example shown in Fig. 5.18, which is the same example we looked at in Fig. 5.12. We have included the corresponding truth table in which we have labeled each of the eight minterms by their minterm number 0 to 7. There are two prime implicants for this function, X and $Y \& !Z$, whose tabular represen-

Minterm	X Y Z	F
0	0 0 0	0
1	0 0 1	0
2	0 1 0	1
3	0 1 1	0
4	1 0 0	1
5	1 0 1	1
6	1 1 0	1
7	1 1 1	1

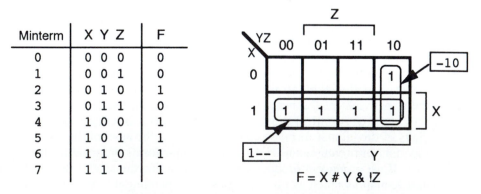

$$F = X \# Y \& !Z$$

Figure 5.18 Example for finding prime implicants.

tations 1-- and -10 are shown in the figure. The following tabulation method will find these prime implicants.

We begin by listing all the minterms in the function (associated with each 1 in the map or each 1 in the F column in the truth table) as shown in the step 1 column of Table 5.3. We list these minterms by their decimal number and by the corresponding binary number or tabular form. We also list these minterms in increasing order of the number of 1's in the tabular, or binary, form, and we have drawn a line between those minterms with one 1, two 1's, and three 1's.

TABLE 5.3   STEPS IN FINDING PRIME IMPLICANTS FOR THE EXAMPLE IN FIGURE 5.18

Step 1	Step 2	Step 3
2 010 √	(2,6) -10	(4,5,6,7) 1--
4 100 √	(4,5) 10- √	(4,6,5,7) 1--
5 101 √	(4,6) 1-0 √	
6 110 √	(5,7) 1-1 √	
7 111 √	(6,7) 11- √	

The next step is to compare each minterm in column 1 of Table 5.3 with the other minterms in this same column to find pairs that differ by only a single binary digit. Because of our ordering of the minterms, we only need to compare minterms in adjacent regions (separated by the lines). For example, minterm 2 and 6 differ only in the first digit. We therefore replace this first digit with a - and enter the new tabular form -10 in the next column labeled step 2. We also place a check mark, √, next to minterm 2 and 6 in column 1 to indicate that we have used these minterms. In the step 2 column, we also include the two minterms (2,6) that contributed to this first entry in column 2.

We continue this process until we have compared all minterms in the first column of Table 5.3. This will lead to the tabular form entries shown in the middle column. Note that we have drawn another line between those new entries with a single 1 and those with two 1's. Also note that all the minterms in the first column are checked, meaning that they all contributed to one or more of the entries in the second column.

We now repeat the process in going from the second column to the third column. In this case we compare each entry above the line in the second column with the entries below the line. We are looking for two entries that differ by only a single digit and whose dashes line up. We see that the (4,5) entry 10- can be combined with the (6,7) entry 11- to produce the first entry (4,5,6,7) 1-- in the last column. Again we replace the two differing digits with another dash. We also see that the (4,6) entry 1-0 combines with the (5,7) entry 1-1 to produce the second entry (4,6,5,7) 1-- in the step 3 column. Note that we have checked the entries in column 2 that took part in the creation of column 3.

Now all the unchecked entries in Table 5.3 are *prime implicants*. Note that there are two: -10 from column 2 and 1-- from column 3. (This last form occurs twice in column 3, but it is only the one prime implicant 1--). These are the two prime implicants shown in Fig. 5.18, which we set out to find.

In this example, all the prime implicants that we found were used to produce the minimum term function shown in Fig. 5.18. This isn't always the case. Sometimes there are redundant prime implicants that are not needed to cover all the minterms in the function. We will next look at an example in which we will not need to use all the prime implicants to produce the minimum term function.

Essential Prime Implicants

Consider the Boolean function represented by the K-map in Fig. 5.19. Before proceeding you should try to write an expression for this function containing the minimum number of product terms by circling the 1's in the best way. We will now go through the *Quine-McCluskey method* for simplifying this function.

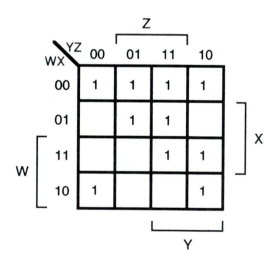

Figure 5.19 Example function for finding essential prime implicants.

The first step is to find all the prime implicants using the same technique we used in Table 5.3. These steps are shown in Table 5.4. Note that there are six prime implicants in this example given by all the unique unchecked entries in Table 5.4. These six prime implicants are listed in the first column of Table 5.5. The second column of Table 5.5 lists all the minterms that were covered by each prime implicant. These are just the minterm numbers adjacent to each prime implicant in Table 5.4.

The remaining columns in Table 5.5 represent each minterm in the original function. We place an × under each minterm in the row of the prime implicant that covers that minterm. Note that many minterms are covered by more than one prime implicant. This means that any of these prime implicants can be used

TABLE 5.4   STEPS IN FINDING PRIME IMPLICANTS FOR THE EXAMPLE IN FIGURE 5.19

Step 1	Step 2	Step 3
0 0000 √	(0,1) 000- √	(0,1,2,3) 00--
1 0001 √	(0,2) 00-0 √	(0,2,1,3) 00--
2 0010 √	(0,8) -000 √	(0,2,8,10) -0-0
8 1000 √	(1,3) 00-1 √	(0,8,2,10) -0-0
3 0011 √	(1,5) 0-01 √	(1,5,3,7) 0--1
5 0101 √	(2,3) 001- √	(1,3,5,7) 0--1
10 1010 √	(2,10) -010 √	
7 0111 √	(8,10) 10-0 √	
14 1110 √	(3,7) 0-11 √	
15 1111 √	(5,7) 01-1 √	
	(10,14) 1-10	
	(7,15) -111	
	(14,15) 111-	

in the final expression of the function to cover that particular minterm. Only if a minterm has a single × in its column will that particular prime implicant be required as part of the final function. We call such a prime implicant an *essential prime implicant*. Note from Table 5.5 that there are only two minterms, 5 and 8, that have a single × in their column. These ×'s correspond to the two prime implicants 0--1 and -0-0, which we have checked in Table 5.5 to indicate that they are *essential prime implicants*.

We therefore know that we need at least these two essential prime implicants in our final function. How many of the other minterms will these two essential prime implicants cover? We can see this by placing a check mark in Table 5.5 under each column of ×'s in which at least one of the ×'s is in the row of one of the two essential prime implicants. Note from Table 5.5 that when we do this we cover all the minterms except 14 and 15. We will therefore need to add at

TABLE 5.5   FINDING ESSENTIAL PRIME IMPLICANTS FOR THE EXAMPLE IN TABLE 5.4

Prime implicants	Covered minterms	Minterms									
		0	1	2	3	5	7	8	10	14	15
1-10	10, 14								×	×	
-111	7, 15						×				×
111-	14, 15									×	×
00--	0, 1, 2, 3	×	×	×	×						
√ -0-0	0, 2, 8, 10	×		×				×	×		
√ 0--1	1, 3, 5, 7		×		×	×	×				
		√	√	√	√	√	√	√	√		

least one more prime implicant to cover these two minterms. From Table 5.5 it
is clear that the prime implicant 111- will cover both minterms 14 and 15, so we
will add this prime implicant to our two essential prime implicants to obtain the
final reduced function:

```
F =     !X & !Z       [-0-0]
    #  !W & Z        [0--1]
    #  W & X & Y     [111-]
```

Is this the function that you obtained when you circled the 1's in Fig. 5.19? If
not (and your function contained four terms), you may not have realized that,
when the right and left and top and bottom of a K-map wrap around, the four
corners represent a 4 × 4 array of 1's that can be circled as shown in Fig. 5.20.
Note that this is the -0-0 prime implicant, and the other two prime implicants
found by the tabulation method are indicated in Fig. 5.20.

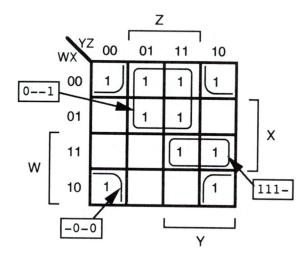

Figure 5.20 The four corners of a K-map can be circled.

Experiment 3: A 2-Bit Comparator

Consider four input values *B1*, *B0*, *A1*, and *A0*, where *B1* and *B0* are the 2 bits
of a 2-bit number *B*, which can have values of 0, 1, 2, or 3. Similarly, *A1* and *A0*
are the 2 bits of the 2-bit number *A*. The following truth table is for a 2-bit comparator with three output variables, *A_EQ_B*, *A_GT_B*, and *A_LT_B*. The variable *A_EQ_B* is 1 if *A* = *B*. The variable *A_GT_B* is 1 if *A* > *B*, and the variable
A_LT_B is 1 if *A* < *B*.

B1	B0	A1	A0	A_EQ_B	A_GT_B	A_LT_B
0	0	0	0	1	0	0
0	0	0	1	0	1	0
0	0	1	0	0	1	0
0	0	1	1	0	1	0
0	1	0	0	0	0	1
0	1	0	1	1	0	0
0	1	1	0	0	1	0
0	1	1	1	0	1	0
1	0	0	0	0	0	1
1	0	0	1	0	0	1
1	0	1	0	1	0	0
1	0	1	1	0	1	0
1	1	0	0	0	0	1
1	1	0	1	0	0	1
1	1	1	0	0	0	1
1	1	1	1	1	0	0

a. Make a Karnaugh map for each output variable A_EQ_B, A_GT_B, and A_LT_B, and write a reduced Boolean expression for each of these output variables.

b. Write a CUPL program for the GAL 16V8 that will assign B to pins 2 and 3, A to pins 4 and 5, and the outputs A_EQ_B, A_GT_B, and A_LT_B to pins 17 to 19, respectively.

c. Program the GAL 16V8 from the fuse map produced in part (b).

d. Make a printout of the chip diagram from the .DOC file. Wire the chip on a prototype breadboard by connecting the four output lines from the PC logic analyzer, *Out3*, *Out2*, *Out1*, and *Out0*, to the PLD input lines *B1*, *B0*, *A1*, and *A0*, respectively. Connect the output PLD signals A_EQ_B, A_GT_B, and A_LT_B to the PC logic analyzer input lines *In4*, *In3*, and *In2*, respectively. Test the circuit by pressing function key *F1* and printing out the resulting truth table.

Note: CUPL allows you to use the following shorthand notation for assigning pin numbers:

```
Pin [2,3] = [B1..0];
Pin [4,5] = [A1..0];
```

These statements are equivalent to the following pin assignment statements:

```
Pin 2 = B1;
Pin 3 = B0;
Pin 4 = A1;
Pin 5 = A0;
```

If you had 4-bit numbers instead of 2-bit numbers, you could assign the four pins 2, 3, 4, and 5 to *A0*, *A1*, *A2*, and *A3* using the single statement

```
Pin [2..5] = [A0..3]
```

If you wanted pin 2 to be *A3* and pin 5 to be *A0*, you would write

```
Pin [2..5] = [A3..0]
```

Simulation

The CUPL program CSIM can be used to run a functional simulation of your design. You must first produce a set of test vectors in a file called *exp3.si* that will give the expected output values for a given set of input values. Listing 5.1 shows what the *.SI* file will look like for this experiment.

First, copy the same header from the *.PLD* file. The next statement

```
ORDER: B1..0,%2,A1..0,%5,A_EQ_B,%6,A_GT_B,%6,A_LT_B;
```

lists the order of the variables (defined in your *.PLD* file) that will be used in this simulation. In this case the order will be

```
B1,B0,A1,A0,A_EQ_B,A_GT_B,A_LT_B
```

that is, the four input variables followed by the three output variables. The entries %2, %5, and %6 in the *ORDER:* statement are used to indicate that 2, 5, and 6 spaces are to be left between the values of these variables in the output file.

The word *VECTORS:* in the *.SI* file is followed by a list of the test vectors. Before listing the test vectors, you can include as many *$msg* lines as you want, which will simply print the message between the following double quotes (" ") to the output file. In Listing 5.1, we print out a heading for our output table. This is followed by 16 test vectors corresponding to the truth table at the beginning of Experiment 3. The four inputs are designated as 0 or 1, and the corresponding output is designated as *H* (high or 1) or *L* (low or 0).

The *.SI* file shown in Listing 5.1 becomes the input to the simulation program CSIM. Remember, to use CSIM you must have compiled the *.PLD* file with CUPL using the *-a* option as in *-fax*. To run the simulation, type

```
csim -l exp3
```

The *-l* ("el") option will produce a listing of any errors in the *.SO* output file. The output file *exp3.so* produced by running CSIM with the input file shown in Listing 5.1 is shown in Listing 5.2. Compare the simulation results shown in this listing with the original truth table for Experiment 3. This shows that the

Listing 5.1   *Exp3.si*

```
Name              Exp3;
Partno            OU0002;
Revision          01;
Date              7/25/91;
Designer          R. E. Haskell;
Company           Oakland University;
Location          Rochester, MI;
Assembly          CSE 171;
Device            G16V8;
Format            j;

/***************************************************************/
/*        2-bit comparator                                     */
/***************************************************************/
/*        Target Device:   G16V8                               */
/***************************************************************/

ORDER: B1..0,%2,A1..0,%5,A_EQ_B,%6,A_GT_B,%6,A_LT_B;

VECTORS:
$msg "       B    A    A_EQ_B A_GT_B A_LT_B";
$msg "       ---  ---  ------ ------ ------";

0000 HLL
0001 LHL
0010 LHL
0011 LHL
0100 LLH
0101 HLL
0110 LHL
0111 LHL
1000 LLH
1001 LLH
1010 HLL
1011 LHL
1100 LLH
1101 LLH
1110 LLH
1111 HLL
```

design equations used in the *.PLD* file produce the expected output. If they didn't, then the incorrect outputs would be flagged in Listing 5.2.

    If you run CSIM by typing

```
csim -w exp3
```

Listing 5.2   *Exp3.so*

```
CSIM: CUPL Simulation Program
Version 4.0a Serial# MD-40A-7985
Copyright (C)  1983,1990 Logical Devices, Inc.
CREATED Thu Jul 25 13:15:00 1991

LISTING FOR SIMULATION FILE: exp3.si

    1: Name           Exp3;
    2: Partno         OU0002;
    3: Revision       01;
    4: Date           7/25/91;
    5: Designer       R. E. Haskell;
    6: Company        Oakland University;
    7: Location       Rochester, MI;
    8: Assembly       CSE 171;
    9: Device         G16V8;
   10: Format         j;
   11:
   12: /***********************************************/
   14: /*         2-bit comparator                   */
   16: /***********************************************/
   17: /*         Target Device:  G16V8              */
   18: /***********************************************/
   19:
   20: ORDER: B1..0,%2,A1..0,%5,A_EQ_B,%6,A_GT_B,%6,A_LT_B;
   21:

===================================================================
                       Simulation Results
===================================================================
        B    A    A_EQ_B A_GT_B A_LT_B
       ---  ---   ------ ------ ------
0001: 00   00       H      L      L
0002: 00   01       L      H      L
0003: 00   10       L      H      L
0004: 00   11       L      H      L
0005: 01   00       L      L      H
0006: 01   01       H      L      L
0007: 01   10       L      H      L
0008: 01   11       L      H      L
0009: 10   00       L      L      H
0010: 10   01       L      L      H
0011: 10   10       H      L      L
0012: 10   11       L      H      L
0013: 11   00       L      L      H
0014: 11   01       L      L      H
0015: 11   10       L      L      H
0016: 11   11       H      L      L
```

the simulation results will be displayed as a waveform on the screen. Press function keys *F1* and *F2* to change the scale and press *F4* to exit.

Once you have run a valid simulation, you can add these test vectors to the JEDEC file produced by CUPL by running CSIM again with the *-j* option. If you do this by typing

```
csim -j exp3
```

the original JEDEC file shown in Listing 5.3 will be changed to that shown in Listing 5.4. Each of these 16 test vectors (starting with *V at the beginning of the line) has 20 characters in it, one for each pin in the GAL 16V8 chip. The first

Listing 5.3   *exp3.jed* file before adding test vectors

```
CUPL               4.0a  Serial# MD-40A-7985
Device             g16v8s  Library DLIB-h-26-9
Created            Thu Jul 25 12:17:43 1991
Name               Exp3
Partno             OU0002
Revision           01
Date               7/25/91
Designer           R. E. Haskell
Company            Oakland University
Assembly           CSE 171
Location           Rochester, MI
*QP20
*QF2194
*G0
*F0
*L00000 11110111101110111111111111111111
*L00032 01110111111110111111111111111111
*L00064 01111111101111111111111111111111
*L00256 10111011111101111111111111111111
*L00288 11110110111101111111111111111111
*L00320 10111111011111111111111111111111
*L00512 10111011101110111111111111111111
*L00544 10110111101101111111111111111111
*L00576 01110111011101111111111111111111
*L00608 01111011011110111111111111111111
*L02048 11100000010011000000110000001100
*L02080 00001100101010101111001000000000
*L02112 00000000000111111111111111111111
*L02144 11111111111111111111111111111111
*L02176 111111111111111110
*C309E
*CB85
```

Listing 5.4   *exp3.jed* file after adding test vectors

```
CUPL          4.0a  Serial# MD-40A-7985
Device        g16v8s  Library DLIB-h-26-9
Created       Thu Jul 25 12:17:43 1991
Name          Exp3
Partno        OU0002
Revision      01
Date          7/25/91
Designer      R. E. Haskell
Company       Oakland University
Assembly      CSE 171
Location      Rochester, MI
*QP20
*QF2194
*QV16
*G0
*F0
*L00000 111101111011101111111111111111111
*L00032 011101111111110111111111111111111
*L00064 011111111011111111111111111111111
*L00256 101110111111011111111111111111111
*L00288 111110110111011111111111111111111
*L00320 101111101111111111111111111111111
*L00512 101110111011101111111111111111111
*L00544 101101111011101111111111111111111
*L00576 011101110111011111111111111111111
*L00608 011110110111101111111111111111111
*L02048 111000000100110000001100000011100
*L02080 000011001010101011100100000000000
*L02112 000000000011111111111111111111111
*L02144 111111111111111111111111111111111
*L02176 11111111111111110
*C309E
*P 1 2 3 4 5 6 7 8 9 10 11 12 13 14 15 16 17 18 19 20
*V0001 X0000XXXXNXXXXXXHLLN
*V0002 X0001XXXXNXXXXXXLHLN
*V0003 X0010XXXXNXXXXXXLHLN
*V0004 X0011XXXXNXXXXXXLHLN
*V0005 X0100XXXXNXXXXXXLLHN
*V0006 X0101XXXXNXXXXXXHLLN
*V0007 X0110XXXXNXXXXXXLHLN
*V0008 X0111XXXXNXXXXXXLHLN
*V0009 X1000XXXXNXXXXXXLLHN
*V0010 X1001XXXXNXXXXXXLLHN
*V0011 X1010XXXXNXXXXXXHLLN
*V0012 X1011XXXXNXXXXXXLHLN
*V0013 X1100XXXXNXXXXXXLLHN
```

Listing 5.4   (*cont.*)

```
*V0014  X1101XXXXNXXXXXXLLHN
*V0015  X1110XXXXNXXXXXXLLHN
*V0016  X1111XXXXNXXXXXXHLLN
*  4E54
```

character corresponds to pin 1 and the last character to pin 20. Each character has the following meaning:

X	don't care
0	drive input low (0 volts)
1	drive input high ($+5$ volts)
H	test output HI ($+5$ volts)
L	test output LO (0 volts)
N	output not tested

A programmer that receives a JEDEC file with test vectors appended to the fuse map will program the chip and then test the chip with these test vectors.

EXERCISES

5.1. Verify theorem (4b) in Table 5.2 using Venn diagrams.

5.2. Verify theorem (6b) in Table 5.2 using Venn diagrams.

5.3. Make truth tables to verify the absorption theorems (5a), (5b), (6a), and (6b) in Table 5.2.

5.4. a. Write the complete sum of products form for the function given by the K-map in Fig. 5.19.

   b. Write a CUPL program to compile this function by writing the function as

$$F = a\ \#\ b\ \#\ c\ \#\ d\ \#\ e$$
$$\#\ f\ \#\ g\ \#\ h\ \#\ i\ \#\ j$$

where $a - j$ are the minterms found in (a). Use the default minimization and find the expanded

product terms for F in the .*DOC* file. Circle the set of 1's in the Karnaugh map of Fig. 5.19 corresponding to these product terms.

   c. Compile the program again using the CUPL *m2* minimization option. Find the expanded product terms for F in the .*DOC* file and circle the set of 1's in the Karnaugh map of Fig. 5.19 corresponding to these product terms.

5.5. Use switching algebra theorems to simplify the following Boolean expressions:

   a. !X & !Y # !X & Y
      # X & Y

   b. (X # Y) & (!X # Y)

   c. !X & (X # Y)

   d. (!X & Y) # !X

   e. Y & (X # !Y)

5.6. Use Karnaugh maps to simplify the following Boolean functions expressed in the *sum of minterms* notation [see Eq. (5.5)].

   a. $F(X,Y,Z) = \sum(0,1,2,3)$
   b. $F(X,Y,Z) = \sum(0,2,4,6)$
   c. $F(X,Y,Z) =$
         $\sum(0,1,2,4,5,6)$
   d. $F(X,Y,Z) =$
         $\sum(1,3,4,5,6,7)$
   e. $F(X,Y,Z) =$
         $\sum(0,2,3,4,6,7)$

5.7. Use Karnaugh maps to simplify the following Boolean functions expressed in the *sum of minterms* notation (see Eq. 5.5):

   a. $F(W,X,Y,Z) =$
         $\sum(0,1,4,5,10,11,14,15)$
   b. $F(W,X,Y,Z) =$
         $\sum(5,7,9,11,13,15)$
   c. $F(W,X,Y,Z) =$
         $\sum(0,2,5,7,8,10,13,15)$
   d. $F(W,X,Y,Z) =$
         $\sum(2,3,6,7,8,10,11,12,$
             $14,15)$

   e. $F(W,X,Y,Z) =$
         $\sum(4,5,6,7,8,9,10,11,$
             $12,13)$

5.8. Use the tabulation method to find the essential prime implicants of the Boolean functions given in Exercise 5.7.

5.9. a. Write an equation for F in the given truth table using a sum-of-products design.

X	Y	Z	F
0	0	0	1
0	0	1	1
0	1	0	0
0	1	1	1
1	0	0	0
1	0	1	0
1	1	0	0
1	1	1	1

   b. Draw a Karnaugh map for F and simplify the expression for F as much as possible.
   c. Draw a logic diagram for this design.

6

Combinational Logic

In the last chapter you obtained the background needed to design some real logic circuits. In this chapter you will learn to design a variety of combinational logic circuits, including:

- Equality and magnitude comparators
- Adders and subtractors
- Decoders and encoders
- Multiplexers and demultiplexers
- Code converters

You will also learn how to use some more features of the CUPL language, including:

- Sets and the FIELD statement
- Equality operator
- Range operations
- TABLE keyword and the function table format

A combinational logic circuit is a logic circuit of the type we have been considering thus far in which the outputs depend only on the current state of the inputs. In the next chapter we will consider logic circuits, called *sequential circuits*, in which the outputs depend not only on the current inputs, but also on past inputs. As we will see, these sequential circuits will need to contain some type of memory device.

6.1 COMPARATORS

We will begin by looking at comparators. In Experiment 3 in Chapter 5 you designed a 2-bit comparator. From the Karnaugh map of the equality output *A_EQ_B* you found that you could not reduce the logic equation, and each of the four terms contained all four input variables (see the truth table in Experiment 3). This is characteristic of equality comparators, which we will look at first.

Equality Comparators

The XNOR gate shown in Fig. 6.1 can be considered to be an equality detector. Note that the output *Z* is 1 when *X* = *Y*.

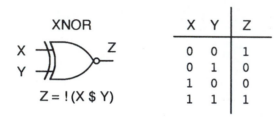

XNOR

$$Z = !(X \$ Y)$$

X	Y	Z
0	0	1
0	1	0
1	0	0
1	1	1

Figure 6.1 The XNOR gate is an equality detector.

Four of these XNOR gates can be combined with an AND gate to produce a 4-bit equality detector, as shown in Fig. 6.2. Only when all four bits of *A* are equal to the corresponding four bits of *B* will *A_EQ_B* be 1. Let's try to implement this design on the GAL 16V8 PLD. The program shown in Listing 6.1 should do this.

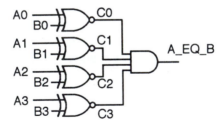

Figure 6.2 A 4-bit equality detector.

Note that we used the shorthand notation introduced in Experiment 3 for assigning the input pin numbers to *A0* to *A3* and *B0* to *B3*. We can treat the four values *A0* to *A3* as a set *A* that we define by the statement

```
FIELD A = [A0..3];
```

The value *A* is now associated with the set [*A0, A1, A2, A3*]. Similarly, the statements

```
FIELD B = [B0..3];
FIELD C = [C0..3];
```

define the two sets *B* and *C*, which contain the elements [*B0*, *B1*, *B2*, *B3*] and [*C0*, *C1*, *C2*, *C3*], respectively. The elements of the set *B* are associated with four

---

Listing 6.1   *eqcomp1.pld*

```
Name                 eqcomp1;
Partno               OU0004;
Revision             01;
Date                 7/26/91;
Designer             R. E. Haskell;
Company              Oakland University;
Location             Rochester, MI;
Assembly             CSE 171;
Device               G16V8;
Format               j;

/**************************************************************/
/*                                                            */
/*        This is a 4-bit equality comparator                 */
/*        using the ANDing of 4 XOR gates                     */
/*                                                            */
/**************************************************************/
/*        Target Device:   G16V8                              */
/**************************************************************/

/* Inputs: */

Pin [2..5] =  [A0..3];
Pin [6..9] =  [B0..3];

/* Outputs: */

Pin 19 = A_EQ_B;

/* Intermediate variables */

FIELD A = [A0..3];
FIELD B = [B0..3];
FIELD C = [C0..3];

/* Logic equations */

C = !(A $ B);

A_EQ_B = C0 & C1 & C2 & C3;
```

of the input pins, while the elements of the set *C* are intermediate variables associated with the outputs of the XNOR gates shown in Fig. 6.2.

We can save writing logic equations for each variable by using the set names in the logic equations. For example, the logic equation

```
C = !(A $ B);
```

shown in Listing 6.1 is expanded by CUPL to be equivalent to

```
C0 = !(A0 $ B0);
C1 = !(A1 $ B1);
C2 = !(A2 $ B2);
C3 = !(A3 $ B3);
```

These four values are then ANDed to produce the output *A_EQ_B*.

If we try to compile the program in Listing 6.1 we obtain the screen display shown in Fig. 6.3. Note that the compiling failed due to an excessive number of product terms.

To find out what happened, look at the expanded product terms in the *.DOC* file as shown in Fig. 6.4. We see that *A_EQ_B* has 16 product terms, and the maximum number that we can have at any output pin of the GAL 16V8 is 8. Look

```
C:\CUPL\CSE171 >cupl -fax eqcomp1
CUPL: Universal Compiler for Programmable Logic
Version 4.0a   Serial# MD-40A-7985
Copyright (C)  1983,1990 Logical Devices, Inc.
Licensed to OAKLAND UNIVERSITY

cuplx
time: 1 secs
cupla
time: 1 secs
cuplb
time: 2 secs
cuplm
time: 1 secs
cuplc
[0006cc] excessive number of product terms:  A_EQ_B
time: 2 secs
total time: 8 secs

CUPL errors encountered!

C:\CUPL\CSE171 >
```

Figure 6.3   Screen display when compiling Listing 6.1.

```
===================================================
               Expanded Product Terms
===================================================


A =>
    A0 , A1 , A2 , A3

A_EQ_B =>
     !A0 & !A1 & !A2 & !A3 & !B0 & !B1 & !B2 & !B3
   #  A0 & !A1 & !A2 & !A3 &  B0 & !B1 & !B2 & !B3
   # !A0 &  A1 & !A2 & !A3 & !B0 &  B1 & !B2 & !B3
   #  A0 &  A1 & !A2 & !A3 &  B0 &  B1 & !B2 & !B3
   # !A0 & !A1 &  A2 & !A3 & !B0 & !B1 &  B2 & !B3
   #  A0 & !A1 &  A2 & !A3 &  B0 & !B1 &  B2 & !B3
   # !A0 &  A1 &  A2 & !A3 & !B0 &  B1 &  B2 & !B3
   #  A0 &  A1 &  A2 & !A3 &  B0 &  B1 &  B2 & !B3
   # !A0 & !A1 &  A2 &  A3 & !B0 & !B1 &  B2 &  B3
   #  A0 & !A1 &  A2 &  A3 &  B0 & !B1 &  B2 &  B3
   # !A0 &  A1 &  A2 &  A3 & !B0 &  B1 &  B2 &  B3
   #  A0 &  A1 &  A2 &  A3 &  B0 &  B1 &  B2 &  B3
   # !A0 &  A1 & !A2 &  A3 & !B0 &  B1 & !B2 &  B3
   #  A0 &  A1 & !A2 &  A3 &  B0 &  B1 & !B2 &  B3
   # !A0 & !A1 & !A2 &  A3 & !B0 & !B1 & !B2 &  B3
   #  A0 & !A1 & !A2 &  A3 &  B0 & !B1 & !B2 &  B3

B =>
    B0 , B1 , B2 , B3

C =>
    C0 , C1 , C2 , C3

C0 =>
    A0 & B0
  # !A0 & !B0

C1 =>
    A1 & B1
  # !A1 & !B1

C2 =>
    A2 & B2
  # !A2 & !B2

C3 =>
    A3 & B3
  # !A3 & !B3
```

Figure 6.4   Expanded product terms from *eqcomp1.doc*.

back at Experiment 3 and note that there were four product terms for A_EQ_B, one for each possible equality. Inasmuch as each input was only 2 bits, there were four possible (2^2) equalities. In Figure 6.2 each input has 4 bits, so there are $2^4 = 16$ possible equalities. This will lead to the 16 product terms shown in Fig. 6.4. In general, an n-bit equality detector will require 2^n product terms.

What can we do to fit our equality detector into a GAL 16V8? Recall from our discussion of the GAL 16V8 in Chapter 4 that the second pair of vertical lines in each group of four in Fig. 4.5 is connected to the output pins. The signal from an output pin can then be fed back to become an input to one of the AND gate arrays of some other output pin. We can use some of these extra output pins to produce intermediate products that we can then feed back to become part of the input to our output pin A_EQ_B. This will lead to a multilevel implementation of the circuit in Fig. 6.2, as shown in Fig. 6.5.

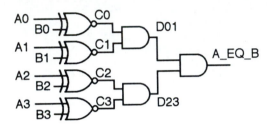

Figure 6.5 A multilevel implementation of Fig. 6.2.

The intermediate values *D01* and *D23* are each the outputs of a 2-bit comparator of the type considered in Experiment 3. We know that these will each use four product terms, which will now fit. The output A_EQ_B will now need only the two product terms *D01* and *D23*. We must define *D01* and *D02* to be output pins as shown in Listing 6.2. The logic equations in Listing 6.2 implement the logic diagram in Fig. 6.5.

```
============================================================
                       Chip Diagram
============================================================

                        _____
                       |   eqcomp2      |
              x---|1              20|---x Vcc
         A0   x---|2              19|---x A_EQ_B
         A1   x---|3              18|---x D01
         A2   x---|4              17|---x D23
         A3   x---|5              16|---x
         B0   x---|6              15|---x
         B1   x---|7              14|---x
         B2   x---|8              13|---x
         B3   x---|9              12|---x
         GND  x---|10             11|---x
                       |_____|
```

Figure 6.6 Chip diagram from *eqcomp2.doc*.

Listing 6.2   *eqcomp2.pld*

```
Name              eqcomp2;
Partno            OU0005;
Revision          01;
Date              7/26/91;
Designer          R. E. Haskell;
Company           Oakland University;
Location          Rochester, MI;
Assembly          CSE 171;
Device            G16V8;
Format            j;

/**************************************************************/
/*                                                            */
/*      This is a 4-bit equality comparator                   */
/*      using intermediate pin outputs                        */
/*                                                            */
/**************************************************************/
/*      Target Device:  G16V8                                 */
/**************************************************************/

/* Inputs: */

Pin [2..5] =  [A0..3];
Pin [6..9] =  [B0..3];

/* Outputs: */

Pin 19 = A_EQ_B;
Pin 18 = D01;          /* Intermediate pin output */
Pin 17 = D23;          /* Intermediate pin output */

/* Intermediate variables */

FIELD A = [A0..3];
FIELD B = [B0..3];
FIELD C = [C0..3];

/* Logic equations: */

C = !(A $ B);
D01 = C0 & C1;
D23 = C2 & C3;
A_EQ_B = D01 & D23;
```

```
==================================================
              Expanded Product Terms
==================================================

A =>
    A0 , A1 , A2 , A3


A_EQ_B =>
    D01 & D23


B =>
    B0 , B1 , B2 , B3


C =>
    C0 , C1 , C2 , C3
C0 =>
    A0 & B0
  # !A0 & !B0


C1 =>
    A1 & B1
  # !A1 & !B1


C2 =>
    A2 & B2
  # !A2 & !B2


C3 =>
    A3 & B3
  # !A3 & !B3


D01 =>
    !A0 & !A1 & !B0 & !B1
  # A0 & !A1 & B0 & !B1
  # !A0 & A1 & !B0 & B1
  # A0 & A1 & B0 & B1


D23 =>
    !A2 & !A3 & !B2 & !B3
  # A2 & !A3 & B2 & !B3
  # !A2 & A3 & !B2 & B3
  # A2 & A3 & B2 & B3


A_EQ_B.oe  =>
    1


D01.oe  =>
    1


D23.oe  =>
    1
```

Figure 6.7   Expanded product terms from *eqcomp2.doc*.

The program in Listing 6.2 compiles and produces the chip diagram shown in Fig. 6.6 and the expanded product terms shown in Fig. 6.7. Note that everything now "fits," and the variables *D01* and *D23* each contain four product terms.

Magnitude Comparators

Suppose we want to modify the program in Listing 6.2 so that it will contain the two additional output pins *A_GT_B* and *A_LT_B* that we had in Experiment 3 for our 2-bit comparator. How can we do this? The truth table method used in Experiment 3 is getting out of hand because there are a total of eight input variables, so the truth table will contain 2^8 or 256 rows!

Consider what it means if $A > B$. If the most significant bit of *A*, *A3*, is 1 and the most significant bit of *B*, *B3*, is 0, then *A* will definitely be greater than *B* regardless of what the other bits in *A* and *B* are. Therefore, *A3 & !B3* will be one of the product terms in *A_GT_B*.

If $A3 = B3$, then *C3* in Fig. 6.5 will be equal to 1. In this case we need to look at *A2* and *B2* to see if *A* is greater than *B*. If $A2 = 1$ and $B2 = 0$ (with *C3* = 1), then *A* will be greater than *B*. This will lead to the product term *C3 & A2 & !B2*.

Following the same reasoning with the remaining bits, *A1* and *A0*, we can write the complete logic equation for *A_GT_B* as

```
A_GT_B  =      A3 & !B3

           #  C3 & A2 & !B2

           #  C3 & C2 & A1 & !B1

           #  C3 & C2 & C1 & A0 & !B0

        =      A3 & !B3

           #  C3 & A2 & !B2

           #  D23 & A1 & !B1

           #  D23 & C1 & A0 & !B0
```

Listing 6.3   *magcomp4.pld*

```
Name              magcomp4;
Partno            DU0006;
Revision          01;
Date              7/25/91;
Designer          R. E. Haskell;
Company           Oakland University;
Location          Rochester, MI;
Assembly          CSE 171;
Device            G16V8;
Format            j;
```

Listing 6.3   *(cont.)*

```
/**************************************************************/
/*                                                            */
/*        This is a 4-bit magnitude comparator               */
/*                                                            */
/**************************************************************/
/*        Target Device:  G16V8                              */
/**************************************************************/

/* Inputs:  */

Pin [2..5] =   [A0..3];
Pin [6..9] =   [B0..3];

/* Outputs:  */

Pin 19 = A_EQ_B;
Pin 18 = D01;
Pin 17 = D23;
Pin 16 = A_GT_B;
Pin 15 = A_LT_B;
Pin 14 = C1;
Pin 13 = C3;

/* Intermediate variables */

FIELD A = [A0..3];
FIELD B = [B0..3];
FIELD C = [C0..3];

/* Logic equations:  */

C = !(A $ B);
D01 = C0 & C1;
D23 = C2 & C3;

A_EQ_B = D01 & D23;

A_GT_B =  A3 & !B3
   # C3 & A2 & !B2
   # D23 & A1 & !B1
   # D23 & C1 & A0 & !B0;

A_LT_B =  !A3 & B3
   # C3 & !A2 & B2
   # D23 & !A1 & B1
   # D23 & C1 & !A0 & B0;
```

This equation is shown in Listing 6.3, where we have used the output pin *D23* for *C2 & C3* and also defined *C1* and *C3* to be output pins in order to reduce the number of product terms in *A_GT_B*. In Listing 6.3 the logic equation for *A_LT_B* is equivalent to

```
A_LT_B =    !A3 & B3

         #  C3 & !A2 & B2

         #  C3 & C2 & !A1 & B1

         #  C3 & C2 & C1 & !A0 & B0

       =    !A3 & B3

         #  C3 & !A2 & B2

         #  D23 & !A1 & B1

         #  D23 & C1 & !A0 & B0
```

Do you see how this ensures that *A* will be less than *B*?

The chip diagram corresponding to the program in Listing 6.3 is shown in Fig. 6.8. An experiment using this chip is described in Experiment 4 at the end of this chapter.

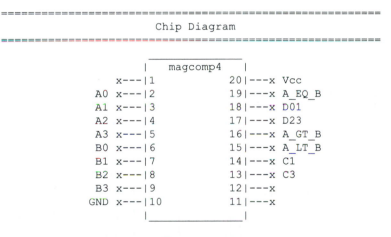

Figure 6.8   Chip diagram from *magcomp4.doc*.

TTL Comparators

The pinouts of two TTL comparators are shown in Fig. 6.9. The 74LS85 is a 4-bit magnitude comparator similar to the one we just designed. It has <, =, and > input pins that allow the chip to be cascaded to form an *n*-bit magnitude comparator, where *n* is a multiple of 4. Figure 6.10 shows how you can connect the

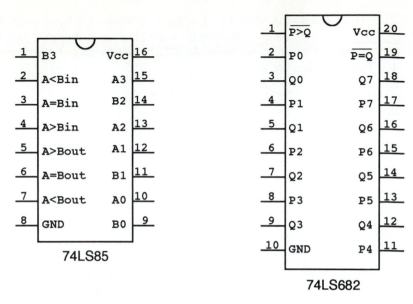

Figure 6.9   Two TTL magnitude comparators.

output of one 74LS85 to the input of a second 74LS85 (called cascading) to produce an 8-bit magnitude comparator.

The 74LS682 shown in Fig. 6.9 is an 8-bit magnitude comparator that can't be cascaded. It has only an active low (0 when *true*) $P = Q$ and an active low $P > Q$ output. With a few external gates you could produce active high outputs for these signals, as well as a $P < Q$ signal. (See Exercise 6.2.)

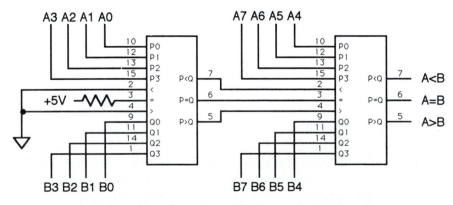

Figure 6.10   Cascading two 74LS85 4-bit magnitude comparators.

6.2 ADDERS AND SUBTRACTORS

In this section we will look at circuits that can add and subtract binary numbers. We will write PLD programs for a 4-bit adder, a 4-bit subtractor, and a circuit that will combine the two.

Half Adder

The truth table for a half adder is shown in Fig. 6.11. In this table, bit A_0 is added to bit B_0 to produce the sum bit S_0 and the carry bit C_1. Note that if you add 1 to 1 you get 2, which in binary is 10 or 0 with a carry bit. The logic diagram for a half adder is also shown in Fig. 6.11. Note that the sum S_0 is just the Exclusive-OR of A_0 and B_0, and the carry C_1 is just A_0 & B_0.

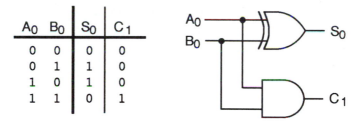

A_0	B_0	S_0	C_1
0	0	0	0
0	1	1	0
1	0	1	0
1	1	0	1

Figure 6.11   Truth table and logic diagram for a half adder.

Full Adder

When adding binary numbers, we need to consider the carry from one bit to the next. Thus, at any bit position we will be adding three bits: A_i, B_i, and the carry-in C_i from the addition of the 2 bits to the right of the current bit position. The sum of these 3 bits will produce a sum bit, S_i, and a carry-out, C_{i+1}, which will be the carry-in to the next bit position to the left. This is called a *full adder* and its truth table is shown in Fig. 6.12. The results of the first seven rows in this

C_i	A_i	B_i	S_i	C_{i+1}
0	0	0	0	0
0	0	1	1	0
0	1	0	1	0
0	1	1	0	1
1	0	0	1	0
1	0	1	0	1
1	1	0	0	1
1	1	1	1	1

Figure 6.12   Truth table for a full adder.

truth table can be inferred from the truth table for the half adder given in Fig. 6.11. In all these rows, only two 1's are ever added together. The last row in Fig. 6.12 adds three 1's. The result is 3, which in binary is 11, or 1 plus a carry.

From the truth table in Fig. 6.12 we can write a sum of products expression for S_i as

$$
\begin{aligned}
S_i = \quad & !C_i \ \& \ !A_i \ \& \ B_i \\
\# \ & !C_i \ \& \ A_i \ \& \ !B_i \\
\# \ & C_i \ \& \ !A_i \ \& \ !B_i \\
\# \ & C_i \ \& \ A_i \ \& \ B_i
\end{aligned}
\qquad (6.1)
$$

We will now show that S_i can also be written as

$$
S_i \ = \ C_i \ \$ \ (A_i \ \$ \ B_i) \qquad (6.2)
$$

Expanding the first Exclusive-OR in Eq. (6.2), we can write

$$
S_i \ = \ !C_i \ \& \ (A_i \ \$ \ B_i) \ \# \ C_i \ \& \ !(A_i \ \$ \ B_i) \qquad (6.3)
$$

From Fig. 6.1, the XNOR operation can be written as

$$
!(A_i \ \$ \ B_i) \ = \ !A_i \ \& \ !B_i \ \# \ A_i \ \& \ B_i \qquad (6.4)
$$

Substituting Eq. (6.4) into Eq. (6.3) and expanding the first Exclusive-OR, we obtain

$$
\begin{aligned}
S_i = \quad & !C_i \ \& \ (!A_i \ \& \ B_i \ \# \ A_i \ \& \ !B_i) \\
\# \ & C_i \ \& \ (!A_i \ \& \ !B_i \ \# \ A_i \ \& \ B_i)
\end{aligned}
\qquad (6.5)
$$

which is equivalent to Eq. (6.1).

Figure 6.13 shows the K-map for C_{i+1} from the truth table in Fig. 6.12. The map shown in Fig. 6.13a leads to the reduced form for C_{i+1} given by

$$
C_{i+1} \ = \ A_i \ \& \ B_i \ \# \ C_i \ \& \ B_i \ \# \ C_i \ \& \ A_i \qquad (6.6)
$$

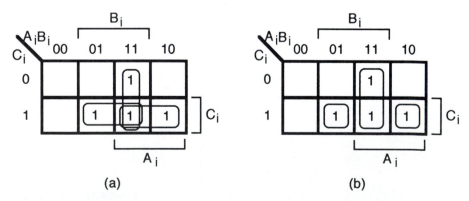

(a)   (b)

Figure 6.13   K-maps for C_{i+1} for the full adder in Fig. 6.12.

While this is the reduced form, a more convenient form can be written from Fig. 6.13b, as follows:

$$C_{i+1} = A_i \ \& \ B_i \ \# \ C_i \ \& \ !A_i \ \& \ B_i \ \# \ C_i \ \& \ A_i \ \& \ !B_i$$

$$= A_i \ \& \ B_i \ \# \ C_i \ \& \ (!A_i \ \& \ B_i \ \# \ A_i \ \& \ !B_i)$$

$$= A_i \ \& \ B_i \ \# \ C_i \ \& \ (A_i \ \$ \ B_i) \qquad\qquad (6.7)$$

From Eqs. (6.2) and (6.7), we can draw the logic diagram for a full adder, as shown in Fig. 6.14. Comparing this diagram to that for a half adder in Fig. 6.11, it is clear that a full adder can be made from two half adders plus an OR gate, as shown in Fig. 6.15.

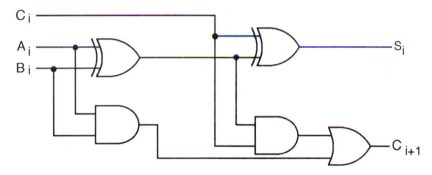

Figure 6.14   Logic diagram for a full adder.

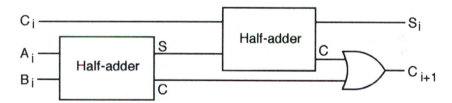

Figure 6.15   A full adder can be made from two half adders.

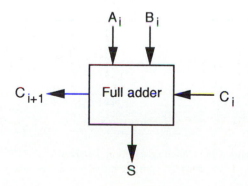

Figure 6.16   Block diagram for a full adder.

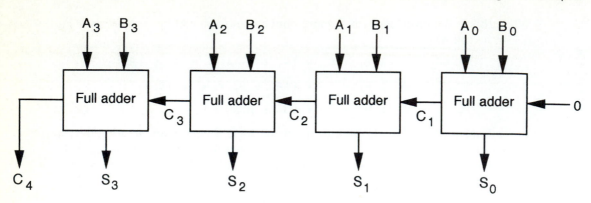

Figure 6.17 Block diagram for a 4-bit adder.

A block diagram of the full adder in Fig. 6.14 is shown in Fig. 6.16. Four of these full adders can be combined to form a 4-bit adder, as shown in Fig. 6.17. Note that the full adder for the least significant bit has a carry-in of zero, while the remaining bits get their carry-in from the carry-out of the previous bit. The final carry-out, C_4, is the carry for the 4-bit addition.

The GAL 16V8 design for this 4-bit adder is given in Listing 6.4. The logic equations used in Listing 6.4 are taken from Eqs. (6.2) and (6.7). Note that we have defined the intermediate carries, $C1$, $C2$, and $C3$, to be pin outputs to reduce the number of product terms in our final expressions. The chip diagram for this 4-bit adder is shown in Fig. 6.18.

```
==============================================================
                        Chip Diagram
==============================================================


                    |      adder4      |
            x---|1              20|---x Vcc
         A3 x---|2              19|---x S0
         A2 x---|3              18|---x S1
         A1 x---|4              17|---x S2
         A0 x---|5              16|---x S3
         B3 x---|6              15|---x C1
         B2 x---|7              14|---x C2
         B1 x---|8              13|---x C3
         B0 x---|9              12|---x Carry
        GND x---|10             11|---x
                    |_____|
```

Figure 6.18 Chip diagram from *adder4.doc*.

Listing 6.4   *adder4.pld*

```
Name             adder4;
Partno           OU0007;
Revision         01;
Date             7/27/91;
Designer         R. E. Haskell;
Company          Oakland University;
Location         Rochester, MI;
Assembly         CSE 171;
Device           G16V8;
Format           j;

/*****************************************************************/
/*        This is a 4-bit adder                                  */
/*****************************************************************/
/*        Target Device:  G16V8                                  */
/*****************************************************************/

/**   Inputs   **/

Pin [2..5]   = [A3..0];              /* 4-bit operand */
Pin [6..9]   = [B3..0];              /* 4-bit operand */

/**   Outputs   **/

Pin [19..16] = [S0..3];              /* 4-bit sum */
Pin 12       = Carry;             /* carry */
Pin [13..15] = [C3..1];              /* intermediate carry */

/** Declarations and Intermediate Variable Definitions **/

C1 = A0 & B0 ;
C2 = C1 & (A1 $ B1) # A1 & B1 ;
C3 = C2 & (A2 $ B2) # A2 & B2 ;

/**   Logic Equations   **/

S0 = A0 $ B0 ;
S1 = C1 $ A1 $ B1 ;
S2 = C2 $ A2 $ B2 ;
S3 = C3 $ A3 $ B3 ;
Carry = C3 & (A3 $ B3) # A3 & B3 ;
```

Half Subtractor

The truth table for a half subtractor is shown in Fig. 6.19. In this table, bit B_0 is subtracted from bit A_0 to produce the difference bit D_0 and the borrow bit C_1. Note that if you subtract 1 from 0 you need to borrow a 1 from the bit to the left (which is really borrowing a 2), so the difference will be $2 - 1 = 1$ with a borrow bit, C_1. The logic diagram for a half subtractor is also shown in Fig. 6.19. Note that the difference D_0 is exactly the same as for the half adder, the Exclusive-OR of A_0 and B_0. Note also that the borrow bit C_1 is $!A_0 \& B_0$. The half subtractor differs from the half adder only in the fact that A_0 is inverted before going to the AND gate to produce the borrow.

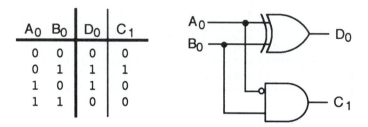

A_0	B_0	D_0	C_1
0	0	0	0
0	1	1	1
1	0	1	0
1	1	0	0

Figure 6.19 Truth table and logic diagram for a half subtractor.

Full Subtractor

The truth table for a full subtractor is shown in Fig. 6.20. In this table the difference D_i is given by

$$D_i = A_i - B_i - C_i \qquad (6.8)$$

All the entries in this table except the third from the bottom can be inferred directly from the truth table of the half subtractor in Fig. 6.19. When $C_i = 1$, $A_i = 0$, and $B_i = 1$, then D_i is equal to $0 - 1 - 1$. The first $0 - 1$ gives 1 with a borrow,

C_i	A_i	B_i	D_i	C_{i+1}
0	0	0	0	0
0	0	1	1	1
0	1	0	1	0
0	1	1	0	0
1	0	0	1	1
1	0	1	0	1
1	1	0	0	0
1	1	1	1	1

Figure 6.20 Truth table for a full subtractor.

and subtracting the second 1 gives 0 with no borrow. Therefore, the net effect of $0 - 1 - 1$ is a difference of 0 and a borrow. (The borrow really borrowed 2, and subtracting a total of 2 gives 0.)

Note that the truth table for the difference D_i is exactly the same as for the sum S_i in the full adder in Fig. 6.12. Therefore, the only difference between a full adder and a full subtractor will be in the logic for the carry and borrow. Figure 6.21 shows the K-map for the borrow C_{i+1} from the truth table in Fig. 6.20. The map shown in Fig. 6.21a leads to the reduced form for C_{i+1} given by

$$C_{i+1} \; = \; !A_i \; \& \; B_i \; \# \; C_i \; \& \; B_i \; \# \; C_i \; \& \; !A_i \qquad\qquad (6.9)$$

While this is the reduced form, a more convenient form can be written from Figure 6.21b as follows:

$$C_{i+1} \; = \; !A_i \; \& \; B_i \; \# \; C_i \; \& \; !A_i \; \& \; !B_i \; \# \; C_i \; \& \; A_i \; \& \; B_i$$

$$= \; !A_i \; \& \; B_i \; \# \; C_i \; \& \; (!A_i \; \& \; !B_i \; \# \; A_i \; \& \; B_i) \qquad (6.10)$$

$$= \; !A_i \; \& \; B_i \; \# \; C_i \; \& \; !(A_i \; \$ \; B_i)$$

where we used Eq. (6.4) in the last step.

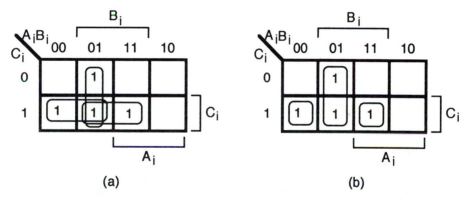

Figure 6.21   K-maps for C_{i+1} for full subtractor in Fig. 6.20.

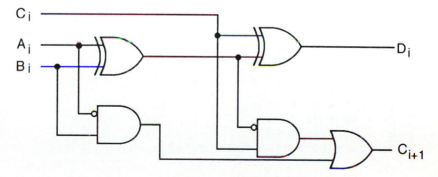

Figure 6.22   Logic diagram for a full subtractor.

Listing 6.5   *subtract.pld*

```
Name             subtract;
Partno           DU0008;
Revision         01;
Date             7/27/91;
Designer         R. E. Haskell;
Company          Oakland University;
Location         Rochester, MI;
Assembly         CSE 171;
Device           G16V8;
Format           j;

/****************************************************************/
/*        This is a 4-bit subtractor                           */
/****************************************************************/
/*        Target Device:  G16V8                                */
/****************************************************************/

/**   Inputs   **/

Pin [2..5]   = [A3..0];              /* 4-bit operand */
Pin [6..9]   = [B3..0];              /* 4-bit operand */

/**   Outputs   **/

Pin [19..16] = [D0..3];              /* 4-bit difference */
Pin [12      = Borrow;               /* borrow */
Pin [13..15] = [C3..1];              /* intermediate borrows */

/** Declarations and Intermediate Variable Definitions **/

C1 = !A0 & B0 ;
C2 = C1 & !(A1 $ B1) # !A1 & B1 ;
C3 = C2 & !(A2 $ B2) # !A2 & B2 ;

/**   Logic Equations   **/

D0 = A0 $ B0 ;
D1 = C1 $ A1 $ B1 ;
D2 = C2 $ A2 $ B2 ;
D3 = C3 $ A3 $ B3 ;
Borrow = C3 & !(A3 $ B3) # !A3 & B3 ;
```

```
================================================================
                          Chip Diagram
================================================================


              |      subtract      |
       x---|1                    20|---x Vcc
   A3  x---|2                    19|---x D0
   A2  x---|3                    18|---x D1
   A1  x---|4                    17|---x D2
   A0  x---|5                    16|---x D3
   B3  x---|6                    15|---x C1
   B2  x---|7                    14|---x C2
   B1  x---|8                    13|---x C3
   B0  x---|9                    12|---x Borrow
  GND  x---|10                   11|---x
              |_____|
```

Figure 6.23   Chip diagram from *subtract.doc*.

From Eqs. (6.2) and (6.10) we can draw the logic diagram for a full subtractor as shown in Fig. 6.22. Comparing this diagram to that for a half subtractor in Fig. 6.19, it is clear that a full subtractor can be made from two half subtractors plus an OR gate. Compare the logic diagram for the full subtractor in Fig. 6.22 with that for the full adder in Fig. 6.14. Note that the only difference is that one of the inputs to the two AND gates is negated.

Four full subtractors can be combined as we did with the full adders in Fig. 6.17 to produce a 4-bit subtractor. It is easy to modify Listing 6.4 to be a 4-bit subtractor, as shown in Listing 6.5, where we used Eqs. (6.2) and (6.10) for the logic equations. The chip diagram for this listing is shown in Fig. 6.23.

An Adder/Subtractor Circuit

It is possible to design a single logic circuit that can serve as both a 4-bit adder and a 4-bit subtractor. There are a couple of ways to do this. For example, the circuit shown in Fig. 6.24 reduces to the half adder in Fig. 6.11 when $E = 0$ and reduces to the half subtractor in Fig. 6.19 when $E = 1$. By adding this Exclusive-OR gate to one of the inputs on each of the two AND gates in logic diagrams for

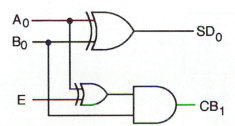

Figure 6.24   Circuit for a half adder ($E = 0$) or a half subtractor ($E = 1$).

C_i	A_i	B_i	S_i	C_{i+1}
1	0	1	0	1
1	0	0	1	0
1	1	1	1	1
1	1	0	0	1
0	0	1	1	0
0	0	0	0	0
0	1	1	0	1
0	1	0	1	0

Figure 6.25 Truth table for a full adder; C_i and B_i in Fig. 6.12 have been complemented.

the full adder and full subtractor (see Figs. 6.14 and 6.22), you can produce a full adder/subtractor that is controlled by the signal E. Combining four such full adder/subtractors will produce a 4-bit adder/subtractor circuit. (See Experiment 5.)

An alternate way to produce a 4-bit adder/subtractor circuit is to note that the truth table for a full adder can be rewritten as shown in Fig. 6.25, where we have just rearranged the order of the rows by complementing the C_i and B_i columns in Fig. 6.12. Note that the carry bits, C_{i+1}, in Fig. 6.25 for the full adder are the complement of the corresponding borrow bits, C_{i+1}, in Fig. 6.20 for the full subtractor. This means that we can use a full adder for a full subtractor if we complement B_i and the incoming carry (borrow), C_i, and then complement the outgoing carry (borrow), C_{i+1}. This is illustrated in Fig. 6.26.

If we connect four of the blocks shown in Fig. 6.26 to form a 4-bit subtractor, the complementing of the output carry and the next input carry will cancel, so the net result will be that only the initial input carry, C_0, will need to be complemented. Since this value is 0 for the full adder, complementing it will make it 1 for a subtraction. This is equivalent to adding 1 to the sum of the A_i's and $!B_i$'s. But this is just the way we took the two's complement of a binary number in Chapter 2: complement all the bits and add 1. Therefore, to subtract with an adder, we can just take the two's complement of the subtrahend and add. A circuit for doing both addition and subtraction using full adders is shown in Fig. 6.27. Note

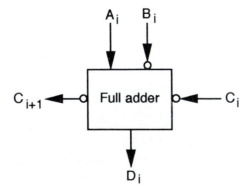

Figure 6.26 A full adder used as a full subtractor.

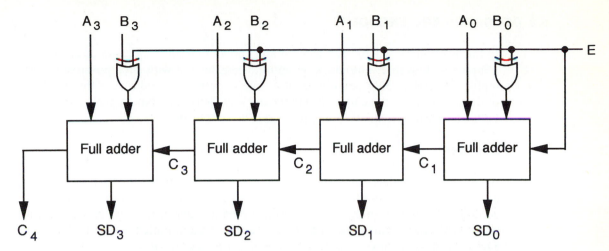

Figure 6.27   A 4-bit adder ($E = 0$)–subtractor ($E = 1$) circuit.

that, when used as a subtractor ($E = 1$), the output carry C_4 will be the complement of the output borrow.

TTL Adder

The pinout for a 74LS283 4-bit binary adder is shown in Fig. 6.28. This chip uses a carry lookahead technique in which the high-order full adders don't have to wait for the carry to be generated by the low-order adders to know what their input carry will be. This means that this chip can avoid the propagation delays involved in generating the carries at each stage and will therefore compute the sum faster than the circuit shown in Fig. 6.17.

74LS283

Figure 6.28   Pinout for the 74LS283 4-bit binary adder.

6.3 DECODERS AND ENCODERS

In this section we will look at decoder and encoder circuits. Decoder circuits have n inputs and up to 2^n outputs. One output is associated with each possible binary input. Generally, only one output at a time is active. Encoders are the opposite of decoders. They have up to 2^n inputs and n outputs. The binary code associated with one particular input line appears on the output pins.

Decoders

An example of a decoder is the 2-to-4 decoder shown in Fig. 6.29. This decoder has two input lines and four outputs. Each output is associated with one possible combination of the inputs, as shown in the truth table in Fig. 6.29. The output associated with a particular code can be either 1 (active high) or 0 (active low). The pins of active low outputs can be designated as $!Y_i$, as shown in Fig. 6.29.

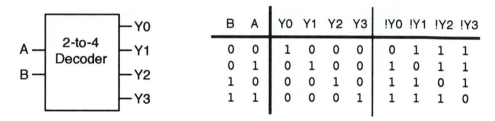

B	A	Y0	Y1	Y2	Y3	!Y0	!Y1	!Y2	!Y3
0	0	1	0	0	0	0	1	1	1
0	1	0	1	0	0	1	0	1	1
1	0	0	0	1	0	1	1	0	1
1	1	0	0	0	1	1	1	1	0

Figure 6.29   Diagram and truth table for a 2-to-4 decoder.

```
==========================================================
                       Chip Diagram
==========================================================

                   |¯¯¯¯¯¯¯¯¯¯¯¯¯|
                   |   24decode  |
           x---|1            20|---x Vcc
      B  x---|2            19|---x !Y0
      A  x---|3            18|---x !Y1
           x---|4            17|---x !Y2
           x---|5            16|---x !Y3
           x---|6            15|---x
           x---|7            14|---x
           x---|8            13|---x
           x---|9            12|---x
    GND  x---|10            11|---x
                   |_____|
```

Figure 6.30   Chip diagram from *24decode.doc*.

The logic equations for the outputs Y_i can be easily written from the truth table in Fig. 6.29 as

$$
\begin{aligned}
Y0 &= \ !B \ \& \ !A \\
Y1 &= \ !B \ \& \ A \\
Y2 &= \ B \ \& \ !A \\
Y3 &= \ B \ \& \ A
\end{aligned}
\qquad (6.11)
$$

The CUPL *.pld* file for this 2-to-4 decoder is given in Listing 6.6. Note that the active high versions of the logic equations given in (6.11) are used in Listing 6.6. However, the output pins are defined to be active low, using the pin defining equation

```
Pin [19..16] = ![Y0..3];
```

Listing 6.6   *24decode.pld*

```
Name            24decode;
Partno          OU0011;
Revision        01;
Date            7/28/91;
Designer        R. E. Haskell;
Company         Oakland University;
Location        Rochester, MI;
Assembly        CSE 171;
Device          G16V8;
Format          j;


/*****************************************************************/
/*    2-to-4 Decoder                                           */
/*****************************************************************/
/*    Target Device: G16V8                                     */
/*****************************************************************/
/**   Inputs  **/

Pin 2 = B;
Pin 3 = A;

/**   Outputs  **/

Pin [19..16] = ![Y0..3];

/**   Logic Equations  **/

Y0 = !B & !A;
Y1 = !B & A;
Y2 = B & !A;
Y3 = B & A;
```

which is equivalent to

$$Pin \; 19 \; = \; !Y0;$$

$$Pin \; 18 \; = \; !Y1;$$

$$Pin \; 17 \; = \; !Y2;$$

$$Pin \; 16 \; = \; !Y3;$$

This will lead to the second set of outputs shown in Fig. 6.29. The chip diagram for the 2-to-4 decoder is shown in Fig. 6.30. Note that the labels on the output

```
Pin #19  02048  Pol x  02120  Acl x
 00000 -x---x-----------------------
 00032 xxxxxxxxxxxxxxxxxxxxxxxxxxxxxxxx
 00064 xxxxxxxxxxxxxxxxxxxxxxxxxxxxxxxx
 00096 xxxxxxxxxxxxxxxxxxxxxxxxxxxxxxxx
 00128 xxxxxxxxxxxxxxxxxxxxxxxxxxxxxxxx
 00160 xxxxxxxxxxxxxxxxxxxxxxxxxxxxxxxx
 00192 xxxxxxxxxxxxxxxxxxxxxxxxxxxxxxxx
 00224 xxxxxxxxxxxxxxxxxxxxxxxxxxxxxxxx
Pin #18  02049  Pol x  02121  Acl x
 00256 -x--x------------------------
 00288 xxxxxxxxxxxxxxxxxxxxxxxxxxxxxxxx
 00320 xxxxxxxxxxxxxxxxxxxxxxxxxxxxxxxx
 00352 xxxxxxxxxxxxxxxxxxxxxxxxxxxxxxxx
 00384 xxxxxxxxxxxxxxxxxxxxxxxxxxxxxxxx
 00416 xxxxxxxxxxxxxxxxxxxxxxxxxxxxxxxx
 00448 xxxxxxxxxxxxxxxxxxxxxxxxxxxxxxxx
 00480 xxxxxxxxxxxxxxxxxxxxxxxxxxxxxxxx
Pin #17  02050  Pol x  02122  Acl x
 00512 x----x-----------------------
 00544 xxxxxxxxxxxxxxxxxxxxxxxxxxxxxxxx
 00576 xxxxxxxxxxxxxxxxxxxxxxxxxxxxxxxx
 00608 xxxxxxxxxxxxxxxxxxxxxxxxxxxxxxxx
 00640 xxxxxxxxxxxxxxxxxxxxxxxxxxxxxxxx
 00672 xxxxxxxxxxxxxxxxxxxxxxxxxxxxxxxx
 00704 xxxxxxxxxxxxxxxxxxxxxxxxxxxxxxxx
 00736 xxxxxxxxxxxxxxxxxxxxxxxxxxxxxxxx
Pin #16  02051  Pol x  02123  Acl x
 00768 x---x------------------------
 00800 xxxxxxxxxxxxxxxxxxxxxxxxxxxxxxxx
 00832 xxxxxxxxxxxxxxxxxxxxxxxxxxxxxxxx
 00864 xxxxxxxxxxxxxxxxxxxxxxxxxxxxxxxx
 00896 xxxxxxxxxxxxxxxxxxxxxxxxxxxxxxxx
 00928 xxxxxxxxxxxxxxxxxxxxxxxxxxxxxxxx
 00960 xxxxxxxxxxxxxxxxxxxxxxxxxxxxxxxx
 00992 xxxxxxxxxxxxxxxxxxxxxxxxxxxxxxxx

LEGEND    X : fuse not blown
          - : fuse blown
```

Figure 6.31 Fuse map from *24decode.doc.*

pins indicate that they are active low. The fuse map for this decoder as given in the .DOC file is shown in Fig. 6.31. Note that the fuse map represents the logic equations as written in Listing 6.6, and the active low pin outputs are accomplished by not blowing the output polarity fuse.

   As another example, the truth table for a 3-to-8 decoder is shown in Fig. 6.32. The eight outputs, Y0 to Y7, are active low. The CUPL program for this decoder is shown in Listing 6.7.

C	B	A	Y0	Y1	Y2	Y3	Y4	Y5	Y6	Y7
0	0	0	0	1	1	1	1	1	1	1
0	0	1	1	0	1	1	1	1	1	1
0	1	0	1	1	0	1	1	1	1	1
0	1	1	1	1	1	0	1	1	1	1
1	0	0	1	1	1	1	0	1	1	1
1	0	1	1	1	1	1	1	0	1	1
1	1	0	1	1	1	1	1	1	0	1
1	1	1	1	1	1	1	1	1	1	0

Figure 6.32   Truth table for a 3-to-8 decoder.

   Note that just as in Listing 6.6 we have written the logic equations as if the outputs were active high and made them active low by defining pins 12 to 19 as ![Y0..7]. The chip diagram for this 3-to-8 decoder is shown in Fig. 6.33.

```
============================================================
                         Chip Diagram
============================================================


                    |      38decode     |
             x---|1                20|---x  Vcc
         C   x---|2                19|---x  !Y0
         B   x---|3                18|---x  !Y1
         A   x---|4                17|---x  !Y2
             x---|5                16|---x  !Y3
             x---|6                15|---x  !Y4
             x---|7                14|---x  !Y5
             x---|8                13|---x  !Y6
             x---|9                12|---x  !Y7
       GND   x---|10               11|---x
                    |                   |
```

Figure 6.33   Chip diagram from 38decode.pld.

Listing 6.7   *38decode.pld*

```
Name               38decode;
Partno             OU0012;
Revision           01;
Date               7/28/91;
Designer           R. E. Haskell;
Company            Oakland University;
Location           Rochester, MI;
Assembly           CSE 171;
Device             G16V8;
Format             j;

/*********************************************************/
/*   3-to-8 Decoder                                      */
/*********************************************************/
/*    Target Device: G16V8                               */
/*********************************************************/

/**   Inputs   **/

Pin 2 = C;
Pin 3 = B;
Pin 4 = A;

/**   Outputs   **/

Pin [19..12] = ![Y0..7];

/**   Logic Equations   **/

Y0 = !C & !B & !A;
Y1 = !C & !B & A;
Y2 = !C & B & !A;
Y3 = !C & B & A;
Y4 = C & !B & !A;
Y5 = C & !B & A;
Y6 = C & B & !A;
Y7 = C & B & A;
```

The eight logic equations in Listing 6.7 are just the eight minterms involving the logic variables [*C, B, A*]. The CUPL *equality operator* (:) can be used to produce a particular minterm as shown in Listing 6.8. If we define the set *input* using the *FIELD* statement

```
FIELD input = [C,B,A];
```

Listing 6.8   *38dcode2.pld*

```
Name              38dcode2;
Partno            OU0013;
Revision          01;
Date              7/28/91;
Designer          R. E. Haskell;
Company           Oakland University;
Location          Rochester, MI;
Assembly          CSE 171;
Device            G16V8;
Format            j;

/*************************************************************/
/*   3-to-8 Decoder demonstrating equality operation    */
/*************************************************************/
/*   Target Device: G16V8                               */
/*************************************************************/

/**   Inputs   **/

Pin 2 = C;
Pin 3 = B;
Pin 4 = A;

/**   Outputs   **/

Pin [19..12] = ![Y0..7];

/**   Intermediate Variables   **/

FIELD input = [C,B,A];

/**   Logic Equations   **/

Y0 = input:0;
Y1 = input:1;
Y2 = input:2;
Y3 = input:3;
Y4 = input:4;
Y5 = input:5;
Y6 = input:6;
Y7 = input:7;
```

then the equation

$$Y5 = \text{input:5}$$

is equivalent to

$$Y5 = C \,\&\, !B \,\&\, A;$$

Note that the equality operator (:) operates on a set, $[C, B, A]$, to produce a single Boolean value. The value is formed by ANDing together all elements in the set, where an element is negated if the corresponding bit position in the constant following the equality operator (:) is 0. This can be seen by comparing the logic equations in Listing 6.8 with their expanded product terms shown in Fig. 6.34.

The default constant following the equality operator (:) is a hexadecimal constant. Different number bases can be used by including the prefix '*b*' for binary, '*o*' for octal, '*d*' for decimal, or '*h*' for hexadecimal. For example, *Y5* in Listing

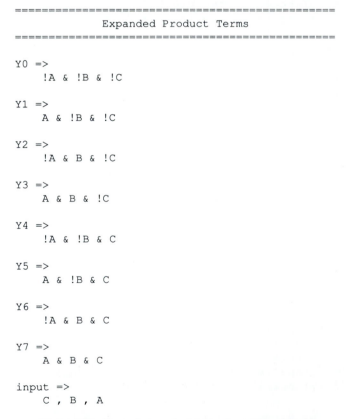

```
=================================================
                Expanded  Product  Terms
=================================================

Y0 =>
     !A & !B & !C

Y1 =>
     A & !B & !C

Y2 =>
     !A & B & !C

Y3 =>
     A & B & !C

Y4 =>
     !A & !B & C

Y5 =>
     A & !B & C

Y6 =>
     !A & B & C

Y7 =>
     A & B & C

input =>
     C , B , A
```

Figure 6.34 Expanded product terms from *38dcode2.pld*.

6.8 could also be written as

$$Y5 = \texttt{input:'b'101;}$$

TTL decoders.   There are several different kinds of TTL decoders. Two examples are shown in Figs. 6.35 and 6.36. The 74LS139 shown in Fig. 6.35 is a dual 2-to-4 decoder. It has two copies of the 2-to-4 decoder we designed in Listing 6.6 in a single chip. Note that the outputs are active low and the enable G must be low to enable an output.

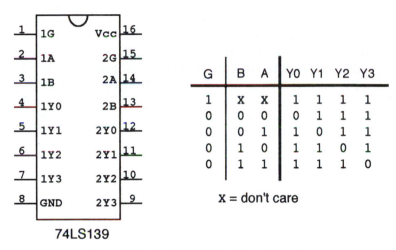

G	B	A	Y0	Y1	Y2	Y3
1	X	X	1	1	1	1
0	0	0	0	1	1	1
0	0	1	1	0	1	1
0	1	0	1	1	0	1
0	1	1	1	1	1	0

X = don't care

74LS139

Figure 6.35   The 74LS139 dual 2-to-4 decoder.

G1	G2	C	B	A	Y0	Y1	Y2	Y3	Y4	Y5	Y6	Y7
X	1	X	X	X	1	1	1	1	1	1	1	1
0	X	X	X	X	1	1	1	1	1	1	1	1
1	0	0	0	0	0	1	1	1	1	1	1	1
1	0	0	0	1	1	0	1	1	1	1	1	1
1	0	0	1	0	1	1	0	1	1	1	1	1
1	0	0	1	1	1	1	1	0	1	1	1	1
1	0	1	0	0	1	1	1	1	0	1	1	1
1	0	1	0	1	1	1	1	1	1	0	1	1
1	0	1	1	0	1	1	1	1	1	1	0	1
1	0	1	1	1	1	1	1	1	1	1	1	0

74LS138

G2 = G2A # G2B
x = don't care

Figure 6.36   The 74LS138 3-to-8 decoder.

The 74LS138 shown in Fig. 6.36 is a popular 3-to-8 decoder that also has active low outputs. It has three enable pins, *G1*, *G2A*, and *G2B*. For the outputs to be enabled, *G1* must be high and both *G2A* and *G2B* must be low.

Address decoders.   One of the most popular uses of PLDs is for address decoding in computer systems. As we will see in Chapter 8, memory devices have chip select lines such as *CS* that must be high to select the memory chip or *!CS* that must be low. Combinational logic is used to cause these lines to go high (or low) only when the specific address range associated with that memory chip is put on the address lines.

The 74LS138 3-to-8 decoder is often used for this purpose. Suppose a computer system has 16 address lines, *A0* to *A15*. If each memory location contains 8 bits, or one *byte*, of data, then this means the computer can address $2^{16} = 65,536$ bytes of memory. We call this 64 Kbytes of memory where 1K = 1,024 bytes. Usually, the high address lines are used to decode relatively large blocks of memory. We will use the lower six address lines to illustrate the process.

Suppose address lines *A3*, *A4*, and *A5* are used as the *A*, *B*, and *C* inputs to the 74LS138 shown in Fig. 6.36. Each of the eight output lines, *Y0* to *Y7*, will then correspond to one of the eight-byte address ranges shown in Table 6.1. In this table, the ×'s are don't cares, which means that address lines *A0* to *A2* can take on the values 000 to 111. In this case the address range 00 to 3F is divided into eight equal parts of 8 bytes each.

TABLE 6.1   ADDRESS DECODING TABLE

A5	A4	A3	A2	A1	A0	Address range
0	0	0	×	×	×	00–07
0	0	1	×	×	×	08–0F
0	1	0	×	×	×	10–17
0	1	1	×	×	×	18–1F
1	0	0	×	×	×	20–27
1	0	1	×	×	×	28–2F
1	1	0	×	×	×	30–37
1	1	1	×	×	×	38–3F

Suppose we wanted to divide the 64 bytes between 00 and 3F into the three *unequal* ranges shown in Table 6.2. The first range between 00 and 1F contains 32 bytes, or half of the 64. The second range between 20 and 3B contains 28 bytes, and the third range between 3C and 3F contains only 4 bytes. We could not produce chip select lines for these ranges with a single 74LS138, but it is a simple matter to do so with our PLD using the CUPL program shown in Listing 6.9, which produces the chip diagram shown in Fig. 6.37. Note from Table 6.2 that the four address lines *A2* to *A5* are needed to distinguish these three address

TABLE 6.2 EXAMPLE ADDRESS RANGES

A5	A4	A3	A2	A1	A0	Address range
0	0	0	0	0	0	00
0	1	1	1	1	1	–1F
1	0	0	0	0	0	20
1	1	1	0	1	1	–3B
1	1	1	1	0	0	3C
1	1	1	1	1	1	–3F

Listing 6.9   *addecode.pld*

```
Name            addecode;
Partno          OU0014;
Revision        01;
Date            7/28/91;
Designer        R. E. Haskell;
Company         Oakland University;
Location        Rochester, MI;
Assembly        CSE 171;
Device          G16V8;
Format          j;

/*****************************************************************/
/*   Example of address decoding using the range operation   */
/*****************************************************************/
/*   Target Device: G16V8                                    */
/*****************************************************************/

/**   Inputs   **/

Pin [2..5] = [A5..2];

/**   Outputs   **/

Pin [19..17] = ![CS0..2];

/**   Intermediate Variables   **/

FIELD address = [A2..5];

/**   Logic Equations   **/

CS0 = address:[00..1F];
CS1 = address:[20..3B];
CS2 = address:[3C..3F];
```

```
============================================================
                        Chip Diagram
============================================================

                        |    addecode   |
                x---|1                20|---x Vcc
          A5    x---|2                19|---x !CS0
          A4    x---|3                18|---x !CS1
          A3    x---|4                17|---x !CS2
          A2    x---|5                16|---x
                x---|6                15|---x
                x---|7                14|---x
                x---|8                13|---x
                x---|9                12|---x
         GND    x---|10               11|---x
                        |_____|
```

Figure 6.37 Chip diagram from *addecode.doc*.

ranges. These four address lines become the inputs to the chip in Fig. 6.37, and the three chip select signals, *!CS0, !CS1*, and *!CS2* for the three address ranges are the outputs.

In Listing 6.9 we use the CUPL *range operation* in the logic equations. We will illustrate how the range operation works by expanding the equation for *CS2* in detail. When using the range operation, CUPL adds all lower-order address variables to the set name even though they are not defined in the *FIELD* statement. Thus, the equation for *CS2* is equivalent to

$$CS2 \ = \ [A5,A4,A3,A2,A1,A0]:[3C..3F]; \qquad (6.12)$$

Now the equality operator (:) is applied to each address in the range, and the

```
=================================================
             Expanded Product Terms
=================================================

CS0 =>
     !A5

CS1 =>
       !A4 & A5
     # !A3 & A5
     # !A2 & A5

CS2 =>
     A2 & A3 & A4 & A5

address =>
     A2 , A3 , A4 , A5
```

Figure 6.38 Expanded product terms from *addecode.doc*.

resulting Boolean values are ORed. Therefore, Eq. (6.12) is expanded as follows:

```
CS2  =    A5 & A4 & A3 & A2 & !A1 & !A0

      #   A5 & A4 & A3 & A2 & !A1 & A0

      #   A5 & A4 & A3 & A2 & A1 & !A0

      #   A5 & A4 & A3 & A2 & A1 & A0;
```

CUPL then reduces this equation to

```
CS2  =  A5 & A4 & A3 & A2 & (!A1 & !A0

                          #  !A1 & A0

                          #  A1 & !A0

                          #  A1 & A0);                (6.13)

     =  A5 & A4 & A3 & A2 & (!A1 & (!A0 # A0)

                          #  A1 & (!A0 # A0));

     =  A5 & A4 & A3 & A2 & (!A1 # A1);

     =  A5 & A4 & A3 & A2;
```

as shown in the expanded product terms in Fig. 6.38. It is a good idea to use the minimization option *m2* when compiling CUPL programs with the range operation so that the maximum minimization will take place.

Compare the expanded product terms in Fig. 6.38 with the address variables in Table 6.2 and note how these logic equations, in fact, separate the three address ranges. For a further study of this address decoder, see Experiment 6 at the end of the chapter.

Encoders

An encoder is the opposite of a decoder. There can be up to 2^n inputs and n outputs. It is assumed that only one input at a time is active (that is, has the value 1 for active high inputs or a 0 for active low inputs). For example, the truth table for a 4-to-2 encoder is shown in Fig. 6.39. Note that in each row of the truth table

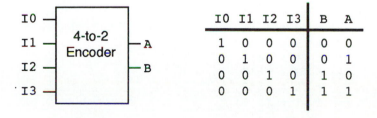

I0	I1	I2	I3	B	A
1	0	0	0	0	0
0	1	0	0	0	1
0	0	1	0	1	0
0	0	0	1	1	1

Figure 6.39 Diagram and truth table for a 4-to-2 encoder.

only one input is a 1 and all the rest are zeros. The remaining 12 possible combinations of input values (where more than one input is 1, or they are all zero) are assumed not to occur and will produce unpredictable outputs.

Given these assumptions, the outputs *A* and *B* can be written simply as

$$A = I1 \ \# \ I3$$
$$B = I2 \ \# \ I3$$

(6.14)

Listing 6.10   *encoder.pld*

```
Name            encoder;
Partno          OU0015;
Revision        01;
Date            7/29/91;
Designer        R. E. Haskell;
Company         Oakland University;
Location        Rochester, MI;
Assembly        CSE 171;
Device          G16V8;
Format          j;

/*******************************************************/
/*   8-to-3 binary encoder                             */
/*******************************************************/
/*    Target Device: G16V8                             */
/*******************************************************/

/**   Inputs   **/

Pin [2..9] = [I0..7];      /* 8 input lines */

/**   Outputs   **/

Pin [16..18] = [Y0..2];    /* 3-bit binary output */
Pin 19 = valid;            /* valid = 1 for valid binary output */

/**   Logic Equations   **/

[Y2..0] =    I7 & 'o'7
        #  I6 & 'o'6
        #  I5 & 'o'5
        #  I4 & 'o'4
        #  I3 & 'o'3
        #  I2 & 'o'2
        #  I1 & 'o'1;

valid = [I0..7]:#;
```

These equations can be implemented with the two OR gates shown in Fig. 6.40.

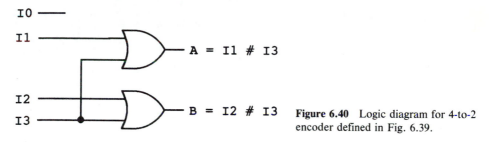

Figure 6.40 Logic diagram for 4-to-2 encoder defined in Fig. 6.39.

The truth table for an 8-to-3 encoder is shown in Fig. 6.41. It should be clear that the three outputs $Y0$, $Y1$, and $Y2$ can be implemented with three 4-input OR gates. Let's implement this encoder on our GAL 16V8. The CUPL program for this encoder is given in Listing 6.10 and the corresponding chip diagram is shown in Fig. 6.42.

I0	I1	I2	I3	I4	I5	I6	I7	Y2	Y1	Y0
1	0	0	0	0	0	0	0	0	0	0
0	1	0	0	0	0	0	0	0	0	1
0	0	1	0	0	0	0	0	0	1	0
0	0	0	1	0	0	0	0	0	1	1
0	0	0	0	1	0	0	0	1	0	0
0	0	0	0	0	1	0	0	1	0	1
0	0	0	0	0	0	1	0	1	1	0
0	0	0	0	0	0	0	1	1	1	1

Figure 6.41 Truth table for a 8-to-3 encoder.

```
=================================================================
                          Chip Diagram
=================================================================


                     |     encoder       |
              x---|1                  20|---x Vcc
          I0  x---|2                  19|---x valid
          I1  x---|3                  18|---x Y2
          I2  x---|4                  17|---x Y1
          I3  x---|5                  16|---x Y0
          I4  x---|6                  15|---x
          I5  x---|7                  14|---x
          I6  x---|8                  13|---x
          I7  x---|9                  12|---x
         GND  x---|10                 11|---x
                     |_____|
```

Figure 6.42 Chip diagram from *encoder.doc*.

Note that we have written the logic equations for *Y0, Y1*, and *Y2* as the single set equation

$$
\begin{aligned}
[\text{Y2..0}] =\;\; & \text{I7 \& 'o'7} \\
\# & \text{I6 \& 'o'6} \\
\# & \text{I5 \& 'o'5} \\
\# & \text{I4 \& 'o'4} \qquad\qquad (6.15) \\
\# & \text{I3 \& 'o'3} \\
\# & \text{I2 \& 'o'2} \\
\# & \text{I1 \& 'o'1}
\end{aligned}
$$

Each variable on the right side of this equation is ANDed with an octal number. This is equivalent to ANDing the variable with each bit of the octal number, where each bit represents the corresponding position in the set [*Y2, Y1, Y0*]. Equation (6.15) therefore expands to

$$
\begin{aligned}
[\text{Y2, Y1, Y0}] =\;\; & [\text{I7,I7,I7}] \\
\# & [\text{I6,I6, 0}] \\
\# & [\text{I5, 0,I5}] \\
\# & [\text{I4, 0, 0}] \qquad\qquad (6.16) \\
\# & [\ 0,\text{I3,I3}] \\
\# & [\ 0,\text{I2, 0}] \\
\# & [\ 0,\ 0,\text{I1}]
\end{aligned}
$$

The logic variable *Y2* is then just the ORing of the first element in each set on the right, that is,

$$
\text{Y2 = I7 \# I6 \# I5 \# I4}
$$

as shown in the expanded product terms in Fig. 6.43. Note that Eq. (6.16) also agrees with the expanded product terms in Fig. 6.43 for *Y1* and *Y0*.

The output variable *valid* was also included in Listing 6.10 and was defined by the logic equation

$$
\text{valid = [I0..7]:\#} \qquad\qquad (6.17)
$$

When a logical operator (#, &, or \$) follows the equality operator as in Eq. (6.17), then the logical operator operates identically on all variables in the set. Thus, Eq. (6.17) is equivalent to

$$
\text{valid = I0 \# I1 \# I2 \# I3 \# I4 \# I5 \# I6 \# I7} \quad (6.18)
$$

as shown in the expanded product terms in Fig. 6.43.

Priority encoder.   The encoder given by the truth table in Fig. 6.41 assumes that only one input has the logical value 1 at any instant. Encoders are

```
=================================================
                Expanded Product Terms
=================================================

     Y0 =>
             I7
        #  I1
        #  I5
        #  I3

     Y1 =>
             I7
        #  I6
        #  I2
        #  I3

     Y2 =>
             I7
        #  I6
        #  I5
        #  I4

     valid =>
             I0
        #  I1
        #  I2
        #  I3
        #  I4
        #  I5
        #  I6
        #  I7
```

Figure 6.43   Expanded product terms from *encoder.doc*.

often used to tell which of several external devices are signaling to the computer that it wants to interrupt the computer for service. What if two external devices signal the computer at the same time by bringing two of the input lines to the decoder high at the same time? Priority encoders are used in this situation to select the external device with the highest priority to receive service.

The truth table for an 8-input priority encoder is given in Fig. 6.44. Note that in any row the zeros to the left of the 1 have been replaced with don't cares

I0	I1	I2	I3	I4	I5	I6	I7	Y2	Y1	Y0
1	0	0	0	0	0	0	0	0	0	0
X	1	0	0	0	0	0	0	0	0	1
X	X	1	0	0	0	0	0	0	1	0
X	X	X	1	0	0	0	0	0	1	1
X	X	X	X	1	0	0	0	1	0	0
X	X	X	X	X	1	0	0	1	0	1
X	X	X	X	X	X	1	0	1	1	0
X	X	X	X	X	X	X	1	1	1	1

Figure 6.44   Truth table for an 8-input priority encoder.

Listing 6.11   *pencoder.pld*

```
Name                pencoder;
Partno              OU0016;
Revision            01;
Date                7/29/91;
Designer            R. E. Haskell;
Company             Oakland University;
Location            Rochester, MI;
Assembly            CSE 171;
Device              G16V8;
Format              j;

/**************************************************************/
/*    8-input priority encoder                              */
/**************************************************************/
/*    Target Device: G16V8                                  */
/**************************************************************/

/**   Inputs  **/

Pin [2..9] = [I0..7];     /* 8 input lines */

/**   Outputs  **/

Pin [16..18] = [Y0..2];   /* 3-bit binary output */
Pin 19 = valid;           /* valid = 1 for valid binary output */

/**   Declarations and Intermediate Variable Definitions  **/

L7 =   I7;
L6 = !I7 &   I6;
L5 = !I7 & !I6 &   I5;
L4 = !I7 & !I6 & !I5 &   I4;
L3 = !I7 & !I6 & !I5 & !I4 &   I3;
L2 = !I7 & !I6 & !I5 & !I4 & !I3 &   I2;
L1 = !I7 & !I6 & !I5 & !I4 & !I3 & !I2 &   I1;

/**   Logic Equations  **/

[Y2..0] =   L7 & 'o'7
          # L6 & 'o'6
          # L5 & 'o'5
          # L4 & 'o'4
          # L3 & 'o'3
          # L2 & 'o'2
          # L1 & 'o'1;

valid = [I0..7]:#;
```

```
========================================================
                 Expanded Product Terms
========================================================


L1 =>
    I1 & !I2 & !I3 & !I4 & !I5 & !I6 & !I7


L2 =>
    I2 & !I3 & !I4 & !I5 & !I6 & !I7


L3 =>
    I3 & !I4 & !I5 & !I6 & !I7


L4 =>
    I4 & !I5 & !I6 & !I7


L5 =>
    I5 & !I6 & !I7


L6 =>
    I6 & !I7


L7 =>
    I7


Y0 =>
    I7
  # I1 & !I2 & !I3 & !I4 & !I5 & !I6 & !I7
  # I5 & !I6 & !I7
  # I3 & !I4 & !I5 & !I6 & !I7


Y1 =>
    I7
  # I6 & !I7
  # I2 & !I3 & !I4 & !I5 & !I6 & !I7
  # I3 & !I4 & !I5 & !I6 & !I7


Y2 =>
    I7
  # I6 & !I7
  # I5 & !I6 & !I7
  # I4 & !I5 & !I6 & !I7


valid =>
    I0
  # I1
  # I2
  # I3
  # I4
  # I5
  # I6
  # I7
```

Figure 6.45 Expanded product terms from *pencoder.doc*.

($\times$'s). This means that if any of these $\times$'s are really 1's, it doesn't matter. The output encoding is that for the 1 on the main diagonal in the truth table. This means, for example, that *I4* has a higher priority than *I3* (or *I2*, *I1*, or *I0*). The input *I7* has the highest priority.

We can implement this priority encoder on our GAL 16V8 using the CUPL program shown in Listing 6.11. The only difference between this program and the one in Listing 6.10 is that we have added eight intermediate variables *L0* to *L7* corresponding to the eight input variables *I0* to *I7*. These intermediate variables are defined to require the higher-priority inputs to be zero when a particular input is 1. These intermediate variables are then used in the same logic equation for the three outputs that we used in Listing 6.10. The expanded product terms for this program are shown in Fig. 6.45. Note how the outputs *Y0, Y1*, and *Y2* are expanded. Compare these expanded logic terms with those in Fig. 6.43 and note how they implement the truth table in Fig. 6.44. You can study the behavior of this priority encoder in Experiment 7.

TTL encoders.   The pinout and truth table for the 74LS148 priority encoder are shown in Fig. 6.46. Note that for this chip the inputs are active low (they assert a zero to be recognized), and input 7 is the highest priority. The output code for input 7 is 000. That is, the outputs are active low as well. There is also an enable input pin, *EI*, and an enable output pin, *EO*. The output pin, *EO*, is designed to be connected to the *EI* pin of another cascaded 74LS148. The *group select* output pin, *GS*, is an active low *valid* pin that goes low when any of the input lines is selected.

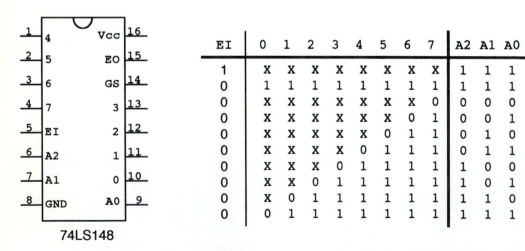

EI	0	1	2	3	4	5	6	7	A2	A1	A0	GS	EO
1	X	X	X	X	X	X	X	X	1	1	1	1	1
0	1	1	1	1	1	1	1	1	1	1	1	1	0
0	X	X	X	X	X	X	X	0	0	0	0	0	1
0	X	X	X	X	X	X	0	1	0	0	1	0	1
0	X	X	X	X	X	0	1	1	0	1	0	0	1
0	X	X	X	X	0	1	1	1	0	1	1	0	1
0	X	X	X	0	1	1	1	1	1	0	0	0	1
0	X	X	0	1	1	1	1	1	1	0	1	0	1
0	X	0	1	1	1	1	1	1	1	1	0	0	1
0	0	1	1	1	1	1	1	1	1	1	1	0	1

74LS148

Figure 6.46   The 74LS148 priority encoder.

6.4 MULTIPLEXERS AND DEMULTIPLEXERS

Multiplexers

An n-input multiplexer (called a *MUX*) is an n-way digital switch that switches one of n inputs to the output. A 4-input multiplexer is shown in Fig. 6.47. The switch is controlled by the two control lines $s0$ and $s1$. The 2 bits on these control lines select one of the four inputs to be "connected" to the output. This means that the logical value of the output Y will be the same as the logical value of the selected input.

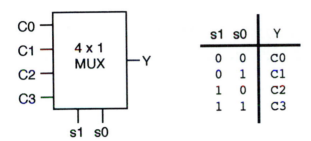

s1	s0	Y
0	0	C0
0	1	C1
1	0	C2
1	1	C3

Figure 6.47   A 4-line-to-1 multiplexer.

From the truth table in Fig. 6.47 we can write the logic equation for Y as

$$Y = \quad C0 \ \& \ !s0 \ \& \ !s1$$
$$\# \ C1 \ \& \ s0 \ \& \ !s1$$
$$\# \ C2 \ \& \ !s0 \ \& \ s1 \qquad (6.19)$$
$$\# \ C3 \ \& \ s0 \ \& \ s1$$

The CUPL program for this *4 × 1* multiplexer is given in Listing 6.12, and the chip diagram is shown in Fig. 6.48. We have used the set name *s_ctrl* for [*s1*,

```
=============================================================
                         Chip Diagram
=============================================================

                        |      41mux       |
               x---|1                 20|---x Vcc
         C0    x---|2                 19|---x
         C1    x---|3                 18|---x
         C2    x---|4                 17|---x
         C3    x---|5                 16|---x
         s1    x---|6                 15|---x  Y
         s0    x---|7                 14|---x
               x---|8                 13|---x
               x---|9                 12|---x
         GND   x---|10                11|---x
                        |_____|
```

Figure 6.48   Chip diagram from *41mux.doc*.

Listing 6.12   *41mux.pld*

```
Name              41mux;
Partno            OU0017;
Revision          01;
Date              7/29/91;
Designer          R. E. Haskell;
Company           Oakland University;
Location          Rochester, MI;
Assembly          CSE 171;
Device            G16V8;
Format            j;


/***************************************************************/
/*    4 line to 1 multiplexer                                  */
/***************************************************************/
/*    Target Device: G16V8                                     */
/***************************************************************/

/**   Inputs   **/

Pin [2..5] = [C0..3];    /* 4 input lines    */
Pin [6,7]  = [s1..0];    /* 2 control lines */

/**   Outputs   **/

Pin 15 = Y;                    /* multiplexed output */

/**   Intermediate variables **/

FIELD s_ctrl = [s1..0];

/**   Logic Equations   **/

Y =    s_ctrl:'b'00 & C0
  #  s_ctrl:'b'01 & C1
  #  s_ctrl:'b'10 & C2
  #  s_ctrl:'b'11 & C3;
```

s0] together with the equality operator to define the logic equation for *Y*. Note from the expanded product terms in Fig. 6.49 that this logic equation reduces to Eq. (6.19).

Demultiplexers

A demultiplexer is the opposite kind of digital switch from a multiplexer. It has one input that is "connected" to one of *n* outputs. A *1 × 4* demultiplexer is shown

```
==================================================
             Expanded Product Terms
==================================================

Y =>
      C0 & !s0 & !s1
    # C1 & s0 & !s1
    # C2 & !s0 & s1
    # C3 & s0 & s1

s_ctrl =>
      s1 , s0
```

Figure 6.49 Expanded product terms
from *41mux.doc*.

in Fig. 6.50. The two control lines *d0* and *d1* determine to which of four outputs,
Y0 to *Y3*, the input *YIN* is connected.

The logic equations for the demultiplexer in Fig. 6.50 are similar to those
for the multiplexer and are given in the CUPL program shown in Listing 6.13.
Note that the expanded product terms in Fig. 6.51 are what you would expect

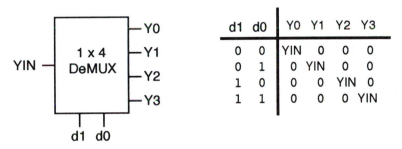

d1	d0	Y0	Y1	Y2	Y3
0	0	YIN	0	0	0
0	1	0	YIN	0	0
1	0	0	0	YIN	0
1	1	0	0	0	YIN

Figure 6.50   A 1-line-to-4 demultiplexer.

```
==================================================
             Expanded Product Terms
==================================================

Y0 =>
     YIN & !d0 & !d1

Y1 =>
     YIN & d0 & !d1

Y2 =>
     YIN & !d0 & d1

Y3 =>
     YIN & d0 & d1

d_ctrl =>
      d1 , d0
```

Figure 6.51 Expanded product terms
from *14demux.doc*.

Listing 6.13   *14demux.pld*

```
Name                14demux;
Partno              DU0018;
Revision            01;
Date                7/29/91;
Designer            R. E. Haskell;
Company             Oakland University;
Location            Rochester, MI;
Assembly            CSE 171;
Device              G16V8;
Format              j;


/******************************************************************/
/*    1 line to 4 demultiplexer                                   */
/******************************************************************/
/*    Target Device: G16V8                                        */
/******************************************************************/

/**   Inputs   **/

Pin 8 = YIN;                    /* input line */
Pin [9,11]  = [d1..0];          /* 2 control lines */

/**   Outputs   **/

Pin [16..19] = [Y3..0];         /* 4 output lines */

/**   Intermediate variables **/

FIELD d_ctrl = [d1..0];

/**   Logic Equations   **/

Y0 = d_ctrl:'b'00 & YIN;
Y1 = d_ctrl:'b'01 & YIN;
Y2 = d_ctrl:'b'10 & YIN;
Y3 = d_ctrl:'b'11 & YIN;
```

from the truth table in Fig. 6.50. The chip diagram for this *1 × 4* demultiplexer is shown in Fig. 6.52.

A multiplexer/demultiplexer combination can be used to connect any of the *n* inputs of the multiplexer to any of the *n* outputs of the demultiplexer. For example, if we connect our *4 × 1* multiplexer to our *1 × 4* demultiplexer as shown in Fig. 6.53, then, by changing our source control lines *s0, s1* and our destination control lines *d0, d1*, we can connect any of the inputs *C0* to *C3* to any of the outputs *Y0* to *Y3*. Notice from Figs. 6.48 and 6.52 that the pinouts for the two

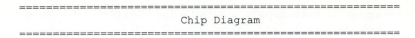

```
=============================================================
                       Chip Diagram
=============================================================

                   _____
                  |    14demux     |
            x---|1                20|---x  Vcc
            x---|2                19|---x  Y0
            x---|3                18|---x  Y1
            x---|4                17|---x  Y2
            x---|5                16|---x  Y3
            x---|6                15|---x
            x---|7                14|---x
      YIN   x---|8                13|---x
      d1    x---|9                12|---x
      GND   x---|10               11|---x  d0
                  |_____|
```

Figure 6.52   Chip diagram from *14demux.doc*.

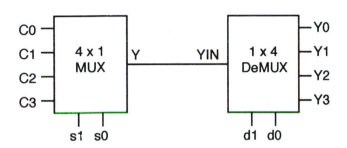

Figure 6.53   Connecting C0–Y3 using a multiplexer and demultiplexer.

```
=============================================================
                       Chip Diagram
=============================================================

                   _____
                  |   muxdemux     |
            x---|1                20|---x  Vcc
      C0    x---|2                19|---x  Y0
      C1    x---|3                18|---x  Y1
      C2    x---|4                17|---x  Y2
      C3    x---|5                16|---x  Y3
      s1    x---|6                15|---x  Y
      s0    x---|7                14|---x
      YIN   x---|8                13|---x
      d1    x---|9                12|---x
      GND   x---|10               11|---x  d0
                  |_____|
```

Figure 6.54   Combining the multiplexer from Fig. 6.48 with the demultiplexer from Fig. 6.52 in a single chip.

programs we have already written for the multiplexer and the demultiplexer will both fit on a single GAL 16V8! This will lead to the chip diagram shown in Fig. 6.54.

In Fig. 6.54, if you connect an external wire between pin 15 (Y) and pin 8 (YIN), you will have the circuit shown in Fig. 6.53. You can study this circuit in more detail in Experiment 8.

TTL Multiplexers/Demultiplexers

There are several different kinds of TTL multiplexers and demultiplexers. Two examples are shown in Figs. 6.55 and 6.56. The 74LS153 shown in Fig. 6.55 is a

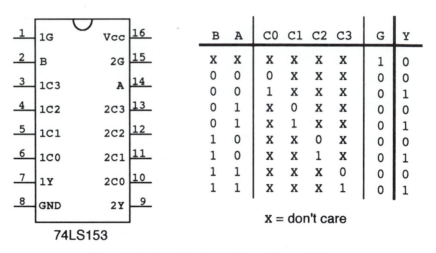

B	A	C0	C1	C2	C3	G	Y
X	X	X	X	X	X	1	0
0	0	0	X	X	X	0	0
0	0	1	X	X	X	0	1
0	1	X	0	X	X	0	0
0	1	X	1	X	X	0	1
1	0	X	X	0	X	0	0
1	0	X	X	1	X	0	1
1	1	X	X	X	0	0	0
1	1	X	X	X	1	0	1

X = don't care

Figure 6.55   The 74LS153 dual 4-to-1-line multiplexer.

G	C	B	A	Y0	Y1	Y2	Y3
1	X	X	X	1	1	1	1
0	1	0	0	0	1	1	1
0	1	0	1	1	0	1	1
0	1	1	0	1	1	0	1
0	1	1	1	1	1	1	0
X	0	X	X	1	1	1	1

X = don't care

Figure 6.56   The 74LS155 dual 1-to-4-line demultiplexer.

dual 4-to-1-line multiplexer. It has two copies of the 4-to-1-line multiplexer we designed in Listing 6.12 in a single chip. In this chip, *A* and *B* are the select lines. The strobe input *G* must be low to connect the inputs to the output.

The 74LS155 shown in Fig. 6.56 is a dual 1-to-4-line demultiplexer. In this chip, *C* is the input data line and *A* and *B* are the select lines. Note that the outputs, *Y0* to *Y3*, are inverting outputs. That is, if *C* is 1, the selected output is 0, while if *C* is 0, the selected output is 1. Again the strobe input *G* must be low to connect the input to the outputs.

6.5 CODE CONVERTERS

Code converters take a certain input code and convert it to a different output code. Often the easiest way to do this is to use a table lookup in some type of memory chip. However, certain code converter problems can be implemented as combinational logic using a PLD. Some of these code converters also exist as TTL chips. We will illustrate code converters with two examples that we can program on our GAL 16V8: a binary-to-BCD converter and a 7-segment decoder.

Binary-to-BCD Converter

A binary coded decimal (BCD) number is the decimal number 0 to 9 represented by their binary equivalent 0000 to 1001. The decimal number 14 would then be represented by the two BCD numbers 0001 0100. On the other hand, the hex

	Binary				Binary Coded Decimal (BCD)					
HEX	C3	C2	C1	C0	E	D	C	B	A	BCD
0	0	0	0	0	0	0	0	0	0	00
1	0	0	0	1	0	0	0	0	1	01
2	0	0	1	0	0	0	0	1	0	02
3	0	0	1	1	0	0	0	1	1	03
4	0	1	0	0	0	0	1	0	0	04
5	0	1	0	1	0	0	1	0	1	05
6	0	1	1	0	0	0	1	1	0	06
7	0	1	1	1	0	0	1	1	1	07
8	1	0	0	0	0	1	0	0	0	08
9	1	0	0	1	0	1	0	0	1	09
A	1	0	1	0	1	0	0	0	0	10
B	1	0	1	1	1	0	0	0	1	11
C	1	1	0	0	1	0	0	1	0	12
D	1	1	0	1	1	0	0	1	1	13
E	1	1	1	0	1	0	1	0	0	14
F	1	1	1	1	1	0	1	0	1	15

Figure 6.57   Truth table for a binary-to-BCD converter.

(binary) representation of the decimal number 14 would be E (1110). A truth table for converting the 16 binary (hex) digits, 0000 to 1111 (0 to F), to the equivalent two BCD numbers, 00 to 15, is shown in Fig. 6.57.

  We could write sum of products logic equations directly from the truth table in Fig. 6.57 and then try to simplify the expressions. Alternatively, we could let

Listing 6.14   *bin2bcd.pld*

```
Name               bin2bcd;
Partno             OU0020;
Revision           01;
Date               7/30/91;
Designer           R. E. Haskell;
Company            Oakland University;
Location           Rochester, MI;
Assembly           CSE 171;
Device             G16V8;
Format             j;

/********************************************************************/
/*    Binary to BCD code converter                                 */
/*    using the TABLE command                                      */
/********************************************************************/
/*    Target Device: G16V8                                         */
/********************************************************************/

/**   Inputs   **/

Pin [2..5] = [C0..3];            /* 4 binary input lines */

/**   Outputs   **/

Pin [15..19] = [A,B,C,D,E];   /* 2 output BCD digits E DCBA */

/**   Intermediate variables **/

FIELD input = [C3..0];
FIELD output = [E,D,C,B,A];

/**   Logic Equations   **/

TABLE input => output{
  0=>00;   1=>01;   2=>02;   3=>03;
  4=>04;   5=>05;   6=>06;   7=>07;
  8=>08;   9=>09;   A=>10;   B=>11;
  C=>12;   D=>13;   E=>14;   F=>15;
  }
```

```
===========================================================
                       Chip Diagram
===========================================================


                    |    bin2bcd    |
          x---|1                20|---x Vcc
     C0   x---|2                19|---x E
     C1   x---|3                18|---x D
     C2   x---|4                17|---x C
     C3   x---|5                16|---x B
          x---|6                15|---x A
          x---|7                14|---x
          x---|8                13|---x
          x---|9                12|---x
    GND   x---|10               11|---x
                    |_____|
```

Figure 6.58   Chip diagram from *bin2bcd.doc*.

CUPL do the work by expressing the relationships between the binary inputs and the BCD outputs in the form of a table using the CUPL *TABLE* command. The way to use this command for this problem is shown in the CUPL program in Listing 6.14. The chip diagram for this program is shown in Fig. 6.58.

The sets *input* and *output* are defined with the *FIELD* command in Listing 6.14. The *TABLE* command is of the following form:

```
TABLE input => output{
     0=>00;   1=>01;   2=>02;   3=>03;
     4=>04;   5=>05;   6=>06;   7=>07;
     8=>08;   9=>09;   A=>10;   B=>11;
     C=>12;   D=>13;   E=>14;   F=>15;
     }
```

In this table, the relationship between the input and output is specified explicitly in table form between the two brackets { and }. CUPL reduces this form to the expanded product terms shown in Fig. 6.59. Compare these expanded product terms with the truth table in Fig. 6.57 and see if you can verify each logic equation.

7-Segment Displays

A *light-emitting diode* (LED) emits light when current flows through it in the positive direction, as shown in Fig. 6.60. Current flows through the LED when the voltage on the *anode* side (the wide side of the black triangle) is made higher than the voltage on the *cathode* side (the straight line connected to the point of the black triangle). When current flows through a lighted LED, the forward voltage

```
====================================================
                Expanded Product Terms
====================================================

A =>
    C0

B =>
     !C1 & C2 & C3
   # C1 & !C3

C =>
     C2 & !C3
   # C1 & C2

D =>
     !C1 & !C2 & C3

E =>
     C2 & C3
   # C1 & C3

input =>
     C3 , C2 , C1 , C0

output =>
     E , D , C , B , A
```

Figure 6.59   Expanded product terms from *bin2bcd.doc*.

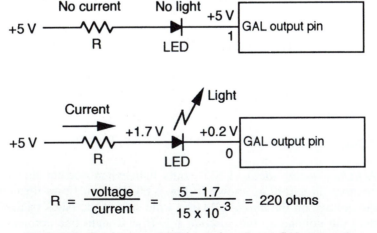

Figure 6.60   Turning on an LED by storing a 0 on a GAL output pin.

across the LED is typically about +1.5 volts (V). We can turn an LED on and off using an output pin of the GAL 16V8 with the circuit shown in Fig. 6.60. When the pin output is high (+5 V), no current can flow through the LED and therefore no light will be emitted. If we bring the GAL output pin low (assume about 0.2 V), then current will flow from the +5-V power supply through the resistor R and the LED. The resistor is used to limit the amount of current that flows through the LED. A typical current would be 15 milliamperes (mA) or 15×10^{-3} amperes (A). Using Ohm's law, we can compute the resistor size needed as shown in Fig. 6.60. The maximum current that should flow into a GAL 16V8 output pin when the output is low is 24 mA. Thus, limiting the current to 15 mA will be a safe choice.

Seven LEDs can be arranged in a pattern to form different digits as shown in Fig. 6.61. Digital watches use similar 7-segment displays using liquid crystals rather than LEDs. The red digits on digital clocks are LEDs. Seven-segment displays come in two types: common anode and common cathode. A common anode 7-segment display has all the anodes tied together as shown in Fig. 6.61. A common cathode 7-segment display would have all the cathodes tied together. In Fig. 6.61 we should really connect a separate resistor to each of the seven LEDs so that each lighted LED would have the same current and therefore the same brightness. For experimental purposes it is easier to cheat and put a single resistor from the common anode to +5 V. This will mean that an 8, which has all LEDs lit, will be dimmer (because the current is split between all 8 LEDs) than a 1, which has only two LEDs lit.

The 7-segment display shown in Fig. 6.61 comes in an integrated package with a common anode pin and separate pins for each segment *a* to *g*. These seven segment pins are connected to seven of the output lines on the GAL 16V8. Then, by bringing different output lines low, we can form any digit by lighting the ap-

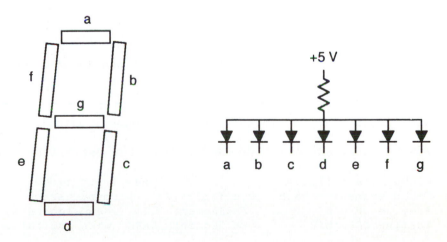

Figure 6.61   A 7-segment display contains seven light-emitting diodes (LEDs).

Listing 6.15   *7seg.pld*

```
Name            7seg;
Partno          OU0021;
Revision        01;
Date            7/30/91;
Designer        R. E. Haskell;
Company         Oakland University;
Location        Rochester, MI;
Assembly        CSE 171;
Device          G16V8;
Format          j;


/*****************************************************************/
/*                                           a             */
/* This is a Hex-to-seven-segment           -----          */
/* decoder capable of driving common-anode  |     |        */
/* LEDs.                                    f|     |b       */
/*                                           |  g  |        */
/*                                           -----          */
/*                                           |     |        */
/*                                          e|     |c       */
/*                                           |     |        */
/*                                           -----          */
/*                                             d            */
/*                                                         */
/*****************************************************************/
/*    Target Device: G16V8                                 */
/*****************************************************************/


/**   Inputs   **/

pin [2..5] = [D0..3];    /* Data input lines to display */

/**   Outputs   **/

pin [19..13] = ![a,b,c,d,e,f,g];   /* Segment output lines */

/** Declarations and Intermediate Variable Definitions **/

FIELD data = [D3..0];               /* Hex input field */
FIELD segment = [a,b,c,d,e,f,g];  /*  Display segment field*/
$define ON  'b'1       /* Segment LIT when logically "ON" */
$define OFF 'b'0       /* Segment DARK when logically "OFF"*/

/** Logic Equations **/
```

Listing 6.15   *(cont.)*

```
                    /*   a       b       c       d       e       f       g    */
segment     =
/* 0 */             [ ON,   ON,   ON,   ON,   ON,   ON,   OFF] & data:0
/* 1 */        #    [OFF,   ON,   ON,   OFF,  OFF,  OFF,  OFF] & data:1
/* 2 */        #    [ ON,   ON,   OFF,  ON,   ON,   OFF,  ON ] & data:2
/* 3 */        #    [ ON,   ON,   ON,   ON,   OFF,  OFF,  ON ] & data:3
/* 4 */        #    [OFF,   ON,   ON,   OFF,  OFF,  ON,   ON ] & data:4
/* 5 */        #    [ ON,   OFF,  ON,   ON,   OFF,  ON,   ON ] & data:5
/* 6 */        #    [ ON,   OFF,  ON,   ON,   ON,   ON,   ON ] & data:6
/* 7 */        #    [ ON,   ON,   ON,   OFF,  OFF,  OFF,  OFF] & data:7
/* 8 */        #    [ ON,   ON,   ON,   ON,   ON,   ON,   ON ] & data:8
/* 9 */        #    [ ON,   ON,   ON,   ON,   OFF,  ON,   ON ] & data:9
/* A */        #    [ ON,   ON,   ON,   OFF,  ON,   ON,   ON ] & data:A
/* B */        #    [OFF,   OFF,  ON,   ON,   ON,   ON,   ON ] & data:B
/* C */        #    [ ON,   OFF,  OFF,  ON,   ON,   ON,   OFF] & data:C
/* D */        #    [OFF,   ON,   ON,   ON,   ON,   OFF,  ON ] & data:D
/* E */        #    [ ON,   OFF,  OFF,  ON,   ON,   ON,   ON ] & data:E
/* F */        #    [ ON,   OFF,  OFF,  OFF,  ON,   ON,   ON ] & data:F;
```

propriate LEDs. The CUPL program shown in Listing 6.15 is a hex-to-seven-segment decoder that converts a 4-bit input hex digit, *0* to *F*, to the appropriate 7-segment codes, *a* to *g*, for driving the common anode 7-segment display shown in Fig. 6.61.

In Listing 6.15, note that the output pins 13 to 19 are defined to be active low so that a logical *true* value (1) will actually produce 0 V at the output pin to turn the LED on. The CUPL statements

```
$define ON    'b'1
$define OFF   'b'0
```

define the variables *ON* and *OFF* to be equal to the binary values 1 and 0, respectively.

The chip diagram for this 7-segment decoder is shown in Fig. 6.62. A particular hex value on the input data lines *data* = [*D3, D2, D1, D0*] will produce the segment values on the output pins *segment* = [*a, b, c, d, e, f, g*]. Note how we have written the function table in Listing 6.15 to graphically show in table form which segments are *ON* and *OFF* to produce a particular digit. For example, digit 5 will have segments *a, c, d, f,* and *g ON* and the others *OFF*.

In the logic equation for *segment* in Listing 6.15, each row contributes one possible product term to each output pin *a* to *g*. For example, in row 5 each output segment labeled *ON* will have the minterm *data:5* = *!D3 & D2 & !D1 & D0* added to its sum of products logic equation. The resulting logic equations for each output

```
================================================================
                          Chip Diagram
================================================================

                    |‾‾‾‾‾‾‾‾‾‾‾‾‾‾‾‾‾|
                    |      7seg       |
           x---|1                20|---x Vcc
       D0  x---|2                19|---x !a
       D1  x---|3                18|---x !b
       D2  x---|4                17|---x !c
       D3  x---|5                16|---x !d
           x---|6                15|---x !e
           x---|7                14|---x !f
           x---|8                13|---x !g
           x---|9                12|---x
      GND  x---|10               11|---x
                    |_____|
```

Figure 6.62   Chip diagram from *7seg.doc*.

pin are then minimized to produce the expanded product terms shown in Fig.
6.63. You should be able to verify these expanded product terms by drawing a
Karnaugh map for each output pin from the table given in Listing 6.15. Each *ON*
in a given column corresponds to a 1 in the K-map.

For example, the K-map for the segment *e* is shown in Fig. 6.64. From the
logic equation table in Listing 6.15, we can write the equation for *e* as the sum
of the following 10 minterms.

$$e = \text{!D3 \& !D2 \& !D1 \& !D0}$$

$$\# \text{ !D3 \& !D2 \& D1 \& !D0}$$

$$\# \text{ !D3 \& D2 \& D1 \& !D0}$$

$$\# \text{ D3 \& !D2 \& !D1 \& !D0}$$

$$\# \text{ D3 \& !D2 \& D1 \& !D0}$$

$$\# \text{ D3 \& !D2 \& D1 \& D0}$$

$$\# \text{ D3 \& D2 \& !D1 \& !D0}$$

$$\# \text{ D3 \& D2 \& !D1 \& D0}$$

$$\# \text{ D3 \& D2 \& D1 \& !D0}$$

$$\# \text{ D3 \& D2 \& D1 \& D0}$$

From the Karnaugh map in Figure 6.64, we can write this in the reduced form

$$e = \text{!D2 \& !D0}$$

$$\# \text{ D3 \& D2}$$

$$\# \text{ D3 \& D1}$$

$$\# \text{ D1 \& !D0}$$

```
=================================================
          Expanded Product Terms
=================================================


a =>
      D1 & D2
  #  !D0 & !D2
  #  !D0 & D3
  #  D1 & !D3
  #  !D1 & !D2 & D3
  #  D0 & D2 & !D3

b =>
      !D0 & !D2
  #  !D1 & !D2
  #  D0 & !D1 & D3
  #  D0 & D1 & !D3
  #  !D0 & !D1 & !D3

c =>
      D0 & !D1
  #  D0 & !D2
  #  !D1 & !D2
  #  !D2 & D3
  #  D2 & !D3

d =>
      !D1 & D3
  #  !D0 & D1 & D2
  #  D0 & !D1 & D2
  #  D0 & D1 & !D2
  #  !D0 & !D2 & !D3

data =>
      D3 , D2 , D1 , D0

e =>
      !D0 & D1
  #  !D0 & !D2
  #  D1 & D3
  #  D2 & D3

f =>
      !D0 & !D1
  #  !D0 & D2
  #  D1 & D3
  #  !D2 & D3
  #  !D1 & D2 & !D3

g =>
      !D0 & D1
  #  D1 & !D2
  #  D0 & D3
  #  !D2 & D3
  #  !D1 & D2 & !D3

segment =>
      a , b , c , d , e , f , g
```

Figure 6.63 Expanded product terms from *7seg.doc*.

151

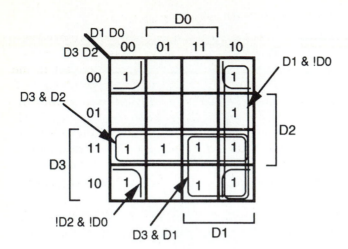

Figure 6.64   K-map for segment *e* in the 7-segment decoder.

which is the same as given in the expanded product terms shown in Fig. 6.63. See Experiment 9 for further study of 7-segment displays.

Experiment 4: Magnitude Comparator

1. Compile the program given in Listing 6.3. Make a set of test vectors and test the program by running CSIM. (See Experiment 3 in Chapter 5.) Add your verified test vectors to the JEDEC file produced by compiling the program with CUPL.
2. Program a GAL 16V8 to produce the chip shown in Fig. 6.8.
3. Use the PLD logic analyzer to test the chip. Connect the eight output lines of the logic analyzer to the *A* and *B* input lines of the chip. Connect the three chip outputs *A_EQ_B*, *A_GT_B*, and *A_LT_B* to the three logic analyzer input lines, *In4, In3*, and *In2*. Change bits 4 to 7 in the output column manually and then press function key *F1* to compare this value with all possible values of the lower 4 bits.
4. Record the results for four different values of *Out4* to *Out7* by printing the resulting truth table. Discuss the results.

Experiment 5: Adder/Subtractor

1. Write a CUPL program called *addsub.pld* that will produce the 4-bit adder/subtractor whose chip diagram follows. Use the method suggested by Fig. 6.24.
2. Make a set of test vectors and test the program by running CSIM. (See Experiment 3 in Chapter 5.)

3. Use the JEDEC file produced in (2) to program a GAL 16V8.

4. Use the PLD logic analyzer to test the chip. Connect the four output lines, *Out4* to *Out7*, of the logic analyzer to the input lines, *A0* to *A3*, of the chip. Connect the four output lines, *Out0* to *Out3*, of the logic analyzer to the input lines, *B0* to *B3*, of the chip. Connect the four chip outputs *SD0* to *SD3* to the four logic analyzer input lines, *In1* to *In4*. Connect the *Carry_Borrow* chip output pin to the logic analyzer input *In0*. Connect the *E* input (pin 11) directly to ground for addition tests and to +5 volts for subtraction tests. Change bits 4 to 7 in the output column manually and then press function key *F1* to add ($E = 0$) all possible values of the lower 4 bits to these upper 4 bits. Repeat with $E = 1$ to subtract the lower four output bits from the upper four.

5. Record the results for four different values of *Out4* to *Out7* by printing the resulting truth table. Indicate the current value of *E*. Discuss the results.

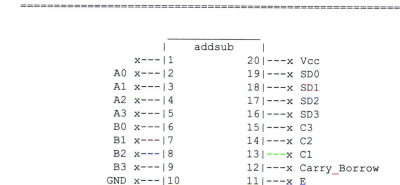

```
============================================================
                      Chip Diagram
============================================================

                    _____
                   |     addsub     |
           x---|1              20|---x Vcc
    A0     x---|2              19|---x SD0
    A1     x---|3              18|---x SD1
    A2     x---|4              17|---x SD2
    A3     x---|5              16|---x SD3
    B0     x---|6              15|---x C3
    B1     x---|7              14|---x C2
    B2     x---|8              13|---x C1
    B3     x---|9              12|---x Carry_Borrow
    GND    x---|10             11|---x E
                   |_____|
```

Experiment 6: Address Decoder

1. Write a CUPL program based on Listing 6.9 that will produce the chip diagram shown in Fig. 6.37. The three outputs *!CS0*, *!CS1*, and *!CS2* should go low in the following address ranges:

Output	Address range
!CS0	00–04
!CS1	10–17
!CS2	20–3F

2. Make a set of test vectors and test the program by running CSIM. (See Experiment 3 in Chapter 5.)

3. Use the JEDEC file produced in (2) to program a GAL 16V8.

4. Use the PLD logic analyzer to test the chip. Connect the four output lines, *Out2* to *Out5*, of the logic analyzer to the input lines, *A2* to *A5*, of the chip. Connect the three chip outputs *!CS0* to *!CS2* to the three logic analyzer input lines, *In2* to *In4*. Note that when you press function key *F1* to produce a truth table the values of *Out4* and *Out5*, connected to *A4* and *A5*, remain the same. Change these manually to 00, 01, 10, and 11 so as to cover the entire address range 00 to 3F in your tests.

5. Record the results for the entire 64-byte address range by printing the resulting four truth tables. Discuss the results.

Experiment 7: Priority Encoder

1. Compile the program given in Listing 6.11. Make a set of test vectors and test the program by running CSIM. (See Experiment 3 in Chapter 5.) Add your verified test vectors to the JEDEC file produced by compiling the program with CUPL.

2. Program a GAL 16V8 to produce a chip with the same chip diagram as shown in Fig. 6.42.

3. Use the PLD logic analyzer to test the chip. Connect the eight output lines of the logic analyzer to the eight input lines, *I0* to *I7*, of the chip. Connect the three chip outputs *Y0, Y1*, and *Y2* to the three logic analyzer input lines, *In0, In1*, and *In2*. Connect the valid output pin to the logic analyzer input line *In4*. Change bits 4 to 7 in the output column manually and then press function key *F1* to produce a truth table for various inputs. Verify that the priority encoder is giving the proper encoded output for different inputs.

4. Record the results by printing the resulting truth tables. Discuss the results.

Experiment 8: Multiplexer/Demultiplexer

1. Write a CUPL program to produce the multiplexer/demultiplexer shown in Fig. 6.54 by combining the programs given in Listings 6.12 and 6.13. Compile the program to produce a JEDEC file.

2. Use the JEDEC file produced in (1) to program a GAL 16V8.

3. Connect an external wire between pin 15 (*Y*) and pin 8 (*YIN*) of your GAL chip to produce the circuit shown in Fig. 6.53.

4. Use the PLD logic analyzer to test the chip. Connect the four output lines, *Out0* to *Out3*, of the logic analyzer to the input lines, *C0* to *C3*, of the GAL chip. Connect the two logic analyzer outputs *Out4* and *Out5* to the GAL input lines, *d0* and *d1*. Connect the two logic analyzer outputs *Out6* and *Out7* to the GAL input lines, *s0* and *s1*. Connect the four GAL outputs *Y0* to *Y3* to the four logic analyzer input lines, *In0* to *In3*. Note that when you press function key *F1* to produce a truth table the values of *Out4* to *Out7* connected to *d0*, *d1*, *s0*, and *s1* remain the same. Change these manually to select different connections between *C0* to *C3* and *Y0* to *Y3*. Verify the operation of the multiplexer/demultiplexer by pressing function key *F1* and noting that the selected input *C* is connected to the selected output *Y*.

5. Record the results for four different input/output selection combinations by printing the resulting four truth tables. Discuss the results.

Experiment 9: 7-Segment Display

1. Compile the program given in Listing 6.15.
2. Program a GAL 16V8 to produce a chip with the chip diagram shown in Fig. 6.62.
3. The MAN 72 is a common anode 7-segment display whose pinout follows. Connect the 7-segment outputs of your GAL chip to the corresponding segment pins (*a* to *g*) of the MAN 72. Connect the three anode pins of the MAN 72 through a single 220-ohm resistor to +5 volts as shown in Fig. 6.61.
4. Use the PLD logic analyzer to test the chip. Connect the four output lines, *Out4* to *Out7*, of the logic analyzer to the four input lines, *D0* to *D3*, of the GAL chip. Manually change the 4 bits *D0* to *D3* from 0000 to 1111 to see if the MAN 72 displays the hex digits *0* to *F*.

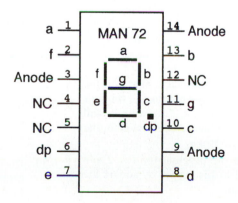

EXERCISES

6.1. a. Modify Fig. 6.2 to make a 2-bit equality detector.

   b. Modify the program in Listing 6.3 to make a 2-bit magnitude comparator based on the circuit in (a).

   c. Compile the program in (b) using the default minimization ($-fax$) and find the expanded product terms for A_EQ_B, A_GT_B, and A_LT_B in the *.DOC* file. Circle the set of 1's in the three Karnaugh maps from Experiment 3 corresponding to these product terms.

   d. Compile the program in (b) again using the CUPL *m2* minimization option ($-faxm2$). Find the expanded product terms for A_EQ_B, A_GT_B, and A_LT_B in the *.DOC* file and circle the set of 1's in the three Karnaugh maps from Experiment 3 corresponding to these product terms.

6.2. Draw a logic diagram that uses the 74LS682 magnitude comparator shown in Fig. 6.9 and produces the signals $P > Q$, $P = Q$, $P < Q$, $!(P > Q)$, $!(P = Q)$, and $!(P < Q)$.

6.3. a. Using the half adder/subtractor shown in Fig. 6.24, draw a logic diagram for a full adder/subtractor that will be a full adder if $E = 0$ and a full subtractor if $E = 1$.

   b. Using the logic diagram drawn in (a), write the logic equations for a 4-bit adder/subtractor.

   c. Draw a Karnaugh map for the carry/borrow in terms of the four variables E, C_i, A_i, and B_i and write a reduced expression for the carry/borrow.

6.4 Rewrite the program for the 2-to-4 decoder in Listing 6.6 by adding the statement

```
FIELD input = [B,A];
```

and writing the logic equations for $Y0$ to $Y3$ using the CUPL equality operator (:).

6.5. Consider the following CUPL equations:

```
FIELD data = [D3..0];

A = data:5;
B = data:8;
C = data:A;
D = data:F;
```

Write the expanded expressions for A, B, C, and D in terms of $D0$, $D1$, $D2$, and $D3$.

6.6. Draw a logic diagram using basic gates for the 2-to-4 decoder described in Listing 6.6.

6.7. Draw a logic diagram using basic gates for the 3-to-8 decoder described in Listing 6.7.

6.8. Expand the following CUPL equations for Z.

```
FIELD X = [X2..0];
FIELD Y = [Y2..0];
FIELD Z = [Z2..0];
```

   a. Z = X & Y;
   b. Z = X # Y;
   c. Z = !(X & Y);
   d. Z = !(X # Y);

6.9. Define CUPL bit field variables A, B, C, and D and write the following logic equations for $D0$, $D1$, $D2$, and $D3$ as a single logic equation for D.

```
D0 = A0 & B0 & C0;
D1 = A1 & B1 & C1;
D2 = A2 & B2 & C2;
D3 = A3 & B3 & C3;
```

6.10. Draw a logic diagram using basic gates for the address decoder described by the expanded product terms in Fig. 6.38.

6.11. Draw a logic diagram using basic gates for the 8-to-3 binary encoder described in Listing 6.10.

6.12. Expand the following CUPL equations:

   a. Z = [X0..3]:&
   b. Z = [X0..4]:#
   c. Z = [Y0..2]:$

6.13. Expand the following CUPL equation:

```
[Y2..0] =    I7 & 'b'111
          #  I6 & 'b'110
          #  I5 & 'b'101
          #  I4 & 'b'100
          #  I3 & 'b'011
          #  I2 & 'b'010
          #  I1 & 'b'001
```

6.14. Expand the logic equations in Listing 6.11 and show that $Y2$, $Y1$, and $Y0$ are given by the expressions in Fig. 6.45.

6.15. Draw a logic diagram using basic gates for the 4-line-to-1 multiplexer described in Listing 6.12.

6.16. Draw a logic diagram using basic gates for the 1-line-to-4 demultiplexer described in Listing 6.13.

6.17. What values of $s1$, $s0$, $d1$, and $d0$ will make the following connections in Figure 6.53?

   a. $C0$ to $Y2$
   b. $C1$ to $Y0$
   c. $C2$ to $Y3$
   d. $C3$ to $Y1$
   e. $C2$ to $Y2$

6.18. **a.** Draw a symbol and truth table for an 8-line-to-1 multiplexer (see Fig. 6.47).

   b. Modify the program in Listing 6.12 to produce an 8-line-to-1 multiplexer.

6.19. **a.** Draw a symbol and truth table for a 1-line-to-8 demultiplexer (see Fig. 6.50).

   b. Modify the program in Listing 6.13 to produce a 1-line-to-8 demultiplexer.

6.20. Derive the logic equations in Fig. 6.59 from the truth table in Fig. 6.57 by drawing a Karnaugh map for each output variable, E, D, C, B, and A.

6.21. Derive the logic equations in Fig. 6.63 from the function table in Listing 6.15 by drawing a Karnaugh map for each output variable, a, b, c, d, e, f, and g.

7

Sequential Logic

In all the logic circuits we have discussed thus far the outputs at any instant depend on only the values of the current inputs. The outputs of most useful logic circuits, however, depend on not only the current inputs, but also on past inputs. This means that the circuit must have some type of memory to remember these past input values. Such circuits are called *sequential circuits*.

In this chapter you will learn:

- How latches and flip-flops can store binary data
- The difference between an S-R latch, a D latch, a D flip-flop and a J-K flip-flop
- How eight D flip-flops are included in the GAL 16V8
- How to use the GAL 16V8 to design the following:
  a. Divide-by-2 counter
  b. Divide-by-8 counter
  c. Modulo-5 counter
  d. 3-Bit down counter with preload and timeout capability
  e. Shift register
  f. Ring counter

7.1 LATCHES AND FLIP-FLOPS

Figure 7.1 shows that two inverters, with the output of one connected to the input of the other, can exist in two different states. The output of the top inverter can

158

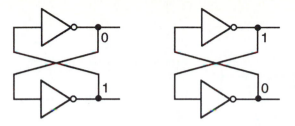

Figure 7.1 Two cross-coupled inverters can exist in two different states.

be either 0 or 1, and the output of the bottom inverter has the opposite logical value. This circuit isn't very useful because we can't change the output values once the circuit is in a particular state. By using NAND gates instead of inverters, we can change the state and have a useful circuit for storing binary data.

!S-!R Latch

Consider the circuit shown in Fig. 7.2. We call this a *!S-!R latch*. The two inputs *!S* and *!R* can have the four possible values shown in the truth table. The four possible states of this circuit are shown in Fig. 7.3. The "normal" state for this circuit is when both *!S* and *!R* are high (1). Suppose that this is the case and that the output Q is 0 and $!Q$ is 1. This is a stable state because if $!Q = 1$ and $!S = 1$ then the output of the upper NAND gate, Q, will be 0. Inasmuch as this 0 value will be an input to the bottom NAND gate, the output, $!Q$, must be 1.

Now suppose that *!S* is brought low while *!R* remains high. This will cause the output of the top NAND gate to go high. This in turn will cause both inputs to the lower NAND gate to be high, so the output, *!Q*, will go low. This is still consistent with the output of the top NAND gate being high (both inputs are now low). We call this the *set* condition. If *!S* is now brought back high, *no change will take place* because the low value of *!Q* will mean that the output of the top NAND gate still remains high. We call this the *store* condition. That is, both Q and $!Q$ have the same value that they had before we brought *!S* back high.

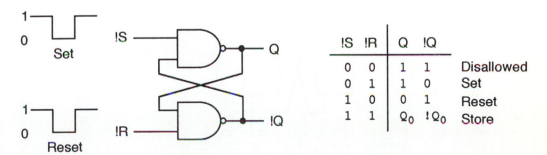

!S	!R	Q	!Q	
0	0	1	1	Disallowed
0	1	1	0	Set
1	0	0	1	Reset
1	1	Q_0	$!Q_0$	Store

Figure 7.2 A !S-!R latch using NAND gates.

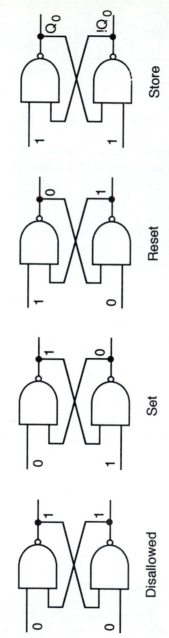

Figure 7.3 The four states of the !S-!R latch.

With both $!S$ and $!R$ high, suppose we bring $!R$ low. This will cause the output of the bottom NAND gate to go high. This in turn will cause both inputs to the upper NAND gate to be high, so the output, Q, will go low. This is still consistent with the output of the bottom NAND gate being high (both inputs are now low). We call this the *reset* condition. If $!R$ is now brought back high, *no change will take place* because the low value of Q will mean that the output of the bottom NAND gate still remains high. We are now in the *store* state where both Q and $!Q$ have the same values (denoted by Q_0 and $!Q_0$ in the truth table in Fig. 7.2) that they had before we brought $!R$ back high.

Therefore, to set the output Q to 1, $!S$ is brought low and back high as indicated by the set pulse shown in Fig. 7.2. Similarly, to reset the output Q to 0, $!R$ is brought low and back high as indicated by the reset pulse shown in Fig. 7.2.

If both $!S$ and $!R$ are low, then both outputs will be high. This is a disallowed state because we always want $!Q$ to be the complement of Q. Only one input at a time is brought low, then high. Pulsing $!S$ low will set Q to 1, and pulsing $!R$ low will reset Q to 0.

The $!S$-$!R$ latch shown in Fig. 7.2 will be set or reset any time $!S$ or $!R$ is brought low. By adding two more NAND gates, we can convert this to an S-R latch that is enabled by a clock signal.

S-R Latch

Figure 7.4 shows an *S-R latch* in which we have added two additional NAND gates to the $!S$-$!R$ latch in Fig. 7.2. In this case, both S and CLK must be high for $!S$ to go low. This is the new set condition. Similarly, both R and CLK must be high for $!R$ to go low. This is the new reset condition. If both S and R are low, then both $!S$ and $!R$ will be high, which is the store state. If S, R, and CLK are all high, then both $!S$ and $!R$ will be low, which is the disallowed state. Note that the clock signal must be high for a set or reset operation to occur.

D Latch

One way to eliminate the disallowed state in Fig. 7.4 is to make sure that S and R always have opposite logical values. We can do this by adding the inverter

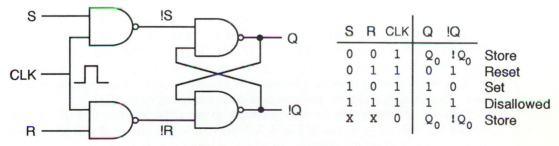

S	R	CLK	Q	!Q	
0	0	1	Q_0	$!Q_0$	Store
0	1	1	0	1	Reset
1	0	1	1	0	Set
1	1	1	1	1	Disallowed
X	X	0	Q_0	$!Q_0$	Store

Figure 7.4   An S-R latch with clock enable.

shown in Fig. 7.5. The resulting circuit is called a *D latch*. In this circuit, *D* is the same as *S* in Fig. 7.4, and *!D* is the same as *R*. Therefore, when *D* and *CLK* are both high, the output *Q* will be high (set). Similarly, when *D* is 0 and *CLK* is 1, *!D* (corresponding to *R* in Fig. 7.4) will be 1 and *Q* will be reset to 0. Note that, since the equivalent *S* and *R* now always have the opposite state, the only way to get to the *store* state is to bring the clock low.

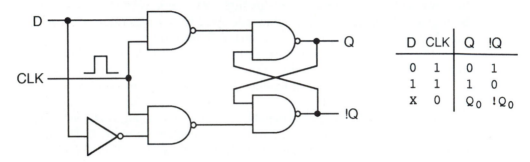

D	CLK	Q	!Q
0	1	0	1
1	1	1	0
X	0	Q_0	$!Q_0$

Figure 7.5   A D latch.

Thus, in a *D* latch the output *Q* will follow the input *D* as long as the enable clock is high. As soon as the clock goes low, the output is latched to the value of *D* when the clock went low. Note that, as long as the clock is high, changes in *D* will be reflected as changes in the output *Q*. Only when the clock goes low will the *last* value of *D* be latched in *Q*.

Often we want to latch *Q* to the value of *D* at a particular instant, such as the rising edge of a clock signal. This will lead to an *edge-triggered flip-flop*.

D Flip-Flop

Suppose that we could make the clock pulse in Fig. 7.5 very narrow. Then the change in *Q* would occur essentially at the time the pulse occurred. An inverter and an AND gate can be used to produce a very narrow pulse (about 10^{-8} second or 10 nanoseconds), as shown in Fig. 7.6. It uses the *propagation delay* through the gates, which is the time it takes a change at the input of the gate to be felt at the output. This is typically about 10 nanoseconds (ns).

Suppose that the input to the inverter *X* in Fig. 7.6 goes high. Due to the propagation delay, this change won't affect the output for about 10 ns. During this time, both inputs to the AND gate are high. Therefore, the output of the AND gate will be high for this length of time (after being delayed by its own propagation delay). Note that no such narrow pulse is generated when *X* goes from high to low. Thus, a single narrow pulse occurs near the rising edge of *X*.

If we add this pulse-narrowing circuit to the *D* latch given in Fig. 7.5, we obtain the *D flip-flop* shown in Fig. 7.7. Note that in this circuit *Q* will be latched to the value of *D* on the positive, or rising, edge of the clock signal.

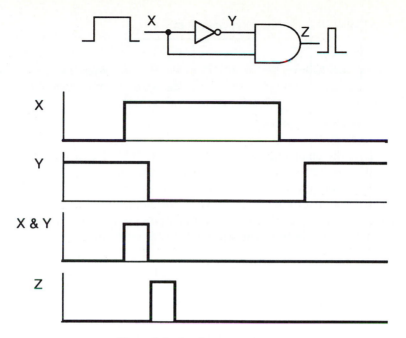

Figure 7.6   A pulse-narrowing circuit.

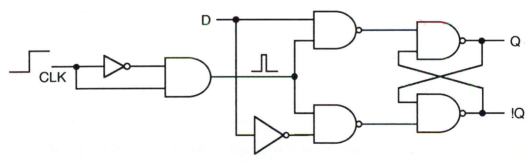

Figure 7.7   A positive edge-triggered D flip-flop.

We call the circuit shown in Fig. 7.7 a *positive edge-triggered D flip-flop*. Some people refer to the latches that we have discussed above as flip-flops. However, we will use the term flip-flop for a device whose output changes only as the result of the input being sampled at a specific time by a clock signal.

The logic diagram and truth table for a positive edge-triggered D flip-flop are shown in Fig. 7.8. The upward arrow for the *CLK* signal in the truth table indicates that it is a positive edge-triggered flip-flop. This is also indicated by the arrow-type symbol next to the *CLK* input in the logic diagram. A negative edge-triggered flip-flop would have a bubble added to the *CLK* input.

D	CLK	Q	!Q
0	↑	0	1
1	↑	1	0
X	0	Q_0	$!Q_0$

Figure 7.8 Logic diagram and truth table for an edge-triggered D flip-flop.

GAL 16V8 D Flip-Flops

Each of the eight output pins of the GAL 16V8 has a positive edge-triggered D flip-flop as part of its output circuit, as shown in Fig. 7.9. Up to this point we have simply bypassed this flip-flop by connecting the output of the polarity Exclusive-OR gate to the output inverter through a multiplexer. This is automatically done for you by CUPL when you compile your CUPL program. We will see in the next example how you tell CUPL that you want to use the D flip-flop.

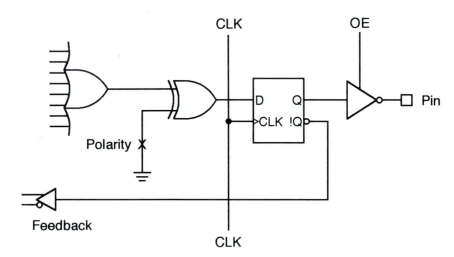

Figure 7.9 Registered mode output pins on the GAL 16V8 contain a D flip-flop.

Divide-by-2 counter.   Suppose we connect the *!Q* output of a D flip-flop to the *D* input as shown in Fig. 7.10. What will happen? On each rising edge of the clock, the value at *D* will be latched (after some propagation delay) to *Q*. We will label the output *Q* as *Q0* and the output *!Q* as *!Q0*. Suppose that *Q0* is initially 0. This means that *!Q0* will be 1. At the first clock, this *!Q0* value of 1 (which is at *D*) will be latched to *Q0*. Therefore, *Q0* will go from 0 to 1 and *!Q0* will go from 1 to 0. This means that *D* will now be 0, so on the next rising edge of the clock the value of *Q0* will go back to 0, and *!Q0* will go back to 1. This process will continually repeat itself, resulting in the frequency of *Q0* being just one-half of the frequency of the clock. We call this a *divide-by-2 counter* because it divides the frequency of the clock by 2.

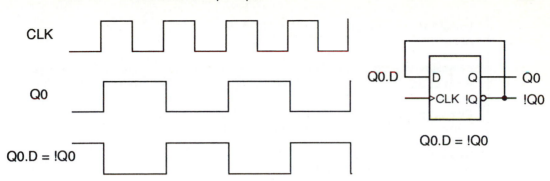

Figure 7.10 Using a D flip-flop as a divide-by-2 counter.

The CUPL program for this divide-by-2 counter is given in Listing 7.1. Note that we tell CUPL that we are using a D flip-flop by using the suffix *.D* on the left side of a logic equation. Thus, the statement

```
q0.d = !q0
```

means "the *D* input to the flip-flop whose output is *q0* is to be equated (connected) to *!q0*." The chip diagram for this program is shown in Fig. 7.11. When using the D flip-flops in the GAL 16V8, *the clock signal must come in pin 1*. This is a common clock signal that goes to all eight D flip-flops.

```
============================================================
                       Chip Diagram
============================================================

               _____
              |      div2cnt      |
   clock x---|1                 20|---x Vcc
         x---|2                 19|---x q0
         x---|3                 18|---x
         x---|4                 17|---x
         x---|5                 16|---x
         x---|6                 15|---x
         x---|7                 14|---x
         x---|8                 13|---x
         x---|9                 12|---x
   GND   x---|10                11|---x
              |_____|
```

Figure 7.11 Chip diagram from *div2cnt.doc*.

The expanded product terms for this program are shown in Fig. 7.12. Note that only the fourth column is connected. This corresponds to the *inverted* feedback of *!Q* as shown in Fig. 7.13. Why is this inverted? Doesn't the equation say

Listing 7.1   *div2cnt.pld*

```
Name              div2cnt;
Partno            OU0022;
Revision          01;
Date              8/05/91;
Designer          R. E. Haskell;
Company           Oakland University;
Location          Rochester, MI;
Assembly          CSE 171;
Device            G16V8;
Format            j;

/********************************************************/
/*      This example demonstrates the use of a D-type   */
/*      flip-flop to design a divide-by-2 counter       */
/*                                                      */
/*              _____    _____    _____    _____     */
/*      clock  __|    |____|    |____|    |____|    |_   */
/*              ___       _____       _____     */
/*      q0     |_____|           |_____|            */
/********************************************************/
/*      Target Device:   G16V8                          */
/********************************************************/

/* Input:   */

Pin 1 =   clock;

/* Outputs:   */

Pin 19 = q0;

/* Logic equations */

q0.d = !q0;
```

to connect *!Q* to *D*? Yes, but note that there is an output inverter between the *Q* output of the flip-flop and the output pin. We have defined pin 19 to be *Q0*, and that is what we are using in our equations. This pin will always contain the opposite polarity of what is really at the *Q* output of the flip-flop. But CUPL has already taken care of this for us by blowing the *polarity* fuse. Therefore, the *D* input to the flip-flop is itself the opposite polarity of the output of the OR gate. Therefore, everything comes out in the wash—as long as the inverted feedback of *!Q* is used.

Normally, you will not have to worry about these internal details. You can think of the pin output as being the *Q* output that is in your equations. You will

```
Pin #19  02048  Pol -   02120  Ac1 x
00000  ---x-------------------------
00032  xxxxxxxxxxxxxxxxxxxxxxxxxxxxxxxx
00064  xxxxxxxxxxxxxxxxxxxxxxxxxxxxxxxx
00096  xxxxxxxxxxxxxxxxxxxxxxxxxxxxxxxx
00128  xxxxxxxxxxxxxxxxxxxxxxxxxxxxxxxx
00160  xxxxxxxxxxxxxxxxxxxxxxxxxxxxxxxx
00192  xxxxxxxxxxxxxxxxxxxxxxxxxxxxxxxx
00224  xxxxxxxxxxxxxxxxxxxxxxxxxxxxxxxx
```

Figure 7.12 Expanded product terms from *div2cnt.doc*.

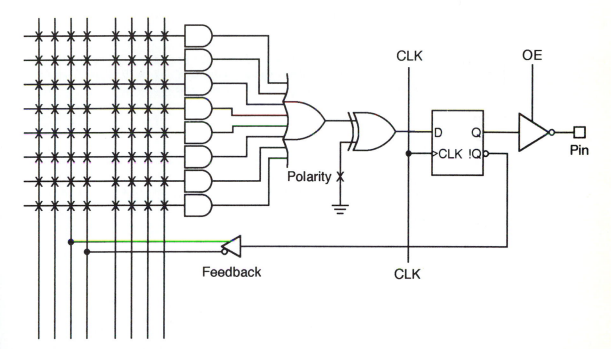

Figure 7.13   Detail of registered feedback in the GAL 16V8.

have to be aware of the output inverter if you use power-up default values. The power-up default values of all flip-flop *Q* outputs are zero. This means that all registered output pins (connected to flip-flops) will initially have high outputs.

Let's test the program in Listing 7.1 by making the simulation file *div2cnt.si* shown in Listing 7.2. The *ORDER* statement contains the two logic variables *clock* and *q0*. In the test vectors, a *C* means "drive the clock *LO*, then *HI*, then *LO*." The simulation will assume that the power-on default values are the initial values. Therefore, the output *q0* will initially be high. The first clock pulse will bring it *LO*. Our first test vector must therefore be *C L*.

Listing 7.2   *div2cnt.si*

```
Name                 div2cnt;
Partno               OU0022;
Revision             01;
Date                 8/05/91;
Designer             R. E. Haskell;
Company              Oakland University;
Location             Rochester, MI;
Assembly             CSE 171;
Device               G16V8;
Format               j;

/******************************************************/
/*      This example demonstrates the use of a D-type  */
/*      flip-flop to design a divide-by-2 counter      */
/*                _____   _____       _____        */
/*    clock      __!     !___!     !___!   !___!     !_ */
/*                ___               _____         _____ */
/*      q0        !_____!               !_____! */
/******************************************************/
/*      Target Device:  G16V8                          */
/******************************************************/

ORDER:  clock,%2,q0;

VECTORS:
  C L
  C H
  C L
  C H
  C L
  C H
  C L
  C H
```

To run this simulation, first compile Listing 7.1 by typing

```
cupl -fax div2cnt
```

Then run the simulation in Listing 7.2 by typing

```
csim -w div2cnt
```

The *-w* option will generate the simulation listing file *div2cnt.so* and display the results in waveform output on the screen. When the output waveforms are displayed, you can expand and contract the scale by pressing function keys *F1* and *F2*. Press *F4* to return to DOS.

A 1-bit register.   As a second example of using the D flip-flop in the GAL 16V8, suppose you want to store a bit from the input pin *IN0* in the flip-flop output *Q*. Another input line called *LOAD* is brought high, and on the next clock cycle the value of *IN0* is stored in *Q*. The circuit shown in Fig. 7.14 will do this. The clock signal is assumed to be running continuously, and so to keep the current value of *Q* unchanged at each clock cycle, this *Q* value is fed back and gated into the OR gate with *!LOAD*. This means that when the *LOAD* signal is *LO* the value of *Q* is continually reloaded and therefore does not change.

When *LOAD* is brought *HI*, the value *IN0* is gated to the OR gate, so on the next clock cycle *Q0* becomes equal to *IN0*. When the *LOAD* signal goes *LO* again, this value then remains at *Q0*.

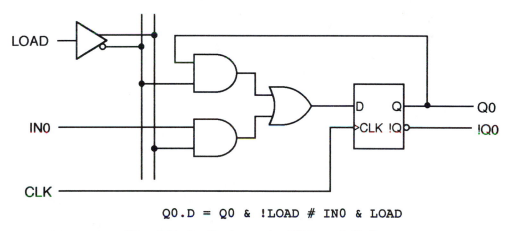

$$Q0.D = Q0 \ \& \ !LOAD \ \# \ IN0 \ \& \ LOAD$$

Figure 7.14   Loading input value IN0 into a D flip-flop.

J-K Flip-Flops

The S-R latch shown in Fig. 7.4 has a disallowed state. We showed one way to eliminate this disallowed state in Fig. 7.5 by making a D latch. Another way is to feed back the *!Q* output to *S* and the *Q* output to *R*. This leads to a *J-K flip-flop*. If we add our pulse-narrowing circuit, we have the *positive edge-triggered J-K flip-flop* shown in Fig. 7.15. The logic diagram and truth table for this J-K flip-flop are shown in Fig. 7.16. Note that *J* plays the role of the *set* input and *K* plays the role of the *reset* input.

Suppose that *J* and *K* are both 0 and that *Q* = 0 and *!Q* = 1. Now let *J* go *HI*. On the next clock pulse all three inputs to the J NAND gate will be *HI*, so the output (*!S*) will be *LO* and *Q* will be set to 1. This will cause *!Q* to go *LO* so

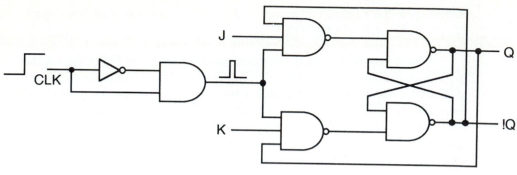

Figure 7.15   A positive edge-triggered J-K flip-flop.

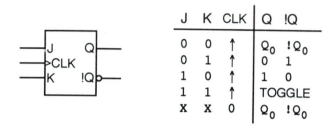

J	K	CLK	Q	!Q
0	0	↑	Q_0	$!Q_0$
0	1	↑	0	1
1	0	↑	1	0
1	1	↑	TOGGLE	
X	X	0	Q_0	$!Q_0$

Figure 7.16   Logic diagram and truth table for a positive edge-triggered J-K flip-flop.

that the output of the *J* NAND gate will stay *HI*. When *J* goes back to 0, the output *Q* will keep its value of 1.

Now, if *K* is brought *HI*, then on the next clock pulse all three inputs to the *K* NAND gate will be *HI*, so the output (*!R*) will be *LO*, and *Q* will be reset to 0. This will cause the output of the *K* NAND gate to stay *HI*. When *K* goes back to 0, the output *Q* will keep its value of 0.

Suppose that both *J* and *K* are brought *HI*. This was the disallowed state in the S-R latch. If *Q* = 0 and *!Q* = 1, then on the next clock pulse all three inputs to the *J* NAND gate will be *HI*, so *Q* will be set to 1 and *!Q* will go to 0. On the next clock pulse all three inputs to the *K* NAND gate will be *HI*, so *Q* will be reset to 0. This process will continue as long as *J* and *K* are both 1. That is, the output *Q* will toggle between 1 and 0.

Yet another method of solving the disallowed state problem is shown in Fig. 7.17, where essentially two S-R flip-flops are concatenated with the outputs *Q* and *!Q* fed back in a J-K format. This is called a *master-slave J-K flip-flop*. The input flip-flop is the master and the output flip-flop is the slave.

The clock signal connected to the slave is inverted from the clock signal connected to the master. This means that when the master is enabled (the clock is *HI*), the slave is disabled. The outputs of the master labeled *S* and *R* in Fig. 7.17 will behave like a J-K flip-flop; *S* will go to 1 if *J* is 1 and *!Q* is 1. When the clock goes *LO*, the master becomes disabled, but the slave becomes enabled. The

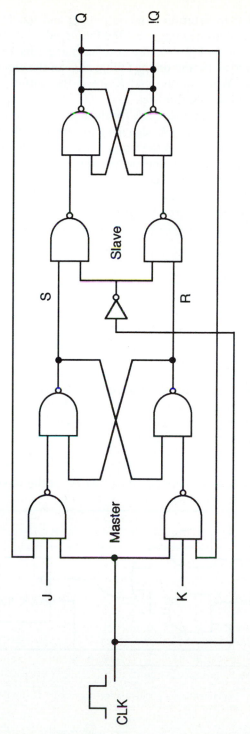

Figure 7.17 Master-slave J-K flip-flop.

values on S and R then determine the outputs Q and $!Q$. Thus, if S had been set to 1, this will cause Q to become 1 on the falling edge of the clock.

If $K = 1$, $J = 0$, and $Q = 1$, then on the rising edge of the clock the master is reset ($S = 0$ and $R = 1$), and on the falling edge of the clock the slave is enabled and Q is reset to 0. When both J and K are 1, the outputs Q and $!Q$ will toggle as in the edge-triggered J-K flip-flop.

The logic diagram and truth table for the master-slave J-K flip-flop are shown in Fig. 7.18. Note that the CLK signal in the truth table is shown as a pulse, indicating that the value of Q is determined by the values of J and K, while the pulse is high and becomes latched on the falling edge of the clock pulse. The values of J and K should remain constant during the time the clock is high. Note that the CLK label on the logic diagram does not have the arrow symbol, which would indicate an edge-triggered flip-flop.

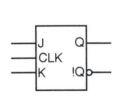

J	K	CLK	Q	!Q
0	0	⊓	Q_0	$!Q_0$
0	1	⊓	0	1
1	0	⊓	1	0
1	1	⊓	TOGGLE	
X	X	0	Q_0	$!Q_0$

Figure 7.18 Logic diagram and truth table for a master-slave J-K flip-flop.

Implementing a J-K flip-flop on a GAL 16V8. The GAL 16V8 has only D flip-flops. However, you can stimulate the behavior of a J-K flip-flop by using the circuit shown in Fig. 7.19. Note that this circuit implements the following equation for the input to the D flip-flop.

$$Q.D = J \ \& \ !Q \ \# \ !K \ \& \ Q \tag{7.1}$$

This is called the *characteristic equation* and gives the next state in terms of the

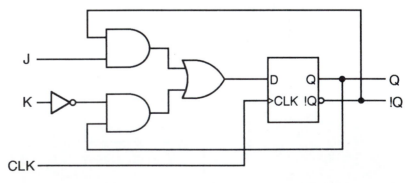

Figure 7.19 Implementing a positive edge-triggered J-K flip-flop with a D flip-flop.

current state and the inputs. Note that Eq. (7.1) leads to the following four cases for different values of J and K:

J	K	Eq. (7.1)
0	0	Q.D = Q
0	1	Q.D = 0
1	0	Q.D = !Q # Q = 1
1	1	Q.D = !Q

Note that this is the behavior of a J-K flip-flop.

7.2 COUNTERS

Earlier in this chapter we showed how a divide-by-2 counter could be implemented on the GAL 16V8. In this section we will take a closer look at counters and consider a divide-by-8 counter, a modulo-5 counter, and a 3-bit down counter. We will see how to add a clear and load function to these counters and how to use the CUPL state machine syntax for designing counters.

Divide-by-8 Counter

A divide-by-8 counter is a 3-bit binary counter that can count from 0 to 7, as shown in Fig. 7.20.

Note that this counter needs three flip-flops to hold the 3 bits $Q0$ to $Q2$. The inputs to these three flip-flops will be $Q0.D$, $Q1.D$, and $Q2.D$. The design process

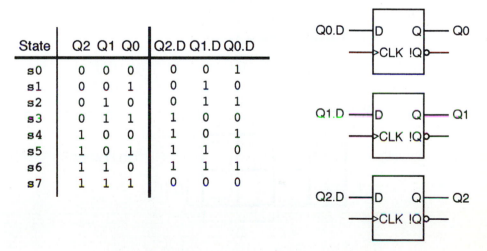

State	Q2	Q1	Q0	Q2.D	Q1.D	Q0.D
s0	0	0	0	0	0	1
s1	0	0	1	0	1	0
s2	0	1	0	0	1	1
s3	0	1	1	1	0	0
s4	1	0	0	1	0	1
s5	1	0	1	1	1	0
s6	1	1	0	1	1	1
s7	1	1	1	0	0	0

Figure 7.20   Truth table for a 3-bit divide-by-8 counter.

is to determine expressions for *Q0.D*, *Q1.D*, and *Q2.D* that will cause the next state to count from 000 to 111 and then wrap around.

This is easy to do because we know that on the next clock pulse whatever is on the *D* inputs to the three flip-flops will be latched to the three outputs. Therefore, we just need to make sure that the *D* inputs contain the next state in the sequence. This is shown in the truth table in Fig. 7.20. Note that in each row the three values under *Q2.D*, *Q1.D*, and *Q0.D* are just the values in the next row under *Q2*, *Q1*, and *Q0*. Note that the last row cycles back to the first row.

We can now use our standard Karnaugh map method to find the logic equations for *Q2.D*, *Q1.D*, and *Q0.D*, as shown in Fig. 7.21. Using these equations,

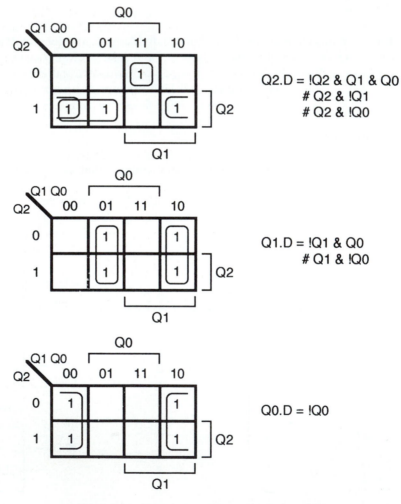

Q2.D = !Q2 & Q1 & Q0
     # Q2 & !Q1
     # Q2 & !Q0

Q1.D = !Q1 & Q0
     # Q1 & !Q0

Q0.D = !Q0

Figure 7.21   K-maps for a 3-bit divide-by-8 counter.

we can write the CUPL program for this divide-by-8 counter as shown in Listing 7.3. The chip diagram for this program is shown in Fig. 7.22. Note that there is only a clock input, and the three outputs will just continually cycle through the count 000 to 111 as long as the clock input continues.

     To test this program, we can create the simulation file shown in Listing 7.4. Recall that the power-up reset will cause all output pins to be high, so the first clock will change the output values to all zeros.

Listing 7.3   *div8cnt.pld*

```
Name              div8cnt;
Partno            DU0023;
Revision          01;
Date              8/05/91;
Designer          R. E. Haskell;
Company           Oakland University;
Location          Rochester, MI;
Assembly          CSE 171;
Device            G16V8;
Format            j;

/********************************************************************/
/*                                                                  */
/*      This example demonstrates the use of D-type flip-flops      */
/*      to design a divide-by-8 counter                             */
/*                                                                  */
/********************************************************************/
/*      Target Device:   G16V8                                      */
/********************************************************************/

/* Inputs:   */

Pin 1 =   clock;

/* Outputs:   */

Pin [19..17] = [q0..2];

/* Logic equations */

q0.d = !q0;
q1.d = !q1 & q0
     # q1 & !q0;
q2.d = !q2 & q1 & q0
     # q2 & !q1
     # q2 & !q0;
```

```
=============================================================
                         Chip Diagram
=============================================================

                    _____
                   |   div8cnt     |
      clock x---|1              20|---x Vcc
            x---|2              19|---x q0
            x---|3              18|---x q1
            x---|4              17|---x q2
            x---|5              16|---x
            x---|6              15|---x
            x---|7              14|---x
            x---|8              13|---x
            x---|9              12|---x
        GND x---|10             11|---x
                   |_____|
```

Figure 7.22 Chip diagram from *div8cnt.doc*.

After compiling Listing 7.3 by typing

```
cupl -fax div8cnt
```

you can run the simulation in Listing 7.4 by typing

```
csim -w div8cnt
```

This will produce the output waveforms on the screen in a graphical format.

In Listing 7.3 we wrote the logic equations as we had derived them from the Karnaugh maps in Fig. 7.21. CUPL provides a state-machine syntax that makes it easy to design such a counter using a high-level language approach. Listing 7.5 shows the design of the same divide-by-8 counter using this state-machine syntax.

Note that we define the set variable *count* to be the three output bits [*q2*, *q1*, *q0*]. We then define the eight states *s0* to *s7* to be the eight bit patterns defined in Fig. 7.20. The logic equations are then of the self-explanatory form:

```
sequence count {
present state_n   next state_n;
- - - - - - - - - - - - - - -
- - - - - - - - - - - - - - -
}
```

When you compile Listing 7.5 using the statement

```
cupl -faxm2 div8cnts
```

Listing 7.4   *div8cnt.si*

```
Name             div8cnt;
Partno           OU0023;
Revision         01;
Date             8/05/91;
Designer         R. E. Haskell;
Company          Oakland University;
Location         Rochester, MI;
Assembly         CSE 171;
Device           G16V8;
Format           j;


/*******************************************************************/
/*                                                                 */
/*      This example demonstrates the use of D-type flip-flops     */
/*      to design a divide-by-8 counter                            */
/*                                                                 */
/*******************************************************************/
/*       Target Device:   G16V8                                    */
/*******************************************************************/

ORDER:  clock,%2,q0,%2,q1,%2,q2;

VECTORS:
  C LLL
  C HLL
  C LHL
  C HHL
  C LLH
  C HLH
  C LHH
  C HHH
  C LLL
  C HLL
  C LHL
  C HHL
  C LLH
  C HLH
  C LHH
  C HHH
```

Listing 7.5   *div8cnts.pld*

```
Name            div8cnts;
Partno          OU0024;
Revision        01;
Date            8/05/91;
Designer        R. E. Haskell;
Company         Oakland University;
Location        Rochester, MI;
Assembly        CSE 171;
Device          G16V8;
Format          j;

/****************************************************************/
/*                                                              */
/*      This example demonstrates the use of state-machine      */
/*      syntax to design a divide-by-8 counter                  */
/*                                                              */
/****************************************************************/
/*      Target Device:   G16V8                                  */
/****************************************************************/

/* Inputs:  */

Pin 1 =  clock;

/* Outputs:  */

Pin [19..17] = [q0..2];

/** Declarations and Intermediate Variable Definitions **/

FIELD count = [q2..0];          /*   declare  counter  bitfield */
$define S0 'b'000               /*   define counter states */
$define S1 'b'001
$define S2 'b'010
$define S3 'b'011
$define S4 'b'100
$define S5 'b'101
$define S6 'b'110
$define S7 'b'111

/** Logic Equations **/

sequence count {                /*   free running counter */

present S0     next S1;
present S1     next S2;
```

Listing 7.5   (*cont.*)

```
present S2        next S3;
present S3        next S4;
present S4        next S5;
present S5        next S6;
present S6        next S7;
present S7        next S0;
}
```

to get the maximum reduction of product terms, the expanded product terms will be as shown in Fig. 7.23. Note that these are the same as the ones we found from the Karnaugh maps in Fig. 7.21.

```
================================================
              Expanded Product Terms
================================================

count =>
     q2 , q1 , q0

q0.d   =>
        !q0

q1.d   =>
          q0 & !q1
     #  !q0 & q1

q2.d   =>
          q0 & q1 & !q2
     #  !q1 & q2
     #  !q0 & q2
```

Figure 7.23   Expanded product terms from *div8cnts.doc*.

As a further example of using the state-machine syntax, suppose we wish to add a *clear* input pin that will clear the output count to 000 on the next clock pulse whenever this pin is high. We call this a *synchronous clear* because the clear will occur only at the clock pulse. Some flip-flops have an *asynchronous clear* that will clear the output to zero whenever the clear signal is active (either HI or LO) independently of the clock signal.

The program shown in Listing 7.6 will accomplish this clearing function. Note that we have made each *next* statement conditional. For example, the statement

```
present S2      if !clear      next S3;
                if  clear      next S0;
```

Listing 7.6   *div8cntc.pld*

```
Name              div8cntc;
Partno            OU0025;
Revision          01;
Date              8/05/91;
Designer          R. E. Haskell;
Company           Oakland University;
Location          Rochester, MI;
Assembly          CSE 171;
Device            G16V8;
Format            j;


/********************************************************************/
/*                                                                  */
/*      This example demonstrates the use of state-machine          */
/*      syntax to clear a divide-by-8 counter                       */
/*                                                                  */
/********************************************************************/
/*        Target Device:    G16V8                                   */
/********************************************************************/

/* Inputs:  */

Pin 1 =   clock;
Pin 2 =   clear;

/* Outputs:  */

Pin [19..17] = [q0..2];

/** Declarations and Intermediate Variable Definitions **/

field count = [q2..0];          /* declare counter bit field */
$define S0 'b'000               /* define counter states */
$define S1 'b'001
$define S2 'b'010
$define S3 'b'011
$define S4 'b'100
$define S5 'b'101
$define S6 'b'110
$define S7 'b'111

/** Logic Equations **/

sequence count {                /* free running counter */
present S0       if !clear   next S1;
                 if clear    next S0;
```

Listing 7.6   (*cont.*)

```
present S1         if !clear    next S2;
                   if clear     next S0;
present S2         if !clear    next S3;
                   if clear     next S0;
present S3         if !clear    next S4;
                   if clear     next S0;
present S4         if !clear    next S5;
                   if clear     next S0;
present S5         if !clear    next S6;
                   if clear     next S0;
present S6         if !clear    next S7;
                   if clear     next S0;
present S7         next S0;
}
```

means that if the present state is *s2* = 010 and if clear = 0 then the next state will be *s3* = 011. On the other hand, if *clear* = 1, then the next state will be *s0* = 000. The resulting chip diagram for this program is shown in Fig. 7.24. Note that pin 2 is the *clear* input.

```
=============================================================
                         Chip Diagram
=============================================================

                        _____
                       |     div8cntc    |
           clock  x---|1                 20|---x Vcc
           clear  x---|2                 19|---x q0
                  x---|3                 18|---x q1
                  x---|4                 17|---x q2
                  x---|5                 16|---x
                  x---|6                 15|---x
                  x---|7                 14|---x
                  x---|8                 13|---x
                  x---|9                 12|---x
             GND  x---|10                11|---x
                       |_____|
```

Figure 7.24   Chip diagram from *div8cntc.doc*.

How does this program convert into logic equations? Figure 7.25 shows the expanded product terms for this program. Note that each of the previous product terms is simply ANDed with *!clear*. Thus, as long as *clear* = 0, the counter will count as usual. On the other hand, if *clear* = 1, then *!clear* will be zero and all the product terms will be zero, and thus the output will be zero. Figure 7.26 shows the logic diagram based on the logic equations in Fig. 7.25.

```
==================================================
                 Expanded Product Terms
==================================================

count =>
    q2 , q1 , q0

q0.d  =>
    !clear & !q0

q1.d  =>
    !clear & q0 & !q1
 # !clear & !q0 & q1

q2.d  =>
    !clear & q0 & q1 & !q2
 # !clear & !q1 & q2
 # !clear & !q0 & q2
```

Figure 7.25 Expanded product terms from *div8cntc.doc*.

To test the program in Listing 7.6, make a simulation file similar to the one in Listing 7.4. Add the *clear* variable following *clock* in the *ORDER* statement. Then make the first two test vectors *C1 LLL* and *C0 HLL*. Continue in the order shown in Listing 7.4. Repeat the sequence again in the middle of the count to show that the counter clears when *clear* = 1.

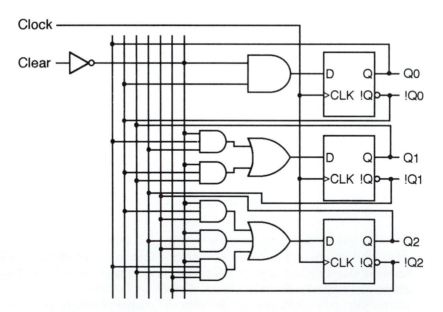

Figure 7.26 Logic diagram for counter in Listing 7.6 and Fig. 7.25.

Modulo-5 Counter

Suppose you want the 3-bit counter to count from 0 to 4 repeatedly. The truth table given in Fig. 7.20 for the divide-by-8 counter must then be modified as shown in Fig. 7.27. Note that only states $s0$ to $s4$ are active, and the count will cycle through these five states. This is sometimes called a *modulo-5 counter*.

Note that the values of $Q2.D$, $Q1.D$, and $Q0.D$ for the last three states are "don't cares." This means that we don't care if they are either 0 or 1 because we don't expect to be using any of these states. This will simplify our logic equations, as shown by the Karnaugh maps in Fig. 7.28. Note that we can circle any ×'s that will help to simplify our equations. Since these are "don't cares," we can assume that they are 1 for our purposes.

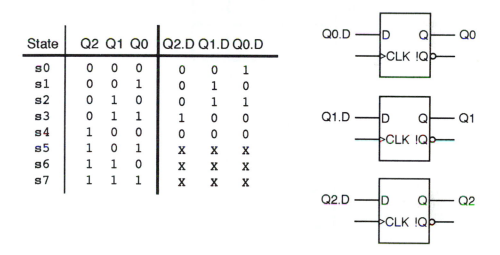

State	Q2	Q1	Q0	Q2.D	Q1.D	Q0.D
s0	0	0	0	0	0	1
s1	0	0	1	0	1	0
s2	0	1	0	0	1	1
s3	0	1	1	1	0	0
s4	1	0	0	0	0	0
s5	1	0	1	X	X	X
s6	1	1	0	X	X	X
s7	1	1	1	X	X	X

Figure 7.27   Truth table for a modulo-5 counter.

Using the logic equations in Fig. 7.28, we can write the CUPL program for the modulo-5 counter as shown in Listing 7.7. Note that we have to add a qualifying *!clear* signal in all our product terms so that the counter can be put into the 000 state to start the count. This is necessary because the power-up initial state will have all output pins *HI*. This is state $s7$, which is a "don't care" state in our truth table, and our logic equations do not guarantee that this state will clock to the $s0$ state (it won't!).

Listing 7.8 shows a simulation file that can be used to test the modulo-5 counter. Note that the *clear* signal is used in the first test vector to get the counter into a known state.

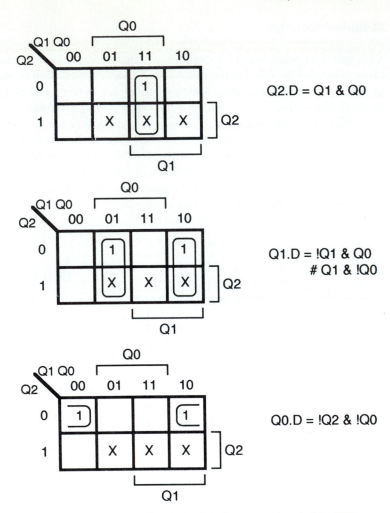

Figure 7.28   K-maps for the modulo-5 counter given in Fig. 7.27.

Listing 7.7   *mod5cnt.pld*

```
Name            mod5cnt;
Partno          OU0026;
Revision        01;
Date            8/06/91;
Designer        R. E. Haskell;
Company         Oakland University;
Location        Rochester, MI;
Assembly        CSE 171;
Device          G16V8;
Format          j;
```

Listing 7.7   *(cont.)*

```
/***************************************************************/
/*      This example demonstrates the use of D-type flip-flops */
/*      to design a modulo-5 counter                           */
/***************************************************************/
/*      Target Device:  G16V8                                  */
/***************************************************************/

/* Inputs:  */

Pin 1 =   clock;
Pin 2 =   clear;

/* Outputs:  */

Pin [19..17] = [q0..2];

/* Logic equations */

q0.d =   !clear & !q2 & !q0;
q1.d =   !clear & !q1 & q0
     #   !clear & q1 & !q0;
q2.d =   !clear & q1 & q0;
```

Listing 7.8   *mod5cnt.si*

```
Name           mod5cnt;
Partno         OU0026;
Revision       01;
Date           8/06/91;
Designer       R. E. Haskell;
Company        Oakland University;
Location       Rochester, MI;
Assembly       CSE 171;
Device         G16V8;
Format         j;

/ *************************************************************/

/***************************************************************/
/*      This example demonstrates the use of D-type flip-flops */
/*      to design a modulo-5 counter                           */
/***************************************************************/
/*      Target Device:  G16V8                                  */
/***************************************************************/
```

Listing 7.8   (*cont.*)

```
ORDER:   clock,%2,clear,%2,q0,%2,q1,%2,q2;

VECTORS:
  C1 LLL
  C0 HLL
  C0 LHL
  C0 HHL
  C0 LLH
  C0 LLL
  C0 HLL
  C0 LHL
  C0 HHL
  C0 LLH
  C0 LLL
  C0 HLL
  C0 LHL
  C0 HHL
  C0 LLH
```

3-Bit Down Counter

As a final example of a counter, we will modify the counter in Fig. 7.20 to make it count down rather than count up. We will also add a clear and parallel load capability to this counter. To make a down counter, we just change the truth table in Fig. 7.20 to that shown in Fig. 7.29. Note that at each clock pulse the current state is changed to the next lower state. The 000 state will wrap around to the 111 state.

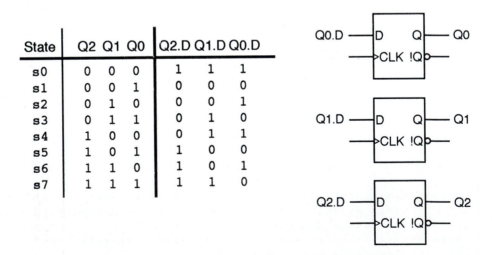

State	Q2	Q1	Q0	Q2.D	Q1.D	Q0.D
s0	0	0	0	1	1	1
s1	0	0	1	0	0	0
s2	0	1	0	0	0	1
s3	0	1	1	0	1	0
s4	1	0	0	0	1	1
s5	1	0	1	1	0	0
s6	1	1	0	1	0	1
s7	1	1	1	1	1	0

Figure 7.29   Truth table for a 3-bit down counter.

The K-maps for *Q2.D*, *Q1.D*, and *Q0.D* are shown in Fig. 7.30. Compare these maps with those shown in Fig. 7.21. We will add a clear input signal (pin 2) that will clear the outputs to 000 the same as we did in Figs. 7.24 and 7.25. We will also use pin 3 as a *load* input that, when *HI*, will load the three values *I0*, *I1*, and *I2* (from pins 4, 5, and 6) into *Q0*, *Q1*, and *Q2*.

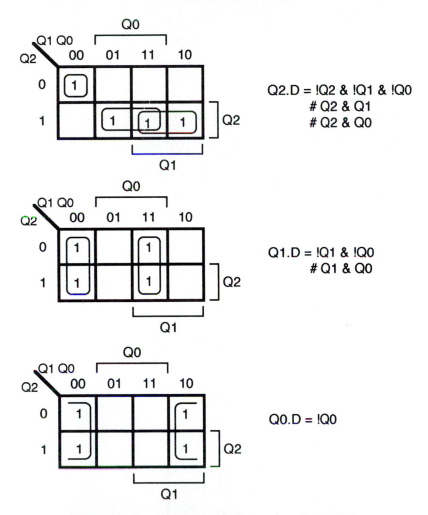

Figure 7.30   K-maps for the 3-bit down counter in Fig. 7.29.

The CUPL program for this down counter is given in Listing 7.9. Note that each product term for the counter is qualified with *!clear & !load*. This means that the counter will count down as long as *clear* and *load* are both *LO*. In addition, each equation for *qi.d* has the term *load & Ii* added (ORed) to it. This means that when *load* is *HI* the values *I0*, *I1*, and *I2* will appear on the *D* inputs to the three

Listing 7.9   *dncnt3ld.pld*

```
Name            dncnt3ld;
Partno          OU0029;
Revision        01;
Date            8/07/91;
Designer        R. E. Haskell;
Company         Oakland University;
Location        Rochester, MI;
Assembly        CSE 171;
Device          G16V8;
Format          j;

/ *****************************************************************/
/*      This is a 3-bit down counter                            */
/*      with clear and parallel load                            */
/ *****************************************************************/
/*      Target Device:  G16V8                                   */
/ *****************************************************************/

/* Inputs:  */

Pin 1 =  clock;
Pin 2 =  clear;
Pin 3 =  load;
Pin [4..6] = [I0..2];

/* Outputs:  */

Pin [19..17] = [q0..2];
Pin 16 = timeout;

/** Logic Equations **/

q0.d =  !clear & !load & !q0
     #  load & I0;

q1.d =  !clear & !load & !q0 & !q1
     #  !clear & !load & q0 & q1
     #  load & I1;

q2.d =  !clear & !load & !q0 & !q1 & !q2
     #  !clear & !load & q1 & q2
     #  !clear & !load & q0 & q2
     #  load & I2;

timeout = ![q0..2]:&;
```

flip-flops. On the next rising edge of the clock, these three values will be loaded into *Q0*, *Q1*, and *Q2*.

We have also included a *timeout* output signal (pin 16) that will go *HI* when the output is 000. Note that the equation for *timeout* is

```
timeout = ![q0..2]:&
```

which is equivalent to

```
timeout = !q0 & !q1 & !q2
```

The chip diagram for this down counter is shown in Fig. 7.31.

```
=============================================================
                       Chip Diagram
=============================================================

                    |     dncnt3ld    |
         clock  x---|1              20|---x  Vcc
         clear  x---|2              19|---x  q0
          load  x---|3              18|---x  q1
            I0  x---|4              17|---x  q2
            I1  x---|5              16|---x  timeout
            I2  x---|6              15|---x
                x---|7              14|---x
                x---|8              13|---x
                x---|9              12|---x
           GND  x---|10             11|---x
                    |_____|
```

Figure 7.31   Chip diagram from *dncnt3ld.doc.*

To test this program, you can use the simulation file given in Listing 7.10. If you run this simulation by typing

```
csim -w dncnt3ld
```

the output waveforms will be displayed on the screen in a graphical format.

If you include *!timeout* with the *!clear & !load* terms in Listing 7.9 and then add the additional term *timeout & Ii* similar to the *load & Ii* term in each logic equation, you will obtain a down counter that automatically reloads the values on pins *I0*, *I1*, and *I2* after each timeout. Using this technique, you can make a modulo-*N* counter by just putting the value *N − 1* on the parallel load input pins (see Exercise 7.5).

Listing 7.10   *dncnt3ld.si*

```
Name           dncnt3ld;
Partno         OU0029;
Revision       01;
Date           8/07/91;
Designer       R. E. Haskell;
Company        Oakland University;
Location       Rochester, MI;
Assembly       CSE 171;
Device         G16V8;
Format         j;


/ **************************************************************/
/*       This is a 3-bit down counter                         */
/*       with clear and parallel load                         */
/ **************************************************************/
/*       Target Device:  G16V8                                */
/ **************************************************************/

ORDER:
  clock,%2,clear,load,%3,I2..0,%3,q0,%2,q1,%2,q2,%2,timeout;

VECTORS:
  C10 XXX LLL H        /* clear counter */
  C00 XXX HHH L
  C00 XXX LHH L
  C00 XXX HLH L
  C00 XXX LLH L
  C00 XXX HHL L
  C01 101 HLH L        /* load 101 into counter */
  C00 XXX LLH L
  C00 XXX HHL L
  C00 XXX LHL L
  C00 XXX HLL L
  C00 XXX LLL H        /* timeout */
  C00 XXX HHH L
  C00 XXX LHH L
  C00 XXX HLH L
  C00 XXX LLH L
  C00 XXX HHL L
  C00 XXX LHL L
  C00 XXX HLL L
  C00 XXX LLL H        /* timeout */
  C00 XXX HHH L
```

7.3 SHIFT REGISTERS

An *n*-bit shift register contains *n* flip-flops. At each clock pulse, data are shifted from one flip-flop to the next. A 4-bit shift register is shown in Fig. 7.32. Serial data in the form of a string of bits is fed into the leftmost flip-flop via *data_in*. At each clock pulse, whatever is at *data_in* is moved to *Q0*, the value at *Q0* goes to *Q1*, the value at *Q1* goes to *Q2*, and the value at *Q2* goes to *Q3*.

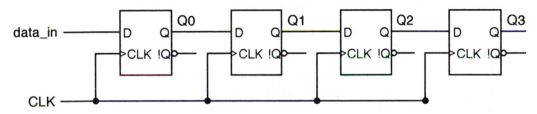

Figure 7.32   A 4-bit shift register.

This 4-bit shift register is easily programmed into a GAL 16V8 using the program shown in Listing 7.11. Note that a *HI clear* signal on pin 2 will set all of the flip-flops to zero. The chip diagram for this shift register is shown in Fig. 7.33.

This shift register can be tested using the simulation file shown in Listing 7.12. Note that the *data_in* value in each test vector is the value that is clocked to *Q0* by the clock in that test vector. If you run this simulation by typing

```
csim -w 4shift
```

the output waveforms displayed on the screen will illustrate the behavior of the shift register.

```
========================================================
                    Chip Diagram
========================================================

                  |      4shift      |
        clock x---|1               20|---x Vcc
        clear x---|2               19|---x q0
              x---|3               18|---x q1
     data_in x---|4               17|---x q2
              x---|5               16|---x q3
              x---|6               15|---x
              x---|7               14|---x
              x---|8               13|---x
              x---|9               12|---x
          GND x---|10              11|---x
                  |_____|
```

Figure 7.33   Chip diagram from *4shift.doc*.

Listing 7.11   *4shift.pld*

```
Name              4shift;
Partno            OU0031;
Revision          01;
Date              8/07/91;
Designer          R. E. Haskell;
Company           Oakland University;
Location          Rochester, MI;
Assembly          CSE 171;
Device            G16V8;
Format            j;

/ ***************************************************************/
/*        This is a 4-bit shift register                      */
/ ***************************************************************/
/*        Target Device:  G16V8                               */
/ ***************************************************************/

/* Inputs:  */

Pin 1 =  clock;
Pin 2 =  clear;
Pin 4 =  data_in;

/* Outputs:  */

Pin [19..16] = [q0..3];

/** Logic Equations **/

q0.d =   !clear & data_in;
q1.d =   !clear & q0;
q2.d =   !clear & q1;
q3.d =   !clear & q2;
```

Listing 7.12   *4shift.si*

```
Name              4shift;
Partno            OU0031;
Revision          01;
Date              8/07/91;
Designer          R. E. Haskell;
Company           Oakland University;
Location          Rochester, MI;
Assembly          CSE 171;
```

Listing 7.12   (*cont.*)

```
Device            G16V8;
Format            j;


/***************************************************************/
/*        This is a 4-bit shift register                       */
/***************************************************************/
/*        Target Device:  G16V8                                */
/***************************************************************/

ORDER:  clock,%2,clear,%2,data_in,%2,q0,%2,q1,%2,q2,%2,q3;

VECTORS:
  C10 LLLL              /* clear register */
  C01 HLLL
  C00 LHLL
  C00 LLHL
  C00 LLLH
  C00 LLLL
  C01 HLLL
  C00 LHLL
  C01 HLHL
  C00 LHLH
  C01 HLHL
  C00 LHLH
  C00 LLHL
  C00 LLLH
  C00 LLLL
```

Ring Counter

If the output *Q3* in the shift register in Fig. 7.32 is connected back to the input of the *Q0* flip-flop, and if only a single 1 is present in the four flip-flops, we have what is called a *ring counter*, as shown in Fig. 7.34. The single 1 in this ring counter is continuously cycled around all four flip-flops. This means that the

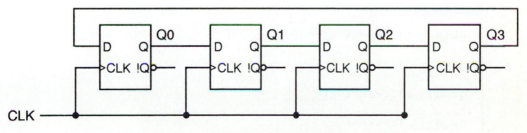

Figure 7.34   A ring counter.

output *Q* on each flip-flop will go *HI* once every four clock cycles, but this impulse will be out of phase by one clock cycle from one flip-flop to the next. We will therefore have generated a four-phase clock that can be used as the basis for various timing circuits.

The CUPL program for this ring counter is given in Listing 7.13. Note that the *clear* input signal is used to provide an initial 1 on *Q3*. When *clear* = *0*, this

Listing 7.13   *ring4.pld*

```
Name              ring4;
Partno            OU0032;
Revision          01;
Date              8/07/91;
Designer          R. E. Haskell;
Company           Oakland University;
Location          Rochester, MI;
Assembly          CSE 171;
Device            G16V8;
Format            j;

/ ************************************************************** /
/ *        This is a 4-bit ring counter                        * /
/ ************************************************************** /
/ *        Target Device:  G16V8                               * /
/ ************************************************************** /

/ * Inputs:   * /

Pin 1 =   clock;
Pin 2 =   clear;

/ * Outputs:   * /

Pin [19..16] = [q0..3];

/ ** Logic Equations ** /

q0.d =   !clear & q3;

q1.d =   !clear & q0;

q2.d =   !clear & q1;

q3.d =   !clear & q2
       # clear;
```

1 will cycle around the ring counter. The simulation file shown in Listing 7.14 can be used to test this ring counter. If you run this simulation by typing

```
csim -w ring4
```

it will be clear from the displayed waveforms what this ring counter does.

Listing 7.14   *ring4.si*

```
Name            ring4;
Partno          OU0032;
Revision        01;
Date            8/07/91;
Designer        R. E. Haskell;
Company         Oakland University;
Location        Rochester, MI;
Assembly        CSE 171;
Device          G16V8;
Format          j;

/ ************************************************************ /
/*         This is a 4-bit ring counter                      */
/ ************************************************************ /
/*         Target Device:  G16V8                             */
/ ************************************************************ /

ORDER:  clock,%2,clear,%2,q0,%2,q1,%2,q2,%2,q3;

VECTORS:
  C1 LLLH
  C0 HLLL
  C0 LHLL
  C0 LLHL
  C0 LLLH
  C0 HLLL
  C0 LHLL
  C0 LLHL
  C0 LLLH
  C0 HLLL
  C0 LHLL
  C0 LLHL
  C0 LLLH
  C0 HLLL
  C0 LHLL
  C0 LLHL
  C0 LLLH
```

Experiment 10: Flip-Flops

1. Write a CUPL program that will put both a D flip-flop and a J-K flip-flop in a single GAL 16V8. Make pin 2 the *D* input to the D flip-flop and pins 3 and 4 the *J* and *K* inputs to the J-K flip-flop. Use pins 19 and 18 for the outputs of the D flip-flop, *Q0* and *!Q0*. Use pins 17 and 16 for the outputs of the J-K flip-flop, *Q1* and *!Q1*. Compile the program to produce a JEDEC file.
2. Make a set of test vectors and test the program by running CSIM.
3. Use the JEDEC file produced in (2) to program a GAL 16V8.
4. Use the PLD logic analyzer to test the chip. Connect the three output lines, *Out0* to *Out3*, and the four input lines, *In1*, *In2*, *In3*, and *In4*, of the logic analyzer to the following pins of the GAL chip.

Logic analyzer	GAL pin no.	Signal
Out0	1	clock
Out1	2	D
Out3	3	J
Out4	4	K
In1	18	!Q0
In2	19	Q0
In3	16	!Q1
In4	17	Q1

5. Verify the operation of the two flip-flops by pressing function key *F1* and observing what happens when the clock signal goes from 0 to 1. Record the results by printing the truth table on the printer. Press function key *F2* to display the waveform. Discuss the results.
6. Switch the *J* and *K* signals by connecting *Out3* to *K* (pin 4) and *Out4* to *J* (pin 3). Repeat (5).

Experiment 11: 4-Bit Divide-by-16 Counter

1. Design a 4-bit divide-by-16 counter for the GAL 16V8 by modifying the program for the divide-by-8 counter given in Listing 7.3. Use pins [19..16] for [*Q0*..3]. Draw the Karnaugh maps for each of the four flip-flop inputs. Compile the program to produce a JEDEC file.
2. Make a set of test vectors and test the program by running CSIM using the -*w* option.
3. Use the JEDEC file produced in (2) to program a GAL 16V8.

4. Use the PLD logic analyzer to test the chip. Connect the output line, *Out0*, and the four input lines, *In1* to *In4*, of the logic analyzer to the following pins of the GAL chip.

Logic analyzer	GAL pin no.	Signal
Out0	1	clock
In1	19	Q0
In2	18	Q1
In3	17	Q2
In4	16	Q3

5. Verify the operation of the counter by pressing function key *F2* to display the waveform. Record the results by printing the waveform on the printer. Discuss the results.

Experiment 12: Modulo-12 Counter

1. Design a 4-bit modulo-12 counter for the GAL 16V8 including a *clear* input signal by following the design of the modulo-5 counter given in Listing 7.7. Use pins [19..16] for [*Q0*..3] and pin 2 for *clear*. Draw the Karnaugh maps for each of the four flip-flop inputs. Compile the program to produce a JEDEC file.

2. Make a set of test vectors and test the program by running CSIM using the -*w* option.

3. Use the JEDEC file produced in (2) to program a GAL 16V8.

4. Use the PLD logic analyzer to test the chip. Connect the output line, *Out0* and *Out7*, and the four input lines, *In1* to *In4*, of the logic analyzer to the following pins of the GAL chip.

Logic analyzer	GAL pin no.	Signal
Out0	1	clock
Out7	2	clear
In1	19	Q0
In2	18	Q1
In3	17	Q2
In4	16	Q3

5. Clear the outputs of the counter manually by setting *Out7* to 1, setting *Out0* to 1 and then resetting it back to 0, and then resetting *Out7* to 0. Verify the operation of the counter by pressing function key *F2* to display the waveform. Record the results by printing the waveform on the printer. Discuss the results.

Experiment 13: 3-Bit Modulo-*N* Down Counter

1. Design a 3-bit modulo-*N* down counter with parallel load for the GAL 16V8 including a *clear* input signal and a *timeout* output signal that automatically reloads the parallel inputs after each timeout (see Exercise 7.5). Use pins [19..17] for [*Q0*..2] and pin 16 for *timeout*. Use pin 2 for clear, pin 3 for load, and pins [4..6] for the parallel inputs [*I0*..2]. Draw the Karnaugh maps for each of the four flip-flop inputs. Compile the program to produce a JEDEC file.

2. Make a set of test vectors and test the program by running CSIM using the -*w* option.

3. Use the JEDEC file produced in (2) to program a GAL 16V8.

4. Use the PLD logic analyzer to test the chip. Connect the output line, *Out0* and *Out4* to *Out7*, and the four input lines, *In1* to *In4*, of the logic analyzer to the pins of the GAL chip shown in the following table.

Logic analyzer	GAL pin no.	Signal
Out0	1	clock
Out7	3	load
Out4	4	I0
Out5	5	I1
Out6	6	I2
In1	19	Q0
In2	18	Q1
In3	17	Q2
In4	15	timeout

5. Load the initial value of *N* − 1 manually by setting *Out7* to 1, *Out4* to *Out6* to *N* − 1, setting *Out0* to 1 and then resetting it back to 0, and then resetting *Out7* to 0. Verify the operation of the counter by pressing function key *F2* to display the waveform. Record the results by printing the waveform on the printer. Discuss the results.

Experiment 14: Shift Register with Parallel Load

1. Design a 3-bit circular shift register with parallel load for the GAL 16V8 including a *clear* input signal. Use pins [19..17] for [*Q0*..2]. Use pin 2 for clear, pin 3 for load, and pins [4..6] for the parallel inputs [*I0*..2]. Compile the program to produce a JEDEC file.

2. Make a set of test vectors and test the program by running CSIM using the -*w* option.

3. Use the JEDEC file produced in (2) to program a GAL 16V8.

4. Use the PLD logic analyzer to test the chip. Connect the output line, *Out0* and *Out4* to *Out7*, and the three input lines, *In1* to *In3*, of the logic analyzer to the pins of the GAL chip shown in the following table.

Logic analyzer	GAL pin no.	Signal
Out0	1	clock
Out7	3	load
Out4	4	I0
Out5	5	I1
Out6	6	I2
In1	19	Q0
In2	18	Q1
In3	17	Q2

5. Load an initial value *N* into the shift register manually by setting *Out7* to 1, *Out4* to *Out6* to *N*, setting *Out0* to 1 and then resetting it back to 0, and then resetting *Out7* to 0. Verify the operation of the circular shift register by pressing function key *F2* to display the waveform. Record the results by printing the waveform on the printer. Discuss the results.

EXERCISES

7.1. Show that if you replace the two NAND gates in Fig. 7.2 with two NOR gates you will obtain an S-R latch with the following truth table.

S	R	Q	!Q	
0	0	Q_0	$!Q_0$	Store
0	1	0	1	Reset
1	0	1	0	Set
1	1	0	0	Disallowed

7.2. Show that a D flip-flop with the same truth table as in Fig. 7.4 can be made by replacing the NAND gates in that figure with NOR gates and AND gates.

7.3. Define pin 19 in Listing 7.1 to be active low by writing the pin statement as

```
Pin 19 = !q0;
```

Compile the program using CUPL and explain the fuse map for pin 19 in the *.DOC* file.

7.4. Design the modulo-5 counter given in Listing 7.7 using state-machine syntax. Compile the program using the *-faxm2* options and compare the expanded product terms with the logic equations in Listing 7.7. Test the program by making a simulation file similar to Listing 7.8.

7.5. Modify Listing 7.9 by having the timeout signal reload the outputs *Q0*, *Q1*, and *Q2* with the input signals *I0*, *I1*, and *I2*. *Hint:* Include *!timeout* and the *!clear & !load* terms in Listing 7.9 and then add the additional term *timeout & Ii* similar to the *load & Ii* term in each logic equation. Test the design by making a modulo-5 counter by putting the values *I0* =

0, $I1 = 0$, and $I2 = 1$ on the parallel load input pins. Make a simulation file to test the design.

7.6. Modify Listing 7.10 to be a 4-bit down counter. Test the program by making a simulation file and running CSIM with the *-w* option.

7.7. Modify the ring counter shown in Fig. 7.34 by connecting *!Q3* to the *D* input of the *Q0* flip-flop, rather than *Q3*. This forms the basis of a *Johnson counter*. Make a table showing what eight consecutive states of *Q0* to *Q3* will be starting with all zeros. Write a CUPL program for this modified ring counter and test your program by making a simulation file.

7.8. Write a CUPL program that will store 4 bits of input data in a 4-bit register when a *load* signal goes *HI*. Test your program by making a simulation file and running CSIM.

7.9. Design a circuit using a 4-bit shift register that will detect the signal 1011 in the input stream. *Hint:* Make the output pin *found* go high when this bit pattern occurs on the four flip-flops. Write a CUPL program for this bit detector and test your program by making a simulation file and running CSIM.

7.10. Using a 3-bit counter, design a circuit whose output pin *pulse1* is high during states *s1* to *s6* and low during states *s0* and *s7*. Write a CUPL program for this pulse generator and test your program by making a simulation file and running CSIM.

8

Computer Memory

Storing data and instructions in some type of memory is a central role for any computer system. In Chapter 7 we saw that flip-flops can be used to store individual bits of data. A collection of flip-flops can be used to form a register that can hold a word of data containing a certain number of bits. The ENIAC developed during World War II used flip-flops made from vacuum tubes to store data in 20 registers. In an attempt to increase the storage capability of a memory, J. P. Eckert, in the mid-1940s, invented an ultrasonic delay line that could store 1,000 binary digits as a circulating sound wave in a tube of mercury. Early computers also stored data as electrostatic charges on the phosphor of cathode ray tubes (CRTs), much the same way as image data are stored on your TV screen. However, the magnetic core memory, invented by J. W. Forrester at MIT in the late 1940s, became the most common type of computer memory until the development of solid-state integrated circuits in the 1960s. Today almost all computer memories use some type of solid-state integrated circuit as the basic memory device.

The memory devices we have just described were and are used for what we call *main memory*. This is memory in which we want to access any memory location as quickly as possible. There has always been an inverse relationship between the number of bits we can store in a memory and the speed at which we can access those bits. The cost per bit is always lower for slow memories. In the early days this led to the development of magnetic drums and later magnetic disks for storing data that could be brought into the faster main memory as needed. The floppy disks and hard disks that we have in our PCs today are descendants of this magnetic storage technology.

Semiconductor memories used today can be divided into two main categories: *read-only memories* (ROMs) and *read-write memories* (RAMs). The data in a ROM can only be read; you can't change their value. The data in a ROM are stored in the ROM when the chip is manufactured. A special type of ROM that can be programmed by the user is called a *programmable read-only memory*, or PROM. A particularly useful version of a PROM is the *erasable programmable read-only memory* or EPROM (sometimes referred to as just a PROM). This EPROM can be erased by exposing the window on the chip to ultraviolet light for about a half-hour. A more recent development is the *electrically erasable programmable read-only memory* or EEPROM, which uses the same technology as in the electrically erasable GAL 16V8 that you have been using in the experiments in this book.

The word RAM stands for *random-access memory*, which is really a misnomer because a ROM is also random access. That is, any memory location can be accessed by providing the address to either the RAM or ROM. A RAM is really a read-write memory, which means that you can write data to the memory as well as read data stored in the memory. However, the word RAM has been used to mean read-write memory as opposed to ROMs, whose data you can only read. The data in most RAMs are lost when you turn off the power to the computer (unless the RAM contains a battery backup). The data in ROMs and PROMs on the other hand do not go away when the power to the chip is removed. RAMs also come in two types: static and dynamic. The data in a static RAM will remain as long as power is provided to the chip. On the other hand, the data in a dynamic RAM will leak away (in a matter of a few milliseconds) unless the data are constantly refreshed.

In this chapter you will learn:

- How to make a 2-word, 2-bit RAM using the GAL 16V8
- How popular EPROMs are programmed
- How static RAMs are addressed in a computer
- How data in a dynamic RAM are accessed

8.1 A 2-WORD, 2-BIT PLD RAM

In this section we will design a 2-word, 2-bit RAM in our GAL 16V8. We begin by designing a single memory cell that can store a single bit of data. We showed how to make a 1-bit register using a D flip-flop in Fig. 7.14. We will modify the circuit in that figure by adding a select line that must be high to either read or write data to the cell, as shown in Fig. 8.1. Note that we have changed the *LOAD* signal to a *read* signal that is high to read the data and low to write data from *data_in* into the cell. The output of the cell is *data_out* and is equal to Q if *read* and *select* are both high. Otherwise, the value of *data_out* will be zero regardless of the value of Q. Note that if *select* is low the current value of Q is continuously

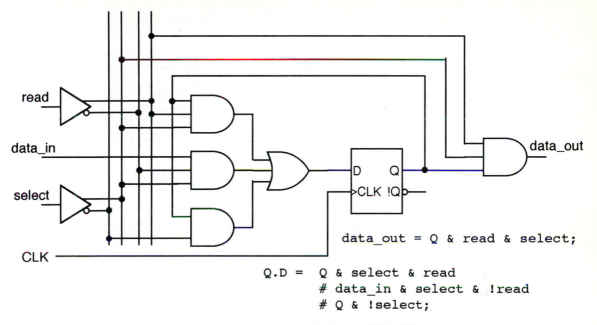

$$\text{data\_out} = Q\ \&\ \text{read}\ \&\ \text{select;}$$

$$Q.D\ =\quad Q\ \&\ \text{select}\ \&\ \text{read}$$
$$\#\ \text{data\_in}\ \&\ \text{select}\ \&\ !\text{read}$$
$$\#\ Q\ \&\ !\text{select;}$$

Figure 8.1   A memory cell using the GAL 16V8.

fed back (through the bottom AND gate) to the D input of the flip-flop. The logic equations for *data_out* and *Q.D* are shown in Fig. 8.1.

The memory cell shown in Fig. 8.1 can be represented by the block diagram symbol shown in Fig. 8.2. This cell has three inputs and one output. If *read* = 0 and *select* = 1, then at the next clock pulse the value of *data_in* will be stored in the memory cell. When *select* = 0, the data stay in the memory cell. If *read* = 1 and *select* = 1, then the value stored in the memory cell will appear on the output *data_out*.

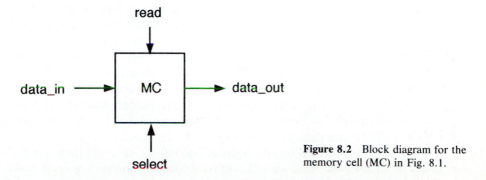

Figure 8.2   Block diagram for the memory cell (MC) in Fig. 8.1.

Four of these memory cells can be combined to form a 2-word, 2-bit RAM as shown in Fig. 8.3. The lower two memory cells form the 2 bits of *word a* and

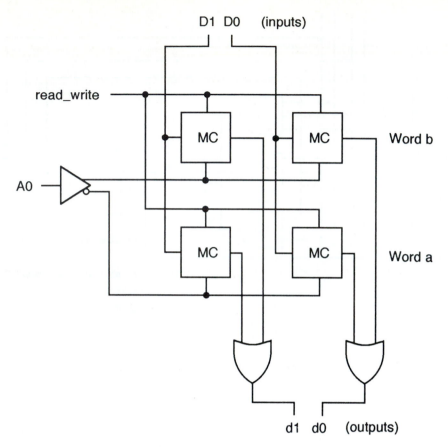

Figure 8.3 A 2-word, 2-bit RAM.

the upper two memory cells form the 2 bits of *word b*. The *data_in* lines of the rightmost bits in each word are connected to the data input line *D0*. The *data_in* lines of the leftmost bits in each word are connected to the data input line *D1*. The *data_out* lines of the rightmost bits in each word are connected through an OR gate to the data output line *d0*. The *data_out* lines of the leftmost bits in each word are connected through an OR gate to the data output line *d1*. Recall that the *data_out* line of a memory cell will be zero if the memory cell in not selected. Therefore, if *word a* is selected in Fig. 8.3, the output data (*d1, d0*) will be the data stored in *word a*. Similarly, if *word b* is selected in Fig. 8.3, the output data (*d1, d0*) will be the data stored in *word b*.

A word is selected by the address line *A0*. If *A0* = 0, then *word a* will be selected. If *A0* = 1, then *word b* will be selected. Finally, the *read_write* line is connected to the read input to each memory cell. If *read_write* is high, the data in the selected word will appear on the output lines (*d1, d0*). If *read_write* is low, the data on the input lines (*D1, D0*) will be stored in the selected word. The

```
============================================================
                        Chip Diagram
============================================================
                         _____
                        |      ram2         |
            clock  x---|1                20|---x Vcc
              !cs  x---|2                19|---x qa0
                   x---|3                18|---x qa1
               A0  x---|4                17|---x qb0
               D1  x---|5                16|---x qb1
               D0  x---|6                15|---x
       read_write  x---|7                14|---x
                   x---|8                13|---x d1
                   x---|9                12|---x d0
              GND  x---|10               11|---x
                        |_____|
```

Figure 8.4   Chip diagram from *ram2.doc*.

program for putting this 2-word, 2-bit RAM into a GAL 16V8 is shown in Listing 8.1, and the corresponding chip diagram is shown in Fig. 8.4.

Note in this program that we have added an active low chip select input, *!cs*, on pin 2. When this input is low, the output buffers of the two data output pins, *d0* and *d1*, are enabled using the two logic equations

```
d0.oe  =  cs  &  read_write;
                                                            (8.1)
d1.oe  =  cs  &  read_write;
```

When the suffix *.oe* is added to an output pin variable name on the left side of a CUPL equation, the output enable line, *OE*, which enables the output inverter shown in Fig. 4.10, is controlled by the logic expression on the right side of the equation. This variable control of the *OE* line is possible only if the D flip-flop for that pin is *not* being used. If the D flip-flop is being used, then the *OE* line is controlled by pin 11. When the output inverter is disabled, its output is put in a

Listing 8.1   *ram2.pld*

```
Name            ram2;
Partno          OU0033;
Revision        01;
Date            8/20/91;
Designer        R. E. Haskell;
Company         Oakland University;
Location        Rochester, MI;
Assembly        CSE 171;
Device          G16V8;
Format          j;
```

Listing 8.1   (*cont.*)

```
/ ************************************************************ /
/*          This is a 2-word, 2-bit RAM                        */
/ ************************************************************ /
/*          Target Device:  G16V8                             */
/ ************************************************************ /

/* Inputs:  */

Pin 1 =  clock;
Pin 2 =  !cs;                    /* chip select */
Pin 4 = A0;                      /* address lines */
Pin [5,6] = [D1..0];             /* data lines */
Pin 7 = read_write;             /* R/!W line */

/* Outputs:  */

Pin [19..18] = [qa0..1];        /* word a data */
Pin [17..16] = [qb0..1];        /* word b data */
Pin 12 = d0;                     /* output data bit 0 */
Pin 13 = d1;                     /* output data bit 1 */

/** Intermediate Equations **/

select_a = !A0;
select_b = A0;
FIELD Qa = [qa1..0];
FIELD Qb = [qb1..0];
FIELD data = [D1..0];

/** Logic Equations **/

Qa.d =  Qa & select_a & read_write
      # data & select_a & !read_write
       # Qa & !select_a;

Qb.d =  Qb & select_b & read_write
       # data & select_b & !read_write
       # Qb & !select_b;

d0 =  qa0 & read_write & select_a
    # qb0 & read_write & select_b;

d1 =  qa1 & read_write & select_a
    # qb1 & read_write & select_b;

d0.oe = cs & read_write;
d1.oe = cs & read_write;
```

high-impedance state. This means that the output pin is effectively disconnected from the circuit. For example, the output data lines (*d1, d0*) in Fig. 8.4 could be connected to the output data lines from a similar RAM chip to form a data bus. Only the memory chip whose chip select line, *!cs*, was low would have its data show up on the data bus.

In Listing 8.1 we have defined the three bit field variables, *Qa, Qb*, and *data* using the statements

```
FIELD Qa = [qa1..0];
FIELD Qb = [qb1..0];                                              (8.2)
FIELD data = [D1..0];
```

The variable *Qa* represents the 2 bits in *word a*, while the variable *Qb* represents the 2 bits in *word b*. The variable *data* represents the 2-bit input data. The equations

```
select_a = !A0;                                                   (8.3)
select_b = A0;
```

define the variables *select_a* and *select_b*, which are high when *word a* and *word b* are selected, respectively.

The logic equation

```
Qa.d =    Qa & select_a & read_write

     # data & select_a & !read_write                             (8.4)

     # Qa & !select_a;
```

is based on the equation for *Q.D* given in Fig. 8.1. From Fig. 8.5 we see that this equation expands to the two equations

```
qa0.d =    !A0 & qa0 & read_write

      # !A0 & D0 & !read_write                                   (8.5)

      # A0 & qa0

qa1.d =    !A0 & qa1 & read_write

      # !A0 & D1 & !read_write                                   (8.6)

      # A0 & qa1
```

A similar set of equations is obtained from the *Qb.d* equation. The two equations

```
================================================
            Expanded Product Terms
================================================

Qa =>
    qa1 , qa0

Qb =>
    qb1 , qb0

d0 =>
    !A0 & qa0 & read_write
  # A0 & qb0 & read_write

d0.oe  =>
    cs & read_write

d1 =>
    !A0 & qa1 & read_write
  # A0 & qb1 & read_write

d1.oe  =>
    cs & read_write

data =>
    D1 , D0

qa0.d  =>
    !A0 & qa0 & read_write
  # !A0 & D0 & !read_write
  # A0 & qa0

qa1.d  =>
    !A0 & qa1 & read_write
  # !A0 & D1 & !read_write
  # A0 & qa1

qb0.d  =>
    A0 & qb0 & read_write
  # A0 & D0 & !read_write
  # !A0 & qb0

qb1.d  =>
    A0 & qb1 & read_write
  # A0 & D1 & !read_write
  # !A0 & qb1

select_a =>
    !A0

select_b =>
    A0
```

Figure 8.5 Expanded product terms from *ram2.doc*.

for the output data lines are given by

```
d0  =    qa0 & read_write & select_a

     # qb0 & read_write & select_b;                            (8.7)

d1  =    qa1 & read_write & select_a

     # qb1 & read_write & select_b;                            (8.8)
```

and follow from the equation for *data_out* in Fig. 8.1 and the circuit in Fig. 8.3.

After compiling this program using CUPL, we can test the design by using the simulation file shown in Listing 8.2. The first two test vectors in Listing 8.2 write the data 10 to *word a* (*A0 = 0*) and the data 01 to *word b* (*A0 = 1*). Recall from Eq. (8.1) that the output pins *d0* and *d1* will be in the high-impedance state when the *read_write* input is low, that is, during a write operation. Therefore, in

Listing 8.2   *ram2.si*

```
Name            ram2;
Partno          OU0033;
Revision        01;
Date            8/20/91;
Designer        R. E. Haskell;
Company         Oakland University;
Location        Rochester, MI;
Assembly        CSE 171;
Device          G16V8;
Format          j;

/ ****************************************************************/
/*        This is a 2-word, 2-bit RAM                           */
/ ****************************************************************/
/*        Target Device:  G16V8                                 */
/ ****************************************************************/

ORDER:  clock,%2,A0,D1,D0,read_write,!cs,%2,d1,d0;

VECTORS:
    C01000 ZZ
    C10100 ZZ
    C0XX10 HL
    C1XX10 LH
    C00000 ZZ
    C11100 ZZ
    C0XX10 LL
    C1XX10 HH
```

the simulation file we use the letter *Z* to indicate that the output pin should be tested for a high impedance.

The third and fourth test vectors in Listing 8.2 read the data in *word a* (*A0 = 0*) and *word b* (*A0 = 1*). Note that the input data is × (don't care) in this case. The outputs should be the data stored by the first two test vectors.

The last four test vectors write the data 00 to *word a* and 11 to *word b* and then read back this data. To run this simulation, type

```
csim -w ram2
```

This will produce the waveforms shown in Fig. 8.6. Note how the data written in from *D1* and *D0* are then read out through *d1* and *d0*. For a further study of this circuit, see Experiment 15 at the end of this chapter.

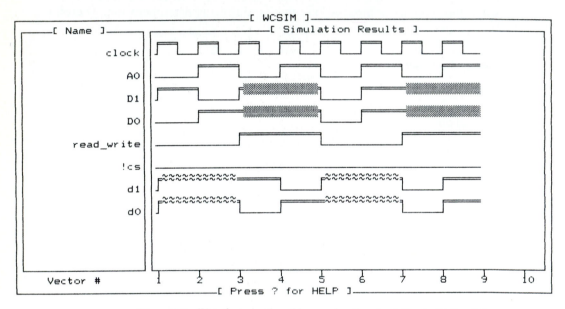

Figure 8.6 Waveform produced by running the simulation in Listing 8.2.

8.2 ROMS AND PROMS

As mentioned earlier in this chapter, read-only memories, or ROMS, contain data that can only be read. The data cannot be changed. A ROM contains a certain number of bytes of data. For example, the diagram for a fictitious 16-byte ROM is shown in Fig. 8.7. The four input address lines, *A0* to *A3*, select one of 16 memory locations, and the contents of the selected address appears on the eight output pins, *D0* to *D7*.

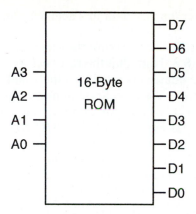

Figure 8.7 A 16-byte ROM containing four input address lines.

Now, whereas the RAM we designed in the previous section had a flip-flop associated with each bit that was stored in the memory, a ROM is just a combinational circuit in which the bits are not really "stored" as they are in a RAM. All that is necessary is that when a particular 4-bit address is applied to the ROM inputs in Fig. 8.7 the data "stored" at that address appear on the eight output pins.

For example, suppose we wanted to have a 16-byte ROM like that shown in Fig. 8.7 that contains the 16 bytes of data shown in Table 8.1. We have already made this ROM! It is the same as the 7-segment decoder we designed in Listing

TABLE 8.1   ROM DATA

Hex address	Hex data
0	7E
1	30
2	6D
3	79
4	33
5	5B
6	5F
7	70
8	7F
9	7B
A	77
B	1F
C	4E
D	3D
E	4F
F	47

6.15. Notice that the 1's in the hex data in Table 8.1 correspond to the *ON* bits in Listing 6.15.

We can test this "ROM" by making the simulation file for the 7-segment decoder shown in Listing 8.3. Note that the test vectors are written as hex digits enclosed in quotes. Single quotes are used for inputs and double quotes are used for outputs. When hex numbers are enclosed in quotes in the test vectors, CSIM will expand each hex digit to 4 bits. For example, the input '5' is equivalent to 0101 and the output "5B" is equivalent to *HLHHLHH*. Note that because the bit field variable *segment* contains only the 7 bits [*a, b, c, d, e, f, g*] the output "5B" is interpreted as only the lower 7 bits of this hex number.

If you run this simulation by typing

```
csim -l 7seg
```

the results will be displayed in the file *7seg.so* shown in Listing 8.4. Note that each address found the proper data "stored" in the ROM.

Listing 8.3   *7seg.si*

```
Name            7seg;
Partno          0U0021;
Revision        01;
Date            7/30/91;
Designer        R. E. Haskell;
Company         Oakland University;
Location        Rochester, MI;
Assembly        CSE 171;
Device          G16V8;
Format          j;

/***************************************************************/
/*                                                      a       */
/* This is a Hex-to-seven-segment                     -----     */
/* decoder capable of driving common-anode          |       |   */
/* LEDs.                                           f |       | b */
/*                                                   |   g   |   */
/*                                                    -----      */
/*                                                   |       |   */
/*                                                 e |       | c */
/*                                                   |       |   */
/*                                                    -----      */
/*                                                      d        */
/*                                                               */
/***************************************************************/
/*      Target Device: G16V8                                   */
/***************************************************************/
```

Listing 8.3   (*cont.*)

```
ORDER:   data,%2,segment;

VECTORS:
$msg "        data  abcdefg";
$msg "        ----  -------";

'0' "7E"
'1' "30"
'2' "6D"
'3' "79"
'4' "33"
'5' "5B"
'6' "5F"
'7' "70"
'8' "7F"
'9' "7B"
'A' "77"
'B' "1F"
'C' "4E"
'D' "3D"
'E' "4F"
'F' "47"
```

Listing 8.4   *7seg.so*

```
CSIM: CUPL Simulation Program
Version 4.0a Serial# MD-40A-7985
Copyright (C)  1983,1990 Logical Device  s, Inc.
CREATED Tue Sep 24 17:22:14 1991

LISTING FOR SIMULATION FILE: 7seg.si

    1: Name           7seg;
    2: Partno         OU0021;
    3: Revision       01;
    4: Date           7/30/91;
    5: Designer       R. E. Haskell;
    6: Company        Oakland University;
    7: Location       Rochester, MI;
    8: Assembly       CSE 171;
    9: Device         G16V8;
   10: Format         j;
   11:
```

Listing 8.4   *(cont.)*

```
12: /**********************************************************/
13: /*                                                  a      */
14: /* This is a Hex-to-seven-segment                 -----    */
15: /* decoder capable of driving common-anode        ¦     ¦  */
16: /* LEDs.                                         f¦     ¦b  */
17: /*                                                ¦  g  ¦   */
18: /*                                                 -----    */
19: /*                                                ¦     ¦   */
20: /*                                              e¦     ¦c   */
21: /*                                                ¦     ¦    */
22: /*                                                 -----    */
23: /*                                                  d      */
24: /*                                                         */
25: /**********************************************************/
26: /*     Target Device: G16V8                                */
27: /**********************************************************/
28:
29: ORDER:  data,%2,segment;
30:


=============================================================
                    Simulation Results
=============================================================
       data   abcdefg
       ----   -------
0001:  0000   HHHHHHL
0002:  0001   LHHLLLL
0003:  0010   HHLHHLH
0004:  0011   HHHHLLH
0005:  0100   LHHLLHH
0006:  0101   HLHHLHH
0007:  0110   HLHHHHH
0008:  0111   HHHLLLL
0009:  1000   HHHHHHH
0010:  1001   HHHHLHH
0011:  1010   HHHLHHH
0012:  1011   LLHHHHH
0013:  1100   HLLHHHL
0014:  1101   LHHHHLH
0015:  1110   HLLHHHH
0016:  1111   HLLLHHH
```

EPROMs

Real ROMs "store" their data in various ways depending on the particular technology used to make the ROM. EPROMs (erasable, programmable read-only memories) store their bits as electric charges on "floating" gates in transistors within the chip. These EPROMs can be programmed by using a PROM programming device similar to the one you use to program the GAL 16V8. (Some programmers can program both PLDs and PROMs.) An erased PROM may have all its bits set to 1 or 0, depending on the particular type of PROM. The 27xxx family of EPROMs shown in Table 8.2 have all their erased bits set to 1. The programming process involves applying a high voltage to a certain pin when the desired address and data are shown to the chip. This causes electrons to be ac-

TABLE 8.2 COMMON EPROMS

Number	Size
2716	2K × 8
2732	4K × 8
2764	8K × 8
27128	16K × 8
27256	32K × 8
27512	64K × 8

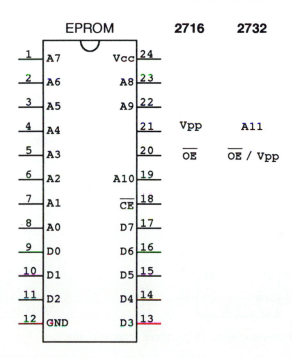

Figure 8.8 Pinouts for the 24-pin 27xx EPROM family.

cumulated on the floating gate. This charge on the floating gate will remain for years and the EPROM will therefore contain the programmed data. Exposing the chip to ultraviolet light for about half an hour will cause the charge on the floating gate to leak away and the EPROM will be erased.

The 2716 and 2732 are 24-pin chips with the pinouts shown in Fig. 8.8. The 2716 contains 2K (2,048) bytes of memory and therefore must have 11 address lines, $A0$ to $A10$ (2^{11} = 2,048). The 2732 contains 4K (4,096) bytes of memory and therefore must add one additional address line, $A11$. This address line is brought into pin 21, which contained the programming voltage V_{pp} in the 2716. In the 2732 this programming voltage is combined with the output enable function on pin 20. By keeping most of the pin functions the same, it is possible, by the judicious use of jumpers, to use the same socket for both 2716 and 2732 EPROMs.

As higher-density EPROMs were developed, this philosophy was maintained as shown by the pinouts in Fig. 8.9. Note that this is a 28-pin chip, but that the lower 24-pins have the same functions as those shown in Fig. 8.8. Each time the amount of memory is doubled in Table 8.2 a new address line must be added to the chip. The way this is done is shown in Fig. 8.9. Note that the 27512 contains 64K (65,536) bytes of memory and has 16 address lines, $A0$ to $A15$ (2^{16} = 65,536).

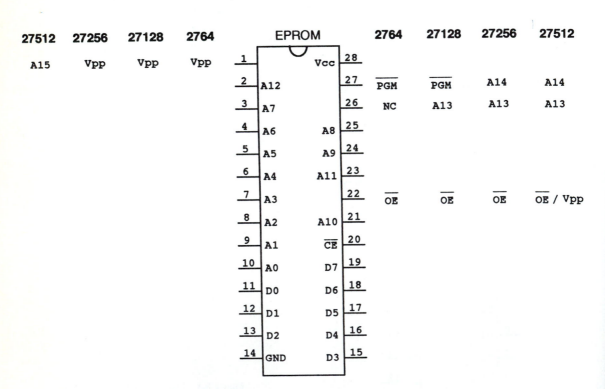

Figure 8.9   Pinouts for the 28-pin 27xxx EPROM family.

While EPROMs are normally used to store programs and data in a computer system, they could also be used to perform a combinational logic function. For example, by storing the data shown in Table 8.1, we could use an EPROM as a 7-segment decoder. (See Experiment 16.) Generally, this is an overkill inasmuch as a large part of the EPROM will be unused.

8.3 STATIC RAMS

The pinouts for a typical 32K × 8 static RAM are shown in Fig. 8.10. Comparing these pinouts with those of a 27256 EPROM in Fig. 8.9, we see that most of the pin functions are the same. The ones that are different can be switched on a printed circuit board by using jumpers. Therefore, it is possible to use a static RAM in a particular socket while a program is being developed and then burn an EPROM of this program and substitute the EPROM for the static RAM. The program will then be fixed at that location in memory and will not go away when power to the computer is turned off.

Pin 27 in Fig. 8.10 is the write enable pin. When this pin is low, the data on the data lines $D0$ to $D7$ will be written into RAM at the address given on the

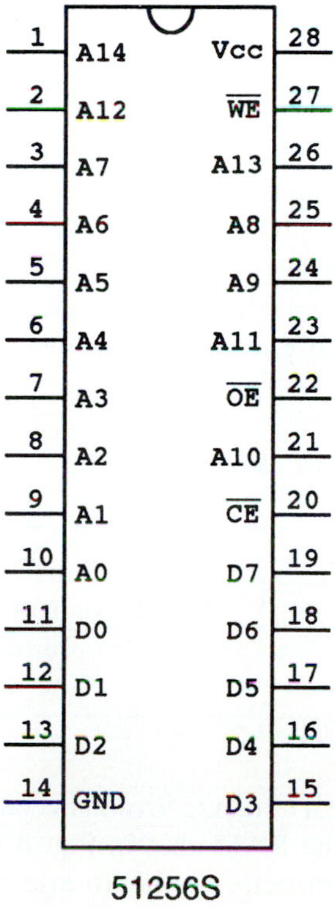

1	A14	Vcc	28
2	A12	$\overline{WE}$	27
3	A7	A13	26
4	A6	A8	25
5	A5	A9	24
6	A4	A11	23
7	A3	$\overline{OE}$	22
8	A2	A10	21
9	A1	$\overline{CE}$	20
10	A0	D7	19
11	D0	D6	18
12	D1	D5	17
13	D2	D4	16
14	GND	D3	15

51256S

Figure 8.10 Pinouts for a 32K × 8 static RAM.

address lines, *A0* to *A14*. When the write enable pin is high, the data at the address on the address lines will be read from the memory and put on the eight data lines.

To access the static RAM at all, the chip enable signal on pin 20 must be low. This is the chip select signal that is generated by some type of address decoding as described in Section 6.3. (See Experiment 17.)

Address Decoding for RAMs and ROMs

The Motorola 68000 microprocessor has 16 data lines that go to memory. This means that it can read and write 2 bytes at a time. The 23 address lines, *A1* to *A23*, of the 68000 can address 2^{23} = 8 Mword (8,388,608 words) or 16 Mbytes (16,777,216 bytes) of memory. Two of the RAM chips shown in Fig. 8.10 could be used to store 32 Kwords of data. The lower byte of each word would be stored in one chip, and the upper byte of each word would be stored in the other. This means that the eight data lines from one chip would be connected to the data lines *D0* to *D7* of the microprocessor, and the eight data lines from the other chip would be connected to data lines *D8* to *D15* of the microprocessor. The address lines *A1* to *A15* from the 68000 would be connected to the address pins *A0* to *A14* of the memory chip. This means that only even addresses from the 68000 can address a 16-bit word. A lower data strobe (*LDS*) line and an upper data strobe (*UDS*) line from the 68000 can be used to address the lower byte or the upper byte in a word. These signals play the role of address line *A0* from the 68000.

Suppose that we want to make a 68000 computer system that will contain 128 Kbytes of static RAM and 128 Kbytes of EPROM. We will use four of the 32K × 8 static RAM chips shown in Fig. 8.10 and two of the 27512 EPROMs shown in Fig. 8.9. These chips will be used in pairs, one for the high byte and one for the low byte, for the word at each even address. The two chips in each pair will be selected at the same time (by bringing their chip enable pins, *CE*, low) when the address lines carry an address in their address range. We will choose the address ranges for each pair of chips given by the memory map shown in Table 8.3.

TABLE 8.3   MEMORY MAP

Device	Memory size (bytes)	Address range
RAM0	64K	000000–00FFFF
RAM1	64K	010000–01FFFF
ROM	128K	C00000–C1FFFF

The 15 address lines *A1* to *A15* from the 68000 will be connected directly to the 15 address lines of the RAM chip in Fig. 8.10, and the 16 address lines *A1* to *A16* will be connected directly to the 16 address lines of the 27512 EPROM

chip in Fig. 8.9. We will use the high-order address lines, *A16* to *A23*, as inputs
to a GAL 16V8 to produce the three chip select signals *ROM_CS, RAM_CS0,*
and *RAM_CS1*. Using the address decoding method described in Chapter 6 (see
Listing 6.9), we can write the CUPL program shown in Listing 8.5 based on the
memory map given in Table 8.3. Note that we have added the read/write line,

Listing 8.5   *ramrom.pld*

```
Name             ramrom;
Partno           OU0041;
Revision         01;
Date             10/3/91;
Designer         R. E. Haskell;
Company          Oakland University;
Location         Rochester, MI;
Assembly         CSE 171;
Device           G16V8;
Format           j;

/ ************************************************************ /
/ *                                                          * /
/ *       RAM & ROM  address  decoder  for  68000  system    * /
/ *                                                          * /
/ ************************************************************ /
/ *         Target Device:   G16V8                            * /
/ ************************************************************ /

/* Inputs:  */

Pin [1..8] =  [A16..23];
Pin 9 =  RW;

/* Outputs:  */

Pin 19 = !ROM_CS;
Pin 18 = !RAM_CS0;
Pin 17 = !RAM_CS1;

/* Intermediate variables */

FIELD address = [A23..16];

/* Logic equations:  */

RAM_CS0 = address:[000000..00FFFF];
RAM_CS1 = address:[010000..01FFFF];
ROM_CS  = RW & address:[C00000..C1FFFF];
```

RW, from the 68000 as an input to the GAL 16V8. This line is high during a read operation and low during a write operation. We include this signal in the logic equation for *ROM_CS* so that the ROM will not be selected during a write operation to a ROM address.

If you compile the program shown in Listing 8.5 and look at the expanded product terms in the *.DOC* file, you will see that CUPL has reduced the logic equations for *RAM_CS0, RAM_CS1,* and *ROM_CS* to the following three equations:

```
RAM_CS0 = !A16 & !A17 & !A18 & !A19 & !A20 &

          !A21 & !A22 & !A23

RAM_CS1 = A16 & !A17 & !A18 & !A19 & !A20 &

          !A21 & !A22 & !A23

ROM_CS  = !A17 & !A18 & !A19 & !A20 &

          !A21 & A22 & A23 & RW
```

Note that address lines *A22* and *A23* distinguish between the addresses of the ROM and the RAMs. The address ranges for the two RAMs are distinguished by address line *A16*.

The output pins for *RAM_CS0, RAM_CS1,* and *ROM_CS* are defined to be active low outputs in Listing 8.5 to correspond to the active low chip enable pins on the RAM and EPROM chips in Figs. 8.10 and 8.9. The chip diagram resulting from the program in Listing 8.5 is shown in Fig. 8.11.

```
===========================================================
                      Chip Diagram
===========================================================

                    _____
                   |     ramrom    |
         A16  x---|1              20|---x  Vcc
         A17  x---|2              19|---x  !ROM_CS
         A18  x---|3              18|---x  !RAM_CS0
         A19  x---|4              17|---x  !RAM_CS1
         A20  x---|5              16|---x
         A21  x---|6              15|---x
         A22  x---|7              14|---x
         A23  x---|8              13|---x
          RW  x---|9              12|---x
         GND  x---|10             11|---x
                   |_____|
```

Figure 8.11 Chip diagram from *ramrom.doc*.

8.4 DYNAMIC RAMS

The 28-pin static RAM shown in Fig. 8.10 contains 256 Kbits of memory organized as 32K 8-bit bytes. If you wanted a 1 Mbyte (1,048,576 bytes) memory, you would have to use 32 of these 28-pin chips. Alternatively, you could use just eight (one for each bit in a byte) of the 1 Mbyte × 1 bit dynamic RAMs shown in Fig. 8.12. This is only an 18-pin chip, compared with the 28-pin static RAM in Fig. 8.10. The cost of these two chips will be roughly the same, so the cost of the eight dynamic RAMS will be substantially less than the cost of 32 static RAMs. However, there is an additional price you have to pay for using these dynamic RAMs.

1	D		Vss	18
2	$\overline{W}$		Q	17
3	$\overline{RAS}$		$\overline{CAS}$	16
4	TF		A9	15
5	A0		A8	14
6	A1		A7	13
7	A2		A6	12
8	A3		A5	11
9	Vcc		A4	10

Figure 8.12 Pinouts for a 1 Mbyte (1,048,576) × 1 bit dynamic RAM.

First, how could we fit 1 Mbit of memory into an 18-pin chip? We would need 20 address lines (2^{20} = 1,048,576) to address 1,048,576 different memory locations. In Fig. 8.12 the chip contains only 10 address lines, *A0* to *A9*. We have to present the 20 address lines to this chip in two steps: first, the lower 10 address lines are connected to the 10 address pins on the chip (using a multiplexer) and the *row address strobe, RAS* (pin 3), is brought low; then the multiplexer switches to connect the upper 10 address lines to the same 10 address pins on the chip and the *column address strobe, CAS* (pin 16), is brought low. A single bit of data is written to the chip through pin 1 (*D*) and is read from the chip through pin 17 (*Q*).

In addition to having to multiplex the address lines onto the chip, there is a further complication when using dynamic RAMs. Whereas in a static RAM the data are stored in a flip-flop made up of several transistors, in a dynamic RAM the data are stored as a charge on a capacitor associated with a single transistor. This is why for a given chip area more bits of data can be stored in a dynamic RAM than in a static RAM. However, the charge stored on the capacitors in a dynamic RAM will leak away within a few milliseconds unless this charge is constantly being restored. The process of reading data from a dynamic RAM automatically writes the data back, which restores (or refreshes) the charge. It is therefore necessary to constantly read all the data in a dynamic RAM or else you will lose it! It turns out that if you read a given row (one of the 10 address line combinations in Fig. 8.12) then all the (1,024) bits in that row will be refreshed. This means that additional circuitry will be needed that will constantly cycle through all the row addresses, refreshing the data stored in the chip. Even with this additional circuitry it is usually cheaper to use dynamic RAM in large systems where a lot of memory is required. For smaller systems involving a modest amount of memory that can fit into a few static RAMs, it will be easier and cheaper to use static RAMs.

Dynamic RAM Controller

In this section we will look at one part of a dynamic RAM controller: how you might generate the *RAS* and *CAS* signals needed to multiplex the address lines onto the dynamic RAM chip. We'll assume that we have a *clear* signal that will go low to initiate an address access cycle as shown in Fig. 8.13. On the rising edge of the next clock cycle (following *clear* going low), the signal *RAS* will go low. In a dynamic RAM system this will latch the row addresses into the chip. On the next rising edge of the clock, the signal *MUX* will go low. This signal would be used to switch to the column addresses. On the next rising edge of the

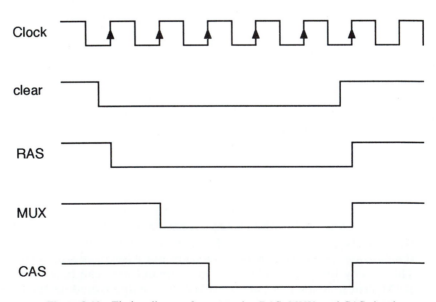

Figure 8.13   Timing diagram for generating RAS, MUX, and CAS signals.

clock, the signal *CAS* will go low. This would be used to latch the column addresses into the chip. When clear goes back high, all three signals, *RAS, MUX*, and *CAS*, will go high.

The various states of the signals *RAS, MUX,* and *CAS* in Fig. 8.13 can be summarized by means of the *state table* shown in Table 8.4. Given the *present state* of these three signals together with the input *clear*, the table shows what the *next state* will be after the next clock pulse. Note that this state table contains all possible states as indicated by the waveforms in Fig. 8.13.

TABLE 8.4 STATE TABLE FOR SIGNALS IN FIGURE 8.13

Present state			Input	Next state		
RAS	MUX	CAS	Clear	RAS	MUX	CAS
1	1	1	1	1	1	1
1	1	1	0	0	1	1
0	1	1	0	0	0	1
0	0	1	0	0	0	0
0	0	0	0	0	0	0
0	0	0	1	1	1	1

We can implement this state table in our GAL 16V8 by making the *next state* the inputs to three D flip-flops. Using a sum of products design from Table 8.4, we can, after reducing the equations by using Karnaugh maps (see Exercise 8.4), write the logic equations as

```
RAS.d  =   RAS & MUX & CAS & clear

       #  !RAS & !MUX & !CAS & clear                          (8.9)

MUX.d  =   RAS & MUX & CAS

       #  !RAS & !MUX & !CAS & clear                          (8.10)

CAS.d  =   RAS & MUX & CAS

       #   MUX & CAS & !clear                                 (8.11)

       #  !RAS & !MUX & !CAS & clear
```

Listing 8.6 shows the CUPL program to produce the *RAS, MUX,* and *CAS* signals. After compiling this program you can test it by using the simulation file

Listing 8.6   *dramctl.pld*

```
Name            dramctl;
Partno          OU0033;
Revision        01;
Date            9/24/91;
Designer        R. E. Haskell;
Company         Oakland University;
Location        Rochester, MI;
Assembly        CSE 171;
Device          G16V8;
Format          j;

/ ****************************************************************/
/*      This example demonstrates the generation               */
/*      of RAS, MUX and CAS signals for a                      */
/*      dynamic RAM controller                                 */
/ ****************************************************************/
/*      Target Device:  G16V8                                  */
/ ****************************************************************/

/* Inputs:  */

Pin 1 =  clock;
Pin 2 =  clear;

/* Outputs:  */

Pin 19 = RAS;
Pin 18 = CAS;
Pin 17 = MUX;

/** Logic Equations **/

RAS.d =  RAS & MUX & CAS & clear
 # !RAS & !MUX & !CAS & clear;

MUX.d =  RAS & MUX & CAS
 # !RAS & !MUX & !CAS & clear;

CAS.d =  RAS & MUX & CAS
 # MUX & CAS & !clear
 # !RAS & !MUX & !CAS & clear;
```

given in Listing 8.7. The test vectors in this file will go through two memory access cycles. If you run this simulation file by typing

```
csim -w dramctl
```

the waveform results shown in Figure 8.14 will be generated.

Listing 8.7   *dramctl.si*

```
Name              dramctl;
Partno            OU0033;
Revision          01;
Date              9/24/91;
Designer          R. E. Haskell;
Company           Oakland University;
Location          Rochester, MI;
Assembly          CSE 171;
Device            G16V8;
Format            j;

/ ******************************************************************/
/*        This example demonstrates the generation              */
/*        of RAS, MUX, and CAS signals for a                    */
/*        dynamic RAM controller                                */
/ ******************************************************************/
/*        Target Device:  G16V8                                 */
/ ******************************************************************/

ORDER:  clock,%2,clear,%2,RAS,%2,MUX,%2,CAS;

VECTORS:
    C1 HHH
    C0 LHH
    C0 LLH
    C0 LLL
    C0 LLL
    C0 LLL
    C1 HHH
    C1 HHH
    C0 LHH
    C0 LLH
    C0 LLL
    C0 LLL
    C0 LLL
    C1 HHH
```

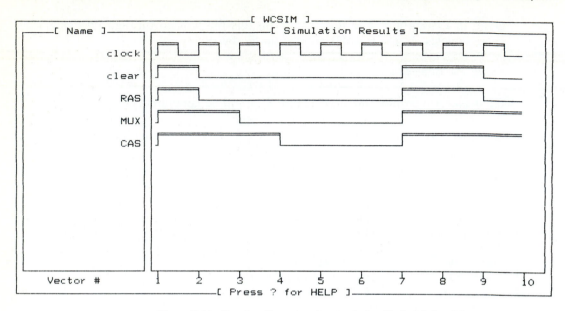

Figure 8.14   Results of running the simulation file in Listing 8.7.

Experiment 15: 2-Word, 2-Bit RAM

1. Compile the program for a 2-word, 2-bit RAM given in Listing 8.1.
2. Modify the test vectors in Listing 8.2 to (1) write the data 01 and 10 to *word a* and *word b*, respectively, and then read back these data, and (2) write the data 11 and 00 to *word a* and *word b*, respectively, and then read back these data. Test the program by running CSIM using the *-w* option.
3. Use the JEDEC file produced in (1) to program a GAL 16V8.
4. Use the PLD logic analyzer to test the chip. Connect the output lines *Out0, Out2, Out3, Out6,* and *Out7* and the two input lines *In3* and *In4* of the logic analyzer to the pins of the GAL chip shown in the following table.

Logic analyzer	GAL pin no.	Signal
Out0	1	clock
ground	2	!cs
Out2	4	A0
Out7	5	D1
Out6	6	D0
Out3	7	read_write
In3	12	d0
In4	13	d1

5. Manually load the input data 10 into *D1* and *D0* by setting *Out7* to 1 and *Out6* to 0. Then press function key *F1*. Note that the first eight rows of the truth table correspond to a read operation (*read_write* = 0) and the last eight rows correspond to a write operation (*read_write* = 1). Rows 0 to 3 and 8 to 11 correspond to *word a* (*A0* = 0), and rows 4 to 7 and 12 to 15 correspond to *word b* (*A0* = 1). A positive edge of the clock signal occurs each time that *Out0* goes from 0 to 1. Note that each read and write operation to a given address occurs twice when you press *F1*. After pressing *F1* the first time, the data value 10 should be written to the two words by the last eight rows in the truth table.

6. Now manually load the input data 01 into *D1* and *D0* by setting *Out7* to 0 and *Out6* to 1 and then press function key *F1* again. The previously stored data, 10, should be read from the two words during the first eight rows of the truth table and then the new data, 10, will be written into the two words by the last eight rows in the truth table. Print the truth table. Continue the process by writing the values 00 and 11 to both words. Print out the truth table each time you press function key *F1*. Discuss the results.

7. Repeat parts (5) and (6) using function key *F2* to display the waveforms.

Experiment 16: Programming an EPROM

1. Program the hex data shown in Table 8.1 in the first 16 locations of one of the EPROMs given in Table 8.2. PROM programming devices will read data to be programmed into the PROM from a file typically stored as a disk file on a PC. The data to be programmed can be stored on the disk in a number of different data file formats. The most popular formats include the *Intel hex format, Motorola hex format, ASCII hex format, Tektronix hex format, straight hex format*, and *binary format*. The easiest one to use for our purposes is the *straight hex format*, which is just hex bytes to be programmed stored on the file as ASCII hex digits (that is, readable text), where each byte is separated by a space as shown in the following figure for the data in Table 8.1.

```
7E  30  6D  79  33  5B  5F  70  7F  7B  77  1F  4E  3D  4F  47
```

The steps in reading this file from disk and programming the PROM will vary depending on the programming device you are using.

2. Use the EPROM programmed in (1) to control a 7-segment display by connecting the output data lines, *D6* to *D0*, to the seven segments *a* to *g* of a MAN 72 (see Experiment 9) through a 7416 open-collector hex inverter. Connect the outputs *Out0* to *Out3* of the PLD logic analyzer to address lines

A0 to *A3* of the EPROM and ground the remaining address lines. This will allow you to manually access the first 16 bytes of the EPROM, which should display the hex digits *0* to *F* on the 7-segment display. Make sure the chip enable pin on the EPROM is connected to ground.

Experiment 17: Decoding a Computer Memory Map

1. Write a CUPL program for a GAL 16V8 that will produce five active low chip select lines corresponding to the memory map shown. Assume you are using a 68000 microprocessor system of the type described in Section 8.3.

Device	Memory size (bytes)	Address range
RAM0	64K	000000–00FFFF
RAM1	64K	080000–08FFFF
RAM2	64K	090000–09FFFF
ROM0	128K	A00000–A1FFFF
ROM1	128K	A20000–A3FFFF

2. Make a simulation file containing a set of test vectors that will test the program written in (1). Test the program by running CSIM.
3. Use the JEDEC file produced in (1) to program a GAL 16V8.
4. Design an experiment using the PLD logic analyzer to test the chip.

Experiment 18: Dynamic RAM Controller Signals

1. Compile the program for the dynamic RAM controller given in Listing 8.5.
2. Test the program using the simulation file given in Listing 8.6 by running CSIM using the *-w* option.
3. Use the JEDEC file produced in (1) to program a GAL 16V8.
4. Use the PLD logic analyzer to test the chip. Connect the output line *Out0* and the three input lines *In2*, *In3*, and *In4* of the logic analyzer to the pins of the GAL chip shown in the following table.

Logic analyzer	GAL pin no.	Signal
Out0	1	clock
Ground	2	clear
In2	17	MUX
In3	18	CAS
In4	19	RAS

5. Press function key *F1*. A positive edge of the clock signal occurs each time that *Out0* goes from 0 to 1. Note that on power-up the three pin outputs *RAS*, *CAS*, and *MUX* will be high. Print the truth table. Discuss the results.
6. Press function key *F2*. Print the waveform and discuss the results.

EXERCISES

8.1. Redraw the circuit in Figure 8.3 to represent a 4-word, 4-bit RAM. Use a decoder to select one of four words from the two address lines *A1* and *A0*.

8.2. Show how jumpers could be used on a printed circuit board so that the same 24-pin socket could be used for both a 2716 and a 2732 EPROM.

8.3. Show how jumpers could be used on a printed circuit board so that the same 28-pin socket could be used for a 2764, a 27128, a 27256, and a 27512 EPROM.

8.4. Derive the logic equations (8.9), (8.10), and (8.11) by drawing Karnaugh maps for *RAS.d, MUX.d*, and *CAS.d* using the state table in Table 8.4.

8.5. Draw a logic diagram in terms of D flip-flops and basic gates that will implement the timing signals shown in Fig. 8.13. See Eqs. (8.9), (8.10), and (8.11).

9

A Look inside the 8086

In this chapter we will begin our look at the 8086 microprocessor by using the TUTOR monitor to see what goes on inside the 8086 and how it executes programs.

In this chapter you will learn:

- The basic components of a computer system
- The internal register structure of the 8086
- How the 8086 microprocessor addresses different memory locations
- How to load and execute simple programs using the TUTOR monitor
- How ASCII data can be entered from the keyboard and displayed on the screen.

9.1 BASIC STRUCTURE OF A COMPUTER

The basic structure of a computer system is shown in Fig. 9.1. Although computers may seem complicated, at the basic level they really do only three different things:

1. Store data
2. Move data from one place to another
3. Perform some basic arithmetic and logical operations

By combining these basic operations in sophisticated ways, it is the software, or computer program, that gives a computer its apparent power.

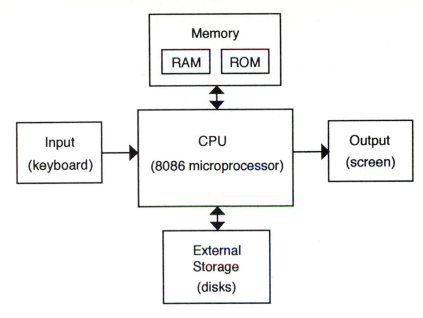

Figure 9.1   Basic structure of a computer system.

In Fig. 9.1, data can be stored in external devices such as floppy disks or hard disks. Data can also be stored temporarily in the internal registers of the central processing unit, or CPU. In the next section we will look at the internal registers of the 8086 microprocessor. Data can also be stored in read-only memory (ROM) and in read-write memory (RAM). Read-only memory is permanent memory in which data are retained when the power to the computer is turned off. The typical PC will contain a BIOS (basic input-output system) ROM that contains basic input/output (I/O) routines for accessing the computer hardware such as the keyboard and video screen. RAM (which stands for random-access memory) is really read-write memory, which means that the program can change the contents of RAM, whereas it cannot change the contents of ROM. In most cases the contents of RAM are lost when you turn off the power to the computer. However, it is possible to have battery-backed RAM whose data are preserved with a battery when the main power to the computer is turned off.

The input and output boxes in Fig. 9.1 are how data get into and out of the computer. For the PC, this is usually a keyboard for input (and possibly a mouse for pointing on the screen) and a video screen for output. You will also generally have some type of printer as an output device. These I/O devices will have some type of RAM associated with them for storing data. For example, when you type keys on the keyboard, the data associated with each key pressed is stored in a section of RAM called the keyboard buffer. Similarly, when you display characters on the screen, the data associated with each character are stored in a section of

RAM called the video buffer. Thus, we can think of data as being stored in all the boxes in Fig. 9.1.

The arrows in Fig. 9.1 show how the computer moves data from one place to another. A large part of all computer programs consists of moving data from the CPU registers to memory, from memory to the CPU registers, from the input to the CPU registers, and from the CPU registers to the output, and to and from external disk drives. Once data have been moved into the internal registers, the CPU can perform simple arithmetic and logical operations on these data. We will look at some examples of these operations later in this chapter. First, we will take a look at the internal registers of the 8086 microprocessor.

9.2 INTERNAL 8086 REGISTERS

The 8086 microprocessor has several internal registers that can store binary data. These are shown in Fig. 9.2. All the registers are 16-bit registers. The general

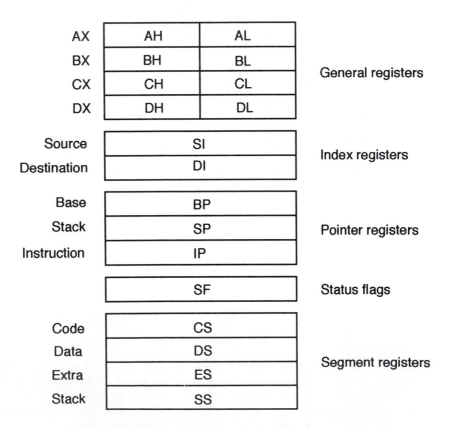

Figure 9.2 The internal registers in the 8086 microprocessor.

registers *AX*, *BX*, *CX*, and *DX* can each be divided into an 8-bit high-order byte and an 8-bit low-order byte. For example, *AX* is made up of the high-order byte *AH* and the low-order byte *AL*. We will look at these registers in more detail in Chapter 10.

If you run the TUTOR monitor program, you will obtain the screen display shown in Fig. 9.3. The contents of the general registers *AX*, *BX*, *CX*, and *DX* are displayed in the upper-left part of the screen.

The white horizontal line across the bottom of the screen is called the command line. When you press the key containing the slash (/), the following message will appear on the command line:

```
COMMAND: ABDEFGIJLMPRSTUQXZ
```

The computer is now waiting for you to press a key containing one of the letters following the word COMMAND. You will learn what all these letters do as we progress through the book. For now, press the key *R*. This will produce

```
        8086 Microprocessor TUTOR              Press F7 for Help

     AH AL      BH BL      CH CL      DH DL     DATA SEG    08 19 2A 3B 4C 5D 6E 7F
  AX 00 00   BX 13 A3   CX 00 C5   DX 3A B3    174F:0000   A1 76 57 FF 06 76 57 3D
                                               174F:0008   00 04 72 0E B8 97 00 50
     SP 0FFF        SI 0000        IP 0000      174F:0010   B8 84 09 50 E8 86 1A 83
     BP 0000        DI 0000                     174F:0018   C4 04 E8 66 3B 88 86 78
     SS 174F        DS 174F        CS 174F      174F:0020   FF 2A E4 50 8D 86 79 FF
  SP+SS 184EF    SI+DS 174F0       ES 174F      174F:0028   50 E8 4C 23 83 C4 04 B8
  BP+SS 174F0    DI+DS 174F0    IP+CS 174F0     174F:0030   FF 7F 50 2B C0 50 E8 B7
  STATUS FLAGS 7202 0111001000000010            174F:0038   23 83 C4 04 2B C0 50 B8
                       ODITSZ A P C             174F:0040   03 00 50 8D 86 78 FF 50
  174F:0000 A17657       MOV    AX,[5776]       174F:0048   E8 17 FC 83 C4 06 8B F0

  SEG 174F:    08 19 2A 3B 4C 5D 6E 7F                          174F: STACK
       FFE8    05 55 4E 41 53 34 20 00     . U N A S 4   .         0FFF
       FFF0    F0 5E 00 00 C0 5E FF FF     . ^ . . . ^ . .
       FFF8    01 00 78 09 96 1D 27 00     . . x . . . ' .
       0000   >A1 76 57 FF 06 76 57 3D     . v W . . v W =
       0008    00 04 72 0E B8 97 00 50     . . r . . . . P
       0010    B8 84 09 50 E8 86 1A 83     . . . P . . . .
       0018    C4 04 E8 66 3B 88 86 78     . . . f ; . . x
  _____   / : Command      > : Go To Memory
                                            Use Cursor Keys to Scroll thru Memory
```

Figure 9.3   Initial screen display of the TUTOR monitor.

the message

REGISTER CHANGE: G P I S F

on the command line. Pressing one of the letters *G*, *P*, *I*, *S*, or *F* will allow you to change a register within one of the following groups:

G, General registers	*A B C D*	(*AX, BX, CX, DX*)
P, Pointer registers	*S B I*	(*SP, BP, IP*)
I, Index registers	*S D*	(*SI, DI*)
S, Segment registers	*S D C E*	(*SS, DS, CS, ES*)
F, Status flags		

For example, to change the contents of general register *AX*, press key *G*. This will produce the message

CHANGE GENERAL REG: A B C D

Press key *A*. This will produce the entry *AX* = followed by a blinking cursor on the bottom line of the screen (this is called the entry line). Type in any four-digit hexadecimal number. When you press the ENTER key, this new number will be stored in the general register *AX*. Try it. If you enter more than 4 digits, the last 4 will be used. If you enter a digit other than *0* to *9* or *A* to *F*, the computer will ignore your request, sound a beep, and clear the command and entry lines. You can then type /*R* again to change a register value. If you make a mistake while entering a hexadecimal value on the entry line, you can back the cursor up (and thereby erase the most recently entered value) by pressing the backspace key.

9.3 COMPUTER MEMORY

In this section we will look at how the 8086 addresses the RAM and ROM in Fig. 9.1. In Chapter 1 we saw that the 8086 had a 20-bit *address bus*, which produces a 20-bit address. This means that the 8086 can address one of 2^{20} = 1,048,576 possible memory locations. Each memory location contains one 8-bit byte of data. Thus, the 8086 can address 1 Mbyte of memory.

The 20-bit address can be represented by a 5-digit hexadecimal number in the range 00000 to FFFFF. The internal registers of the 8086, however, are only 16 bits or 4 hex digits long. Some of these registers are used to point to various memory locations. How can a 16-bit register be used to point to an address in a 20-bit address range? The answer is that the 20-bit address is broken up into two parts, a 16-bit *segment address* and a 16-bit *offset address*, which are offset from each other by 4 bits, as shown in Fig. 9.4.

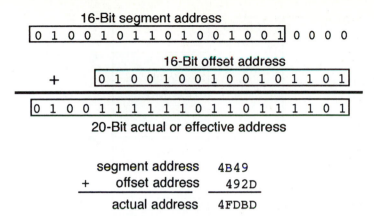

Figure 9.4   An actual 20-bit address is formed by adding a 16-bit segment address to a 16-bit offset address that is shifted 4 bits to the right.

The 1-Mbyte address range can be thought of as broken up into 64-Kbyte segments, as shown in Fig. 9.5. The starting address of a segment is given by the segment address *XXXX0*. Note that this address must be a multiple of 16 in the actual address space. We call this a *paragraph boundary*. The offset address *0YYYY* is the 16-bit address (64K) within a given segment. The actual address is found by adding the segment address to the offset address.

On the TUTOR display, five actual addresses are displayed: *SP* + *SS*, *BP* + *SS*, *SI* + *DS*, *DI* + *DS*, and *IP* + *CS*. These actual addresses are formed by adding the segment addresses in *SS*, *DS*, or *CS* to the offset addresses in *SP*, *BP*, *SI*, *DI*, or *IP*. Note that on the screen the segment addresses are shifted 4 bits (one hex digit) to the left of the offset addresses.

The 8086 has four segment registers (*CS*, *DS*, *SS*, and *ES*) that define four different segments within the 1-Mbyte address range. These four segments may partially or completely overlap. The uses of the four segment registers will be described in Chapter 10. For now, let us see how we can use the TUTOR monitor to examine the contents of any memory location.

TUTOR's Memory Display

When you run the TUTOR monitor program, the screen display is as shown in Fig. 9.3. Along the lower-left side of the screen are seven rows of reverse video 4-digit hexadecimal addresses.[1] Note that the addresses of adjacent rows differ by eight. These are *offset addresses* relative to the *segment address* labeled *SEG* just above the offset addresses. In Fig. 9.3 the value of this segment address is

---

[1] The memory display in the upper-right section of the screen is a part of the data segment. We will look at this data segment display in Chapter 11.

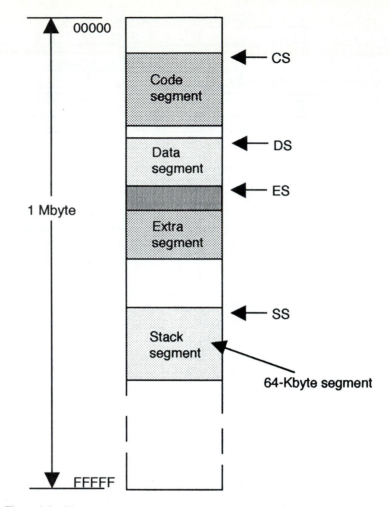

Figure 9.5   The actual 1-Mbyte address range is divided into 64-Kbyte segments.

174FH. Your segment address value may be different from this. When TUTOR
is executed, it displays the first available free memory in the memory display.
This means that you should be able to change these memory values without crash-
ing the system. The fourth row of offset addresses contains the address 0000H.
The 8 bytes following this address (remember that each byte is represented by a
2-digit hexadecimal number) are the contents of offset addresses 0000H to 0007H.
The 8 bytes in the next row (following the address 0008H) are the contents of
offset addresses 0008H to 000FH.

The white bar at the top of the memory display contains the digits

```
08 19 2A 3B 4C 5D 6E 7F
```

This is a guide that gives the last digit of a memory address. Note that the starting address on each line ends with either a 0 or an 8. If it ends with a 0, then the addresses of the 8 bytes on that line end with the *first* digit in each pair (0 to 7) of the guide line shown above. If the starting address ends with an 8, then the addresses of the 8 bytes on that line end with the *second* digit in each pair (8 to F) of the guide line shown above.

A position cursor, $>$, points to the contents of offset address 0000H. Note that the preceding line begins with address FFF8H and ends with FFFFH. Thus, this display shows the contents of the beginning of a segment from offset addresses 0000H to 00018H and the top of the segment from offset addresses FFE8H to FFFFH. It is possible to look at the contents of any offset address in between by scrolling the display.

The cursor keys can be used to scroll through memory. Table 9.1 gives the function of each cursor key.

TABLE 9.1   CURSOR KEYS TO SCROLL THROUGH MEMORY

Key	Function
Right cursor	Advance 1 byte
Left cursor	Back up 1 byte
Down cursor	Advance 1 row
Up cursor	Back up 1 row
PgDn	Advance 7 rows
PgUp	Back up 7 rows
Home	Go to offset address 0000H

Press the right cursor key containing the right arrow $\rightarrow$ (located on key 6 of the numeric key pad at the right of the keyboard or in a separate group of cursor keys) and watch the position cursor $>$. Note that it moves to offset address 0001H. Press the right cursor key several more times. Note that when you get to the end of the line (offset address 0007H) and advance to offset address 0008H all the memory locations scroll up one line, and a new line containing addresses 0020H to 0027H appears at the bottom of the display.

Press all the cursor keys given in Table 9.1 until you become familiar with how they work. Note that if you hold down one of the cursor keys the function will repeat continuously (until the keyboard buffer becomes full and the computer beeps at you).

Scrolling through memory is not a convenient way to get to a memory location that is a long way off. You can use the $>$ symbol to go to any memory location within a segment or to go to the beginning of another segment. Press the key containing the symbol $>$. It is not necessary to hold down the shift key. Typing a period (without the shift key) or the $>$ symbol (with the shift key) will both cause the following message to appear on the command line:

`goto: Offset or Seg address`

You now go to any offset address within the current segment by pressing key *O* ("oh," not "zero"), or you can go to the beginning of a new segment by pressing key *S*. Press key *O*. The message

`ENTER OFFSET ADDRESS`

will appear on the command line and a blinking cursor will appear on the entry line. Enter any address and press ENTER. The position cursor will immediately move to the memory address that you entered. You do not have to type leading zeros when entering the address. For example, if you enter *B*, the position cursor will move to offset address 000BH.

   If you make a mistake while entering an address, pressing the backspace key will move the blinking cursor back one space and erase the most recently entered digit. Try this. If you back up the blinking cursor beyond the starting position, the command line will clear and you will return to the TUTOR monitor. Note that you may enter the hex digits *A* to *F* with or without pressing the shift key. They will always be displayed in uppercase. If you type an invalid address (any digits other than *0* to *F*), the command line will clear, a beep will sound, and you will return to the TUTOR monitor.

   To go to the beginning of a new segment, type >*S*. The message

`ENTER SEGMENT ADDRESS`

will appear on the command line and a blinking cursor will appear on the entry line. Enter the address 2100 and press ENTER. Note that the value of the SEG address displayed near the left center of the screen has changed to 2100 and the offset address has returned to 0000, as shown in Fig. 9.6. The position cursor > is really pointing to the actual address 21000 formed by adding the segment address 2100 and the offset address 0000 as follows:

$$
\begin{array}{ll}
2100 & \text{segment address} \\
\underline{0000} & \underline{\text{offset address}} \\
21000 & \text{actual address}
\end{array}
$$

   We sometimes indicate the actual address by writing it in the form

`segment_address:offset_address`

Thus the address 2100:0000 is the actual address 21000 shown in Fig. 9.6.

```
        8086 Microprocessor TUTOR              Press F7 for Help

     AH AL       BH BL      CH CL      DH DL    DATA SEG    08 19 2A 3B 4C 5D 6E 7F
  AX 00 00   BX 11 C5   CX 00 C5   DX 3A EE    1574:0000   FF 7F 50 2B C0 50 E8 B7
                                                1574:0008   23 83 C4 04 2B C0 50 B8
     SP 0FFF       SI 0000       IP 0000        1574:0010   03 00 50 8D 86 78 FF 50
     BP 0000       DI 0000                      1574:0018   E8 17 FC 83 C4 06 8B F0
     SS 1574       DS 1574       CS 2100        1574:0020   0B F6 74 03 E9 CE 00 E8
  SP+SS 1673F   SI+DS 15740       ES 1574       1574:0028   29 3B 89 86 76 FF 3D 61
  BP+SS 15740   DI+DS 15740   IP+CS 21000       1574:0030   00 74 5D 3D 62 00 74 05
  STATUS FLAGS 7206 0111001000000110            1574:0038   E8 FB 22 EB 11 E8 DD FD
                    ODITSZ A P C                1574:0040   89 46 F8 89 56 FA 2B C0
  2100:0000 2B4353       SUB    AX,[BP+DI+5      1574:0048   89 46 FE 89 46 FC B8 FF
  3H]
  SEG 2100:    08 19 2A 3B 4C 5D 6E 7F                       1574: STACK
      FFE8  66 6C 61 67 00 00 00 00     f l a g . . . .         0FFF
      FFF0  00 00 00 00 09 00 01 31     . . . . . . . 1
      FFF8  61 62 63 64 65 66 67 68     a b c d e f g h
      0000 >2B 43 53 53 54 41 54 55     + C S S T A T U
      0008  53 20 46 4C 41 47 53 00     S   F L A G S .
      0010  4F 44 49 54 53 5A 20 41     O D I T S Z   A
      0018  20 50 20 43 00 30 38 20     P   C . 0 8

                                     / : Command      > : Go To Memory
                                     Use Cursor Keys to Scroll thru Memory
```

Figure 9.6   The address 2100:0000 contains the value 2B.

Note that there are many different ways that an actual address can be divided between a segment address and an offset address. For example, memory location 21000 shown in Fig. 9.6 can be expressed as

$$2000:1000$$

That is, the segment address could be 2000 and the offset address could be 1000. To verify this change, go to the *SEG* address to 2000 by typing >*S* and entering 2000. Then go to the offset address 1000 by typing >*O* and entering 1000. Note that the same value of 2B (the value in your computer may be different) is in location 21000, as shown in Fig. 9.7.

Notice that the offset addresses between FFE8H and FFFFH in Fig. 9.6 are *not* the same as the corresponding offset addresses in Fig. 9.7. This is because the offset addresses 0000H to FFFFH wrap around within a given segment. Thus, for example, the address 2100:FFF8 is the actual address 30FF8:

$$\begin{array}{r} 2100 \\ \underline{FFF8} \\ 30FF8 \end{array}$$

```
        8086 Microprocessor TUTOR              Press F7 for Help

     AH AL     BH BL      CH CL      DH DL     DATA SEG    08 19 2A 3B 4C 5D 6E 7F
  AX 00 00  BX 11 C5  CX 00 C5  DX 3A EE      1574:0000   FF 7F 50 2B C0 50 E8 B7
                                               1574:0008   23 83 C4 04 2B C0 50 B8
     SP 0FFF      SI 0000       IP 0000        1574:0010   03 00 50 8D 86 78 FF 50
     BP 0000      DI 0000                      1574:0018   E8 17 FC 83 C4 06 8B F0
     SS 1574      DS 1574      CS 2000         1574:0020   0B F6 74 03 E9 CE 00 E8
  SP+SS 1673F  SI+DS 15740     ES 1574         1574:0028   29 3B 89 86 76 FF 3D 61
  BP+SS 15740  DI+DS 15740  IP+CS 20000        1574:0030   00 74 5D 3D 62 00 74 05
  STATUS FLAGS 7206 0111001000000110           1574:0038   E8 FB 22 EB 11 E8 DD FD
                    ODITSZ A P C               1574:0040   89 46 F8 89 56 FA 2B C0
  2000:1000 2B4353        SUB   AX,[BP+DI+5    1574:0048   89 46 FE 89 46 FC B8 FF
  3H]
  SEG 2000:   08 19 2A 3B 4C 5D 6E 7F                            1574: STACK
     0FE8   45 47 53 50 2B 53 53 53    E G S P + S S S           0FFF
     0FF0   49 2B 44 53 42 50 2B 53    I + D S B P + S
     0FF8   53 44 49 2B 44 53 49 50    S D I + D S I P
     1000  >2B 43 53 53 54 41 54 55    + C S S T A T U
     1008   53 20 46 4C 41 47 53 00    S   F L A G S .
     1010   4F 44 49 54 53 5A 20 41    O D I T S Z   A
     1018   20 50 20 43 00 30 38 20      P   C . 0 8

  _____  / : Command    > : Go To Memory
                                           Use Cursor Keys to Scroll thru Memory
```

Figure 9.7 The address 2000:1000 contains the same value 2B as address 2100:0000 in Fig. 9.6.

On the other hand, the address 2000:0FF8 is the actual address 20FF8:

$$\begin{array}{r} 2000 \\ \underline{0FF8} \\ 20FF8 \end{array}$$

Verify that the value 61 (or whatever value is in your computer) shown stored at 2100:FFF8 in Fig. 9.6 is really stored at address 30FF8. Note that this address is outside the segment starting at 2000 shown in Fig. 9.7. Go to the segment starting at 30FF and note that address 30FF:0008 is the same as address 2100:FFF8, as shown in Figs. 9.6 and 9.8.

9.4 YOUR FIRST COMPUTER PROGRAM

We have seen how data are stored in the 8086 registers and in memory. As we saw in Section 9.1, the other two basic functions of a computer are to move data

```
        8086 Microprocessor TUTOR           Press F7 for Help

     AH AL     BH BL      CH CL      DH DL   DATA SEG   08 19 2A 3B 4C 5D 6E 7F
  AX 00 00  BX 11 C5   CX 00 C5   DX 3A EE   1574:0000  FF 7F 50 2B C0 50 E8 B7
                                             1574:0008  23 83 C4 04 2B C0 50 B8
     SP 0FFF       SI 0000       IP 0000     1574:0010  03 00 50 8D 86 78 FF 50
     BP 0000       DI 0000                   1574:0018  E8 17 FC 83 C4 06 8B F0
     SS 1574       DS 1574      CS 30FF      1574:0020  0B F6 74 03 E9 CE 00 E8
  SP+SS 1673F  SI+DS 15740      ES 1574      1574:0028  29 3B 89 86 76 FF 3D 61
  BP+SS 15740  DI+DS 15740   IP+CS 30FF0     1574:0030  00 74 5D 3D 62 00 74 05
  STATUS FLAGS 7206 0111001000000110         1574:0038  E8 FB 22 EB 11 E8 DD FD
                       ODITSZ A P C          1574:0040  89 46 F8 89 56 FA 2B C0
  30FF:0008 61           ???                 1574:0048  89 46 FE 89 46 FC B8 FF

  SEG 30FF:   08 19 2A 3B 4C 5D 6E 7F                     1574: STACK
      FFF0   00 00 00 00 00 00 00 00     . . . . . . . .     0FFF
      FFF8   00 00 00 00 00 00 00 00     . . . . . . . .
      0000   00 00 00 00 09 00 01 31     . . . . . . . 1
      0008  >61 62 63 64 65 66 67 68     a b c d e f g h
      0010   10 00 10 00 69 6E 69 31     . . . . i n i 1
      0018   3A 09 63 61 6C 6C 09 69     : . c a l l . i
      0020   6E 69 74 32 00 00 00 00     n i t 2 . . . .

                                     / : Command      > : Go To Memory
  _____   Use Cursor Keys to Scroll thru Memory
```

Figure 9.8 The address 30FF:0008 contains the same value 61 as address 2100:
FFF8 in Fig. 9.6.

from one place to another and to perform certain arithmetic and logical operations. We will illustrate these functions by executing the simple program shown in Fig. 9.9, which is a sample of a typical assembly language program listing.

The numbers on the left side of Fig. 9.9 are the offset addresses at which the first byte of each instruction in the program is stored. This address is followed by the bytes that make up each instruction. The assembly language instructions themselves are given on the right side of Fig. 9.9. For example, the instruction *mov ax,1234h* is stored in memory starting at offset address 0000 as the 3 bytes *B8 34 12*. The first byte is the opcode for the instruction "move into *ax* the two following bytes." Note that the 16-bit value 1234H is stored in memory low-byte

```
0000   B8 34 12        mov    ax,1234h
0003   8B D8           mov    bx,ax
0005   F7 D8           neg    ax
0007   03 C3           add    ax,bx
0009   F7 D3           not    bx
000B   CC              int    3
```

Figure 9.9 Your first sample program.

first; that is, the low-byte 34 is stored at address 0001 and the high-byte 12 is stored at address 0002. This is the way that Intel always stores 16-bit values in memory—low-byte first. (Motorola microprocessors do just the opposite; they store the high-byte first.)

It is easy to enter this program into memory using the TUTOR monitor. This can be done by using the command /M. Go to offset address 0000 within TUTOR's initial segment. (If you have changed the segment address, press *Ctrl F6* to restart TUTOR.) Then type /M. This will produce the following message on the command line:

```
MEMORY CHANGE:   H A
```

You have two choices at this point. You can enter *hex* data by pressing key *H*, or you can enter ASCII data by pressing key *A*. We will consider ASCII data in the next section. For now, press key *H*. The message *ENTER HEX VALUES* will appear on the command line. Type the bytes making up the program in Fig. 9.9, that is,

```
B8 34 12 8B D8 F7 D8 03 C3 F7 D3 CC
```

Note that you do not have to type a space between each byte. Each time you type a byte it appears on the entry line and is stored in the memory location pointed to by the position cursor. The position cursor is then automatically advanced to the next memory location and a space is added on the entry line. You can enter as many hex bytes as you want. When you come to the end of the entry line, it will automatically clear and start again at the beginning of the line. When you finish entering hex values, press *Enter*. Pressing any nonhex key while entering hex values will clear the command line, sound a beep, and return to the TUTOR monitor.

After you have entered these program bytes into memory, move the position cursor back to offset address 0000 by pressing the *Home* key. Then type /UP. This will disassemble the code you just typed in and display the program in the upper-right part of the screen, as shown in Fig. 9.10. This will verify that you typed in all the bytes correctly. Note also that the first instruction pointed to by the position cursor is disassembled directly above the memory display near the center of the screen.

You can execute this instruction by pressing function key *F1*. Do it. Note that the 16-bit value 1234H is moved from the 2 bytes following the opcode into register *AX*, and the position cursor moves to the next instruction at offset address 0003, as shown in Fig. 9.11. The code for this next instruction is disassembled, and the instruction *MOV BX,AX* is displayed directly above the memory guide near the center of the screen.

This second instruction, *MOV BX,AX*, moves the contents of the register *AX* to the register *BX*. To execute this instruction, press function key *F1* again.

```
8086 Microprocessor TUTOR           Press F7 for Help

     AH AL     BH BL     CH CL     DH DL
AX  00 00  BX 11 C5  CX 00 C5  DX 3A EE    1574:0000 B83412      MOV   AX,1234H
                                           1574:0003 8BD8        MOV   BX,AX
      SP 0FFF       SI 0000        IP 0003  1574:0005 F7D8       NEG   AX
      BP 0000       DI 0000                 1574:0007 03C3       ADD   AX,BX
      SS 1574       DS 1574     CS 1574     1574:0009 F7D3       NOT   BX
   SP+SS 1673F   SI+DS 15740     ES 1574    1574:000B CC         INT3
   BP+SS 15740   DI+DS 15740  IP+CS 15743   1574:000C 2BC0       SUB   AX,AX
   STATUS FLAGS 7246 0111001001000110       1574:000E 50         PUSH  AX
                   ODITSZ A P C             1574:000F B80300     MOV   AX,0003H
   1574:0000 B83412       MOV   AX,1234H    1574:0012 50         PUSH  AX


SEG 1574:   08 19 2A 3B 4C 5D 6E 7F                          1574: STACK
    FFE8    00 00 00 00 00 00 00 00      . . . . . . . .         0FFF
    FFF0    00 00 00 00 00 00 00 00      . . . . . . . .
    FFF8    00 00 00 00 00 00 00 00      . . . . . . . .
    0000   >B8 34 12 8B D8 F7 D8 03      . 4 . . . . . .
    0008    C3 F7 D3 CC 2B C0 50 B8      . . . . + . P .
    0010    03 00 50 8D 86 78 FF 50      . . P . . x . P
    0018    E8 17 FC 83 C4 06 8B F0      . . . . . . . .

                                      / : Command      > : Go To Memory
                                      Use Cursor Keys to Scroll thru Memory
```

Figure 9.10 /UP will disassemble the code at the position cursor.

Note that *BX* now contains the value 1234H. The next instruction, *NEG AX*, will take the two's complement of *AX* and leave the result in *AX*. The value in *AX* is 1234H. What will its two's complement be? Press function key *F1* and see if you predicted the correct value. Remember from Chapter 2 that if you add the two's complement of a 16-bit hex number to the number itself you should get 10000H. The instruction *ADD AX,BX* will add the original number in *BX* to the two's complement of that number in *AX* and leave the sum in *AX*. Press function key *F1* to execute this next instruction. Note that the value in *AX* is now 0000H, and the 1 is in the carry bit (the rightmost bit in the status flags near the center of the screen). The next instruction is *NOT BX*. This will take the one's complement of the value 1234H that is in *BX*. Execute this instruction by pressing *F1*. What value do you get in *BX*? How is this value related to the two's complement?

The last instruction in the program in Fig. 9.9 is the software interrupt instruction *INT 3*. This instruction has the opcode *CCH* and produces a breakpoint instruction in TUTOR that will prevent us from single stepping beyond this instruction. We will discuss software interrupts and breakpoints in detail in later chapters.

```
          8086 Microprocessor TUTOR              Press F7 for Help

        AH AL    BH BL    CH CL    DH DL
   AX  12 34  BX 11 C5  CX 00 C5  DX 3A EE   1574:0000 B83412      MOV   AX,1234H
                                             1574:0003 8BD8        MOV   BX,AX
        SP 0FFF      SI 0000      IP 0003    1574:0005 F7D8        NEG   AX
        BP 0000      DI 0000                 1574:0007 03C3        ADD   AX,BX
        SS 1574      DS 1574   CS 1574       1574:0009 F7D3        NOT   BX
   SP+SS 1673F  SI+DS 15740    ES 1574       1574:000B CC          INT3
   BP+SS 15740  DI+DS 15740  IP+CS 15743     1574:000E 2BC0        SUB   AX,AX
   STATUS FLAGS 7246 0111001001000110        1574:000F 50          PUSH  AX
                     ODITSZ A P  C           1574:000F B80300      MOV   AX,0003H
   1574:0003 8BD8          MOV   BX,AX       1574:0012 50          PUSH  AX


  SEG 1574:   08 19 2A 3B 4C 5D 6E 7F                           1574: STACK
      FFE8    00 00 00 00 00 00 00 00     . . . . . . . .        0FFF
      FFF0    00 00 00 00 00 00 00 00     . . . . . . . .
      FFF8    00 00 00 00 00 00 00 00     . . . . . . . .
      0000    B8 34 12>8B D8 F7 D8 03     . 4 . . . . . .
      0008    C3 F7 D3 CC 2B C0 50 B8     . . . . + . P .
      0010    03 00 50 8D 86 78 FF 50     . . P . . x . P
      0018    E8 17 FC 83 C4 06 8B F0     . . . . . . . .

                                          / : Command      > : Go To Memory
                                          Use Cursor Keys to Scroll thru Memory
```

Figure 9.11 Press function key *F1* to single step an instruction.

This simple example has shown us how data can be moved around within a computer and how simple operations such as *ADD, NEG*, and *NOT* can change the values in a register. In Chapter 10 we will look at some additional instructions and begin to write some simple programs. Before doing that, however, let's look a little closer at our input and output blocks in Fig. 9.1 and see how we can get characters from the keyboard and display them on the screen.

9.5 KEYBOARD INPUT AND SCREEN OUTPUT

I/O in the PC can be carried out at three different levels. At the lowest level the program controls the hardware directly. This often involves programming certain peripheral chips that are part of the hardware system. We will look at some examples of this type of programming in later chapters. At the next higher level we can use the built-in BIOS ROM routines for accessing the hardware. These are written in the form of software interrupts that are easy to access. The highest level of I/O processing is to use the various DOS commands that are part of the disk operating system. Each of these levels of processing has its advantages and disadvantages. The lowest level is the most difficult to program but gives you the most control over the hardware and the most potential speed of execution of your program. It is, however, very dependent on the particular type of hardware you are using, and therefore the programs are the least portable from one type of computer to another. At the other end of the spectrum the idea of an operating system such as DOS is to hide all these grubby details from the user and to provide a consistent I/O interface that a programmer can use on potentially different types of hardware. The problem with some of the DOS I/O routines is that they hide too much from the user and you often can't do exactly what you want to do. Also, many of the DOS routines do a lot of error checking (good), which makes their execution somewhat slow and sluggish (bad).

In the middle level are the BIOS ROM routines, which are relatively fast and generally give you access to what you need. While different PCs and PC compatibles may use different BIOS ROMs, they all perform the same basic I/O functions by calling the same software interrupts. Thus, programs that call the BIOS ROM routines are generally just as portable (from one PC compatible to another) as those that call the DOS routines. We will show you how to call both types of I/O routines. We will use the DOS routines to do all our disk I/O. However, we will generally use the BIOS routines for keyboard and screen I/O because it will give us better control over exactly what we want to do. Before looking at how to get data from the keyboard or to the screen, let us first look at the form that these data usually take.

ASCII Data

The name ASCII stands for *American Standard Code for Information Interchange*. In this standard code a certain 7-bit binary number is associated with each character (letter, digit, or special character). This code is used extensively throughout the industry for sending information from one computer to another or for sending data from a terminal to a computer. The hex values for the ASCII codes of all characters are shown in Table 9.2. To use this chart, read the first hex digit across the top and the second hex digit along the left side of the chart. For example, the ASCII code for A is 41H.

Note that only the hex digits 0 to 7 are listed across the top of the chart. This means that bit 7 is assumed to be zero. This is because the standard ASCII codes use only 7 bits (0 to 6). The eighth bit (bit 7) is often used as an error-checking parity bit when sending data from a terminal to a computer.

The IBM PC uses an enhanced ASCII code that is slightly different from the standard. The ASCII codes for the characters that are displayed on the IBM PC are shown in Table 9.3.

The characters corresponding to the ASCII codes stored in the 56 memory bytes on the TUTOR screen are displayed to the right of the memory section at

TABLE 9.2 STANDARD ASCII CODES

Dec	→	0	16	32	48	64	80	96	112
↓	Hex	0	1	2	3	4	5	6	7
0	0	NUL	DLE	blank	0	@	P		p
1	1	SOH	DC1	!	1	A	Q	a	q
2	2	STX	DC2	"	2	B	R	b	r
3	3	ETX	DC3	#	3	C	S	c	s
4	4	EOT	DC4	$	4	D	T	d	t
5	5	ENQ	NAK	%	5	E	U	e	u
6	6	ACK	SYN	&	6	F	V	f	v
7	7	BEL	ETB	'	7	G	W	g	w
8	8	BS	CAN	(	8	H	X	h	x
9	9	HT	EM	)	9	I	Y	i	y
10	A	LF	SUB	*	:	J	Z	j	z
11	B	VT	ESC	+	;	K	[	k	{
12	C	FF	FS	,	<	L	\	l		
13	D	CR	GS	-	=	M	]	m	}
14	E	SO	RS	.	>	N	^	n	~
15	F	SI	US	/	?	O	_	o	DEL

the bottom of the screen. Typing /A will toggle these ASCII characters on and off. You can enter ASCII codes directly into memory by typing /MA. The message

PRESS ASCII KEY

will be displayed on the command line. Press keys A, B, C, D, and E. Note that the normal ASCII codes for the lowercase letters a to d (61H to 65H) are stored in consecutive memory locations, and the ASCII characters a to d are displayed to the right of the memory display. They are also displayed on the entry line (the bottom line of the screen).

    You can enter IBM PC ASCII codes into particular memory locations associated with the video screen. As an example, if you're using the monochrome display, go to memory location B000:0000 by typing >SB000. If you're using a graphics monitor (such as VGA), go to memory location B800:0000 by typing >SB800. Memory location B0000 is the first memory location of the *video RAM* for the monochrome display, and memory location B8000 is the first memory location of the video RAM for a graphics monitor display. Every 2 bytes in the video RAM correspond to a particular location on the video screen. The first byte of each pair contains the ASCII code for the character that is currently being displayed at that location on the screen. The second byte of each pair contains the attribute of the displayed character. The attribute byte determines if the char-

TABLE 9.3 IBM PC ASCII CODES

DECIMAL VALUE	HEXA DECIMAL VALUE	0 / 0	16 / 1	32 / 2	48 / 3	64 / 4	80 / 5	96 / 6	112 / 7	128 / 8	144 / 9	160 / A	176 / B	192 / C	208 / D	224 / E	240 / F
0	0	BLANK (NULL)	►	BLANK (SPACE)	0	@	P	`	p	Ç	É	á	░	└	╨	∝	≡
1	1	☺	◄	!	1	A	Q	a	q	ü	æ	í	▒	┴	╤	β	±
2	2	☻	↕	"	2	B	R	b	r	é	Æ	ó	▓	┬	╥	Γ	≥
3	3	♥	‼	#	3	C	S	c	s	â	ô	ú	│	├	╙	π	≤
4	4	♦	¶	$	4	D	T	d	t	ä	ö	ñ	┤	─	╘	Σ	∫
5	5	♣	§	%	5	E	U	e	u	à	ò	Ñ	╡	┼	╒	σ	∫
6	6	♠	▬	&	6	F	V	f	v	å	û	ª	╢	╞	╓	µ	÷
7	7	•	↨	'	7	G	W	g	w	ç	ù	º	╖	╟	╫	τ	≈
8	8	◘	↑	(	8	H	X	h	x	ê	ÿ	¿	╕	╚	╪	Φ	°
9	9	○	↓	)	9	I	Y	i	y	ë	Ö	⌐	╣	╔	┘	θ	∙
10	A	◎	→	*	:	J	Z	j	z	è	Ü	¬	║	╩	┌	Ω	·
11	B	♂	←	+	;	K	[	k	{	ï	¢	½	╗	╦	█	δ	√
12	C	♀	∟	,	<	L	\	l	¦	î	£	¼	╝	╠	▄	∞	ⁿ
13	D	♪	↔	─	=	M	]	m	}	ì	¥	¡	╜	═	▌	φ	²
14	E	♫	▲	.	>	N	^	n	~	Ä	₧	«	╛	╬	▐	∈	■
15	F	☼	▼	/	?	O	_	o	△	Å	ƒ	»	┐	╧	▀	∩	BLANK

Reprinted by permission from the IBM PC Technical Reference Manual. © 1981 by International Business Machines Corporation.

acter is underlined, blinking, or displayed in reverse video or increased intensity. These details will be described in Chapter 13.

Memory location B000:0000 for the monochrome display or B800:0000 for the graphics monitor display corresponds to the upper-left corner of the video screen. Note that it contains the hex value 20. From Table 9.3 you see that this is the ASCII code for a blank (black), which is what is being displayed at the upper-left corner of the screen. You can change this value by typing /MA. The message PRESS ASCII KEY is displayed on the command line. Press key A. Note that the normal ASCII code for a lower case *a*, 61H, is stored in memory location B000:0000 (or B800:0000), which causes the *a* to be displayed in the upper-left corner of the screen. Note that it is displayed in normal video, which is controlled by the byte at address B000:0001.

The *a* is also displayed on the entry line, and the position cursor advances to memory location B000:0001, which is the attribute byte 07h for the *a* displayed in the upper-left corner of the screen. You can continue to enter ASCII values. For example, type the letter *p*, which will change the attribute value to 70H. Note that this causes the displayed *a* in the upper-left corner of the screen to be displayed in reverse video. Continue to type *b p c p*. Note that the letters *abc* appear in reverse video on the top line of the screen as the ASCII codes and attribute value for each letter are stored in memory locations B000:0000 to B000:0005 (or B800:0000 to B800:0005). We will take a closer look at how characters are displayed on the screen in Chapter 13.

Keyboard Input

A built-in BIOS software interrupt routine can be used to read the keyboard. The following two instructions will wait for a key to be pressed and then return the ASCII code of the key in AL and the scan code of the key in AH.

```
B4 00   MOV   AH,0
CD 16   INT   16H
```

The scan codes and ASCII codes associated with each key are given in Table 9.4. The program shown in Fig. 9.12 can be used to verify all the scan and ASCII codes in Table 9.4. Enter this program at offset address 0000 using /MH. This time single step through this program using function key *F2* instead of *F1*. When you single step the instruction *INT 16H* using function key *F2*, the program will go and execute the entire BIOS routine and then return to offset address 0004. However, when executing the BIOS routine, the program will be waiting for you to press a key. Therefore, after you press *F2* when the position cursor is at offset address 0002, press any other key on the keyboard. The value of the scan code for that key will be stored in *AH*, and the value of the ASCII code will be stored in *AL*. The position cursor will move to the *JMP KEYIN* instruction, which will just jump back to offset address 0000 when you press *F2* again. Keep single stepping through this program, checking the codes for a number of keys. We will look at keyboard input routines in more detail in Chapter 13.

```
0000   B4 00      KEYIN:   MOV   AH,0
0002   CD 16               INT   16H
0004   EB FA               JMP   KEYIN
```

Figure 9.12   Program to find the scan and ASCII codes of any key pressed.

Screen Output

We have already seen that data are stored on the screen by writing an ASCII code and an attribute byte to a particular location in the video RAM. This is an example of low-level I/O. We can also write to the screen by using BIOS or DOS calls. We will look in more detail at doing screen I/O in Chapter 13, where we will write a series of very useful subroutines that will allow you to do whatever you want on the screen. For now we will give you two DOS calls and one BIOS call that will allow you to get characters stored on the screen.

TABLE 9.4 KEYBOARD SCAN/ASCII HEX CODES

Function keys	Unshifted	Shifted	Ctrl	Alt
F1	3B/00	54/00	5E/00	68/00
F2	3C/00	55/00	5F/00	69/00
F3	3D/00	56/00	60/00	6A/00
F4	3E/00	57/00	61/00	6B/00
F5	3F/00	58/00	62/00	6C/00
F6	40/00	59/00	63/00	6D/00
F7	41/00	5A/00	64/00	6E/00
F8	42/00	5B/00	65/00	6F/00
F9	43/00	5C/00	66/00	70/00
F10	44/00	5D/00	67/00	71/00

Numeric keypad		Unshifted	Shifted	Ctrl	Alt
Ins	0	52/00	52/30		
End	1	4F/00	4F/31	75/00	00/01
↓	2	50/00	50/32		00/02
PgDn	3	51/00	51/33	76/00	00/03
←	4	4B/00	4B/34	73/00	00/04
	5		4C/35		00/05
→	6	4D/00	4D/36	74/00	00/06
Home	7	47/00	47/37	77/00	00/07
↑	8	48/00	48/38		00/08
PgUp	9	49/00	49/39	84/00	00/09
−		4A/2D	4A/2D		
+		4E/2B	4E/2B		
Del	.	53/00	53/2E		

Key	Unshifted	Shifted	Ctrl	Alt
A	1E/61	1E/41	1E/01	1E/00
B	30/62	30/42	30/02	30/00
C	2E/63	2E/43	2E/03	2E/00
D	20/64	20/44	20/04	20/00
E	12/65	12/45	12/05	12/00
F	21/66	21/46	21/06	21/00
G	22/67	22/47	22/07	22/00
H	23/68	23/48	23/08	23/00
I	17/69	17/49	17/09	17/00
J	24/6A	24/4A	24/0A	24/00
K	25/6B	25/4B	25/0B	25/00
L	26/6C	26/4C	26/0C	26/00

(continued)

TABLE 9.4   *(cont.)*

Key		Unshifted	Shifted	Ctrl	Alt
M		32/6D	32/4D	32/0D	32/00
N		31/6E	31/4E	31/0E	31/00
O		18/6F	18/4F	18/0F	18/00
P		19/70	19/50	19/10	19/00
Q		10/71	10/51	10/11	10/00
R		13/72	13/52	13/12	13/00
S		1F/73	1F/53	1F/13	1F/00
T		14/74	14/54	14/14	14/00
U		16/75	16/55	16/15	16/00
V		2F/76	2F/56	2F/16	2F/00
W		11/77	11/57	11/17	11/00
X		2D/78	2D/58	2D/18	2D/00
Y		15/79	15/59	15/19	15/00
Z		2C/7A	2C/5A	2C/1A	2C/00
Space		39/20	39/20	39/20	39/20
ESC		01/1B	01/1B	01/1B	
1	!	02/31	02/21		78/00
2	@	03/32	03/40	03/00	79/00
3	#	04/33	04/23		7A/00
4	$	05/34	05/24		7B/00
5	%	06/35	06/25		7C/00
6	ˆ	07/36	07/5E	07/1E	7D/00
7	&	08/37	08/26		7E/00
8	*	09/38	09/2A		7F/00
9	(	0A/39	0A/38		80/00
0	)	0B/30	0B/29		81/00
—	—	0C/2D	0C/5F	0C/1F	82/00
=	+	0D/3D	0D/2B		83/00
[	{	1A/5B	1A/7B	1A/1B	
]	}	1B/5D	1B/7D	1B/1D	
Backspace		0E/08	0E/08	0E/7F	
;	:	27/3B	27/3A		
'	"	28/27	28/22		
`	~	29/60	29/7E		
,	<	33/2C	33/3C		
.	>	34/2E	34/3E		
/	?	35/2F	35/3F		
Enter		1C/0D	1C/0D	1C/0A	
Tab		0F/09	0F/00		
\	|	2B/5C	2B/7C	2B/1C	

To print a character on the screen, you can use the following DOS routine:

```
        DOS Character Output

   DL = ASCII code of character

   B4 02          MOV AH,2
   CD 21          INT 21H
```

This DOS routine will print the character in *DL* at the current cursor position on the screen and increment the cursor position. The only question is where is the cursor to begin with. If you want to display characters at a particular location on the screen, you must first set the cursor to that location. You can do this by calling the following BIOS routine:

```
            Set Cursor

   DH = row          DL = column

   B7 00          MOV BH,0
   B4 02          MOV AH,2
   CD 10          INT 10H
```

Finally, to print a string of characters on the screen, the ASCII codes of the character string are stored in memory starting at *DS:DX*, and the string must be terminated with a *$* character (ASCII code 24H). Then you execute the following code:

```
          String Output

   $ terminated string at DS:DX

   B4 09          MOV AH,9
   CD 21          INT 21H
```

As an example of using these routines, go to offset address 0000 and enter the word *Hello$* by typing */MA* followed by *Hello$*. Note that the data segment *DS* is the same as *CS* and your current segment, *SEG*. Then enter the program shown in Fig. 9.13 starting at offset address 0008h. Verify that you typed it in correctly by pressing */UP* to disassemble the code. This program should set the cursor at the beginning of the bottom line on the screen and then print the word *Hello* there. To execute this entire program, move the position cursor to offset address 0008h and type */EG*. This will execute the program and display the word *Hello*, as shown in Fig. 9.14.

```
0008   B7 00          mov bh,0       set the cursor
000A   B2 00          mov dl,0       at column 0
000C   B6 18          mov dh,24      row 24 = 18h
000E   B4 02          mov ah,2
0010   CD 10          int 10h
0012   BA 00 00       mov dx,0       set string address to 0000h
0015   B4 09          mov ah,9       DOS string output function
0017   CD 21          int 21h
0019   CC             int 3          stop program with breakpoint
```

Figure 9.13 Program to print the string at DS:0000 on the bottom line of the screen.

```
        8086 Microprocessor TUTOR          Press F7 for Help

     AH AL    BH BL     CH CL     DH DL
  AX 09 24  BX 00 C5  CX 00 C5  DX 00 00   1574:0008 B700      MOV    BH,00H
                                           1574:000A B200      MOV    DL,00H
     SP 0FFF      SI 0000       IP 0019     1574:000C B618      MOV    DH,18H
     BP 0000      DI 0000                   1574:000E B402      MOV    AH,02H
     SS 1574      DS 1574       CS 1574     1574:0010 CD10      INT    10H
  SP+SS 1673F  SI+DS 15740      ES 1574     1574:0012 BA0000    MOV    DX,0000H
  BP+SS 15740  DI+DS 15740   IP+CS 15759    1574:0015 B409      MOV    AH,09H
  STATUS FLAGS 7246 0111001001000110        1574:0017 CD21      INT    21H
                     ODITSZ A P C           1574:0019 CC        INT3
  1574:0019 CC          INT3               1574:001A 42        INC    DX

  SEG 1574:   08 19 2A 3B 4C 5D 6E 7F                           1574: STACK
      0000    48 65 6C 6C 6F 24 D8 03     H e l l o $ . .       0FFF
      0008    B7 00 B2 00 B6 18 B4 02     . . . . . . . .
      0010    CD 10 BA 00 00 B4 09 CD     . . . . . . . .
      0018    21>CC 42 B4 02 CD 21 CC     ! . B . . . ! .
      0020    0B F6 74 03 E9 CE 00 E8     . . t . . . . .
      0028    29 3B 89 86 76 FF 3D 61     ) ; . . v . = a
      0030    00 74 5D 3D 62 00 74 05     . t ] = b . t .

                                          / : Command      > : Go To Memory
  Hello                                   Use Cursor Keys to Scroll thru Memory
```

Figure 9.14 Tutor display after executing the program in Fig. 9.13.

Experiment 19: 8086 Registers and Memory

1. Run the TUTOR monitor by typing *tutor*. Use the /R command described in Section 9.2 to set the 8086 registers to the following hex values:

```
AX = 1234  BX = 5678  CX = 89AB  DX = CDEF
SI = 1111  DI = 2222
```

2. Go to offset address 1000 within the current segment by typing >*O1000*. Enter 8 bytes into memory by typing /*MH* followed by

```
11 22 33 44 55 66 77 88 <Enter>
```

3. Enter the ASCII codes for letters *A* to *H* in the next eight memory locations (offset addresses 1008 to 100F) by typing /*MA* followed by

```
A B C D E F G H <Enter>
```

Print the TUTOR screen on the printer by pressing *Shift-Print Screen*.

4. Go to a new segment (by typing >*S*...) in which the data you have just typed in starting at offset address 1000 will be stored at offset address 0000. Print the TUTOR screen on the printer. Go to the segment in which you can find your data at offset address 100. Print the TUTOR screen on the printer.

5. Enter the bytes of the program shown in Fig. 9.9 starting at offset address 0000. Move the cursor to the beginning of the program (by pressing the *Home* key), disassemble the code by typing /*UP*, and then single step each instruction by pressing function key *F1*. Observe the registers after you execute each instruction. After executing all the instructions, print the TUTOR screen on the printer.

6. Go to the segment address of the video RAM in your computer (either B000 or B800) and write the inverse video letters *abc* in the upper-right corner of the screen by typing /*MA* followed by

```
a p b p c p <Enter>
```

Print the TUTOR screen on the printer.

7. Type in the program shown in Fig. 9.12 starting at offset address 0000. Single step through the program using function key *F2*. When you execute the instruction at offset address 0002, you will need to press any key to continue. The scan code and ASCII code for this key will be stored in *AH* and *AL*. Check several of the scan codes and ASCII codes given in Table 9.4.

8. Modify the program in Fig. 9.13 so as to display your first name on the bottom row of the screen starting in column 10. Print the TUTOR screen on the printer.

Experiment 20: TUTOR Commands

1. Go to memory location 2000:0000 and enter the eight hex values

```
11 22 33 44 55 66 77 88
```

Transfer these 8 bytes to locations 2C00:0FF8 to 2C00:0FFF using the TUTOR command /T described in Appendix B. Transfer the same bytes to locations 2D00:1010 to 2D00:1017. (Make sure segment address 2C00 is higher than the initial value of SEG on the TUTOR screen. If not, choose a higher segment address to which to transfer the data.)

2. Go to memory location 2000:0003 and insert the 3 bytes *AA BB CC* between 33 and 44 using the TUTOR command /I (see Appendix B).

3. Delete the 3 bytes you inserted in step 2 using the TUTOR command /D (see Appendix B).

4. Save the 8 bytes from locations 2000:0000 to 2000:0007 on a disk using the TUTOR command /SS described in Appendix B. Type /QD to exit to DOS and list the directory (*dir*) to see the file you saved. Run TUTOR again and load the 8 bytes you saved at memory location 2000:0100 using the /SL command (see Appendix B).

5. When you first run TUTOR, observe the value stored in *BX* and *CX*. The value in *BX* is the segment address that contains the tutor program. The value in *CX* is the starting offset address of TUTOR. Go to this starting address and press /UP. The beginning of the tutor program will be disassembled on the right side of the screen. Now press /LP. This will disassemble a page of code on the entire screen. To print disassembled code on the printer, type /P. Press P and a page of disassembled code will be printed. You can use the command /PB to print a specified block of code.

EXERCISES

9.1. To change the value in the index register *SI*, type /R I S. Then enter a 4-digit hexadecimal value. To change the value in the base pointer register *BP*, type /R P B, and enter a 4-digit hexadecimal value. Change the contents of the following registers to the indicated hex values:

```
AX = 003F    SI = 4444
SS = 0F13    BX = 142C
DI = 5555    DS = 0413
CX = 7777    SP = 0FFF
ES = 0F11    DX = 000F
BP = ABCD    IP = 1000
```

9.2. To change the value in the status register *SF*, type /R F. Then enter a 4-digit *hexadecimal value*. Note that this hex value will be displayed on the screen as both a 4-digit hexadecimal number and as the corresponding 16-bit *binary value*. What 4-digit hexadecimal number must you enter on the entry line in order for each of the following 16 bits to be displayed in the status register *SF*? Verify your answers by changing the contents of *SF* on the screen to each of the following values:

a. 01110010 11000011
b. 11101000 10101010
c. 00011111 00001111
d. 10110100 11101100
e. 11001101 11001100
f. 10100101 10101110
g. 00111001 01010101
h. 00000110 00000011

9.3. What 16-bit binary number is equivalent to each of the following hexadecimal numbers? Verify your answers by changing the contents of the status register to each of these values and noting its binary value on the screen.

a. 65AB
b. 0A0B
c. 4872
d. BE17
e. 9DA4
f. C3E2
g. F2AC
h. 1703

9.4. Fill in the missing offset addresses.

a. 152F:29D2 = 1000: _____
b. 0300:155A = 0000: _____
c. 1380:FFFF = 2000: _____

9.5. Fill in the missing segment addresses.

a. 117F:49C3 = _____ :3333
b. 1728:3821 = _____ :4321
c. 0E10:0300 = _____ :0000

10

8086 Instructions

In Chapter 9 we took a look inside the 8086 and saw how basic instructions are executed. In this chapter we will take a closer look at some of the 8086 instructions that we will need to understand before we can begin to write our own programs. All 8086 instructions are related in one way or another to the register structure that we looked at in Chapter 9. Therefore, we will begin this chapter with a closer look at the functions of these 8086 registers.

In this chapter you will learn:

- The function of each of the 8086 registers, including the meaning of the bits in the status register
- How the instructions *MOV* and *XCHG* can transfer and exchange data between two registers
- How the 8086 shift and rotate instructions work
- To use the immediate and register addressing modes
- The basic arithmetic instructions
- The basic logical instructions

10.1 A CLOSER LOOK AT THE 8086 REGISTERS

In Chapter 9 we saw that the 8086 microprocessor contains the set of registers shown in Fig. 10.1. We will take a closer look at each of these register groups in this section.

256

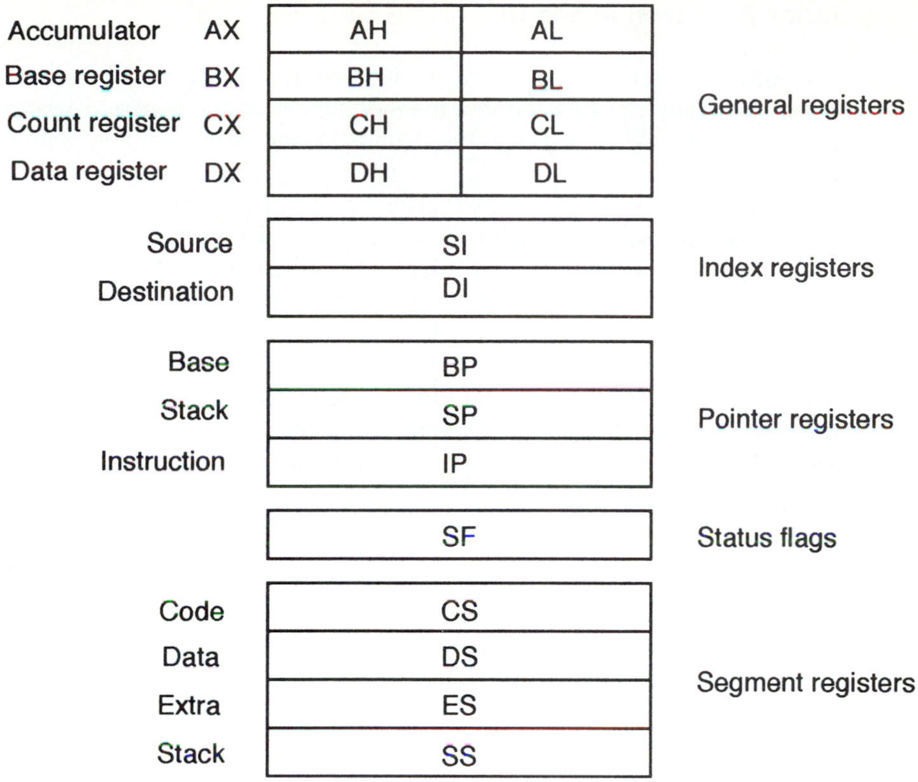

Accumulator	AX	AH	AL
Base register	BX	BH	BL
Count register	CX	CH	CL
Data register	DX	DH	DL

General registers

Source	SI
Destination	DI

Index registers

Base	BP
Stack	SP
Instruction	IP

Pointer registers

	SF

Status flags

Code	CS
Data	DS
Extra	ES
Stack	SS

Segment registers

Figure 10.1   The 8086 registers.

General Registers

The registers *AX*, *BX*, *CX*, and *DX* are general-purpose 16-bit registers. The upper halves of each of these registers are called *AH*, *BH*, *CH*, and *DH*. These are 8-bit registers that can be accessed directly. Similarly, the lower halves of these registers are called *AL*, *BL*, *CL*, and *DL*. These registers are shown in Fig. 10.1. Although all the general registers can be used interchangeably for many operations, each of the registers are used for certain specific purposes. This is what gives rise to the names *accumulator, base, count,* and *data* for the registers *AX, BX, CX,* and *DX* shown in Fig. 10.1. All general registers are used for storing intermediate results. When you want to move a byte (8 bits) or word (16 bits) from one memory location to another, you must first load the byte or word into one of the registers such as *AX* (with a *MOV* instruction) and then store the byte in the other memory location (with a second *MOV* instruction). The details of how to address various memory locations will be described in Chapter 12.

Index Registers, SI and DI

The index registers *SI* and *DI* are 16-bit registers that are used for several different purposes. They can be used in a manner similar to the general registers for temporary storage when moving 16-bit data to and from memory using the *MOV* instruction.

The main use of the index registers *SI* and *DI* is in conjunction with various modes of addressing. An addressing mode is what specifies where a particular data item is to be found. For example, the instruction *MOV AX,1234H* that we used in Chapter 9 is an example of the *immediate addressing mode*. This means that the data 1234H immediately follow the opcode in memory. The instruction *NEG AX* that we also used in the last chapter is an example of the *register addressing mode*. This means that the data of interest is in the register *AX*. One of the most important addressing modes associated with the index registers *SI* and *DI* is register indirect addressing. For example, the instruction

```
MOV   AL,[SI]
```

means move into *AL* the byte in the data segment at the offset address that is in *SI*. We say that *SI* is pointing to a byte in the data segment. We will look in detail at this and related addressing modes in Chapter 12.

Pointer Registers

Stack pointer, SP, and base pointer, BP.   The stack is a region of memory that is set aside for storing temporary data. The stack pointer *SP* is a 16-bit register that contains the offset address of the top of the stack. The actual address is found by adding the segment address stored in the stack segment register, *SS*. The stack is used by the 8086 to save the return address when a subroutine is called. It is also used to save register values when an interrupt is called. Subroutines will be discussed in Chapter 11, and interrupts will be described in Chapters 11 and 14.

The stack can be used to save the contents of any register using the *PUSH* instruction. Data are removed from the stack using the *POP* instruction. Examples of using these instructions together with a discussion of subroutines will be given in Chapter 11, where the operation of the stack will be described in detail.

The base pointer, *BP*, is a 16-bit register that is used to access data in the stack segment. The stack segment register, *SS*, is used to find the actual address associated with an offset address in *BP*. Addressing modes involving *BP*, including the method of passing subroutine parameters on the stack, will be discussed in Chapter 12.

Instruction Pointer, IP.   The instruction pointer, *IP*, is a 16-bit register that contains the offset address of the next instruction to be executed. When an instruction is executed, the instruction pointer is automatically incremented the number of times needed to point to the next instruction. Instructions may be from 1 to 6 bytes long. Therefore, the program counter may be incremented by 1 to 6, depending on the instruction being executed.

You can change the value stored in the instruction pointer by pressing /RPI and then entering a new 4-digit hex value. Normally, however, the instruction pointer will automatically change itself as a program is executed.

For example, go back to Chapter 9 and reenter the program given in Fig. 9.9. As you single step through this program by pressing function key *F1*, note how the instruction pointer, *IP*, is automatically incremented to the offset address of the next instruction to be executed.

The *NOP* instruction (opcode 90) does nothing except advance the instruction pointer by one. The *NOP* instruction takes three clock cycles to execute, and it is sometimes used when short delays of a few microseconds are required.

Status Register

The 8086 has a status register that contains six status flags and three control flags. The six status flags are the carry flag (*C*), the zero flag (*Z*), the sign flag (*S*), the overflow flag (*O*), the auxiliary flag (*A*), and the parity flag (*P*). The three control flags are the interrupt enable flag (*I*), the direction flag (*D*), and the trap flag (*T*). Each flag is 1 bit in the status register. The location of each flag is shown in Fig. 10.2, and the value of each flag is displayed in the status register shown near the center of the TUTOR screen.

You can change the contents of the status register by typing /RF and then entering a *hexadecimal* value. For example, if you enter 9C1, then the bit pattern

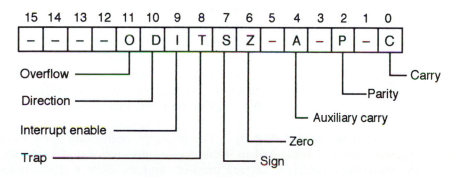

Figure 10.2   The status register.

0000100111000001 will be displayed in the status register. We will now look at the meaning of each flag.

Carry flag (C).   The carry flag is bit 0 of the status register. It can be considered to be an extension of a register or a memory location operated on by an instruction. The carry bit is changed by three different types of instructions. The first type is arithmetic instructions such as addition and subtraction. These include *ADD* and *ADC* (add with carry) or *SUB* and *SBB* (subtract with borrow) described in Section 10.4 and compare instructions (*CMP*) described in Chapter 11.

The second group of instructions that can change the carry bit are the shift and rotate instructions (such as *SAL, SHL, RCL,* and *RCR*), which will be described in Section 10.3.

Finally, the carry bit can be set to 1 with the instruction *STC* (set carry, opcode = F9), cleared to zero with the instruction *CLC* (clear carry, opcode = F8), and complemented with the instruction *CMC* (complement carry, opcode = F5).

Zero flag (Z).   The zero flag is bit 6 of the status register. This flag is set to 1 when the result of an instruction is zero. If the result of an instruction is not zero, the Z flag is cleared to zero. This Z flag is tested by the branching instruction *JE* (jump if equal to zero, $Z = 1$) and *JNE* (jump if not equal to zero, $Z = 0$). We will describe how these branching instructions work in Chapter 11.

Sign flag (S).   The sign flag is bit 7 of the status register. Negative numbers are stored in 8086 computers using the two's complement representation. In this representation a negative number is indicated when bit 7 (the leftmost bit) of a byte is set to 1. When the result of an instruction leaves the sign bit set (bit 7 of a byte or bit 15 of a word), the S flag is set to 1. If the result of an instruction is positive (the sign bit is 0), the S flag is cleared to 0. The S flag is tested by the branching instruction *JS* (jump on sign, $S = 1$) and *JNS* (jump on not sign, $S = 0$). We will discuss branching instructions in Chapter 11.

Overflow flag (O).   The overflow flag is bit 11 of the status register. It is set any time the result of a signed (two's complement) operation is out of range. Its relationship to the carry flag will be described in Section 10.4. The O flag is tested by the branching instructions *JO* (jump overflow, $O = 1$) and *JNO* (jump on not overflow, $O = 0$). We will discuss branching instructions in Chapter 11.

Interrupt enable flag (I).   The interrupt enable flag is bit 9 of the status register. When it is cleared to 0, hardware interrupts entering the *INTR* pin of the microprocessor (pin 18) are masked, and the 8086 will not respond to an interrupt. When the I flag is set to 1, interrupts are enabled and the 8086 will service hardware interrupts.

The *I* flag is set to 1 with the instruction *STI* (set interrupt enable flag, opcode = FB) and is cleared to zero with the instruction *CLI* (clear interrupt enable flag, opcode = FA). A detailed discussion of interrupts will be given in Chapter 14.

Auxiliary carry flag (A).   The auxiliary carry flag is bit 4 of the status register. It contains the carry from bit 3 to bit 4 resulting from an 8-bit addition or subtraction operation. The auxiliary carry flag is used by the microprocessor when performing binary-coded decimal (BCD) addition.

Parity flag (P).   The parity flag is bit 2 of the status register. It is set to 1 if the low-order 8 bits of the result of an instruction contain an even number of 1 bits. The parity flag will be 0 if an instruction produces an 8-bit result with an odd number of 1 bits.

Direction flag (D).   The direction flag is bit 10 of the status register. This bit determines whether the index registers *SI* and *DI* are automatically incremented or decremented in certain string manipulation instructions. If $D = 0$, then *SI* and *DI* are incremented. If $D = 1$, then *SI* and *DI* are decremented. These string manipulation instructions will be described in Chapter 12. The *D* flag is cleared to 0 with the instruction *CLD* (clear direction flag, opcode = FC) and is set to 1 with the instruction *STD* (set direction flag, opcode = FD).

Trap flag (T).   The trap flag is bit 8 of the status register. When set to 1, it will produce an interrupt after a single instruction is executed. This is how the TUTOR monitor executes a single instruction when you press the *F1* key. A description of how this works will be given in Chapters 11 and 14.

Segment Registers, CS, DS, SS, and ES

In Chapter 9 you saw how an 8086 memory address is made up of two parts: a segment address and an offset address. The TUTOR monitor displays an offset address relative to the segment address displayed on the screen as *SEG*.

The 8086 microprocessor has four registers that contain segment addresses. These are called the code segment register, *CS*, the data segment register, *DS*, the stack segment register, *SS*, and the extra segment register, *ES*. This means that at any instant four different 64-Kbyte segments are defined. These were shown in Fig. 9.5. Note that these four segments may partially or completely overlap. For example, if *CS*, *DS*, *ES*, and *SS* all contain the same value, then a single 64-Kbyte segment is defined.

The code segment defined by *CS* contains the program that is being executed. The instruction pointer, *IP*, that points to the next instruction uses the code segment register *CS* to form the actual address of the next instruction.

The data segment defined by *DS* contains data used by the program. Most of the data addressing modes to be described in Chapter 12 use the data segment register to form the effective address of the data.

The segment defined by *SS* contains the stack. The pointer registers, *SP* and *BP*, described above use the stack segment register to form the actual address of the data. A complete discussion of the stack will be given in Chapter 11.

The extra segment defined by *ES* is used for a variety of useful purposes. Sometimes you need to access data that are not properly defined relative to the current data segment. The extra segment register is also used by certain string manipulation instructions to be described in Chapter 12.

10.2 MOVE AND EXCHANGE INSTRUCTIONS

We saw in Chapter 9 that the instructions

```
B8 34 12   MOV AX,1234H
B6 18      MOV DH,24
```

will move the hex value 1234H into *AX* and the decimal value 24 (18H) into *DH*. These are examples of *immediate addressing*. The opcodes B8 and B6 are always used to move 16-bit immediate data into *AX* and 8-bit immediate data into *DH*, respectively. The opcodes to move immediate data into the other general registers are given in Table 10.1.

The opcodes in Table 10.1 can be found from the instruction opcode map shown in Table A.2a in Appendix A. The opcodes are read from this table by reading the first hex digit from the left column and the second hex digit from the

TABLE 10.1   MOVE IMMEDIATE DATA INSTRUCTIONS FOR GENERAL REGISTERS

Opcode	Instruction	Operation
B0	MOV AL, imm8	imm8 → AL
B1	MOV CL, imm8	imm8 → CL
B2	MOV DL, imm8	imm8 → DL
B3	MOV BL, imm8	imm8 → BL
B4	MOV AH, imm8	imm8 → AH
B5	MOV CH, imm8	imm8 → CH
B6	MOV DH, imm8	imm8 → DH
B7	MOV BH, imm8	imm8 → BH
B8	MOV AX, imm16	imm16 → AX
B9	MOV CX, imm16	imm16 → CX
BA	MOV DX, imm16	imm16 → DX
BB	MOV BX, imm16	imm16 → BX

imm8 = 8-bit data byte

imm16 = 16-bit immediate data (low byte, high byte)

top row. Note that the row labeled *B* includes all the instructions shown in Table 10.1. It also includes four additional instructions (opcodes BC to BF) for moving immediate data into the pointer and index registers.

Figure 10.3 defines the *MOV* instruction that can be used to transfer data between any two 8-bit registers or between any two 16-bit registers. The *MOV* instructions in Fig. 10.3 are 2-byte instructions in which the first byte is the opcode (88 or 8A for 8-bit byte registers and 89 or 8B for 16-bit word registers), and the second byte is a postbyte that defines the two registers involved in the transfer according to Fig. 10.3.

Machine Code	Assembly Language Instruction	Operation
88 PB	MOV RB1, RB2	move RB2 to RB1
89 PB	MOV RW1, RW2	move RW2 to RW1
8A PB	MOV RB2, RB1	move RB1 to RB2
8B PB	MOV RW2, RW1	move RW1 to RW2

PB = postbyte

1	1					

RB2   RB1
RW2   RW1

RB1,2	RW1,2
000 = AL	000 = AX
001 = CL	001 = CX
010 = DL	010 = DX
011 = BL	011 = BX
100 = AH	100 = SP
101 = CH	101 = BP
110 = DH	110 = SI
111 = BH	111 = DI

Figure 10.3   Form of MOV instructions to transfer register contents.

For example, suppose you want to transfer the value in accumulator *AL* to register *CH*. The postbyte (for the 88 opcode) would be

1	1	0	0	0	1	0	1	= C5H

AL   CH

Therefore, the instruction to transfer *AL* to *CH* is

88 C5   MOV CH,AL

Note from Figure 10.3 that this instruction can also use the opcode 8A together with the postbyte

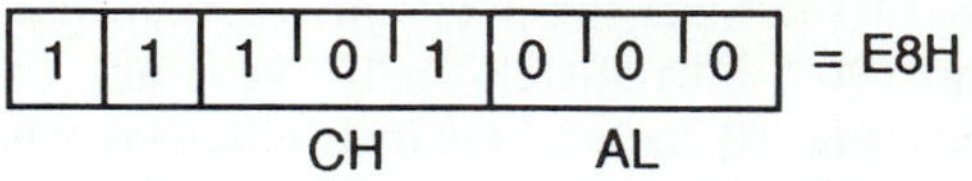

| 1 | 1 | 1 | 0 | 1 | 0 | 0 | 0 | = E8H |

         CH   AL

and be written as

```
8A E8   MOV CH,AL
```

The reason that there are two ways to do apparently the same thing is that the postbyte really has the following more general form:

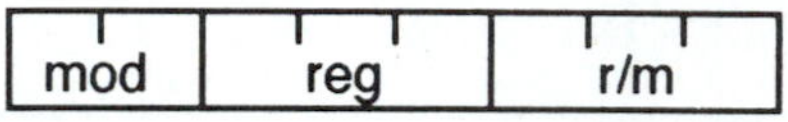

| mod | reg | r/m |

If the first 2 bits (*mod*) in the postbyte are 11 as in Fig. 10.3, then the last 3 bits in the postbyte (*r/m*) represent a register. If the value of *mod* is not 11 then the last 3 bits in the postbyte will define some memory location rather than a register. In this case the opcode 88 will move a byte from a memory location to a register, while the opcode 8A will move a byte from a register to a memory location. We will look at these *MOV* instructions in Chapter 12.

    Figure 10.4 defines the exchange instruction, *XCHG*. There are two forms of the *XCHG* instruction shown in Fig. 10.4. The first will exchange the 16-bit contents of *AX* with any of the 16-bit registers given in Fig. 10.4. This is a 1-byte instruction with an opcode *9X*, where *X* depends on the register involved ac-

Machine Code	Assembly Language Instruction	Operation
9X	XCHG reg	Exchange AX and reg
86 PB	XCHG RB1,RB2	Exchange RB1 and RB2
87 PB	XCHG RW1,RW2	Exchange RW1 and RW2

X	reg	X	reg
000	AX	100	SP
001	CX	101	BP
010	DX	110	SI
011	BX	111	DI

PB, RB1,2 and RW1,2 same as in Figure 10.3

Figure 10.4 XCHG instruction.

cording to Figure 10.4. For example, the instruction

    93   XCHG BX

will exchange the contents of *AX* and *BX*.

The second form of the *XCHG* instruction involves the same postbyte as in Fig. 10.3. For example, the instruction

    87 FE   XCHG SI,DI

will exchange the contents of *SI* and *DI*.

10.3 SHIFT AND ROTATE INSTRUCTIONS

There are 14 instructions that allow you to move bits around in registers or in any memory location. We will study these instructions by using the general registers. Similar results can be obtained on registers *SP*, *BP*, *SI*, and *DI* or any memory location by using some of the addressing modes described in Chapter 12.

Shift Left, SHL or SAL

The *SHL AL,1* instruction with an opcode of *D0 E0* will cause the 8 bits in accumulator *AL* to be shifted 1 bit to the left. The leftmost bit (bit 7) will be shifted into the carry bit. A zero will be shifted into the rightmost bit (bit 0).

Figure 10.5 Result of executing SHL AL,1 instruction eight times.

To see how this instruction works, store the hex value *AAH* in accumulator *AL* by typing /*RGA AA*, and store the instruction *D0 E0* at offset addresses 0000 to 000F by typing

```
/MH   D0 E0 D0 E0 D0 E0 D0 E0 D0 E0 D0 E0 D0 E0 D0 E0
```

Now move the position cursor back to offset address 0000H by pressing the *Home* key and single step (*F1*) eight times. You should observe the shifting of the bits in accumulator *AL* as shown in Figure 10.5. Note how the carry bit in the status register is changed each time you execute *SHL AL,1*. The opcodes for shifting the 8-bit general registers are given in Table 10.2.

Shift Right, SHR

The *SHR AL,1* instruction with an opcode of *D0 E8* will cause the 8 bits in accumulator *AL* to be shifted 1 bit to the right. The rightmost bit (bit 0) will be

TABLE 10.2 8-BIT REGISTER SHIFT AND ROTATE INSTRUCTIONS

	AL	CL	DL	BL	AH	CH	DH	BH	
ROL	D0 C0	D0 C1	DO C2	D0 C3	D0 C4	D0 C5	D0 C6	D0 C7	Rotate left
ROR	D0 C8	D0 C9	D0 CA	D0 CB	D0 CC	D0 CD	D0 CE	D0 CF	Rotate right
RCL	D0 D0	D0 D1	D0 D2	D0 D3	D0 D4	D0 D5	D0 D6	D0 D7	Rotate through carry left
RCR	D0 D8	D0 D9	D0 DA	D0 DB	D0 DC	D0 DD	D0 DE	D0 DF	Rotate through carry right
SHL/SAL	D0 E0	D0 E1	D0 E2	D0 E3	D0 E4	D0 E5	D0 E6	D0 E7	Shift left
SHR	D0 E8	D0 E9	D0 EA	D0 EB	D0 EC	D0 ED	D0 EE	D0 EF	Shift right
SAR	D0 F8	D0 F9	DO FA	D0 FB	D0 FC	D0 FD	DO FE	D0 FF	Shift arithmetic right
ROL reg,CL	D2 C0	D2 C1	D2 C2	D2 C3	D2 C4	D2 C5	D2 C6	D2 C7	Rotate left CL bits
ROR reg,CL	D2 C8	D2 C9	D2 CA	D2 CB	D2 CC	D2 CD	D2 CE	D2 CF	Rotate right CL bits
RCL reg,CL	D2 D0	D2 D1	D2 D2	D2 D3	D2 D4	D2 D5	D2 D6	D2 D7	Rotate through carry left CL bits
RCR reg,CL	D2 D8	D2 D9	D2 DA	D2 DB	D2 DC	D2 DD	D2 DE	D2 DF	Rotate through carry right CL bits
SHL reg,CL	D2 E0	D2 E1	D2 E2	D2 E3	D2 E4	D2 E5	D2 E6	D2 E7	Shift left CL bits
SHR reg,CL	D2 E8	D2 E9	D2 EA	D2 EB	D2 EC	D2 ED	D2 EE	D2 EF	Shift right CL bits
SAR reg,CL	D2 F8	D2 F9	D2 FA	D2 FB	D2 FC	D2 FD	D2 FE	D2 FF	Shift arithmetic right CL bits

shifted into the carry bit. A zero will be shifted into the leftmost bit (bit 7). A picture of what this instruction does is shown in Fig. 10.6.

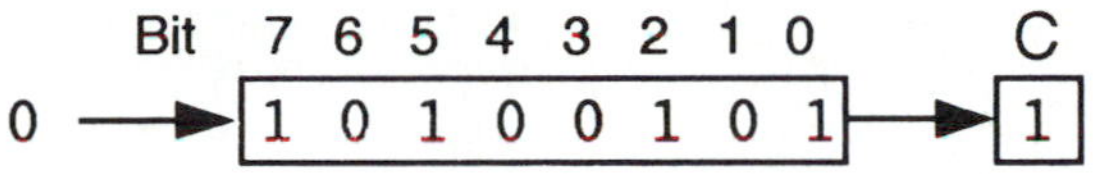

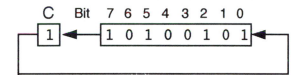

Figure 10.6   The shift right, SHR, instruction.

Rotate through Carry Left, RCL

The rotate through carry left instruction *RCL* differs from the shift left instruction in that the carry bit is shifted into the rightmost bit rather than a zero, as shown in Fig. 10.7. Each time that the instruction is executed, all bits are shifted 1 bit to the left. Bit 7 is shifted into the carry, and the carry bit is shifted into bit 0.

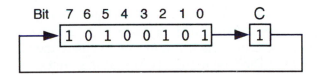

Figure 10.7   The rotate through carry left, RCL, instruction.

Rotate through Carry Right, RCR

The rotate through carry right instruction *RCR* is just the opposite of rotate through carry left. As shown in Fig. 10.8, each bit is shifted 1 bit to the right. Bit 0 is shifted into the carry, and the carry bit is shifted into bit 7.

Figure 10.8   The rotate through carry right, RCR, instruction.

Rotate Left and Rotate Right, ROL and ROR

In addition to the two rotate instructions *RCL* and *RCR* that rotate the bits through the carry bit, the 8086 has two rotate instructions that do *not* rotate through the carry. These two instructions are shown in Fig. 10.9. The rotate left instruction, *ROL*, shifts the leftmost bit into the carry *and* into the rightmost bit position. Similarly, the rotate right instruction, *ROR*, shifts the rightmost bit into the carry *and* into the leftmost bit position. Note carefully the difference between the instructions *RCL* and *RCR* in Figs. 10.7 and 10.8 and the instructions *ROL* and *ROR* in Fig. 10.9.

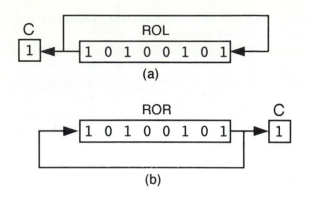

(a)

(b)

Figure 10.9 The rotate left, ROL, and rotate right, ROR, instructions do not rotate the bits through the carry.

Shift Arithmetic Right, SAR

The shift arithmetic right instruction, *SAR*, differs from the shift right instruction, *SHR*, shown in Fig. 10.6 in that the sign bit (the leftmost bit) remains the same. This means that if the sign bit is a 1 (corresponding to a negative number) this 1 will continually be shifted to the right. A picture of what this instruction does is shown in Fig. 10.10.

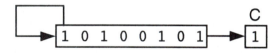

Figure 10.10 Shift arithmetic right, SAR, instruction.

Shift and Rotate with Count Instructions

The shift and rotate instructions described above shift all bits in a register one bit. These instructions are shown in the top half of Table 10.2. The instructions shown in the bottom half of Table 10.2 allow you to shift or rotate the bits in a register a given number of bits. The number of bits to shift is stored in register *CL*.

For example, the two instructions

```
0000 B1 03   MOV CL,3
0002 D2 E0   SHL AL,CL
```

will shift the contents of *AL* left 3 bits. This is equivalent to multiplying the contents of *AL* by $2^3 = 8$.

As a second example, the two instructions

```
0000 B1 0A   MOV CL,10
0002 D3 EA   SHR DX,CL
```

will shift the contents of *DX* right 10 bits. This is equivalent to dividing the contents of *DX* by $2^{10} = 1024$.

Note that all the shift and rotate instructions in Table 10.2 contain 2 bytes and that the first byte is *D0* in the first seven rows of the table and the first byte is *D2* for all the instructions in the last seven rows. If you look up the opcodes *D0* and *D2* in Table A.2a in Appendix A, you will see that there is an asterisk (*) for that opcode. This means that you must go to Table A.2b to find the form of a postbyte for this instruction. Note that in the row labeled *D0* there are seven different shift and rotate instructions. The 3-bit code at the top of each column is the postbyte opcode (*PBOC*) that must be put into the following postbyte:

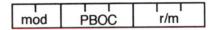

If you are shifting or rotating the contents of a register, then the value of *mod* in this postbyte is 11, and the *r/m* value is the register value using the same three bit codes given in Fig. 10.3 for the *MOV* instruction. For example, the postbyte opcode (PBOC) for the instruction *RCR CH,1* (fourth column in Table A.2b) is 011. Therefore, the complete postbyte is

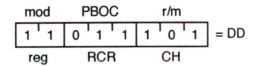

and the instruction code

```
D0 DD   RCR CH,1
```

agrees with the entry in Table 10.2. In fact, this is how Table 10.2 was generated. You should be able to verify any of the entries in Table 10.2.

10.4 BASIC ARITHMETIC INSTRUCTIONS

In this section we will take a look at the basic addition, subtraction, multiplication, and division instructions that are available in the 8086.

Binary Addition

The addition of binary numbers is carried out bit by bit starting with the least significant bit (the rightmost bit) according to Table 10.3. This is the same as the truth table for a full adder given in Fig. 6.12. The 8086 addition instructions are shown in Table 10.4.

TABLE 10.3 BINARY ADDITION

Carry(in)	A	B	A + B + Carry	Carry(out)
0	0	0	0	0
0	0	1	1	0
0	1	0	1	0
0	1	1	0	1
1	0	0	1	0
1	0	1	0	1
1	1	0	0	1
1	1	1	1	1

TABLE 10.4 ADDITION INSTRUCTIONS

Mnemonic	Meaning
ADD ac,data	Add immediate data to AX or AL register
ADD mem/reg, data	Add immediate data to register or memory location
ADD mem/reg1,mem/reg2	Add register to register, register to memory, or memory to register
ADC ac,data	Add with carry immediate data to AX or AL register
ADC mem/reg,data	Add with carry immediate data to register or memory location
ADC mem/reg1,mem/reg2	Add with carry register to register, register to memory, or memory to register

Consider the following binary addition:

```
                  Binary     Hex  Decimal
        Carry 0   01100010
            A     00110101    35    53
            B     00011001    19    25
                  01001110    4E    78
```

Note that the initial carry bit is zero and the final carry bit (0) is shown in the box. This is the carry bit that is displayed in the status register after an instruction such as *ADD ac,data* is executed. The intermediate carry bits are determined according to Table 10.3.

The binary values of *A* and *B* shown above are equivalent to the hexadecimal numbers 35H and 19H. These can be added directly (in hexadecimal) as shown above. The equivalent decimal addition (53 + 25 = 78) is also shown.

Carry and overflow.   The program shown in Fig. 10.11 adds the hexadecimal numbers 35H and 19H. Enter this program at offset address 0000 using

```
0000   B0 35     MOV   AL,35H      ;AL = 35H
0002   04 19     ADD   AL,19H      ;AL = AL + 19H
```

Figure 10.11   Program to add 35H and 19H.

the TUTOR monitor. The result of this addition is shown in Fig. 10.12. Single step through this program. Note that when the addition instruction at address 0002 is executed the carry flag C and the overflow flag O are both cleared to zero.

Decimal	Hex		Binary
53	35		00110101
+25	+19		00011001
78	4E	**C** [0]	01001110
		O [0]	

Figure 10.12   There is no carry from bit 6 to bit 7 and no carry from bit 7 to **C**.

Now modify this program by changing the 19 at offset address 0003 to 5BH. This is equivalent to adding the decimal numbers 53 and 91 as shown in Fig. 10.13. Single step through this new program and note that when the addition instruction at address 0002 is executed the carry flag C is cleared to zero, but the overflow flag O is set to one. There is an overflow because the answer 90H is really the *negative* (two's complement) value -112_{10}. (Verify this.) Although 90H is equivalent to the positive value 144_{10} when thinking about the result as an 8-bit unsigned number, the overflow flag, O, in the status register always thinks of the result as a signed number between -128 and $+127$. If the correct result is outside this range (144 in Fig. 10.13), then the overflow flag O is set to 1.

Decimal	Hex		Binary
53	35		00110101
+91	+5B		01011011
144	90	**C** [0]	10010000
		O [1]	

Figure 10.13   An overflow occurs (**O** = 1) when there is a carry from bit 6 to bit 7 and no carry from bit 7 to **C**.

Now modify the program again by changing the 5BH offset address 0003 to D3H. The hex value D3H represents the negative decimal number -45, as can be seen by taking the two's complement of D3H.

$$D3H = 11010011$$

$$\text{two's complement} = 00101101 = 2DH = 45_{10}$$

Therefore, adding D3H to 35H is the same as subtracting 45_{10} from 53_{10}, as shown in Fig. 10.14. Single step through this program and note that when the addition instruction at address 0002 is executed the carry flag C is set to 1, but the overflow

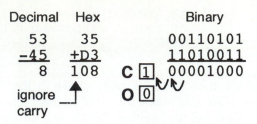

Figure 10.14 The overflow flag **O** is cleared to zero when there is a carry from bit 6 to bit 7 *and* a carry from bit 7 to **C**.

flag *O* is cleared to zero. There is no overflow because the binary addition result (08H) is correct. The result will always be correct (and therefore *O* will be cleared to zero) if there is a carry from bit 7 to *C* *and* a carry from bit 6 to bit 7.

Finally, change the value at address 0001 from 35H to 9EH. The hex value 9EH is equivalent to the negative decimal value −98:

$$9EH = 10011110$$

$$\text{two's complement} = 01100010 = 62H = 98_{10}$$

Figure 10.15 shows that adding −98 and −45 produces the decimal value −143 and the hex value 71H, which is incorrect. The *O* flag and the carry are both set to 1. Verify this by single stepping through the program.

```
Decimal   Hex          Binary
  -98      9E         10011110
  -45     +D3         11010011
 -143     171    C 1   01110001
ignore  ↑        O 1
carry
```

Figure 10.15 The overflow flag **O** is set to 1 when there is a carry from bit 7 to **C** but no carry from bit 6 to bit 7.

The results illustrated in Figs. 10.12 to 10.15 show that the overflow flag, *O*, is set to 1 if there is a carry from bit 6 to bit 7 with no carry from bit 7 to *C* (Fig. 10.13) *or* if there is a carry from bit 7 to *C* with no carry from bit 6 to bit 7 (Fig. 10.15). If there is no carry from bit 6 to bit 7 *and* no carry from bit 7 to *C* (Fig. 10.12), *or* if there is a carry from bit 6 to bit 7 *and* a carry from bit 7 to *C* (Fig. 10.14), then there is no overflow and *O* = 0. This can be summarized by saying that the overflow flag, *O*, is the *Exclusive OR* of a carry from bit 6 to bit 7 and a carry from bit 7 to *C*. That is,

$$O = (\text{carry from bit 6 to bit 7}) \ \$ \ (\text{carry from bit 7 to } C)$$

where the *Exclusive-OR* operation *A $ B* is given in Table 10.5.

Binary Subtraction

The subtraction of binary numbers can be carried out bit by bit starting with the least-significant bit according to Table 10.6, which is the same as the truth table

TABLE 10.5 EXCLUSIVE-OR OPERATION $

A	B	A $ B
0	0	0
0	1	1
1	0	1
1	1	0

TABLE 10.6 BINARY SUBTRACTION

Borrow (in)	A	B	A − B − Borrow	Borrow (out)
0	0	0	0	0
0	0	1	1	1
0	1	0	1	0
0	1	1	0	0
1	0	0	1	1
1	0	1	0	1
1	1	0	0	0
1	1	1	1	1

for a full subtractor given in Fig. 6.20. The first four rows have no borrow in.
The results in rows 1, 3, and 4 are obvious and result in no borrow out. In row
2 we are subtracting a 1 from a 0. This means that we need to borrow from the
bit to our left in a binary number. Because we are in base 2, this means that we
are really borrowing a 2, and therefore the result in row 2 of the table is $2 - 1$
$= 1$ plus a borrow. In a similar way you should convince yourself that the last
four rows in the table make sense.

An example is shown in Fig. 10.16. Note how a borrow may be required
when subtracting bits. The 8086 uses the carry flag as a borrow flag.

```
   Decimal            Hex                     Binary
          Borrow = 0 1      Borrow = 0 1   111
   181                B5                    10110101
  -111               -6F                   -01101111
    70                46                     01000110
```

Figure 10.16 Example of binary subtraction.

The subtraction shown in Fig. 10.16 is equivalent to taking the two's complement of the subtrahend and adding, as shown in Fig. 10.17. Note that this
addition causes the carry bit C to be set. However, there is no borrow. The 8086

```
  B5         B5        10110101
 -6F        +91        10010001        Figure 10.17  Binary subtraction is
  46  C 1    46  C 1   01000110        equivalent to taking the two's
                                       complement of the subtrahend and
          Borrow = 0                   adding.
```

complements the carry bit after a subtraction and uses the carry flag as the borrow flag. Therefore, the carry bit in the status register will not be set following this subtraction.

The 8086 subtraction instructions are given in Table 10.7. The subtraction illustrated in Figs. 10.16 and 10.17 can be performed by executing the instructions shown in Fig. 10.18. Type in this program using TUTOR and observe the contents of accumulator *AL* and the status register as you single step through the program.

TABLE 10.7 SUBTRACTION INSTRUCTIONS

Mnemonic	Meaning
SUB ac,data	Subtract immediate data from AL or AX register
SUB mem/reg, data	Subtract immediate data from register or memory location
SUB mem/reg1,mem/reg2	Subtract register from register, register from memory, or memory from register
SBB ac,data	Subtract with borrow immediate data from AL or AX register
SBB mem/reg,data	Subtract with borrow immediate data from register or memory location
SBB mem/reg1,mem/reg2	Subtract with borrow register from register, register from memory, or memory from register

Note that after the subtraction the carry bit is zero, indicating *no borrow*. The carry will always be zero if the magnitude (0 to 255) of the minuend (B5H in Fig. 10.18) is larger or equal to the magnitude of the subtrahend (6FH in Fig. 10.18). If the magnitude (0 to 255) of the minuend is *less than* the magnitude of the subtrahend, the carry flag will be set to 1 (corresponding to a borrow).

```
0000   B0 B5      MOV AL,B5H    ;AL = B5H
0002   2C 6F      SUB AL,6FH    ;AL = AL- 6FH-C
```

Figure 10.18 Program to subtract 6FH from B5H.

The overflow flag *O* only has meaning when you are subtracting signed (two's complement) numbers. As in addition, the overflow flag *O* is set to 1 when the result is outside the range -128 through $+127$ for an 8-bit subtraction.

16-Bit Addition and Subtraction

The instructions *ADD* and *SUB* can be used to add and subtract 16-bit data using the 16-bit registers. For example, suppose you want to add the two hex values 37FAH and 82C4H. The result is BABEH, as shown by the following hexadecimal addition.

$$
\begin{array}{r}
37FAH \\
+82C4H \\
\hline
BABEH
\end{array}
$$

The program shown in Fig. 10.19 will add these two 16-bit numbers. Note that the instruction *MOV AX,37FAH* loads a 16-bit value into register *AX*, and the instruction *ADD AX,82C4H* adds a 16-bit value to *AX* with the result in *AX*. Enter this program and single step the two instructions.

```
0000   B8 FA 37      MOV   AX,37FAH      ;AX = 37FAH
0002   05 C4 82      ADD   AX,82C4H      ;AX = AX + 82C4H
```

Figure 10.19   Program to add 37FAH and 82C4H.

The carry flag is set if there is a carry from bit 15 of *AX* (bit 7 of AH). Bit 15 (the leftmost bit) of *AX* is the sign bit of *AX*. Negative numbers are represented as two's complement 16-bit numbers. Signed 16-bit numbers can have values ranging from 8000H ($-32,768$) to 7FFFH ($+32,767$).

Suppose you want to add the negative number FBH (-5) to the positive number 123AH. You can load the value FBH into accumulator *AL* (the low byte of *AX*), but what should be in accumulator *AH* (the high byte of *AX*)? Bit 7 of *AL* is the sign bit of the 8-bit number in *AL*. This bit must be extended through *AH* to give the proper 16-bit signed value in *AX*. If bit 7 of *AL* is 0, then *AH* should contain 00H; if bit 7 of *AL* is 1, then *AH* should contain FFH. The 8086 instruction *CBW* (convert byte to word) will extend the sign bit of *AL* into *AH*. For example, the program shown in Fig. 10.20 will add FBH to 123AH. Note that the answer, 1235H, is in register *AX*. Enter this program and single step the three instructions.

```
0000   B0 FB         MOV   AL,0FBH        AL = -5
0002   98            CBW                  ;AX = -5
0003   05 3A 12      ADD   AX,123AH       ;AX = AX + 123AH
```

Figure 10.20   Program to add FBH to 123AH.

Suppose you want to *subtract* the 16-bit value 8315H from A1C9H. The result is 1EB4H, as shown by the following hexadecimal subtraction:

$$
\begin{array}{r}
A1C9H \\
-8315H \\
\hline
1EB4H
\end{array}
$$

The program shown in Fig. 10.21 will subtract these two 16-bit numbers. Type in this program and single step the two instructions. After executing the *SUB* instruction with a 16-bit register, the carry bit will be set to 1 if the magnitude of the 16-bit minuend is *less than* the magnitude of the 16-bit subtrahend.

In addition to *ADD* and *SUB*, the instructions *INC* and *DEC* can be used to increment by 1 or decrement by 1 the contents of an 8- or 16-bit register or memory.

```
0000   B8 C9 A1      MOV   AX,A1C9H      ;AX = A1C9H
0003   2D 15 83      SUB   AX,8315H      ;AX = AX - 8315H
```

Figure 10.21   Program to subtract 8315H from A1C9H.

Binary Multiplication

Binary multiplication can be carried out bit by bit, in a manner similar to decimal multiplication, using Table 10.8.

TABLE 10.8   BINARY MULTIPLICATION TABLE

	0	1
0	0	0
1	0	1

Consider the multiplication example shown in Fig. 10.22. Note that as 1101 is multiplied by each binary digit in 1100 the partial product is shifted 1 bit to the left before adding the result. This is the same as in decimal multiplication. The binary multiplication example just given is equivalent to the hexadecimal multiplication

$$
\begin{array}{r}
D \\
\times\ C \\
\hline
9C
\end{array}
$$

Decimal	Binary
13	1101
x 12	1100
26	0000
13	0000
156	1101
	1101
	10011100

$$9 \quad C_{16} = 156_{10}$$

Figure 10.22   Example of binary multiplication.

TABLE 10.9   HEXADECIMAL MULTIPLICATION TABLE

	0	1	2	3	4	5	6	7	8	9	A	B	C	D	E	F
0	0	0	0	0	0	0	0	0	0	0	0	0	0	0	0	0
1		1	2	3	4	5	6	7	8	9	A	B	C	D	E	F
2			4	6	8	A	C	E	10	12	14	16	18	1A	1C	1E
3				9	C	F	12	15	18	1B	1E	21	24	27	2A	2D
4					10	14	18	1C	20	24	28	2C	30	34	38	3C
5						19	1E	23	28	2D	32	37	3C	41	46	4B
6							24	2A	30	36	3C	42	48	4E	54	5A
7								31	38	3F	46	4D	54	5B	62	69
8									40	48	50	58	60	68	70	78
9										51	5A	63	6C	75	7E	87
A											64	6E	78	82	8C	96
B												79	84	8F	9A	A5
C													90	9C	A8	B4
D														A9	B6	C3
E															C4	D2
F																E1

where the result can be read from the hexadecimal multiplication table given in Table 10.9.

Multiplying two 8-bit binary numbers is equivalent to multiplying two 2-digit hex numbers. The example in Fig. 10.23 shows how to do this using Table 10.9.

The 8086 instruction *MUL* (opcode = F6) will multiply the contents of accumulator *AL* by the contents of an 8-bit register or memory location specified by a postbyte and store the result in register *AX*. To try this instruction, type in the program shown in Fig. 10.24 and single step through it. This program loads the value 3DH into *AL* and the value 5AH into *BL* and then multiplies them. The result, 1572H, should be displayed in register *AX*.

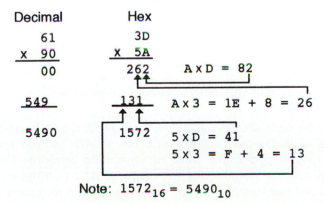

Figure 10.23 Performing binary multiplication using Table 10.9.

```
0000    B0 3D       MOV    AL,3DH              ;AL = 3DH
0002    B3 5A       MOV    BL,5AH              ;BL = 5AH
0004    F6 E3       MUL    BL                  ;AX = AL x BL
```

Figure 10.24   Program to multiply 3DH by 5AH.

The postbyte E3 given in Fig. 10.24 can be determined from the description of the *MUL* instruction given in Fig. 10.25. The form of the postbyte shown in Fig. 10.25 can be used to multiply the contents of *AL* or *AX* by an 8- or 16-bit register, respectively. The more general form of the postbyte

mod	PBOC	r/m

can be used to multiply the contents of *AL* or *AX* by a value in memory. In Chapter 12 we will show how different values of *mod* and *r/m* in this postbyte correspond to different addressing modes. Also note from Table A.2b in Appendix A that the value of *PBOC* in the postbyte for the *MUL* instruction is 100. This is the value used in Fig. 10.25.

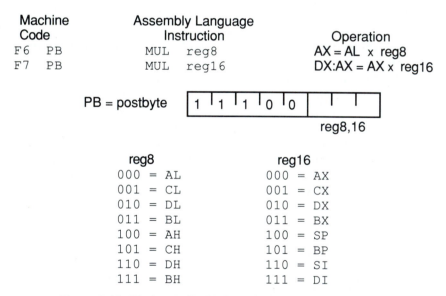

Figure 10.25   The instruction MUL performs unsigned multiplication.

When performing 8-bit multiplication using the form *MUL reg8*, the 16-bit product is stored in *AX*, with the most significant 8 bits in *AH* and the least significant 8 bits in *AL*. When performing 16-bit multiplication using the form *MUL reg16*, the 32-bit product is stored in registers *DX* and *AX*, with the most significant 16 bits in *DX* and the least significant 16 bits in *AX*. As an example, consider the following hex multiplication:

```
      31A4
    ×1B2C
    253B0
     6348
    2220C
     31A4
   544D430
```

The program shown in Fig. 10.26 will perform this multiplication. Type in the program and single step through it. Note that the result is stored in registers *DX* and *AX*.

```
0000   B8 A4 31      MOV   AX,31A4H    ;AX = 31A4H
0003   BB 2C 1B      MOV   BX,1B2CH    ;BX = 1B2CH
0006   F7 E3         MUL   BX          ;DX:AX = AX x BX
```

Figure 10.26   Program to multiply 31A4H by 1B2CH.

Signed multiplication.   Consider the following multiplication:

Decimal	*Hex*
165	A5
×36	×24
990	294
495	14A
5940	1734

Note that $5940_{10} = 1734_{16}$. This is an example of *unsigned* multiplication. The *MUL* instruction given in Fig. 10.25 applies only to unsigned multiplication. To check this, multiply the values A5H and 24H using the program in Fig. 10.26. The result should be 1734H stored in *AX*.

Now the value A5H could be interpreted as a two's complement value:

$$A5H = 10100101$$

$$\text{two's complement} = 01011011 = 5BH = 91_{10}$$

In this case A5H represents -91_{10}. The multiplication given above should then be as follows:

Decimal

```
  -91
  ×36
  546
  273
-3276
```

$$3276_{10} = 0CCC_{16}$$
$$= 0000\ 1100\ 1100\ 1100$$
$$\text{two's complement} = 1111\ 0011\ 0011\ 0100$$
$$= F334H$$

Therefore, considered as *signed* multiplication, the result of multiplying A5H by 24H should be F334H.

The program shown in Fig. 10.27 will multiply A5H (-91_{10}) by 24H (36_{10}) using the *signed* multiplication instruction, *IMUL*, given in Fig. 10.28. The (signed) result is F334H (-3276_{10}) and is stored in *AX*. Note that the machine code difference between *MUL* and *IMUL* occurs in the postbyte. Type in this program and single step through it.

```
0000   B0 A5        MOV   AL,A5H        ;AL = A5H
0002   B3 24        MOV   BL,24H        ;BL = 24H
0004   F6 EB        IMUL  BL            ;AX = AL x BL
```

Figure 10.27 Program to multiply (signed) A5H by 24H.

Machine Code	Assembly Language Instruction	Operation
F6 PB	IMUL reg8	AX = AL x reg8
F7 PB	IMUL reg16	DX:AX = AX x reg16

PB = postbyte

```
┌───┬───┬───┬───┬───┬───┬───┬───┐
│ 1 │ 1 │ 1 │ 0 │ 1 │   │   │   │
└───┴───┴───┴───┴───┴───┴───┴───┘
                            reg8,16
```

reg8	reg16
000 = AL	000 = AX
001 = CL	001 = CX
010 = DL	010 = DX
011 = BL	011 = BX
100 = AH	100 = SP
101 = CH	101 = BP
110 = DH	110 = SI
111 = BH	111 = DI

Figure 10.28 The instruction IMUL performs signed multiplication.

Binary Division

The 8086 has two instructions for performing binary division: *DIV* performs *unsigned* binary division and *IDIV* performs *signed* binary division. These instructions, involving 8- or 16-bit registers, are shown in Fig. 10.29. The more general form of the postbyte described earlier for the multiply instruction can be used to replace *reg8* and *reg16* with memory locations. Note that the first byte of the opcode is the same as the corresponding *MUL* (or *IMUL*) instruction. Only the postbyte distinguishes these different instructions, as is clear from Table A.2b in Appendix A.

Machine Code	Assembly Language Instruction	Operation
F6 PB	DIV reg8	AL = AX/reg8 (unsigned) AH = remainder
F7 PB	DIV reg16	AX = DX:AX/reg16 (unsigned) DX = remainder
F6 PBI	IDIV reg8	AL = AX/reg8 (signed) AH = remainder
F7 PBI	IDIV reg16	AX = DX:AX/reg16 (signed) DX = remainder

PB = postbyte (DIV)

1	1	1	1	1	0			

reg8,16

PBI = postbyte (IDIV)

1	1	1	1	1	1			

reg8,16

reg8	reg16
000 = AL	000 = AX
001 = CL	001 = CX
010 = DL	010 = DX
011 = BL	011 = BX
100 = AH	100 = SP
101 = CH	101 = BP
110 = DH	110 = SI
111 = BH	111 = DI

Figure 10.29   The 8086 binary division instructions.

As an example of using the *DIV* instruction, consider the following hexa-decimal long division where you can use Table 10.9 to help guess the next hex digit in the quotient and to perform hex multiplication of the divisor by the quotient digits.

```
                           CA = quotient
           divisor = EE )BC2F = dividend
                         B28
                          9AF
                          94C
                           63 = remainder
```

The program shown in Fig. 10.30 will perform this division. After executing this program, the quotient (CAH) should be stored in *AL* and the remainder (63H) should be stored in *AH*.

```
0000   B8 2F BC      MOV   AX,OBC2FH      ;AX = BC2FH
0003   B3 EE         MOV   BL,OEEH        ;BL = EEH
0005   F6 F3         DIV   BL             ;AL = AX/BL
```

Figure 10.30 Program to divide (unsigned) BC2FH by EEH.

Note that the instruction *DIV* involves dividing a 16-bit number by an 8-bit number (or a 32-bit number by a 16-bit number) with the quotient being an 8-bit number (or a 16-bit number). If the divisor is too small, the quotient may be larger than FFH (or FFFFH for a 16-bit number). If this happens, a divide-by-zero interrupt occurs. We will discuss interrupts in Chapters 11 and 14.

Packed BCD Arithmetic

Whereas computers add and subtract binary numbers, the people using the computers are more familiar with dealing with decimal numbers. For this reason, decimal numbers are normally entered through the keyboard and displayed on the screen. This means that the computer must convert a decimal number entered from the keyboard to a binary number, perform a calculation, and then convert the binary result to a decimal number before displaying it on the screen.

An alternative is to do the calculation in *decimal*, thus avoiding the conversion to binary. The 8086 microprocessor uses the decimal adjust instructions *DAA* (after addition) and *DAS* (after subtraction), to convert the result of a binary addition or subtraction to a packed *binary coded decimal (BCD)* result. A BCD digit is one of the decimal digits 0 to 9. These digits are coded using the 4-bit binary equivalent representations 0000 to 1001. The 4-bit combinations corresponding to the hex digits A to F are not allowed. An 8-bit byte can contain 2 BCD digits. Thus, the decimal number 35 is stored in packed BCD format as 35H = 00110101. Note that as a BCD number this is interpreted as 35_{10} and *not* as $35_{16} = 53_{10}$.

BCD addition. An example of the difference between binary and decimal addition is shown in Fig. 10.31. Note that the *hex values* 35H and 47H are used in both cases. The 8086 instruction *ADD AL,data* will always perform the binary addition shown on the left in Fig. 10.31. However, if this addition instruction is followed by the decimal adjust instruction, *DAA* (opcode = 27H), the binary result (7CH) will be changed to the corresponding decimal result (82H). To see this,

```
         Binary                          Decimal

     35H   00110101                  35H   00110101
   + 47H   01000111                + 47H   01000111
     7CH   01111100                  82H   10000010
```

Figure 10.31 Binary and decimal addition.

enter the program shown in Fig. 10.32 and single step through the three instructions. Following the *DAA* instruction, the carry will be set when the result of the decimal addition exceeds 99.

```
0000   B0 35          MOV  AL,35H        ;AL = 35H
0002   04 47          ADD  AL,47H        ;AL = AL + 47H
0004   27             DAA                ;Decimal adjust
```

Figure 10.32 Program to add BCD numbers.

Note that packed BCD numbers use all 8 bits in a byte (4 bits for each of 2 digits). Therefore, no sign bit is associated with BCD numbers. You must keep track of the sign of BCD numbers separately. The decimal adjust instruction, *DAA*, can only be used after an *addition to accumulator AL*.

BCD subtraction.   The statement *DAS* (opcode = 2FH), *decimal adjust accumulator after subtraction*, can be used following a binary subtraction from *AL* to convert the binary result to a BCD result. As an example, the program shown in Fig. 10.33 will subtract the BCD number 25 from 52. Type in this program and single step through it. Note particularly the effect of the *DAS* instruction.

```
0000   B0 52          MOV  AL,52H        ;AL = 52H
0002   2C 25          SUB  AL,25H        ;AL = AL - 25H
0004   2F             DAS                ;Decimal adjust
```

Figure 10.33 Program to subtract BCD numbers.

Unpacked BCD Arithmetic

The decimal adjust instructions *DAA* and *DAS* described above assume that the data are stored in packed BCD format, that is, 2 BCD digits per byte. When data are entered from the keyboard, for example, the data are initially stored as an ASCII code. That is, the BCD digits 0 to 9 are stored, 1 digit per byte, as the hex ASCII values 30H to 39H. Note that the low-order 4 bits in these ASCII codes are the correct BCD digits for the corresponding decimal value. If multiple-digit BCD numbers are stored 1 digit per byte (in the low-order 4 bits), we call this an *unpacked BCD format*.

The 8086 has four instructions that can be used in conjunction with unpacked BCD arithmetic. These are given in Fig. 10.34. The first two instructions (*AAA*

Machine Code	Assemble Language Instruction	Operation
37	AAA	Adjust result of ASCII addition
3F	AAS	Adjust result of ASCII subtraction
D4 0A	AAM	Adjust result of BCD multiplication
D5 0A	AAD	Adjust AX for BCD division

Figure 10.34 ASCII adjust instructions for unpacked BCD arithmetic.

and *AAS*) are used in a similar manner to *DAA* and *DAS* except that they assume unpacked BCD data. The instruction *AAM* is used following a binary multiply instruction when the original data are in unpacked BCD form. The instruction *AAD* is used *before* a binary division instruction to convert a BCD number in *AX* to a corresponding binary value. We will look at examples that use each of these instructions.

ASCII addition.   Consider the following decimal and ASCII addition:

	Decimal	*ASCII*
	9	39
	+6	+36
	15	01 05
		AH AL

If the ASCII code for 9 (39H) is stored in *AL* (unpacked BCD) and the ASCII code for 6 (36H) is added to *AL* using the instruction *ADD AL,36H*, the result (6FH) will be stored in *AL*. If the instruction *AAA* is then executed, the correct unpacked BCD result (15) will be stored in *AH* (01) and *AL* (05). (This assumes that the initial value of *AH* is 00.) To test this, type in the program in Fig. 10.35 and single step through it. Note that the result following the *AAA* instruction is stored in unpacked BCD form in *AH* and *AL*. If *AH* contained an initial value other than 00, then this initial value would simply have the 01 added to it. Following the execution of the *AAA* instruction, the carry flag, *C*, will be set to 1 if the BCD sum is greater than 9. Note that this is the case in Fig. 10.35.

```
0000   B8 39 00     MOV   AX,0039H      ;AL = 39H
0003   04 36        ADD   AL,36H        ;AL = AL + 36H
0005   37           AAA                 ;ASCII adjust
```

Figure 10.35   Example of unpacked BCD addition using ASCII adjust for addition, AAA.

ASCII subtraction.   Consider the following decimal and ASCII subtraction:

	Decimal	*ASCII*
	6	36
	-9	-39
borrow = 1	7	FF 07 carry flag = 1
		AH AL

The program in Fig. 10.36 will perform this subtraction. Following the *AAS* instruction, the contents of *AL* will contain the unpacked BCD result of the subtraction. If a borrow is required, the carry flag will be set and 1 will be subtracted from the *AH* register. Type in this program and single step through it.

```
0000   B8 36 00      MOV   AX,0036H      ;AL = 36H
0003   2C 39         SUB   AL,39H        ;AL = AL - 39H
0005   3F            AAS                 ;ASCII adjust
```

Figure 10.36 Example of unpacked BCD subtraction using ASCII adjust for subtraction, AAS.

BCD multiplication.   Consider the following decimal, binary (hex), and BCD multiplication:

Decimal	Binary (Hex)	BCD
8	08	08
×7	×07	×07
56	38	05 06
		AH AL

The *AAM* instruction can be used following an unsigned multiplication of two unpacked BCD numbers (with the high-order 4 bits equal to 0) to produce a BCD result with the high-order unpacked BCD digit in *AH* and the low-order unpacked BCD digit in *AL*.

The program in Fig. 10.37 will multiply 08 (in *AL*) by 07 (in *BL*) using the instruction *MUL BL* at offset address 0004. The result of this binary multiplication will be 38H, which is the binary representation of the decimal value 56. The instruction *AAM* divides this result by 10 (this is the value 0A in the machine code D4 0A) and stores the quotient (05) in *AH* and the remainder (06) in *AL*. These are the unpacked BCD digits of the decimal product. Type in this program and single step through it. Note that the final result is stored in *AH* (05) and *AL* (06).

```
0000   B0 08         MOV   AL,08H        ;AL = 08H
0002   B3 07         MOV   BL,07H        ;BL = 07H
0004   F6 E3         MUL   BL            ;AL = AL x BL
0006   D4 0A         AAM                 ;ASCII adjust
```

Figure 10.37 Example of unpacked BCD multiplication using ASCII adjust for multiplication, AAM.

BCD division.   Consider the following decimal division:

```
         9 = quotient
     6)56
        54
         2 = remainder
```

Recall that the unsigned binary division instruction *DIV* divides the (binary) contents of *AX* by *reg8* (for example, *BL*) and stores the quotient in *AL* and the remainder in *AH*. If you store the decimal value 56 as two unpacked BCD digits in *AH* and *AL* (05 in *AH* and 06 in *AL*), then the ASCII adjust instruction *AAD* (D5 0A) will convert this value in *AX* (0506) to the corresponding binary value (0036H). If the BCD divisor 06 is stored in *BL*, then the normal (unsigned) binary division will produce the correct quotient (09) and remainder (02) in *AL* and *AH*, respectively.

The program shown in Fig. 10.38 will perform this BCD division. Note that unlike the ASCII adjust for addition, subtraction, and multiplication, which are executed *after* the arithmetic operation, the ASCII adjust for division instruction, *AAD*, is executed *before* the *DIV* instruction. Single step the program in Fig. 10.36 and note how the *AAD* instruction modifies the contents of *AX* and how the final quotient is in *AL* and the remainder is in *AH*.

```
0000   B8 06 05      MOV   AX,0506H      ;AX = 0506H
0003   B3 06         MOV   BL,06         ;BL = 06H
0005   D5 0A         AAD                 ;Adjust AX for
                                         ;   BCD div
0007   F6 F3         DIV   BL            ;divide
```

Figure 10.38   Example of unpacked BCD division using ASCII adjust for division, AAD.

10.5 BASIC LOGICAL INSTRUCTIONS

The basic logical operators are *AND*, *OR*, and *NOT*. The *Exclusive-OR* operation (which can be defined in terms of the basic three logical operators) was defined earlier in this chapter in the section on carry and overflow. In Chapter 9, we saw that the 8086 *NOT* instruction took the one's complement of a byte or word; that is, it changed the state of each bit. The 8086 instructions *AND*, *OR*, and *XOR* perform the logical operations *AND*, *OR*, and *XOR* on a bit-by-bit basis according to Table 10.10. In this table, b_R represents a register bit and b_M can be a memory or a register bit. We can also *AND*, *OR*, and *XOR* immediate data with the contents of a register or memory.

TABLE 10.10   LOGICAL OPERATIONS

b_R	b_M	b_R AND b_M	b_R OR b_M	b_R XOR b_M
0	0	0	0	0
0	1	0	1	1
1	0	0	1	1
1	1	1	1	0

For example, the instruction

```
24 F0    AND AL,0F0H
```

will *AND* the value in accumulator *AL* with the value F0H. Notice that we have written F0H as 0F0H in the instruction. This is because the assembler (to be described in Chapter 11) requires all immediate values to begin with a digit (0 to 9). Otherwise, it will treat F0H as a possible label or variable name.

The opcodes associated with all instructions can be found from Table A.2 in Appendix A. This table shows the opcode space for the 8086. For example, the opcode for *AND AL,0F0H* is found from the entry *AND AL,imm* in row 2, column 4. Thus, the opcode is 24. Therefore, the two program bytes 24 F0 will AND accumulator *AL* with the immediate value 0F0H. Note from Table A.2 that some of the instructions are byte (*b*) instructions that involve 8-bit data and registers. Others are word (*w*) instructions that involve 16-bit data and registers.

The instruction *AND* performs a bit-by-bit AND operation of the contents of register *R* with the contents of memory location *M*, where *M* is specified by the addressing mode. In general, the result may be stored in the register *R* or memory location *M*. For the immediate mode, *M* will be the byte following the opcode and the result will be stored in the register *R*. Type in the two instructions in Fig. 10.39 and execute them in the single-step mode. Note that after executing the instruction *AND AL,0F0H* the value in accumulator *AL* will be 50H. That is, the lower nibble (the 4 bits 1010 = A) has been masked to zero. This is because ANDing anything with a zero produces a zero, while ANDing any bit with a 1 leaves the bit unchanged (see Table 10.10).

```
0000   B0 5A         MOV   AL,5AH
0002   24 F0         AND   AL,0F0H
```

Figure 10.39   ANDing a byte with F0H will mask the lower nibble.

A particular bit can be set to 1 by using the *OR* instruction. For example, the instructions in Fig. 10.40 will set bit 7 of accumulator *AL* by ORing the contents of *AL* (13H) with 80H. The resulting value of *AL* will be 93H. Type in these two instructions and execute them by single stepping. Do you see where the opcode 0C comes from in Table A.2?

```
0000   B0 13         MOV   AL,13H
0002   0C 80         OR    AL,80H
```

Figure 10.40   Bit 7 of accumulator A can be set by executing OR AL,80H.

Note from Table 10.10 that *0 XOR 1 = 1* and *1 XOR 1 = 0*. Thus, if you Exclusive-OR the contents of *AL* with FFH, you will obtain the one's complement of *AL*. For example, type in the two instructions in Fig. 10.41 and execute them

```
0000   B0 55        MOV   AL,55H
0002   34 FF        XOR   AL,0FFH
```

Figure 10.41 The one's complement of AL can be found by executing XOR AL,0FFH.

by single stepping. Note that the value 55H becomes AAH when Exclusive-ORed with FFH. The same result is achieved with the 2-byte instruction *NOT AL* (F6 D0).

Experiment 21: 8086 Instructions

1. Fill in the column labeled *Machine code* in the following table by looking up the opcodes in Appendix A.

Instruction	Machine code	Register value after execution		
		Binary	Hex	Carry
MOV AL,0A7H	B0 A7	AL = 10100111	A7	---
SHL AL,1		AL =		
RCL,AL,1		AL =		
NOT AL		AL =		
NEG AL		AL =		
SAR AL,1		AL =		
MOV AH,AL		AX =		
INC AX		AX =		
DEC AH		AX =		
MOV CX,AX		CX =		
SHR AH,1		AX =		
MOV SI,AX		SI =		
XCHG SI,CX		SI =		
MOV AX,CX		AX =		
MOV CL,4		CX =		
ROR AX,CL		AX =		
SHL AL,1		AX =		
RCR AX,1		AX =		
MOV DI,AX		DI =		
INC DI		DI =		
XCHG DI,AX		AX =		

2. Enter all the machine code into the computer starting at offset address 0000 using the TUTOR command */MH*. After entering the code, go to offset address 0000 and then type */UP*. This will disassemble your code on the right side of the screen and you can easily check to make sure you didn't make any errors in entering the code. To disassemble a longer block of code, you can type */LP*. This will replace the TUTOR memory display with the dis-

assembled code. Press the right arrow key (on the keypad digit 6) to disassemble another page. Press *Enter* to go back to TUTOR.

3. Fill in the *binary* and *hex* values of the indicated registers that will result when each instruction is executed. Also fill in the resulting value of the carry flag C. Verify each result by single stepping the instructions using the *F1* function key and observing the registers on the TUTOR screen.

Experiment 22: 8086 Arithmetic

1. Key in and single step through the program in Fig. 10.11. Modify the program so as to perform the additions in Figs. 10.13, 10.14, and 10.15. Explain the value of the carry and overflow flags in each case.

2. Key in and single step through the programs in Figs. 10.18, 10.19, 10.20, and 10.21. Key in a program that will subtract the hex number B3CF from 73D9. Single step the program and observe the value of the carry and overflow flags. Explain the results. Verify the subtraction by doing it by hand.

3. Key in and single step through the multiplication and division programs in Figs. 10.24, 10.26, 10.27, and 10.30. Modify the program in Fig. 10.30 to perform *signed* division by using *IDIV*. Use this program to carry out the following divisions:

$$26/7 \qquad -26/7 \qquad 26/-7 \qquad -26/-7$$

What is the relationship between the sign of the remainder and the sign of the dividend and/or divisor?

4. One high-resolution graphics screen on a PC is made up of a rectangular array of 640×200 dots. The horizontal or x coordinate increases from left to right (0 to 639). The vertical or y coordinate increases from top to bottom (0 to 199). Thus, the upper-left corner of the screen is coordinate (0,0). A rectangular box on the screen can be defined by giving its top-left and bottom-right coordinates. Assume that *AX* contains the value of *TOP*, *BX* contains *LEFT*, *CX* contains *BOTTOM*, and *DX* contains *RIGHT*. Write a routine that will leave the area of the rectangle in *DX:AX*. Assume that the area *contains* the coordinate points *TOP*, *LEFT*, *BOTTOM*, and *RIGHT*. For example, the width of the rectangle is $(RIGHT - LEFT + 1)$.

Test your program by entering the following values in the four general registers using /R:

```
TOP        AX = 0015H
LEFT       BX = 0022H
BOTTOM     CX = 00BDH
RIGHT      DX = 01FAH
```

Single step through your program and find the hex value of the area of the rectangle.

EXERCISES

10.1. Find the machine code instructions corresponding to the following assembly language instructions:

```
MOV    DL,CH
XCHG   AX,SI
XCHG   BL,DH
MOV    CX,DI
XCHG   DX,BX
```

Type in these instructions and single step through them.

10.2. Single step through a program that loads the hex value 2C into accumulator *AL*, transfers the value to register *AH*, and then exchanges the contents of *AX* and *BP*.

10.3. The opcodes for *STC* and *CLC* are F9 and F8, respectively. Enter the following bytes in memory starting at offset address 0000.

```
F9 F8 F9 F8 F9 F8 F9 F8
```

Single step through these instructions (by pressing key *F1*) and watch the carry flag.

10.4. Repeat the exercise shown in Fig. 10.5 using register *BL*. The opcode for *SHL BL,1* is D0 E3 (see Table 10.2).

10.5. Store the hex value 7B in accumulator *AL* and execute the instruction *SHL AL,1* eight times. What is the value of the carry bit and the hex value in accumulator *AL* after executing each instruction?

10.6. Store the hex value D5 in accumulator *AL* and execute the instruction *SHR AL,1* (D0 E8) eight times. What is the value in the carry bit and the hex value in accumulator *AL* after executing each instruction? Repeat using register *DL* (D0 EA).

10.7. Store the hex value 2C in accumulator *AL* and a 1 in the carry bit. (You can store a 1 in the carry bit by typing /*RF* 0001.) Execute the instruction *RCL AL,1* (D0 D0) eight times. What is the value in the carry bit and the hex value in accumulator *AL* after executing each instruction? Repeat using register *CL* (D0 D1).

10.8. Store the hex value 69 in accumulator *AL* and a 1 in the carry bit. Execute the instruction *RCR AL,1* (D0 D8) eight times. What is the value in the carry bit and the hex value in accumulator *AL* after executing each instruction? Repeat using register *BH* (D0 DF).

10.9. Store the hex value 85 in accumulator *AL*. Execute the instruction *ROL AL,1* (D0 C0) eight times. What is the value in the carry bit and the hex value in accumulator *AL* after executing each instruction? Repeat using the instruction *ROR AL,1* (D0 C8).

10.10. Store the hex value B1 in accumulator *AL* and execute the instruction *SAR AL,1* (D0 F8) eight times. What is the value in the carry bit and the hex value in accumulator *AL* after executing each instruction? Repeat using register *BH* (D0 FF).

10.11. Store the hex value 05 in *AL* and execute the two instructions

```
MOV    CL,3
SHL    AL,CL
```

Do these two instructions multiply by 8?

10.12. Store the hex value 6A34 in *DX* and execute the two instructions

```
MOV   CL,0AH
SHR   DX,CL
```

Do these two instructions divide by 1024?

10.13. Modify the program in Fig. 10.18 to perform the following subtractions. In each case explain the answer in accumulator *AL* and the value of the carry flag *C* and the overflow flag *O*.

   a. 73H − A1H
   b. BBH − F2H
   c. D3H − 47H
   d. E1H − C3H

10.14. Modify the programs in Figs. 10.19 and 10.21 to perform the following additions and subtractions.

   a. 31A4H + B120H
   b. 4BCFH − 182AH
   c. ABCDH − 813CH
   d. 015DH + 3AFFH

10.15. Single step through a program that will perform each of the following multiplications and divisions. Verify the results in each case.

   a. 4FH × 31H
   b. 4217H / AAH

   c. 183CH × 209FH
   d. 135A2C1BH / D1C4H

10.16. Modify the program in Fig. 10.32 to perform the following decimal additions. In each case indicate the answer in accumulator *AL* and the value of the carry flag *C*.

   a. 49 + 34
   b. 73 + 47
   c. 20 + 36
   d. 55 + 69

10.17. Modify the program in Fig. 10.33 to perform the following decimal subtractions. In each case indicate the answer in accumulator *AL* and the value of the carry flag *C*.

   a. 89 − 35
   b. 63 − 27
   c. 46 − 63
   d. 23 − 47

10.18. Modify the programs in Figs. 10.35 through 10.38 to perform the following unpacked BCD arithmetic operations.

   a. 4 + 8
   b. 7 − 5
   c. 8 × 6
   d. 37 / 5

11

8086 Programs

In Chapter 10 you became familiar with a number of the 8086 instructions. You were able to execute these instructions in short programs that you entered using the TUTOR monitor. We now want to see how these instructions can be used to form larger programs. For a program to be useful we need to be able to alter the order of execution of the instructions based on what has previously occurred in the program. In 8086 programs we use branching instructions to accomplish this, and we will look at these instructions in Section 11.1.

The secret to writing large assembly language programs is to break the program into lots of little programs that are written in terms of modules. One form of module is the subroutine that we will look at in Section 11.2. Another type of module is the software interrupt call, such as the BIOS and DOS calls. We will see how these work in Section 11.3.

You will learn the most about assembly language programming by debugging your own programs. In Section 11.4 we will see how the TUTOR monitor makes it easy for you to debug programs that are assembled using a macro assembler.

In this chapter you will learn:

- The 8086 conditional and unconditional jump instructions
- How to calculate branching displacements
- How to use the *LOOP* instruction
- How a stack works
- How to use the *PUSH* and *POP* instructions
- How subroutines and software interrupts work

- The general structure of an 8086 assembly language program
- How to load .EXE files into TUTOR, set breakpoints, and debug programs
- How to generate an object file using a macro assembler and to link one or more of these object modules to produce an executable .EXE file.

11.1 BRANCHING INSTRUCTIONS

A computer program achieves its apparent power by being able to conditionally branch to different parts of a program. The 8086 microprocessor uses branching or conditional jump instructions for this purpose. A conditional jump instruction can cause a branch in the program to occur, depending on the state of one or more of the bits in the status register. In this section we will look at the 8086 instructions related to branching.

Conditional Jump Instructions

The 8086 has a large number of conditional branching instructions. The instructions shown in Table 11.1 test the state of one of the status flags. Other branching instructions described later in this section test some combination of the status flags.

TABLE 11.1   SOME CONDITIONAL JUMP INSTRUCTIONS

Operation	Mnemonic	Opcode	Branch test
Jump on equal zero	JE/JZ	74	$Z = 1$
Jump on not equal zero	JNE/JNZ	75	$Z = 0$
Jump on not sign	JNS	79	$S = 0$
Jump on sign	JS	78	$S = 1$
Jump on not below (not carry)	JNB/JAE/JNC	73	$C = 0$
Jump on below (carry)	JB/JNAE/JC	72	$C = 1$
Jump on overflow	JO	70	$O = 1$
Jump on not overflow	JNO	71	$O = 0$
Jump on parity (even)	JP/JPE	7A	$P = 1$
Jump on not parity (odd)	JNP/JPO	7B	$P = 0$

A branching instruction will cause a branch to occur if the branch test is true. For example, the branching instruction *JE* (jump on equal) will cause a branch in the program if the *Z* flag in the status register is 1. This will be the case if the result of the previous instruction produced a result of zero.

The conditional jump instructions shown in Table 11.1 are all 2 bytes long. The first byte is the opcode, whose values for the eight branching instructions shown in Table 11.1 are given in the table. The second byte of the instruction is the *relative displacement* of the branch destination. This is the two's complement number that must be added to the value of the instruction pointer + 2 (the offset address of the next instruction) to obtain the offset address of the instruction to be executed if the branch test is *true*. If the branch test is *false*, then the instruction following the branching instruction is executed. This is illustrated in Fig. 11.1. Note that if $Z = 1$ when the *JE* instruction is executed, the program will branch to the offset address formed by adding the displacement (06) to the offset address of the next instruction (0014), that is, to offset address 001A = 0014 + 06.

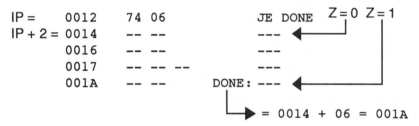

Figure 11.1 The displacement (06) in a branching instruction is added to the instruction pointer + 2 to obtain the destination offset address of the branch.

If a branching instruction branches backward in memory, the displacement must be negative. It is just the two's complement of the number of bytes between the offset address of the next instruction ($IP + 2$) and the branch destination offset address. Note that, since the branch displacement is a single 8-bit byte, a branching instruction can only branch forward a maximum of 127 bytes (7FH) and backward a maximum of -128 bytes (80H). The counting of these bytes always begins at the offset address of the instruction *following* the branching instruction. These displacements are automatically calculated by the assembler. Note that all conditional jumps take place within a given segment.

Unconditional Jump Instructions

The instructions in Table 11.1 are *conditional* jump instructions that may or may not cause a branch to occur depending on the value of one of the status flags. Sometimes you may want to jump no matter what. This is called an unconditional jump. Three different versions of the unconditional jump instruction are shown in Table 11.2.

The short *JMP* instruction (opcode = EB) has an 8-bit displacement as an operand. This is the same two's complement displacement described above for conditional jump instructions. It will allow an unconditional jump a maximum of 127 bytes forward or 128 bytes backward.

If you need to jump a farther distance within a segment, you can use the long form of the *JMP* instruction (opcode = E9). This requires a 2-byte operand

TABLE 11.2 SOME UNCONDITIONAL JUMP INSTRUCTIONS

Operation	Mnemonic	Opcode	Operand
Short jump	JMP	EB	8-Bit displacement
Long jump	JMP	E9	16-Bit displacement
Absolute jump	JMP	EA	Segment address: offset address

that represents a 16-bit two's complement number that must be added to the offset address of the next instruction to obtain the destination offset address.

All the branching instructions described so far use a *relative* displacement in the operand. This will allow a branch to any offset address within a given segment. Most conditional branch instructions are to nearby addresses, so a 1-byte (8-bit) displacement is sufficient. If, on occasion, you need to jump conditionally to a distant location within the segment, you can use the long *JMP* instruction. For example, the instruction

```
        JE distant
next:   -----
```

can be replaced with

```
        JNE next
        JMP distant
next:   -----
```

where *distant* is a 16-bit displacement. A 16-bit displacement can have values between +32,767 (7FFFH) and −32,728 (8000H). These displacements, when added to the value in the instruction pointer + 2, will produce an offset address that will wrap around within the current segment. That is, branching instructions that use relative displacements in the operand cannot jump out of the current segment.

To jump to a new segment, you must use a different form of the *JMP* statement. One version is the absolute *JMP* instruction (opcode = EA) shown in Table 11.2. The operand for this instruction contains a new offset address plus a new segment address. For example, suppose you want to jump to the absolute address 0123:4567. The following instruction will do this.

```
EA 67 45 23 01    JMP 0123:4567
```

Note that the opcode (EA) is followed first by the destination offset address (low byte, high byte) and then by the destination segment address (low byte, high byte).

Within a given segment, both short and long jump instructions use a *relative* displacement in the instruction. Since this is the number that is *added* to the offset address of the following instruction, it is independent of the destination offset address. This means that, if the entire program is moved within the segment, this relative displacement does not change. The use of relative displacements for determining a destination address will allow you to write *position-independent code*. This means that a program within a given segment can be moved to any location in memory and still run.

Calculating branching displacements. If you are entering short programs using the TUTOR monitor, you can either calculate the branching displacements by hand or automatically using the /J TUTOR monitor command. Suppose a branching instruction is to branch backward -8 bytes from the address of the next instruction. Since -8 is represented as a two's complement hexadecimal number by F8H, the branching displacement will be F8, as shown in Fig. 11.2. Note that this subtraction is done by subtracting the address of the next instruction ($IP + 2$) from the destination offset address. The result, FFF8H, is the 16-bit hexadecimal representation of -8_{10}. When a two's complement, 8-bit hexadecimal number such as F8 is stored as a 16-bit number, the sign bit (1 in this case) is extended to the left through the high-order byte. Thus, F8H and FFF8H both represent the negative number -8_{10}. When using a short jump instruction, the displacement F8H is used; when using a long jump instruction, the displacement FFF8H is used.

```
             000C      --              LOOP1:  ---
             000D      -- --                   ---
             000F      -- -- --                 ---
  IP =       0012      75 F8                   JNE LOOP1
  IP + 2 =   0014      -- --                   ---
             0016      -- -- --

                                        000C   LOOP1
                                       -0014   IP + 2
                                        FFF8
```

Figure 11.2 Negative branches can be found by subtracting the offset address of the next instruction from the destination offset address.

If you are entering a machine language program into memory using TUTOR and you don't know the branching displacements, you can have TUTOR calculate these displacements for you. When you enter a machine language program with TUTOR (by using /MH) and you come to the location of a jump displacement, just type 00 if it is a short jump instruction and 00 00 if it is a long jump instruction. These will leave 1 or 2 bytes where the displacement is to go. Then go back to each of these displacement locations and type /J. The command line will display

```
JUMP DISPLACEMENT:   L S
```

Type *L* for a long jump or *S* for a short jump. The command line will then display

ENTER DESTINATION OFFSET ADDRESS

Enter the destination offset address and the correct displacement will automatically be inserted at the current position cursor location (that is, at the location of the displacement byte) when you press the ENTER key. If you had pressed *S*, one displacement byte is inserted. If you had pressed *L*, two displacement bytes are inserted.

Try this by going to location 0013. Then type */JS 000C*. The displacement F8H should be inserted at 0013, as shown in Fig. 11.2. If you now type */JS 001A*, the displacement 06H will be inserted at 0013, as shown in Fig. 11.1.

Branching Examples

The following short examples will illustrate branching on the state of the *Z*, *S*, and *C* flags.

Branching on the zero flag Z.   Type in the program shown in Fig. 11.3 starting at offset address 0000. You should verify the displacements FD (at offset address 0004) and F8 (at offset address 0007) by using the */J* displacement calculation feature of the TUTOR monitor described above.

```
0000   B9 03 00        LOOP1:   MOV   CX,3
0003   49              LOOP2:   DEC   CX
0004   75 FD                    JNE   LOOP2
0006   74 F8                    JE    LOOP1
```

Figure 11.3   JNE and JE branch on Z = 0 and Z = 1, respectively.

Now single step through this program starting at offset address 0000. After executing the instruction *DEC CX* (at 0003) the first time, the value of *CX* is 02H and the value of the zero flag *Z* is zero. Therefore, the *JNE* instruction at address 0004 will branch back to address 0003 and execute *DEC CX* again. The value of *CX* will now be 01H and the *Z* flag will still be zero. Therefore, the *JNE* instruction will branch back to address 0003 again. This time the *DEC CX* instruction will cause the value of *CX* to go to zero. This will cause the *Z* flag to be set to 1. The test *Z* = 0 of the *JNE* instruction will fail, so another branch will not occur. The next instruction at address 0006 will therefore be executed. This is a *JE* instruction that will branch if *Z* = 1. But the *Z* flag will be equal to 1 (otherwise, the *JNE* instruction would have jumped), and therefore the program will jump to address 0000 and you can single step through the program again. Single step through this program several times, observing the value of the *Z* flag and the contents of *CL*.

Branching on the sign flag S.   The program shown in Fig. 11.4 will test the branching instructions *JNS* and *JS*. Type in this program and single step through it. The value in *CL* is set to 7DH at address 0000 and then incremented by 1 (to 7EH) at address 0002. The *S* flag will be zero (7EH is a positive number), so the JNS instruction will branch back to address 0002. Register *CL* will then be incremented to 7FH (still positive), so the *JNS* instruction will branch back again to the *INC CL* instruction. This time *CL* will be incremented to 80H, which is a negative number (-128_{10}) because bit 7 is set to 1. This will cause the sign flag *S* in the status register to be set to 1, so the *JNS* test ($S = 0$) will fail. The *JS* instruction at address 0006 will then be executed, which will always (because $S = 1$) branch back to address 0000. Single step through this program several times and observe the value of the *S* flag and the contents of *CL*.

```
0000   B1  7D      LOOP1:   MOV   CL,7DH
0002   FE  C1      LOOP2:   INC   CL
0004   79  FC               JNS   LOOP2        Figure 11.4   JNS and JS branch on
0006   78  F8               JS    LOOP1        S = 0 and S = 1, respectively.
```

Branching on the carry flag C.   The example given in Fig. 11.3 decrements register *CL* until it becomes zero. The example given in Fig. 11.4 increments register *CL* until it becomes negative (equal to 80H). Suppose you wanted to decrement register *AL* until it became less than a particular value, say 2BH. The program shown in Fig. 11.5 will do this. Type in the program and single step through it.

```
0000   B0  2E      LOOP1:   MOV   AL,2EH
0002   FE  C8      LOOP2:   DEC   AL
0004   3C  2B               CMP   AL,2BH
0006   73  FA               JNB   LOOP2        Figure 11.5   JNB and JB branch on
0008   72  F6               JC    LOOP1        C = 0 and C = 1, respectively.
```

The *CMP* (compare) instruction at address 0004 will subtract the value 2BH from the current value of *AL*. Recall from Section 10.4 that the carry flag, *C*, will be set to 1 if the magnitude of *AL* (considered to be an 8-bit positive number from 0 to 255_{10}) is less than 2BH. If *AL* is greater than or equal to 2BH, then the carry flag will be cleared to zero. Thus, the *JNB* (jump on not below or jump on not carry) instruction at address 0006 will branch if the value of *AL* is "not below" 2BH. That is, if *AL* is larger than or equal to 2BH, a branch will occur. The *JC* (jump on carry or jump on below) instruction at address 0008 will always branch because the carry flag will have to be set to get to the instruction. Single step through this program several times and observe the value of the *C* flag and the contents of accumulator *AL*.

An example that branches on the *overflow flag* is left as an exercise at the end of the chapter.

Other Conditional Jump Instructions

The conditional jump instructions given in Table 11.1 are the ones most commonly used. In fact, you can get by using only these. However, sometimes it is convenient to use the additional conditional jump instructions given in Tables 11.3 and 11.4. You must, however, be careful. It is very easy to make a mistake when using these conditional jump instructions. The instructions in Table 11.3 must only be used when you are thinking about *unsigned* numbers, that is, 8-bit numbers with decimal values between 0 and 255 (00H to FFH) or 16-bit numbers with decimal values between 0 and 65,535 (0000H to FFFFH).

The branching instructions in Table 11.4 must only be used when you are thinking about *signed* numbers, that is, 8-bit signed numbers with decimal values between -128 (80H) and $+127$, (7FH) or 16-bit signed numbers with decimal values between $-32,768$ (8000H) and $+32,767$ (7FFFH).

It is very easy to confuse the instructions in Tables 11.3 and 11.4. This can lead to execution errors that are sometimes hard to find. For example, suppose register *CL* is used as a counter and you want to go through a loop 200_{10} (C8H)

TABLE 11.3   CONDITIONAL JUMP INSTRUCTIONS TO USE FOLLOWING A COMPARISON OF *UNSIGNED* NUMBERS

Operation	Mnemonic	Opcode	Branch test
Jump on above (not below or equal)	JA/JNBE	77	C # Z = 0
Jump on below or equal (not above)	JBE/JNA	76	C # Z = 1
Jump on above or equal (not below, not carry)	JAE/JNB/JNC	73	C = 0
Jump on below (carry) (not above or equal)	JB/JNAE/JC	72	C = 1

TABLE 11.4   CONDITIONAL JUMP INSTRUCTIONS TO USE FOLLOWING A COMPARISON OF *SIGNED* NUMBERS

Operation	Mnemonic	Opcode	Branch test
Jump on greater than or equal (not less)	JGE/JNL	7D	S $ O = 0
Jump on less than (not greater or equal)	JL/JNGE	7C	S $ O = 1
Jump on greater than (not less than or equal)	JG/JNLE	7F	Z # (S $ O) = 0
Jump on less than or equal (not greater)	JLE/JNG	7E	Z # (S $ O) = 1

times. You might think that the following loop will work:

```
      MOV  CL,0        ;set CL = 0
LOOP: INC  CL          ;increment CL
      CMP  CL,C8H      ;compare CL to C8H
      JL   LOOP        ;loop if CL<200
```

It won't! The branching instruction *JL LOOP* will fail the first time. This is because the value of *CL* is 1 and the value of C8H is not 200_{10} but is -56_{10}. Remember that the *JL* instruction (and all the instructions in Table 11.4) consider all numbers to be two's complement *signed* numbers. Inasmuch as 1 (the value of *CL*) is greater than -56_{10}, the instruction *JL* will not branch.

The instruction you really want to use is *JB* (jump on below). This instruction and all instructions in Table 11.3 treat all numbers as unsigned numbers, so C8H is considered to be 200_{10} and not -56_{10}.

In Table 11.3 note that the instructions *JAE/JNB* and *JB/JNAE* test only the carry flag. All other instructions in Tables 11.3 and 11.4 use branch tests that involve more than one status flag.

Loop Instructions

The 8086 has three versions of a *LOOP* instruction that make it easy to form loops. These loop instructions are given in Table 11.5. The statement

```
LOOP   disp8
```

decrements *CX* and jumps if $CX \neq 0$. The value of *disp8* is an 8-bit two's complement displacement calculated the same as for the conditional jump instructions.

As an example, the program in Fig. 11.6 is equivalent to the program in Fig. 11.3. Note that the *LOOP* instruction loops on itself. This is okay because *CX* is

TABLE 11.5 LOOP INSTRUCTIONS

Opcode	Assembly language instruction	Operation
E2	Loop disp8	Dec CX and jump if $CX \neq 0$
E1	LOOPZ disp8 or LOOPE disp8	Dec CX and jump if $CX \neq 0$ and $Z = 1$
E0	LOOPNZ disp8 or LOOPNE disp8	Dec CX and jump if $CX \neq 0$ and $Z = 0$
E3	JCXZ disp8	Jump if $CX = 0$

```
0000   B9 03 00       L1:     MOV    CX,3
0003   E2 FE          L2:     LOOP   L2
0005   EB F9                  JMP    L1
```

Figure 11.6 Using a LOOP instruction to form an equivalent loop to that in Fig. 11.3.

decremented by 1 each time the *LOOP* instruction is executed. Type in this program and single step through it several times.

The *LOOP* instruction can be thought of as implementing a *repeat while CX* $\neq$ 0 or a *repeat until CX* = 0 loop, as shown in Fig. 11.7. Sometimes you would like to implement a *do while* loop, which is not executed at all if *CX* is equal to 0 at the beginning of the loop. The *JCXZ* instruction in Table 11.5 can be used at the beginning of a loop to accomplish this, as shown in Fig. 11.8.

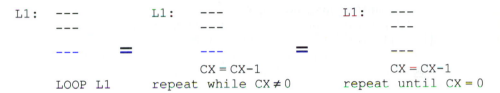

Figure 11.7 The LOOP instruction can implement a *repeat while* or *repeat until* loop.

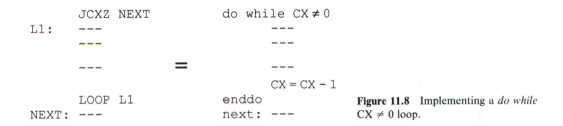

Figure 11.8 Implementing a *do while* CX $\neq$ 0 loop.

Two other forms of the *LOOP* instruction are shown in Table 11.5. The *LOOPZ* (or *LOOPE*) instruction will decrement *CX* and jump if *CX* $\neq$ 0 *and Z* = 1. Thus, an early exit from the loop will occur if the instruction preceding *LOOPZ* produced a nonzero result.

The *LOOPNZ* (or *LOOPNE*) instruction will decrement *CX* and jump if *CX* $\neq$ 0 *and Z* = 0. That is, an early exit from the loop will occur if the instruction preceding *LOOPNZ* produced a zero result.

11.2 THE STACK AND SUBROUTINES

The stack is a group of memory locations in which temporary data can be stored. A stack is different from any other collection of memory locations in that data are put on and taken from the *top* of the stack. The process is similar to stacking dinner plates on top of one another, where the last plate put on the stack is always the first one removed from it. We sometimes refer to this as a *last in, first out* or LIFO stack.

The offset memory address corresponding to the top of the stack (the last full location) is stored in the stack pointer, *SP*. The actual stack address is found by combining the offset address in the stack pointer with the segment address in the stack segment register, *SS*. When data are put on the stack, the stack pointer is *decremented*. This means that the stack grows *backward* in memory. As data values are put on the stack, they are put into memory locations with lower addresses. Data can be put on and taken off the stack 2 bytes at a time using *PUSH* and *POP* instructions.

PUSH and POP Instructions

The *PUSH* and *POP* instructions of the 8086 are given in Table 11.6. The *PUSH* and *POP* instructions always move 2 bytes (16 bits) at a time to and from the stack. As shown in Table 11.6, any 16-bit register can be pushed on (or popped from) the stack using a 1-byte opcode. A 2-byte opcode can be used to push (or pop) data directly from (or to) a memory location. The postbytes | *mod* | 110 | *r/m* | and | *mod* | 000 | *r/m* | determine the memory locations involved using the addressing modes described in Chapter 12. In this chapter we will illustrate pushing and popping the contents of registers.

TABLE 11.6 PUSH AND POP INSTRUCTIONS

Operation	Mnemonic	Opcode encoding
Push register on stack	PUSH reg	01010rrr
Push segment reg on stack	PUSH segreg	000ss110
Push status reg on stack	PUSHF	9C
Push 16 bits from memory	PUSH mem	FF |mod|110|r/m|
Pop register from stack	POP reg	01011rrr
Pop segment reg from stack	POP segreg	000ss111
Pop status reg from stack	POPF	9D
Pop 16 bits to memory	POP mem	8F |mod|000|r/m|

rrr	reg	ss	segreg
000	AX	00	ES
001	CX	01	CS (cannot POP to CS)
010	DX	10	SS
011	BX	11	DS
100	SP		
101	BP		
110	SI		
111	DI		

For example, suppose you want to push the value of register *AX* on the stack. From Table 11.6 the opcode for *PUSH AX* is 50H. When you first run TUTOR, the stack pointer, *SP*, contains the value 0FFF. The stack segment, *SS*, will be the same as the code segment in which the current memory is being displayed. These values are displayed on the far right side of the TUTOR screen beside the word STACK. Note that the stack is empty (no values are displayed under the word STACK).

The program shown in Fig. 11.9 will load *AX* with the value 1234H and then push *AX* on the stack. Type in this program and single step through it. Note that when the *PUSH AX* instruction at address 0003 is executed the value 1234H is pushed on the stack and the value of the stack pointer (the address on the top of the stack) has been decremented to 0FFD, as shown in Fig. 11.10. When the

```
0000   B8 34 12       MOV  AX,1234H
0003   50             PUSH AX
```

Figure 11.9   Program to push AX on the stack.

```
     8086 Microprocessor TUTOR          Press F7 for Help

   AH AL    BH BL     CH CL      DH DL    DATA SEG    08 19 2A 3B 4C 5D 6E 7F
AX 12 34  BX 11 C5  CX 00 C5  DX 3A EE    1574:0000   B8 34 12 50 00 00 00 00
                                          1574:0008   00 00 00 00 00 00 00 00
   SP 0FFD      SI 0000      IP 0004      1574:0010   00 00 00 00 00 00 00 00
   BP 0000      DI 0000                   1574:0018   00 00 00 00 00 00 00 00
   SS 1574      DS 1574      CS 1574      1574:0020   00 00 00 00 00 00 00 00
SP+SS 1673D  SI+DS 15740     ES 1574      1574:0028   00 00 00 00 00 00 00 00
BP+SS 15740  DI+DS 15740  IP+CS 15744     1574:0030   00 00 00 00 00 00 00 00
STATUS FLAGS 7206 0111001000000110        1574:0038   00 00 00 00 00 00 00 00
               ODITSZ A P C               1574:0040   00 00 00 00 00 00 00 00
1574:0004 0000        ADD   [BX+SI],AL    1574:0048   00 00 00 00 00 00 00 00

SEG 1574:   08 19 2A 3B 4C 5D 6E 7F                        1574: STACK
   FFE8   00 00 00 00 00 00 00 00    . . . . . . . .       0FFD   1234
   FFF0   00 00 00 00 00 00 00 00    . . . . . . . .
   FFF8   00 00 00 00 00 00 00 00    . . . . . . . .
   0000   B8 34 12 50>00 00 00 00    . 4 . P . . . .
   0008   00 00 00 00 00 00 00 00    . . . . . . . .
   0010   00 00 00 00 00 00 00 00    . . . . . . . .
   0018   00 00 00 00 00 00 00 00    . . . . . . . .

                                          / : Command    > : Go To Memory
                                          Use Cursor Keys to Scroll thru Memory
```

Figure 11.10   Screen display after executing the program in Fig. 11.9.

instruction *PUSH AX* is executed, the following steps occur:

1. The stack pointer *SP* is decremented by 1 (to 0FFEH).
2. The contents of *AH* are stored at the address in *SP* (0FFEH).
3. The stack pointer *SP* is decremented by 1 again (to 0FFDH).
4. The contents of *AL* are stored at the address in *SP* (0FFDH).

The result is that the value in *AH* (12H) is stored in location 0FFEH and the value in *AL* (34H) is stored in location 0FFDH, and the value of *SP* has been decremented by 2 to 00FDH, as shown in Fig. 11.11. Go to offset address 0FFDH in the current segment and verify that, in fact, this is where the value 1234H was stored.
    If the statement

```
0004   5B      POP   BX
```

is added to the program in Fig. 11.9, then the same two values pushed on the stack will be popped off the stack and stored in register *BX*. This statement causes the following steps to occur:

1. The value at the offset address stored in *SP* is loaded into register *BL*.
2. The stack pointer is incremented by 1.
3. The value at the new address stored in *SP* is loaded into register *BH*.
4. The stack pointer is incremented by 1.

Therefore, the final value of *SP* will be 0FFF.
    Note that the values pushed on the stack in Fig. 11.9 can be popped off into another register. Try this by adding the above statement to the program in Fig. 11.9 and then single step this one statement (assuming that the value 1234H is still on the stack from single stepping the statements in Fig. 11.9).

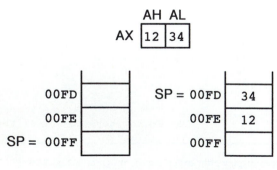

Figure 11.11 Pushing AX on the stack.

Subroutines

A subroutine is a segment of code that is normally written to perform a particular function or task. A subroutine is called by executing a *CALL* instruction. A subroutine is exited by executing a *return from subroutine* (*RET*) instruction. This will cause the program to return to the instruction following the *CALL* instruction that called the subroutine.

The computer knows where to go when a *RET* instruction is executed because it stored the return address on the stack when the *CALL* instruction was executed. To see how this works, key in all the instructions shown in Fig. 11.12.

```
0000    E8 05 00              CALL  0008H
0003    E8 0A 00              CALL  0010H
0006    CC                    INT   3
---------------------------------------------
0008    E8 05 00              CALL  0010H
000B    C3                    RET
---------------------------------------------
0010    C3                    RET
```

Figure 11.12 Illustrating the CALL and RET instructions.

```
        8086 Microprocessor TUTOR          Press F7 for Help

     AH AL     BH BL     CH CL     DH DL    DATA SEG    08 19 2A 3B 4C 5D 6E 7F
  AX 00 00  BX 11 C5  CX 00 C5  DX 3A EE    1574:0000   E8 05 00 E8 0A 00 CC 00
                                            1574:0008   E8 05 00 C3 00 00 00 00
     SP 0FFD      SI 0000      IP 0008       1574:0010   C3 00 00 00 00 00 00 00
     BP 0000      DI 0000                    1574:0018   00 00 00 00 00 00 00 00
     SS 1574      DS 1574      CS 1574       1574:0020   00 00 00 00 00 00 00 00
  SP+SS 1673D  SI+DS 15740      ES 1574      1574:0028   00 00 00 00 00 00 00 00
  BP+SS 15740  DI+DS 15740  IP+CS 15748      1574:0030   00 00 00 00 00 00 00 00
  STATUS FLAGS 7206 0111001000000110         1574:0038   00 00 00 00 00 00 00 00
                    ODITSZ A P C             1574:0040   00 00 00 00 00 00 00 00
  1574:0008 E80500      CALL   0010H         1574:0048   00 00 00 00 00 00 00 00

  SEG 1574:   08 19 2A 3B 4C 5D 6E 7F                          1574: STACK
       FFF0   00 00 00 00 00 00 00 00    . . . . . . . .         0FFD   0003
       FFF8   00 00 00 00 00 00 00 00    . . . . . . . .
       0000   E8 05 00 E8 0A 00 CC 00    . . . . . . . .
       0008  >E8 05 00 C3 00 00 00 00    . . . . . . . .
       0010   C3 00 00 00 00 00 00 00    . . . . . . . .
       0018   00 00 00 00 00 00 00 00    . . . . . . . .
       0020   00 00 00 00 00 00 00 00    . . . . . . . .

                                     / : Command     > : Go To Memory
                                     Use Cursor Keys to Scroll thru Memory
```

Figure 11.13 Screen display after executing CALL 0008H at address 0000.

Note that this shows three separate modules: a main program starting at offset address 0000 and two subroutines starting at offset addresses 0008 and 0010.

The first instruction is *CALL 0008H*. This form of the *CALL* statement (opcode = E8) uses a 16-bit relative displacement as an operand. This is the same type of two's complement relative displacement used in the long *JMP* instruction described in Section 11.1. You can use the */JL* TUTOR command to calculate the displacement 0005 stored at offset address 0001 in Fig. 11.12. This displacement (0005) is added to the offset address of the next instruction (0003) to obtain the destination offset address 0008 = 0003 + 0005. If you single step this instruction, the program will jump to offset address 0008H, and the offset address 0003H will be pushed on the stack, as shown in Fig. 11.13.

The offset address of the next instruction is 0003H. This is the address stored on the stack. When a *RET* instruction (opcode = C3) is executed, it pops the top offset address from the stack and puts it in the instruction pointer. This will cause the program to return to the instruction following the *CALL* instruction that called the subroutine.

The first instruction of the subroutine at offset address 0008H is another

```
        8086 Microprocessor TUTOR          Press F7 for Help

      AH AL     BH BL     CH CL     DH DL    DATA SEG    08 19 2A 3B 4C 5D 6E 7F
   AX 00 00  BX 11 C5  CX 00 C5  DX 3A EE    1574:0000   E8 05 00 E8 0A 00 CC 00
                                             1574:0008   E8 05 00 C3 00 00 00 00
      SP 0FFB      SI 0000      IP 0010      1574:0010   C3 00 00 00 00 00 00 00
      BP 0000      DI 0000                   1574:0018   00 00 00 00 00 00 00 00
      SS 1574      DS 1574      CS 1574      1574:0020   00 00 00 00 00 00 00 00
   SP+SS 1673B  SI+DS 15740      ES 1574     1574:0028   00 00 00 00 00 00 00 00
   BP+SS 15740  DI+DS 15740  IP+CS 15750     1574:0030   00 00 00 00 00 00 00 00
   STATUS FLAGS 7206 0111001000000110        1574:0038   00 00 00 00 00 00 00 00
                        ODITSZ A P C         1574:0040   00 00 00 00 00 00 00 00
   1574:0010 C3          RET                 1574:0048   00 00 00 00 00 00 00 00

   SEG 1574:   08 19 2A 3B 4C 5D 6E 7F                       1574: STACK
      FFF8   00 00 00 00 00 00 00 00    . . . . . . . .      0FFB  000B
      0000   E8 05 00 E8 0A 00 CC 00    . . . . . . . .      0FFD  0003
      0008   E8 05 00 C3 00 00 00 00    . . . . . . . .
      0010  >C3 00 00 00 00 00 00 00    . . . . . . . .
      0018   00 00 00 00 00 00 00 00    . . . . . . . .
      0020   00 00 00 00 00 00 00 00    . . . . . . . .
      0028   00 00 00 00 00 00 00 00    . . . . . . . .

   _____  / : Command    > : Go To Memory
                                        Use Cursor Keys to Scroll thru Memory
```

Figure 11.14 Screen display after executing CALL 0010H at address 0003.

CALL instruction that jumps to offset address 0010H. If you single step this instruction, the screen display will be as shown in Fig. 11.14. Note that the program jumps to offset address 0010H and the return offset address 000BH is pushed on the stack.

The instruction at offset address 0010H is *RET*. If you single step this instruction, the program will return to offset address 000BH, as shown in Fig. 11.15. Note that the most recent return offset address has been popped from the stack.

If you single step the *RET* instruction at offset address 000BH, the program will return to offset address 0003H. Note that the program found its way back to offset address 0003H by popping the last return offset address from the stack.

The instruction at offset address 0003H is another *CALL 0010H* instruction. Single step this instruction and note how the *RET* instruction at 0010H will return this time to offset address 0006H.

Table 11.7 shows all the different forms of the *CALL* and *RET* instructions. The form of the *CALL* statement illustrated in Fig. 11.12 is

CALL *disp16*

```
        8086 Microprocessor TUTOR          Press F7 for Help

     AH AL     BH BL     CH CL     DH DL    DATA SEG   08 19 2A 3B 4C 5D 6E 7F
 AX 00 00   BX 11 C5   CX 00 C5   DX 3A EE   1574:0000  E8 05 00 E8 0A 00 CC 00
                                             1574:0008  E8 05 00 C3 00 00 00 00
     SP 0FFD      SI 0000      IP 000B       1574:0010  C3 00 00 00 00 00 00 00
     BP 0000      DI 0000                    1574:0018  00 00 00 00 00 00 00 00
     SS 1574      DS 1574      CS 1574       1574:0020  00 00 00 00 00 00 00 00
 SP+SS 1673D  SI+DS 15740      ES 1574       1574:0028  00 00 00 00 00 00 00 00
 BP+SS 15740  DI+DS 15740  IP+CS 1574B       1574:0030  00 00 00 00 00 00 00 00
 STATUS FLAGS 7206 0111001000000110          1574:0038  00 00 00 00 00 00 00 00
                      ODITSZ A P C           1574:0040  00 00 00 00 00 00 00 00
 1574:000B C3         RET                    1574:0048  00 00 00 00 00 00 00 00

 SEG 1574:   08 19 2A 3B 4C 5D 6E 7F                         1574: STACK
     FFF0  00 00 00 00 00 00 00 00     . . . . . . . .       0FFD  0003
     FFF8  00 00 00 00 00 00 00 00     . . . . . . . .
     0000  E8 05 00 E8 0A 00 CC 00     . . . . . . . .
     0008  E8 05 00>C3 00 00 00 00     . . . . . . . .
     0010  C3 00 00 00 00 00 00 00     . . . . . . . .
     0018  00 00 00 00 00 00 00 00     . . . . . . . .
     0020  00 00 00 00 00 00 00 00     . . . . . . . .

_____    / : Command    > : Go To Memory
                                          Use Cursor Keys to Scroll thru Memory
```

Figure 11.15   Screen display after executing RET at location address 0010H.

TABLE 11.7 CALL AND RET INSTRUCTIONS

Operation	Mnemonic	Opcode encoding
Intrasegment		
Call subroutine	CALL *disp16*	E8 disp_lo disp_hi
Call subroutine	CALL *mem*	FF |mod|010|r/m|
Return from subroutine	RET	C3
Return and add to SP	RET *disp16*	C2 disp_lo disp_hi
Intersegment		
Call subroutine	CALL *mem*	FF |mod|011|r/m|
Call subroutine	CALL *addr*	9A segment:offset
Return from subroutine	RET	CB
Return and add to SP	RET *disp16*	C2 disp_lo disp_hi

where *disp16* is the 16-bit relative displacement. This means that you can jump to a subroutine anywhere within the current segment (intrasegment or near). Suppose you want to jump to a subroutine in a different segment (intersegment or far). In this case you could use the form

```
CALL addr
```

shown in Table 11.7. For example, to call a subroutine at the absolute memory location 1234:5678, you could use the following instruction:

```
9A 78 56 34 12    CALL 1234:5678
```

Note that the operand contains 4 bytes. The first two are the destination offset address and the next two are the destination segment address. This instruction jumps to the destination address by storing the first 2 bytes of the operand in *IP* and the next 2 bytes in *CS*. How can the program find its way back to the statement following *CALL*? This *CALL* statement must not only store the offset address of the next instruction but also the current contents of *CS*. It pushes *CS* on the stack first; then it pushes *IP* + 5 (the offset address of the next instruction) on the stack.

To return from an intersegment subroutine, the program must pop 4 bytes off the stack. The first two go into *IP* and the next two go into *CS*. The *RET* statement (opcode = C3) used in Fig. 11.12 only popped 2 bytes off the stack. This is the one to use for intrasegment or near CALLs. The intersegment or far *RET* statement (opcode = CB) shown in Table 11.7 will pop 4 bytes off the stack and return to the segment from which the CALL was made.

Table 11.7 shows an intersegment and intrasegment CALL of the form

```
CALL mem
```

This is an indirect call to a memory location using the addressing modes described in Chapter 12.

The return statement of the form

```
RET disp16
```

shown in Table 11.7 adds the 16-bit value *disp16* to the stack pointer after the return has occurred. This is sometimes useful as a method of adjusting the stack pointer if parameters were passed to the subroutine on the stack. An example of this will be given in Chapter 12.

11.3 SOFTWARE INTERRUPTS

Another type of software module, similar to subroutines, is the software interrupt such as the *INT 16H* BIOS call we used to read the keyboard in Chapter 9 or the *INT 21H* DOS call we used to display a character on the screen. Where does the program jump when these instructions are executed? The answer is that the programmer must have stored the address of the software interrupt routine in a special table of interrupt routine addresses, called interrupt vectors. This interrupt vector table occupies the first 1024 bytes of memory in the computer, that is, addresses 0000:0000 to 0000:03FF. Each entry in the table occupies 4 bytes: the first 2 bytes contain the offfset address to be loaded into the instruction pointer, *IP*, and the next 2 bytes contain the segment address to be loaded into the segment register *CS*. This means that there can be a total of 256 (FFH) interrupt vectors in the table, as shown in Fig. 11.16. The *CS:IP* pairs in the interrupt vector table represent the starting addresses of the various interrupt routines.

Software interrupts are called using the instruction

```
INT n
```

where *n* is the interrupt type number (00H to FFH) given in Fig. 11.16. When *INT n* is executed, the following interrupt sequence takes place:

1. The current status register is pushed on the stack.
2. The interrupt enable flag, *I*, and the trap flag, *T*, in the status register are cleared to mask further hardware interrupts.
3. The current values of *CS* and *IP* are pushed on the stack.
4. New values for CS_n and IP_n are loaded from the interrupt vector table.

Thus, after executing *INT n*, the 6 bytes shown in Fig. 11.17 will be pushed on the stack and the interrupt service routine at $CS_n:IP_n$ will start executing. This

Offset address   **Type number**

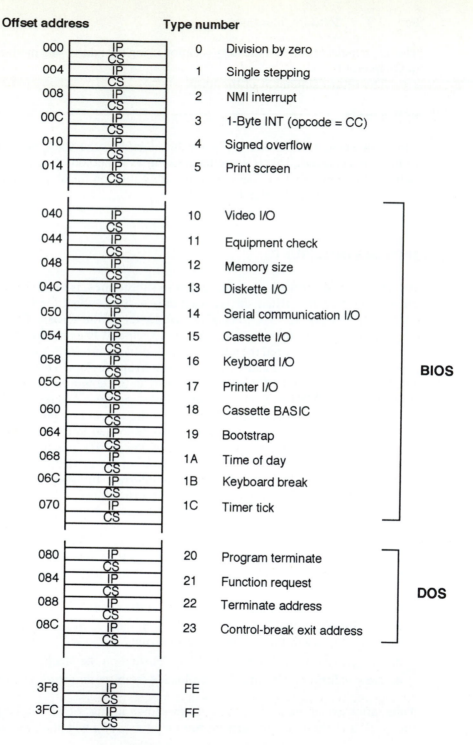

000	0	Division by zero
004	1	Single stepping
008	2	NMI interrupt
00C	3	1-Byte INT (opcode = CC)
010	4	Signed overflow
014	5	Print screen
040	10	Video I/O
044	11	Equipment check
048	12	Memory size
04C	13	Diskette I/O
050	14	Serial communication I/O
054	15	Cassette I/O
058	16	Keyboard I/O
05C	17	Printer I/O
060	18	Cassette BASIC
064	19	Bootstrap
068	1A	Time of day
06C	1B	Keyboard break
070	1C	Timer tick
080	20	Program terminate
084	21	Function request
088	22	Terminate address
08C	23	Control-break exit address
3F8	FE	
3FC	FF	

BIOS (for types 10–1C)

DOS (for types 20–23)

Figure 11.16 Interrupt vector table.

310

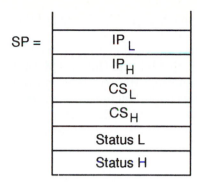

SP =

| IP$_L$ |
| IP$_H$ |
| CS$_L$ |
| CS$_H$ |
| Status L |
| Status H |

Figure 11.17 Interrupts push the status register *CS* and *IP* onto the stack.

same sequence occurs for hardware interrupts, which we will describe in Chapter 14.

The address CS_n:IP_n is called an interrupt vector and you must store this address in the special locations shown in Fig. 11.16. This would be the starting address of your interrupt service routine. The last statement in an interrupt service routine must be the *IRET* (return from interrupt) instruction (opcode = CF). This statement pops the instruction pointer (first 2 bytes), the *CS* register (next 2 bytes), and the status register (next 2 bytes) off the stack. The program will therefore continue at the point in the program where the interrupt occurred. For a software interrupt, this would be the statement following the *INT n* statement.

Each entry in the interrupt vector table shown in Fig. 11.16 has an interrupt type number associated with it. This is a number between 0 and 255 (00H to FFH). The address of the interrupt vector is found by multiplying the interrupt type number by 4. For example, interrupt type number 5 has its interrupt vector located at address 5 × 4 = 20 = 014H, as shown in Fig. 11.16. Note that each interrupt vector consists of 4 bytes, the first two contain *IP* and the next two contain *CS*.

The first few entries in the interrupt vector table are used for special purposes, as indicated in Fig. 11.16. The type 0 interrupt is automatically requested if a division instruction results in a quotient that is too large to fit into the quotient register (*AL* or *AX*). This is called a *divide-by-zero* error even though you don't have to divide by zero to produce this interrupt. The type 1 interrupt is a special interrupt used for single stepping, which we will describe below. The type 2 interrupt is always the vector address for the nonmaskable hardware interrupt (NMI), which we will describe in Chapter 14. If you want an interrupt to occur when the overflow flag is set (see Chapter 10), you can follow the arithmetic instruction with the instruction *INTO*, interrupt on overflow (opcode = CE). This will cause a type 4 interrupt.

Interrupt types 10H to 1CH shown in Fig. 11.16 are the BIOS ROM routines for handling basic I/O operations. We have already used *INT 16H* for reading the keyboard and *INT 10H* for setting the screen cursor. We will consider the video

I/O routines in more detail in Chapter 13 and some of the other BIOS routines in Chapters 14 to 17.

In addition to the interrupt routines that are built into the BIOS ROM, the disk operating system, DOS, that is loaded into RAM when you boot up the system also contains a number of interrupt routines that you can use. Some of these are shown in Fig. 11.16. The most important one is *INT 21H*. This is a function request that handles many useful DOS functions depending on the value in *AH* when *INT 21H* is called. A list of these functions is given in Appendix D. We have already used the character output and string output routines in Chapter 9. We will cover a number of the most important DOS calls related to disk I/O in Chapter 15.

Software interrupts can be used much like subroutines where the starting address of the routine, *CS:IP*, is stored in the interrupt vector table. The other difference between an interrupt service routine and a subroutine is that a software interrupt saves the status flag as well as *CS* and *IP* on the stack. As a result, three words must be popped from the stack at the end of an interrupt service routine (using *IRET*) rather than one (for a near *RET*) or two (for a far *RET*) for a subroutine. We will show you how to write your own interrupt service routines in Chapter 14.

Breakpoints and Single Stepping

Note that software interrupts require 2 bytes: CD, the opcode for *INT*, plus the type number. When setting a breakpoint as we do in the TUTOR monitor (by typing /*BS*), you need to be able to replace only a single byte. A special software interrupt, *INT 3*, uses the single opcode, CC (see Fig. 11.16). We have used this instruction to end many of our programs. This is because the TUTOR monitor has an interrupt service routine, whose vector address is stored in the type 3 location of the interrupt vector table, that displays the current register contents and then jumps back to the TUTOR monitor.

The single-stepping feature of the TUTOR monitor uses the type 1 interrupt, which will occur one instruction after the trap flag, *T*, if the status register is set to 1. The *T* flag can be set to 1 by pushing the status register on the stack (perhaps as the result of an interrupt) and ORing the high byte of the status register (in the stack) with 10H. Assuming that *CS* and *IP* have also been pushed on the stack, then an *IRET* instruction will cause the modified status register (with $T = 1$) to be popped from the stack. After one instruction is executed, a type 1 interrupt will occur.

In the TUTOR monitor this interrupt service routine resets to zero the *T* flag that was just pushed onto the stack. (The 8086 automatically resets the *T* flag in the actual status register to zero after it pushes it on the stack. Otherwise, you would single step each instruction in the interrupt service routine!) It then displays the current contents of all the registers.

11.4 WRITING AND DEBUGGING COMPLETE PROGRAMS

We will now take a look at complete programs: how to write them, assemble them, link them, run them, and debug them. To write a program, you will need some type of text editor or word processor. Any kind that will generate straight ASCII text files will do. A full screen editor such as EMACS will work just fine. You will also need a macro assembler such as the IBM PC Macro Assembler (MASM), Microsoft's Macro Assembler (MASM), or Borland's Turbo Assembler (TASM). We will describe how to use a macro assembler later in this section.

If you don't have an editor or assembler handy, you can still learn a lot about assembly language programming by studying, running, and debugging the programs in this book that we have already edited and assembled for you. The source listings (.ASM files), object code (.OBJ files), and executable (.EXE) files for many of the programs in this book are included on the TUTOR disk. We will show you in this section how you can load these .EXE files into TUTOR, set breakpoints, and execute part or all of the programs.

General Structure of an 8086 Assembly Language Program

The general structure of an 8086 assembly language program is shown in Fig. 11.18. The program is made up of a collection of segments that begin with the assembler directive *SEGMENT* and end with the *ENDS* directive. A stack segment is required to produce a valid .EXE file that can be run. The data segment will contain the definitions of data variables.

The code segment will contain the main program and subroutines, which must begin with the assembler directive *PROC* and end with the directive *ENDP*. The directive *PROC* is followed by either *NEAR* or *FAR*, which determines the version of *RET* to be used in that procedure. The attribute *NEAR* will use the intrasegment version of *RET* (opcode = C3) and the attribute *FAR* will use the intersegment version (opcode = CB; see Table 11.7).

The assembly language program must end with the *END* directive. This can be followed by an optional expression that identifies the label corresponding to the starting offset address of the program.

Note from Fig. 11.18 that the labels associated with each *SEGMENT* directive must be the same labels used with the corresponding *ENDS* directive. Similarly, the labels associated with each *PROC* directive must also be used with the corresponding *ENDP* directive.

The main program is normally given the type attribute *FAR* in the *PROC* directive. This means that you can end the main program with an intersegment *RET* instruction that will transfer control to another segment. Of course, you must have pushed the destination code segment (*CS*) and instruction pointer (*IP*) on the stack so that they will be popped off the stack when the *RET* instruction is

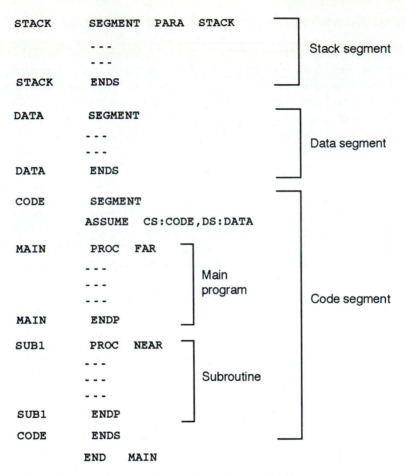

Figure 11.18   General structure of an 8086 assembly language program.

executed. While this is somewhat awkward, it was the standard way to quit programs in earlier versions of DOS. With DOS versions 2.0 and above, it is better
(and easier) to return to DOS from the main program by executing the following
DOS function call:

```
MOV  AX,4C00H     ;quit to DOS
INT  21H
```

Consider the program shown in Listing 11.1a for finding the two's complement of a double (32-bit) word. This program is designed to be run only from
TUTOR, so we will end the main program with the *INT 3* breakpoint instruction.
Listing 11.1a is exactly as you would type it using an editor such as EMACS and
is stored on the TUTOR disk under the filename *neg2word.asm*. All your assembly

Listing 11.1a   *neg2word.asm*

```
title   Two's complement of a double word

stack   segment     para   stack
        db     64 dup(?)
stack   ends

data    segment
dnum    dd     12345678h
negnum  dd     ?
data    ends
code    segment public
        assume cs:code,ds:data

main    proc    far
        mov     ax,data
        mov     ds,ax               ;set ds=data
        mov     ax,word ptr dnum    ;ax=low word
        mov     dx,word ptr dnum+2  ;dx=high word
        call    dnegate             ;2's compl
        mov     word ptr negnum,ax    ;store lo word
        mov     word ptr negnum+2,dx ;store hi word
        int     3
main    endp

;       negate double word dx:ax
dnegate proc    near
        push    bx               ;save regs
        push    cx
        mov     bx,dx            ;bx=hi word
        mov     cx,ax            ;cx=lo word
        xor     ax,ax            ;ax=0
        mov     dx,ax            ;dx=0
        sub     ax,cx            ;dx:ax =
        sbb     dx,bx            ; 0:0 - bx:cx
        pop     cx               ;restore regs
        pop     bx
        ret
dnegate endp

code    ends
        end     main
```

language source files must have the filename extension *asm*. This file becomes the input to the macro assembler.

The assembler will produce two output files: *neg2word.obj* and *neg2word.lst*. The .OBJ file is the object file that will be the input to the linker. The .LST file is shown in Listing 11.1b.

The .LST file is the same source listing as the .ASM file in Listing 11.1a with the addition of the offset addresses (within the code segment) and the machine code displayed to the left of each assembly language instruction. In addition, there is a symbol table at the end of the .LST file that gives the offset addresses of all variables and labels. This .LST file will help you find any particular instruction when the machine code has been loaded into TUTOR.

Note that in the stack segment in Listing 11.1 the statement

```
db      64 dup(?)
```

will reserve 64 bytes of memory for the stack. This stack segment will be located immediately following the program starting at the next paragraph (16-byte increments) boundary.[1] (This is the meaning of the *PARA* option in the stack *SEGMENT* directive.)

The statement

```
assume      cs:code,ds:data
```

must appear at the beginning of a code segment to tell the assembler to assume that the code segment register, *CS*, will contain the address of the segment *CODE* and the data segment register, *DS*, will contain the address of the segment *DATA*. The program must explicitly set the data segment register *DS* to *DATA*, and this is done with the first two statements in the program:

```
0000   B8 ---- R     mov   ax,data
0003   8E D8         mov   ds,ax        ;set ds=data
```

Note that the first statement is assembled as a *MOV ax,immed* instruction (opcode = B8H), but the immediate value to move into *AX* isn't known and is left in the listing as two unknown bytes ---- *R*. Even after the linker produces the executable file *neg2word.exe* from the object file *neg2word.obj* (we will describe how to do this later in this section), this immediate value of *DATA* will still not be known. This value represents the segment address of the data segment for this program. But this data segment value can't be known until the program is loaded into

---

[1] The stack segment may not always immediately follow the code segment. It will depend on the names of the segments. Unless overridden, the linker will arrange the segments alphabetically in memory. The .MAP file, to be described later in this chapter, will show you where all the segments in a given program are located.

Listing 11.1b *neg2word.lst*

```
IBM Personal Computer MACRO Assembler    Version 2.00      Page  1-1
Two's complement of a double word                          07-12-91

                          title   Two's complement of a double word

0000                      stack segment       para   stack
0000      40 [                    db    64 dup(?)
                   ??
                    ]

0040                      stack ends

0000                      data segment
0000  78 56 34 12         dnum          dd     12345678h
0004  ????????            negnum        dd     ?
0008                      data ends

0000                      code segment public
                              assume cs:code,ds:data

0000                      main proc   far
0000  B8 ---- R               mov    ax,data
0003  8E D8                   mov    ds,ax                  ;set ds=data
0005  A1 0000 R               mov    ax,word ptr dnum       ;ax=low word
0008  8B 16 0002 R            mov    dx,word ptr dnum+2     ;dx=high word
000C  E8 0017 R               call   dnegate               ;2's compl
000F  A3 0004 R               mov    word ptr negnum,ax     ;store lo word
0012  89 16 0006 R            mov    word ptr negnum+2,dx   ;store hi word
0016  CC                      int    3
0017                      main endp

                          ;      negate double word dx:ax
0017                      dnegate proc   near
0017  53                     push   bx               ;save regs
0018  51                     push   cx
0019  8B DA                  mov    bx,dx            ;bx=hi word
001B  8B C8                  mov    cx,ax            ;cx=lo word
001D  33 C0                  xor    ax,ax            ;ax=0
001F  8B D0                  mov    dx,ax            ;dx=0
0021  2B C1                  sub    ax,cx            ;dx:ax =
0023  1B D3                  sbb    dx,bx            ; 0:0 - bx:cx
0025  59                     pop    cx               ;restore regs
0026  5B                     pop    bx
0027  C3                     ret
0028                      dnegate    endp

0028                      code ends
                              end    main
```

memory. When you execute an .EXE file from DOS by typing its name (such as *neg2word*), DOS will load in the file and then compute and insert all the relocatable addresses, such as the value of *DATA* in the above example, before it executes the program. We will now show you how TUTOR can do the same thing, which will allow you to load, execute, and debug any .EXE program.

Debugging .EXE Programs Using TUTOR

The TUTOR monitor can be used to explore the structure of .EXE files and to debug programs that you have written as .EXE files. With the position cursor of TUTOR set to offset address 0000 in a free memory segment (such as the one displayed when you first execute TUTOR), load the file *neg2word.exe* using */SL*. The header of the .EXE file will be loaded at offset address 0000. This header will always begin with the 2 bytes 4D 5A. The meanings of the other bytes in the header are given in Fig. 11.19. Note that the header contains information from the linker about where the code segment and stack segment should be (relative to where the .EXE file was loaded into memory) and the values of the stack pointer and instruction pointer. When DOS loads an .EXE file, it sets *CS*, *SS*, *SP*, and *IP* using these values. It creates a 256-byte *program segment prefix* (PSP) in front of the program and sets *DS* and *ES* to the segment address of this program segment prefix. The .EXE header also contains relocation information needed, for example, to locate the data segment relative to the code segment.

.EXE File Header

	08 19	2A 3B	4C 5D	6E 7F
0000	4D 5A	last page size	file size	#reloc items
0008	header size	min alloc	max alloc	SS offset
0010	initial SP	checksum	initial IP	CS offset
0018	reloc tbl offset	overlay #		
0020				
	offset	segment	offset	segment

Figure 11.19 Description of an .EXE file header.

The .EXE header in the file *neg2word.exe* that you have just loaded into memory contains 512 (200H) bytes. Go to offset address 0200 and you should find the object code for the program shown in Listing 11.1b. However, the first statement will be

```
MOV   AX,0003H
```

This value of 0003H is not going to be the final value for *DATA*. Note the value of the current segment address *SEG*. Go back to offset address 0000 and *press function key F10*. Note that the segment address has changed and the position cursor is pointing to the first instruction of the program at offset address 0000. In addition, the value to be moved into *AX* in the first instruction has also been changed and is equal to the current segment address *SEG* plus 0003 (this was the 0003 that was in the original .EXE file). Pressing function key *F10* has just performed the loading function that DOS does everytime you run an .EXE program. It has computed the real value of the data segment once we know where you actually loaded it in the program.

The program needs to actually set the data segment register, *DS*, to this value by executing the first two instructions. Single step these two instructions by pressing function key *F1* twice. Note that the data segment memory displayed in the upper-right part of the screen changes to this new value of *DS* and displays the values

```
78 56 34 12
```

in the first 4 bytes of the data segment. This is just the 32-bit value 12345678H that was defined in the program by the statement

```
dnum    dd   12345678h
```

in Listing 11.1a. Note from the listing file in Listing 11.1b that the assembler actually stores this 32-bit number in memory at offset address 0000 in the data segment. We have just found these data using TUTOR!

The assembler directive *dd* means *define double word* and will reserve 32 bits in the data segment for the variable we have called *dnum* and will assign an initial value of 12345678H to this variable. The second statement in the data segment portion of Listing 11.1 is

```
negnum    dd   ?
```

This statement defines a second variable called *negnum* that also contains 32 bits (*dd*), but has an unspecified initial value (?). The contents of this variable are stored at offset addresses 0004 to 0007 in the data segment. These will be the last 4 bytes in the top row of the data segment memory in TUTOR and may contain all zeros at this point. The program is going to compute the two's complement of 12345678H and store the result in this second variable *negnum*.

The third statement in the main program of Listing 11.1b is

```
0005   A1 0000 R    mov   ax,word ptr dnum    ;ax=low word
```

This statement will load the low word of *dnum* (5678H) into *ax*. Because we have defined *dnum* as a 32-bit value using *dd*, we cannot just load *dnum* into the 16-bit register *ax*. The assembler expects only 16-bit variables (defined with the directive *dw*, *define word*) to be loaded into 16-bit registers and only 8-bit variables (defined with the directive *db*, *define byte*) to be loaded into 8-bit registers. We can tell the assembler to load the 16-bit value starting at the address of *dnum* (0000) into *ax* by including the assembler directive *word ptr* before the variable *dnum*, as shown. This tells the assembler that, notwithstanding the fact that we defined *dnum* to be 32 bits, for this operation treat it as a 16-bit value starting at *dnum*. Therefore, if we execute this instruction, the value 5678H (stored low byte first at offset address 0000 in the data segment) should be loaded into *ax*. Single step this instruction with *F1* and see if it does.

The next statement is

```
0008  8B 16 0002 R    mov  dx,word ptr dnum+2    ;dx=high word
```

This will move the 16-bit value at dnum + 2 (1234H) into *dx*. Verify this by pressing *F1* again.

The next statement is

```
000C  E8 0017 R     call dnegate    ;2's compl
```

This is a call to the subroutine *dnegate*, which will take the two's complement of the 32-bit number in *dx:ax* and leave the result in *dx:ax*. If you press *F1* at this point, you will enter this subroutine and could single step through each instruction in the subroutine. You can do this later. For now press function key *F2*, which will execute the entire subroutine and return to the instruction following *call dnegate*. The two's complement of 12345678H should now be stored in *dx:ax* (the high word will be in *dx* and the low word in *ax*). You should verify that this is the correct two's complement.

The next two statements will move this 32-bit value in *dx:ax* into the variable *negnum*. Press *F1* twice and watch it go! Note the order in which the bytes are stored in *negnum*.

The subroutine *dnegate* in Listing 11.1 takes the two's complement of *dx:ax* by subtracting this value from 0:0. It does this by first moving *dx:ax* into *bx:cx* and then setting *dx:ax* = 0:0. Note that the statement

```
xor   ax,ax
```

will set *ax* to zero. Verify this. Also note that the second subtraction in this subroutine must be a *subtract with borrow* instruction in order to handle a possible borrow from the first subtraction.

Go back to the beginning of the program by pressing *Home* and single step the program again, this time single stepping through the subroutine by pressing *F1*. Make sure you understand how the program works.

Suppose you had single stepped through the program using *F2* and when you called the subroutine it produced the wrong answer. Inasmuch as the values in *ax* and *dx* going into the subroutine were correct, the problem must have been within the subroutine. Perhaps we mistyped the instruction at offset address 001FH and typed *mov ax,dx* instead of *mov dx,ax*. This would have produced the machine code 8B C2 at this offset address instead of 8B D0. Change D0 to C2 at offset address 0020 using */MH*.

To find this mistake, we will set a breakpoint at offset address 0019H. This is within the subroutine but before where we expect the error to be. To set the breakpoint, move the position cursor to address 0019H and then type */BS*. This will set a breakpoint by replacing the opcode with CCH. Now press *Home* to go to the beginning of the program and execute the program by pressing */EG*. Note that the program will execute up to the breakpoint and replace the original opcode at that address. You can now begin to single step from here. Note that at this point the correct values are in *ax* and *dx*, but when you single step the incorrect instruction, it will be obvious that the zero in *ax* is not being moved to *dx* and you will have discovered the error.

This technique of setting a breakpoint as far into the program as possible without causing the error and then single stepping until the error is discovered is an important debugging tool. By using this technique you should be able to discover most run time errors in your programs.

When you load an .EXE file into TUTOR and then press function key *F10*, the program will be ready to execute. In addition to fixing up all the relocation addresses, TUTOR stores the correct values of *CS*, *DS*, *ES*, *SS*, *SP*, and *IP* for this .EXE file in these registers.

You can therefore load any .EXE file into any convenient place in memory, press key *F10*, and execute the program. You can therefore use TUTOR to debug your programs by setting breakpoints and single stepping. When the program is completely debugged, it should work from DOS without change.

If you press key *F10*, set a breakpoint, and then execute the program, the program will stop with the data segment register and the stack pointer in general changed to some values that are different from their initial values. If you want to go back and execute the program again from the beginning, these values should be restored to their original values. This can normally be done by pressing function key *F9*.

Using a Macro Assembler

When using the IBM PC macro assembler (or similar assembler), you will carry out the following steps:

1. Create a source code file with a filename extension .ASM using any convenient editor.
2. Use the assembler to convert the .ASM file to an object file (with an .OBJ extension) and to produce a listing file (with an extension .LST).

3. Use the linker to produce an executable file (with an extension .EXE) from one or more .OBJ files.

4. Run the program by typing the name of the .EXE file.

We will consider each of these steps by means of the example program shown in Listing 11.2a. This program will clear the screen and then display on the screen any key you type from the keyboard. The cursor will automatically be advanced

Listing 11.2a   *typescn.asm*

```
title    Type characters to screen

;        LINK with screen
stack    segment para stack
         db    64 dup(?)
stack    ends
;        screen subroutines
         extrn clrscn:near,chrout1:near
         extrn crlf:near,getkey:near

code     segment       public
         assume cs:code
main     proc    far
         call    clrscn        ;clear screen
keyscn:  call    getkey        ;wait for key
         cmp     al,1bh        ;if esc key
         jne     chkcr
         call    escape        ;quit to DOS
         int     21h
chkcr:   cmp     al,0dh        ;if enter key
         jne     dspchr
         call    crlf          ;do cr lf
         jmp     keyscn        ; & loop back
dspchr:  call    chrout1       ;else display char
         jmp     keyscn        ; & do again
main     endp

;        return to DOS
escape   proc    near
         call    clrscn        ;clear screen
         mov     ax,4C00h      ;terminate
         int     21h           ; process
escape   endp

code     ends
         end     main
```

one space as each character is typed. If you press the *Enter* key, the cursor will advance to the beginning of the next line. (We call this a carriage return, *CR*, and a line feed, *LF*.) If you press the *ESC* key, the screen will clear and the program will return to DOS.

The program in Listing 11.2 uses four external subroutines that are stored in the file *screen.asm* that is on your TUTOR disk. We will study how all these subroutines work in Chapter 13. For now, we will use only the four given in Table 11.8.

TABLE 11.8   SOME *SCREEN.ASM* SUBROUTINES

Subroutine	Input	Output	Registers Modified	Description
clrscn	None	None	None	Clear screen
getkey	None	AL = ASCII code of key	AX	Wait for key and get key value
crlf	None	None	None	Carriage return line feed
chroutl	AL = ASCII code of character to display	None	None	Output a character to screen with current attribute

The file *screen.asm* has been assembled to produce the object file *screen.obj*. This object file must be linked with the object file produced by assembling Listing 11.2a. We will show you how to do this later in this section. To use the subroutines in Table 11.8, we must include the statements

```
extrn clrscn:near,chrout1:near
extrn crlf:near,getkey:near
```

at the beginning of the program as shown in Listing 11.2a. These statements tell the assembler to consider the subroutines *clrscn,chrout1,crlf,* and *getkey* as near subroutines whose actual offset address won't be resolved until the two object files *typescn.obj* and *screen.obj* are linked. The main program in Listing 11.2a calls these four external subroutines as well as the internal subroutine *escape,* which will return to DOS when the *ESC* key is pressed. Note in the main program that ordinary labels used for branching must end with a colon (:), while segment and procedure names do not.

We will assume that the assembler is on the hard disk drive *C* and that you will write your programs to a floppy disk in drive *A*. First, type in the program shown in Listing 11.2a using any text editor. You should use the tab key to tab to the various columns. Start typing the labels in the leftmost column on the screen.

The directory containing the macro assembler MASM should be in the *PATH* command in the *AUTOEXEC.BAT* file. This will mean that DOS can always find MASM regardless of your current directory. Assuming you have the file *typescn.asm* on your disk in drive *A* and the current directory is *A>*, then type

```
masm typescn
```

This will load the assembler from drive *C* and prompt you. Respond to each prompt with

```
a:
```

or simply press *Enter* as shown in Fig. 11.20. If there are any errors in the source program, they will be listed on the screen. At the end of the assembly process, the number of errors will be displayed, as shown in Fig. 11.20.

```
A:\ >masm typescn
IBM Personal Computer MACRO Assembler    Version 2.00
(C)Copyright IBM Corp 1981, 1984
(C)Copyright Microsoft Corp 1981, 1983, 1984

Object filename [typescn.OBJ]: a:
Source listing  [NUL.LST]: a:
Cross reference [NUL.CRF]:

50092 Bytes free

Warning Severe
Errors  Errors
0       0

A:\ >
```

Figure 11.20   Example of using the assembler.

In addition to the object file *testprog.obj*, you have also created the listing file *typescn.lst*. shown in Listing 11.2b. You can see the contents of this file by typing

```
type testprog.lst
```

Press the two keys *Ctrl PrtSc* before typing the line above to get the listing sent to the printer. Press *Ctrl PrtSc* again to stop the printing.

Note that the machine code is printed in the *.lst* listing. However, the machine code in this listing is not exactly the same as the executable code that is stored in memory. For example, the value 001D at offset address 000B will actually

Listing 11.2b   *typescn.lst*

```
IBM Personal Computer MACRO Assembler    Version 2.00        Page   1-1
Type characters to screen                             07-14-91

                          title   Type characters to screen

                      ;        LINK with screen
0000                  stack  segment para stack
0000      40 [                          db     64 dup(?)
                ??
                      ]

0040                  stack        ends
                      ;    screen subroutines
                            extrn    clrscn:near,chrout1:near
                            extrn    crlf:near,getkey:near

0000                  code     segment       public
                      assume cs:code
0000                  main     proc     far
0000  E8 0000 E               call     clrscn        ;clear screen
0003  E8 0000 E       keyscn: call     getkey        ;wait for key
0006  3C 1B                   cmp      al,1bh        ;if esc key
0008  75 05                   jne      chkcr
000A  E8 001D R               call     escape        ;quit to DOS
000D  CD 21                   int      21h
000F  3C 0D           chkcr:  cmp      al,0dh        ;if enter key
0011  75 05                   jne      dspchr
0013  E8 0000 E               call     crlf          ;do cr lf
0016  EB EB                   jmp      keyscn        ; & loop back
0018  E8 0000 E       dspchr: call     chrout1       ;display char
001B  EB E6                   jmp      keyscn        ; & do again
001D                  main     endp

                      ;    return to DOS
001D                  escape  proc     near
001D  E8 0000 E               call     clrscn        ;clear screen
0020  B8 4C00                 mov      ax,4C00h      ;terminate
0023  CD 21                   int      21h           ; process
0025                  escape  endp

0025                  code     ends
                      end      main
```

be stored in memory as 1D 00. Similarly, the value 4C00 at offset address 0021 will actually be stored in memory as 00 4C. Any 16-bit value written in the listing file without a space, such as 1234, will be stored in memory "backward" as 34 12.

Before you can run the program you must link it using the linker.

Using the linker LINK.   The linker is stored in the DOS file LINK.EXE. The directory containing this file should also be in the *PATH* command in the *AUTOEXEC.BAT* file. You will need to copy the object file *screen.obj* from the TUTOR disk to your current directory containing your assembled object file *typescn.obj*. Then type

```
link
```

The linker will be executed and will prompt you. Respond to the first prompt (for the .OBJ filename) with the two object files

```
typescn screen
```

Simply press *Enter* for the last three prompts, as shown in Fig. 11.21. This will create the default executable file *typescn.exe*. You are now ready to run the program.

```
A:\ >link

Microsoft (R) Personal Computer Linker   Version 2.40
Copyright (C) Microsoft Corp 1983, 1984, 1985.  All rights reserved.

Object Modules [.OBJ]: typescn screen
Run File [TYPESCN.EXE]:
List File [NUL.MAP]:
Libraries [.LIB]:

A:\ >
```

Figure 11.21   Linking the subroutines in *screen.obj* to your program *typescn.obj*.

You must always use the linker to produce an .EXE file even if you are not linking in any external subroutines. You would just list your own program name when asked for the .OBJ file to link.

Running the program.   To run the program *typescn.exe*, simply type

```
typescn
```

This will cause the file *typescn.exe* to be loaded into memory, a program segment prefix to be created, and any relocation to be done. The program will then be executed beginning at the start address (as specified in the *END* statement of the assembly language program).

When you run *typescn.exe* you should be able to type anything you want on the screen and return to DOS by pressing the *ESC* key, as shown in Fig. 11.22.

```
The program typescn.exe is now running.  Anything you type on the keyboard will
be displayed on the screen.  When you press the enter key the cursor will move t
o the beginning of the next line like this.
If you reach the end of the screen line, the typing will automatically continue
on the next line.
If you press the ESC key the screen will clear and you will return to DOS.
```

Figure 11.22   An example of running the program *typescn.exe*.

In Listing 11.2 the statement

```
code        segment     public
```

defines the code segment to have the name *code* and to be *public*. The file *screen.asm* has this same statement for its code segment. The public declaration in each statement means that these two code segments will be concatenated in memory by the linker in the order that you specified them when running the linker. In the example shown in Fig. 11.21, the object code for *typescn.obj* will be stored in memory first, followed by the object code for *screen.obj*. If you load the file *typescn.exe* into TUTOR and press *F10*, you will be at the beginning of the program *typescn*. The subroutines in *screen.asm* will follow this code in memory.

In the file *screen.asm* the statements

```
public      clrscn,chrout1,crlf,getkey
```

must be included to make the addresses of these subroutines available to the linker so that they can be linked with other programs.

Experiment 23: Mixed Double Multiply

In this programming problem you will write an 8086 subroutine that will multiply an unsigned 32-bit multiplicand by an unsigned 16-bit multiplier and produce a 32-bit product.

1. The 8086 instruction *MUL* can multiply a 16-bit integer in *AX* by another 16-bit integer, producing a 32-bit product in *DX:AX*. Sometimes we need to multiply a 32-bit value (double word) by a 16-bit value (word). In general,

this could produce a 48-bit product as follows, where A, B, C, D and E are 16-bit values.

$$
\begin{array}{rrr}
 & A & B \\
\times & & C \\
\hline
 & BCH & BCL \\
ACH & ACL & \\
\hline
D & E & F
\end{array}
$$

The values *BCH* and *BCL* are the high word and low word of the partial product $B \times C$, and the values *ACH* and *ACL* are the high word and low word of the partial product $A \times C$. Even though this product can contain 48 bits, we often know that the result will, in fact, fit in 32 bits. That is, the product will be less than 4,294,967,296. If this is the case, then $D = ACH$ will equal zero, and the 32-bit product will consist of the high word $PH = E = BCH + ACL$ and the low word $PL = F = BCL$. Write a subroutine called *mdmul* that will multiply *dx:ax* by *bx* and leave the 32-bit product in *dx:ax*.

2. Write a main program module that includes a stack segment, a data segment and a code segment. The data segment should be as follows

```
data        segment
prod        dd    ?
oper1       dd    123456h
oper2       dw    100h
data        ends
```

The first two statements of your main program should be

```
mov ax,data
mov ds,ax
```

This will establish the value *ds* to be your data segment. Write a main program that will read the values of *oper1* and *oper2* from the data segment, calculate the mixed double product by calling the subroutine *mdmul*, and store the result in the variable *prod* in the data segment. Stop the program by executing *INT 3*.

3. Load the .EXE file of your program into TUTOR at offset address 0000. The position cursor will be pointing to the beginning of the .EXE file header, which starts with 4D 5A. Press function key *F10*. Single step the first two instructions and note that your data segment will be displayed. Single step the remainder of your program and watch 123456H × 100H being calculated. What is the answer?

4. Change the values in *oper1* and *oper2* so as to calculate ABCDEFH × ABH. What is the answer?

Experiment 24: Double Word Division

In this programming problem you will write an 8086 subroutine that will divide an unsigned 32-bit dividend by an unsigned 16-bit divisor and produce a 32-bit quotient and a 16-bit remainder.

1. The 8086 instruction *DIV* can divide a 32-bit integer in *DX:AX* by a 16-bit integer, leaving the 16-bit quotient in *AX* and the 16-bit remainder in *DX*. If the 32-bit dividend is too large or the 16-bit divisor is too small, the quotient may not fit into 16 bits. If this occurs, a divide-by-zero trap (interrupt) will occur. To keep this from happening, what is needed is a divide routine that will return a 32-bit quotient, rather than a 16-bit quotient. This is easy to do by using multiple-word division. When doing long division, you divide the divisor into the "high part" of the dividend to get the "high part" of the quotient. The "high remainder" becomes part of the remaining dividend that is divided by the divisor to yield the "low part" of the quotient and the final remainder.

    In particular, if *num* is a 32-bit numerator with high word *numH* and low word *numL*, then to divide *num* by the 16-bit denominator *denom*, first divide *0:numH/denom* to give *quotH* and *remH*. Then divide *remH:numL/denom* to give *quotL* and *rem*.

    Write a subroutine called *ddiv* that will divide *dx:ax* by *bx* and leave the quotient in *dx:ax* and the remainder in *bx*.

2. Write a main program module that includes a stack segment, a data segment, and a code segment. The data segment should be as follows:

```
data        segment
num         dd   12345678h
denom       dw   10h
rem         dw   ?
quot        dd   ?
data        ends
```

The first two statements of your main program should be

```
mov ax,data
mov ds,ax
```

This will establish the value *ds* to be your data segment. Write a main program that will read the values of the numerator and denominator from the data segment, calculate the double division by calling the subroutine *ddiv*, and store the result in the variables *quot* and *rem* in the data segment. Stop the program by executing *INT 3*.

3. Load the .EXE file of your program into TUTOR at offset address 0000. The position cursor will be pointing to the beginning of the .EXE file header, which starts with 4D 5A. Press function key *F10*. Single step the first two instructions and note that your data segment will be displayed. Single step the remainder of your program and watch 12345678H/10H being calculated. What is the answer?

4. Change the values in *num* and *denom* so as to calculate ABCDEF12H/ BADH. What is the answer?

Experiment 25: Keyboard Inputs

The subroutine *getkey* in Table 11.8 returns the ASCII code of the key pressed. However, if you look at Table 9.4, you will note that the function keys and some of the keys on the numeric keypad have keyboard ASCII codes of zero. When this occurs, the subroutine *getkey* adds (or ORs) the hex value 80H to the scan code given in Table 9.4. For example, if you press the *Del* key (with scan code = 53H), the subroutine *getkey* will return the value 53H + 80H = D3H.

Modify Listing 11.2a so that if you press the *Del* key the program will clear the screen and you can begin typing in characters again. Assemble, link, and run this new program.

EXERCISES

11.1. Type in the following program and single step through it several times. Explain how each instruction affects the contents of accumulator *AL* and the value of the carry flag *C*.

```
0000   B0 13   LOOP1:  MOV   AL,13H
0002   FE C0   LOOP1:  INC   AL
0004   3C 16           CMP   AL,16H
0006   72 FA           JB    LOOP2
0008   73 F6           JNB   LOOP1
```

11.2. Type in the following program and single step through it several times. Explain how each instruction affects the accumulator *AL* and the value of the overflow flag *O*.

```
0000   B0 7A   LOOP1:  MOV   AL,7AH
0002   04 02   LOOP2:  ADD   AL,2
0004   71 FC           JNO   LOOP2
0006   70 F8           JO    LOOP1
```

11.3. Type in the following program and single step through it several times. Explain what you observe.

```
0000   B0 83   LOOP1:  MOV   AL,83H
0002   FE C8   LOOP2:  DEC   AL
0004   3C 7E           CMP   AL,7EH
0006   77 FA           JA    LOOP2
0008   76 F6           JBE   LOOP1
```

Change the instructions *JA* to *JG* and *JBE* to *JLE* and single step through the program several times. Explain what you observe.

11.4.
```
L1:   MOV   CX,5
      MOV   BX,3
L2:   DEC   BX
      LOOPNE L2
      JMP   L1
```

a. Write the machine code for the program given above.

b. Type in the program starting at offset address 0000 and single step through it several times. Explain what you observe.

c. Change the first statement to *MOV CX,2* and repeat (b).

d. Change the statement *LOOPNE L2* to *LOOPE L2* and repeat (b).

11.5. Write a program that will push the values of *AX* and *CX* on the stack and then *POP* these values into *SI* and *DI*.

12

More Addressing Modes

In previous chapters we have executed a number of 8086 instructions, either by single stepping (using key *F1*) or by executing a program using /*E*. Most 8086 instructions operate on some kind of data. For example, the contents of accumulator *AX* may be incremented. This is an example of a single operand instruction. Some instructions, such as *ADD*, contain two operands. The operands specify where the data to be used in the instruction are to be obtained. There are many different forms that these operands can take. These are known as the *operand addressing modes*.

   You have already learned to use register addressing and immediate addressing in Chapter 10. In this chapter you will learn to use the following 8086 addressing modes:

- Direct
- Register indirect
- Indexed, with possible displacement
- Based, with possible displacement
- Indexed plus based, with possible displacement
- Stack addressing

12.1 ADDRESSING MODE POSTBYTE

Many 8086 instructions include a *postbyte* in addition to the primary opcode byte. This postbyte, as we saw in Chapter 10, can have one of the two forms shown

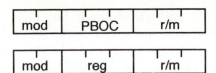

Figure 12.1 Two forms of the 8088 addressing mode postbyte.

in Fig. 12.1. In the first of the two forms, PBOC is a 3-bit postbyte opcode that, together with the primary opcode, determines the instruction. For example, in Table A.2a in Appendix A, an asterisk in a particular opcode location indicates that a secondary postbyte opcode is needed to specify the instructions. These are listed in Table A.2b of Appendix A. The postbyte opcodes are only 3 of the bits that form the entire postbyte. The remaining 5 bits are divided between a 2-bit *mod* field and a 3-bit *r/m* field, as shown in Fig. 12.1. The meanings of these two fields are given in Table 12.1. Although this table looks complicated, it, together with Table 12.2, defines all the 8086 addressing modes. Tables 12.1 and 12.2 are reproduced in Appendix A as Tables A.3 and A.4.

TABLE 12.1 POSTBYTE *MOD, R/M* FIELDS

r/m	mod = 11 Byte	mod = 11 Word	mod = 00	mod = 01	mod = 11
000	AL	AX	BX + SI	BX + SI + disp8	BX + SI + disp16
001	CL	CX	BX + DI	BX + DI + disp8	BX + DI + disp16
010	DL	DX	BP + SI	BP + SI + disp8	BP + SI + disp16
011	BL	BX	BP + DI	BP + DI + disp8	BP + DI + disp16
100	AH	SP	SI	SI + disp8	SI + disp16
101	CH	BP	DI	DI + disp8	DI + disp16
110	DH	SI	Direct	BP + disp8	BP + disp16
111	BH	DI	BX	BX + disp8	BX + disp16

TABLE 12.2 POSTBYTE *REG* FIELD

Register	Byte (b)	Word (w)
000	AL	AX
001	CL	CX
010	DL	DX
011	BL	BX
100	AH	SP
101	CH	BP
110	DH	SI
111	BH	DI

The second form of the postbyte shown in Fig. 12.1 includes the field *reg* instead of a postbyte opcode. The meaning of *reg* is shown in Table 12.2. When *mod* = 11, the *r/m* code refers to a register. This means that the instruction is a *register to register* instruction, such as the *MOV* instructions we looked at in Section 10.2. If *mod* is *not* 11, then one of the operands in the instruction will refer to a memory location. Table 12.1 is rearranged in Table 12.3 to give the names of these operand addressing modes. We will look at each of these addressing modes in the following sections. Before doing that, however, let's look at a few more examples of the addressing mode postbyte for some register and immediate addressing.

TABLE 12.3   8086 OPERAND ADDRESSING MODES

Addressing mode	r/m	mod = 00	mod = 01	mod = 10
Direct	110	Direct		
Register Indirect	100	SI		
	101	DI		
	111	BX		
Indexed	100		SI + disp8	SI + disp16
	101		DI + disp8	DI + disp16
Based	111		BX + disp8	BX + disp16
Based stack	110		BP + disp8	BP + disp16
Based + indexed	000	BX + SI	BX + SI + disp8	BX + SI + disp16
	001	BX + DI	BX + DI + disp8	BX + DI + disp16
Based + indexed	010	BP + SI	BP + SI + disp8	BP + SI + disp16
Stack	011	BP + DI	BP + DI + disp8	BP + DI + disp16

Immediate Addressing

To see how Table 12.1 is used with the immediate mode instructions in Table A.2, suppose you want to code the instruction

```
ADD   BL,19H
```

From Table A.2 you see that the only single opcode immediate *ADD* instruction involves registers *AL* or *AX*. The instruction

```
ADD b r/m,imm
```

uses the opcode 80 plus the postbyte

mod	0 0 0	r/m

From Table 12.1 you see that a value of *mod* = 11 corresponds to an operation on a *register*. The value of *r/m* then specifies the register. A value of *r/m* = 011 corresponds to *BL* for a byte instruction. Therefore, the postbyte for the instruction

```
ADD   BL,19H
```

is

or C3H. Therefore, the coding for the instruction will be

```
80 C3 19    ADD BL,19H
```

To try this, type in the program shown in Fig. 12.2. This is the same program as in Fig. 10.11 that adds 35H to 19H, except that register *BL* is used in Fig. 12.2. Single step this instruction and observe the result (4E) in *BL*.

```
0000   B3 35        MOV   BL,35H
0002   80 C3 19     ADD   BL,19H
```
Figure 12.2 Program to add 35H and 19H using *BL*.

Register Addressing

In *register addressing* the data are found in a register. For example, the instruction

```
DEC CL
```

decrements the contents of register *CL*. This is an example of a single-operand instruction. From Table A.2a in Appendix A, you see that there is no single opcode for this instruction. You can *DEC* the 16-bit register *CX* with the opcode 49, but to *DEC CL* you must use the opcode FE plus a postbyte. The postbyte can be found from Tables A.2b and A.3 to be

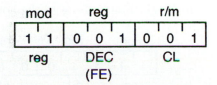

or C9H. Therefore, the coding for *DEC CL* is FE C9.

Register addressing can also involve two operands, as we saw in Chapter 10. For example, the instruction

```
MOV   AX,SI
```

moves the contents of register *SI* to register *AX*. Opcodes 88 to 8B in Table A.2 correspond to the instructions shown in Table 12.4. These instructions can be used to move data from one register to another register, from a register to a memory location, or from a memory location to a register. The second form of the postbyte shown in Fig. 12.1 is used to determine the source and destination in this instruction.

TABLE 12.4 GENERAL MOVE INSTRUCTIONS

Opcode	Instruction
88	MOV b r/m,reg
89	MOV w r/m,reg
8A	MOV b reg,r/m
8B	MOV w reg,r/m

For example, to code

```
MOV   AX,SI
```

you can choose *AX* to be the *reg* and *SI* to be the *r/m* (with *mod* = 11). You would then choose the form *MOV w reg,r/m* with the primary opcode 8B and the postbyte (see Tables 12.1 and 12.2)

or C6H. Therefore, the coding of the instruction is

```
8B C6      MOV   AX,SI
```

Note that this instruction could also be coded as

```
89 F0      MOV   AX,SI
```

by using *r/m* as the destination and *reg* as the source. In this case the postbyte is

or F0H.

The reason that there are two ways to code the same instruction is that both the source and destination in this example are registers. However, in Table 12.4 the operand *r/m* can, in general, be a *memory* location. The operand *reg* is always a register. We will now look at how to move data between a register and a memory location.

12.2 DIRECT ADDRESSING MODE

The direct addressing mode uses a 2-byte operand that can represent any offset address. This offset address is combined with the value in the *data segment register, DS*, to form the actual address of the data.

An example of using the direct addressing mode was given in Listing 11.1. In that example, *dnum* and *negnum* were defined to be 32-bit values in the data segment using the assembler directive *dd*. As another example, consider the program shown in Listing 12.1. This program stores the value FDH in memory location *joe* (direct mode) and then increments this memory location (direct mode) until the value becomes 00 (is no longer negative). The offset address 0000 within

Listing 12.1   *joe.lst*

```
                             title   Direct addressing example

0000                         stack   segment para stack
0000      40 [                       db       64 dup(?)
                 ??
                       ]
0040                         stack   ends

0000                         data    segment public
0000    ??                   joe     db       ?
0001                         data    ends

0000                         code    segment public
                                     assume cs:code,ds:data
0000                         main    proc    far
0000    B8 ---- R                    mov     ax,data         ;set ds
0003    8E D8                        mov     ds,ax
0005    C6 06 0000 R FD  m1:         mov     joe,0fdh        ;joe = fd
000A    FE 06 0000 R     m2:         inc     joe             ;joe = joe + 1
000E    78 FA                        js      m2              ;repeat until joe=0
0010    74 F3                        je      m1              ;do again
0012                         main    endp

0012                         code    ends
                                     end     main
```

the data segment is given the name *joe* using the *define-byte (DB)* assembler directive. This means that *joe* is a variable name whose offset address within the data segment is 0000. The value of *joe* will be the byte stored at this address. The *?* in the *DB* statement means that the assembler doesn't have to assign an initial value to *joe*.

Linking the assembly language program shown in Listing 12.1 will produce the executable file *joe.exe*. Load this .EXE file into TUTOR (using */SL*) and then press function key *F10*. Single step the first two instructions by pressing function key *F1* twice. This will set *DS* to the data segment containing *joe* and will display the contents of *joe* in the first byte of the data segment displayed in the upper-right part of the screen. When you press *F1* again, you will execute the instruction *mov joe,0fdh*, which will store the hex value FD in offset address 0000 in the data segment as shown in Fig. 12.3.

Continue to single step through this program several times while watching the contents of DS:0000. Note that the instruction

```
MOV   JOE,0FDH
```

```
        8086 Microprocessor TUTOR            Press F7 for Help

      AH AL     BH BL     CH CL     DH DL    DATA SEG   08 19 2A 3B 4C 5D 6E 7F
   AX 15 85  BX 10 00  CX 00 C5  DX 3A EE    1585:0000  FD 50 E8 AB 21 83 C4 04
                                             1585:0008  8B D8 D1 E3 8B 3E 1A 58
      SP 0040      SI 0000      IP 000A       1585:0010  8B 01 89 46 F2 A1 56 59
      BP 0000      DI 0000                    1585:0018  48 50 2B C0 50 E8 90 21
      SS 1586      DS 1585      CS 1583        1585:0020  83 C4 04 89 46 DC 0B C0
   SP+SS 158A0  SI+DS 15850      ES 1573       1585:0028  74 71 8B F0 D1 E6 03 36
   BP+SS 15860  DI+DS 15850  IP+CS 1583A       1585:0030  1A 58 A1 E0 5D 39 04 74
   STATUS FLAGS 7202 0111001000000010         1585:0038  62 C6 06 CC 5A FF B8 FF
                          ODITSZ A P C         1585:0040  FF 50 B8 08 85 15 85 15
   1583:000A FE060000      INC   [0000H]      1585:0048  D9 16 0A 00 83 15 02 72

   SEG 1583:   08 19 2A 3B 4C 5D 6E 7F                         1586: STACK
      FFF0   00 00 00 00 00 00 00 00    . . . . . . . .           0040
      FFF8   00 00 00 00 00 00 00 00    . . . . . . . .
      0000   B8 85 15 8E D8 C6 06 00    . . . . . . . .
      0008   00 FD>FE 06 00 00 75 FA    . . . . . u .
      0010   74 F3 00 00 00 00 00 00    t . . . . . . .
      0018   00 00 00 00 00 00 00 00    . . . . . . . .
      0020   FD 50 E8 AB 21 83 C4 04    . P . . ! . . .

   _____  / : Command    > : Go To Memory
                                             Use Cursor Keys to Scroll thru Memory
```

Figure 12.3   TUTOR display illustrating direct addressing.

will move the value FDH into memory location DS:0000. Similarly, the instruction

```
INC   JOE
```

will increment the contents of memory location DS:0000.
    The second instruction in Fig. 12.3 is

```
MOV   DS,AX
```

which moves the contents of *AX* to the segment register *DS*. The segment registers are not included in the register lists in Tables 12.1 and 12.2 and therefore cannot be used for *reg* or *r/m* in the postbytes in Fig. 12.1. Rather, special instructions are required that involve the segment registers. Table 12.5 shows the *MOV* instructions that use the segment registers. The postbyte D8 in Listing 12.1 is found as follows:

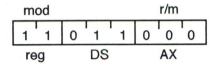

You can move the contents of *CS* to *r/m*, but you *cannot* move the contents of *r/m* to *CS*. The only way you should change the contents of *CS* is with the instructions *JMP*, *CALL*, *RET*, *IRET*, and *INT*.

TABLE 12.5   SEGMENT REGISTER MOVE INSTRUCTIONS

Operation	Mnemonic	Opcode encoding
Move segment register to register or memory	MOV r/m,segreg	8C |mod|0ss|r/m|
Move register or memory to segment register	MOV segreg,r/m	8E |mod|0ss|r/m|

ss	segreg
00	ES
01	CS (MOV CS,r/m *not* allowed)
10	SS
11	DS

Note that there are no instructions for loading immediate data directly into the segment registers. The immediate data must first be moved into another register (such as *AX*) and then into the segment register, as shown by the first two instructions in Listing 12.1.

The coding of the third instruction in Listing 12.1,

```
C6 06 0000 FD     m1:     mov     joe,0fdh
```

is determined as follows. The opcode C6 is for the general instruction

```
C6     MOV b   r/m,imm
```

We want *r/m* to be *direct addressing*. From Table 12.1 this requires a postbyte with *mod* = 00 and *r/m* = 110. The three *reg* bits in the middle are not used and are just set to 000. Thus, the postbyte is

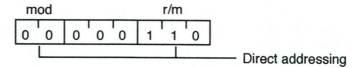

or 06H. For direct addressing the postbyte is followed by the 16-bit offset address in the low-byte, high-byte format. The immediate data will then follow these bytes. Thus, the complete coding will be

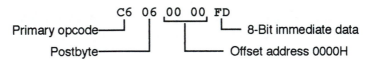

If *joe* had been given a *word* type by using the *DW* (*define word*) assembler directive in Listing 12.1, then the instruction

```
MOV   JOE,0FDH
```

would store the value FDH in *joe* and the value 00H in *joe* + 1. The assembler now considers *joe* to be a 16-bit value. When the value FDH is incremented, it will change to FEH, but this is now considered to be the positive value 00FDH and not a negative value. Therefore, the sign flag will not be set, and the JS instruction in Listing 12.1 will fail. This is an example where changing the type attribute of *joe* from *byte* to *word* makes the program bomb.

When *joe* is given the type *word*, the assembler will code the instruction

```
MOV   JOE,0FDH
```

as follows:

```
              C7  06  00  00  FD  00
Primary opcode───┘   │        │    └── 16-Bit immediate data
      Postbyte───────┘        └── Offset address 0000H
```

If *joe* has been defined as type *word*, but you really want to store FDH only in a single byte, you can type

```
MOV   BYTE PTR JOE,0FDH
```

This will override the declared type and assemble the byte opcode C6, rather than the word opcode C7. On the other hand, if *joe* has been defined as type *byte*, you can override this declaration by typing

```
MOV   WORD PTR JOE,0FDH
```

In this case the value FDH will be stored in *joe*, and the value 00H will be stored in *joe* + 1.

Table 12.6 shows the instructions that can be used to directly increment or decrement a memory location. When applied to direct addressing, the postbyte for *INC* will be 06.

TABLE 12.6   INC AND DEC INSTRUCTIONS FOR REGISTER OR MEMORY

Opcode	Postbyte	Instruction
FE	|mod|000|r/m|	INC BYTE PTR r/m
FF	|mod|000|r/m|	INC WORD PTR r/m
FE	|mod|001|r/m|	DEC BYTE PTR r/m
FF	|mod|001|r/m|	DEC WORD PTR r/m

When word (*WORD PTR*) instructions are applied to direct addressing, 2 bytes are used at the offset address. For example, the instruction

```
FF 06 00 00      INC  WORD PTR JOE
```

will increment the 16-bit word stored at the offset addresses 0000H (low-byte) and 0001H (high-byte).

If *joe* has been defined as type *byte* using DB and you then type the instruction

```
MOV   AX,JOE
```

the assembler will produce the error message *operand types must match*. Both parts of the operand must be of the same type, *byte* or *word*. You could correct this error by typing

```
MOV   AX,WORD PTR JOE
```

which would move the value of *joe* into *AL* and the value of *joe* + 1 into *AH*.

Suppose that instead of the *contents* of *joe* and *joe* + 1 you want to store the *offset address* of *joe* in *AX*. The statement

```
MOV   AX,OFFSET JOE
```

will do this, and the assembler will use the immediate mode of addressing. For example, if *joe* is at offset address 0000H, then the above instruction will be coded as follows:

```
B8 00 00      MOV   AX,OFFSET JOE
```

Note that the offset address 0000H is stored as immediate data in the program.

The *load effective address*, LEA, instruction can also be used to produce the same result. The general form of the LEA instruction is

```
LEA   reg,r/m
```

where the offset address associated with *r/m* (as given in Table 12.1) is stored in *reg* (as given in Table 12.2).

For example, the instruction

```
8D 06 00 00      LEA   AX,JOE
```

will produce the same result as

```
B8 00 00      MOV   AX,OFFSET JOE
```

where 0000H is the offset address of *JOE*.

12.3 REGISTER INDIRECT ADDRESSING

Register indirect addressing stores the *address* of a data item in a register. The 8086 index registers *SI* and *DI* and the *base* register *BX* can be used to point to various memory locations. The actual address pointed to by these registers is formed by using the contents of the data segment register *DS* as the segment address and the contents of *SI*, *DI*, or *BX* as the offset address.

As an example of using register indirect addressing, the program shown in Listing 12.2 will move *CX* (4) bytes from the offset address pointed to by *SI* (*source*) to the offset address pointed to by *DI* (*dest*). The first two instructions set *DS* to point to the data segment. The next three instructions load *CX* with 4, *SI* with the offset address of *source* (0000), and *DI* with the offset address of *dest* (0004). The instruction

```
ml:    move    al,[si]
```

Listing 12.2   *movbyte1.lst*

```
                              title   Register Indirect Addressing

0000                          stack   segment para stack
0000        40 [                      db      64 dup(?)
                  ??
                        ]

0040                          stack   ends

0000                          data    segment public
0000    11 22 33 44           source  db      11h,22h,33h,44h
0004        04 [              dest    db      4 dup(?)
                  ??
                        ]
0008                          data    ends

0000                          code    segment         public
                                      assume cs:code,ds:data
0000                          main    proc    far
0000    B8 ---- R                     mov     ax,data      ;set ds
0003    8E D8                         mov     ds,ax
0005    B9 0004                       mov     cx,4         ;4 bytes
0008    BE 0000 R                     mov     si,offset source
000B    BF 0004 R                     mov     di,offset dest
000E    8A 04             m1:         mov     al,[si]      ;get next byte
0010    88 05                         mov     [di],al      ;& move it
0012    46                            inc     si
0013    47                            inc     di
0014    E2 F8                         loop    m1           ;do 4 times
0016    CC                            int     3
0017                          main    endp

0017                          code    ends
                                      end     main
```

will move the contents of 0000H (the offset address stored in *SI*) into accumulator *AL*. The coding of this instruction can be found from Tables 12.4 and 12.1 as follows:

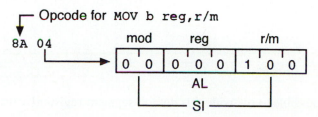

The instruction

```
88 05      mov   [di],al
```

will move the contents of *AL* to the memory location pointed to by *DI* (initially 0004H). The coding of this instruction can also be found from Tables 12.4 and 12.1 as follows:

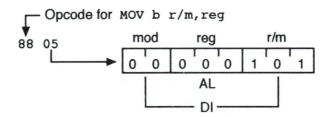

The next two instructions in Listing 12.2 increment *SI* and *DI* so that they will point to offset addresses 0001H and 0005H, respectively. The *loop m1* instruction will decrement *CX* and branch back to *m1* if *CX* is not equal to zero. Thus, this loop will be executed four times, with *SI* and *DI* incremented each time through the loop.

The executable file for this program, *movbyte1.exe*, is on the TUTOR disk. Load the program into TUTOR (using */SL*) and press function key *F10*. Press *F1* twice to single step the first two instructions. This will set *DS* and display the data segment at the upper-right part of the screen. Note that the initial values, 11 22 33 44, specified for *source* in the data segment of Listing 12.2 are already stored at offset addresses 0000 to 0003, as shown in Fig. 12.4. Now continue to single step through this program and note how the four values 11 22 33 44 get moved to offset addresses 0004 to 0007.

Segment Override Prefix

In the example in Listing 12.2, the default segment used with the register indirect addressing mode is *DS*. That is, the contents of *DS* are used as the segment address together with the offset addresses in *SI* and *DI* to determine the actual address of the data in the instructions

```
MOV   AL,[SI]
```

and

```
MOV   [DI],AL
```

It is possible to override this default segment register by using a *segment override*

```
        8086 Microprocessor TUTOR              Press F7 for Help

    AH AL      BH BL      CH CL      DH DL     DATA SEG    08 19 2A 3B 4C 5D 6E 7F
 AX 15 85   BX 10 00   CX 00 C5   DX 3A EE     1585:0000   11 22 33 44 00 00 00 00
                                               1585:0008   04 89 46 FC F6 46 FA 08
    SP 0040      SI 0000      IP 0005           1585:0010   74 18 8B 76 FA 81 E6 03
    BP 0000      DI 0000                        1585:0018   00 8A 84 F2 50 98 89 46
    SS 1586      DS 1585      CS 1583           1585:0020   F6 8A 84 66 51 88 46 F8
 SP+SS 158A0  SI+DS 15850      ES 1573          1585:0028   EB 18 8A 46 FA 24 03 88
 BP+SS 15860  DI+DS 15850  IP+CS 15835          1585:0030   46 F8 B8 00 04 50 2B C0
 STATUS FLAGS 7202 0111001000000010             1585:0038   50 E8 64 30 83 C4 04 89
                     ODITSZ A P C               1585:0040   46 F6 80 7E 85 15 85 15
 1583:0005 B90400      MOV   CX,0004H           1585:0048   D9 16 05 00 83 15 02 72

 SEG 1583:   08 19 2A 3B 4C 5D 6E 7F                          1586: STACK
    FFE8   00 00 00 00 00 00 00 00     . . . . . . . .          0040
    FFF0   00 00 00 00 00 00 00 00     . . . . . . . .
    FFF8   00 00 00 00 00 00 00 00     . . . . . . . .
    0000   B8 85 15 8E D8>B9 04 00     . . . . . . . .
    0008   BE 00 00 BF 04 00 8A 04     . . . . . . . .
    0010   88 05 46 47 E2 F8 CC 00     . . F G . . . .
    0018   00 00 00 00 00 00 00 00     . . . . . . . .

                                       / : Command     > : Go To Memory
                                       Use Cursor Keys to Scroll thru Memory
```

Figure 12.4   Initial values specified in the data segment of Listing 12.2.

prefix given in Figure 12.5. For example, the instruction

```
26 88 05      MOV  ES:[DI],AL
```

will use the extra segment register *ES* instead of *DS* in forming the actual address from the offset address in *DI*.

Segment register	Segment override prefix
ES	26
CS	2E
SS	36
DS	3E

Figure 12.5   Segment override prefixes.

String Primitive Instructions

The 8086 has a number of *string primitive instructions* that makes it easy to manipulate a sequence of bytes in memory. For example, the entire *m1* loop in Listing

12.2 can be replaced with the *single instruction*

```
F3 A4       REP MOVSB
```

The instruction *MOVSB* is one of the string primitive instructions given in Table 12.7. It will move a byte of data from the offset address pointed to by *SI* in the *data* segment to an offset address pointed to by *DI* in the *extra* segment. The values of *SI* and *DI* will then either be incremented or decremented depending on whether the direction flag *D* in the status register is a 0 (increment) or a 1 (decrement).

TABLE 12.7 STRING PRIMITIVE INSTRUCTIONS

Opcode	Instruction	Meaning
A4	MOVS b	Move byte of data from [SI] in the *data* segment (DS) to [DI] in the *extra* segment (ES). Adjust SI and DI.
A5	MOVS w	Move word of data from [SI] in the *data* segment (DS) to [DI] in the *extra* segment (ES). Adjust SI and DI.
A6	CMPS b	Compare byte of data at [SI] in the *data* segment (DS) with byte of data at [DI] in the *extra* segment (ES). Adjust SI and DI.
A7	CMPS w	Compare word of data at [SI] in the *data* segment (DS) with word of data at [DI] in the *extra* segment (ES). Adjust SI and DI.
AA	STOS b	Store contents of AL in [DI] in the *extra* segment (ES). Adjust DI.
AB	STOS w	Store contents of AX in [DI] in the *extra* segment (ES). Adjust DI.
AC	LODS b	Load byte from [SI] in the *data* segment (DS) into AL. Adjust SI.
AD	LODS w	Load word from [SI] in the *data* segment (DS) into AX. Adjust SI.
AE	SCAS b	Compare contents of AL with byte of data at [DI] in the *extra* segment (ES). Adjust DI.
AF	SCAS w	Compare contents of AX with word of data at [DI] in the *extra* segment (ES). Adjust DI.

The *REP* prefix, when used before the string primitive instruction *MOVS* (or *LODS* or *STOS*), repeats the string primitive instruction *CX* times. Following each execution of the string primitive instruction, *CX* is decremented by 1 and the *REP* prefix tests *CX*. If *CX* = 0, then the program continues with the instruction following the string primitive instruction.

As an example of using a string primitive instruction, the program shown in Listing 12.3 performs the same operation as the program in Listing 12.2. Note that the instruction

```
rep movsb
```

has replaced the entire *m1* loop in Listing 12.2. Also note that the data segment address *data* has to be moved into the *extra* segment register *ES* because the *DI* register used by the string primitive instructions *always* uses the extra segment

Listing 12.3   *movbyte2.lst*

```
                                title String Primitive Example

0000                            stack  segment para stack
0000      40 [                      db       64 dup(?)
              ??
                   ]

0040                            stack  ends

0000                            data   segment       public
0000   11 22 33 44               source db      11h,22h,33h,44h
0004      04 [                   dest   db       4 dup(?)
              ??
                   ]
0008                            data   ends

0000                            code   segment   public
                                assume    cs:code,ds:data
0000                            main   proc      far
0000   B8 ---- R                     mov      ax,data      ;set ds
0003   8E D8                         mov      ds,ax
0005   8E C0                         mov      es,ax        ;es = ds
0007   B9 0004                       mov      cx,4         ;4 bytes
000A   BE 0000 R                     mov      si,offset source
000D   BF 0004 R                     mov      di,offset dest
0010   FC                            cld                   ;inc si and di
0011   F3/ A4                        rep movsb             ;move 4 bytes
0013   CC                            int      3
0014                            main   endp

0014                            code   ends
                                end      main
```

register. It cannot be overridden with a segment override prefix. The instruction
CLD will clear the direction flag in the status register so that the values of *SI* and
DI will automatically be *incremented* each time *MOVSB* is executed.

The executable file for this program, *movbyte2.exe*, is on the TUTOR disk.
Load the program into TUTOR (using */SL*) and press function key *F10*. Press *F1*
twice to single step the first two instructions. This will set *DS* and display the
initial values, 11 22 33 44, in the data segment at the upper-right part of the screen.
Now continue to single step through this program. Note that you must single step
the instruction

```
F3 A4       rep movsb
```

four times in order to move all 4 bytes.

When used before the string primitive instructions *CMPS* and *SCAS*, two forms of the *REP* prefix are possible, as shown in Fig. 12.6. As an example, the program shown in Listing 12.4 will scan the 8 bytes starting at offset address 0000 in the data segment (also the extra segment) looking for the byte 55H (stored in *AL*). This is all done by the instruction

```
F2 AE        repne scasb
```

This loop can terminate in one of two ways. If the byte 55H is not one of the bytes from 0000 to 0007, then the loop will end because *CX* went to zero. No match will be found, so the Z-flag will be 0.

Opcode	Instruction	Meaning
F2	REPNE/REPNZ	Following CMPS or SCAS loop will terminate if Z-flag is 1
F3	REPE/REPZ	Following CMPS or SCAS loop will terminate if Z-flag is 0

Figure 12.6   REP prefix will affect the Z-flag when used before CMPS or SCAS.

On the other hand, suppose that the byte 55H is at offset address 0004 in the data segment (as it is in Listing 12.4). In this case the loop will terminate because the *Z*-flag goes to 1 when the match is found (*DI* = 0004). After that *SCASB* instruction is executed, *DI* will automatically be incremented by 1. That is, *DI* will point to the byte following the one where a match was found. A *JE* branching instruction can be used following the instruction

```
F2 AE        repne scasb
```

to jump to a particular section of code if a match is found.

The executable file for this program, *scan8.exe*, is on the TUTOR disk. Load the program into TUTOR (using */SL*) and press function key *F10*. Press *F1* twice to single step the first two instructions. This will set *DS* and display the initial values, 11 22 33 44 55 66 77 88, in the data segment at the upper-right part of the screen. Now continue to single step through this program. Note that after you single step the instruction

```
F2 AE        repne scasb
```

five times the loop exits with the Z-flag in the status register equal to 1 and *DI* = 0005 (the byte following the match).

Now change the value in location DS:0004 to 00. (To do this, remember the code segment, *CS*, and change the segment *SEG* to the data segment using >*S*. Make the change using */MH* and then return to the code segment.) Single step

Listing 12.4   *scan8.lst*

```
                               title  Scan String Example

0000                           stack  segment para stack
0000        40 [                       db      64 dup(?)
                    ??
                         ]

0040                           stack  ends

0000                           data   segment public
0000    11 22 33 44             buff   db      11h,22h,33h,44h
0004    55 66 77 88                    db      55h,66h,77h,88h
0008                           data   ends

0000                           code   segment        public
                                      assume cs:code,ds:data
0000                           main   proc    far
0000    B8 ---- R                      mov     ax,data          ;set ds
0003    8E D8                          mov     ds,ax
0005    8E C0                          mov     es,ax            ;es = ds
0007    B9 0008                        mov     cx,8             ;8 bytes
000A    BF 0000 R                      mov     di,offset buff   ;di -> 1st byte
000D    FC                             cld                      ;inc di
000E    B0 55                          mov     al,55h           ;look for 55h
0010    F2/ AE                         repne   scasb            ;scan bytes
0012    CC                             int     3
0013                           main   endp

0013                           code   ends
                                      end     main
```

through the program again. Note that this time you will execute the instruction

```
F2 AE        repne scasb
```

eight times after which the value of *DI* will be 0008 and the *Z*-flag in the status register will be 0, indicating that no match was found.

12.4 INDEXED ADDRESSING

The 8086 has a number of addressing modes that makes it easy to access data elements within an array. The *indexed addressing mode* uses *SI* or *DI* to index into an array starting at the offset address *disp8* or *disp16* within the data segment (*DS*). This is illustrated in Fig. 12.7.

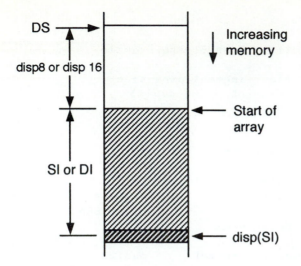

Figure 12.7 Accessing an array element disp(SI) or disp(DI).

For example, consider the array of weights (given in hex) shown in Fig. 12.8. These are stored in the data segment of the program in Listing 12.5 using the statements

```
0008   86 7B C5 CD        wt     db      134,123,197,205
000C   6E 9B B7 AF               db      110,155,183,175
```

I	WT(I)
0	86
1	7B
2	C5
3	CD
4	6E
5	9B
6	B7
7	AF

Figure 12.8 An array of weights WT(I).

Note that the weights are entered in decimal (without the H) following the *define byte* directive. The assembler will convert the values to hex as shown. The first weight is stored at offset address 0008. This is the offset address of the label *wt*. You can use *SI* (or *DI*) to index into the array to find a particular weight. For example, in Listing 12.5 the two statements

```
BE 0004             mov   si,4        ;index = 4
8A 84 0008 R        mov   al,wt[si]   ;get wt[4]
```

will move the value of *wt*(4) = 6E into *AL* (Fig. 12.9).

Listing 12.5   *weights.lst*

```
                                     title Indexed Addressing Example

0000                                 stack segment para stack
0000        40 [                           db      64 dup(?)
                          ??
                                ]

0040                                 stack ends

0000                                 data  segment public
0000    11 22 33 44          buff    db      11h,22h,33h,44h
0004    55 66 77 88                  db      55h,66h,77h,88h
0008    86 7B C5 CD          wt      db      134,123,197,205
000C    6E 9B B7 AF                  db      110,155,183,175
0010                                 data  ends

0000                                 code  segment public
                                           assume cs:code,ds:data
0000                                 main  proc    far
0000    B8 ---- R                          mov     ax,data         ;set ds
0003    8E D8                              mov     ds,ax
0005    BE 0004                            mov     si,4            ;index = 4
0008    8A 84 0008 R                       mov     al,wt[si]       ;get wt[4]
000C    CC                                 int     3
000D                                 main  endp

000D                                 code  ends
                                           end     main
```

The postbyte 84H used in the second statement is found from Tables 12.2 and 12.3 as follows:

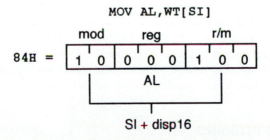

Note that the array name, *wt*, is associated with the displacement, *disp16*, and has the value 0008 in the example shown.

```
      8086 Microprocessor TUTOR              Press F7 for Help

    AH AL     BH BL     CH CL      DH DL    DATA SEG    08 19 2A 3B 4C 5D 6E 7F
 AX 15 6E  BX 10 00  CX 00 C5  DX 3A EE    1584:0000   11 22 33 44 55 66 77 88
                                            1584:0008   86 7B C5 CD 6E 9B B7 AF
    SP 0040       SI 0004       IP 000C     1584:0010   2B C0 50 E8 9A 30 83 C4
    BP 0000       DI 0000                   1584:0018   04 89 46 FC F6 46 FA 08
    SS 1585       DS 1584      CS 1583      1584:0020   74 18 8B 76 FA 81 E6 03
 SP+SS 15890  SI+DS 15844      ES 1573      1584:0028   00 8A 84 F2 50 98 89 46
 BP+SS 15850  DI+DS 15840   IP+CS 1583C     1584:0030   F6 8A 84 66 51 88 46 F8
 STATUS FLAGS 7202 0111001000000010         1584:0038   EB 18 8A 46 FA 24 03 88
                     ODITSZ A P C           1584:0040   46 F8 B8 00 6E 15 84 15
 1583:000C CC        INT3                   1584:0048   D9 16 0C 00 83 15 02 72

 SEG 1583:    08 19 2A 3B 4C 5D 6E 7F                      1585: STACK
    FFF0   00 00 00 00 00 00 00 00    . . . . . . . .        0040
    FFF8   00 00 00 00 00 00 00 00    . . . . . . . .
    0000   B8 84 15 8E D8 BE 04 00    . . . . . . . .
    0008   8A 84 08 00>CC 00 00 00    . . . . . . . .
    0010   11 22 33 44 55 66 77 88    . " 3 D U f w .
    0018   86 7B C5 CD 6E 9B B7 AF    . { . . n . . .
    0020   2B C0 50 E8 9A 30 83 C4    + . P . . 0 . .

 _____   / : Command      > : Go To Memory
                                           Use Cursor Keys to Scroll thru Memory
```

Figure 12.9 The value 6E at offset address 0008 + 0004 is moved to *AL*.

The executable file for this program, *weights.exe*, is on the TUTOR disk. Load the program into TUTOR (using */SL*) and press function key *F10*. Press *F1* twice to single step the first two instructions. This will set *DS* and display the weights, 86 7B C5 CD 6E 9B B7 AF, on the second line of the data segment (starting at offset address 0008) at the upper-right part of the screen. Continue to single step through this program and note how the byte at *wt*[4] (6E) gets loaded into *AL*. Change the value of *SI* at offset address 0006 in the program from 04 to 07 and see if the weight value AFH gets loaded into *AL* when the instruction *mov al,wt[si]* is executed. Try some different values of *SI*.

Sometimes it is more convenient to use the value in a register as the *base* address of an array and to use a displacement such as *disp8* or *disp16* as the index into the array. This is called *based addressing*.

12.5 BASED ADDRESSING

A *record* is a collection of data items, possibly of different types (ASCII data, integer data, and the like) that are related in some way. For example, suppose you want to store an address book in the computer. Each entry (different person) in the book would be a record. This record would contain the person's name, address, and phone number, as shown in Table 12.8. Note that each record is 40H bytes long and is made up of the six record items shown in Table 12.9.

TABLE 12.8   RECORD LAYOUT FOR AN ADDRESS BOOK

	00	0F	10	1F	20	2C	2D	30	31	35	36	3F
Record 0	Name		Street		City		State		Zip		Phone	
Record 1												
Record 2												
.												
.												
.												
.												
Record n												

TABLE 12.9   LOCATION OF RECORD ITEMS WITHIN RECORD

Record item	Displacement within record	Length of record item	Type of data
Name	00H	10H	ASCII
Street	10H	10H	ASCII
City	20H	0DH	ASCII
State	2DH	04H	ASCII
Zip	31H	05H	ASCII
Phone	36H	0AH	ASCII

The important point in Table 12.8 is that the starting location of a particular record item (for example, *PHONE*) is at the same relative displacement from the beginning of the record for all records in the address book. Suppose that register *BX* contains the starting address (base address) of a particular record. The *PHONE* number associated with that record will always be found by adding 36H (the displacement of *PHONE*) to the contents of *BX*. To find the phone number of a different record, you only have to change the contents of *BX*. This is called *based addressing.*

Note that, whereas the indexed addressing form *disp(SI)* uses the *disp* as the starting address of an array, the based addressing form *BX(disp)* uses *disp* as the displacement into a record whose starting address is in *BX*.

From Tables 12.1, 12.2, and 12.3, the first digit of the phone number can be loaded into *AL* using the statement

```
8A 47 36    MOV AL,PHONE[BX]
  │  │  └─────displacement PHONE
  │  └────────postbyte for AL,BX + disp8
  └───────────opcode for MOV reg,r/m
```

The postbyte 47H is determined as follows:

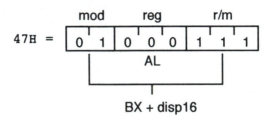

More powerful methods of accessing the data in Table 12.8 can be obtained by combining indexed and based addressing.

12.6 INDEXED PLUS BASED ADDRESSING

It is possible to use *SI* and *DI* as an index variable into a based array of the form *BX(SI)* or *BX(DI)*. These forms of addressing are listed as *BX + SI* and *BX + DI* in the *mod* = 00 column in Table 12.3. In addition, you can add either an 8- or 16-bit displacement, as shown in the last two columns of Table 12.3.

As an example of when you may want to do this, consider the address book records shown in Table 12.8. A collection of such records is sometimes called a *file*. You may have more than one such file. For example, you might have a Christmas list address book and perhaps others for different members of the family. Each address book would start at a different offset address in memory (within a given data segment). The base address stored in *BX* would select a particular address book. Since each record is 40H bytes long, record *n* will start at 40H × *n* bytes from the base address. This value could be stored in *SI*. A constant displacement can then access a particular record item.

An example of using this addressing mode is shown in Listing 12.6. This listing illustrates the use of a assembler directive called *STRUC*. The purpose of *STRUC* is to define a particular data structure that can be duplicated at other locations within the program. We will use *STRUC* to define the structure of a particular record in Listing 12.6. The two statements *adbook struc* and *adbook ends* at the beginning of Listing 12.6 define a dummy segment in which the labels *name*, *street*, *city*, *state*, *zip*, and *phone* define the lengths of each of these fields within the record. Later in the data segment we can duplicate these records by using *adbook* as a assembler directive in the form *rec0 adbook* or *rec1 adbook*.

Listing 12.6   *adbook.lst*

```
                            title   Address Book

0000                        stack   segment para stack
0000      40 [                      db      64 dup(?)
               ??
                   ]

0040                        stack   ends

                            adbook  struc
0000   20 20 20 20 20 20    name    db      '                       '
       20 20 20 20 20 20
       20 20 20 20
0010   20 20 20 20 20 20    street  db      '                       '
       20 20 20 20 20 20
       20 20 20 20
0020   20 20 20 20 20 20    city    db      '                   '
       20 20 20 20 20 20
       20
002D   20 20 20 20          state   db      '     '
0031   20 20 20 20 20        zip    db      '      '
0036   20 20 20 20 20 20    phone   db      '              '
       20 20 20 20
0040                        adbook  ends

0000                        data    segment public
0000      0A [              phbuff  db      10 dup(0)
               00
                   ]

000A   4A 6F 65 20 44 6F    rec0    adbook <'Joe Doe','123 Main St.','Roch
       65 20 20 20 20 20            ester','Mich'>
       20 20 20 20
001A   31 32 33 20 4D 61
       69 6E 20 53 74 2E
       20 20 20 20
002A   52 6F 63 68 65 73
       74 65 72 20 20 20
       20
0037   4D 69 63 68
003B   20 20 20 20 20
0040   20 20 20 20 20 20
       20 20 20 20
```

Listing 12.6 *(cont.)*

```
004A   4D 61 72 79 20 20  rec1    adbook <'Mary',,,,,'521-8934'>
       20 20 20 20 20 20
       20 20 20 20
005A   20 20 20 20 20 20
       20 20 20 20 20 20
       20 20 20 20
006A   20 20 20 20 20 20
       20 20 20 20 20 20
       20
0077   20 20 20 20
007B   20 20 20 20 20
0080   35 32 31 2D 38 39
       33 34 20 20


008A   4A 6F 68 6E 20 20  rec2    adbook <'John',,,,,'831-4321'>
       20 20 20 20 20 20
       20 20 20 20
009A   20 20 20 20 20 20
       20 20 20 20 20 20
       20 20 20 20
00AA   20 20 20 20 20 20
       20 20 20 20 20 20
       20
00B7   20 20 20 20
00BB   20 20 20 20 20
00C0   38 33 31 2D 34 33
       32 31 20 20


00CA                      data    ends

0000                      code    segment public
                                  assume cs:code,ds:data,es:data
0000                      main    proc    far
0000   B8 ---- R                  mov     ax,data             ;set ds
0003   8E D8                      mov     ds,ax
0005   8E C0                      mov     es,ax               ; and es
0007   FC                         cld                         ;di increases
0008   BB 000A R                  mov     bx,offset rec0      ;start of file
000B   B9 000A                    mov     cx,10               ;phone = 10 char
000E   B0 02                      mov     al,2                ;record 2
0010   B4 40                      mov     ah,64               ;64 char/rec
0012   F6 E4                      mul     ah
0014   8B F0                      mov     si,ax               ;si=64*rec#
0016   BF 0000 R                  mov     di,offset phbuff    ;di-> buffer
0019   8A 40 36          m1:      mov     al,phone[bx][si]    ;get digit
```

Listing 12.6   *(cont.)*

```
001C   46                        inc     si
001D   AA                        stosb                    ;move to buffer
001E   E2 F9                     loop    m1               ;get all digits
0020   CC                        int     3
0021                     main    endp
0021                     code    ends
                                 end     main
```

Look at the data segment in Listing 12.6 and notice how the three records *rec0*, *rec1*, and *rec2* have been defined. The definition of *adbook* using the *STRUC* assembler directive has initialized all the bytes to ASCII blanks. The lengths of each field were adjusted by using the DB assembler directive with an ASCII string of blanks of the proper length. When defining a specific instance of the address book record in the data segment using *adbook*, any or all of these blank fields may be overwritten by using the *angle bracket* operand, as shown in Listing 12.6. The angle bracket operand contains parameter fields separated by commas, corresponding to each field defined by *STRUC* to be in *adbook*. For example, *rec0* is defined to have the initial name, *Joe Doe*, the street, *123 Main St.*, the city, *Rochester*, and the State, *Mich*. All the other fields will maintain their default blank values. You can leave any field within the record with its default value by including commas within the angle bracket operand. For example, in *rec1* the operand <'*Mary*',,,,,'*521-8934*'> will define the name field to be *Mary* and the phone field to be *521-8934*. All other fields will remain blank.

The program in Listing 12.6 will get the phone number in record 2 (831-4321) and store this phone number in the 10-byte phone buffer, *phbuff*, at the beginning of the data segment. The start of the address book is at offset address *rec0* within the data segment. This offset address (000AH) is stored in *BX* in the instruction at offset address 0008 within the code segment. The start of record 2 is found by adding 40H × 2 to *BX*. The value 40H × 2 is stored in *SI* in the instruction at location *CS:0014*. The statement

```
8A 40 36      MOV   AL,PHONE[BX][SI]
```

at location *CS:0019* moves the first digit (ASCII code) of the phone number into *AL*. Note that it adds the contents of *BX* (the start of the address book), *SI* (the beginning of record 2), and 36H (the beginning of *PHONE*) to get the final offset address of *PHONE*. This value is stored at address *ES:DI* using the *STOSB* instruction at *CS:001D*. The *m1* loop will transfer the entire phone number (the length of *PHONE*, 0AH, is in *CX*) from the address book to the phone buffer at location *DS:0000–DS:0009*.

    You could have used the *REP MOVSB* instruction to perform the entire loop in Listing 12.6 if you had moved the starting address of *PHONE* into *SI*. However, this example is to illustrate the use of the based plus indexed addressing mode.

    The executable file for this program, *adbook.exe*, is on the TUTOR disk. Load the program into TUTOR (using */SL*) and press function key *F10*. Press *F1* twice to single step the first two instructions. This will set *DS* and display the beginning of the data segment at the upper-right part of the screen. Note that the first 10 bytes are zeros, corresponding to the initial values in *phbuff*, and the following bytes contain the contents of rec0 as shown in the TUTOR screen display in Fig. 12.10. The program will move the phone number from *rec2* that begins at offset address 008A in the data segment. This part of the data segment isn't visible on the TUTOR screen. However, you can display any part of memory in the upper-right part of the screen by using the TUTOR command */G*. If you type */G*, the command line will display

```
DATA SEGMENT: S O D
```

```
        8086 Microprocessor TUTOR              Press F7 for Help

     AH AL     BH BL     CH CL     DH DL     DATA SEG    08 19 2A 3B 4C 5D 6E 7F
  AX 15 86  BX 10 00  CX 00 C5  DX 3A EE     1586:0000   00 00 00 00 00 00 00 00
                                             1586:0008   00 00 4A 6F 65 20 44 6F
     SP 0040       SI 0000      IP 0005       1586:0010   65 20 20 20 20 20 20 20
     BP 0000       DI 0000                    1586:0018   20 20 31 32 33 20 4D 61
     SS 1593       DS 1586      CS 1583       1586:0020   69 6E 20 53 74 2E 20 20
  SP+SS 15970   SI+DS 15860     ES 1573       1586:0028   20 20 52 6F 63 68 65 73
  BP+SS 15930   DI+DS 15860  IP+CS 15835      1586:0030   74 65 72 20 20 20 20 4D
  STATUS FLAGS 7202 0111001000000010          1586:0038   69 63 68 20 20 20 20 20
                         ODITSZ A P C         1586:0040   20 20 20 20 20 20 20 20
  1583:0005 8EC0        MOV    ES,AX          1586:0048   20 20 4D 61 72 79 20 20

  SEG 1583:   08 19 2A 3B 4C 5D 6E 7F                        1593: STACK
        FFE8   00 00 00 00 00 00 00 00     . . . . . . . .        0040
        FFF0   00 00 00 00 00 00 00 00     . . . . . . . .
        FFF8   00 00 00 00 00 00 00 00     . . . . . . . .
        0000   B8 86 15 8E D8>8E C0 FC     . . . . . . . .
        0008   BB 0A 00 B9 0A 00 B0 02     . . . . . . . .
        0010   B4 40 F6 E4 8B F0 BF 00     . @ . . . . . .
        0018   00 8A 40 36 46 AA E2 F9     . . @ 6 F . . .

                                      / : Command     > : Go To Memory
                                      Use Cursor Keys to Scroll thru Memory
```

Figure 12.10 The first 10 bytes of the data segment (*phbuff*) initially contain all zeros.

```
                8086 Microprocessor TUTOR              Press F7 for Help

        AH AL      BH BL      CH CL      DH DL    DATA SEG    08 19 2A 3B 4C 5D 6E 7F
    AX 15 86   BX 10 00   CX 00 C5   DX 3A EE    1586:008A   4A 6F 68 6E 20 20 20 20
                                                 1586:0092   20 20 20 20 20 20 20 20
        SP 0040        SI 0000        IP 0005    1586:009A   20 20 20 20 20 20 20 20
        BP 0000        DI 0000                   1586:00A2   20 20 20 20 20 20 20 20
        SS 1593        DS 1586        CS 1583    1586:00AA   20 20 20 20 20 20 20 20
    SP+SS 15970   SI+DS 15860        ES 1573     1586:00B2   20 20 20 20 20 20 20 20
    BP+SS 15930   DI+DS 15860   IP+CS 15835      1586:00BA   20 20 20 20 20 20 38 33
    STATUS FLAGS 7202 0111001000000010           1586:00C2   31 2D 34 33 32 31 20 20
                          ODITSZ A P C           1586:00CA   51 0A 50 FF 76 F6 E8 4D
    1583:0005 8EC0        MOV    ES,AX            1586:00D2   DF 83 C4 06 0A C0 74 04

    SEG 1583:   08 19 2A 3B 4C 5D 6E 7F                          1593: STACK
        FFE8   00 00 00 00 00 00 00 00    . . . . . . . .           0040
        FFF0   00 00 00 00 00 00 00 00    . . . . . . . .
        FFF8   00 00 00 00 00 00 00 00    . . . . . . . .
        0000   B8 86 15 8E D8>8E C0 FC    . . . . . . . .
        0008   BB 0A 00 B9 0A 00 B0 02    . . . . . . . .
        0010   B4 40 F6 E4 8B F0 BF 00    . @ . . . . . .
        0018   00 8A 40 36 46 AA E2 F9    . . @ 6 F . . .

    _____    / : Command     > : Go To Memory
                                                 Use Cursor Keys to Scroll thru Memory
```

Figure 12.11   The phone number of *rec2* starts at offset address 00C0 in the data segment.

Type *O* and then enter the offset address 8A. This will display the data segment starting at offset address 008A, and you will be able to see the phone number starting at offset address 00C0, as shown in Fig. 12.11.

Type */GD* to go back to the beginning of the current data segment where *phbuff* is located (*/GS* will allow you to display a different segment in the upper-right part of the screen.) Now continue to single step through this program and note how each byte of the phone number of *rec2* is moved to *phbuff*.

12.7 STACK ADDRESSING

The *based* and *based plus indexed* addressing described in the previous two sections involves the use of the base register *BX*. When this register is used, the actual address is found in the data segment. That is, the data segment register *DS* is used to calculate the actual address.

Sometimes it is useful to use these addressing modes when accessing data in the stack segment rather than the data segment. This may occur, for example, when passing parameters on the stack to subroutines. The base pointer register, *BP*, can be used instead of *BX* to hold a base address within the stack segment. Table 12.3 shows the *based stack* and *based plus indexed stack* addressing modes that are available on the 8086. These modes work just like the *based* and *based plus indexed* modes just described except that *BP* replaces *BX* and *SS* replaces *DS*. That is, the data are accessed in the *stack segment*.

As an example of passing parameters on the stack, we will modify the program shown in Listing 11.1a that uses the subroutine *neg2word* to find the two's complement of a double word. Instead of passing the double word to the subroutine in the registers *dx:ax*, we will push the double word on the stack before calling the subroutine *dneg2*, as shown in the main program in Listing 12.7. The instruction *call dneg2* will push the return (offset) address on the stack before jumping to the subroutine *dneg2*. The first four instructions of *dneg2* will push *bp* on the stack, set *bp* to *sp*, and then push *bx* and *cx* on the stack. At this point the stack will therefore look like Figure 12.12.

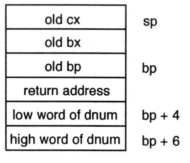

Figure 12.12   Stack picture after executing the first four instructions in the subroutine *dneg2*.

The double word, *dnum*, is now on the stack at location *bp* + 4 and *bp* + 6. We can move these values into *bx* and *cx* using the instructions

```
mov    bx,6[bp]    ;bx=hi word
mov    cx,4[bp]    ;cx=lo word
```

as shown in Listing 12.7. When using this stack addressing mode, note that the data are accessed in the stack segment. This subroutine will pass the answer (the two's complement of *dnum*) back to the main program in the registers *dx:ax*.

After executing the three *pop* instructions at the end of the subroutine *dneg2*, the stack pointer will be pointing to the word containing the return address. If we execute the instruction *ret* at this point, the program will return to the main program, but the stack pointer will be pointing to the address *bp* + 4 in Fig. 12.12. The main program should then add 4 to the stack pointer to put it back to its location prior to pushing the parameters on the stack. Alternatively, the subroutine

Listing 12.7   *stkpara.asm*

```
title   Two's complement of a double word
;       Example of passing parameters on the stack
stack   segment para stack
 db     64 dup(?)
stack   ends

data    segment
dnum    dd     12345678h
negnum  dd     ?
data    ends

code    segment public
assume  cs:code,ds:data

main    proc    far
        mov     ax,data
        mov     ds,ax                 ;set ds=data
        mov     ax,word ptr dnum      ;ax=low word
        mov     dx,word ptr dnum+2    ;dx=high word
        push    dx                    ;push high word
        push    ax                    ;push low word
        call    dneg2                 ;2's compl
        mov     word ptr negnum,ax    ;store lo word
        mov     word ptr negnum+2,dx  ;store hi word
        int     3
main    endp

;       negate double word passed on stack
dneg2   proc    near
        push    bp            ;save bp
        mov     bp,sp         ;index with bp
        push    bx            ;save regs
        push    cx
        mov     bx,6[bp]      ;bx=hi word
        mov     cx,4[bp]      ;cx=lo word
        xor     ax,ax         ;ax=0
        mov     dx,ax         ;dx=0
        sub     ax,cx         ;dx:ax =
        sbb     dx,bx         ; 0:0 - bx:cx
        pop     cx            ;restore regs
        pop     bx
        pop     bp            ;restore bp
        ret     4             ;fix stack
dneg2   endp

code    ends
        end     main
```

itself can fix up the stack by using the form of the return statement given by

```
ret   4             ;fix stack
```

which will add 4 to the stack pointer after popping the return address from the stack.

This technique of passing parameters to a subroutine on the stack is used by most high-level languages when they want to access an assembly language routine. Languages differ in the order that their parameters are pushed on the stack and whether the calling program or the subroutine should be responsible for fixing up the stack after the return. If the subroutine is passing no more than 4 bytes of information back to the calling program, it will normally use registers *ax* and *dx* for this purpose. Otherwise, it may pass the segment and offset addresses of the returned data in *dx:ax* (as in C), or the calling program may have included the offset address (within the data segment) where the resulting data are to be deposited as the last parameter pushed on the stack prior to the subroutine call (as in FORTRAN, BASIC, and Pascal).

Experiment 26: Macros and Threaded Languages

In this experiment you will learn how to use *macros* and how a stack-oriented, threaded interpretive language works. You will also see a good example of register indirect addressing associated with the *PUSH* and *POP* instructions.

1. Programming is made easier if you break up your routines into small modules. You can do this by using lots of subroutines. Your program might then look something like this:

```
call  sub1
call  sub2
call  sub3
call  sub4
```

Suppose that *every* statement in your program was of this form. Then you wouldn't really need to include the opcode for the *CALL* statement since every statement would be understood to be a *CALL* statement. This would save you a byte of memory for every statement, and the program would reduce to a list of addresses of the subroutines:

```
sub1
sub2
sub3
sub4
```

This is the idea behind threaded interpretive languages such as *Forth*. The language is made up entirely of *words* (which are like subroutines), which are made up of a list of other words (that you have previously defined). This list of words is just a list of the addresses to be executed when the word is called or executed. Thus, in the list above, *sub1* might itself consist of another list of *word* addresses that must be "executed" every time *sub1* is called. Of course, eventually some real 8086 machine code must be executed for anything to happen. Words that contain real machine code, rather than just a list of addresses of other words, are called *primitive* or *kernel* words.

2. Data are passed from one word to the next on the stack. Every word has a stack picture associated with it that shows the items on the stack before the word is called and after the word is called. The stack picture looks like this:

```
( stack items before -- stack items after )
```

For example, the word *DUP* duplicates the top stack item and the stack picture looks like this:

```
DUP  ( w -- w w )
```

This means that before *DUP* is executed a value *w* is on the stack, and after *DUP* has been executed there are two values of *w* on the stack. In these pictures the top of the stack is on the right. The word *DUP* is a primitive that can be implemented in 8086 assembly language as

```
dup:    mov   bx,sp
        push  0[bx]
```

The word *OVER* (*w1 w2 -- w1 w2 w1*) copies the second stack item to the top of the stack. It can be implemented as

```
over:  mov   bx,sp
       push  2[bx]
```

The word *DROP* (*w --*) discards the top stack item. It can be implemented as

```
drop:  inc  sp
       inc  sp
```

The word *SWAP* (*w1 w2 -- w2 w1*) exchanges the top two stack items. It can be implemented as

```
swap:  pop   bx
       pop   ax
       push  bx
       push  ax
```

3. Write assembly language code that will implement the following words:

store (w a --)   Store the word *w* at offset address *a*. (This word
                        is written as ! in Forth.)

at (a -- w)   Fetch the word value *w* stored at the address *a*.
                        (This word is written as @ in Forth.)

plus (w w -- w)   Add the top two items on the stack. (This word
                        is written as + in Forth.)

4. The word *PSTOR* (*n a* --) adds *n* to the contents of address *a*. In Forth
this word is written as +! and pronounced "plus store." Note that *PSTOR*
can be defined in terms of our previous words as

```
:   pstor     ( n a -- )
              swap            (                    )
              over            (                    )
              at              (                    )
              plus            (                    )
              swap            (                    )
              store   ;       (                    )
```

Fill in the stack picture following each word in the definition of *pstor*.

5. In assembly language we can implement *pstor* by writing

```
pstor:        dw      swap,over,at
              dw      plus,swap,store
```

The assembler will assemble this word as a list of the offset addresses of
the six words making up the definition. Suppose that *si* is pointing to *pstor*
(that is, it is pointing to an address that contains the address of *swap*). The
two statements

```
lodsw
jmp   ax
```

will load *ax* with the address of *swap* and then jump to this address (that is,
swap will be executed). The value of *si* will automatically be incremented
by 2 (by *lodsw*) and will therefore be pointing to the word containing the
address of *over*. After executing each of the words in *pstor*, we need to
execute the above two statements to go to the next word. We can do this
by introducing the following *macro*:

```
$next   macro
           lodsw
           jmp   ax
        endm
```

We would then include this macro at the end of each primitive definition. For example,

```
dup: mov   bx,sp
     push  0[bx]
     $next
```

When this code is assembled, the actual code in the macro *$next* is inserted at the end of the definition of *dup*.

6. Write a program that includes the following:
   a. The statement

```
spp   equ   3e7eh
```

   b. The macro definition of *$next*.
   c. A single code segment containing the assume statement

```
assume    cs:code,ds:code,ss:code
```

   d. The following main program:

```
main:      mov   ax,cs
           mov   ds,ax
           mov   ss,ax
           mov   sp,ssp
           cld
again:     mov   ax,2
           push  ax
           mov   ax,offset  addr1
           push  ax
           mov   si,offset  pstor
           $next

addr1      dw    0
```

   e. Add definitions for all the primitives discussed above as well as the definition of *pstor*. Add the statement

```
dw     again
```

   to the definition of *pstor*.

7. Assemble, link, and load this program into TUTOR. Single step through the program and watch the value 2 be added to the contents of *addr1* as all the words in *pstor* are executed.

EXERCISES

12.1. Use Tables A.2a and A.2b to code the following instructions:

   a. SUB   AX,1234H
   b. MOV   DX,5432H
   c. XOR   CH,3CH
   d. CMP   AH,0CH

12.2. Code the following instructions:

   a. MOV   DH,CL
   b. MOV   DI,AX
   c. MOV   SP,AX
   d. MOV   BL,AH

12.3. Code the following instructions assuming that *SAM* is a label at offset address 0005H.

   a. DEC   BYTE PTR SAM
   b. MOV   BYTE PTR SAM,13H
   c. MOV   ES,AX
   d. MOV   SS,SAM

12.4. Write a program that will store the value AAH in 256 consecutive memory locations starting at location *DS:0100*. *Hint:* The instruction *REP STOSB* will store the same value in consecutive memory locations.

12.5. After executing the program in Exercise 12.4, write and execute a program that will transfer 256 bytes starting at location *DS:0100* to another location starting at location *DS:0200*.

12.6. The word *CAT* can be stored in memory as the three ASCII bytes 43 41 54. Store these values at some location between DS:0100 and DS:0200. Write and execute a program that will search for the word *CAT* in this memory range and determine the address where it is stored.

12.7. Enter three names, addresses, and phone numbers in *rec0*, *rec1*, and *rec2* in Listing 12.6. Change *phbuff* to be a 16-byte buffer. Modify the program in Listing 12.6 to move the following data to this new buffer region.
   a. Name in record 1
   b. Street in record 0
   c. Zip code in record 0
   d. State in record 2
   e. City in record 2
   f. Phone number in record 1

13

Screen Display

The PC screen display is controlled by a plug-in board in the PC. When IBM introduced the first PC in 1981, it provided two different types of screen display boards: a *monochrome display adapter* (MDA) and a *color graphics adapter* (CGA). Each adapter required its own separate monitor. The monochrome monitor displayed only text (25 rows of 80 characters each). The color graphics adapter could display either 40 characters per row or 80 characters per row of text, as well as limited color graphics. In 1982, Hercules Computer Technology introduced its first graphics card, which allowed monochrome graphics to be displayed on the monochrome monitor. We will study how this is done in Chapter 16. A number of other companies introduced color graphics cards that provided better resolution and more colors than CGA graphics. In 1984, IBM introduced its *enhanced graphics adapter* (EGA) and later brought out its *video graphics array* (VGA) board, both of which provided high-resolution color graphics and text.

This chapter will be concerned with text display. The use of graphics will be covered in Chapter 16.

In this chapter you will learn:

- How a raster scan display works
- How character data are stored in a video RAM
- How to display characters using BIOS routines
- How to write a number of useful subroutines for controlling the screen display and keyboard inputs
- How to allocate and deallocate memory

13.1 RASTER SCAN DISPLAYS

A video monitor screen works by causing an electron beam to scan the screen in a raster format, that is, in a series of horizontal lines moving down the screen. The electron beam impinging on a phosphor-coated screen causes light to be emitted. The electron beam scans the entire screen in $\frac{1}{60}$ (or sometimes $\frac{1}{50}$) second. Home TV images are displayed in an *interlaced* format in which every other scan line is displayed in the first $\frac{1}{60}$ second, and the remaining alternate scan lines are displayed in the next $\frac{1}{60}$ second. It therefore takes $\frac{1}{30}$ second to display the entire image. Although only one spot on the screen is being hit by the electron beam at any instant of time, if the entire screen is rewritten every $\frac{1}{30}$ second, the eye will retain the image from one screen scan to the next. It will therefore look as if an image fills the entire screen, even though only one spot is really being displayed.

When using a color graphics adapter (CGA), the PC scans the same 200 horizontal lines every $\frac{1}{60}$ second. Eight consecutive horizontal lines are used to display a single character. Therefore, 25 (200/8) lines of text can be displayed on the screen. Each character displayed on the screen is in the form of a 5 × 7 dot matrix located within an 8 × 8 dot area on the screen.

The IBM monochrome monitor will display 25 rows of 80 characters each. The monochrome characters are a 7 × 9 dot matrix within a 9 × 14 character box, as shown in Fig. 13.1. Therefore, 350 (25 × 14) horizontal lines are scanned every $\frac{1}{50}$ second on the monochrome display.

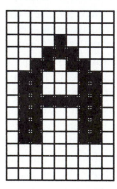

Figure 13.1 A 7 × 9 dot matrix character within a 9 × 14 dot area on the screen.

A dot will be displayed on the screen if the electron beam is turned on when it is at the location on the screen where the dot is to be displayed. If the electron beam is turned off, then no dot will be displayed on the screen. The video signal that is fed into the video monitor is a signal that turns the electron beam on and off at the proper timing to produce the desired effect on the screen.

For example, to display the A shown in Fig. 13.1, we must control the electron beam for 14 consecutive scan lines. The third scan line (the top of the A) contains a single dot surrounded by four blanks on each side. If we represent a dot by 1 and a blank by 0, then the top of the A is represented by 000010000.

The next two scan lines of the A would be represented by 000111000 and 001101100, respectively.

With the color graphics adapter (CGA) the PC can display either 40 or 80 characters per line. If we use 40 characters per line, 320 (40 × 8) dot positions will occur on each line. To display an entire line of 40 characters, we must display the top row of each character, then the second row of each character, then the third row, and so on. It will take eight horizontal scan lines to display one line of 40 characters.

The way that this is done is shown in Fig. 13.2. Suppose that you want to display the three characters *T H E* at the upper-left corner of the screen. The

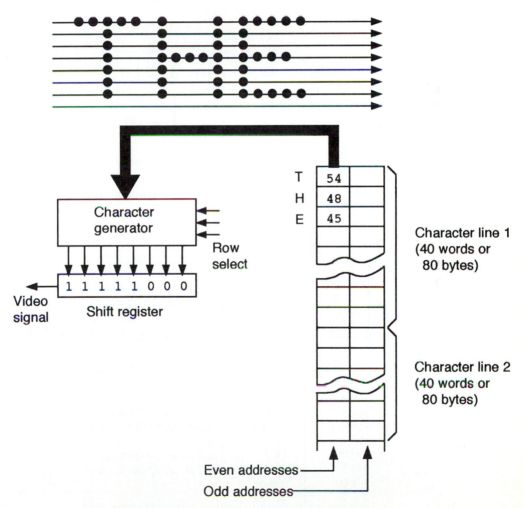

Figure 13.2 ASCII codes for characters to be displayed on the screen are stored in a video RAM.

screen ASCII codes for these characters are stored in the first three even address locations of a video RAM. Each byte containing a screen ASCII code is followed by a byte containing a character attribute code. To display the top bar of the *T* (in row 0), the ASCII code for *T* (54) and the row number (00) are used to form an input address to the character generator. The character generator is really a read-only memory (ROM) that contains the dot patterns used to form the various characters. For example, the top of the *T* is represented by the dot pattern 11111000. This will be the output of the character generator when the input is the ASCII code for *T* and the row select value 00. This dot pattern code is put into a shift register from which it is shifted out 1 bit at a time to form the video signal as shown in Fig. 13.2. This video signal goes to the video monitor where it controls the electron beam.

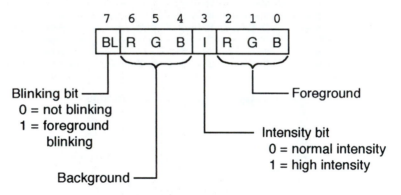

Background	Foreground	Monochrome Display	Color Graphics Display
0 0 0	1 1 1	normal display	normal display
1 1 1	0 0 0	reverse video	reverse video
0 0 0	0 0 0	non display (black)	non display (black)
1 1 1	1 1 1	non display (white)	non display (white)
0 0 0	0 0 1	underline	blue character

Foreground/Background Color Codes

R G B	Color	
0 0 0	Black	
0 0 1	Blue	Setting the I-bit
0 1 0	Green	will result in 8
0 1 1	Cyan	additional shades of
1 0 0	Red	these 8 colors for
1 0 1	Magenta	the foreground color.
1 1 0	Yellow	
1 1 1	White	

Figure 13.3   The attribute byte.

After the top of the *T* is displayed, the top of the *H* must be displayed next. The ASCII code for *H* (stored in the next even address of the video RAM) is moved to the input of the character generator. The row select input remains at 00. The output of the character generator will be 10001000, corresponding to the top part of the *H*. This code then gets shifted out of the shift register and becomes the next part of the video signal.

This process continues until the first 40 ASCII codes, stored in the first 40 even bytes of the video RAM, have all been cycled to the character generator. At this point the top of all characters will have been displayed. This will all have taken place in less than one ten-thousandth of a second. The row select input is then incremented by 1 and the same 40 ASCII codes stored in the first 40 even bytes of the video RAM are recycled to the character generator. This will cause the proper dot pattern for row 1 of all 40 characters to be displayed on the screen.

After eight rows of dots have been displayed (corresponding to row select inputs of 0–7), a complete line of 40 characters will have been displayed. To display the next line of 40 characters, the same process is repeated using 40 new bytes in the video RAM. These 40 bytes will contain the ASCII codes for the 40 characters to be displayed on line 2 of the video screen.

Each ASCII code stored in the video RAM has an associated *attribute byte* stored in the following odd address. For a monochrome display, this attribute byte determines whether the character will be displayed in normal or reverse video and if the character will be underlined, blinking and/or displayed in high intensity. For a color display the attribute will determine the foreground and background color of each character. The definitions of the bits within this attribute byte are shown in Fig. 13.3.

It is important to note that the attribute byte must contain some nonzero value. If the attribute byte is zero, then the character will not be displayed on the screen regardless of the value of the ASCII code. If you want to display a blank on the screen, you should store the ASCII code for a blank (20H) followed by the normal attribute byte (07H).

13.2 THE VIDEO RAM

You saw in Section 9.5 that the video RAM for storing text on a PC screen begins at memory location B000:0000 for a monochrome display and at memory location B800:0000 for a graphics monitor display. Each character location on the screen is associated with two consecutive bytes in memory. The first byte (even memory address) contains the ASCII code for the character to be displayed. The second byte (odd memory address) contains the attribute byte given in Fig. 13.3. The segment address of the video RAM and the size of the character cell depend on the particular video mode you are using. The standard text modes available on a PC are shown in Table 13.1.

TABLE 13.1 TEXT MODES

Mode	Type	Columns × Rows	Video RAM segment address	Character cell size
0	CGA	40 × 25	B800	8 × 8
	EGA			8 × 14
	VGA			9 × 16
1	CGA	40 × 25	B800	8 × 8
	EGA			8 × 14
	VGA			9 × 16
2	CGA	80 × 25	B800	8 × 8
	EGA			8 × 14
	VGA			9 × 16
3	CGA	80 × 25	B800	8 × 8
	EGA			8 × 14
	VGA			9 × 16
7	MDA	80 × 25	B000	9 × 14
	VGA			9 × 16

The first graphics board provided with the early IBM PCs was a color graphics adapter (CGA) that allowed you to display text in either black and white (modes 0 and 2) or color (modes 1 and 3). The color graphics adapter will display text in either a 40 × 25 format or an 80 × 25 format. Since each character requires 2 bytes (one for the ASCII code and one for the attribute), the video RAM must contain either 2000 bytes (40 × 25 × 2) or 4000 bytes (80 × 25 × 2). The original color graphics adapter board contained 16K bytes of RAM used for the video RAM. This means that either eight pages of a 40 × 25 screen or four pages of an 80 × 25 screen could simultaneously be stored in the computer. Which page is being displayed depends on the starting address of the video RAM. This can be changed under software control. The starting segment address of each page is given in Fig. 13.4. Within each page the offset address associated with each screen

	40 x 25 Screen		80 x 25 Screen	
Page	Starting Segment Address	Page	Starting Segment Address
0	B800	0	B800
1	B880	1	B900
2	B900	2	BA00
3	B980	3	BB00
4	BA00		
5	BA80		
6	BB00		
7	BB80		

Figure 13.4 Starting segment addresses for the video RAM in a color graphics adapter.

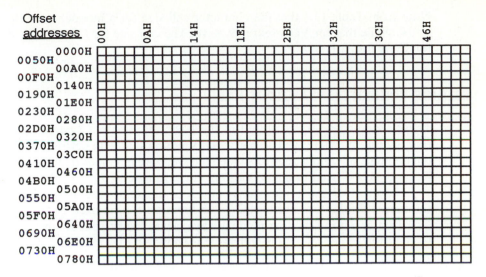

Figure 13.5 Memory map for video RAM associated with a 40-column text screen.

position is shown in Fig. 13.5 for a 40-column display and Fig. 13.6 for an 80-column display.

The monochrome display adapter (MDA) always displays 80 × 25 characters. The MDA video RAM starts at segment address B000H. The offset addresses for the various characters on the screen are those shown in Fig. 13.6.

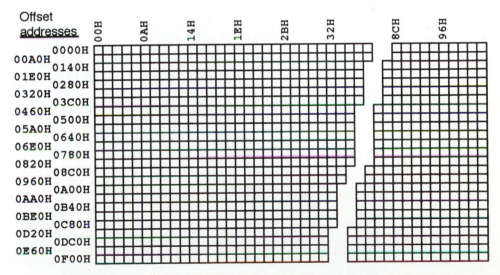

Figure 13.6 Memory map for video RAM associated with an 80-column text screen.

Note from Table 13.1 that the character cell size for a monochrome display is 9 × 14, while that for VGA text is 9 × 16. The cell size for CGA text is 8 × 8 and for EGA text it is 8 × 14.

13.3 BIOS SCREEN DISPLAY ROUTINES

These video routines are stored in the basic input/output system (BIOS) ROM that is built into the PC. The particular function that gets performed depends on the contents of various registers when the software interrupt *INT 10H* is executed. Register *AH* is used to define various video functions.

Figure 13.7 shows the values of *AX* to use to set the text mode and select the active display page. The *AH* = 15 function can be used to find the current video state. Setting the text mode always clears the screen. A simple subroutine to clear the screen using this technique is shown in Fig. 13.8. The subroutine first

AH = 0	*Set text mode* Input: AL (See Table 13.1) 0 - 40x25 BW 1 - 40x25 COLOR 2 - 80x25 BW 3 - 80x25 COLOR 7 - Monochrome
AH = 5	*Select active display page* Input: AL = new page value 0-7 (modes 0-1) 0-3 (modes 2-3)
AH = 15 (0FH)	*Get current video state* Output: AL = current mode (see AH=0) AH = number of characters per row BH = current active display page

Figure 13.7   Setting the text mode using INT 10H.

```
;          clear screen
clrscn     proc   near
           push   ax
           mov    ah,15              ;read vid mode
           int    10h
           mov    ah,0               ;and set again
           int    10h
           pop    ax
           ret
clrscn     endp
```

Figure 13.8   Subroutine to clear the screen.

reads the current video state and then sets it again. This will clear the screen and it is quite fast.

As you saw in Chapter 9, you can print a character on the screen simply by storing the ASCII code and attribute for the character in the proper location in the video RAM. The built-in video routines called by *INT 10H* do a lot of these details for you.

First, to display a character at a particular location, you must know the address in the video RAM associated with that location. The PC has a *cursor* that can be positioned anywhere on the screen. All characters are then printed at the current cursor position. The cursor can be controlled using the *INT 10H* routines given in Fig. 13.9.

AH = 1	*Set cursor type* Input: CH = start line of cursor CL = stop line of cursor

AH = 2	*Set cursor position*
	Input: DH = row number
	        DL = column number
	        BH = page number

AH = 3	*Read cursor position*
	Input: BH = page number
	Output: DH = row number of current cursor
	        DL = column number of current cursor
	        CH = start line of current cursor
	        CL = stop line of current cursor

Figure 13.9   Cursor control options using INT 10H.

The form or type of the cursor can be controlled using the *AH* = 1 instruction in Fig. 13.9. The cursor is always blinking. Normally it looks like an underline. When using a monochrome monitor, this is really a double line in rows 11 and 12 of the 9 × 14 character box in each character location. You can change this cursor form by specifying the start line and stop line for the cursor in *CH* and *CL*. For example, if you make the start line 0 (*CH* = 00H) and the stop line 13 (*CL* = 0DH), then the cursor will be a 9 × 14 blinking rectangle rather than an underline.

The position of the cursor is set by using *AH* = 2 before calling *INT 10H*, as shown in Fig. 13.9. The row number is stored in *DH* (00H is the top row and 18H is the bottom row), and the column number is stored in *DL* (00H is the leftmost column). The page number defined in Fig. 13.4 is stored in *BH*. Using *AH* = 3 when calling *INT 10H* allows you to read the current cursor position as shown in Fig. 13.9.

A number of useful subroutines can be written using the cursor control BIOS routines in Fig. 13.9. For example, the subroutine *setcur* shown in Fig. 13.10 will set the cursor at row *dh* and column *dl*. The subroutine *rdcurs* in Fig. 13.10 will

```
;              set cursor at dx=row:col
setcur         proc  near
               push  ax
               push  bx
               mov   bh,0              ;page 0
               mov   ah,2
               int   10h              ;set cursor
               pop   bx
               pop   ax
               ret
setcur         endp


;              read cursor
;              output: dh=row   dl=col
rdcurs         proc  near
               push  ax
               push  bx
               push  cx
               mov   bh,0              ;page 0
               mov   ah,3
               int   10h              ;read cursor
               pop   cx
               pop   bx
               pop   ax
               ret
rdcurs         endp
```

Figure 13.10 Subroutines to set and read the cursor.

read the current cursor position and leave the row in *dh* and the column in *dl*. These subroutines can then be used to write the subroutines *inccur* and *deccur* shown in Fig. 13.11, which will increment and decrement the cursor. Note that these subroutines do not check for the end or the beginning of the line. We will see later how to perform a carriage return/line feed when the end of the line is reached.

The subroutine *home* shown in Fig. 13.12 will set the cursor to the upper-left corner of the screen (row 0, column 0). The subroutine *tab* shown in Fig. 13.12 will increment the cursor by five column spaces. Again note that this subroutine does not check for the end of a line.

Character Output Routines

Once the cursor position is set, you can read or write characters and attribute bytes using the video routines shown in Fig. 13.13. The *AH* = 9 routine allows you to write at the current cursor position the character whose ASCII code is in *AL* and whose attribute is in *BL*. The value in *CX* determines how many of these characters to write. If you want to display only one character (the normal case),

```
;         inc cursor
inccur    proc   near
          push   dx
          call   rdcurs           ;read cursor
          inc    dl               ;inc dl
          call   setcur           ;set cursor
          pop    dx
          ret
inccur    endp


;         dec cursor
deccur    proc   near
          push   dx
          call   rdcurs           ;read cursor
          dec    dl               ;inc dl
          call   setcur           ;set cursor
          pop    dx
          ret
deccur    endp
```

Figure 13.11   Subroutines to increment and decrement the cursor.

```
;         home cursor
home      proc   near
          push   dx
          mov    dx,0             ;row=0 col=0
          call   setcur
          pop    dx
          ret
home      endp


;         tab
tab       proc   near
          push   ax
          push   bx
          push   dx
          mov    bh,0
          mov    ah,3             ;read cursor
          int    10h
          add    dl,5             ;mov cursor +5
          mov    ah,2
          int    10h              ;set cursor
          pop    dx
          pop    bx
          pop    ax
          ret
tab       endp
```

Figure 13.12   Subroutines to home and tab the cursor.

AH = 8	Read character/attribute at current cursor position
	Input: BH = page number
	Output: AL = ASCII code of character read
	AH = Attribute of character read
AH = 9	Write character/attribute at current cursor position
	Input: BH = page number
	CX = count of characters to write
	AL = ASCII code of character to write
	BL = attribute of character to write
AH = 10 (0AH)	Write character only at current cursor position
	Input: BH = page number
	CX = count of characters to write
	AL = ASCII code of character to write
AH = 14 (0EH)	Write character (teletype mode)
	Input: AL = ASCII code of character to write
	BL = foreground color (in graphics mode)
	BH = page number
	Cursor position is automatically incremented and screen width is specified by most recent mode set.

Figure 13.13   Character-handling routines using INT 10H.

you must set $CX = 1$. On the other hand, you could draw a dashed line all the way across an 80-column screen by setting $CX = 50H$ and putting the ASCII code for a dash (2DH) in AL.

The subroutine *chrout* shown in Fig. 13.14 will print a character (with a given attribute) at the current cursor position and then advance the cursor one character position on the screen. The subroutine uses the $AH = 3$ option in Fig. 13.9 to read the current cursor position. When calling this subroutine, the ASCII code of the character to write is in AL and the attribute of the character is in BL (see the $AH = 9$ option in Fig. 13.13). After writing the character/attribute at the current cursor position, the column number of the cursor (in DL) is incremented. If it exceeds the line length (taken as 80 in Fig. 13.14), then DL is set to 0 (a carriage return) and the row number (in DH) is incremented (a line feed). When the row number exceeds 24, the entire screen is scrolled up one line using the $AH = 6$ scroll option given in Fig. 13.15.

A simple character output subroutine, called *chrprt*, is given in Fig. 13.16. This routine uses the teletype mode option ($AH = 0EH$) in Fig. 13.13. This option will print a character whose ASCII code is in AL at the current cursor position. It automatically increments the cursor position after each character is written. The screen width (either 40 or 80) is determined by the most recent mode set, and the screen will scroll when the cursor increments past the bottom line. The subroutine in Fig. 13.16 seems to do everything that the one in Fig. 13.14 does. The difference is that the attribute of individual characters can be set (in BL) by the subroutine in Fig. 13.14. On the other hand, characters printed using the

```
            ;       character output
chrout     proc near
           push  ax
           push  bx                  ;save regs
           push  cx
           push  dx
           push  ax
           mov   bh,0
           mov   ah,3
           int   10h                 ;read cursor
           mov   cx,1
           pop   ax                  ;get char
           cmp   al,0dh              ;check for CR
           je    chr1
           cmp   al,20h              ;ignore ctrl
           jb    chr3                ; characters
           mov   ah,9
           int   10h                 ;write char/att
           inc   dl                  ;inc cursor
           cmp   dl,80               ;if end of line
           jb    chr2
chr1:      mov   dl,0                ;do CR
           inc   dh                  ; LF
           cmp   dh,25               ;if end of
           jb    chr2                ; screen
           mov   cx,0                ;scroll
           mov   dx,184fh            ; entire
           mov   bh,07h              ; screen
           mov   ax,0601h            ; up
           int   10h                 ; 1 line
           mov   dx,1800h            ;CR
           mov   bh,0                ;reset page no.
chr2:      mov   ah,2
           int   10h                 ;set new cursor
chr3:      pop   dx                  ;restore regs
           pop   cx
           pop   bx
           pop   ax
           ret
chrout     endp
```

Figure 13.14   A character output subroutine.

AH = 6	*Scroll active page up*
	Input: AL = number of lines to scroll
	(e.g. AL=1 scrolls page up 1 line)
	AL=0 will blank entire window
	(CH,CL) = row,column of upper left corner of scroll
	(DH,DL) = row,column of lower right corner of scroll
	BH = attribute to use on blank bottom line
AH = 7	*Scroll active page down*
	Input: AL = number of lines to scroll
	(e.g. AL=1 scrolls page down 1 line)
	AL=0 will blank entire window
	(CH,CL) = row,column of upper left corner of scroll
	(DH,DL) = row,column of lower right corner of scroll
	BH = attribute to use on blank top line

Figure 13.15   Scroll options using INT 10H.

```
;           print a char using teletype mode
chrprt      proc    near
            push    ax
            push    bx
            mov     bh,0              ;page 0
            mov     ah,0eh            ;write char in
            int     10h               ; al on screen
            pop     bx
            pop     ax
            ret
chrprt      endp
```

Figure 13.16   Alternative subroutine to print a character at the current cursor location.

subroutine in Fig. 13.16 will acquire whatever attribute has previously been assigned to that screen location. If the attribute byte happens to be 00 (non-display;
see Fig. 13.3), then the subroutine in Fig. 13.16 will appear *not* to print a character.
You must be careful about this. In addition, you can easily modify the subroutine
in Fig. 13.14 to write characters in a predefined window on the screen and scroll
the characters only within that window.

   We can write our own subroutine to print a character on the screen at the
current cursor position with the current attribute by first reading the character
and attribute at the current cursor location using the *AH = 8* function in Fig.
13.13, storing that attribute value in *BL*, and then calling the *chrout* routine in
Fig. 13.14. The subroutine *chrout1* shown in Fig. 13.17 will do this. This subroutine
will be convenient to use when you want to write a character on the screen using
the current attribute at the cursor location. All you need to do is load the ASCII
code of the character to write into *AL* and then call *chrout1*.

The subroutine *clrwin* shown in Fig. 13.18 will clear a window on the screen by using the $AL = 0$ option of the scroll *INT 10H* function ($AH = 6$) given in Fig. 13.15. This subroutine is useful if you need to blank only a portion of the screen.

```
;          display char with current attribute
chrout1    proc   near
           push   ax
           push   bx
           push   ax                ;save char
           mov    bh,0              ;page 0
           mov    ah,8
           int    10h               ;read attribute
           mov    bl,ah
           pop    ax                ;get char
           call   chrout            ;& display
           pop    bx
           pop    ax
           ret
chrout1    endp
```

Figure 13.17   Subroutine to print a character with the current attribute.

```
;          clear window
;          ch:cl = row:col of upper left corner
;          dh:dl = row:col of lower right corner
clrwin     proc   near
           push   ax
           push   bx
           mov    bh,7              ;normal attr
           mov    ah,6              ;scroll func
           mov    al,0              ;blank window
           int    10h
           pop    bx
           pop    ax
           ret
clrwin     endp
```

Figure 13.18   Subroutine to clear a rectangular area on the screen.

13.4 SCREEN SUBROUTINES

In the last section we wrote a number of subroutines to clear the screen, set and move the cursor, and write a character on the screen. These subroutines were based on the *INT 10H* video BIOS routines. All these subroutines are included

TABLE 13.2 SCREEN SUBROUTINES

Subroutine	Function
stvseg	Set video RAM segment address, *vidseg*, to B000H or B800H
chrout	Output a character to the screen at the current cursor position
mess	Display a message on the screen
chrout1	Character output with the current attribute
mess2	Display a message on the screen at the current cursor position
fmess	Fast message display by writing directly to the screen
setcur	Set cursor at *row, col*
rdcurs	Read cursor position
inccur	Increment cursor position
deccur	Decrement cursor position
clrscn	Clear screen
home	Move cursor to upper-left corner of screen
crlf	Carriage return, line feed
tab	Move cursor five positions to the right
getatt	Get the attribute of character at the current cursor position
chgatt	Change attribute of character at the current cursor position
invatt	Invert attribute of word at the current cursor position
togatt	Invert attribute of character at the current cursor position
invline	Invert line of text at current cursor position
blank	Blank one row
clrwin	Clear window
curoff	Hide cursor
chrprt	Print a character on the screen using the teletype mode
hexasc	Hex to ASCII conversion for single hex digit
pbyte	Print a byte as two hex digits
delay	Delay *ax* ticks (18.2 ticks per second)
tone	Make a tone
beep	Beep a tone
getkey	Wait for key and get key value
dokey	Process a key
query	Buffered keyboard input at current cursor position
svinit	Allocate save screen buffer (16000 bytes for four screens)
resize	Resize memory
relssb	Release save screen buffer
savescr	Save screen (can be nested four deep)
restscr	Restore screen
quit	Quit to DOS

in the file *screen.asm*, which is included on the TUTOR disk. A list of all the subroutines included in this file is given in Table 13.2. A complete listing of this file is given as Listing C.1 in Appendix C. In this section we will look at some of the other screen subroutines that are included in the *screen.asm* file.

You can use any of these subroutines in your own programs by assembling the file *screen.asm* to produce the object file *screen.obj*. You would then link this object file with the object file of your program as described in Section 11.4. You would need to include an *extrn* statement in your program for each screen subroutine that you use, as illustrated in the example in Listing 11.2a.

Printing a Message

Suppose you want to print a message, consisting of a string of characters, at some arbitrary location on the screen. The first thing to do is to store the message as a sequence of ASCII codes in consecutive memory locations. The message can be printed on the screen by moving this block of ASCII codes into the proper area of the video RAM.

The subroutine *mess* shown in Fig. 13.19 will write a message on the screen starting at location *DH* (row), *DL* (col) using the character output subroutine *chrout* given in Fig. 13.14. The message must end with a byte containing 00H.

```
;          message display
mess       proc  near
           push  ax
           push  bx
           push  cx
           push  si
           mov   bh,0          ;page 0
           mov   ah,2          ;set cursor
           int   10h           ; at dh,dl
           mov   cx,1          ;1 character
           cld                 ;si increases
ms1:       lodsb               ;[si]-->al
           cmp   al,0          ;message done?
           je    ms2           ;if so, return
           call  chrout        ;display char
           jmp   ms1           ;and continue
ms2:       pop   si
           pop   cx
           pop   bx
           pop   ax
           ret
mess       endp
```

Figure 13.19   Subroutine to print message from *[SI]* at row = *DH*, col = *DL* with attribute in *BL*.

The starting address of the message must be stored in *SI*, and the attribute to be used for each character in the message must be stored in *BL*.

As an example, the program shown in Listing 13.1 will print the message *Hello World* in reverse video near the center of a cleared screen. Note that the message *Hello World* is stored in a separate data segment using the *db* assembler directive. If the message is included between single quotes, the ASCII code for each character in the message will be stored in consecutive bytes in memory. The

Listing 13.1   *messtest.lst*

```
                                title Message test
                        ;       LINK with screen

0000                            stack  segment para stack
0000     40 [                          db      64 dup(?)
              ??
                      ]
0040                            stack  ends

0000                            data   segment public
0000     48 65 6C 6C 6F 20 msg1 db      'Hello World',0
         57 6F 72 6C 64 00
000C                            data   ends

                        ;       screen subroutines
                                extrn mess:near,clrscn:near

0000                            code   segment public
                                       assume cs:code,ds:data
0000                            main   proc   far
0000     B8 ---- R                     mov    ax,data         ;set ds
0003     8E D8                         mov    ds,ax
0005     E8 0000 E                     call   clrscn          ;clear screen
0008     B6 0B                         mov    dh,11           ;row 11
000A     B2 20                         mov    dl,32           ;column 32
000C     B3 70                         mov    bl,70h          ;reverse video
000E     BE 0000 R                     mov    si,offset msg1  ;si -> message
0011     E8 0000 E                     call   mess            ;print message
0014     B4 00                         mov    ah,0            ;wait for
0016     CD 16                         int    16h             ; any key
0018     E8 0000 E                     call   clrscn          ;clear screen
001B     B8 4C00                       mov    ax,4C00h
001E     CD 21                         int    21h             ;return to DOS
0020                            main   endp
0020                            code   ends
                                       end    main
```

message must end with a byte containing 00H. Note that this program must be linked with the *screen.obj* file to produce an executable .EXE file.

An alternate message display subroutine is shown in Fig. 13.20. The subroutine *mess2* will display a message on the screen at the *current cursor position* with the *current attribute*. The message must be stored at *si* in the data segment. Note that this subroutine first reads the current cursor position and the current attribute and then calls the subroutine *mess*.

```
;           message display with current attribute
;           at current cursor position
mess2       proc    near
            push    ax
            push    bx
            push    dx
            call    rdcurs          ;read cursor
            mov     bh,0            ;page 0
            mov     ah,8
            int     10h             ;read attribute
            mov     bl,ah
            call    mess            ;& display mess
            pop     dx
            pop     bx
            pop     ax
            ret
mess2       endp
```

Figure 13.20 Subroutine to display a message with the current attribute at the current cursor position.

Fast message-printing subroutine.   Sometimes it is necessary to write to the screen at a faster rate than is possible by using the BIOS (or DOS) routines. This is the case if data are being updated continuously. For example, in the logic analyzer program, *logic2.asm*, that you used in earlier chapters, the input lines from the printer port are displayed on the screen in real time. If the subroutine *mess* given above is used to display these input bits, the cursor will be observed jumping around under these bits. This is because the cursor constantly has to be moved from the output bits to the input bits while the program continually prints the input bits and waits for the cursor in the output bits to be moved.

An alternative is to replace the subroutine *mess* with the subroutine *fmess*, which will write directly to the screen. In this case the cursor is never actually moved to the location on the screen where the message is printed. Rather, the row (*DH*) and column (*DL*) values are used to compute the offset address (to be stored in *DI*) in the video RAM where the message is to start. From Fig. 13.6, this offset address will be given by the equation

$$offset\ address\ =\ 160 * row\ +\ 2 * col$$

or

$$di = 160 * dh + 2 * dl \qquad (13.1)$$

To compute the value *di* in Eq. (13.1) as fast as possible, we will not use the *MUL* instruction, but rather will use the subroutine *setdi* shown in Fig. 13.21. Note that to compute 160 * *dh* we use the fact that

$$160 * dh = 128 * dh + 32 * dh$$

where we can compute 128 * *dh* and 32 * *dh* by fast shifting operations. Note that we can always use this technique to multiply by any constant because we can write the constant as the sum of numbers that are powers of 2 (its binary representation). In Fig. 13.21 we put the row value in *ax* and then shift it left 5 bits (to multiply by 32) and then two more bits (to multiply by 128). These two values are added to get the value 160 * *row*.

```
;           set di to video RAM offset address
;           di = row * 160 + col
setdi       proc   near
            push   cx
            mov    ah,0
            mov    al,dh              ;ax=row
            mov    cl,5
            shl    ax,cl              ;ax=32*row
            mov    di,ax              ;di=32*row
            shl    ax,1
            shl    ax,1               ;ax=128*row
            add    di,ax              ;di=160*row
            mov    ah,0
            mov    al,dl              ;ax=col
            shl    ax,1               ;ax=2*col
            add    di,ax              ;di=video offset
            pop    cx
            ret
setdi       endp
```

Figure 13.21   Fast subroutine to compute video RAM offset address.

The subroutine *fmess* is shown in Fig. 13.22. After storing the video RAM offset address of the first character of the message in *di* (by calling *setdi*), the attribute of the message (in *bl*) is stored in *ah*. The instruction *lodsb* in the *fms1* loop will read each ASCII code of the message from the string in the data segment, and the instruction *stosw* will store both the ASCII code (in *al*) and the attribute (in *ah*) at the next location in the video RAM. The loop will terminate when the zero at the end of the message is read.

```
;             fast message routine
;             si -> message in data segment
;             dh = row, dl = col
;             bl = attribute of message
fmess      proc   near
           push   ax
           push   di
           call   setdi              ;di->vidRAM offset
           mov    ah,bl              ;ah=attribute
           mov    es,vidseg          ;es->video RAM
           cld
fms1:      lodsb
           cmp    al,0
           je     fms2
           stosw
           jmp    fms1
fms2:      pop    di
           pop    ax
           ret
fmess      endp
```

Figure 13.22 Message subroutine that writes directly to the screen.

When writing directly to the screen, the segment address of the video RAM must be known and stored in the variable *vidseg*. This can be done by calling the subroutine *stvseg* shown in Fig. 13.23. This subroutine first gets the current video state using the *INT 10H* (*AH* = 15) BIOS call and then sets the variable *vidseg* to B000H for a monochrome monitor or to B800H for all others (such as VGA).

```
;             set video RAM segment address
stvseg     proc   near
           push   ax
           mov    ah,15
           int    10h                ;get video state
           cmp    al,7               ;if monochrome
           jne    svg1
           mov    vidseg,0b000h      ; vidseg=b000
           jmp    svg2               ;else
svg1:      mov    vidseg,0b800h      ; vidseg=b800
svg2:      pop    ax
           ret
stvseg     endp
```

Figure 13.23 Subroutine to set the video RAM segment address.

Keyboard Control

In Chapter 9 you saw that *INT 16H* can be used to read the keyboard. All the options available with this interrupt call are given in Fig. 13.24. In addition to waiting for a key to be pressed (*AH* = 0), you can check to see if a key has been pressed (*AH* = 1), and, if so (*Z* = 0), read the value in *AX*, or, if not (*Z* = 1), go do something else. This would be useful, for example, in a terminal emulation program where you want to alternate between checking the keyboard and checking the RS-232 serial port (see Chapter 17).

AH = 0	*Wait for key to be pressed* Output: AH = scan code of key pressed AL = ASCII code of key pressed
AH = 1	*Check to see if key has been pressed and set Z-flag* Output: Z = 1 no key was pressed Z = 0 key has been pressed and AH = scan code AL = ASCII code
AH = 2	*Check special keys* Output: AL = kb_flag (0040:0017)

Figure 13.24 Keyboard control options using INT 16H.

The third option in Fig. 13.24 (*AH* = 2) allows you to interrogate the state of some special keys. Memory location 0040:0017 is called the *kb_flag*, and the bits in this byte are set according to the state of certain special keys as indicated in Fig. 13.25.

To see how these bits get set, go to location 0040:0017 in the TUTOR monitor. The memory locations (and registers) in TUTOR get updated only when you make a change, such as moving the position cursor (>) forward or backward. Move the position cursor forward and backward and watch memory location 0040:0017 as you press the following keys: *Ins, Caps Lock, Num Lock, Scroll*

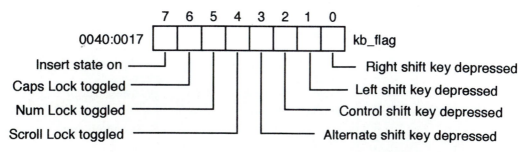

Figure 13.25 Definition of the *kb_flag* at location 0040:0017.

Lock, *Left Shift*, *Right Shift*. Note that the forward and backward cursor keys will not work while pressing the *Ctrl* or *Alt* keys.

From Table 9.4, note that the ASCII codes for certain keys such as the function keys and the cursor keys are all zero. This means that the scan code is the only way to distinguish between these keys. It will be useful to assign these keys a modified ASCII code that is formed by ORing their scan code with 80H. This will provide a unique ASCII code inasmuch as all "normal" ASCII codes are 7-bit codes with values between 00H and 7FH. The subroutine *getkey* shown in Fig. 13.26 will do this. Note from Table 9.4 that pressing the alternate key with a key on the numeric keypad produces a scan code of zero. These keys are ignored in the subroutine *getkey*.

```
;              wait for key and get key value
;              output: al = ascii code of key
;                      function & cursor keys have
;                      al = scan code OR 80H
getkey    proc   near
gk1:      mov    ah,0
          int    16h            ;wait for key
          cmp    ah,0           ;ignore Alt-keypd
          je     gk1
          cmp    al,0
          jne    gk2            ;if ascii = 0
          mov    al,ah          ;use scan code
          or     al,80h         ; OR 80h
gk2:      ret
getkey    endp
```

Figure 13.26   The subroutine *getkey*.

Use of a Jump Table

Many programs will wait for a key to be pressed and then execute a particular subroutine depending on the key pressed. For example, the use of pop-up menus is described in the experiments at the end of this chapter. In this program, certain keys such as the cursor keys and some of the letter keys perform particular tasks.

In programs of this sort, a jump table made up of a list of key ASCII codes and subroutine offset addresses is a useful technique for executing the appropriate routine. For example, the subroutine *dokey* shown in Fig. 13.27 will process a key whose ASCII code (as obtained from the subroutine *getkey* in Fig. 13.26) is stored in register *al*. Before calling the subroutine *dokey*, register *di* contains the offset address of a jump table in the code segment and *dx* contains the offset address of the default subroutine to call if the key ASCII code is not in the jump table. Note that the jump table is made up of bytes (*db*) containing the key ASCII code of different keys followed by a word (*dw*) containing the label (offset address)

```
;           process a key
;           input: al = ascii code of key
;                  di -> jump table
;                  dx -> default subroutine
dokey   proc    near
dk1:    cmp     al,cs:[di]              ;chk next code
        jne     dk2                     ;if a match
        call    word ptr cs:1[di]       ;call sub
        ret                             ;and quit
dk2:    cmp     byte ptr cs:[di],0      ;if not
        je      dk3                     ;end of table
        add     di,3                    ;chk next entry
        jmp     dk1                     ; in table
dk3:    call    dx                      ;else call
        ret                             ;default sub
dokey   endp


;           jump table
jmptbl  db      key1                    ; <-- di points here
        dw      sub1
        db      key2
        dw      sub2
        db      key3
        dw      sub3
        db      0


;           default subroutine
deflt   proc    near                    ; <-- dx points here
        ---
        ---
        ---
        ret
deflt   endp
```

Figure 13.27 Processing a key using a jump table.

of the subroutine to call if that key is pressed. For example, if the key with an
ASCII code *key1* is pressed, then the subroutine *sub1* will be called. Similarly,
if the key with an ASCII code *key2* is pressed, then the subroutine *sub2* will be
called. The jump table ends with a byte containing 00H.

The subroutine *dokey* compares the ASCII code in *al* with each entry in the
jump table until a match is found (at which point the following subroutine in the
jump table is executed, after which the subroutine *dokey* is exited). If no match
is found in the jump table, the program jumps to *dk3*, which will call the subroutine
whose offset address is in register *dx*. Study the subroutine *dokey* and make sure
you understand how it works.

The advantage of using a jump table like the one shown in Fig. 13.27 is that it is easy to add new key functions and change what keys do by simply adding or changing the entries in the jump table. To assemble a jump table without errors, you must tell the assembler the location of all the subroutines in the jump table. You could just use the *extrn* assembler directive to indicate that the subroutine will be assembled in a separate module. Regardless of whether the subroutine is an internal or external subroutine, you can begin by just making a stub for each subroutine of the form

```
sub1   proc   near
       ret
sub1   endp
```

You can then assemble and link all modules to produce an executable file that you can begin to debug. You can then write and debug each subroutine one by one. This is an example of *top-down programming*.

Buffered Keyboard Input

In many programs it is necessary to type a string of characters into a buffer for further processing. We will look at two ways to do this. The first is a DOS function call, and the second is the subroutine *query* that is part of our screen subroutine file, *screen.asm*.

Function call 0AH (that is, $AH = 0AH$ in *INT 21H*) is used for a buffered keyboard input. The setup for using this function is shown in Fig. 13.28. Load *DS* and *DX* such that *DS:DX* points to the beginning of an input buffer. Store the length of this buffer in the first byte. After calling *INT 21H*, characters typed on the keyboard will be stored in the buffer starting with the third byte, as shown in Fig. 13.28. Some basic editing features can be used while filling this buffer.

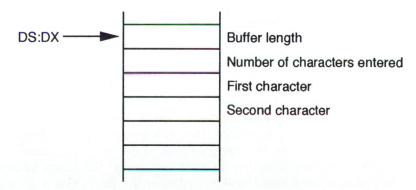

Figure 13.28   Setup for using the buffered keyboard input ($AH = 0AH$) in *INT 21H*.

The interrupt function exits when you press *ENTER*. At that point the second byte of the buffer will contain the number of characters actually stored in the input buffer. If you try to type past the next to last byte in the buffer, the bell will sound and the extra characters will be ignored.

The subroutine *query* in the file *screen.asm* is a buffered keyboard input routine that stores the input characters in the buffer *kbuf*, which is an 80-byte buffer defined in the data segment in the *screen.asm* file as shown in Fig. 13.29. The label *bufend* in Fig. 13.29 defines the byte following the end of the input keyboard buffer.

```
data      segment  public
kbuf      db       80 dup(?)
bufend    db       ?
span      dw       ?
sisave    dw       ?
svseg     dw       0
data      ends
```

Figure 13.29 The data segment used by the screen subroutines in the file *screen.asm*.

The subroutine *query* is shown in Fig. 13.30. The subroutine *dokey* given in Fig. 13.27 is used together with the jump table *jmptbq* to process each key pressed. The jump table handles the *backspace*, *Enter*, and *ESC* keys, while the subroutine *tobuff* is the default subroutine that stores any other key in the buffer *kbuf* and displays the character on the screen. Note that in the subroutine *tobuff* the index register *si* gets incremented to point to the next available byte in the keyboard input buffer, *kbuf*. In the jump table in Fig. 13.30 the variables *_bksp*, *_enter*, and *_esc* have been equated to the key ASCII codes 8, 13 and 27, respectively. These three keys will call the subroutines *backsp*, *enterq*, and *quit*, respectively. These three subroutines are given in Fig. 13.31.

The subroutine *backsp* in Fig. 13.31 decrements the *kbuf* pointer, *si* (unless the buffer is empty), and stores a blank ASCII code (20H) in that byte. It also decrements the cursor on the screen and erases the character by writing a blank character on the screen. Note that after calling the subroutine *chrout1*, which advances the cursor, the cursor needs to be decremented again.

The subroutine *enterq* in Fig. 13.31 is a little tricky. This is the subroutine that is called when the *Enter* key is pressed while you are typing characters into *kbuf* in *query*. We therefore want to leave *query* at this point. But note in Fig. 13.30 that the subroutine *query* does not have any *RET* statement. It is just a continuous loop that calls *getkey* and *dokey*. We must rely on *dokey* to exit *query* when the *Enter* key is pressed. How can we do this? Remember that every time we call a subroutine the return address of the next instruction is pushed on the stack. Therefore, when we execute *call query*, the return address of the next instruction (call it *addr1*) will be pushed on the stack. This is the address we want to get back to when we press the *Enter* key. When we press the *Enter* key, we will execute the statement *call dokey* in the subroutine *query* in Fig. 13.30. This

```
;              buffered keyboard input
;              at current cursor position
;              input asciiz string is at kbuf
;              # of character entered at span
;              output: none
query   proc   near
        mov    sisave,si
        mov    si,offset kbuf      ;si->kbuf
qy1:    call   getkey              ;get key
        mov    di,offset jmptbq
        mov    dx,offset tobuff    ;default
        call   dokey               ;process key
        jmp    qy1
query   endp


;              query jump table
jmptbq  db     _bksp               ;backspace
        dw     backsp
        db     _enter              ;enter
        dw     enterq
        db     _esc                ;esc
        dw     quit
        db     0


;              display & store char in kbuf
tobuff  proc   near
        cmp    si,offset bufend
        jb     tb1                 ;if end.of.buf
        call   beep                ; beep &
        ret                        ; quit
tb1:    mov    [si],al             ;store char
        inc    si                  ;inc ptr
        call   chrout1             ;display char
        ret
tobuff  endp
```

Figure 13.30 The subroutine *query*.

will push the return address of the next instruction (call it *addr2*) on the stack. At this point the two addresses *addr1* and *addr2* are on the stack. But the subroutine *dokey* given in Fig. 13.27 will call the subroutine *enterq* in Fig. 13.31 by executing the statement *call word ptr cs:1[di]*. This will push the return address of the next instruction (call it *addr3*) on the stack. At this point the three addresses *addr1*, *addr2*, and *addr3* will be on the stack. The *RET* instruction in *enterq* will normally return to *addr3*, which is the address on the top of the stack. But we really want to return to *addr1* (the address following the *call query* instruction), which is the third address on the stack. To get to this address, we just pop the

```
;               backspace
backsp    proc    near
          cmp     si,offset kbuf
          ja      bk1                    ;if 1st char
          call    beep                   ;beep & ret
          ret
bk1:      dec     si                     ;back up & put
          mov     byte ptr [si],20h      ;20h in kbuf
          call    deccur                 ;back up & put
          mov     al,20h                 ;blank on
          call    chrout1                ;screen
          call    deccur
          ret
backsp    endp


;               enter from query
;               exits from query
enterq    proc    near
          mov     byte ptr [si],0        ;make asciiz
          sub     si,offset kbuf         ;store #char
          mov     span,si                ;in span
          mov     si,sisave              ;restore si
          pop     ax                     ;>enterq
          pop     ax                     ;>dokey
          ret                            ;>query
enterq    endp


;               quit to dos
quit      proc    near
          mov     ax,4C00h
          int     21h
quit      endp
```

Figure 13.31 *Query* jump table subroutines.

top two addresses from the stack using the two *pop ax* instructions just before the *RET* instruction in the subroutine *enterq* in Fig. 13.31. The *RET* instruction will then pop the address *addr3* into the instruction pointer and return to the instruction following the *call query* instruction. Before leaving *enterq*, a zero is inserted at the end of the string in *kbuf* to make it an ASCIIZ string. In addition, the number of characters entered into *kbuf* by *query* is stored in the variable *span*, which is defined in the data segment in Fig. 13.29. Also note that the value of *si* that was saved in the variable *sisave* at the beginning of the subroutine *query* is restored in *enterq*.

The subroutine *quit* in Fig. 13.31, executed when the *ESC* key is pressed, just returns to DOS using the *AH* = 4C function call. You could add a *call clrscn* instruction to the beginning of this subroutine if you wanted the screen to be cleared before returning to DOS.

Typing characters on the screen.   As an example of using the subroutine *query*, consider the program shown in Listing 13.2, which will type any characters on the screen. Note that after assembling this program the object file *typscn.obj* must be linked with *screen.obj* to make available the subroutines *clrscn*, *query*, and *crlf*.

Listing 13.2   *typscn.asm*

```
        title type characters to screen

;       LINK with screen
stack   segment para stack
        db    64 dup(?)
stack   ends

data    segment  public
data    ends

;       screen subroutines
        extrn clrscn:near,query:near
        extrn crlf:near

code    segment  public
        assume cs:code,ds:data
main    proc  far
        mov   ax,data      ;set ds
        mov   ds,ax
        call  clrscn       ;clear screen
mn1:    call  query        ;type next line
        call  crlf         ;carriage return
        jmp   mn1          ;keep going
main    endp

code    ends
        end   main
```

The subroutine *query* allows you to type any characters on a single line of the screen and use the *backspace* key to make any corrections. When you press the *Enter* key, the subroutine *query* will be exited as described above, and the subroutine *crlf*, shown in Fig. 13.32, will be executed. This subroutine will cause the cursor to move to the beginning of the next line and scroll the screen when the bottom of the screen is reached.

```
;          carriage return line feed
crlf       proc   near
           push   ax
           push   bx
           push   cx
           push   dx
           call   rdcurs            ;read cursor
           mov    dl,0              ;do CR
           inc    dh                ; LF
           cmp    dh,25             ;if end of
           jb     cr1               ; screen
           mov    cx,0              ;scroll
           mov    dx,184fh          ; entire
           mov    bh,07h            ; screen
           mov    ax,0601h          ; up
           int    10h               ; 1 line
           mov    dx,1800h          ;CR
           mov    bh,0              ;page 0
cr1:       call   setcur            ;set cursor
           pop    dx
           pop    cx
           pop    bx
           pop    ax
           ret
crlf       endp
```

Figure 13.32 Subroutine to perform a screen carriage return/line feed.

Note that the main program is just a loop that continually calls the two subroutines *query* and *crlf*. When the *ESC* key is pressed, the subroutine *query* causes the program to return to DOS using the subroutine *quit* in Fig. 13.31.

Attribute Control

Sometimes it is useful to know the attribute of a particular character on the screen and to be able to change the attribute of any character. The subroutines *getatt* and *chgatt* shown in Fig. 13.33 will do this. These subroutines use the basic *INT 10H* BIOS calls given in Fig. 13.13.

The subroutine *togatt* shown in Fig. 13.34 will toggle the attribute of the character at the current cursor position between normal and inverse. Suppose you want to toggle the attribute of an entire word. You can do this by toggling the attribute of each character in the word until a blank character on the screen is encountered. The subroutine *invatt* shown in Fig. 13.35 will do this. This sub- routine might be useful if you are selecting menu items by moving the cursor up and down and the selected item is displayed in reverse video. However, suppose

```
;               get attribute of character at
;               dx = row:col and store in bl
getatt    proc  near
          push  ax
          call  setcur            ;set cursor
          mov   bh,0              ;page 0
          mov   ah,8              ;read char/attr
          int   10h
          mov   bl,ah             ;bl = attrib
          pop   ax
          ret
getatt    endp


;               change attribute of character at
;               current cursor position to bl
chgatt    proc  near
          push  ax
          push  bx
          push  cx
          mov   bh,0              ;page 0
          mov   ah,8              ;read char/attr
          int   10h
          mov   cx,1
          mov   ah,9
          int   10h               ;write char/att
          pop   cx
          pop   bx
          pop   ax
          ret
chgatt    endp
```

Figure 13.33 Subroutines to get and change the attribute of characters on the screen.

the menu items contain more than one word. How can you invert a line of text containing more than one word? You could continue to invert words (together with the blanks between them) until two consecutive blanks are encountered. The subroutine *invline* shown in Fig. 13.36 will do this.

Note that the subroutine *invatt* leaves the cursor at the first blank following the word. The subroutine *invline* calls *invatt* (which inverts the attribute of a word) and *togatt* (which inverts the blank following the word) until a second blank following a word is found. In this way, *invline* will invert the attribute of a group of words including a blank at the end of the line of text. This will be useful in making menus, including pop-up menus. (See Experiments 27 and 28 at the end of this chapter.)

```
;           toggle attribute of character
;           at current cursor position
togatt      proc   near
            push   ax
            push   bx
            push   cx
            mov    bh,0              ;page 0
            mov    ah,8              ;read char/attr
            int    10h
            cmp    ah,07h            ;if normal
            jne    ta1
            mov    bl,70h            ;make inverse
            jmp    ta2               ;else
ta1:        mov    bl,07h            ;make normal
ta2:        mov    cx,1
            mov    ah,9
            int    10h               ;write char/att
            pop    cx
            pop    bx
            pop    ax
            ret
togatt      endp
```

Figure 13.34 Subroutine to toggle the attribute of a character from normal to inverse.

```
;           invert attribute of word at current
;           cursor position
invatt      proc   near
            push   ax
            push   bx
            push   cx
            mov    bh,0              ;page 0
ia1:        mov    ah,8              ;read char/attr
            int    10h
            cmp    al,20h            ;if blank
            je     ia4               ; quit
            cmp    ah,07h            ;if normal
            jne    ia2
            mov    bl,70h            ;make inverse
            jmp    ia3               ;else
ia2:        mov    bl,07h            ;make normal
ia3:        mov    cx,1
            mov    ah,9
            int    10h               ;write char/att
            call   inccur            ;adv cursor
            jmp    ia1               ;repeat
ia4:        pop    cx
            pop    bx
            pop    ax
            ret
invatt      endp
```

Figure 13.35 Subroutine to toggle the attribute of a word from normal to inverse.

```
;           invert line of text at
;           current cursor position
invline   proc   near
          push   ax
ivl1:     call   invatt          ;invert word
          call   togatt          ;invert blank
          call   inccur          ;inc cursor
          mov    ah,8            ;read chr/attr
          int    10h
          cmp    al,20h          ;repeat until
          jne    ivl1            ;blank
          pop    ax
          ret
invline   endp
```

Figure 13.36 Subroutine to toggle the attribute of a line of text from normal to inverse.

13.5 MEMORY MANAGEMENT

As we have seen, the data segment is used to store variables including arrays, strings, and tables. These are all static data structures that we define (and therefore reserve space for) before we run the program. Sometimes it is more convenient to use dynamic data structures, where we allocate and deallocate memory "on the fly" during the execution of the program. We may not know how much memory we need for some application or we may need to reuse the same physical memory for different purposes in a program because we don't have enough memory to allocate it all ahead of time. Finally, we may simply want to allocate a large block of memory in a separate segment for some special purpose.

We can use certain DOS *INT 21H* function calls to allocate and deallocate memory. These DOS functions are shown in Fig. 13.37. When a program is run, DOS will normally allocate all available memory to the program. There is usually a lot more memory allocated than the program actually needs. This means that if you want to allocate additional memory in your program for some particular function this additional memory will not be available. To make it available, you will need to modify the memory allocation by calling the *AH* = 4AH DOS *INT 21H* function. As shown in Fig. 13.37 this requires that you know how many total paragraphs of memory your program really needs and the segment address corresponding to the beginning of your program.

In memory, your program will consist of a program segment prefix (PSP), the code segment, the data segment, and the stack segment. When the program is first run, the extra segment register will point to the beginning of the program segment prefix and the stack segment register will point to the stack segment. The value *SS − ES* will therefore be the number of paragraphs of memory used by the program excluding the stack. We normally reserve 64 bytes (or four para-

AH = 4AH	*Modify memory allocation*
	Input: BX = new requested block size in paragraphs
	         ES = segment of block to be modified
	Output: If carry = 0, successful
	         If carry = 1, then
	             AX = error codes
	                 7 memory control blocks destroyed
	                 8 insufficient memory
	                 9 invalid segment in ES
	             BX = maximum block size available

AH = 48H	*Allocate memory*
	Input: BX = number of paragraphs of memory needed
	Output: If carry = 0, successful
	             AX = initial segment of allocated block
	         If carry = 1, then
	             AX = error codes
	                 7 memory control blocks destroyed
	                 8 insufficient memory
	             BX = size of largest available block

AH = 49H	*Release memory*
	Input: ES = segment of block to be released
	Output: If carry = 0, successful
	         If carry = 1, then
	             AX = error codes
	                 7 memory control blocks destroyed
	                 9 invalid segment in ES

Figure 13.37 Allocating and deallocating memory using INT 21H.

graphs) of memory for the stack. Therefore, if we add five paragraphs to ($SS -$ ES), we should have a block size larger than is needed by the program. The subroutine *resize* shown in Fig. 13.38 can be called at the beginning of a program (immediately after setting the data segment register) to release all excess memory and make it available to allocate by the user. Note from Fig. 13.37 that if this

```
;             resize memory
resize    proc   near
          mov    ax,es            ;ax=psp seg
          mov    bx,ss            ;bx=stack seg
          sub    bx,ax            ;reserve psp-ss
          add    bx,5             ; + stack size
          mov    ah,4Ah
          int    21h              ;resize mem
          ret
resize    endp
```

Figure 13.38 Subroutine to release excess memory at the beginning of a program.

resize operation is not successful the carry flag will be set to 1, and *AX* will contain one of three possible error codes. You should check this carry flag after calling *resize* to make sure the excess memory got released.

To allocate memory, you set *BX* to the number of paragraphs you want and call *INT 21H* with *AH* = 48H, as shown in Fig. 13.37. If this function call is successful, the carry flag will be zero and *AX* will contain the initial segment address of the block of memory allocated. You can save this segment address in some convenient place (such as a variable name) for future use.

To deallocate memory that has previously been allocated using the *AH* = 48H function call, you set *ES* to the segment address of the block to be released and call *INT 21H* with *AH* = 49H, as shown in Fig. 13.37.

As an example, suppose we want to reserve 16,000 bytes of memory to hold up to four video screens of data. Recall that one screen contains $80 \times 25 = 2,000$ characters, and each character needs 2 bytes, one for the ASCII code and one for the attribute byte. The subroutine *svinit* shown in Fig. 13.39 can be used to allocate this 16,000-byte screen buffer, and the subroutine *relssb* also shown in Fig. 13.39 will release these same 16,000 bytes. Note that the variable *svseg* (defined in the data segment in Fig. 13.29) is used to store the segment address of the 16,000-byte buffer allocated by *svinit*. If the value of this variable is zero, then no bytes are allocated. We will use this 16,000-byte buffer to save up to four different screen images.

```
;               allocate save screen buffer
svinit    proc    near
          mov     svseg,0          ;svseg = 0
          mov     bx,1000          ;request 16000
          mov     ah,48h           ; bytes
          int     21h
          jc      sv1              ;if no error
          mov     svseg,ax         ;svseg = seg
sv1:      ret
svinit    endp


;               release save screen buffer
relssb    proc    near
          cmp     svseg,0          ;if allocated
          je      rel1
          mov     ax,svseg         ;deallocate
          mov     es,ax            ;es = svseg
          mov     ah,49h
          int     21h              ;release mem
rel1:     ret
relssb    endp
```

Figure 13.39   Subroutines to allocate and deallocate memory.

To save a screen to our 16,000-byte buffer, we can just call the subroutine *savescr* shown in Fig. 13.40. This subroutine always moves the 2,000 words of the video RAM to the first 2,000 words (4,000 bytes) of the 16,000-byte save buffer. However, before moving these 2,000 words, it first moves the first 12,000 bytes of the buffer up in memory by 4,000 bytes to make room for the new screen. This means that you can store up to four different screens in the buffer by simply calling *savescr* four times.

The last screen saved can be restored by calling the subroutine *restscr* shown in Fig. 13.41. This subroutine will move the first 2,000 words in the save screen buffer to the video RAM and then move the last 12,000 bytes in the buffer down

```
;            save  screen
savescr      proc  near
             push  ax                    ;save regs
             push  cx
             push  si
             push  di
             push  ds
             push  es
             cmp   svseg,0               ;if buff exists
             je    svsc1
             std                         ;move 12000
             mov   ax,svseg              ; bytes up
             mov   ds,ax                 ; 4000 bytes
             mov   es,ax                 ; to make hole
             mov   cx,6000               ; in buffer
             mov   si,11998
             mov   di,15998
             rep movsw
             mov   ax,vidseg             ;move video ram
             mov   ds,ax                 ; to svseg
             mov   si,0                  ; buffer
             mov   di,0
             mov   cx,2000
             cld
             rep movsw
svsc1:       pop   es                    ;restore regs
             pop   ds
             pop   di
             pop   si
             pop   cx
             pop   ax
             ret
savescr      endp
```

Figure 13.40 The subroutine *savescr*.

```
;          restore screen
restscr   proc   near
          push   ax                    ;save regs
          push   cx
          push   si
          push   di
          push   ds
          push   es
          cmp    svseg,0               ;if buff exists
          je     rsts1
          mov    ax,vidseg             ;move 1st 4000
          mov    es,ax                 ; bytes from
          mov    ax,svseg              ; svseg buffer
          mov    ds,ax                 ; to tv ram
          mov    si,0
          mov    di,0
          mov    cx,2000
          cld
          rep movsw
          mov    ax,data
          mov    ds,ax                 ;ds = data
          mov    ax,svseg              ;move last
          mov    es,ax                 ; 12000 bytes
          mov    ds,ax                 ; in buffer
          mov    si,4000               ; down 4000
          mov    di,0                  ; bytes
          mov    cx,6000
          rep movsw
rsts1:    pop    es                    ;restore regs
          pop    ds
          pop    di
          pop    si
          pop    cx
          pop    ax
          ret
restscr   endp
```

Figure 13.41   The subroutine *restscr*.

by 4,000 bytes. This will put the data of the next to last screen saved at the beginning of the buffer so that, if the subroutine *restscr* is called again, the next to last screen saved will be redisplayed on the screen. This technique can be used in Experiment 28 at the end of this chapter to make pop-up menus. If the subroutine *savescr* is called before a submenu is displayed on top of a main menu, then the subroutine *restscr* will cause the submenu to be erased and the main menu to be redisplayed. You can nest these submenus four deep (that is, call *savescr* four times before you need to call *restscr*).

Experiment 27: Menus and Transaction Control

In this experiment you will learn to use the screen display subroutines in the file *screen.asm* that you can link with your own programs. Write a main program that displays the following initial screen:

```
                        Menu display example
                        First screen display
                        Second screen display
                        Text display



    Press ESC to return to DOS
```

The first menu item, *First screen display*, should be displayed in reverse video. This indicates a *selected* menu item. Pressing the up and down cursor keys should move the *selected* item up and down. Pressing the *Enter* key should cause the selected item (the one displayed in reverse video) to be executed. As an alternate method of selecting a menu item, allow the menu item to be executed by typing the first letter of the item. That is, *F* or *f* should select the first item, *S* or *s* should select the second item, and *T* or *t* should select the third item. The three menu items should perform the following functions when executed:

Item 1: First screen display.   Clear the screen and display the message *This is the first screen* in the center of the screen. The message should be *blinking* in *normal* video. Display the message *Press ESC to return to previous screen* at the bottom of the screen and have the program return to the main menu if you press the *ESC* key.

Item 2: Second screen display.   Clear the screen and display the message *This is the second screen* in the center of the screen. The message should be *blinking* in *reverse* video. Display the message *Press ESC to return to previous screen* at the bottom of the screen and have the program return to the main menu if you press the *ESC* key.

Item 3: Text display.   Clear the screen and display any characters that you type from the keyboard. Pressing the *Enter* key should produce a carriage return and line feed. When you reach the bottom of the screen, the entire screen should scroll up one line. Have the program return to the main menu if you press the *ESC* key.

Experiment 28: Pop-up Menus

In this experiment you will learn to make pop-up menus, to use the *struc* assembler directive, and to use jump tables to control what your program does in response to different key pressings. You should use the subroutines in a file *screen.asm* and link these subroutines with your program.

A menu will be defined by the following data structure:

```
menudat    struc
ulx        db      0       ;upper-left x-coord of menu
uly        db      0       ;upper-left y-coord of menu
wid        db      0       ;width of menu
attrib     db      70h     ;reverse video attribute
no_item    db      0       ;no. of items in menu
curpos     db      0       ;cursor position of selected item
items      dw      0       ;list of message addresses of items
enttbl     dw      0       ;enter table for menu
jmptbl     dw      0       ;jump table for menu
menudat    ends
```

Use character graphics to draw a box around each menu and submenu.

Each menu will have the following behavior:

1. The up and down cursor keys will be used to select a menu item. A selected menu item will appear with its attribute complemented.
2. Pressing the *Enter* key will execute the selected item by calling the appropriate subroutine.
3. Pressing the first letter of a menu item will cause that item to be selected and executed.

Write a main program that displays the following initial menu:

```
┌─────────────────────────┐
│                         │
│   First item            │
│                         │
│   Second item           │
│                         │
│   Quit to DOS           │
│                         │
└─────────────────────────┘
```

This main menu should have its upper-left corner located at column 25, row 6 and have a width of 25. You can define this menu with the statement

```
menu1    menudat  <25,6,25,,3,,,,>
```

The three menu items should perform the following functions when executed:

Item 1: First item.   Display the following submenu at column 30, row 8 superimposed on top of the main menu:

```
First   sub1   item
Second sub1 item
```

Include stubs for these subroutines. Pressing the *ESC* key should remove this submenu and return to the main menu.

Item 2: Second item.   Display the following submenu at column 30, row 10 superimposed on top of the main menu:

```
First   sub2   item
Second sub2 item
```

Include stubs for these subroutines. Pressing the *ESC* key should remove this submenu and return to the main menu.

Item 3: Quit to DOS.   Clear the screen, release any memory you allocated, and go to DOS.

Use the subroutines *savescr* and *restscr* (see Figs. 13.40 and 13.41) from *screen.asm* to save the screen before a submenu is displayed and restore the screen when the submenu is to be erased. You must first call *resize* at the beginning of your program and then call *svinit* to allocate the screen buffer.

Experiment 29: Text Editor

In this experiment you will write a program that will allow you to enter any text you want within a 64 × 16 character text window on the screen. You will then create a full screen editor within this window that will allow you to insert and delete characters and move text to different parts of the window.

The text window will contain 1024 (1 Kbyte) characters. Some versions of the Forth programming language use 1-Kbyte screens to store the source listings of its programs. You could also use such 1-Kbyte blocks to store any kind of useful information. In Chapter 15 we will see how to store these 1-Kbyte blocks of information on disk.

1. The main program for this full screen editor should use the subroutines *getkey* and *dokey* to process the keys using a jump table (see Figs. 13.26 and 13.27). Begin by writing an initial display subroutine that will display the following screen:

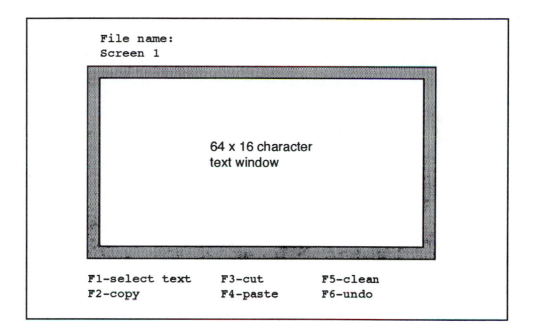

```
File name:
Screen 1



                    64 x 16 character
                    text window




F1-select text      F3-cut          F5-clean
F2-copy             F4-paste        F6-undo
```

Use the subroutine *mess* given in Fig. 13.19 to print the text in the figure. Display the window border using reverse video spaces. Recall from Fig. 13.13 that you can display an entire horizontal bar by using the $AH = 9$, *INT 10H* function call, with *CX* equal to the number of reverse video spaces to print. Pressing the *ESC* key should exit to DOS.

2. Implement the four cursor keys on the numeric keypad and the *Home* key (key 7 of the numeric keypad). The four cursor keys should move the cursor nondestructively to any position within the text editor window. The *up* and *down* cursor keys should cause the cursor to stop at the top and bottom of the window. At the right edge of the window the right cursor key should advance the cursor to the beginning of the following line. At the left edge of the window the left cursor key should move the cursor to the end of the previous line. The *Home* key should move the cursor to the top-left position of the text window.

3. Implement the *default* subroutine called by *dokey* when the key ASCII code is not in the jump table. This routine should *insert* any text typed at the current location of the cursor and advance the cursor to the next location within the text window. To implement this routine, store an image of the text window as 1024 contiguous words (ASCII code, attribute byte) in a text buffer in memory. When a character is to be inserted in the text, insert one word at the cursor position in the text buffer and then rewrite the text buffer to the screen. To work at an acceptable speed, you will need to write directly to the video RAM rather than go through the BIOS ROM. Write a subroutine that will copy row number *row* from the text buffer to the screen window. This subroutine can be used to form other subroutines that will copy to the screen either the remaining characters in the text buffer or the entire text buffer.

Implement the *tab* key by having it insert five spaces at the current cursor location. Implement the *Enter* key by having it insert spaces to the end of the current line and move the cursor to the beginning of the following line.

4. Implement the six function keys shown below the text window in the figure in (1). Pressing *F1* will cause the character at the current cursor position to be displayed in reverse video. Subsequent pressings of the cursor keys will make all text between the original and final cursor positions reverse video. This is called *selecting* text characters. Selected text can be deselected by pressing key *F1* again. Selected text can be erased by pressing the backspace key. Selected text can be copied or cut (erased) to the clipboard (another 1,024-word buffer in memory) by pressing *F1* or *F2*. Text on the clipboard can be inserted (pasted) at the current cursor position by pressing *F4*. Key *F5* will clear the entire window, and key *F6* will undo the most recent change that deleted any characters.

EXERCISES

13.1. Give the hex value of the attribute byte on a monochrome display for each of the following:
   a. normal video
   b. reverse video
   c. blinking normal video
   d. blinking reverse video
   e. high-intensity normal video
   f. high-intensity reverse video

13.2. Give the hex value of the attribute byte on a color display for each of the following:

   a. yellow character on a blue background
   b. yellow character on a black background
   c. red character on a green background
   d. red character on a blue background
   e. white character on a blue background
   f. white character on a red background

13.3. In the video RAM of an 80-character/row display, find the offset address containing the ASCII code of a character located at each of the following screen locations:
   a. column 13, row 0
   b. column 25, row 5
   c. column 0, row 8
   d. column 40, row 15
   e. column 5, row 24

13.4. Using any subroutines in the file *screen.asm* (see Table 13.2), write instructions to set the cursor to column 10, row 5.

13.5. Using any subroutines in the file *screen.asm* (see Table 13.2), write instructions to print the message "8086 Microprocessor" centered on the top row of the screen.

13.6. Using any subroutines in the file *screen.asm* (see Table 13.2), write instructions to blank the lower-right quarter of the screen.

13.7. Write instructions that use the shift and add method of multiplying by a constant (see Fig. 13.21) to compute the following:
   a. $ax = ax * 10$
   b. $ax = ax * 30$
   c. $ax = ax * 50$
   d. $ax = ax * 100$

13.8. Go to address 0040:0017 in TUTOR. You should be able to verify the operation of 6 of the 8 bits shown in Fig. 13.25 by pressing the various keys and moving the TUTOR position cursor back and forth to update the TUTOR screen. Which 2 keys cannot be verified in this way?

13.9. If *al* contains the value *key2* when the subroutine *dokey* in Fig. 13.27 is called, how many times will the instruction *cmp al,cs:[di]* at the label *dk1:* be executed before the subroutine *sub2* is executed?

13.10. Write a subroutine called *query2* that uses the buffered input DOS function ($AH = 0AH$) to perform the same function as the subroutine *query* given in Fig. 13.30.

14

PC Hardware

The user interacts with a personal computer by means of various input/output devices. We have seen how to use the PC keyboard and video screen in Chapters 9 and 13. In Chapter 9 we studied software interrupts. External devices can produce hardware interrupts. When a hardware interrupt occurs, the normal execution of a program is suspended and control is transferred to a special part of the program called an interrupt service routine. After executing this interrupt service routine, control returns to the point at which the program was interrupted. In this chapter we will take a closer look at how the 8086 microprocessor handles interrupts and input/output (I/O) operations.

In particular, in the chapter you will learn:

- How hardware interrupts are generated and processed by the 8086
- How to display a real-time clock on the PC
- The meaning of the 8086 IN and OUT instructions
- The I/O address space associated with the PC
- How to use the parallel printer interface
- How to use the IBM PC speaker interface

14.1 INTERRUPTS

The 8086 microprocessor can handle three different types of interrupts: reset, hardware interrupts, and software interrupts. Software interrupts were described in Chapter 9 and occur when the *INT* instruction (opcode = CC or CD) is executed. In this section we will discuss the reset and hardware interrupts.

Reset

When the *reset* pin on an 8086 goes high, normal microprocessor functions are suspended. When this pin returns low, the microprocessor will set the status register, the instruction pointer, and the segment registers *DS, SS,* and *ES* to 0000H. It will set the code segment register to FFFFH. Execution will therefore begin at location FFFF:0000.

The PC has a power-up reset circuit that causes this reset pin to go high and then low after power (5 volts) has been applied to the 8086. Location FFFF:0000 in the BIOS (basic input output system) ROM contains an intersegment JMP instruction to the code in ROM that is executed when the computer is turned on.

The reset routine is executed only in response to power-on. Pressing the combination *Ctrl, Alt, Del* keys will (normally) execute the equivalent of a system reset (reboot) without the power-on diagnostics.

Hardware Interrupts

There are two hardware interrupt pins on the 8086: INTR and NMI. NMI is a *nonmaskable interrupt*. When this pin goes from low to high, the instruction being executed is completed, and the following interrupt sequence takes place:

1. The status register, code segment register (*CS*), and instruction pointer (*IP*) are pushed on the stack (see Fig. 14.1).

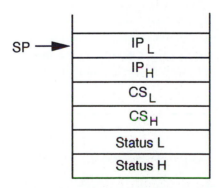

Figure 14.1 Hardware interrupts push the status register, CS, and IP onto the stack.

2. The program jumps to $CS_2{:}IP_2$, where the instruction pointer IP_2 is stored in locations 0000:0008 to 0000:0009 and the code segment CS_2 is stored in locations 0000:000A to 0000:000B. Thus a nonmaskable interrupt is a type 2 interrupt (see Fig. 11.16).

The address $CS_2{:}IP_2$ is called an interrupt vector, and you must store this address in the interrupt vector table shown in Fig. 11.16. This would be the starting address of your interrupt service routine.

The last statement in an interrupt service routine must be the *IRET* (return from interrupt) instruction (opcode = CF). This statement pops the instruction pointer (first 2 bytes), the *CS* register (next 2 bytes), and the status register (next 2 bytes) off the stack. The program will therefore continue at the point in the program where the interrupt occurred.

Only the instruction pointer, the *CS* register, and the status register are saved on the stack when an interrupt occurs. If your interrupt service routine uses other registers, you must also save these values by pushing them on the stack. At the end of the interrupt service routine, you must *POP* any saved registers off the stack.

The *INTR* pin on the 8086 is used for processing *maskable* hardware interrupts. These interrupts can be masked by clearing the interrupt enable flag, *I*, in the status register to zero. This can be done with the *clear interrupt flag* instruction, *CLI* (opcode = FA). To enable hardware interrupts on the *INTR* pin, you must set the interrupt enable flag, *I*, in the status register to 1 by using the instruction *STI* (opcode = FB).

When an enabled *INTR* hardware interrupt occurs, you want a particular interrupt service routine to be executed. You may have several different sources of hardware interrupts, each of which has its own interrupt service routine. This means you will need several different interrupt vectors (*CS:IP* pairs) that point to the starting address of the interrupt service routine. The hardware interrupt vectors are stored in the same interrupt vector table used for software interrupts that is shown in Fig. 11.16. This interrupt vector table occupies the first 1,024 bytes of memory (in segment 0000).

How does the 8086 know which of the 256 interrupt vectors to use when it receives an *INTR* hardware interrupt? The answer is that the interrupting source must send the interrupt type number on the data bus after the 8086 has acknowledged (via the *INTA* pin or status lines *S0* to *S2*) the interrupt. Thus, the device causing the interrupt tells the 8086 where to find the interrupt vector. The 8086

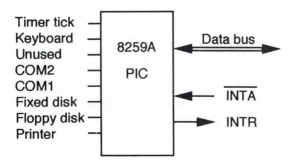

Figure 14.2 The programmable interrupt controller sends one of eight interrupts to the PC.

simply multiplies the type number sent on the data bus by 4 to obtain the address of the interrupt vector.

External circuitry is required to generate these interrupt type numbers when hardware interrupts occur. The PC uses a special programmable interrupt controller (PIC) chip (Intel 8259A) for this purpose (see Fig. 14.2). It can generate eight different hardware interrupts with type numbers from 8 to F. Some of these eight interrupt numbers are used by the PC, while others are available for the user to use. These are shown in Table 14.1.

TABLE 14.1   PC HARDWARE INTERRUPTS

Interrupt type no.	Interrupt vector hex offset address	Name
8	20	Timer tick
9	24	Keyboard
A	28	Unused
B	2C	Reserved for COM2 serial I/O
C	30	Reserved for COM1 serial I/O
D	34	Unused
E	38	Disk I/O
F	3C	Reserved for printer

After an interrupt has been acknowledged and the location of the interrupt vector determined, the interrupt is processed by carrying out the steps shown in Figure 14.3. After pushing the status register onto the stack, the I flag and the T flag are cleared to zero. This has the effect of masking interrupts. (The T flag is associated with single stepping and will be described below.) The instruction pointer, IP, and code segment register, CS, are also pushed onto the stack so that the program can pick up from where it left off. The stack will look like Fig. 14.1. Loading IP and CS from the interrupt vector table will cause execution to begin at the beginning of the interrupt service routine.

1. Push the current status register on the stack.
2. Clear the interrupt enable flag, I, and the trap flag, T, in the status register to mask further interrupts.
3. Push IP and CS on the stack.
4. Load IP and CS from the interrupt vector table.

Figure 14.3   Interrupt sequence that causes a jump to an interrupt service routine.

When the interrupt service routine executes the *return from interrupt* instruction, *IRET*, it pops *IP, CS*, and the *status register* off the stack. These were the values pushed on the stack when the interrupt occurred, so the program will pick up from where it left off. Note that the status register popped from the stack will have the *I* flag set to 1, because that was its value when the status register was pushed on the stack. It is therefore not necessary to execute the statement *STI* before returning from an interrupt service routine. Sometimes (particularly in software interrupt routines) you may want to enable hardware interrupts while the interrupt service routine is being executed. You would then include the *STI* instruction at the beginning of the interrupt service routine.

Single Stepping

A type 1 interrupt will occur one instruction after the trap flag, *T*, in the status register is set to 1. The *T* flag can be set to 1 by pushing the status register on the stack (perhaps as the result of an interrupt) and ORing the high byte of the status register (in the stack) with 10H. Assuming that *CS* and *IP* have also been pushed on the stack, then an *IRET* instruction will cause the modified status register (with $T = 1$) to be popped from the stack. After one instruction is executed, a type 1 interrupt will occur.

In the TUTOR monitor this interrupt service routine resets the *T* flag that was just pushed onto the stack to zero. (The 8086 automatically resets the *T* flag in the actual status register to zero after it pushes it on the stack. Otherwise, you would single step each instruction in the interrupt service routine!) It then displays the current contents of all the registers.

Setting the Interrupt Vector

If you write an interrupt service routine, you must store the segment and offset addresses of your interrupt service routine in the interrupt vector table. Before you do this, it is a good idea to save the current segment and offset addresses that are at that particular interrupt number location in the interrupt vector table so that you can restore these values before you leave your program. The best way to set the interrupt vector is to use the DOS *INT 21H* functions shown in Fig. 14.4. These routines will take care of turning interrupts off while the new values are being stored so that an interrupt won't occur before both the segment

AH = 35H	*Get Interrupt Vector* Inputs: AL = interrupt number Outputs: ES:BX = segment:offset of current Type AL interrupt handler

AH = 25H	*Set Interrupt Vector*
	Inputs: AL = interrupt number
	               DS:DX = segment:offset of interrupt
	                      handler

Figure 14.4   DOS *INT 21H* functions for getting and setting the interrupt vector.

address and the offset address have been changed. Otherwise, the system could crash if the interrupt occurred with the wrong segment or offset address.

As an example, the code shown in Fig. 14.5 will save the interrupt vector currently stored for the type 1CH interrupt and replace it with the interrupt service routine labeled *intser* in the current code segment. We will use this code in the following example of a real-time clock.

```
push    ds                      ;save ds
mov     ah,35h                  ;save 1Ch int vec
mov     al,1Ch
int     21h
mov     vecseg,es
mov     vecoff,bx
push    cs                      ;store int vec
pop     ds
mov     dx,offset intser
mov     ah,25h
int     21h
pop     ds                      ;restore ds
```

Figure 14.5 Code to store the interrupt vector in the type 1CH location.

Real-time Clock

In this section we will write a program that displays a real-time clock on the screen using the hardware interrupt type 8 (see Table 14.1). The 8253-5 Programmable Interval Timer chip produces a hardware interrupt (type 8) approximately 18.2 times per second. The interrupt service routine for this type 8 interrupt is stored in ROM at the segment and offset addresses stored in the interrupt vector table at address 0000:0020. This interrupt service routine increments a 32-bit counter stored in locations 0040:006C to 0040:006D (low word) and 0040:006E to 0040:006F (high word). The built-in software interrupt, *INT 1AH* (time of day), allows you to read and set this 32-bit counter as shown in Fig. 14.6.

AH = 0	*Read the 32-bit counter clock setting* Output: CX = high word of count 　　　　　DX = low word of count 　　　　　AL = 0 if count has not exceeded 　　　　　　　　24 hours since last read 　　　　　　　= 1 if 24 hours has passed
AH = 1	*Set the 32-bit counter clock* Input:　CX = high word of count 　　　　　DX = low word of count

Figure 14.6 Time of day options using INT 1AH.

After incrementing the 32-bit counter, the type 8 hardware interrupt checks for a timeout of the disk drive motor and then calls interrupt type 1CH using *INT 1CH*. This is a user-defined interrupt routine that normally contains only an *IRET* instruction (see Fig. 11.16). You can write any interrupt service routine you like and store the starting address in locations 0000:0070 to 0000:0073 (vector address for a type 1CH interrupt). Your routine will then be executed on every hardware interrupt (18.2 times per second).

We will use the type 1CH interrupt for our interrupt service routine. The algorithm for this interrupt service routine is shown in Fig. 14.7. The time will be displayed in reverse video in the upper-right corner of the screen in the form

```
HOURS:MINS:SECS
```

Since there are 18.2 interrupts per second, we will count 18 interrupts before incrementing the SECS. Every fifth second we will use a count of 19 interrupts. This should make the clock gain only about 1.3 seconds/hour.

```
        dec count (count is initially set to 18)
        if count > 0
        then return from interrupt
        else inc SECS
            if SECS=60
            then inc MINS
                reset SECS=00
                if MINS=60
                then inc HOURS
                    reset MINS=00
                    if HOURS=13
                    then set HOURS=01
                    endif
                endif
            endif
            display time
            set count to 18 (or 19 every 5th time)
        endif
```

Figure 14.7   Algorithm for real-time clock interrupt service routine.

We will write a main program that reads in and displays the current time, stores the interrupt vector address, and then returns to the TUTOR monitor (using *INT 3*) with the hardware interrupts enabled. The clock should continue to tick along on the screen as you go about using the TUTOR monitor.

We will use the buffered keyboard input subroutine *query* available in our *screen.asm* subroutines (see Chapter 13). The keyboard buffer will start at location *data:kbuf* and, after entering the time 10:24:37, the *HOURS, MINS*, and *SECS*

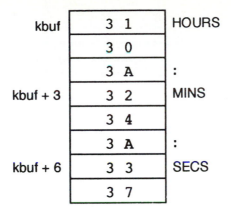

kbuf	3 1	HOURS
	3 0	
	3 A	:
kbuf + 3	3 2	MINS
	3 4	
	3 A	:
kbuf + 6	3 3	SECS
	3 7	

Figure 14.8 Storing the time 10:24:37 in the keyboard buffer.

will be stored in the keyboard buffer as shown in Fig. 14.8. The complete real-time clock program is given in Listing 14.1.

Note that the data entered from the keyboard in Fig. 14.8 are ASCII data. This makes it easy to display these data in the upper-right corner of the screen. The eight bytes from *kbuf* are simply stored in the 8 even bytes of the video RAM starting at offset address 008C (see Fig. 13.6), and the appropriate attribute code (70H for reverse video) is stored in the first 8 odd bytes. The subroutine *dsptim* shown at the end of Listing 14.1 will display the time.

The interrupt service routine is given in Listing 14.1 as the routine *intser*. It follows the algorithm given earlier. Note that since the time data are stored in the keyboard buffer in ASCII form, it is convenient to use the ASCII adjust

Listing 14.1   *clock.asm*

```
title    real-time clock

;        Link with screen

stack    segment para stack
         db    64 dup (?)
stack    ends

         extrn mess2:near,setcur:near
         extrn query:near
         extrn kbuf:byte,blank:near

data     segment      public
msg1     db    'Enter current time '
         db    '<hour:min:sec>: ',0
count    db    ?
cnt5     db    ?
```

Listing 14.1   *(cont.)*

```
vidseg   dw     ?          ;video segment address
vecseg   dw     ?          ;save int vector segment addr
vecoff   dw     ?          ;save int vector offset addr
data     ends
;
code     segment public
         assumecs:code,ds:data

;        turn clock off
clkoff   proc near
         push  ds                        ;save ds
         mov   dx,vecoff                  ;restore old
         mov   ds,vecseg                  ; 1Ch int vec
         mov   al,1Ch
         mov   ah,25h
         int   21h
         pop   ds
         int 3
clkoff   endp

;        main program
clock    proc far
         mov   ax,data
         mov   ds,ax                      ;ds=data
         mov   ah,15                      ;get video state
         int   10h
         cmp   al,7                       ;if mode 7
         jne   clk1
         mov   vidseg,0b000h              ;vidseg=b000
         jmp   clk2                       ;else
clk1:    mov   vidseg,0b800h              ;vidseg=b800
clk2:    mov   dh,24                      ;row=24
         call  blank                      ;blank row 24
         mov   dl,0                       ;col=0
         call  setcur                     ;set cursor
         mov   si,offset msg1
         call  mess2                      ;enter
         call  query                      ; starting time
         call  dsptim                     ;display time
         mov   count,18                   ;count=18
         mov   cnt5,5                      ;cnt5=5
         push  ds                         ;save ds
         mov   ah,35h                     ;save 1Ch int vec
         mov   al,1Ch
         int   21h
         mov   vecseg,es
```

Listing 14.1   *(cont.)*

```
          mov    vecoff,bx
          push   cs                        ;store int vec
          pop    ds
          mov    dx,offset intser
          mov    ah,25h
          int    21h
          pop    ds                        ;restore ds
          int 3                            ; stay in tutor
clock     endp


;         interrupt service routine
intser    proc near
          push   ax                        ;save regs
          push   cx
          push   si
          push   ds
          mov    ax,data
          mov    ds,ax                     ;ds=data
          dec    count                     ;dec count
          jne    out2                      ;if = 0
          mov    si,offset kbuf            ;point to time
          mov    ax,6[si]                  ;ax=secs
          xchg   al,ah
          add    al,1                      ;inc secs
          aaa                              ;ascii adjust
          or     al,30h
          mov    6[si],ah
          mov    7[si],al
          cmp    ax,3630h                  ;if secs=60
          jne    out1                      ;then
          mov    word ptr 6[si],3030h ;   secs=00
          mov    ax,3[si]
          xchg   al,ah
          add    al,1                      ;   inc mins
          aaa
          or     al,30h
          mov    3[si],ah
          mov    4[si],al
          cmp    ax,3630h                  ;   if mins=60
          jne    out1                      ;   then
          mov    word ptr 3[si],3030h ;     mins=00
          mov    ax,[si]
          xchg   al,ah
          add    al,1                      ;     inc hours
          aaa
```

Listing 14.1   *(cont.)*

```
            or     al,30h
            mov    [si],ah
            mov    1[si],al
            cmp    ax,3133h                 ;       if hours=13
            jne    out1                     ;       then
            mov    word ptr [si],3130h      ;         hours=01
out1:       call   dsptim                   ;display time
            mov    count,18                 ;count=18
            dec    cnt5                     ;  (or every
            jne    out2                     ;     5th time,
            inc    count                    ;   count=19)
            mov    cnt5,5                   ; reset cnt5=5
out2:       pop    ds                       ;restore regs
            pop    si
            pop    cx
            pop    ax
out3:       iret
intser      endp

;           display time
dsptim      proc near
            push   ax                       ;save regs
            push   si
            push   di
            push   cx
            push   es
            mov    ax,vidseg                ;point to video
            mov    es,ax                    ; RAM with es
            mov    di,008ch                 ;end of 1st row
            mov    cx,8                     ;move 8 bytes
            mov    si,offset kbuf           ;point to time
            mov    ah,70h                   ;reverse video
            cld
dpt1:       lodsb                           ;load byte
            stosw                           ;store word
            loop   dpt1                     ;do 8 times
            pop    es                       ;restore regs
            pop    cx
            pop    di
            pop    si
            pop    ax
            ret
dsptim      endp

code        ends
            end    clock
```

addition, *AAA*, instruction (see Chapter 10) when incrementing SECS, MINS, and HOURS.

An executable version of the program shown in Listing 14.1 is stored on your TUTOR disk under the file name *clock.exe*. You can load this program into TUTOR by typing */SL* and then entering the filename *clock.exe*. If you press function key *F10*, you will note that the main program starts at offset address 0011. Execute the program starting at this location by typing */EG*. After entering the time, the clock should begin working. While it is keeping time, you can move around in TUTOR.

To stop the clock, you must replace the interrupt vector for the type 1CH interrupt with the values saved in *vecoff* and *vecseg* at the end of the main program. The procedure *clkoff* given at the beginning of Listing 14.1 will do this. Just go to this location by pressing *Home* and execute the code by typing */EG*, and the clock will stop. If you don't stop the clock, it will continue to be displayed even when you return to DOS!

A Delay Subroutine

As mentioned above, a timer tick occurs 18.2 times per second and produces the type 8 hardware interrupt listed in Table 14.1. The *INT 1AH* time of day software

```
;              delay
;              input:  ax = no. of ticks to delay
;                      18.2 ticks per second
delay          proc    near
               push    ax                  ;save regs
               push    cx
               push    dx
               push    ax                  ;push #ticks
               mov     ah,0                ;time of day
               int     1Ah                 ; interrupt
               push    cx                  ;push hi count
               push    dx                  ;push lo count
               mov     bp,sp               ;bp -> lo count
dly1:          mov     ah,0
               int     1Ah                 ;get new count
               sub     dx,[bp]
               sbb     cx,2[bp]            ;calc diff
               cmp     dx,4[bp]            ;repeat until
               jb      dly1                ;diff > #ticks
               add     sp,6                ;fix stack
               pop     dx                  ;restore regs
               pop     cx
               pop     ax
               ret
delay          endp
```

Figure 14.9   A delay subroutine.

interrupt shown in Fig. 14.6 can be used to delay a given number of ticks. The subroutine given in Fig. 14.9 will delay *ax* ticks. After calling this subroutine with the number of ticks to delay in register *ax*, the registers *ax, cx*, and *dx* are saved on the stack. Then *ax* is pushed on the stack again. This is the number of ticks to delay, and this value on the stack will be used as a local variable in the subroutine. The 32-bit counter is then read using the *AH* = 0 option in Fig. 14.6. The high count and low count that are returned in registers *cx* and *dx* are pushed on the stack, and the value of the stack pointer is then stored in register *bp*. At this point the stack will look like that shown in Fig. 14.10.

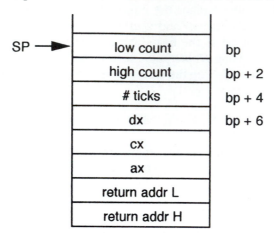

Figure 14.10 Stack contents at instruction labeled *dly1* in Fig. 14.9.

Note that the original low count is stored at [*bp*], the original high count is stored at 2[*bp*], and the number of ticks to delay is stored at 4[*bp*]. These are all local variables that will disappear when we leave the subroutine. The 32-bit counter is then continually read in the *dly1* loop until the new value minus the original value is greater than or equal to the number of ticks to delay. Note that when the loop is exited the stack pointer must be incremented by 6 so as to jump over our three local variables before we pop the three registers from the stack and return from the subroutine.

14.2 IN AND OUT INSTRUCTIONS

As you have seen in previous chapters, the 8086 microprocessor has a large number of instructions that access data in various memory locations. Some memory locations are read-only memory (ROM) and some are read/write memory (RAM).

Personal computers typically access external devices by means of various peripheral interface chips. Some of these are programmable chips that contain various registers. The microprocessor must store data in some of these registers and read data from others. These registers therefore look like memory locations to the microprocessor.

It is possible to connect these peripheral chips in such a way that they occupy the same memory space used by RAM and ROM. This is called *memory-mapped I/O*. The advantage of this method is that all the instructions that access memory can be used to access the I/O registers. No special instructions are needed to do I/O processing. A disadvantage of memory-mapped I/O is that the I/O devices take up memory space that could otherwise be used for RAM or ROM. Some microprocessors, such as those from Motorola, use memory-mapped I/O exclusively.

The 8086 microprocessor has two special instructions, *IN* and *OUT*, that are used only for I/O operations. When one of these instructions is executed, a certain line will go low. This line can be used to ensure that a programmable peripheral chip will respond only to *IN* and *OUT* instructions and not to other memory-access instructions. The 16 address lines used to form the normal memory offset address can also be used to form a 64-Kbyte memory space that is devoted entirely to I/O. This means that *in addition* to the 1-Mbyte address space of the 8086 described in Chapter 9, there is an additional 64-Kbyte I/O address space, with addresses from 0000H to FFFFH that respond only to the *IN* and *OUT* instructions.

The forms of the *IN* and *OUT* instructions for the 8086 are given in Table 14.2. The 2-byte forms involving the I/O port number *data8* can be used to access I/O ports with I/O addresses between 00H and FFH. The forms involving the register *DX* can be used to access any I/O port in the 64-Kbyte I/O address space.

TABLE 14.2   IN AND OUT INSTRUCTIONS

Opcode	Mnemonic		Operation
EC	IN	AL,DX	Input I/O port [DX] to AL
ED	IN	AX,DX	Input I/O ports [DX] and [DX] + 1 to AX
E4 *data8*	IN	AL,*data8*	Input I/O port *data8* to AL
E5 *data8*	IN	AX,*data8*	Input I/O port *data8* and *data8* + 1 to AX
EE	OUT	DX,AL	Output AL to I/O port [DX]
EF	OUT	DX,AX	Output AX to I/O port [DX] and [DX] + 1
E6 *data8*	OUT	*data8*,AL	Output AL to I/O port *data8*
E7 *data8*	OUT	*data8*,AX	Output AX to I/O port *data8* and *data8* + 1

PC I/O Address Space

The I/O address space used in a typical IBM PC is shown in Table 14.3. Note that the addresses in the lower half of the table (>FFH) can be accessed only by using the *DX* form of the *IN* and *OUT* instructions in Table 14.2.

We will describe the operation of some of the programmable peripheral interface devices listed in Table 14.3 in this and subsequent chapters. We will look at the printer interface in the following section and the speaker interface in

TABLE 14.3 IBM PC I/O ADDRESS MAP

Hex addresses	Device
00–0F	8237-2 DMA controller
20–21	8259A Programmable interrupt controller
40–43	8253-5 Programmable interval timer
60–63	8255A-5 Programmable peripheral interface (PPI)
80–83	DMA page register
A0	NMI mask register
200–20F	Game I/O adapter
378–37F	Parallel printer port
3B0–3BF	IBM monochrome display (6845) and parallel printer adapter
3D0–3DF	Color/graphics adapter (6845)
3F0–3F7	NEC PD765 floppy disk controller
3F8–3FF	8250 Universal asynchronous receiver/transmitter

Section 14.4. The use of the 6845 CRT controller chip to create Hercules graphics will be discussed in Chapter 16. The 8250 Universal asynchronous receiver/transmitter and the 8259A Programmable Interrupt Controller will be described in Chapter 17, where we will see how to use these chips to program an interrupt-driven serial communications program.

14.3 PRINTER INTERFACE

The printer interface is a parallel I/O port. This means that data are sent to the printer 1 byte (8 bits) at a time. The printer must have a parallel interface capable of receiving this data. Some printers have serial interfaces and they cannot be used with the PC parallel printer interface. Most printers used with personal computers, however, come with parallel interfaces.

To use a printer, you must have a parallel printer adapter on the board plugged into one of the peripheral I/O slots in the computer. A parallel printer adapter is often included as part of some other board such as a monochrome display board. The parallel printer adapter will have a 25-pin D connector that comes out the back of the computer. The pins on this connector contain the signals shown in Fig. 14.11.

To print a character on the printer, the PC puts the ASCII code for the character to be printed on the data pins 2 to 9. It then checks to see that the *BUSY* line (pin 11) is low (that is, the printer is not busy printing the previous character). If the printer is not busy, then the PC pulses the *STROBE* line (pin 1) low, then high. When this *STROBE* line goes low, the printer will bring the *BUSY* line high, read the data byte, and print the character. After the character has been printed (or stored in the printer buffer waiting to be printed), the printer will bring the

Pin No.	Signal	Direction
1	Strobe	Out
2	Data bit 0	Out
3	Data bit 1	Out
4	Data bit 2	Out
5	Data bit 3	Out
6	Data bit 4	Out
7	Data bit 5	Out
8	Data bit 6	Out
9	Data bit 7	Out
10	Acknowledge	In
11	Busy	In
12	Out of paper	In
13	Select	In
14	Auto feed	Out
15	I/O error	In
16	Initialize printer	Out
17	Select in	Out
18–25	Ground	

Figure 14.11 Connector used for the parallel printer interface.

BUSY line low, indicating that it can receive another data byte. This basic hand-shake operation is shown in Fig. 14.12.

The PC uses three consecutive bytes of I/O memory to communicate with the printer. The I/O address (port number) of the first of these bytes (called *printer base*) is stored in memory locations 0040:0008 to 0040:0009 for printer number 0.

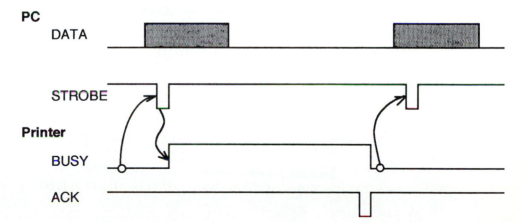

Figure 14.12 Basic handshake used by the parallel printer interface.

You can use up to four printers and locations 0040:0008 to 0040:000F will store the *printer_base* addresses for the four printers.

Go to memory location 0040:0008 using the TUTOR monitor and see what the *printer_base* address is. If it is 0000H, then you have no printer attached. It will be 0378H for the IBM parallel printer adapter and 03BCH for the printer adapter on the IBM monochrome display card.

The 3 bytes starting at the *printer_base* address have the meanings shown in Fig. 14.13. The *Data out* port is the I/O port used to store the data byte being sent to the printer. Bit 7 of the *Printer status byte* port is used to test for the printer being busy. This bit has the opposite polarity of the *Busy* signal in Fig. 14.12. Thus, the printer will not be busy when bit 7 of the *Printer status byte* is high.

The STROBE signal in Fig. 14.12 can be pulsed *low* and then *high* by bringing bit 0 in the *Printer control byte* port in Fig. 14.13 *high*, then *low*. This is because bit 0 in the *Printer control byte* port has the opposite polarity of the STROBE signal in Fig. 14.12.

You can initialize the printer by bringing bit 2 of the *Printer control byte* port low for at least 50 microseconds. The *Acknowledge* signal (pin 10) in Fig.

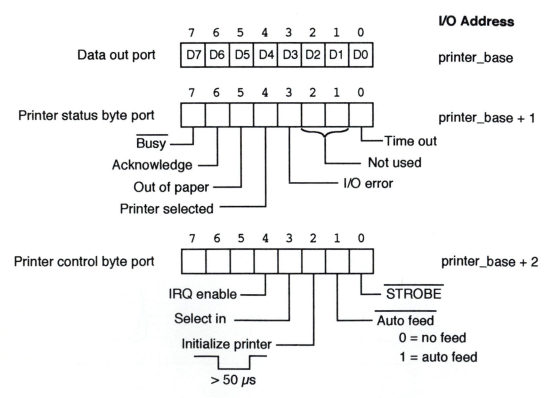

Figure 14.13   The three I/O ports used in the parallel printer interface.

14.11 will pulse *low*, then *high* just before the *Busy* signal goes low. That is, it pulses low after each character is printed. If the IRQ enable bit (bit 4) in the *Printer control byte* port in Fig. 14.13 is set to 1, then a type 0FH interrupt (see Table 14.1) will occur on a high to low transition of the *Acknowledge* signal (pin 10 in Fig. 14.11 or bit 6 in the *Printer status byte* port in Fig. 14.13). Using the above information, you could write your own printer I/O driver routines. The basic algorithm for printing a character is given in Fig. 14.14.

```
Store ASCII code of character to be
      printed in Data Out port.
Wait for bit 7 of the Printer Status Byte
      port (Busy) to go high.
Bring bit 0 of the Printer Control Byte
      (STROBE) high (1) then low (0).
```

Figure 14.14   Algorithm to send a character to the printer.

Alternatively, you can use the built-in BIOS routines, which are called using the software interrupt 17H (see Fig. 11.16). The options available with these printer I/O routines are given in Fig. 14.15. Before calling these routines you must set DX to the printer number (0, 1, 2, or 3) of the printer to use. If you have only one printer, use $DX = 0$. The value of DX used will select one of four possible *printer_base* addresses from the table at locations 0040:0008 to 0040:000F, as shown in Fig. 14.16.

AH = 0	*Print character*
	 Input: AL = ASCII code of character to print
	          DX = printer no. (0 - 3)
	 Output: AH = printer status byte
	          bit 0 = 1 if printer busy (time out)

AH = 1	*Initialize printer port* Input: DX = printer no. (0 - 3) Output: AH = printer status byte
AH = 2	*Read printer status byte* Input: DX = printer no. (0 - 3) Output: AH = printer status byte

Figure 14.15   Printer I/O options used with INT 17H.

As an example of using these printer routines, the program shown in Listing 14.2 will:

1. Clear the screen and ''home'' the cursor.
2. Use the buffered keyboard input subroutine *query* to type a line on the screen.

Listing 14.2   *prntype.asm*

```
                    title type to printer

stack    segment para stack
         db    64 dup(?)
stack    ends

;        screen subroutines
         extrn    crlf:near,quit:near
         extrn    clrscn:near,query:near
         extrn    kbuf:byte,span:word

data     segment public
data     ends

code     segment public
         assume  cs:code,ds:data
prntyp   proc far
         mov    ax,data
         mov    ds,ax                  ;ds=data
         call   clrscn                 ;clear screen
         mov    dx,0
         mov    ah,1
         int    17h                    ;init printer
pt1:     call   query                  ;get line of text
         cmp    span,0                 ; typed
         je     pt3                    ;exit to DOS
         mov    cx,span                ;cx = #char
         mov    dx,0                   ;printer # = 0
         mov    si,offset kbuf         ;point to char
         cld
pt2:     lodsb                         ;al=next char
         mov    ah,0
         int    17h                    ;print char
         test   ah,01h                 ;if time out
         jne    pt3                    ; goto DOS
         loop   pt2
         mov    al,0ah                 ;at end of line
         mov    ah,0
         int    17h                    ;printer cr/lf
         call   crlf                   ;screen cr/lf
         jmp    pt1
pt3:     call   quit                   ;goto DOS
prntyp   endp

code     ends
         end    prntyp
```

DX

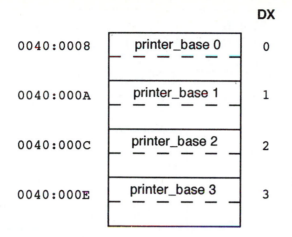

```
0040:0008    | printer_base 0 |   0
             |_____|
0040:000A    | printer_base 1 |   1
             |_____|
0040:000C    | printer_base 2 |   2
             |_____|
0040:000E    | printer_base 3 |   3
             |_____|
```

Figure 14.16 The value of DX will select one of four possible *printer_base* address values for use in the INT 17H printer I/O routines.

3. Print the line just typed on the printer.

4. Repeat steps 2 and 3 until only *Enter* is pressed, which will quit the program and return to DOS.

You can try out this program, which is on your disk. Remember to turn on the printer. If you try to print a character and the printer can't do it within 5 to 15 seconds (depending on the speed of your computer), bit 0 of the *Printer status byte* (Fig. 14.13) will be set to 1. If this occurs in the program in Listing 14.2, the program will return to DOS. Try this by keeping the ON-LINE button on the printer turned off. After entering the first line on the screen, the program will "hang up," but will return to DOS following the timeout.

14.4 SOUND INTERFACE

Two programmable interface chips, a PPI and an interval timer, are involved in the speaker interface, as shown in Fig. 14.17. The basic sound signal sent to the speaker amplifier is a square wave produced by the interval timer. The period of the square wave (or pitch of the sound) depends on a 16-bit value stored in the counter register of the interval timer. This counter register (all 16 bits) has the I/O address 0042H. You have to store 8 bits at a time in this register. Whether the byte you store in I/O port 0042H goes to the least significant byte (LSB) or the most significant byte (MSB) of the counter register depends on how you set up the control register at I/O port 0043H. For the speaker interface, you should store the value B6H in the control register. The meanings of the various bits in this value are given in Fig. 14.18. The interval timer has three 16-bit counters and a control register. The control register is used to select a particular counter and mode of operation. Six different modes of operation are possible, including event

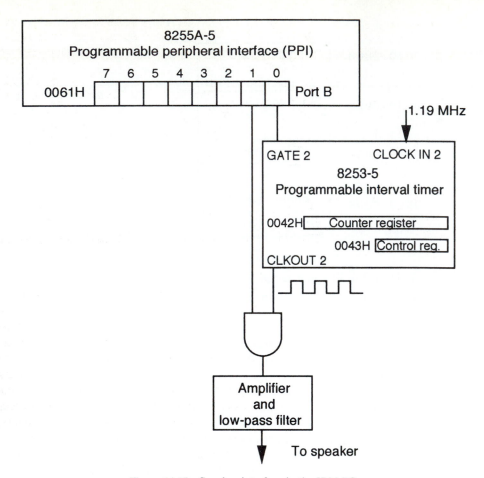

Figure 14.17   Speaker interface in the IBM PC.

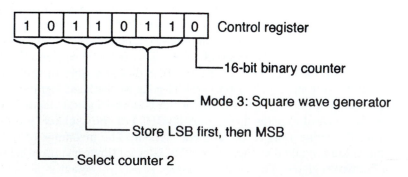

Figure 14.18   Interval timer control register setup used for the speaker interface.

counting, one-shot operation, rate generator, square-wave generator, and software and hardware triggered strobes.

In the square-wave generator mode used in the speaker interface, the output (CLKOUT 2) remains high for half the count and low for half the count (even number counts). The counter register is decremented by 2 on each falling edge of the 1.19-MHz CLOCK IN 2 signal. When the counter register reaches zero, it is reloaded with the original count and the state of the CLKOUT 2 signal is changed.

The counter register can be inhibited from decrementing by means of the *GATE* input. This input must be high for the counter to decrement. As seen in Fig. 14.17, this gate input is connected to bit 0 of port B in the 8255A-5 PPI. The PPI is a programmable parallel interface chip that contains three 8-bit I/O ports. Bits 0 and 1 of port B (I/O address 0061H) must be set to 1 for the speaker to produce a tone. These bits can be used to turn the speaker on and off.

```
;              make a tone
;              dx = pitch of tone
;              bx = length of tone
tone      proc  near
          push  ax               ;save regs
          push  bx
          push  cx
          push  dx
          mov   al,0b6h
          out   43h,al           ;B6 in ctrl reg
          mov   al,dl            ;LSB pitch ->
          out   42h,al           ; counter reg
          mov   al,dh            ;MSB pitch ->
          out   42h,al           ; counter reg
          in    al,61h           ;PPI port B
          mov   ah,al            ; -> AH
          or    al,03h           ;speaker on
          out   61h,al           ;set bits 0,1
          push  ax
          mov   ax,bx            ;delay bx ticks
          call  delay
          pop   ax
          mov   al,ah            ;speaker off
          out   61h,al
          pop   dx               ;restore regs
          pop   cx
          pop   bx
          pop   ax
          ret
tone      endp
```

Figure 14.19 The subroutine *tone*.

```
               beep a tone
     beep      proc  near
               push  bx
               push  dx
               mov   dx,0300h        ;set pitch
               mov   bx,4            ;delay .22 s
               call  tone
               pop   dx
               pop   bx
               ret
     beep      endp
```

Figure 14.20   The subroutine *beep*.

The *tone* subroutine included in the *screen.asm* file is given in Fig. 14.19 with comments describing the meaning of each instruction. Notice how the *IN* and *OUT* instructions are used to access the control and counter registers in the interval timer and the port B register in the PPI. This subroutine uses the value of *DX* as the pitch (the value stored in the counter register) and the value in *BX* as the length of the tone. The *beep* subroutine, also included in the *screen.asm* file, uses a pitch value of 300h and a tone length of four timer ticks, as shown in Fig. 14.20.

Experiment 30: 7-Segment Counter

In this experiment you will write a program to control the 7-segment display from the PC.

1. Program a GAL 16V8 using the 7-segment decoder program shown in Listing 6.15. Wire up the 7-segment display as shown in Experiment 9 at the end of Chapter 6. Connect the four output lines *Out0* to *Out3* to the four input lines, *D0* to *D3*, of the GAL chip.

2. Write a program that will display the digit zero on the 7-segment display when the program is first run and then display the digits 0 to 9 if you press keys 0 to 9. Pressing the *up* cursor key should increment the displayed digit. Pressing the *down* cursor key should decrement the displayed digit.

3. Modify the program so as to include the displays *A, b, C, d, E,* and *F* when you press these keys.

Experiment 31: Morse Code Generator

In this experiment you will write a program to generate and display the Morse code for all the letters in the alphabet. The International Morse Code is

A	.-	E	.	I	..	M	--	Q	--.-	U	..-	Y	-.--
B	-...	F	..-.	J	.---	N	-.	R	.-.	V	...-	Z	--..
C	-.-.	G	--.	K	-.-	O	---	S	...	W	.--		
D	-..	H	....	L	.-..	P	.--.	T	-	X	-..-		

To store the international Morse Code in memory, design a sequential table containing the Morse code for each letter (in order) using the format

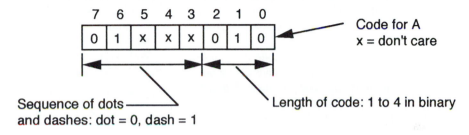

Write an assembly language program for the PC that, for any letter key pressed, will display the letter and corresponding Morse code on the bottom line of the screen in the format shown above and then sound the Morse code. The program should default to uppercase, ignore nonletter keys, and return to DOS when the *ESC* key is pressed.

Use any appropriate subroutines in the file *screen.asm*, including the subroutine *tone* to produce the sound of the Morse code.

EXERCISES

14.1. Using the TUTOR monitor, find the address in ROM that is executed on power-up. Disassemble the first dozen or so instructions that are executed.

14.2. Using the TUTOR monitor, find the address in ROM of the first instruction that is executed when the timer tick hardware interrupt occurs. Disassemble the first dozen or so instructions of this interrupt service routine.

14.3. Using the TUTOR monitor, find the address in ROM of the first instruction that is executed when the keyboard hardware interrupt occurs. Dis-

assemble the first dozen or so instructions of this interrupt service routine.

14.4. Using the TUTOR monitor, find the address in ROM of the first instruction that is executed when an *INT 21H DOS* function call is made. Disassemble the first dozen or so instructions of this software interrupt service routine.

14.5. Using the TUTOR monitor, go to the low byte of the 32-bit timer tick counter at location 0040:006C. Each time you move the position cursor back and forth, the value of the counter will be updated. Do this and observe the contents of the counter. Observe the elapsed tick time if you wait 15 seconds between position cursor moves. What should the value be?

14.6. Modify the *clock.asm* program (included on the TUTOR disk) so that it will display the clock at the beginning of the second row on the screen. Assemble and link the program with *screen.obj* and run the program from TUTOR.

14.7. Write a subroutine called *seconds* that will delay *ax* seconds. How accurate is your delay routine? Make it as accurate as you can.

14.8. The *printer_base* address(es) for any printer ports in your computer will be stored in memory starting at address 0040:0008, as shown in Fig. 14.16. Examine these memory locations using the TUTOR monitor and find the *printer_base* address for the second printer port (if you have one) connected to the logic analyzer.

    a. Write a subroutine called *gtport* that will read the *printer_base* address from location 0040:000A and store the result in the data segment variable *pport*.

    b. Write a subroutine called *output* that will output the byte in *al* to the second printer port.

    c. Write a subroutine called *input* that will read the second printer port status register into *al*.

14.9. The frequencies associated with the musical scale are shown in the following table. Calculate the pitch values to use for *DX* in the tone subroutine in Fig. 14.19 for each note. Write a program that will play the major musical scale when you press keys A, S, D, F, G, H, J, and K on the keyboard.

Note	Frequency, Hz
Middle C	261.6
C# Db	277.2
D	293.7
D# Eb	311.1
E	329.6
F	349.2
F# Gb	370.0
G	392.0
G# Ab	415.3
A	440.0
A# Bb	466.2
B	493.9
C	523.3
C# Db	554.4
D	587.3
D# Eb	622.3
E	659.3

15

Disk Input/Output

The user interacts with a personal computer by means of various input/output devices. We have seen how to use the IBM PC screen and keyboard in Chapters 9 and 13. Interrupts associated with external devices were discussed in Chapter 14, where we also looked at the printer and sound interfaces. In this chapter we will look at how the PC handles input/output (I/O) operations associated with the disk drives.

In particular, in this chapter you will learn:

- The various disk formats used in the PC
- How to access the boot sector using DOS interrupts
- The directory structure of disk files
- How to use DOS functions to:
  a. Open and close files
  b. Read from and write data to disk files
  c. Search the dictionary for a filename
- How to make a *terminate-and-stay resident* (TSR) program that will write the screen to a disk file when you press *Shift-Print Screen*

15.1 DISK FORMATS AND FILE STRUCTURE

Floppy disk drives used in the PC come in two sizes, 5.25 inches and 3.5 inches. The diskettes used in the 5.25-inch drives can be either single or double sided and double density or high density. The 3.5-inch diskettes are double sided and

TABLE 15.1   TYPES OF PC DISKETTES

Size (inches)	Description	No. of tracks per side	No. of sectors per track	Capacity (bytes)
5.25	Single-sided (SS) double-density (DD)	40	8 or 9	160 KB/180 KB
5.25	Double-sided (DS) double-density (DD)	40	8 or 9	320 KB/360 KB
5.25	Double-sided (DS) high-density (HD)	80	15	1.2 MB
3.5	Double-sided (DS)	80	9	720 KB
3.5	Double-sided (DS) high-density (HD)	80	18	1.44 MB

may be high density. This situation leads to five different types of diskettes with different capacities as shown in Table 15.1. A single-sided 5.25-inch drive (now obsolete) can read only single-sided diskettes. A double-density diskette has 40 circular tracks per side with either eight (DOS 1.1 and below) or nine (DOS 2.0 and above) sectors per track. Each sector contains 512 bytes; therefore, each track contains 4,096 (DOS 1.1) or 4,608 (DOS 2.0) bytes, and each side of the diskette contains 163,840 bytes (160 KBytes) for eight sectors/track or 184,320 bytes (180 KBytes) for nine sectors/track. A double-sided disk drive has two separate reading heads, and a double-sided, double-density diskette contains a total of 327,680 bytes (320 KBytes) or 368,640 bytes (360 KBytes). Double-sided drives can read disks formatted on single-sided drives, but not vice versa. High-capacity, 5.25-inch drives can use double-sided, high-density diskettes that have 80 tracks/side and 15 sectors/track with each sector containing 512 bytes. This means that these high-density diskettes can contain 1,228,800 bytes (1.2 MBytes). A high-capacity drive can read double-density or single-sided diskettes, but not vice versa.

The 3.5-inch diskettes contain 80 tracks/side and may have either 9 or 18 sectors/track. With 512 bytes/sector, this means that these diskettes can contain either 737,280 bytes (720 KBytes) or 1,474,560 bytes (1.44 MBytes). A 1.44-MBytes drive can read 720-KByte diskettes, but not vice versa. Given a choice, you should use high-density disk drives, which can access data on diskettes with a lower capacity. Of course, you can't use 5.25-inch diskettes in 3.5-inch drives, or vice versa. The best option is to have both sizes of drives in the same computer.

In addition to floppy disk drives, most PCs today also have some type of fixed or hard disk drive. The capacity of these fixed disk drives varies widely from perhaps 20 Mbytes to hundreds of Mbytes.

The DOS software interrupt statements *INT 25H* and *INT 26H* can be used to read and write specific sectors on a disk using the options shown in Fig. 15.1. When returning from either of these routines, the stack will still contain the status

INT 25H	*Absolute Disk Read*
	Input: CX = no. of sectors to read
	AL = drive no. (0 = A, 1 = B, 2 = C, etc.)
	DX = starting logical sector no.
	DS:BX = buffer address
	Output: carry=0 successful operation
	carry=1 failed operation (reason in AH)
INT 26H	*Absolute Disk Write*
	Input: CX = no. of sectors to write
	AL = drive no. (0 = A, 1 = B, 2 = C, etc.)
	DX = starting logical sector no.
	DS:BX = buffer address
	Output: carry=0 successful operation
	carry=1 failed operation (reason in AH)

Figure 15.1 Absolute disk read and write operations using *INT 25H* and *INT 26H*.

register pushed on the stack by these instructions. Two bytes should therefore be added to *SP* to keep the stack from growing. If the disk access operation is successful, the carry flag will be cleared to zero. Otherwise, the carry flag will be set and the reason for the error is given in *AH* according to the error codes in Table 15.2.

You will seldom use the interrupt calls given in Fig. 15.1 because DOS provides much safer ways to access the disk by using *INT 21H* function calls. We will look in detail at how to use these function calls later in this chapter. However, as an example of using the *INT 25H* absolute disk read routine, suppose you want to read the boot sector, which is sector number 0 on the disk. From the point of view of DOS, all sectors on the disk are numbered sequentially from

TABLE 15.2 DISK ERROR CODES IN AH

Value	Status
01H	Bad command
02H	Bad address mark
03H	Write-protected disk
04H	Sector not found
08H	DMA failure
10H	CRC error
20H	Disk controller error
40H	Seek error
80H	Timeout error

track to track. These logical sector numbers therefore become independent of the number of sectors per track for a particular disk format. The boot sector is logical sector number 0, which is the first sector on track 0 of side 1 on the disk.

The program shown in Listing 15.1 will read this boot sector into the 512-byte buffer *dbuff* in the data segment. An example of running this program when drive A is a 1.2-MByte, 5.25-inch disk drive is shown in Fig. 15.2. The first 80 bytes read from the boot sector are shown in the data segment at the upper-right portion of the screen.

The first 3 bytes in the boot sector are a *JMP* instruction to the bootstrap program, which will read into memory the disk files containing the operating

Listing 15.1   *int25.lst*

```
                              title Absolute disk read
                         ;            read boot sector

0000                          stack segment para stack
0000   40 [                         db      64 dup(?)
              ??
                         ]
0040                          stack ends

0000                          data segment   public
0000   0200 [                        buff db    512 dup(?)        ;disk buffer
              ??                                ]
0200                          data ends

0000                          code segment   public
                              assumecs :code,ds:data
0000                          main proc far
0000   B8 ---- R                    mov    ax,data              ;set ds
0003   8E D8                        mov    ds,ax
0005   BB 0000 R                    mov    bx,offset buff        ;disk transfer area
0008   B9 0001                      mov    cx,1                  ;# sectors to read
000B   B0 01                        mov    al,0                  ;drive # (A)
                                                                 ;use 1 for drive B
                                                                 ;use 2 for drive C
000D   BA 0000                      mov    dx,0                  ;relative sector 0
0010   CD 25                        int    25h                   ;disk read
0012   72 03                        jc     mn1                   ;jump if error
0014   83 C4 02                     add    sp,2                  ;fix stack
0017   CC                    mn1: int  3                         ;breakpoint
0018                          main endp
0018                          code ends
                              end    main
```

```
        8086 Microprocessor TUTOR            Press F7 for Help

     AH AL     BH BL     CH CL     DH DL    DATA SEG   08 19 2A 3B 4C 5D 6E 7F
  AX 01 00  BX 00 00  CX 00 00  DX 00 00    1587:0000  EB 34 90 4D 53 44 4F 53
                                            1587:0008  33 2E 33 00 02 01 01 00
     SP 0040       SI 01B6        IP 0017    1587:0010  02 E0 00 60 09 F9 07 00
     BP 7420       DI 0001                   1587:0018  0F 00 02 00 00 00 00 00
     SS 15A7       DS 1587       CS 1585     1587:0020  00 00 00 00 00 00 00 00
  SP+SS 15AB0   SI+DS 15A26       ES 1575    1587:0028  00 00 00 00 00 00 00 12
  BP+SS 1CE90   DI+DS 15871    IP+CS 15867   1587:0030  00 00 00 00 01 00 FA 33
  STATUS FLAGS 7212 0111001000010010         1587:0038  C0 8E D0 BC 00 7C 16 07
                        ODITSZ A P C         1587:0040  BB 78 00 36 C5 37 1E 56
  1585:0017 CC          INT3                 1587:0048  16 53 BF 2B 7C B9 0B 00


  SEG 1585:  08 19 2A 3B 4C 5D 6E 7F                    15A7: STACK
     FFF8  00 00 00 00 00 00 00 00   . . . . . . . .      0040
     0000  B8 87 15 8E D8 BB 00 00   . . . . . . . .
     0008  B9 01 00 B0 00 BA 00 00   . . . . . . . .
     0010  CD 25 72 03 83 C4 02>CC   . % r . . . . .
     0018  00 00 00 00 00 00 00 00   . . . . . . . .
     0020  EB 34 90 4D 53 44 4F 53   . 4 . M S D O S
     0028  33 2E 33 00 02 01 01 00   3 . 3 . . . . .

                                     / : Command    > : Go To Memory
                                     Use Cursor Keys to Scroll thru Memory
```

Figure 15.2 Example of running the program in Listing 15.1 to read the boot sector.

system. In Fig. 15.2 these 3 bytes are

```
EB 34      JMP    0036H
90         NOP
```

The beginning of the bootstrap program can be seen at offset address 0036H beginning with the instruction FA (*CLI*). The next 8 bytes in the boot sector contain the manufacturer's identification. In Fig. 15.2 these contain the bytes *MSDOS3.3*, as can be seen in the code segment starting at offset address 0023H, which is the same as offset address 0003H in the data segment.

Bytes 000BH to 001DH in the boot sector (shown underlined in the data segment in Fig. 15.2) contain the information in Table 15.3 concerning the physical layout of the disk. Bytes 000BH to 0017H are called the BIOS parameter block (BPB). Note that this disk contains a total of 2,400 sectors. At 512 bytes/sector, this means that the total capacity of the disk is $2,400 \times 512 = 1,228,800$, which agrees with the high-density 5.25-inch diskette given in Table 15.1. The media

TABLE 15.3 BOOT SECTOR INFORMATION

Offset address	Description	Size (bytes)	Fig. 15.2 Example	
			Hex	Dec
000BH	Bytes/sector	2	0200	512
000DH	Sectors/cluster	1	01	1
000EH	Reserved sectors	2	0001	1
0010H	No. of FATs	1	02	2
0011H	No. of root directory entries	2	00E0	224
0013H	Total no. of sectors	2	0960	2400
0015H	Media descriptor byte	1	F9	249
0016H	No. sectors/FAT	2	0007	7
0018H	No. sectors/track	2	000F	15
001AH	No. of heads	2	0002	2
001EH	No. of hidden sectors	2	0000	0

TABLE 15.4 MEDIA DESCRIPTOR BYTE

Descriptor	Media type
0F8H	Fixed disk
0F0H	3.5 inch, 2 sided, 18 sector
0F9H	3.5 inch, 2 sided, 9 sector
0F9H	5.25 inch, 2 sided, 15 sector
0FCH	5.25 inch, 1 sided, 9 sector
0FDH	5.25 inch, 2 sided, 9 sector
0FEH	5.25 inch, 1 sided, 8 sector
0FFH	5.25 inch, 2 sided, 8 sector

descriptor byte (at offset address 0015H) in Table 15.3 indicates the type of media currently in the disk drive according Table 15.4.

DOS files are allocated disk space in file allocation units called *clusters*. A cluster may consist of one or more (two, four or eight) sectors depending on the type of disk. From Table 15.3 we see that the high-density diskette used in the example of Fig. 15.2 uses one sector per cluster. Each cluster is associated with one entry in the *file allocation table* (FAT), which occupies a number of sectors following the boot sector. From Table 15.3 we see that the FAT uses seven sectors on the high-density disk of Fig. 15.2.

Each entry in the FAT consists of 12 bits (fixed disks may have 16-bit FAT entries) containing a link to another FAT entry. This means that every 3 bytes in the FAT contains two FAT entries. The first two entries in the FAT contain information about the type of disk being used. The remaining bytes in the FAT are initially filled with zeros. When a file is created, it is allocated a cluster of disk space, and the FAT entry corresponding to this cluster is filled with FFFH (or any value between FF8H and FFFH), indicating it is the last cluster of a file. The FAT entry number is stored in the directory entry for that file. Each directory entry contains the 32 bytes shown in Fig. 15.3. The root directory occupies space on the disk following the FAT. From Table 15.3 we see that the high-density 5.25-inch disk contains 224 root directory entries (double-sided, double-density disks contain 112 root directory entries). The size of this directory will therefore be 224 × 32 = 7,168 bytes or 14 sectors. When a file is enlarged, it is allocated additional clusters, and the FAT entries corresponding to these clusters are linked into the FAT to form a FAT chain. For example, if a file contains three clusters, the first cluster number will be stored at offset 1AH within the file directory entry, as shown in Fig. 15.3. This first cluster number is also a FAT entry number. The contents of this FAT entry will contain the cluster number of the second cluster in the file, which is also the FAT entry number of the next entry in the chain. This second entry will contain the cluster number of the third cluster in the file, which points to the third FAT entry in the chain. This third FAT entry will contain FFFH, indicating that it is the last cluster in the file.

Bytes	Contents
00H-07H	Filename (E5H in byte 0 means directory entry not used)
08H-0AH	Filename extension
0BH	File attribute
	01H = read only
	02H = hidden file
	04H = system file
	08H = volume label
	10H = subdirectory
	20H = archive bit
0CH-15H	Reserved
16H-17H	Time of last update
	Bits 0-4 2-second increment (binary)
	Bits 5-10 minutes, 0-59 (binary)
	Bits 11-15 hours, 0-23 (binary)
18H-19H	Date of last update
	Bits 0-4 day, 1-31 (binary)
	Bits 5-8 month, 1-12 (binary)
	Bits 9-15 year, 0-119 (1980-2099) (binary)
1AH-1BH	Starting cluster number (points to the logical sector of the start of the file)
1CH-1FH	File size in bytes

Figure 15.3   Format of each directory entry.

Subdirectories

The root directory of the high-density disk given in the example in Table 15.3 can contain a maximum of 224 entries. Some of these entries can be subdirectories. When this is the case, the file attribute byte at offset 0BH in the directory entry has bit 4 set to 1. A subdirectory will have a file size of zero, and its cluster will contain additional directory entries of the form shown in Fig. 15.3. A subdirectory will always contain at least two directory entries. The first has the filename consisting of a single dot (.) (2EH), which refers to the subdirectory itself. The second entry will have the filename consisting of two dots (..) (2EH 2EH) and represents the parent directory.

Subdirectories are only available on versions of DOS of 2.0 and higher. The earlier versions of DOS (1.1) did not allow subdirectories and accessed files using a cumbersome file control block (FCB). This technique has been superseded by a simpler and more general file access method that uses file handles. In this book we will use only the file handle method.

A particular file is specified by an ASCIIZ string, which is a string containing the pathname followed by a zero byte. You can think of the directory as made up of a tree structure in which the primary filenames are attached to a root directory (designated by a backslash, \). Each of these primary filenames can have one or more subdirectories, and these subdirectories can have their own subdirectories. This makes it easy for you to organize all your files in a logical manner. Figure 15.4 shows a simple example of subdirectories. To access the file *neg2word.asm* on a disk in drive *B*, you would specify the pathname with the

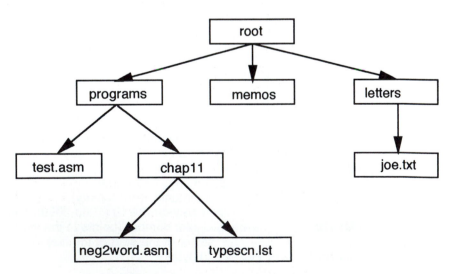

Figure 15.4 An example of subdirectories.

following ASCIIZ string:

```
'b:\programs\chap11\neg2word.asm',0
```

To create, or make, the subdirectory *programs*, you would go to the root directory and type

```
md programs
```

To change the current directory from the root directory to the subdirectory *programs,* you can type

```
cd programs
```

To remove a subdirectory (the subdirectory must contain no files), you can type

```
rd programs
```

The statement

```
prompt $p$g
```

will cause the prompt to look like this.

```
B:\PROGRAMS >
```

This is useful because it will tell you what subdirectory you are in. If you include this statement in the *autoexec.bat* file in the root directory, then the statement will be executed every time you turn on the computer.

Another statement that should be in your *autoexec.bat* file is the *path* statement that will tell DOS what subdirectories to check when searching for a file-

AH = 39H	*Make directory*
	Input: DS:DX points to ASCIIZ string
	Output: AX = standard error codes (3 or 5)
	(see Table 15.5)
	If no errors, carry flag = 0
AH = 3AH	*Remove directory*
	Input: DS:DX points to ASCIIZ string
	Output: AX = standard error codes (3 or 5)
AH = 3BH	*Change current directory*
	Input: DS:DX points to ASCIIZ string
	Output: AX = standard error codes (3)

Figure 15.5   Subdirectory options using INT 21H.

TABLE 15.5   STANDARD ERROR CODES

Error code	Meaning
1	Invalid function number
2	File not found
3	Path not found
4	No handle available; all in use
5	Access denied
6	Invalid handle
7	Memory control blocks destroyed
8	Insufficient memory
9	Invalid memory block address
A	Invalid environment (see DOS SET command)
B	Invalid format
C	Invalid access code
D	Invalid data
E	Not used
F	Invalid drive specification
10	Attempt to remove current directory
11	Not same device
12	No more files to be found

name. For example, if you type the statement

```
path c:\;c:\dos;b:\programs
```

then, if a file is not found in the current or specified directory, DOS will look for the file in the root directory of drive *C*, the subdirectory \DOS in drive *C*, and the subdirectory \PROGRAMS in drive *B*.

The *INT 21H* functions shown in Fig. 15.5 can be used to make, remove, and change subdirectories. If an error occurs when calling one of these *INT 21H* functions, the carry flag will be set to 1 and the value in *AX* will contain a standard error code whose meaning is given in Table 15.5. The error codes in Table 15.5 are available in DOS 2.0 and later versions. Additional error codes were introduced with DOS 3.0 and later versions. These extended error codes also provide suggestions for taking corrective action. (See DOS *INT 21H* function call *AH* = 59H.)

15.2 DISK FILE I/O ROUTINES

DOS provides a series of disk I/O routines that allow you to access files by name without having to worry about where the file is actually stored on the disk. Early versions of DOS (1.1) required that you first set up a *file control block* (FCB) before accessing a file. With the introduction of DOS 2.0, a new method of accessing files using file handles was provided that eliminated the need to set up an FCB. The use of file handles is becoming the standard way of accessing MS DOS disk files, and it is the only method that we will consider in this chapter.

In this section we will study a number of the *INT 21H* DOS function calls that are used to access data in a disk file. Using these DOS function calls, we will write a number of useful subroutines for handling disk I/O. All these subroutines are contained in a file called *disk.asm* whose complete source listing is given as Listing C.2 in Appendix C. This file is on the disk accompanying this book and can be assembled and linked with your own programs.

Opening and Closing Files

Before you can read and write data to a disk file, you must open the file. If the file does not exist, it must first be created. The functions shown in Fig. 15.6 are used to create, open, and close a file. When a file is opened, DOS assigns it a

AH = 3CH	*Open/Create file*
	Input: DS:DX points to ASCIIZ string
	CX = file attribute:
	01H=read only
	02H=hidden
	04H=system
	08H=volume label
	10H=subdirectory
	20H=archive
	Output: AX = file handle
	If carry = 1, then
	AX = standard error codes (3, 4 or 5)
AH = 3DH	*Open file*
	Input: DS:DX points to ASCIIZ string
	AL = access code:
	0=open for reading
	1=open for writing
	2=open for reading and writing
	Output: AX = file handle
	If carry = 1, then
	AX = standard error codes (2, 4, 5 or C)
AH = 3EH	*Close file handle*
	Input: BX = file handle
	Output: AX = standard error codes (6)

Figure 15.6 Open and close functions using INT 21H.

Handle	Use
0	Standard input (normally keyboard)
1	Standard output (normally screen)
2	Standard error output (always screen)
3	Standard auxiliary device
4	Standard printer

Figure 15.7 Standard handles available for all files.

handle, which is just a 16-bit number used to identify the file to other functions. Five standard handles are available for every file. These are given in Fig. 15.7.

The function *AH* = 3CH shown in Fig. 15.6 will create a new file of zero length with a filename given by the ASCIIZ string at *DS:DX*. If a file with this filename already exists, its contents will be lost. On the other hand, the function *AH* = 3DH given in Fig. 15.6 will open an existing file whose filename is an ASCIIZ string at *DS:DX*. If a file with this filename does not exist, a *file not found* error (*error code* = 2) will occur.

The subroutine shown in Fig. 15.8 will open an existing file or, if the file does not exist, will create a new file. When calling this subroutine, *dx* points to

```
      The subroutine shown in Figure 15.8 will open an
            existing file or, if the file does
            not; open or create file
;           input:  dx -> asciiz string
;           output: bx = handle
open        proc  near
            push  cx
            mov   al,2               ;read & write
            mov   ah,3dh
            int   21h                ;open file
            jnc   op2
            cmp   ax,2               ;if file
            jne   op1                ; not found
            mov   ah,3ch             ;create
            mov   cx,0               ; normal attr
            int   21h                ; file
            jnc   op2
op1:        call  open_err           ;error mess
            stc
            jmp   op3
op2:        mov   bx,ax              ;bx=handle
op3:        pop   cx
            ret
open        endp
```

Figure 15.8 Subroutine to open an existing file or create a new one.

```
open_err proc    near
         push    bx
         push    dx
         push    si
         call    beep
         mov     bx,ax           ;bx=err code
         mov     dx,1801h        ;bottom line
         call    setcur
         mov     si,offset em1   ;print
         call    mess2           ; error message
         mov     al,bl
         call    pbyte           ; & error code
         mov     al,'H'
         call    chrprt
         pop     si
         pop     dx
         pop     bx
         ret
open_err endp
```

Figure 15.9   Subroutine to print a disk open error message.

an ASCIIZ string in the data segment containing the pathname of the file. After leaving the subroutine, the handle of the opened file will be in *bx*. Note that the subroutine first tries to open an existing file using the *AH* = 3DH function call. If this is successful, the file handle is put in *bx* and the subroutine is exited. On the other hand, if error code 2 occurs (file not found), a new file is created using the *AH* = 3CH function call. Any other error will produce a call to the subroutine *open_err* shown in Fig. 15.9. The error message, *em1*, called in the subroutine in Fig. 15.9 is contained in the *disk.asm* data segment shown in Fig. 15.10.

The subroutine shown in Fig. 15.11 will ask for a filename to be entered (using *query* from the *screen.asm* subroutines) from the keyboard and will then open the file and store the handle in the word variable *handle* in the data segment of Fig. 15.10.

```
data       segment  public
handle     dw       ?
bytbuf     db       ?
fnmsg      db       'Enter filename: ',0
em1        db       'Disk open error: ',0
em2        db       'Disk close error: ',0
em3        db       'Disk read error: ',0
em4        db       'Disk write error: ',0
em5        db       'Disk file error: ',0
data       ends
```

Figure 15.10   Data segment used by the *disk.asm* subroutines.

```
;              enter filename and open
;              input:  none
;              output: handle is in 'handle'
;                      carry = 1 if not opened
        openfn  proc  near
                push  bx
                push  dx
                push  si
                mov   si,offset fnmsg
                call  mess2               ;display mess
                call  query               ;enter filename
                cmp   span,0              ;if no chars
                jne   of0                 ; set carry
                stc                       ; and quit
                jmp   of1
        of0:    mov   dx,offset kbuf
                call  open                ;open it
                jc    of1                 ;if error,quit
                mov   handle,bx           ;store handle
        of1:    pop   si
                pop   dx
                pop   bx
                ret
        openfn  endp
```

Figure 15.11   Subroutine to enter a filename and open the file.

The subroutine in Fig. 15.12 will close the file whose handle is in *bx* by calling the *AH* = 3EH DOS function call. An error will produce a close error message by calling the subroutine *close_err*, which is similar to the *open_err* subroutine in Fig. 15.9 and is given in the *disk.asm* file in Appendix C.

Sometimes you may need to replace an existing file with a new file of the same name. Calling the subroutine *create* shown in Fig. 15.13 will create a file of zero length which will allow you to write over old data in a previous file of the same name without having any of the old data still around.

```
;              close file
;              input: bx = handle
close   proc  near
        mov   ah,3eh
        int   21h                 ;close file
        jnc   cl1                 ;if error
        call  close_err           ; print it
        stc
cl1:    ret
close   endp
```

Figure 15.12   Subroutine to close a file.

```
;           create file
;           (set length to zero to write over)
;           input:  dx -> asciiz string
;           output: bx = handle
create      proc  near
            push  cx
            mov   ah,3ch           ;create
            mov   cx,0             ; normal attr
            int   21h             ; file
            jnc   ct2
ct1:        call  open_err         ;error mess
            stc
            jmp   ct3
ct2:        mov   bx,ax            ;bx=handle
ct3:        pop   cx
            ret
create      endp
```

Figure 15.13   Subroutine to create a new file.

AH = 3FH	*Read from file or device*
	Input: BX = file handle
	CX = count of bytes to read
	DS:DX points to buffer to receive data
	Output: AX = actual number of bytes read
	(AX=0 means end of file read)
	If carry = 1, then
	AX = standard error codes (5 or 6)
AH = 40H	*Write to file or device*
	Input: BX = file handle
	CX = count of bytes to write
	DS:DX points to buffer containing data
	Output: AX = actual number of bytes written
	(must equal CX for no error)
	If carry = 1, then
	AX = standard error codes (5 or 6)
AH = 42H	*Move file pointer*
	Input: BX = file handle
	CX:DX = offset value (CX is high-order word)
	AL = method code:
	0=move pointer to start of file + offset
	1=increase pointer by offset
	2=move pointer to end of file + offset
	Output: DX:AX = new value of file pointer
	If carry = 1, then
	AX = standard error codes (1 or 6)

Figure 15.14   File read and write options using INT 21H.

Reading and Writing Data to a File

To read or write to a file or device, the functions given in Fig. 15.14 are used. You just specify a file handle (given to you when you opened the file), point to the buffer address with *DS:DX*, and store the number of bytes to read or write in *CX*. This is an example of stream-oriented I/O in which a given number of bytes is sent to or read from the file in a serial fashion. The "file" need not be a file on disk but could be a device associated with one of the standard handles in Fig. 15.7. For example, a serial I/O port could be the standard auxiliary device with a handle of 3. The use of a handle makes it easy to redirect data to different files or devices by simply changing the handle value.

The *read* and *write* subroutines shown in Fig. 15.15 allow you to read *cx* bytes from a file into a buffer at *DS:DX* and to write *cx* bytes from such a buffer to a file. The *read* subroutine will return a value of zero in *AX* if an *end-of-file mark* was read. This will occur if there are no more data bytes in the file. If an error occurs when using these subroutines, an error message similar to the one

```
;           read file
;           input: bx = handle
;                  cx = # of bytes to read
;                  dx -> buffer address
;           output: ax = # of bytes read
;                   ax = 0 if EOF
read    proc    near
        mov     ah,3fh
        int     21h                 ;read file
        jnc     rd1                 ;if error
        call    read_err            ; print it
        stc
rd1:    ret
read    endp


;           write file
;           input: bx = handle
;                  cx = # of bytes to write
;                  dx -> buffer address
write   proc    near
        mov     ah,40h
        int     21h                 ;write file
        jnc     wt1                 ;if error
        call    write_err           ; print it
        stc
wt1:    ret
write   endp
```

Figure 15.15 Subroutines to read and write file data.

```
;               get next byte
;               input:  bx = handle
;               output: al = byte
;                       carry = 1 if EOF
gtbyte     proc    near
           push    cx
           push    dx
           mov     cx,1                ;read 1 byte
           mov     dx,offset bytbuf
           call    read
           cmp     ax,0                ;if EOF
           jne     gb1
           stc                         ; set carry
           jmp     gb2                 ;else
gb1:       mov     al,bytbuf           ;al=byte
           clc                         ;clear carry
gb2:       pop     dx
           pop     cx
           ret
gtbyte     endp
```

Figure 15.16   The subroutine *gtbyte* will read the next byte into *al*.

shown in Fig. 15.9 will be written at the bottom of the screen. The subroutines *read_err* and *write_err* are given in the file *disk.asm* in Appendix C.

The subroutine *gtbyte* shown in Fig. 15.16 is a useful subroutine that returns the next byte in the file in register *al*. It only needs the file handle in *bx* when the subroutine is called. The subroutine indicates an *end-of-file* condition by setting the carry flag.

The subroutine *sndbyte* shown in Fig. 15.17 will write the byte in *al* to a file

```
;               send byte
;               input: bx = handle
;                      al = byte
sndbyte    proc    near
           push    cx
           push    dx
           mov     bytbuf,al           ;bytbuf=byte
           mov     dx,offset bytbuf
           mov     cx,1                ;1 byte
           call    write               ;send it
           pop     dx
           pop     cx
           ret
sndbyte    endp
```

Figure 15.17   The subroutine *sndbyte* will send the byte in *al* to the file whose handle is in *bx*.

```
;            send crlf
sndcrlf   proc   near
          mov    al,13              ;send cr
          call   sndbyte
          mov    al,10              ;send lf
          call   sndbyte
          ret
sndcrlf   endp
```

Figure 15.18 The subroutine *sndcrlf*.

whose handle is in *bx*. An example of using this subroutine is shown in Fig. 15.18 where the subroutine *sndcrlf* will send a carriage return (0DH) and a line feed (0AH) to the disk file.

It is up to you to structure the file in any logical manner you wish. You can position the file pointer (where you begin to read or write) within a file using the *AH* = 42H option given in Fig. 15.14. This function call is incorporated in the general subroutine *movptr* shown in Fig. 15.19. When calling this subroutine, *bx* contains the file handle, *cx:dx* is a 32-bit offset value, and *al* contains the method code. If *al* = 0, the pointer is moved from the start of the file plus the offset. If *al* = 1, the pointer is incremented by the offset from its current location. If *al* = 2, the pointer is moved to the end of the file plus the offset. While this last case may seem useless, it actually is useful in finding the length of a file. Because the DOS function *AH* = 42H returns the new value of the pointer in *dx:ax* if we set the offset *cx:dx* to zero before calling the function with *al* = 2, the length of the file will be returned in *dx:ax*. The subroutine *getlen* shown in Fig. 15.20 will do this.

If an error occurs in *movptr* or *getlen*, an error message similar to the one

```
;            move pointer
;            input: bx = handle
;                   cx:dx = offset value
;                   al = 0 - start of file + offset
;                        1 - inc ptr by offset
;                        2 - end of file + offset
;            output: dx:ax = new value of ptr
movptr    proc   near
          mov    ah,42h             ;move ptr
          int    21h
          jnc    mpt1
          call   ptr_err
          stc
mpt1:     ret
movptr    endp
```

Figure 15.19 The subroutine *movptr* is used to move the file pointer.

```
;              get length of file
;              input:  bx = handle
;              output: dx:ax = length of file
getlen   proc   near
         push   cx
         mov    cx,0
         mov    dx,0              ;offset=0
         mov    al,2             ;mov ptr from
         mov    ah,42h            ; end of file
         int    21h
         jnc    gl1              ;if error
         call   ptr_err          ; print it
         stc
gl1:     pop    cx
         ret
getlen   endp
```

Figure 15.20 The subroutine *getlen* will return the length of a file in *dx:ax*.

shown in Fig. 15.9 will be written at the bottom of the screen. The subroutine *ptr_err* is given in the file *disk.asm* in Appendix C.

If you write data to a file, the file pointer will be pointing to the end of the file where any new data will be added. If you want to read the data that you just wrote to the file, you will first need to move the pointer back to the beginning of the file. The subroutine *rewind* shown in Fig. 15.21 will do this. Note that it calls the move pointer DOS function $AH = 42H$ in Fig. 15.14 with an offset and method code of zero.

```
;              rewind file
;              input: bx = handle
rewind   proc   near
         push   cx
         push   dx
         mov    cx,0
         mov    dx,0              ;offset=0
         mov    al,0             ;mov ptr from
         mov    ah,42h            ; start of file
         int    21h
         jnc    rw1              ;if error
         call   ptr_err          ; print it
         stc
rw1:     pop    dx
         pop    cx
         ret
rewind   endp
```

Figure 15.21 The subroutine *rewind* will move the pointer to the beginning of the file.

Finding Directory Entries

Suppose you want to make a list of the filenames in the directory. To do this you can use the DOS *INT 21H* functions shown in Fig. 15.22. You must first set up a *disk transfer area* (DTA) in the data segment by setting *DX* to the offset address of the DTA and calling *INT 21H* with *AH* = 1AH. To find the first entry in the root directory of drive *C*, you would have *DX* point to the following ASCIIZ file specification in the data segment:

`'C:\*.*'`

If you wanted to find the first entry in subdirectory *programs* of drive *A*, you would use the file specification

`'A:\programs\*.*'`

Then call *INT 21H* with *AH* = 4EH and *CX* equal to the file attribute given in Fig. 15.6. If *CX* is set to zero, then the first ordinary file in the directory will be found and data associated with that file will be stored in the DTA, as shown in Fig. 15.23. The filename found will be located at offset 30 (1EH) within the DTA in the form of an ASCIIZ string with a period inserted between the filename and the extension. If the file attribute, *CX*, contains the value 10H, then both ordinary files and subdirectories will be included in the search.

Once the first match is found (the specification *.* will match all files in the directory), the next match can be found by calling *INT 21H* with *AH* = 4FH.

AH = 1AH	*Set disk transfer area address* Input: DS:DX points to disk transfer area (DTA) Output: none

AH = 4EH	*Search directory for first match*
	Input: CX = attribute to use in search
	            DS:DX points to ASCIIZ file specification
	Output: If carry = 0
	                    DTA contains data in Figure 15.23
	            If carry = 1, then
	                    AX = standard error codes (2 or 12H)

AH = 4FH	*Search directory for next match*
	Input: none
	Output: If carry = 0
	                    DTA contains data in Figure 15.23
	            If carry = 1, then
	                    AX = standard error codes (12H)

Figure 15.22   DOS INT 21H functions for finding directory entries.

Byte offset within DTA	Contents
0 – 20	reserved for future use
21	attribute of matched file
22 – 23	file time
24 – 25	file date
26 – 27	file size (least significant word)
28 – 29	file size (most significant word)
30 – 42	filename and extension (ASCIIZ string)

Figure 15.23   Contents of disk transfer area (DTA) after finding a directory match.

This call will use the same attribute and file specification used in the previous *AH* = 4EH call. Information about the next file will then be found in the DTA. If no more files are found, then the carry flag will be set to 1 and *AX* will contain the error code 12H. This test can be used to find all filenames in the directory.

15.3 SAVING THE SCREEN DISPLAY TO DISK

It is sometimes useful to save everything on the screen to disk. To do this, we will change the *Print Screen* interrupt so that when you press *Shift-Print Screen* the contents of the screen will go to a disk file rather than to the printer. You could then edit these data, move them to another computer, and print them out later. Interrupt type number 5 is used for the print screen interrupt service routine, as shown in Fig. 11.16. We will need to replace the interrupt vector stored in the interrupt table by DOS for sending the screen to the printer with the interrupt vector for our own interrupt service routine for sending the screen to a disk file.

To be useful, this interrupt service routine must be in memory all the time so that, regardless of what program you are currently running, the screen will be sent to disk if you press *Shift-Print Screen*. To do this, we must make our interrupt service routine a *Terminate-and-Stay-Resident* (or TSR) program. We do this by using the DOS *INT 21H* function with *AH* = 31H, as shown in Fig. 15.24. The use of this DOS function is illustrated in Listing 15.2, which is a listing of the file *ss.asm*. This assembled file is linked with the object files *screen.obj* and *disk.obj* to produce the executable file *ss.exe*. When the program *ss* is executed from DOS, it will execute the main program shown at the end of Listing 15.2. Notice that this main program is in a separate code segment called *transient_main*. The pur-

AH = 31H	*Terminate and stay resident*
	Input: AL = return code
	DX = memory size to save (in paragraphs)

Figure 15.24   DOS INT 21H function for terminating a process without releasing its memory.

Listing 15.2   *ss.asm*

```
title    Save screen to disk
;               Terminate and stay resident
;               Use Shift-PrtScn to save screen

;        LINK with screen and disk
data     segment  public
tempbuf dw     80 dup(?)
curpos  dw     ?
data     ends

;        screen subroutines
         extrn setcur:near,rdcurs:near
         extrn stvseg:near,vidseg:word

;        dos subroutines
         extrn close:near,sndbyte:near
         extrn openfn:near,handle:word

code     segment  public
         assume cs:code,ds:data

;        interrupt 5 service routine
scn2fil proc   near
         sti
         push    ax
         push    bx
         push    cx
         push    dx
         push    si
         push    di
         push    es
         push    ds
         assume ds:data
         mov     ax,seg data
         mov     ds,ax
         call    stvseg             ;set vidseg
         call    save24             ;save row 24
         mov     dh,24
         mov     dl,0
         call    setcur
         call    openfn             ;open filename
         call    get24              ;restore row 24
         mov     ax,vidseg          ;save screen
         mov     es,ax
         mov     si,0
         mov     cx,25
         mov     bx,handle
```

Listing 15.2   (*cont.*)

```
s2f3:     call    sndline              ;send 25 lines
          loop    s2f3
          call    close
          pop     ds
          pop     es
          pop     di
          pop     si
          pop     dx
          pop     cx
          pop     bx
          pop     ax
          iret
scn2fil endp

;         save row 24 in tempbuf
save24    proc    near
          push    ds
          push    ds
          pop     es
          mov     ax,vidseg
          mov     ds,ax
          mov     di,offset tempbuf
          mov     si,0f00h
          mov     cx,80
          rep movsw
          assume ds:data
          mov     ax,data
          mov     ds,ax
          call    rdcurs
          mov     curpos,dx            ;save curs pos
          pop     ds
          ret
save24    endp

;         restore row 24 from tempbuf
get24     proc    near
          mov     ax,vidseg
          mov     es,ax
          mov     si,offset tempbuf
          mov     di,0f00h
          mov     cx,80
          rep movsw
          mov     dx,curpos
          call    setcur
          ret
get24     endp
```

Listing 15.2   (*cont.*)

```
;          send line of 80 characters from screen
;          inputs:  bx = handle
;                    es = vidseg
;                    si = offset addr of row to send
;          outputs: si = offset addr of next row
sndline  proc    near
         push    cx
         mov     cx,80                    ;send 80 chars.
sl1:     mov     al,es:[si]
         cmp     al,32                    ;if ascii code
         jb      sl2                      ;is < 20H
         cmp     al,128                   ;or > 7FH
         jb      sl3
sl2:     mov     al,'.'                   ;send a '.'
sl3:     call    sndbyte
         add     si,2
         loop    sl1
         mov     al,13                    ;send crlf
         call    sndbyte
         mov     al,10
         call    sndbyte
         pop     cx
         ret
sndline  endp
code     ends


transient_main segment para public
         assume  cs:transient_main,ss:stack
main     proc    far
         mov     ax,seg scn2fil    ;set int 5
         mov     ds,ax
         mov     dx,offset scn2fil
         mov     al,5
         mov     ah,25h
         int     21h
         mov     dx,cs             ;dx = end of resident portion
         mov     ax,es             ;es = psp segment
         sub     dx,ax             ;dx = size of resident portion
         mov     ax,3100h          ;terminate and stay resident
         int     21h
main     endp
transient_main ends

stack    segment para stack
         db      64 dup(?)
stack    ends
         end     main
```

pose of the main program is to store the address of the interrupt service routine *scn2fil*, which will write the screen to a disk file, in the interrupt vector table (type 5) and then exit to DOS without releasing the memory associated with the interrupt service routine. Note that the current value of *CS* when this main program is being executed will be the segment address of *transient_main*. We don't need to keep this. The value in *ES* will be the segment address of the program segment prefix that precedes our entire program. Therefore, the value $DX = CS - ES$ will be the number of paragraphs to save, which will include all the segments *code*, *data*, and *stack* (including the *code* and *data* segments included in the files *screen.asm* and *disk.asm*). This is because in memory these segments are in alphabetical order, as can be seen from the file *ss.map* (created when calling LINK) shown in Fig. 15.25.

```
Start   Stop    Length  Name
          Class
00000H 00A01H 00A02H  CODE
00A10H 00D0FH 00300H  DATA
00D10H 00D4FH 00040H  STACK
00D50H 00D68H 00019H  TRANSIENT_MAIN
```

Figure 15.25   Contents of the file *ss.map*.

```
Program entry point at 00D5:0000
```

The interrupt service routine, *scn2fil*, will save the current screen to disk. After saving the video RAM segment address in the variable *vidseg* by calling the *screen.asm* subroutine *stvseg*, the program saves the bottom row of the screen in *tempbuf* using the subroutine *save24*. The user is then asked to enter a filename on this bottom row using the *screen.asm* subroutine *openfn*. The subroutine *get24* then restores the bottom row on the screen.

The *s2f3* loop in Listing 15.2 sends the characters on the screen to the disk by calling the subroutine *sndline* 25 times. The subroutine *sndline*, also given in Listing 15.2, will send a single line of 80 characters to the screen using the *disk.asm* subroutine *sndbyte*.

Experiment 32: Typing Characters to a Disk File

The program in Listing 14.2 sent each line typed on the screen to the printer. Write a similar program that will send each line typed on the screen to a disk file. When the program is first run, it should ask for a filename to open. When you press the *Enter* key without typing any characters on the line, the program should close the file before exiting to DOS.

Write a second program that will read the file containing your data and display the contents on the screen. When the program is run, it should ask for a filename to open, read all the data from the disk and display it on the screen, close the file, and exit to DOS.

Experiment 33: Saving Text Editor Files

Modify the program written in Experiment 29 in Chapter 13 by adding the capability to read and save disk files. The disk files will consist of 1,024-byte blocks of data, each of which will fill the 64 × 16 window on the screen. The first block on the disk will contain data for screen 1, the second block will contain data for screen 2, and so on. The screen number should be displayed above the window on the screen, as shown in Experiment 29.

When function key *F7* is pressed, the program should ask for a filename at the top of the screen and create the file if it does not exist. If the file does exist, the first block of 1,024 bytes of data should be loaded into the text buffer and displayed in the window on the screen where it can be edited.

When function key *F8* is pressed, the screen number displayed on the screen should be saved. If no file is open, a new filename should be entered to save the data.

Use the *page up* and *page down* cursor keys to display different blocks of data on the screen. The program should increase or decrease the screen number displayed on the screen by 1 each time the *page up* or *page down* cursor key is pressed. When you press one of these keys, the program should save the current screen data and then load the new screen data from disk.

When you press the *ESC* key, the program should save the current screen, close the file, and exit to DOS.

Experiment 34: Disk Directory and File Display

In this experiment you will write a program that will display the disk directory and allow you to select a particular file to display on the screen.

Write a program that will display the directory on a disk as a list of up to 15 filenames in a window. When the directory is first displayed, the first filename should be displayed in reverse video, with all the others in normal video. This *reverse video cursor* will be moved from filename to filename by using the *up* and *down* cursor keys plus the *home* and *end* keys. When you press the *Enter* key, the screen should print out on the screen the contents of the file whose filename is currently displayed in reverse video. When the file is printed to the screen, have the output pause each time the screen fills up until a key is pressed. Pressing the *ESC* key should take you back to DOS.

Hints:

1. Use a jump table in your main program to handle the cursor keys, the *home* and *end* keys, and the *Enter* key.
2. Display the directory by searching for all files using a *.* pathname. Use the DOS functions 4EH and 4FH to search for a filename.

3. Keep track of the file number corresponding to the filename displayed in reverse video.

Extra credit: Modify the program so as to display subdirectories as well as normal filenames. When you press the *Enter* key with a subdirectory selected, the program should display the directory (filenames) of the subdirectory. Any of these files (including additional subdirectories) should be displayed by selecting with the cursor keys and pressing the *Enter* key. When displaying the files in a subdirectory, pressing function key *F1* should bring you back to the next higher directory in the path.

Experiment 35: Browsing and Printing Text Files

Write a program that is controlled by a menu display (see Experiments 27 or 28 in Chapter 13). One menu item should select a filename from a menu (see Experiment 34) and display the contents of the file on the screen. Display a screenfull at a time and use the *page up* and *page down* cursor keys to scroll through the file.

A second menu item should select a filename from a menu (see Experiment 34) and print the contents of the file to a printer. Use the standard handle number 4 to redirect the file contents to the printer.

EXERCISES

15.1. Modify the program in Listing 15.1 to read the boot sector for a disk in your disk drive. Find the information in Table 15.3 for your disk.

15.2. Modify the program in Listing 15.1 to read sector 1 (the first sector of the FAT). The first byte will be the media descriptor byte and the next 2 bytes will each contain FFH. The next 3 bytes will contain two 12-bit FAT entries. For example, the 3 bytes 03 40 00 correspond to the two FAT entries 003 and 004. An FAT entry of FFF indicates the last cluster in a file. Make a list of the cluster numbers for the first file on your disk.

15.3. Using the boot sector information for your disk found in Exercise 15.1, find the logical sector number for the first file on your disk. The first file will be located after the FAT and the root directory. The number of sectors per FAT, the number of FATs, and the number of root directory entries will tell you how many sectors to skip. (Each directory entry uses 32 bytes, so there can be 16 directory entries per sector.) Modify the program in Listing 15.1 to read the sector corresponding to the first cluster of the first file on your disk.

16

Graphics

You learned how to display text on the screen in Chapter 13. In this chapter we will look at how to display graphics on the PC.

In particular you will learn:

- How to select the CGA, EGA, and VGA graphics modes
- How to plot a dot
- How to plot a line
- How the 6845 CRT controller is used to display Hercules graphics
- How to set the Hercules graphics mode
- How to display characters using Hercules graphics

16.1 GRAPHICS MODES

As discussed in Chapter 13, IBM provided two different types of screen display boards with its first PC in 1981: a monochrome display adapter (MDA) and a color graphics adapter (CGA). The MDA displayed only text on a monochrome monitor. The color graphics adapter could display color graphics on a separate color TV or color monitor. In 1982, Hercules Computer Technology introduced its first graphics card, which allowed monochrome graphics to be displayed on the monochrome monitor. We will show you how to do this later in this chapter. In 1984, IBM introduced its enhanced graphics adapter (EGA) and later brought out its video graphics array (VGA) board, both of which provide high-resolution color graphics and text.

462

TABLE 16.1   GRAPHICS MODES

Mode	Type	Resolution, columns × rows	No. of colors	Video RAM segment address	Character cell size
4	CGA, EGA, VGA	320 × 200	4	B800	8 × 8
5	CGA, EGA, VGA	320 × 200	4	B800	8 × 8
6	CGA, EGA, VGA	640 × 200	2	B800	8 × 8
0D	EGA, VGA	320 × 200	16	A000	8 × 8
0E	EGA, VGA	640 × 200	16	A000	8 × 8
0F	EGA, VGA	640 × 350	2	A000	8 × 14
10	EGA, VGA	640 × 350	16	A000	8 × 14
11	VGA	640 × 480	2	A000	8 × 16
12	VGA	640 × 480	16	A000	8 × 16
13	VGA	320 × 200	256	A000	8 × 8

The graphics modes on the PC are set using *INT 10H* with *AH* = 0 and *AL* set to one of the mode numbers given in Table 16.1. Modes 4, 5, and 6 are the original CGA modes. These modes are also available on the newer EGA and VGA boards. Mode 4 is a medium resolution (320 × 200) mode that supports four colors. Mode 6 has higher resolution (640 × 200), but only two colors (black and white). Note that the video RAM containing this graphics data begins at segment address B800H.

EGA graphics introduced modes 0D, 0E, 0F, and 10, which provided more colors (16) and higher resolution (up to 640 × 350). VGA graphics supports these EGA modes, plus adds modes 11, 12, and 13, which provide even higher resolution (640 × 480), plus a new medium-resolution mode (320 × 200) that can display 256 different colors. Most VGA boards also support some extended VGA modes that can display 132 columns of text and 800 × 600 resolution color graphics with 16 colors. Note that the video RAM for the EGA and VGA graphics modes begins at segment address A000H.

Most high-performance graphics programs require writing the graphics data directly to the video RAM to increase speed. We will show how to do this later in the chapter when we describe Hercules graphics. There are *INT 10H* BIOS routines that allow you to set a graphics mode, select colors, and read and write dots to the screen. In addition, the character display BIOS functions described in Chapter 13 can be used to write text on the screen when in any of the graphics modes in Table 16.1.

The graphics data are stored in the video RAM. In mode 6 there are 640 × 200 = 128,000 picture elements (pixels or pels) displayed on the screen. The information about eight consecutive pixels is stored in a single byte. This means that 128,000/8 = 16,000 bytes of memory are required to contain all the graphics information. Each plot position on the screen is associated with a single *bit* in one of the memory buffer bytes. A 1 in a bit position will produce a white spot on the screen, while a 0 in a bit position will produce a black spot on the screen. Bit position 7 in each byte is plotted first. The graphics memory buffer for mode 6 is actually divided into two 8,000-byte banks. The bank from B800:0000 to B800:1F3F contains data for the even scan lines (0, 2, 4, . . ., 198). The bank from B800:2000 to B800:3F3F contains data for the odd scan lines (1, 3, 5, . . ., 199).

The CGA graphics mode 4 has $320 \times 200 = 64,000$ pixels in an image. Its memory buffer still contains 16,000 bytes, which means that only four pixels are associated with each byte. That is, each pixel uses 2 bits in a byte. These 2 bits are used to encode one of four possible colors to be plotted. If the 2 bits are 00, it means the background color is to be plotted. The background can be one of 16 different colors and the other 3 colors can be selected from one of two color palettes.

The background color and the color palette selection can be done using *INT 10H* with *AH* = 11 (0BH), as shown in Fig. 16.1. Note that one of 16 background colors can be selected using *BH* = 0. Setting *BH* = 1 selects one of two possible color palettes depending on the value in *BL*. For color palette 0, the three possible foreground pixel colors are green, red, and yellow. For color palette 1, the three possible foreground pixel colors are cyan, magenta, and white.

AH = 11 (0BH)	*Select background color and palette*
	Input: BH = 0 *Select background color*
	BL = background color (bits 0 – 3)
	BH = 1 *Select palette*
	BL = 0 palette 0
	BL = 1 palette 1

Background Colors		Color Palettes		
0 0 0 0	Black	Color No.	Palette 0	Palette 1
0 0 0 1	Blue	1	green	cyan
0 0 1 0	Green	2	red	magenta
0 0 1 1	Cyan	3	yellow	white
0 1 0 0	Red			
0 1 0 1	Magenta			
0 1 1 0	Brown			
0 1 1 1	Light gray			
1 0 0 0	Dark gray			
1 0 0 1	Light blue			
1 0 1 0	Light green			
1 0 1 1	Light cyan			
1 1 0 0	Light red			
1 1 0 1	Light magenta			
1 1 1 0	Yellow			
1 1 1 1	White			

Figure 16.1   Color options for CGA mode 4 using INT 10H.

The program shown in Listing 16.1 will switch to graphics mode 4 and display the background as black. Each time you press the space bar the background will cycle through all 16 colors shown in Fig. 16.1. Pressing any other key will return to the text mode and to DOS. This program is included on the TUTOR disk. Alternatively, you can just enter the machine code shown in Listing 16.1 using TUTOR and execute the program from there.

The VGA mode 13 is a medium-resolution graphics mode that can display 256 colors. In this mode the graphics data are stored as 1 byte per pixel, where the byte contains one of 256 possible color values. The other EGA and VGA graphics modes store data for eight pixels in each byte, that is, 1 bit per pixel.

Listing 16.1   *colorb.lst*

```
                        title   CGA color background

0000                    stack   segment para stack
0000      40 [          db          64 dup(?)
              ??   ]
0040                    stack   ends

0000                    code    segment public
                        assume cs:code
0000                    main    proc    far
0000   B4 0F                    mov     ah,15           ;get video mode
0002   CD 10                    int     10h
0004   50                       push    ax              ;and save it
0005   B4 00                    mov     ah,0
0007   B0 04                    mov     al,4            ;switch to
0009   CD 10                    int     10h             ;graphics mode 4
000B   BB 0000                  mov     bx,0            ;start with black
000E   B4 0B          again:    mov     ah,0bh          ;change
0010   CD 10                    int     10h             ;background color
0012   B4 00                    mov     ah,0
0014   CD 16                    int     16h             ;wait for key
0016   3C 20                    cmp     al,20h          ;if space bar
0018   75 04                    jne     done            ;then inc
001A   FE C3                    inc     bl              ;background color
001C   EB F0                    jmp     again           ;& change again
001E   58             done:     pop     ax              ;get text mode
001F   B4 00                    mov     ah,0            ;and reset it
0021   CD 10                    int     10h
0023   B8 4C00                  mov     ax,4c00h        ;quit to DOS
0026   CD 21                    int     21h
0028                    main    endp
0028                    code    ends
                        end     main
```

The way they are able to represent up to 16 different colors is to use up to 4 bit planes, where a given bit (or byte) in each plane can be at the same address but can store different color data. Special map mask and latch registers are used to write different colors to different pixel locations.

16.2 PLOTTING A DOT

To plot a dot on the screen you can use $AH = 12$ (0CH) with *INT 10H*, as given in Fig. 16.2. The row number (0 to 199, 0 to 349, or 0 to 479) and column number (0 to 319 or 0 to 639) are stored in registers *DX* and *CX*, respectively. The color value is stored in *AL*. The EGA/VGA modes 0D, 0E, 0F, and 10 contain 8, 4, 2, and 2 pages of memory, respectively. This means that separate graphic images can be stored simultaneously on these different pages. When plotting a dot in these modes, you must set *BH* to this page number. If you are using only one page, this will be zero.

If bit 7 of *AL* is set to 1 when a dot is plotted, the color value in *AL* will be Exclusive-OR'd with the color value of the current dot. For example, suppose a red dot (color value = 2) is plotted on the screen. If you plot another red dot on top of it, with bit 7 in *AL* set to 1, the actual dot plotted will be 2 *XOR* 2 (10 XOR 10 = 00) or 0. This will plot the background color or erase the red dot.

The program shown in Listing 16.2 will fill the screen with a series of vertical lines (by plotting a dot in each row of a column) using all 16 colors in the EGA/VGA mode 0Dh. The result will be a set of vertical bands of colors. After plotting all the vertical lines, the program will wait for you to press any key before returning to the text mode and to DOS. Running this program will give you a good idea of

AH = 12 (0CH)	*Write dot*
	Input: DX = row number
	CX = column number
	BH = page no. (EGA and VGA only)
	AL = color number
	If bit 7 of AL equals 1, the color value is
	exclusive OR'd with the color value of
	the current dot. If both color values are
	the same, the dot will be erased.
AH = 13 (0DH)	*Read dot*
	Input: DX = row number
	CX = column number
	BH = page no. (EGA and VGA only)
	Output: AL = color value of dot read

Figure 16.2   Reading and writing a graphics dot using INT 10H.

how long it takes to plot dots using these BIOS routines. This program is included on the TUTOR disk. Alternatively, you can just enter the machine code shown in Listing 16.2 using TUTOR and execute the program from there. You can easily modify this program to use different graphics modes with different resolutions. (See the exercises at the end of the chapter.)

Listing 16.2   *colors.lst*

```
                        title       Color graphics

0000           stack        segment para stack
0000    40 [        db          64 dup(?)
             ?? ]
0040           stack        ends

0000           code         segment public
                            assume cs:code
0000           main         proc    far
0000  B4 0F                 mov     ah,15        ;get video mode
0002  CD 10                 int     10h
0004  50                    push    ax           ;and save it
0005  B4 00                 mov     ah,0
0007  B0 0D                 mov     al,0Dh       ;switch to
0009  CD 10                 int     10h          ;graphics mode 0D
000B  B7 00                 mov     bh,0         ;page 0
000D  B9 013F               mov     cx,319       ;cx = col. no.
0010  B0 0F                 mov     al,15        ;al - color no.
0012  BA 00C7       mn1:    mov     dx,199       ;dx = row no.
0015  B4 0C        mn2:     mov     ah,0ch
0017  CD 10                 int     10h          ;plot dot
0019  4A                    dec     dx
001A  79 F9                 jns     mn2          ;plot 1 col.
001C  FE C8                 dec     al           ;change color
001E  79 02                 jns     mn3          ;if < 0
0020  B0 0F                 mov     al,15        ;reset to 15
0022  E2 EE        mn3:     loop    mn1          ;do all cols.
0024  B4 00                 mov     ah,0
0026  CD 16                 int     16h          ;wait for key
0028  58                    pop     ax           ;get text mode
0029  B4 00                 mov     ah,0         ;and reset it
002B  CD 10                 int     10h
002D  B8 4C00               mov     ax,4c00h     ;quit to DOS
0030  CD 21                 int     21h
0032           main         endp
0032           code         ends
                            end     main
```

16.3 LINE DRAWING ROUTINE

The built-in graphics routines associated with *INT 10H* do not include a routine for plotting a line. Suppose you want to plot a straight line from one point on the screen to another. You can plot a straight line by plotting a series of dots between the two points. But how do you know where to plot the dots? You could calculate the slope of the line and use this value to calculate the location of each point. Efficient algorithms involving only addition and subtraction have been developed for this purpose.[1] An alternate approach is described by Beetem in the October 1980 issue of *Byte Magazine*.[2]

The basic idea of the Beetem approach is to calculate the midpoint between the two end points of the line as shown in Fig. 16.3. This operation requires only

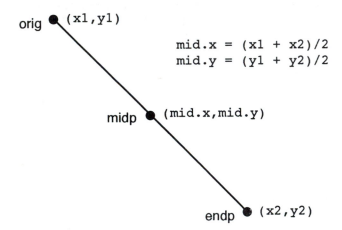

```
mid.x = (x1 + x2)/2
mid.y = (y1 + y2)/2
```

Figure 16.3 Calculating the midpoint of a line segment.

one addition and a divide by 2 (*SHR, 1*) for each component (*x* and *y*). If the midpoint (*mid.x, mid.y*) does not coincide with the origin (*x1, y1*), then the midpoint becomes the new end point and the new half-length line segment is bisected again to form a new midpoint. This process is continued until the midpoint falls on the origin (this will happen using integer arithmetic), and then the origin is plotted. As this subdivision process takes place, the midpoints and end points are saved by pushing them on the stack. After each new origin is plotted, a new origin and end point are popped from the stack, and the process continues until all points along the line have been plotted.

A pseudocode version of the algorithm for plotting this line is given in Fig. 16.4. For the algorithm to work, the *orig* must always be to the left of the *endp*. If it isn't, the algorithm automatically interchanges them at the beginning. When

---

[1] See, for example, J. E. Bresenham, "Algorithm for Computer Control of a Digital Plotter," *IBM Systems J.* **4**, pp. 25–30 (1965).

[2] J. Beetem, "Vector Graphics for Raster Displays," *Byte*, **5**, pp. 286–293 (Oct. 1980).

```
save registers
if orig.x > endp.x
then interchange orig and endp
push endp
push endp
loop: compute midp
        if midp = orig
        then plot orig
                pop orig
                pop endp
        else push endp
                push midp
                endp = midp
repeat until stack is empty
plot orig
restore registers
```

Figure 16.4 Algorithm for plotting a straight line in Fig. 16.3 from x1, y1 to x2, y2.

computing the midpoint, it is necessary to ensure that the values of *mid.x* and *mid.y* are truncated to the *orig* side of *midp*. Since *orig* is always to the left of *endp*, this will be the case for *mid.x*. If *orig.y* < *endp.y* then *mid.y* is truncated; otherwise, *mid.y* is rounded. This is easy to test by checking the carry flag after dividing by 2 (shifting right) when calculating *mid.y*.

An 8086 implementation of this algorithm is given in Listing 16.3. To use this subroutine, the values of *x1, y1, x2,* and *y2* are stored in registers *CX, DX, AX,* and *BX,* respectively. The subroutine *plot* called by *line* in Listing 16.3 must be a subroutine that plots a dot at *x = CX, y = DX*. For example, the subroutine *plot* given at the end of Listing 16.3 will plot a white dot (*AL* = 3) in graphics mode 6. These line and plot subroutines are given in the file *plotline.asm* that is included on the TUTOR disk and can be linked with your own programs.

Listing 16.3   *plotline.asm*

```
        title   plot line subroutine

;       inputs: ax = x2 = endp.x
;               bx = y2 = endp.y
;               cx = x1 = orig.x
;               dx = y1 = orig.y
        public  line
code    segment public
        assume  cs:code

;       plot line
line    proc near
        push    ax                      ;save registers
        push    bx
```

Listing 16.3   (*cont.*)

```
          push    cx
          push    dx
          push    si
          push    di
          push    bp
          push    ax                          ;make space for yflg
          mov     bp,sp                       ;bp=initial sp
          mov     byte ptr 1[bp],0            ;iflg=0
          cmp     cx,ax                       ;if orig.x1>orig.x2
          jb      la                          ;then interchange
          xchg    cx,ax                       ;orig and endp
          xchg    dx,bx
la:       cmp     bx,dx                       ;if bx<dx then set
          ja      lb                          ;  yflg=80h
          mov     byte ptr 1[bp],80h
lb:       push    ax                          ;push endp:x
          push    bx                          ;push endp:y
          push    ax                          ;push endp:x
          push    bx                          ;push endp:y
ln1:      mov     si,cx                       ;compute midp.x
          add     si,ax
          shr     si,1                        ;si=(x1+x2)/2
          mov     di,dx                       ;compute midp.y
          add     di,bx
          shr     di,1                        ;di=(y1+y2)/2
          jnb     ln2                         ;if carry set
          cmp     byte ptr 1[bp],0
          je      ln2                         ;then if yflg set
          inc     di                          ;round midp.y
ln2:      cmp     si,cx                       ;if midp=orig
          jne     ln3
          cmp     di,dx
          jne     ln3                         ;then
          call    plot                        ;plot orig
          pop     dx                          ;pop orig.y
          pop     cx                          ;         .x
          pop     bx                          ;pop endp.y
          pop     ax                          ;         .x
          jmp     ln4
ln3:      push    ax                          ;push endp.x
          push    bx                          ;           .y
          push    si                          ;push midp.x
          push    di                          ;           .y
          mov     ax,si
          mov     bx,di
```

Listing 16.3   (*cont.*)

```
ln4:    cmp      bp,sp
        jne      ln1
        call     plot               ;plot orig
ln5:    pop      ax                 ;restore yflg
        pop      bp                 ;restore regs
        pop      di
        pop      si
        pop      dx
        pop      cx
        pop      bx
        pop      ax
        ret
line    endp

;       plot point at x=cx, y=dx
plot    proc near
        push     ax
        mov      ax,0c03h           ;color=white
        int      10h                ;write dot
        pop      ax
        ret
plot    endp
code    ends
        end
```

As an example of using this line-plotting subroutine, suppose you want to plot the star shown in Fig. 16.5. Store the number of lines to plot (5) followed by the *x, y* pairs of each vertex in a data segment as shown at the beginning of the program in Listing 16.4. In the main program to plot the star, given in Listing

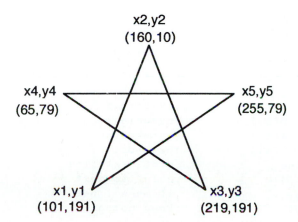

Figure 16.5 To plot the star, store the coordinates of the vertices in a data segment in memory.

Listing 16.4   *star.asm*

```
        title   star
stack segment para stack
        db      64 dup(?)
stack ends

data  segment
points dw       05              ;no. of lines
       dw       101,191         ;x1,y1
       dw       160,10          ;x2,y2
       dw       219,191         ;x3,y3
       dw       65,79           ;x4,y4
       dw       255,79          ;x5,y5
       dw       101,191         ;x1,y1
data   ends


       extrn    line:near
code   segment public
       assume   cs:code,ds:data


;      plot star
star   proc far
       mov      ax,data
       mov      ds,ax           ;ds=data
       mov      ah,15           ;get video mode
       int      10h
       push     ax              ;and save it
       mov      ax,0004h        ;switch to med-res
       int      10h             ;   graphics
       mov      ah,0bh
       mov      bx,0101h
       int      10h             ;select palette 1
       mov      bx,0
       mov      ah,0bh
       int      10h             ;background black
       mov      si,offset points ;star data
       mov      bp,[si]         ;bp=# of lines to plot
       add      si,2            ;point to first point
st1:   mov      cx,[si]         ;cx=orig.x
       mov      dx,2[si]        ;dx=orig.y
       mov      ax,4[si]        ;ax=endp.x
       mov      bx,6[si]        ;bx=endp.y
       call     line            ;plot next line
       add      si,4            ;point to next point
       dec      bp              ;if more lines
       jne      st1             ;keep going
       mov      ah,0
```

Listing 16.4   (*cont.*)

```
          int      16h               ;wait for key
          pop      ax                ;get text mode
          mov      ah,0              ;& switch to it
          int      10h
          mov      ax,4c00h          ;return to DOS
          int      21h
star      endp
code      ends
          end      star
```

16.4, register *SI* points to the beginning of the memory buffer containing the vertex data and is incremented by 4 (2 words per vertex) after each line is plotted.

The *line* subroutine given in Listing 16.3 and the program to plot the star given in Listing 16.4 can be assembled separately and then linked. It is clear that the program in Listing 16.4 can be used to plot any figure whose vertices can be prestored in memory.

16.4 THE MC6845 CRT CONTROLLER

Figure 13.2 illustrated how a raster scan display works. We saw that the ASCII codes of the characters displayed on the screen are stored in a video RAM and continuously cycled to a character generator. This character generator has a set of row select inputs in addition to the character ASCII code and outputs the bit pattern corresponding to the selected row in the character. This output goes to a shift register, which becomes the video signal to the monitor. Graphics displays work in a similar manner except the character generator is bypassed. That is, the bit pattern for each row of eight dots on the screen must be stored in a byte in the video RAM. This means that the video RAM for graphics must be much larger than that for text.

Implementing the raster scan process shown in Fig. 13.2 requires critical timing to read the ASCII codes and generate the proper row select signals at just the right time. This function is performed by a CRT (cathode ray tube) controller chip. The original IBM PC used the Motorola MC6845 CRT controller chip (CRTC) for this purpose. This chip is also used to display Hercules graphics on a monochrome monitor. We will show how this is done in the next section. In this section we will describe the basic function of the MC6845 CRTC and show how it is configured for monochrome text display. EGA and VGA display boards use special graphics display chips with many additional features. However, they also include registers that replicate the functions of the MC6845 CRTC described in this section.

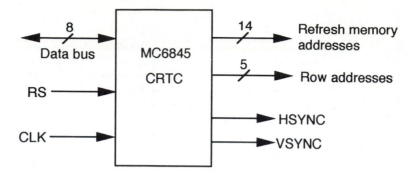

Figure 16.6 Principal signals associated with the MC6845 CRT controller.

The MC6845 CRTC is a 40-pin chip whose principal signals are shown in Fig. 16.6. The data sheet for the MC6845 is included in Appendix F. The MC6845 communicates with the host microprocessor over the 8-bit data bus shown in Fig. 16.6. The register select signal *RS* shown in Fig. 16.6 is connected to address line A0. This means that the MC6845 CRTC looks like two consecutive memory locations to the host processor. In the Hercules graphics examples we will present, these two memory locations are the addresses 03B4H and 03B5H in the I/O space (read and written to with the *IN* and *OUT* instructions). The MC6845 contains 18 internal registers. An indirect addressing scheme is used to address these 18 registers with only two different external addresses. The first address (03B4H) is used to store the register number selected (0 to 17), and then the data to read or write to that register are read from or stored in the second address (03B5H). This process will be illustrated in the next section.

The CLK input signal to the MC6845 CRTC is a *character* clock signal whose period, T_c, is equal to the time it takes to display one row of dots in a character. For a monochrome display with a 9×14 character cell, this will be the time to display nine dots. This character time, T_c, for a monochrome display is 553 nanoseconds (553×10^{-9} seconds), corresponding to a dot frequency of $(9/0.553)$ = 16.27 megahertz.

The 14 refresh memory address lines shown in Fig. 16.6 are used to address up to 2^{14} = 16 Kbytes of video RAM memory. The 5 row address lines shown in Fig. 16.6 are used to select up to 2^5 = 32 row select lines on a character generator. The HSYNC and VSYNC signals are the horizontal and vertical sync signals that are generated by the MC6845 CRTC and used by the video monitor to control the horizontal and vertical scan times.

The MC6845 CRTC is a programmable device in which the user can select such things as the number of characters per row, the number of rows displayed on the screen, and the cell size of the characters. To program the MC6845 for the monochrome text mode (80 characters $\times$ 25 rows), we can store the values shown in Table 16.2 in the first 16 registers in the MC6845 (the last 2 registers are used to read a light pen location). The meanings of most of these registers

TABLE 16.2 CRTC REGISTER VALUES FOR MONOCHROME TEXT MODE

Register number	Register name	Programmed value	
		Decimal	Hex
R0	Horizontal total	97	61H
R1	Horizontal displayed	80	50H
R2	Horizontal sync position	82	52H
R3	Horizontal sync width	15	0FH
R4	Vertical total	25	19H
R5	Vertical scan line adjust	6	06H
R6	Vertical displayed	25	19H
R7	Vertical sync position	25	19H
R8	Interlace mode	2	02H
R9	Maximum scan line address	13	0DH
R10	Cursor start	11	0BH
R11	Cursor end	12	0CH
R12	Start address (H)	0	00H
R13	Start address (L)	0	00H
R14	Cursor (H)	0	00H
R15	Cursor (L)	0	00H

are shown in Fig. 16.7. The first four registers, *R0* to *R3*, control the horizontal timing. The values stored in these registers are multiples of the character time, T_c. The number of characters displayed on a line is stored in *R1*. The total horizontal scan time (including the horizontal retrace) is *R0* + 1. In Fig. 16.7 this corresponds to a time of 98 × 0.553 microseconds = 54.2 microseconds. The position and width of the horizontal sync signal shown in Fig. 16.7 are controlled by registers *R2* and *R3*, respectively.

The vertical scan timing is controlled by registers *R4* to *R7*. The number of rows of characters to display on the screen is stored in register *R6*. The total vertical scan time (including the vertical retrace) is given by (*R4* + 1) *rows* + *R5 scan lines*. This vertical scan time normally corresponds to a vertical scan frequency of 60 hertz (cycles per second) or 50 hertz. The monochrome display uses a vertical scan frequency of 50 hertz. The value stored in register *R5* is the number of horizontal scan lines needed to make the total vertical scan time as close to 1/50 of a second as possible. The position of the vertical sync pulse is stored in register *R7*. Its width is constant and equal to 16 horizontal scan lines.

The other register value shown in Fig. 16.7 is *R9*, which is the maximum scan line address for a given character cell. For a monochrome display with a 9 × 14 character cell, the row addresses for each character are numbered 0 to 13. This last row number is the one that is stored in register *R9*. Register *R8* is an interlace mode, and the value of 2 given in Table 16.2 corresponds to normal

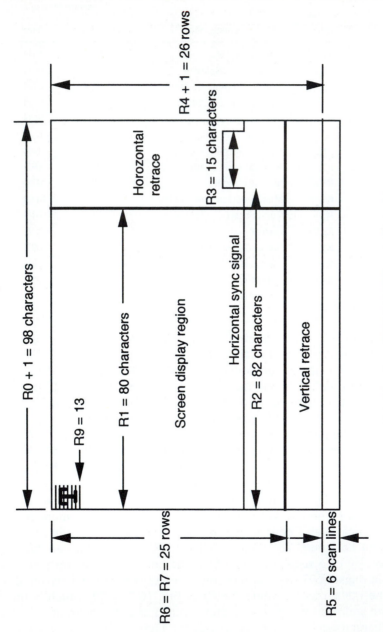

Figure 16.7 Meanings of MC6845 CRT controller registers.

interlace (see the data sheet in Appendix F). The cursor start and cursor end values stored in registers *R10* and *R11* define the shape of the cursor. The values 11 and 12 given in Table 16.2 mean that the cursor will be an underline starting in row 11 of the character cell and ending in row 12. The address within the video RAM (as addressed by the refresh memory addresses of the MC6845 CRTC) corresponding to the upper-left corner of the screen is stored in registers *R12* and *R13*. The initial location of the cursor within the video RAM is stored in registers *R14* and *R15*. The value of zero means that the cursor will be in the upper-right corner of the screen (corresponding to address 0000 in the video RAM).

The process of setting the monochrome text mode (by calling *INT 10H* with *AH* = 0 and *AL* = 7) will include writing the values shown in Table 16.2 to the MC6845 CRTC registers. In the next section we will show how a Hercules graphics display can be produced by changing the values of the MC6845 CRTC registers.

16.5 HERCULES GRAPHICS ROUTINES

In this section we will show you how to set the Hercules graphics mode (by programming the MC6845 CRTC) and to write subroutines to plot and erase dots, draw lines, and display characters on the screen. The resolution of a Hercules graphics screen is 720 × 348, as shown in Fig. 16.8. The 720 dots on a given row are stored in 90 consecutive bytes of memory (90 × 8 = 720), as shown in Fig. 16.8. This means that the video RAM must contain 90 × 348 = 31,320 bytes. This is almost 32 Kbytes of memory, which will require 15 address lines (2^{15} = 32,768). But note from Fig. 16.6 that the MC6845 CRTC has only 14 refresh memory address lines. The solution to this problem is to use some of the five row address lines as video RAM address lines inasmuch as we are no longer using a character generator. Hercules graphics uses the first 13 address lines from the refresh address lines in Fig. 16.6 for the video RAM address lines *A0* to *A12*. The first two row address lines in Fig. 16.6 are then connected to the video RAM address lines *A13* and *A14*. The resulting memory map is shown in Fig. 16.9.

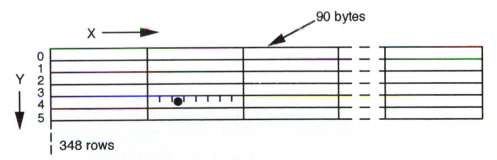

Figure 16.8   Video display layout for Hercules graphics.

A15 A14 A13 A12	A11 A10 A9 A8	A7 A6 A5 A4	A3 A2 A1 A0	Address range
0 0 0 X	X X X X	X X X X	X X X X	0000 - 1FFF
0 0 1 X	X X X X	X X X X	X X X X	2000 - 3FFF
0 1 0 X	X X X X	X X X X	X X X X	4000 - 5FFF
0 1 1 X	X X X X	X X X X	X X X X	6000 - 7FFF

Figure 16.9 Memory map associated with Hercules graphics.

Note that as the row address lines *RA1* and *RA0* (connected to address lines *A14* and *A13*) take on the values 00, 01, 10, and 11 the resulting video RAM address increases by 0000H, 2000H, 4000H, and 6000H, as shown in Fig. 16.9. Using two row address lines is like having a character generator with characters that are four scan lines high. Recalling how a raster scan display works, this means that the row address lines *RA1* and *RA0* will be incremented through the values 00, 01, 10, and 11 on four consecutive scan lines on the screen. Therefore, the video RAM addresses of the first byte of the first four scan lines will be 0000H, 2000H, 4000H, and 6000H. The 90 bytes in row number 0 will have addresses 0000H to 0059H. The 90 bytes in row number 1 will have addresses 2000H to 2059H. Row number 4 (the fifth line on the screen) will begin with video RAM address 005AH. In general, the video RAM address of the first byte in row *Y* is given by

```
first.byte.address                                          (16.1)
    = [2000H * (Y MOD 4)] + [90 * INT(Y/40)]
```

For speed, we will compute these first byte addresses for all 348 rows and store them in a table called *row_table*. This can be done automatically when you assemble a program by including the macro shown in Fig. 16.10. This macro is included in the file *graph.asm*, which contains all the Hercules graphics subroutines described in this section. A listing of the file *graph.asm* is included as Listing C.3 in Appendix C.

```
row_table    label    word                  ;define row add
        line_num = 0
        rept 87                              ;348/4
            dw    line_num * 90
            dw    2000h + line_num * 90
            dw    4000h + line_num * 90
            dw    6000h + line_num * 90
            line_num = line_num + 1          ;next row
        endm
```

Figure 16.10 Macro used to build a table containing the addresses of the first byte in each row.

Inasmuch as each of the 90 bytes in a row contains 8 bits corresponding to 8 consecutive dots on the screen, a dot located at position (X, Y) on the screen will be located in a byte whose address is

```
byte.address = first.byte.address                    (16.2)
             + [INT(X/8)]
```

where *first.byte.address* is given by Eq. (16.1).

To set the Hercules graphics mode, we must store the appropriate values in the 16 MC6845 CRTC registers. The values used for Hercules graphics are given in Table 16.3. Note that the *Horizontal displayed* value in *R1* is 45. This is because Hercules graphics reads 2 bytes at a time into a 16-bit shift register. Therefore, the 90 bytes on each line are like 45 characters that are 16 bits wide. Note that the value in *R9* is 3, which means that the "characters" are four scan lines high. This is because we are using the two row address lines, *RA1* and *RA0*, as described above. The *Vertical displayed* value in *R6* is 87, which means that 87 "characters" that are four lines high are displayed on the screen. Therefore, the number of displayed scan lines is $87 \times 4 = 348$.

In addition to filling the MC6845 registers with the values given in Table 16.3, the two Hercules graphics registers shown in Fig. 16.11 must also be set. The *config switch* at address 03BFH must have bit 0 set to 1 to enable graphics.

TABLE 16.3 CRTC REGISTER VALUES FOR HERCULES GRAPHICS MODE

Register number	Register name	Programmed value	
		Decimal	Hex
R0	Horizontal total	53	35H
R1	Horizontal displayed	45	2DH
R2	Horizontal sync position	46	2EH
R3	Horizontal sync width	7	07H
R4	Vertical total	91	5BH
R5	Vertical scan line adjust	2	02H
R6	Vertical displayed	87	57H
R7	Vertical sync position	87	57H
R8	Interlace mode	2	02H
R9	Maximum scan line address	3	03H
R10	Cursor start	0	00H
R11	Cursor end	0	00H
R12	Start address (H)	0	00H
R13	Start address (L)	0	00H
R14	Cursor (H)	0	00H
R15	Cursor (L)	0	00H

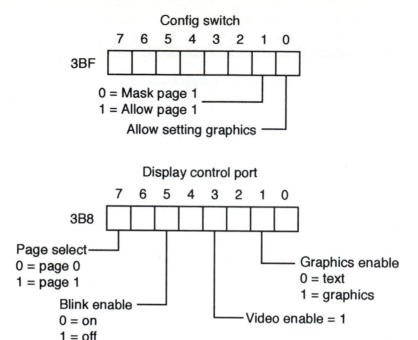

Figure 16.11 Hercules graphics registers.

The *display control port* at address 03B8H must be set to 0AH to enable the video and graphics and select page 0.

The subroutine *stherc* given in Fig. 16.12 will set Hercules graphics. This subroutine is included in the file *graph.asm*. Note that the table *vidtbl* in the data segment contains the 16 values given in Table 16.3 to be stored in the MC6845 registers. This is done in the *sg1* loop, where the consecutive register numbers (*ah*) are stored in the MC6845 address 03B4H and the internal register values (read with *lodsb*) are stored in the MC6845 address 03B5H. Note that the screen is cleared by filling the video RAM with zeros.

To plot a dot on the screen, we simply need to write a 1 to the appropriate bit position in the appropriate byte in the video RAM. The address of this byte is given by Eq. 16.2. The bit position within this byte is given by

```
bit.position = 7 - (X MOD 8)
```
                                                                                    (16.3)

The subroutine *plotad* given in Fig. 16.13 will find the address and bit position of the dot to be plotted. The *X* and *Y* coordinates of the dot to be plotted are stored in *CX* and *DX* before calling the subroutine. The subroutine will return the byte address of the dot in *DI* and the appropriate mask byte in *BL*. For example,

```
data    segment public
vidtbl  db      53,45,46,7,91,2,87,87
        db      2,3,0,0,0,0,0,0
data    ends

code    segment public
        assume cs:code,ds:data
;       set up hercules graphics
stherc  proc    near
        push    ax                      ;save regs
        push    cx
        push    dx
        push    di
        mov     dx,03bfh                ;config switch
        mov     al,1
        out     dx,al                   ;allow graphics
        mov     ax,0b000h               ;seg b000h
        mov     es,ax
        mov     cx,8000h                ;word count
        mov     di,0
        cld
        xor     ax,ax                   ;ax=0
        rep stosw                       ;clear video ram
        mov     dx,03b4h                ;6845 port
        mov     si,offset vidtbl        ;si->values
        mov     cx,16                   ;16 regs
        xor     ax,ax                   ;ah=0
sg1:    mov     al,ah                   ;reg no.
        out     dx,al                   ;select reg
        inc     dx                      ;dx=03b5h
        lodsb                           ;get value
        out     dx,al                   ;store it
        dec     dx                      ;dx=03b4h
        inc     ah                      ;next reg
        loop    sg1                     ;do all 16
        mov     dx,03b8h                ;control port
        mov     al,0ah                  ;enable video
        out     dx,al                   ; & graphics
        pop     di                      ;restore regs
        pop     dx
        pop     cx
        pop     ax
        ret
stherc  endp
code    ends
        end
```

Figure 16.12 Subroutine to set Hercules graphics.

```
;         calculate plot addr at x=cx, y=dx
;         di --> addr  bl=mask  es=B000

plotad proc near
       push    ax
       push    cx
       push    dx
       mov     di,dx                ;y-table
       shl     di,1                 ; index
       mov     di,row_table[di]     ;di->y-table
       mov     ax,cx                ;ax = x
       shr     ax,1
       shr     ax,1
       shr     ax,1                 ;int(x/8)
       add     di,ax                ;byte addr
       mov     bl,80h               ;mask
       and     cx,7                 ;x mod 8
       shr     bl,cl                ;get mask
       mov     ax,0b000h
       mov     es,ax                ;seg b000h
       pop     dx
       pop     cx
       pop     ax
       ret
plotad endp
```

Figure 16.13 Subroutine to find the video RAM plot address.

if bit 5 in the byte corresponds to the dot, then the value of *BL* will be 00100000. The value of *ES* will also be set to the segment address of the video RAM.

The subroutines *plot* and *erase* given in Fig. 16.14 will plot and erase a dot at location *X* = *CX* and *Y* = *DX*. Note that in each case the subroutine *plotad* is called to find the byte (in *DI*) and the mask (in *BL*) corresponding to the dot location. The 1 in the mask is simply ORed into the byte to plot the dot. To erase the dot, the mask is complemented to produce a zero at the dot position, which is then ANDed into the byte.

The subroutine *line* given earlier in this chapter in Listing 16.3 is included in the file *graph.asm*. In this case the plot subroutine called by *line* will be the Hercules graphics plot routine given in Fig. 16.14. To use the Hercules graphics subroutines in *graph.asm*, you must either have a Hercules graphics card installed in your computer or switch to the Hercules monochrome mode that is available on many VGA cards. There is normally a program you run (such as *vgaplus*) that allows you to select the Hercules mode. Once you are in the Hercules mode, you can switch to Hercules graphics by calling the subroutine *stherc* in Fig. 16.12.

Once you switch to the Hercules graphics mode, you are in a bit-mapped environment in which the character generator is no longer available for displaying characters. If you want to display a character, you must plot all the dots that make up the character! While this may seem like a lot of work (and it is), it has the advantage that you can make the character look like anything you want (any

```
;        plot point at x=cx, y=dx
plot     proc    near
         push    bx
         push    di
         push    es
         call    plotad              ;calc addr
         or  es:[di],bl              ;or in 1
         pop     es
         pop     di
         pop     bx
         ret
plot     endp

;        erase point at x=cx, y=dx
erase    proc    near
         push    bx
         push    di
         push    es
         call    plotad              ;calc addr
         not     bl                  ;not mask
         and     es:[di],bl          ;and in 0
         pop     es
         pop     di
         pop     bx
         ret
erase    endp
```

Figure 16.14 Subroutines to plot and
erase a dot.

font), have any size, and be displayed anywhere on the screen. For example, the
monochrome uppercase A has the bit-mapped layout shown in Fig. 16.15, where
the hex byte associated with each row is given on the right. Note that a 1 in the
byte corresponds to a dot being plotted in the character.

The bit-mapped values for all 256 characters in the monochrome character
set are included at the end of the data segment of *graph.asm* in Appendix C as
the table *charset*. The data are stored as 16 bytes per character in the order of

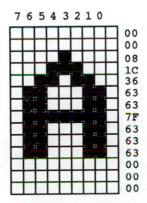

Figure 16.15 Bit-mapped values for
the letter A.

their ASCII code. Groups of 16 characters are labeled separately. If you go to ASCII code 41H, you will find the 14 bytes shown in Fig. 16.15. By modifying this table, you could easily change the font of any character.

To write a character on the screen, you need to move the first 14 bytes from the *charset* table (the ones shown in Fig. 16.15 for the letter A) for the character to be displayed to the appropriate memory in the video RAM. Because there are 90 bytes per row but only 80 monochrome characters per row (9 bits wide), each row of bits in most characters will actually be stored in two consecutive video RAM bytes rather than one. This somewhat complicates the process of writing the characters to the screen. The subroutine for doing this, called *charwt*, is shown in Fig. 16.16 and is included in the file *graph.asm*. Before calling this subroutine, you load *AL* with the ASCII code of the character to write and (*CX, DX*) with the *X* and *Y* coordinate of the upper-left dot in the character. The subroutine will leave *DX* unchanged and *CX* increased by 9. This will be the location of the next adjacent character.

From Table 9.3, note that the graphics characters whose ASCII codes begin with *C* or *D* extend to the rightmost bit position in the 9 × 14 character cell. These are the only characters that are actually nine dots wide. In the subroutine *charwt* in Fig. 16.16, the variable *bit9flg* is set (to FFH) for the character graphics ASCII codes. This flag is checked later in the subroutine to see if a 1 in the eighth pixel should by copied into the ninth pixel location.

The other complication in the subroutine *charwt* is due to the fact that the character data will normally need to be stored in 2 consecutive bytes. The way this is done is that 2 bytes are read into *AX* from the video RAM at the location where the character is to be plotted, and information about the bit position of the leftmost dot in the character is stored in *CL* (*X MOD 8*). The problem is that when

```
;               character write
;               input: al = ascii code of char
;                      cx = x-coord. upper-left
;                      dx = y-coord. upper-left
;               output: cx = cx(input)+9 = x-coord+9
;                       dx = dx(input) = y-coord

charwt      proc    near
            push    ax
            push    bx
            push    si                      ;save regs
            push    di
            push    bp
            mov     bx,cx                   ;bx = x
            mov     es,video_seg            ;es->video ram
            cld
            mov     bit9flg,0               ;default no
            cmp     al,0c0h                 ; line draw
```

Figure 16.16 Subroutines to write a character to the screen.

```
              jb      cw1                  ;check for
              cmp     al,0dfh              ; line draw
              ja      cw1                  ; characters
              not     bit9flg              ;yes, set flag
cw1:          xor     ah,ah                ;ah = 0
              shl     ax,1                 ;mult by 16
              shl     ax,1                 ;16 bytes per
              shl     ax,1                 ; char in table
              shl     ax,1
              mov     si,offset charset    ;si->char set
              add     si,ax                ;offset in tbl
              mov     bp,14                ;char height=14
cw2:          mov     cx,bx                ;cx = x
              mov     di,dx                ;di = y
              shl     di,1                 ;2 bytes/entry
              mov     di,row_table[di]     ;row offset
              mov     ax,cx                ;ax = col
              shr     ax,1
              shr     ax,1
              shr     ax,1                 ;int(x/8)
              add     di,ax                ;char pos byte
              and     cl,7                 ;x mod 8
              mov     ax,es:[di]           ;get 2 bytes
              xchg    ah,al                ;ah = [di]
              rol     ax,cl                ;mov char to al
              mov     ah,byte ptr [si]     ;ah= char line
              cmp     bit9flg,0
              je      cw3
              test    ah,1                 ;if 8th pixel
              je      cw3                  ; on, duplicate
              or      al,80h               ; 8th bit
              jmp     cw4
cw3:          and     al,07fh              ;erase pixel 9
cw4:          ror     ax,cl                ;restore word
              xchg    ah,al                ;restore order
              stosw                        ;write word
              inc     dx                   ;next row
              inc     si                   ;next tbl byte
              dec     bp                   ;do all 14 rows
              jne     cw2
              sub     dx,14                ;restore orig y
              add     bx,9                 ;inc col by 9
              mov     cx,bx
              pop     bp
              pop     di                   ;restore regs
              pop     si
              pop     bx
              pop     ax
              ret
charwt        endp
```

Figure 16.16   *(cont.)*

TABLE 16.4   HERCULES GRAPHICS SUBROUTINES

stherc	*Set up Hercules graphics* input: none output: es = B000H

line	*Plot line*
	input: ax = x coordinate of end point
	        bx = y coordinate of end point
	        cx = x coordinate of origin
	        dx = y coordinate of origin
	output: none

plot	*Plot dot* input: cx = x coordinate of point to plot dx = y coordinate of point to plot output: none
erase	*Erase dot* input: cx = x coordinate of point to erase dx = y coordinate of point to erase output: none

plotad	*Calculate plot addr at coordinate x, y*
	input: cx = x coordinate of point
	        dx = y coordinate of point
	output: di = offset address of byte containing point
	        bl = mask with 1 in bit position of point
	        es = B000H

messg	*Message display*
	input: si = offset address of asciiz message
	        cx = x coordinate of start of message
	        dx = y coordinate of start of message
	output: none

charwt	*Character write*
	input: al = ascii code of char
	        cx = x coordinate, upper left
	        dx = y coordinate, upper left
	output: cx = cx(input)+9 = x coordinate + 9
	        dx = dx(input) = y coordinate

cpconv	*Cursor position conversion*
	input: dl = col = character column position (0 to 79)
	        dh = row = character row position (0 to 24)
	output: cx = x coordinate = 9*column
	        dx = y coordinate = 14*row

sinax	*Compute sin ax* input: ax = degrees output: ax = sine value $\times$ 1000
cosax	*Compute cos ax* input: ax = degrees output: ax = cosine value $\times$ 1000

2 bytes are read from memory into *AX* the low memory byte goes to *AL* and the high memory byte goes to *AH*. To make the pair *AH:AL* contain the dots as they appear on the screen, it is necessary to exchange these 2 bytes. Once this is done *AX* is rotated *CL* bits to get all bits corresponding to dots in other characters (that is, ones we don't want to change) into *AL*. Note that at this point bit 7 in *AL* will correspond to bit 9 (the rightmost bit) in the new character. The new data from the *charset* table are then read into *AH*, and then *AX* is rotated back to its previous position. Finally, *AH* and *AL* are exchanged again, and *AX* is then written back into the video RAM. This will write one row of the character. The process is repeated 14 times in the *cw2* loop in Fig. 16.16 to write each row in the character.

All the Hercules graphics subroutines that are included in the file *graph.asm* are shown in Table 16.4. Note that in addition to the subroutines described above there is a message writing subroutine, *messg*, that will write messages on the screen. The message must be stored in the data segment as an ASCIIZ string, as was done with the subroutine *mess* in *screen.asm*. The subroutine *cpconv* will convert a character cursor position in terms of character rows and columns into a graphics dot location on the screen where the subroutine *charwt* can display the character.

The subroutines *sinax* and *cosax* will return the sine and cosine (times 1000) of the angle *AX* (in degrees) using a table lookup. These subroutines can be useful for plotting graphic figures where you may want to plot a line at some particular angle and you need to compute the end-point coordinates to use the subroutine *line*.

Experiment 36: Drawing Graphic Pictures

In this experiment you will write a program that will allow you to plot graphics figures interactively.

1. Write a program that will set Hercules graphics and display a single dot (the cursor) at the center of the screen. Moving the eight cursor keys around the 5 on the numeric keypad should move the dot in eight possible directions (up, down, left, right, NE, SE, SW, NW). If the *Num Lock* key is on, the dots should remain plotted as you move the cursor. If the *Num Lock* key is off, the dots are not plotted. Pressing the *ESC* key should clear the screen and take you back to DOS.

2. Modify your program so that you type out Hercules graphics characters when you press any key. The graphics dot cursor should be adjusted so that it always follows the character just displayed.

3. Add some additional feature of your own choice. For example, you might move the dot cursor so as to set the two end points of a line and then have the LINE subroutine plot the line between these two points. You could use various function keys for this purpose.

Experiment 37: Plotting Sine and Cosine Waves

1. Using the subroutine *sinax*, plot six cycles of a sine wave on the screen. Include both horizontal and vertical labeled axes. Use the subroutine *line* to plot a line between adjacent points on the graph.

2. Add a plot of a cosine wave to the sine wave plotted in (1).

Experiment 38: Plotting Graphic Figures

1. Write a subroutine called *BOX* that will draw a square box on the screen by starting at location $X = CX$, $Y = DX$ and drawing a line of length BX at an angle AX to the horizontal. Continue plotting the box counterclockwise by adding 90 degrees to AX for each of the other three sides.

2. Plot a figure made up of 18 boxes of the same size. All boxes should share a common vertex at the center of the screen, and the initial angle of each box should be 20 degrees more than the previously drawn box.

3. Plot a figure made up of 10 concentric boxes at a 45-degree angle (diamonds) with sides ranging from 15 dots to 150 in steps of 15.

4. Use multiple calls to the subroutine *BOX* to draw a unique graphic figure of your choice.

EXERCISES

16.1. Modify the program in Listing 16.2 to fill the screen with bands of all 16 colors in the EGA/VGA mode 0EH.

16.2. Modify the program in Listing 16.2 to fill the screen with bands of all 16 colors in the EGA/VGA mode 10H.

16.3. Modify the program in Listing 16.2 to fill the screen with bands of all 16 colors in the VGA mode 12H.

16.4. Modify the program in Listing 16.2 to plot 256 vertical lines on the screen displaying each of the 256 colors in the VGA mode 13H.

16.5. Modify the program in Listing 16.2 to make horizontal bands. Change the program to display horizontal lines for the graphics modes in Exercises 16.1 to 16.4.

16.6. Write 8086 instructions that will plot a green dot on a red background at the center of the screen in graphics mode 04.

16.7. The *line* subroutine in Listing 16.3 is called with the following values in the general registers: $AX = 0065H$, $BX = 002CH$, $CX = 0062H$, $DX = 002FH$. How many times will the subroutine *plot* be executed?

16.8. Modify the program in Listing 16.4 to plot a polygon with:
   a. 5 equal sides
   b. 8 equal sides
   c. 12 equal sides

16.9. Modify the program in Listing 16.4 so that each vertex of the star is connected to all other vertices.

16.10. The MC6845 CRTC register values for monochrome text are given in Table 16.2. Assume that the character time, T_c, is 553 ns. What is the time, T_{sl}, to scan a single line? What is the time, T_{cr}, to display a single row of characters? What is the total time for a single vertical scan?

16.11. Find the Hercules graphics video RAM address and bit position for a dot to be plotted at the following coordinates:

    a. $x = 244$, $y = 139$
    b. $x = 500$, $y = 210$
    c. $x = 125$, $y = 300$
    d. $x = 53$, $y = 25$

16.12. Using the *charset* table in the file *graph.asm* in Appendix C, find the 14 bytes representing the bit-mapped values for the following characters: E, J, q, %, 9.

16.13. Draw a diagram to show the steps used in the subroutine *charwt* to plot each row of a character.

16.14. Write 8086 instructions that will find the Hercules graphics dot coordinates corresponding to a character to plot in character row 10, character column 15. Leave the X coordinate in *CX* and the Y coordinate in *DX*.

17

Serial Communication

Parallel I/O as used in the printer interface described in Chapter 14 requires eight data lines to transmit a byte (8 bits) of data. This becomes expensive when data have to be sent a long distance. It is much less expensive to use a single data line over which the 8 bits are sent 1 bit at a time. This is called *serial communication* and will obviously be considerably slower than sending the 8 bits in parallel.

In this chapter you will learn:

- The basic format of asynchronous serial communication
- The PC BIOS functions that can be used for serial I/O
- To program the 8250 universal asynchronous receiver/transmitter
- How to write an interrupt-driven terminal program

17.1 SERIAL I/O

There are two basic types of serial communication: *synchronous* and *asynchronous*. In synchronous communication, data are normally sent in blocks that often contain error checking. The timing is controlled by a standard clock at both the transmitter and receiver ends. On the other hand, the timing for asynchronous communication is handled one character at a time, and while the clocks at the transmitter and receiver must be approximately the same, they are resynchronized with each character. Because each character requires these additional synchronizing bits, asynchronous communication is slower than synchronous communication. However, it is simpler to implement and is in widespread use. In this chapter we will consider only asynchronous communication.

490

Asynchronous serial communication uses a *start bit* to tell when a particular character is being sent. This is illustrated in Fig. 17.1, which shows the transmitted waveform when the character *T* (ASCII code = 54H) is sent with odd parity. Before a character is sent, the line is in the high or *mark* state. The line is then brought low (called a *space*) and held low for a time *t* called the *bit time*. This first space is called the *start bit*. It is typically followed by 7 or 8 data bits. The least significant bit D0 is transmitted first. For example, in Fig. 17.1 the 7 bits corresponding to the ASCII code 54H (the character *T*) are sent, starting with D0. These 7 bits are followed by a *parity bit*. This bit is set to a 1 or a 0 such that the sum of the number of 1's transmitted is either even or odd. We have used odd parity in Fig. 17.1. Since three 1's were sent (D2, D4, and D6), the parity bit is zero. Sometimes a character is sent with no parity, in which case the parity bit is ignored. The parity bit is followed by 1 or 2 stop bits, which are always high (a *mark*). The next character will be indicated by the presence of the next start bit.

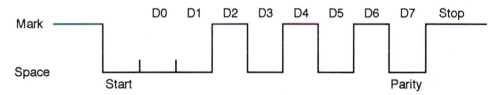

Figure 17.1   ASCII code 54H = 1010100 ("T") sent with odd parity.

The reciprocal of the bit time is called the *baud rate*. Common baud rates used in serial communication are given in Table 17.1. The 110 baud rate uses 2 stop bits. This means that 11 bit times per character are used (7 data bits + 1 parity bit + 1 start bit + 2 stop bits). Therefore, 10 characters per second are transmitted at 110 baud. The remaining baud rates in Table 17.1 use 1 stop bit and therefore use 10 bit times per character.

TABLE 17.1   COMMON ASYNCHRONOUS SERIAL BAUD RATES

Baud rate	Bit time (ms)	No. of stop bits	Character time (ms)	Characters/second
110	9.09	2	100.00	10
150	6.67	1	66.67	15
300	3.33	1	33.33	30
600	1.67	1	16.67	60
1200	0.833	1	8.33	120
2400	0.417	1	4.17	240
4800	0.208	1	2.08	480
9600	0.104	1	1.04	960

17.2 BIOS RS-232 COMMUNICATIONS INTERFACE

The *Asynchronous Communications Adapter* (ACA) was the original serial communications board provided by IBM that plugged into one of the I/O peripheral slots. This card uses a special programmable I/O chip called the *INS8250 Universal Asynchronous Receiver/Transmitter* (UART) manufactured by National Semiconductor. We will describe this chip in more detail in Section 17.3. Many manufacturers provide serial boards for the PC that use this UART chip.

A functional block diagram of the Asynchronous Communications Adapter (ACA) is shown in Fig. 17.2. This communications adapter will have a 25-pin D connector that comes out of the back of the computer. The pins on this connector contain the signals shown in Fig. 17.3. This connector is compatible with the standard RS-232C serial interface. The serial bit patterns sent over the transmit and receive pins (pins 2 and 3) are represented by + 12-volt (bit = 0) and − 12-volt (bit = 1) signals. These voltages are transformed from the corresponding 0- and 5-volt levels used in the computer by the ACA.

In addition to the standard RS-232C voltage interface, a different interface, the EAI 20-milliampere current loop, represents a 0 and 1 bit by the absence or presence of a 20-milliampere current rather than a voltage level. The IBM Asynchronous Communications Adapter board allows you to select either the voltage

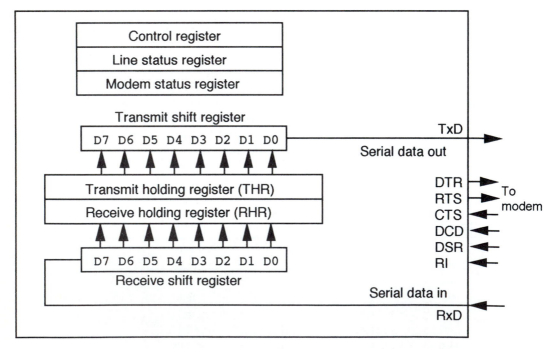

Figure 17.2 Functional diagram of an Asynchronous Communications Adapter (ACA).

Pin No.	Signal	Direction
1	NC	
2	Transmit data (TxD)	Out
3	Receive data (RxD)	In
4	Request to send (RTS)	Out
5	Clear to send (CTS)	In
6	Data set ready (DSR)	In
7	Signal ground	
8	Carrier detect (CD)	In
9	+Transmit current loop return (20 ma)	Out
10	NC	
11	-Transmit current loop data (20 ma)	Out
12-17	NC	
18	+Receive current loop data (20 ma)	In
19	NC	
20	Data terminal ready (DTR)	Out
21	NC	
22	Ring indicate	In
23-24	NC	
25	-Receive current loop return (20 ma)	In

Figure 17.3 Connector used for the RS-232C serial communications interface.

(RS-232C) or current loop option by changing the direction in which you plug in a shunt module.

The main function of the ACA is to transform parallel data from the 8086 into serial data and send it out through the transmit data pin *TxD*, and to receive serial data through the receive data pin *RxD* and transform it to parallel data that can be read by the 8086.

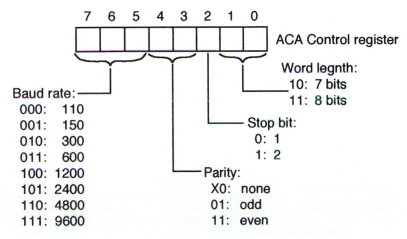

Figure 17.4 Control register used by the communications port.

AH = 0	Initialize communications port Input: AL = ACA control register (Figure 17.4) DX = RS-232 card no. (0 - 3) Output: AH = Line status register (Figure 17.6) AL = Modem status register (Figure 17.7)
AH = 1	Send serial character Input: AL = character to send DX = RS-232 card no. (0 - 3) Output: AH = Line status register (Figure 17.6)
AH = 2	Receive a serial character Input: DX = RS-232 card no. (0 - 3) Output: AL = character received AH = Line status register (Figure 17.6)
AH = 3	Read status register Input: DX = RS-232 card no. (0 - 3) Output: AH = Line status register (Figure 17.6) AL = Modem status register (Figure 17.7)

Figure 17.5   RS-232 communications options used with INT 14H.

You can access the ACA by means of the BIOS software interrupt *INT 14H*. These communications routines make use of a control register and two status registers. The control register is shown in Fig. 17.4. This control register allows you to select the baud rate, the parity, the number of stop bits, and the word length. You initialize the communications port by setting $AH = 0$ and calling *INT 14H* with the appropriate control register in *AL*. This and the other options available with *INT 14H* are shown in Fig. 17.5.

As with the printer I/O routines described in Chapter 14, you must set *DX* to the RS-232C card number you want to use. If you have only one serial port, use $DX = 0$. The starting I/O port addresses for up to four RS-232C adapters are stored at locations 0040:0000 to 0040:0007.

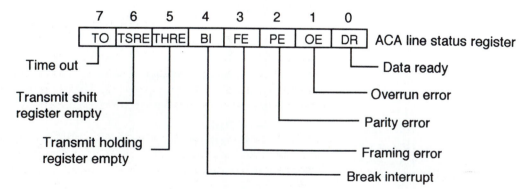

Figure 17.6   Line status register.

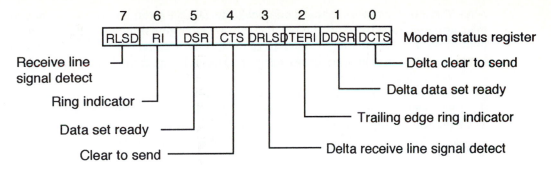

Figure 17.7   Modem status register.

When you initialize an RS-232C communications port by calling *INT 14H* with $AH = 0$, the initialization routine will return with *AH* containing the *line status register* and *AL* containing the *modem status register*. The definitions of these status registers are given in Figs. 17.6 and 17.7.

Bit 0 of the line status register is the *data ready* bit. This bit is set to 1 when the *receive shift register* has filled up with a complete byte and transferred this byte to the *receive holding register* (RHR) (see Fig. 17.2). The receive holding register can then be read by using *INT 14H* with $AH = 2$ (see Fig. 17.5).

Reading the receive holding register will clear the *DR* bit in the line status register. If you call *INT 14H* with $AH = 2$, the software interrupt routine will wait for a serial character to be received. Alternatively, you can poll the *DR* bit to see if the receive holding register is full and, if not, go do something else. A typical polling sequence is shown in Fig. 17.8. If the *DR* bit is set to 1, then the receive holding register is read using *INT 14H* with $AH = 2$. Otherwise, the program branches to *NEXT*, which might check the keyboard and then returns to *RECV* to check the *DR* bit again.

```
recv:  mov   dx,0
       mov   ah,3
       int   14h          ;read status reg.
       shr   ah,1          ;test DR
       jnb   next          ;if DR=0, goto NEXT
       mov   ah,2
       int   14h          ;else, read char.
       ---   ---
       ---   ---
next:  ---   ---
```

Figure 17.8   Polling the receive holding register.

You must make sure that you check the *DR* bit often enough so as not to miss any incoming bytes. If the receive shift register gets full before the previous data in the receive holding register have been read, the overrun error flag (bit 1) in the line status register will be set to 1. The overrun error flag is cleared by reading the line status register.

All asynchronous serial data must end with at least 1 stop bit. If a stop bit does not occur where expected, a framing error is indicated and the *FE* flag (bit 3) in the status register is set to 1. This flag is set or reset after each byte is received. You must therefore test this bit between the time that a character is received and the next character fills the receive shift register.

When a data character has been received in the receive holding register, the parity error flag, *PE* (bit 2), in the line status register will be set to 1 if the number of ones in the byte does not agree with the preselected parity (odd or even). The parity error flag is cleared whenever the line status register is read.

Bit 5 of the line status register is the *transmit holding register empty (THRE)* bit. This bit is set to 1 when data from the *transmit holding register (THR)* is transferred to the *transmit shift register*. These data are then shifted out through *TxD* at the baud rate, preceded by a start bit and ending with a parity bit (if selected) and 1 or 2 stop bits (see Fig. 17.2). While these data are being shifted out, another byte can be stored in the transmit holding register. When this is done, the *THRE* bit is cleared to zero and will remain zero until the transmit shift register has finished shifting out the previous character. When the shift register is free to accept another byte, the *transmit shift register empty* flag (bit 6) will be set to 1, and the contents of the *THR* are transferred to the shift register and the *THRE* flag (bit 5) in the line status register is set to 1 again.

A *BREAK* signal occurs on an asynchronous serial line when a *SPACE* (logic 0) occurs for longer than a full character transmission time. When this occurs, the *break interrupt* flag (bit 4) in the line status register is set to 1.

To send a serial character, all you have to do is store the character in *AL* and call *INT 14H* with *AH* = 1 (see Fig. 17.5). This BIOS routine will take care of checking the transmit holding register empty flag to make sure it is set to 1 before sending your character. If it is unable to send your character, then the *time out* flag (bit 7) in the line status register will be set to 1.

The *modem status register* shown in Fig. 17.7 is associated with the use of a *modem*. A modem is used to modulate (and demodulate) a serial, digital signal so that it can be transmitted over telephone lines.

The *clear to send (CTS)* flag (bit 4) and the *data set ready (DSR)* flag (bit 5) in the modem status register are the complements of the *CTS* and *DSR* signals from a modem. These flags must both be 1 in order to send a character over the communications line.

The *received line signal detect (RLSD)* flag (bit 7) in the modem status register is the complement of the *carrier detect (CD)* signal from the modem. If this flag is 0, it indicates that a carrier is not present at the modem and therefore valid data cannot be sent or received.

When the *ring indicator (RI)* flag (bit 6) in the modem status register is set to 1, it means that a telephone ringing signal has been received by the modem. The *trailing edge ring indicator (TERI)* flag (bit 2) will be set to 1 if the *RI* input to the ACA has changed from on to off. Bits 0, 1, and 3 in the modem status register get set if the *CTS, DSR*, or *RLSD* signals, respectively, change state since the last time the modem status register was read.

A BIOS-based PC Terminal Program

In this section we will write a program that will turn the PC into a dumb terminal. A typical dumb terminal will check to see if a key has been pressed. If it has, it will send the character to the host computer. It will then check to see if the host computer is sending a character. If it is, it will display the character on the screen. Otherwise, it will check the keyboard again.

This algorithm for a dumb terminal is given in Fig. 17.9. This algorithm is for *full-duplex* communication in which the host computer echoes each character that it receives. Therefore, the PC will not display a character typed on the keyboard until the character has been sent to the host computer and returned. The user will think that it is being displayed immediately, but actually it makes a round trip to the host computer. In *half-duplex* communication the PC would display each character as it is typed and the host computer would not echo the characters that it receives.

```
loop:   if key has been pressed
                then send character to host computer
        if host computer has sent character
                then display character
repeat  loop
```

Figure 17.9   Algorithm for a dumb terminal.

The assembly language program for this dumb terminal is shown in Listing 17.1. The program continually alternates between checking the keyboard and checking the asynchronous communications adapter (ACA). The communications port is initialized to 1200 baud, no parity, 1 stop bit, and 8-bit word length by using the control byte 83H in *AL* and calling *INT 14H* with *AH* = 0. The characters are displayed on the screen using the *chrout* subroutine given in the file *screen.asm* (see Chapter 13).

The dumb terminal program given in Listing 17.1 is limited to baud rates below 1,200 baud. The reason for this is that if we don't check the status register before another character is received into the receive holding register the previously received character will be overrun and lost. Therefore, we can't spend too much time in *chrout* displaying the character on the screen. This is generally not a problem if we only display a single character. However, when the characters

Listing 17.1   *dumbterm.asm*

```
                title   PC Dumb Terminal

;               link with screen
stack           segment para stack
                db    64 dup(?)
stack           ends

extrn           clrscn:near,chrout:near,quit:near
code            segment public
                assume cs:code

term            proc far
                call  clrscn               ;clear screen
                mov   dx,0                  ;1200 baud
                mov   ax,0083h              ;no parity
                int   14h                   ;1 stop/8 bits
key:            mov   ah,1                  ;if key not
                int   16h                   ; pressed,
                je    recv                  ; goto recv
                mov   ah,0
                int   16h                   ;read key
                cmp   al,1bh                ;if esc key
                je    done                  ;goto DOS
                mov   ah,1                  ;al=ascii code
                int   14h                   ;send character
recv:           mov   ah,3
                int   14h                   ;read status
                shr   ah,1                  ;if no char
                jnb   key                   ;check keyboard
                mov   ah,2                  ;otherwise,
                int   14h                   ;read character
                and   al,7fh                ;clear parity bit
                mov   bl,7                  ;normal video
                call  chrout                ;display char
                jmp   key                   ;repeat again
done:           call  quit                  ;goto DOS
term            endp
code            ends
                end   term
```

reach the bottom of the screen, the entire screen needs to be scrolled, and this takes enough time so that characters will be lost at baud rates above about 1,200 baud.

The solution to this problem is to have each received character produce a hardware interrupt that will simply read the character from the receive holding register and put it in a circular queue data structure from which it can be read at our leisure. Thus, more than one character could be received during the scrolling operation, but these characters will not be lost because they would be in the queue—put there by the interrupt service routine that interrupted the scrolling process.

We cannot use most of the BIOS *INT 14H* serial I/O functions when using hardware interrupts. This is because some of these explicitly turn off the interrupts. To use interrupts, we must program the 8250 UART chip directly. We will describe how the 8250 is connected to the 8086 in the next section and will then write an interrupt-driven communications program in Section 17.4.

17.3 THE 8250 UNIVERSAL ASYNCHRONOUS RECEIVER/ TRANSMITTER

The INS8250 Universal Asynchronous Receiver/Transmitter (UART) is a 40-pin chip that is used on serial I/O cards for the PC. The functional block diagram for the 8250 UART chip is the same as for the ACA shown in Fig. 17.2. The 8250 UART has the 10 internal registers shown in Table 17.2. The I/O space addresses of these registers for the two serial ports, COM1 and COM2, are given in Table 17.2. Note that the first three registers in Table 17.2 have the same I/O address. If bit 7 of the *line control register* is set to 1, then the address 3F8H (COM1) will be the *divisor low register* (which is used to set the baud rate). On the other hand, if bit 7 of the line control register is zero, then the address 3F8H (COM1) will be the *receive data buffer* for a read operation and the *transmit data buffer* for a write operation. These are the same as the receive and transmit holding registers in Fig. 17.2. The *interrupt enable register* and the *divisor high register* in Table

TABLE 17.2   8250 UART REGISTERS

| Register address | | Bit 7 | Read/ | 8250 Register | |
COM1	COM2	LCR	write	Name	Symbol
3F8H	2F8H	0	R	Receive data buffer	RECDATA
3F8H	2F8H	0	W	Transmit data buffer	TXDATA
3F8H	2F8H	1	R/W	Divisor low register	DIVLOW
3F9H	2F9H	0	R/W	Interrupt enable register	IER
3F9H	2F9H	1	R/W	Divisor high register	DIVHI
3FAH	2FAH	×	R	Interrupt ID register	INTID
3FBH	2FBH	×	R/W	Line control register	LCR
3FCH	2FCH	×	R/W	Modem control register	MCR
3FDH	2FDH	×	R/W	Line status register	LSR
3FEH	2FEH	×	R/W	Modem status register	MSR

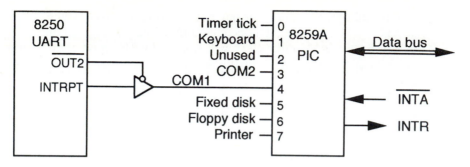

Figure 17.10 The 8250 must have $\overline{\text{OUT2}}$ low to enable COM1 interrupts.

17.2 also share the same I/O address and are distinguished by the value of bit 7 in the *line control register*.

The 8250 UART *line control register* (LCR) is similar to the ACA *control register* shown in Fig. 17.4 except that the baud rate is not set with this register. The lower 5 bits are the same as in Fig. 17.4, and bit 7 is used as a register address discrimination bit as described above. The 8250 UART *line status register* (LSR) is similar to the *ACA line status register* shown in Fig. 17.6 except that bit 7 (timeout) is always zero. The 8250 UART *modem status register* (MSR) is the same as the *ACA modem status register* shown in Fig. 17.7. The INS8250 data sheet is included in Appendix F.

The way in which the 8259A Priority Interrupt Controller (PIC) is used to process hardware interrupts on the PC was discussed in Section 14.1. The interrupt line from the 8250 UART chip is connected to the COM1 (*irq4*) line of the PIC as shown in Fig. 17.10. Note that this interrupt line goes through a buffer that is enabled when the *!OUT2* line of the 8250 goes low. This line is controlled by bit 3 in the 8250 UART modem control register that is shown in Fig. 17.11. This bit must be set to 1 to enable 8250 interrupts. To have a hardware interrupt occur every time the receive data ready bit in the line status register gets set (meaning a new value has been loaded into the receive data buffer), we must set bit 0 of the 8250 *interrupt enable register* shown in Fig. 17.12.

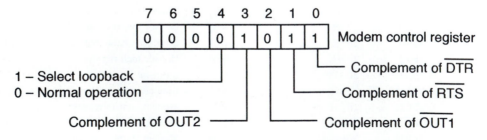

Figure 17.11 The 8250 modem control register.

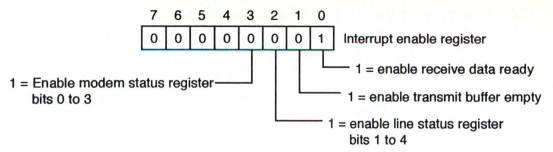

Figure 17.12   The 8250 interrupt enable register.

Even after setting the modem control register and the interrupt enable register to the values shown in Figs. 17.11 and 17.12, the interrupt signal will still not get through the PIC to the 8086 microprocessor. That is because the PIC has an *interrupt mask register* that can mask any of the eight possible hardware interrupts shown in Fig. 17.10. Bit 4 of this interrupt mask register (which has the I/O address 21H) controls the COM1 interrupt signal and must be cleared to zero to enable this interrupt, as shown in Fig. 17.13. The timer, keyboard, and disk drives will normally be enabled already, while the printer and the two serial ports will generally be masked. Therefore, to enable COM1 while keeping all the other bits in the interrupt mask register unchanged, we can use the instructions.

```
in     al,imask
and    al,0efh        ;enable irq4
out    imask,al
```

where *imask* is equated to 21H, the I/O address of the interrupt mask register. To turn off the COM1 interrupt, we can set bit 4 of the interrupt mask register with the following instructions:

```
in     al,imask
or     al,10h         ;disable irq4
out    imask,al
```

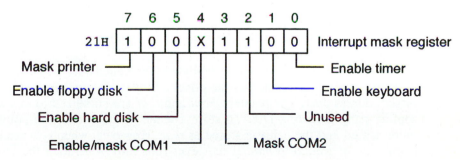

Figure 17.13   The 8259A PIC interrupt mask register.

17.4 AN INTERRUPT-DRIVEN PC TERMINAL PROGRAM

In this section we will write a PC terminal program in which a hardware interrupt occurs each time a character is received in the serial port. The interrupt service routine will read this character and store the value in the *circular queue* shown in Fig. 17.14. Multiple values can be stored in this queue before they are removed (in the same order they were stored). Therefore, characters will not be lost if they are received faster than they can be displayed while scrolling. Of course, if the queue is full and another character is received it will be lost; but we will make the queue big enough so that this will not happen.

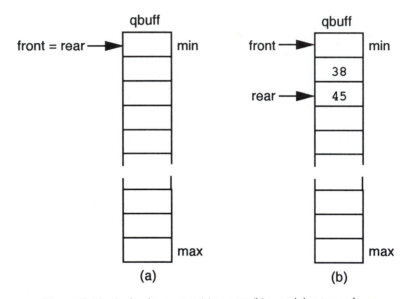

Figure 17.14 A circular queue: (a) empty; (b) containing two values.

Using this queue, the main program will then be that shown at the beginning of Listing 17.2. You should compare the instructions between the labels *key:* and *done:* with those in Listing 17.1 for our dumb terminal using the BIOS functions. Note that instead of checking the line status register to see if a character has been received, we simply check the queue to see if a hardware interrupt has deposited a character for us to read.

The queue is defined to be a 256-byte buffer called *qbuff* in the data segment. The first byte in the queue has the offset address *min*, and the last byte has the offset address *max*. The pointers *front* and *rear* are initialized to *min* in the subroutine *initq* in Listing 17.2. To store a value in the queue, the pointer *rear* is incremented and the value is stored at *rear*. However, when *rear* exceeds *max*, it must wrap around to *min*. If *rear* ever runs into *front*, then the queue is full and we will back up *rear* and not store the new value. The complete algorithm

Listing 17.2   *ibmterm.asm*

```
            title IBM PC terminal using interrupts

stack    segment       para stack
         db    64 dup(?)
stack    ends

data     segment
qbuff    db    256    dup(?)
front    dw    ?
rear     dw    ?
min      dw    ?
max      dw    ?
m0       db    'Select Baud Rate',0
m1       db    '1.   300',0
m2       db    '2.   600',0
m3       db    '3. 1200',0
m4       db    '4. 2400',0
m5       db    '5. 4800',0
m6       db    '6. 9600',0
vecseg   dw    ?                        ;save int vector
vecoff   dw    ?
txdata   equ   3f8h
recdat   equ   3f8h
mcr      equ   3fch
ier      equ   3f9h
lsr      equ   3fdh
intvec   equ   0ch
imask    equ   21h
eoi      equ   20h
ocw2     equ   20h
data     ends

extrn    chrout:near,mess:near
extrn    clrscn:near,quit:near
code     segment   public
         assume cs:code,ds:data

main     proc   far
         mov    ax,data                 ;set ds
         mov    ds,ax
         call   initq                   ;queue init
         call   gtbaud                  ;get baud
         call   isetup                  ;int setup
         in     al,imask
         and    al,0efh                 ;enable irq4
         out    imask,al
```

Listing 17.2   *(cont.)*

```
key:        mov     ah,1                ;if key not
            int     16h                 ; pressed
            je      recv                ; goto recv
            mov     ah,0                ;else
            int     16h                 ;read key
            cmp     ah,1                ;if esc key
            je      done                ;goto DOS
            call    send                ;send character
recv:       call    checkq              ;check queue
            je      key                 ;if empty,rdkey
            mov     bl,07h              ;normal video
            and     al,7fh              ;strip parity
            call    chrout              ;display char
            jmp     key                 ;repeat again
done:       in      al,imask
            or      al,10h              ;disable irq4
            out     imask,al
            push    ds                  ;save ds
            mov     dx,vecoff           ;restore old
            mov     ds,vecseg           ; 0ch int vec
            mov     al,intvec
            mov     ah,25h
            int     21h
            pop     ds                  ;restore ds
            call    quit                ;goto DOS
main        endp

;           display menu
menu        proc    near
            call    clrscn              ;clear screen
            mov     dx,0510h            ;row 5,col 16
            mov     si,offset m0
            mov     bl,07h              ;normal video
            call    mess                ;mess 0
            add     dh,2                ;row=row+2
            add     dl,4                ;col=col+4
            mov     si,offset m1
            call    mess                ;mess 1
            inc     dh                  ;inc row
            mov     si,offset m2
            call    mess                ;mess 2
            inc     dh
            mov     si,offset m3
            call    mess                ;mess 3
            inc     dh
            mov     si,offset m4
```

Listing 17.2   (*cont.*)

```
            call   mess                    ;mess 4
            inc    dh
            mov    si,offset m5
            call   mess                    ;mess 5
            inc    dh
            mov    si,offset m6
            call   mess                    ;mess 6
            mov    dh,5                     ;row=5
            mov    dl,33                    ;col=33
            mov    ah,2
            int    10h                     ;set cursor
            ret
menu        endp

;           get baud rate
gtbaud      proc   near
            call   menu                    ;display menu
gb1:        mov    ah,0                    ;wait for key
            int    16h
            cmp    al,31h                  ; between 1
            jb     gb1
            cmp    al,36h                  ; and 6
            ja     gb1
            and    al,0fh                  ;baud code
            inc    al                      ;between 2-7
            mov    cl,5                     ;move to
            shl    al,cl                    ; bits 5-7
            mov    cl,3                     ;no parity
            or     al,cl                    ; 8 bits
            mov    ah,0
            mov    dx,0
            int    14h                     ;set ACA ctrl reg
            call   clrscn                  ;clear screen
            ret
gtbaud      endp

;           initialize queue
initq       proc   near
            mov    ax,offset qbuff
            mov    front,ax                ;front->qbuff
            mov    rear,ax                 ;rear->qbuff
            mov    min,ax                  ;min->qbuff
            add    ax,255                  ;max ->
            mov    max,ax                  ; qbuff+255
            ret
initq       endp
```

Listing 17.2   (*cont.*)

```
;          check queue
checkq  proc  near
        mov   si,front
        cmp   si,rear              ;if front=rear
        je    cq2                  ;then empty
        cli                        ;disable int
        inc   si                   ;inc front
        cmp   si,max               ;if front>max
        jbe   cq1                  ;then
        mov   si,min               ; front=min
cq1:    mov   front,si             ;get byte
        mov   al,[si]              ; @ front
        test  al,0ffh              ;clear Z flag
        sti                        ;enable int
cq2:    ret
checkq  endp


;          store al in queue
qstore  proc  near
        inc   rear                 ;inc rear
        mov   si,rear              ;if rear>max
        cmp   si,max               ;then
        jbe   qs1
        mov   si,min               ;rear=min
        mov   rear,si
qs1:    cmp   si,front             ;if front=rear
        jne   qs3                  ;then full
        dec   si                   ; dec rear
        cmp   si,min               ; if rear<min
        jae   qs2                  ; then rear=max
        mov   si,max
        mov   rear,si
qs2:    ret                        ;else store
qs3:    mov   [si],al              ; at rear
        ret
qstore  endp


;          send char in al to 8250
send    proc  near
        push  ax                   ;save char
        mov   dx,lsr
sd1:    in    al,dx                ;wait for
        test  al,20h               ; trans buff
        je    sd1                  ; to be empty
        mov   dx,txdata
        pop   ax                   ;get char &
```

Listing 17.2   *(cont.)*

```
        out    dx,al                ; send it
        ret
send    endp

;       interrupt setup
isetup  proc   near
        mov    dx,mcr               ;modem cr
        mov    al,0bh               ;out2 lo
        out    dx,al                ;DTR,RTS lo
        mov    dx,ier
        mov    al,1                 ;enable recv
        out    dx,al                ; interrupts
        push   ds                   ;save ds
        mov    ah,35h               ;save 0Ch int vec
        mov    al,intvec
        int    21h
        mov    vecseg,es
        mov    vecoff,bx
        mov    dx,offset intser
        push   cs
        pop    ds
        mov    ah,25h               ;set int type
        int    21h                  ; vector
        pop    ds
        ret
isetup  endp

;       interrupt service routine
intser  proc   near
        push   ax                   ;save regs
        push   si
        push   dx
        push   ds
        mov    ax,data
        mov    ds,ax                ;ds=data
        mov    dx,lsr               ;if char ready
        in     al,dx
        test   al,01h
        je     ints1
        mov    dx,recdat            ;read it
        in     al,dx
        call   qstore               ;put in queue
ints1:  pop    ds
        pop    dx
        pop    si
        mov    al,eoi               ;8259 EOI
```

Listing 17.2   (*cont.*)

```
        out     ocw2,al
        pop     ax
        iret
intser  endp

code    ends
        end     main
```

for storing a value in the queue is given in Fig. 17.15 and is implemented by the subroutine *qstore* in Listing 17.2, which stores the value in *al* in the queue.

To read a value from the queue, the pointer *front* is incremented and that value is read. This will guarantee that the first value stored in the queue will be the first one read from the queue. The queue will be empty any time that *front = rear*. The algorithm to check the queue is given in Fig. 17.16 and is implemented by the subroutine *checkq* in Listing 17.2.

At the beginning of the main program in Listing 17.2, the baud rate is set using the subroutine *gtbaud*. This subroutine displays a menu from which six different baud rates can be selected. The selected baud rate is set by initializing the communications port (by calling *INT 14H* with *AH* = 0) with the appropriate value in the ACA control register in Fig. 17.4. Inasmuch as this call to the BIOS function *INT 14H* will disable the 8250 interrupts, it is necessary to call the subroutine *gtbaud* before calling the subroutine *isetup*. For the same reason, we

```
inc rear
if rear > max
then rear = min
if front = rear
then queue is full
        dec rear
        if rear < min
        then rear = max
else store value at rear
```

Figure 17.15 Algorithm to store a value in the circular queue in Fig. 17.14.

```
if front = rear
then queue is empty (Z flag = 1)
else  disable interrupts
        inc front
        if front > max
        then front = min
        read byte at front into al
        clear Z flag
        enable interrupts
```

Figure 17.16 Algorithm to check queue for a value.

cannot use the *INT 14H* function ($AH = 1$) to send a character out the serial line. We must therefore write our own *send* subroutine that waits for bit 5 in the line status register in Fig. 17.6 to go high before writing the character to the transmit holding register.

The interrupt service routine, *intser*, given at the end of Listing 17.2, checks to make sure a character is really there, and then reads it from the receive data buffer and stores it in the queue by calling *qstore*. Note that the data segment register, *ds*, must be set to *data* at the beginning of the interrupt service routine because there is no guarantee that it will have this value when the interrupt service routine is called. For example, if a character is being displayed on the screen and is in the middle of an *INT 10H* BIOS call when the interrupt occurs, it is likely that the data segment will have been changed to 0040H, the data segment used by the BIOS routines. Of course, our interrupt service routine must save this value of *ds* and restore it before leaving.

Before leaving the interrupt service routine, we must also execute the two instructions

```
mov   al,eoi            ;8259 EOI
out   ocw2,al
```

where *eoi* is equal to 20H and *ocw2* is the I/O address 20H of the 8259A Priority Interrupt Controller. Whenever a hardware interrupt occurs, a bit associated with that particular interrupt is stored in the 8259A *in-service register*. This bit must be cleared by writing a 20H value to I/O address 20H before leaving the interrupt service routine. This is called the *end of interrupt* (EOI) command. If you fail to do this, the interrupt will still be pending after leaving the interrupt service routine

TABLE 17.3   8250 UART BAUD RATE DIVISORS

Baud rate	Divisor high	Divisor low
110	04H	17H
150	03H	00H
300	01H	80H
600	00H	0CH
1,200	00H	60H
2,400	00H	30H
4,800	00H	20H
9,600	00H	0CH
19,200	00H	06H
38,400	00H	03H
57,600	00H	02H
115,200	00H	01H

and it will be called again immediately. It will appear as if you never get out of the interrupt service routine!

Setting the baud rate by storing a value in the ACA control register in Fig. 17.4 using the *INT 14H* BIOS function will limit you to a maximum baud rate of 9,600 baud. You can also set the baud rate by writing values directly to the 8250 UART *divisor high* and *divisor low* registers given in Table 17.2. The values to store in these registers for various baud rates are given in Table 17.3.

Experiment 39: Communicating between Two Computers

1. Connect two PCs together using a *null modem* between the two COM1 serial ports. A *null modem* is a serial cable in which pins 2 and 3 are crossed. That is, the transmit pin 2 of one computer is connected to the receive pin 3 of the other computer.

2. You will execute the same program on both computers. Modify the program given in Listing 17.2 so that when you press function key *F1* it switches to a double-screen mode. In this mode, whatever you type on the first computer should be displayed on the lower half of the second computer and on the upper half of the first computer (after making a round trip to the second computer). Similarly, anything typed on the second computer should be displayed on the lower half of the first computer and on the upper half of the second computer (after making a round trip to the first computer). Both halves of the screen should scroll independently when they are full.

You need to be able to tell when a received character is one that originated at the other computer or is one that has made a round trip from your computer. To do this use the following algorithm:

```
Send your own character with bit 7 = 0
If    you receive a character with bit 7 = 0
Then display it on the bottom of the screen,
     make bit 7 = 1 and send it back
Else display it on the top of the screen
     and do not send it back
```

Extra credit

3. Modify the program to download a file from one computer to another. That is, read a file from one disk, send it over the serial line, and store it on a disk in the other computer. Design a simple user interface of your choice.

4. Modify the program so as to communicate between the computers at a baud rate of 57,600 baud.

Experiment 40: A Smarter Communications Program

1. Add a pop-up menu front end to the program in Listing 17.2 by combining this program with the results of Experiment 28 in Chapter 13. When the *Select baud rate* menu item is selected, allow the user to select a baud rate from 300 to 9,600 from a pop-up menu.

2. Add additional features to your communications program. These can include:
   a. Automatically logging you on to a main computer or local area network by providing your user ID and password.
   b. Pressing function key *F1 turns capture on*. This will ask you for a filename and then store everything that comes in the serial port to this file on disk as well as being displayed on the screen. Pressing function key *F2* should *turn capture off* by closing the file.

EXERCISES

17.1. Write a printer routine that will send characters to a serial printer using an ACA.

17.2. Write a subroutine, *gtbaud*, that could be used in the program in Listing 17.2 to set the baud rate to any of the values given in Table 17.3. Modify the subroutine *menu* accordingly.

17.3. Discuss what will happen if interrupts are not disabled in the subroutine *checkq* in Listing 17.2 and an interrupt occurs at various locations within the subroutine before and after the variable *front* is changed.

17.4. What will the parity bit be for each of the following examples?
   a. Character Y, even parity
   b. Character K, odd parity
   c. Character S, even parity
   d. Character A, odd parity

17.5. How long will it take to send a page of 4,096 characters over a 9600-baud asynchronous serial line?

17.6. a. How long will it take to send a text file containing 100,000 characters over a 1,200-baud asynchronous serial line?

   b. How long will it take to send this same file between two computers at a baud rate of 57,600?

17.7. What value should you store in the ACA control register to initialize the serial port for 300 baud, 7 bits, and odd parity?

17.8. What value should you store in the ACA control register to initialize the serial port for 9,600 baud, 7 bits, and even parity?

17.9. Write a subroutine that will check the *line status register* for a *parity*, *overrun*, or *framing* error and print the appropriate error message on the screen.

17.10. How would you have to modify the program given in Listing 17.2 to have it use the COM2 serial port?

17.11. Explain how you could write an interrupt service routine that would send a character from a printer buffer to a parallel printer each time an *ACK* signal is received from the printer (see Fig. 14.12). How would you program the PIC *interrupt mask register*?

REFERENCES

ABEL, PETER, *IBM PC Assembly Language and Programming*, Prentice Hall, Englewood Cliffs, N.J., 2nd Ed., 1991.

AUGARTEN, STAN, *Bit by Bit—An Illustrated History of Computers*, Ticknor & Fields, New York, 1984.

BRADLEY, DAVID J., *Assembly Language Programming for the IBM Personal Computer*, Prentice Hall, Englewood Cliffs, N.J., 1984.

BREY, BARRY B., *The Intel Microprocessors—8086/8088, 80186, 80286, 80386, and 80486—Architecture, Programming, and Interfacing*, Merrill/Macmillan Publishing Company, New York, 1991.

CLEMENTS, ALAN, *Principles of Computer Hardware*, PWS-KENT Publishing Company, Boston, Mass., 2nd Ed., 1993.

DUNCAN, RAY, *Advanced MS DOS*, Microsoft Press, Redmond, Wash., 1986.

EVANS, CHRISTOPHER, *The Making of the Micro—A History of Computers*, Van Nostrand Reinhold Company, New York, 1981.

GILES, WILLIAM B., *Assembly Language Programming for the Intel 80XXX Family*, Macmillan Publishing Company, New York, 1991.

GOLDSTINE, HERMAN H., *The Computer from Pascal to von Neumann*, Princeton University Press, Princeton, N.J., 1972.

GRAY, ROBERT L., *Macro Assembler Programming—for the IBM PC and Compatibles*, SRA, Inc., Chicago, Ill., 1989.

JOURDAIN, ROBERT, *Programmer's Problem Solver for the IBM PC, XT & AT*, Brady Communications Company, Inc., New York, 1986.

MANO, M. MORRIS, *Digital Design*, Prentice Hall, Englewood Cliffs, N.J., 2nd Ed., 1991.

McCALLA, THOMAS RICHARD, *Digital Logic and Computer Design*, Merrill/Macmillan Publishing Company, New York, 1992.

MORGAN, CHRISTOPHER L. AND MITCHELL WAITE, *8086/8088 16-Bit Microprocessor Primer*, BYTE/McGraw-Hill, Peterborough, N.H., 1982.

MURRAY, WILLIAM H. III AND CHRIS H. PAPPAS, *80386/80286 Assembly Language Programming*, Osborne, McGraw-Hill, Berkeley, Cal., 1986.

PELLERIN, DAVID AND MICHAEL HOLLEY, *Practical Design Using Programmable Logic*, Prentice Hall, Englewood Cliffs, N.J., 1991.

ROTH, CHARLES H., JR., *Fundamentals of Logic Design*, West Publishing Company, St. Paul, Minn., 4th Ed., 1992.

TRIEBEL, WALTER A. AND AVTAR SINGH, *The 8088 and 8086 Microprocessors—Programming, Interfacing, Software, Hardware, and Applications*, Prentice Hall, Englewood Cliffs, N.J., 1991.

TRIEBEL, WALTER A., *The 80386DX Microprocessor—Hardware, Software, and Interfacing*, Prentice Hall, Englewood Cliffs, N.J., 1992.

WAKERLY, JOHN F., *Digital Design Principles and Practices*, Prentice Hall, Englewood Cliffs, N.J., 1990.

Appendixes

Appendix A

8086 INSTRUCTION SET

TABLE A.1 8086 INSTRUCTION SET

Effective Address (EA) Clock Cycle Values

		Clocks
Displacement only	disp	6
Base or index only	BX, SI, DI	5
Base + displacement	BX + disp, BP + disp	9
Index + displacement	SI + disp, DI + disp	9
Base + index	BP + DI, BX + SI	7
	BP + SI, BX + DI	8
Base + index + displacement	BP + DI + disp, BX + SI + disp	11
	BP + SI + disp, BX + DI + disp	12

Add two clock cycles when segment override is used.

Key to Status Flag Codes

x	Set or reset by instruction
u	Undefined
r	Replaced from memory or register
1	Always set to 1
0	Always cleared to 0
blank	Unchanged

d = 1	"to" register	s = 1	data byte sign extended to form 16-bit operand
d = 0	"from" register	v = 0	"count" = 1
w = 1	word instruction	v = 1	"count" in CL
w = 0	byte instruction	x	don't care

TABLE A.1 (*cont.*)

AAA *ASCII adjust for addition* Flags ODITSZAPC

`0 0 1 1 0 1 1 1`

Clocks = 4

u   uuxux

AAD *ASCII adjust for division* Flags ODITSZAPC

`1 1 0 1 0 1 0 1` `0 0 0 0 1 0 1 0`

Clocks = 60

u   xxuxu

AAM *ASCII adjust for multiply* Flags ODITSZAPC

`1 1 0 1 0 1 0 0` `0 0 0 0 1 0 1 0`

Clocks = 83

u   xxuxu

AAS *ASCII adjust for subtraction* Flags ODITSZAPC

`0 0 1 1 1 1 1 1`

Clocks = 4

u   uuxux

ADC *Add with carry* Flags ODITSZAPC
Register/memory with register to either

`0 0 0 1 0 0 d w` `mod reg r/m`

Clocks: register to register   3
memory to register   9 + EA
register to memory   16 + EA

x   xxxxx

Immediate to register/memory

`1 0 0 0 0 0 s w` `mod 0 1 0 r/m` `data` `data if s:w = 01`

Clocks: immediate to register   4
immediate to memory   17 + EA

Immediate to accumulator

`0 0 0 1 0 1 0 w` `data` `data if w = 1`

Clocks = 4

ADD *Addition* Flags ODITSZAPC
Register/memory and register to either

`0 0 0 0 0 0 d w` `mod reg r/m`

Clocks: register to register   3
memory to register   9 + EA
register to memory   16 + EA

x   xxxxx

Immediate to register/memory

`1 0 0 0 0 0 s w` `mod 0 0 0 r/m` `data` `data if s:w = 01`

Clocks: immediate to register   4
immediate to memory   17 + EA

Immediate to accumulator

`0 0 0 0 0 1 0 w` `data` `data if w = 1`

Clocks = 4

TABLE A.1 (*cont.*)

AND   *Logical AND*   Flags ODITSZAPC
Register/memory and register to either   0   xxux0

0 0 1 0 0 0 d w	mod reg r/m

Clocks: register to register   3
         memory to register   9 + EA
         register to memory   16 + EA

Immediate to register/memory

1 0 0 0 0 0 0 w	mod 1 0 0 r/m	data	data if w = 1

Clocks: immediate to register   4
         immediate to memory   17 + EA

Immediate to accumulator

0 0 1 0 0 1 0 w	data	data if w = 1

Clocks = 4

CALL   *Call a procedure*   Flags ODITSZAPC
Direct within segment

1 1 1 0 1 0 0 0	disp-low	disp-high

Clocks = 19

Indirect within segment

1 1 1 1 1 1 1 1	mod 0 1 0 r/m

Clocks = 21 + EA

Direct intersegment

1 0 0 1 1 0 1 0	offset-low	offset-high
Clocks = 28	segment-low	segment-high

Indirect intersegment

1 1 1 1 1 1 1 1	mod 0 1 1 r/m

Clocks = 37 + EA

CBW   *Convert byte to word*   Flags ODITSZAPC

1 0 0 1 1 0 0 0

Clocks = 2

CLC   *Clear carry flag*   Flags   ODITSZAPC
| 0

1 1 1 1 1 0 0 0

Clocks = 2

CLD   *Clear direction flag*   Flags ODITSZAPC
                                              0

1 1 1 1 1 1 0 0

Clocks = 2

CLI   *Clear interrupt flag*   Flags ODITSZAPC
                                           0

1 1 1 1 1 0 1 0

Clocks = 2

TABLE A.1 (*cont.*)

CMC *Complement carry flag*   Flags ODITSZAPC

| 1 1 1 1 0 1 0 1 |

Clocks = 2

CMP *Compare*   Flags ODITSZAPC
Register/memory and register   x   xxxxx

| 0 0 1 1 1 0 d w | mod reg r/m |

Clocks: register with register 3
         memory with register   9 + EA
         register with memory   9 + EA

Immediate with register/memory

| 1 0 0 0 0 0 s w | mod 1 1 1 r/m | data | data if s:w = 01 |

Clocks: immediate to register 4
         immediate to memory   17 + EA

Immediate with accumulator

| 0 0 1 1 1 1 0 w | data | data if w = 1 |

Clocks = 4

CMPS *Compare string*   Flags ODITSZAPC

| 1 0 1 0 0 1 1 w | x   xxxxx

Clocks = 22

CWD *Convert word to double word*   Flags ODITSZAPC

| 1 0 0 1 1 0 0 1 |

Clocks = 5

DAA *Decimal adjust for addition*   Flags ODITSZAPC

| 0 0 1 0 0 1 1 1 | x   xxxxx

Clocks = 4

DAS *Decimal adjust for subtraction*   Flags ODITSZAPC

| 0 0 1 0 1 1 1 1 | u   xxxxx

Clocks = 4

DEC *Decrement by 1*   Flags ODITSZAPC
Register/memory   x   xxxxx

| 1 1 1 1 1 1 1 w | mod 0 0 1 r/m |

Clocks: register 2
         memory   15 + EA

Register

| 0 1 0 0 1 reg |

Clocks = 2

TABLE A.1 *(cont.)*

D I V *Division (unsigned)*   Flags   ODITSZAPC

| 1 1 1 1 0 1 1 w | mod 1 1 0 r/m |
u   uuuuu

Clocks: 8-bit register   80-90
8-bit memory   (86-96) + EA
16-bit register   144-162
16-bit memory   (150-168) + EA

E S C *Escape to external device*   Flags   ODITSZAPC

| 1 1 0 1 1 x x x | mod x x x r/m |

Clocks = 7 + EA

HLT *Halt*   Flags   ODITSZAPC

| 1 1 1 1 0 1 0 0 |

Clocks = 2

I DIV *Integer division (signed)*   Flags   ODITSZAPC

| 1 1 1 1 0 1 1 w | mod 1 1 1 r/m |
u   uuuuu

Clocks: 8-bit register   101-112
8-bit memory   (107-118) + EA
16-bit register   165-184
16-bit memory   (171-190) + EA

IMUL *Integer multiplication (signed)*   Flags   ODITSZAPC

| 1 1 1 1 0 1 1 w | mod 1 0 1 r/m |
x   uuuux

Clocks: 8-bit register   80-98
8-bit memory   (86-104) + EA
16-bit register   128-154
16-bit memory   (134-160) + EA

I N *Input to AL or AX from port*   Flags   ODITSZAPC
Fixed port

| 1 1 1 0 0 1 0 w | port |

Clocks = 10 (byte) or 14 (word)

Variable port (DX)

| 1 1 1 0 1 1 0 w |

Clocks = 8 (byte) or 12 (word)

INC *Increment by 1*   Flags   ODITSZAPC
Register/memory
x   xxxxx

| 1 1 1 1 1 1 1 w | mod 0 0 0 r/m |

Clocks: register   2
memory   15 + EA

Register

| 0 1 0 0 0 reg |

Clocks = 2

TABLE A.1 (*cont.*)

INT   *Interrupt*   Flags   ODITSZAPC
Type specified   00

1 1 0 0 1 1 0 1	type

Clocks = 51

Type 3

1 1 0 0 1 1 0 0

Clocks = 51

INTO   *Interrupt on overflow*   Flags   ODITSZAPC
                                                                         00
1 1 0 0 1 1 1 0

Clocks = 52 or 4

IRET   *Interrupt return*   Flags   ODITSZAPC
                                                                       rrrrrrrrr
1 1 0 0 1 1 1 1

Clocks = 24

JA/JNBE   *Jump if above/not below or equal*   Flags   ODITSZAPC

0 1 1 1 0 1 1 1	disp

Clocks: jump taken   16
         jump not taken 4

JAE/JNB   *Jump if above or equal/not below*   Flags   ODITSZAPC

0 1 1 1 0 0 1 1	disp

Clocks: jump taken   16
         jump not taken 4

JB/JNAE   *Jump if below/not above or equal*   Flags   ODITSZAPC

0 1 1 1 0 0 1 0	disp

Clocks: jump taken   16
         jump not taken 4

JBE/JNA   *Jump if below or equal/not above*   Flags   ODITSZAPC

0 1 1 1 0 1 1 0	disp

Clocks: jump taken   16
         jump not taken 4

JC   *Jump if carry*   Flags   ODITSZAPC

0 1 1 1 0 0 1 0	disp

Clocks: jump taken   16
         jump not taken 4

JCXZ   *Jump if CX is zero*   Flags   ODITSZAPC

1 1 1 0 0 0 1 1	disp

Clocks: jump taken   18
         jump not taken 6

JE/JZ   *Jump if equal/zero*   Flags   ODITSZAPC

0 1 1 1 0 1 0 0	disp

Clocks: jump taken   16
         jump not taken 4

TABLE A.1 (*cont.*)

JG/JNLE *Jump if greater/not less or equal*   Flags ODITSZAPC

0 1 1 1 1 1 1 1	disp

Clocks: jump taken   16
          jump not taken 4

JGE/JNL *Jump if greater or equal/not less*   Flags ODITSZAPC

0 1 1 1 1 1 0 1	disp

Clocks: jump taken   16
          jump not taken 4

JL/JNGE *Jump if less/not greater or equal*   Flags ODITSZAPC

0 1 1 1 1 1 0 0	disp

Clocks: jump taken   16
          jump not taken 4

JLE/JNG *Jump if less or equal/not greater*   Flags ODITSZAPC

0 1 1 1 1 1 1 0	disp

Clocks: jump taken   16
          jump not taken 4

JMP *Unconditional jump*   Flags ODITSZAPC
Direct within segment

1 1 1 0 1 0 0 1	disp-low	disp-high

Clocks = 15

Direct within segment - short

1 1 1 0 1 0 1 1	disp

Clocks = 21 + EA

Indirect within segment

1 1 1 1 1 1 1 1	mod 1 0 0 r/m

Clocks: memory 18 + EA
          register 11

Direct intersegment

1 1 1 0 1 0 1 0	offset-low	offset-high
	segment-low	segment-high

Clocks = 15

Indirect intersegment

1 1 1 1 1 1 1 1	mod 1 0 1 r/m

Clocks = 24 + EA

JNC *Jump if not carry*   Flags ODITSZAPC

0 1 1 1 0 0 1 1	disp

Clocks: jump taken   16
          jump not taken 4

TABLE A.1 (*cont.*)

JNE/JNZ   *Jump if not equal/not zero*   Flags   ODITSZAPC

0 1 1 1 0 1 0 1	disp

Clocks: jump taken   16
        jump not taken 4

JNO   *Jump if not overflow*   Flags   ODITSZAPC

0 1 1 1 0 0 0 1	disp

Clocks: jump taken   16
        jump not taken 4

JNP/JPO   *Jump if not parity/parity odd*   Flags   ODITSZAPC

0 1 1 1 1 0 1 1	disp

Clocks: jump taken   16
        jump not taken 4

JNS   *Jump if not sign*   Flags   ODITSZAPC

0 1 1 1 1 0 0 1	disp

Clocks: jump taken   16
        jump not taken 4

J O   *Jump if overflow*   Flags   ODITSZAPC

0 1 1 1 0 0 0 0	disp

Clocks: jump taken   16
        jump not taken 4

JP/JPE   *Jump if parity/parity even*   Flags   ODITSZAPC

0 1 1 1 1 0 1 0	disp

Clocks: jump taken   16
        jump not taken 4

J S   *Jump if sign*   Flags   ODITSZAPC

0 1 1 1 1 0 0 0	disp

Clocks: jump taken   16
        jump not taken 4

LAHF   *Load AH from flags*   Flags   ODITSZAPC

1 0 0 1 1 1 1 1

Clocks = 4

LDS   *Load pointer into reg and DS*   Flags   ODITSZAPC

1 1 0 0 0 1 0 1	mod reg r/m

Clocks = 16 + EA

LOCK   *Bus lock prefix*   Flags   ODITSZAPC

1 1 1 1 0 0 0 0

Clocks = 2

TABLE A.1   *(cont.)*

LODS   *Bus lock prefix*   Flags   ODITSZAPC

1 1 1 1 0 0 0 0

Clocks = 2

LOOP   *Loop CX times*   Flags   ODITSZAPC

1 1 1 0 0 0 1 0	disp

Clocks: jump taken   17
         jump not taken 5

LOOPE/LOOPZ   *Loop if equal/zero*   Flags   ODITSZAPC

1 1 1 0 0 0 0 1	disp

Clocks: jump taken   18
         jump not taken 6

LOOPNE/LOOPNZ   *Loop if not equal/hot zero*   Flags   ODITSZAPC

1 1 1 0 0 0 0 0	disp

Clocks: jump taken   19
         jump not taken 5

LEA   *Load effective address to register*   Flags   ODITSZAPC

1 0 0 0 1 1 0 1	mod reg r/m

Clocks = 2 + EA

LES   *Load pointer to register and ES*   Flags   ODITSZAPC

1 1 0 0 0 1 0 0	mod reg r/m

Clocks = 16 + EA

MOV   *Move*   Flags   ODITSZAPC
Register/memory to/from register

1 0 0 0 1 0 d w	mod reg r/m

Clocks: register to register   2
         memory to register   8 + EA
         register to memory   9 + EA

Immediate to register/memory

1 1 0 0 0 1 1 w	mod 0 0 0 r/m	data	data if w = 1

Clocks: immediate to register   4
         immediate to memory   10 + EA

Immediate to register

1 0 1 1 w reg	data	data if w = 1

Clocks = 4

Memory to accumulator

1 0 1 0 0 0 0 w	addr-low	addr-high

Clocks = 10

TABLE A.1 (*cont.*)

Accumulator to memory

1 0 1 0 0 0 1 w	addr-low	addr-high

Clocks = 10

Register/memory to segment register

1 0 0 0 1 1 1 0	mod 0 reg r/m

Clocks: register to register   2
         memory to register   8 + EA

Segment register to register/memory

1 0 0 0 1 1 0 0	mod 0 reg r/m

Clocks: register to register   2
         register to memory   9 + EA

MOVS *Move string*   Flags   ODITSZAPC

1 0 1 0 0 1 0 w

Clocks: byte   18
         word   26
         rep byte   9 + 17/rep
         rep word   9 + 25/rep

MUL   *Multiply (unsigned)*   Flags   ODITSZAPC
                                                                        x   uuuux

1 1 1 1 0 1 1 w	mod 1 0 0 r/m

Clocks: 8-bit register   70-77
         8-bit memory   (76-83) + EA
         16-bit register   118-133
         16-bit memory   (124-139) + EA

NEG   *Negate (change sign)*   Flags   ODITSZAPC
                                                                        x   xxxx1

1 1 1 1 0 1 1 w	mod 0 1 1 r/m

Clocks: register 3
         memory 16 + EA

NOP   *No operation*   Flags   ODITSZAPC

1 0 0 1 0 0 0 0

Clocks = 3

NOT   *Logical NOT*   Flags   ODITSZAPC
                                                                    x   xxxx1

1 1 1 1 0 1 1 w	mod 0 1 0 r/m

Clocks: register 3
         memory 16 + EA

OR   *Logical inclusive OR*   Flags   ODITSZAPC
Register/memory and register to either   0   xxux0

0 0 0 0 1 0 d w	mod reg r/m

Clocks: register to register   3
         memory to register   9 + EA
         register to memory   16 + EA

524

Appendix A

TABLE A.1 (*cont.*)

Immediate to register/memory

1 0 0 0 0 0 0 w	mod 0 0 1 r/m	data	data if w = 1

Clocks: immediate to register   4
         immediate to memory   17 + EA

Immediate to accumulator

0 0 0 0 1 1 0 w	data	data if w = 1

Clocks = 4

OUT   *Output from AL or AX to port*   Flags   ODITSZAPC
Fixed port

1 1 1 0 0 1 1 w	port

Clocks = 10 (byte) or 14 (word)

Variable port (DX)

1 1 1 0 1 1 1 w

Clocks = 8 (byte) or 12 (word)

POP   *Pop word off stack*   Flags   ODITSZAPC
Register/memory

1 0 0 0 1 1 1 1	mod 0 0 0 r/m

Clocks: register   12
         memory   25 + EA

Register

0 1 0 1 1   reg

Clocks = 12

Segment register

0 0 0 reg 1 1 1

Clocks = 12

POPF   *Pop flags off stack*   Flags   ODITSZAPC
                                                            rrrrrrrrr

1 0 0 1 1 1 0 1

Clocks = 12

PUSH   *Push word onto stack*   Flags   ODITSZAPC
Register/memory

1 1 1 1 1 1 1 1	mod 1 1 0 r/m

Clocks: register   15
         memory   24 + EA

Register

0 1 0 1 0   reg

Clocks = 15

Segment register

0 0 0 reg 1 1 0

Clocks = 14

TABLE A.1 *(cont.)*

PUSHF   *Push flags onto stack*   Flags   ODITSZAPC

| 1 0 0 1 1 1 0 0 |

Clocks = 14

RCL   *Rotate through carry left*   Flags   ODITSZAPC

| 1 1 0 1 0 0 v w | mod 0 1 0   r/m | x   x

Clocks: single-bit register   2
         single-bit memory   15 + EA (byte) 23 + EA (word)
         variable-bit register   8 + 4/bit
         variable-bit memory   20 + EA + 4/bit (byte) 28 + EA + 4/bit (word)

RCR   *Rotate through carry right*   Flags   ODITSZAPC

| 1 1 0 1 0 0 v w | mod 0 1 1   r/m | x   x

Clocks: single-bit register   2
         single-bit memory   15 + EA (byte) 23 + EA (word)
         variable-bit register   8 + 4/bit
         variable-bit memory   20 + EA + 4/bit (byte) 28 + EA + 4/bit (word)

REP   *Repeat string operation*   Flags   ODITSZAPC

| 1 1 1 1 0 0 1 0 |

Clocks = 2

REPE/REPZ   *Repeat string operation*   Flags   ODITSZAPC
                  while equal/zero

| 1 1 1 1 0 0 1 1 |

Clocks = 2

REPNE/REPNZ   *Repeat string operation*   Flags   ODITSZAPC
                  while not equal/not zero

| 1 1 1 1 0 0 1 0 |

Clocks = 2

RET   *Return from procedure*   Flags   ODITSZAPC
Within segment

| 1 1 0 0 0 0 1 1 |

Clocks = 20

Within segment, add immediate to SP

| 1 1 0 0 0 0 1 0 | data-low | data-high |

Clocks = 24

Intersegment

| 1 1 0 0 1 0 1 1 |

Clocks = 32

Intersegment, add immediate to SP

| 1 1 0 0 1 0 1 0 | data-low | data-high |

Clocks = 31

TABLE A.1   *(cont.)*

ROL   *Rotate left*   Flags   ODITSZAPC

| 1 1 0 1 0 0 v w | mod 0 0 0   r/m | x   x |

Clocks: single-bit register   2
         single-bit memory   15 + EA (byte) 23 + EA (word)
         variable-bit register   8 + 4/bit
         variable-bit memory   20 + EA + 4/bit (byte) 28 + EA + 4/bit (word)

ROR   *Rotate right*   Flags   ODITSZAPC

| 1 1 0 1 0 0 v w | mod 0 0 1   r/m | x   x |

Clocks: single-bit register   2
         single-bit memory   15 + EA (byte) 23 + EA (word)
         variable-bit register   8 + 4/bit
         variable-bit memory   20 + EA + 4/bit (byte) 28 + EA + 4/bit (word)

SAHF   *Store AH into flags*   Flags   ODITSZAPC

| 1 0 0 1 1 1 1 0 | rrrrr |

Clocks = 4

SAL/SHL   *Shift arithmetic left/logical left*   Flags   ODITSZAPC

| 1 1 0 1 0 0 v w | mod 1 0 0   r/m | x   x |

Clocks: single-bit register   2
         single-bit memory   15 + EA (byte) 23 + EA (word)
         variable-bit register   8 + 4/bit
         variable-bit memory   20 + EA + 4/bit (byte) 28 + EA + 4/bit (word)

SAR   *Shift arithmetic right*   Flags   ODITSZAPC

| 1 1 0 1 0 0 v w | mod 1 1 1   r/m | x   x |

Clocks: single-bit register   2
         single-bit memory   15 + EA (byte) 23 + EA (word)
         variable-bit register   8 + 4/bit
         variable-bit memory   20 + EA + 4/bit (byte) 28 + EA + 4/bit (word)

SBB   *Subtract with borrow*   Flags   ODITSZAPC

Register/memory and register from either   x   xxxxx

| 0 0 0 1 1 0 d w | mod   reg   r/m |

Clocks: register to register   3
         memory to register   9 + EA (byte) 13 + EA (word)
         register to memory   16 + EA (byte) 24 + EA (word)

Immediate from register/memory

| 1 0 0 0 0 0 s w | mod 0 1 1 r/m | data | data if s:w = 01 |

Clocks: immediate to register   4
         immediate to memory   17 + EA (byte) 25 + EA (word)

Immediate from accumulator

| 0 0 0 1 1 1 0 w | data | data if w = 1 |

Clocks = 4

TABLE A.1 (*cont.*)

SCAS *Scan string* Flags ODITSZAPC

| 1 0 1 0 1 1 1 w |

x   xxxxx

Clocks: byte   15
         word   19
         rep byte   9 + 15/rep
         rep word   9 + 19/rep

SHR *Shift logical right* Flags ODITSZAPC

| 1 1 0 1 0 0 v w | mod 1 0 1   r/m |

x   x

Clocks: single-bit register   2
         single-bit memory   15 + EA (byte) 23 + EA (word)
         variable-bit register   8 + 4/bit
         variable-bit memory   20 + EA + 4/bit (byte) 28 + EA + 4/bit (word)

STC *Set carry flag* Flags ODITSZAPC

| 1 1 1 1 1 0 0 1 |

1

Clocks = 2

STD *Set direction flag* Flags ODITSZAPC

| 1 1 1 1 1 1 0 1 |

1

Clocks = 2

STI *Set interrupt enable flag* Flags ODITSZAPC

| 1 1 1 1 1 0 1 1 |

1

Clocks = 2

STOS *Store byte or word string* Flags ODITSZAPC

| 1 0 1 0 1 0 1 w |

Clocks: byte   11
         word   15
         rep byte   9 + 10/rep
         rep word   9 + 14/rep

SUB *Subtractraction* Flags ODITSZAPC
Register/memory and register from either

x   xxxxx

| 0 0 1 0 1 0 d w | mod reg   r/m |

Clocks: register to register   3
         memory to register   9 + EA (byte) 13 + EA (word)
         register to memory   16 + EA (byte) 24 + EA (word)

Immediate from register/memory

| 1 0 0 0 0 0 s w | mod 1 0 1 r/m | data | data if s:w = 01 |

Clocks: immediate to register   4
         immediate to memory   17 + EA (byte) 25 + EA (word)

Immediate from accumulator

| 0 0 1 0 1 1 0 w | data | data if w = 1 |

Clocks = 4

TABLE A.1   *(cont.)*

TEST   *Test (nondestructive logical AND)*   Flags   0DITSZAPC
Register/memory and register   0   xxuxO

1 0 0 0 0 1 0 w	mod reg r/m

Clocks: register and register   3
           register and memory   9 + EA (byte) 13 + EA (word)

Immediate and register/memory

1 1 1 1 0 1 1 w	mod 0 0 0 r/m	data	data if w = 1

Clocks: immediate and register   4
           immediate and memory   11 + EA

Immediate and accumulator

1 0 1 0 1 0 0 w	data	data if w = 1

Clocks = 4

WAIT   *Wait until TEST line active*   Flags   0DITSZAPC

1 0 0 1 1 0 1 1

Clocks = 3 + 5n

XCHG *Exchange*   Flags   0DITSZAPC
Register/memory with register

1 0 0 0 0 1 1 w	mod reg r/m

Clocks: register with register   4
           register with memory   17 + EA (byte) 25 + EA (word)

Register with accumulator

1 0 0 1 0 reg

Clocks = 3

XLAT   *Translate byte to AL*   Flags   0DITSZAPC

1 1 0 1 0 1 1 1

Clocks = 11

XOR   *Logical Exclusive OR*   Flags   0DITSZAPC
Register/memory and register to either   0   xxuxO

0 0 1 1 0 0 d w	mod reg r/m

Clocks: register to register   3
           memory to register   9 + EA (byte) 13 + EA (word)
           register to memory   16 + EA (byte) 24 + EA (word)

Immediate to register/memory

1 0 0 0 0 0 0 w	mod 1 1 0 r/m	data	data if w = 1

Clocks: immediate to register   4
           immediate to memory   17 + EA (byte) 25 + EA (word)

Immediate to accumulator

0 0 1 1 0 1 0 w	data	data if w = 1

Clocks = 4

TABLE A.2a INSTRUCTION OPCODE MAP

	0	1	2	3	4	5	6	7	8	9	A	B	C	D	E	F
0	ADD r/m,reg	ADD r/m,reg	ADD reg,r/m	ADD w reg,r/m	ADD b AL,imm	ADD w AX,imm	PUSH ES	POP ES	OR r/m,reg	OR w r/m,reg	OR reg,r/m	OR reg,r/m	OR b AL,imm	OR w AX,imm	PUSH CS	
1	ADC b r/m,reg	ADC w r/m,reg	ADC b reg,r/m	ADC w reg,r/m	ADC b AL,imm	ADC w AX,imm	PUSH SS	POP SS	SBB b r/m,reg	SBB w r/m,reg	SBB reg,r/m	SBB w reg,r/m	SBB b AL,imm	SBB w AX,imm	PUSH DS	POP DS
2	AND b r/m,reg	AND w r/m,reg	AND b reg,r/m	AND w reg,r/m	AND b AL,imm	AND w AX,imm	SEGMENT ES	DAA	SUB b r/m,reg	SUB w r/m,reg	SUB b reg,r/m	SUB w reg,r/m	SUB b AL,imm	SUB w AX,imm	SEGMENT CS	DAS
3	XOR b r/m,reg	XOR w r/m,reg	XOR b reg,r/m	XOR w reg,r/m	XOR b AL,imm	XOR w AX,imm	SEGMENT SS	AAA	CMP b r/m,reg	CMP w r/m,reg	CMP b reg,r/m	CMP w reg,r/m	CMP b AL,imm	CMP w AX,imm	SEGMENT DS	AAS
4	INC AX	INC CX	INC DX	INC BX	INC SP	INC BP	INC SI	INC DI	DEC AX	DEC CX	DEC DX	DEC BX	DEC SP	DEC BP	DEC SI	DEC DI
5	PUSH AX	PUSH CX	PUSH DX	PUSH BX	PUSH SP	PUSH BP	PUSH SI	PUSH DI	POP AX	POP CX	POP DX	POP BX	POP SP	POP BP	POP SI	POP DI
6																
7	JO	JNO	JB/JNAE JC	JNB/JAE JNC	JE/JZ	JNE/JNZ	JBE/JNA	JNBE/JA	JS	JNS	JP/JPE	JNP/JPO	JL/JNGE	JNL/JGE	JLE/JNG	JNLE/JG
8	*	*	*	*	TEST r/m,reg	TEST r/m,reg	XCHG r/m,reg	XCHG r/m,reg	MOV b r/m,reg	MOV w r/m,reg	MOV b reg,r/m	MOV w reg,r/m	MOV r/m,seg	LEA reg,r/m	MOV seg,r/m	POP r/m
9	NOP	XCHG CX,AX	XCH DX,AX	XCH BX,AX	XCH SP,AX	XCHG BP,AX	XCHG SI,AX	XCHG DI,AX	CBW	CWD	CALL inter	WAIT	PUSHF	POPF	SAHF	LAHF
A	MOV b AL,mem	MOV AX,mem	MOV mem,AL	MOV mem,AX	MOVS b	MOVS w	CMPS b	CMPS w	TEST b AL,imm	TEST w AL,imm	STOS b	STOS w	LODS b	LODS w	SCAS b	SCAS w
B	MOV AL,imm	MOV CL,imm	MOV DL,imm	MOV BL,imm	MOV AH,imm	MOV CH,imm	MOV DH,imm	MOV BH,imm	MOV AX,imm	MOV CX,imm	MOV DX,imm	MOV BX,imm	MOV SP,imm	MOV BP,imm	MOV SI,imm	MOV DI,imm
C			RET intra+	RET intra	LE reg,r/m	LD reg,r/m	MOV b r/m,imm	MOV w r/m,imm			RET inter+	RET inter	INT type	INT	INTO	IRET
D	*	*	*	*	AAM	AAD	*	XLAT	ESC 0	ESC 1	ESC 2	ESC 3	ESC 4	ESC 5	ESC 6	ESC 7
E	LOOPNZ/LOOPNE	LOOPZ/LOOPE	LOOP	JCXZ	IN b AL,port	IN w AX,port	OUT b port,AL	OUT w port,AX	CALL intra	JMP intra	JMP inter	JMP short	IN b AL,DX	IN w AX,DX	OUT b DX,AL	OUT w DX,AX
F	LOCK	*	REP/REPNE REPNZ	REPE/REPZ	HLT	CMC	*	*	CLC	STC	CLI	STI	CLD	STD	*	*

TABLE A2.b INSTRUCTION OPCODE MAP

mod	PBOC	r/m

Postbyte Opcodes (PBOC)

	000	001	010	011	100	101	110	111
80,82	ADD b r/m,imm	OR b r/m,imm	ADC b r/m,imm	SBB b r/m,imm	AND b r/m,imm	SUB b r/m,imm	XOR b r/m,imm	CMP b r/m,imm
81	ADD w r/m,imm	OR w r/m,imm	ADC w r/m,imm	SBB w r/m,imm	AND w r/m,imm	SUB w r/m,imm	XOR w r/m,imm	CMP w r/m,imm
83	ADD se r/m,imm		ADC se r/m,imm	SBB se r/m,imm		SUB se r/m,imm		CMP se r/m,imm
D0	ROL b r/m,1	ROR b r/m,1	RCL b r/m,1	RCR b r/m,1	SHL/SALb r/m,1	SHR b r/m,1		RAR b r/m,1
D1	ROL w r/m,1	RORw r/m,1	RCL w r/m,1	RCR w r/m,1	SHL/SALw r/m,1	SHR w r/m,1		RAR w r/m,1
D2	ROL b r/m,CL	ROR b r/m,CL	RCL b r/m,CL	RCR b r/m,CL	SHL/SALb r/m,CL	SHR b r/m,CL		RAR b r/m,CL
D3	ROL w r/m,CL	ROR w r/m,CL	RCL w r/m,CL	RCR w r/m,CL	SHL/SALw r/m,CL	SHR w r/m,CL		RAR w r/m,CL
F6	TEST b r/m,imm		NOT b r/m	NEG b r/m	MUL b r/m	IMUL b r/m	DIV b r/m	IDIV b r/m
F7	TEST w r/m,imm		NOT w r/m	NEG w r/m	MUL w r/m	IMUL w r/m	DIV w r/m	IDIV w r/m
FE	INC b r/m	DEC b r/m						
FF	INC w r/m	DEC w r/m	CALL intra	CALL inter	JMP intra	JMP inter	PUSH r/m	

TABLE A.3 POSTBYTE *MOD,R/M* FIELDS

r/m	Byte (mod = 11)	Word (mod = 11)	mod = 00	mod = 01	mod = 11
000	AL	AX	BX + SI	BX + SI + disp8	BX + SI + disp16
001	CL	CX	BX + DI	BX + DI + disp8	BX + DI + disp16
010	DL	DX	BP + SI	BP + SI + disp8	BP + SI + disp16
011	BL	BX	BP + DI	BP + DI + disp8	BP + DI + disp16
100	AH	SP	SI	SI + disp8	SI + disp16
101	CH	BP	DI	DI + disp8	DI + disp16
110	DH	SI	Direct	BP + disp8	BP + disp16
111	BH	DI	BX	BX + disp8	BX + disp16

TABLE A.4   POSTBYTE *REG* FIELD

reg	Byte (b)	Word (w)
000	AL	AX
001	CL	CX
010	DL	DX
011	BL	BX
100	AH	SP
101	CH	BP
110	DH	SI
111	BH	DI

TABLE A.5   8086 OPERAND ADDRESSING MODES

Addressing mode	r/m	mod = 00	mod = 01	mod = 10
Direct	110	Direct		
Register indirect	100	SI		
	101	DI		
	111	BX		
Indexed	100		SI + disp8	SI + disp16
	101		DI + disp8	DI + disp16
Based	111		BX + disp8	BX + disp16
Based stack	110		BP + disp8	BP + disp16
Based + indexed	000	BX + SI	BX + SI + disp8	BX + SI + disp16
	001	BX + DI	BX + DI + disp8	BX + DI + disp16
Based + indexed	010	BP + SI	BP + SI + disp8	BP + SI + disp16
Stack	011	BP + DI	BP + DI + disp8	BP + DI + disp16

Appendix B

THE TUTOR MONITOR

The TUTOR monitor will run on a PC-compatible computer containing an 8088, 8086, 80286, 80386, or 80486 microprocessor. The last three microprocessors must be running in the *real* mode (the default) in which they behave like an 8086. The TUTOR monitor is stored in the file *tutor.exe* and can be executed from DOS by typing *tutor*.

When the program is executed, the starting segment address is displayed in *BX* and the starting offset address is displayed in *CX*. In Fig. 9.3, this starting address of TUTOR is shown to be 13A3:00C5. The starting segment address will depend on which version of DOS you are using and whether you have any other resident software in your system. The actual starting address of TUTOR is stored in the type 60H software interrupt vector address. This means that *INT 60H* will execute the TUTOR monitor. The length of the TUTOR monitor is stored in *DX* when TUTOR is first executed. The initial segment of the memory displayed on the TUTOR monitor is the first free memory directly above the memory where TUTOR is stored. This is segment address 174FH in Fig. 9.3, but will likely be different on your computer. However, this will be free memory where you can store your own programs.

Because the TUTOR monitor allows you to look anywhere in memory and change any value you want, you may sometimes inadvertently *bomb* the system. When this happens, you will have to reboot the system. You can usually do this by pressing the *Ctrl-Alt-Del* keys, which will reboot DOS. You will then have to execute the TUTOR monitor again. Sometimes, if you have inadvertently disabled interrupts, the keyboard will be dead and you will have to turn off the computer in order to reboot the system. In this case you will lose all data in RAM, including your program. You should make sure that you always have a copy of your programs on disk before executing any program.

A summary of the TUTOR monitor commands is given at the end of this appendix. The basic operation of the TUTOR monitor is introduced in Chapters 9 to 11. The following commands are described, with examples, at the indicated pages in this book.

/A	Display ASCII characters	page 247
/B	Set breakpoint	page 321
/E	Execute a program	page 251
/G	Change data segment	page 358
/J	Calculate a jump displacement	page 296
/M	Enter hex or ASCII values in memory	page 242
/R	Change the contents of a register	page 233
/S	Store (retrieve) data on disk	page 318
/U	Unassemble a portion of memory on the right side of the display	page 242

The following TUTOR commands are not described elsewhere in the book:

/L   List a disassembled portion of memory

You can disassemble a program on the screen starting at the position cursor by typing /L. The command line will display

```
LIST: P B S
```

If you press *P* (for *Page*), a page of disassembled code will be listed on the screen. Press the forward (right cursor) key → to disassemble a new page. You can continue to press the → key to list a new page. Press the *Enter* key to go back to the TUTOR monitor.

If you want to disassemble only a fixed number of bytes, press */LB*. You will be asked for an ending offset address. This should be the first offset address following the block of memory to be disassembled. When you press *Enter*, only the disassembled block of memory will be displayed on the screen. Press *Enter* to return to the TUTOR monitor.

If you press */LS*, you can scroll through a program by disassembling one line at a time. When you type */LS*, the opcode at the position cursor location is disassembled and displayed on the top of the screen. Pressing the right cursor → key will cause the next instruction to be disassembled. You can continue pressing the → key to disassemble more instructions. Press the *Enter* key to return to the TUTOR monitor.

/P   Print a disassembled portion of memory

Prints a disassembled portion of memory on the printer using the same format as */L*.

/D   Delete a block of bytes

Move the position cursor to the location in memory where bytes are to be deleted. In response to the prompt

```
DELETE: NO. OF BYTES
```

enter the number of bytes to be deleted. The prompt

```
DELETE: ENDING OFFSET ADDRESS
```

will then be displayed. Type the offset address following the last byte to be *moved up* when the deleted bytes are removed. When you press *Enter*, the number of bytes indicated will be deleted, starting at the position cursor, and the remaining bytes up to the ending address will be moved up. Bytes can be deleted only within a single segment.

/F   Find a particular string of bytes

After the prompt

```
FIND: ENTER HEX VALUES
```

enter any number of 2-digit hex values. When you press *Enter*, the cursor will move to the first byte in the sequence. The search occurs only within a single segment.

/I   Insert any number of hex bytes

Move the position cursor to the location in memory where bytes are to be inserted. In response to the prompt

```
INSERT: ENDING OFFSET ADDRESS
```

enter the offset address of the last byte that is to be shifted up in memory as bytes are inserted. Succeeding bytes will be overwritten as bytes are inserted.

After entering the ending address, the prompt

```
ENTER HEX VALUES
```

will appear on the command line. Enter any number of 2-digit hex values. As each byte is entered, it is inserted in memory, all bytes up to the ending address are moved up 1 byte in memory, and the position cursor is advanced to the next byte. Bytes can be inserted only within a single segment.

/T   Transfer a block of bytes

Move the position cursor to the location in memory of the first byte of the block to be transferred. In response to the prompt

```
TRANSFER: DESTINATION SEGMENT ADDRESS
```

enter the *segment* address of the destination. In response to the prompt

```
TRANSFER: DESTINATION OFFSET ADDRESS
```

enter the *offset* address of the destination. The destination address (*segment: offset*) is the address to which the first byte in the block (at the position cursor) is to be moved. After entering the destination address, the prompt

```
TRANSFER: NO. OF BYTES
```

will appear on the command line. Enter the number of bytes to be moved. When you press *Enter*, the block of bytes will be transferred to the new location and the cursor will move to the first byte of this new block. Any number of bytes can be moved either forward or backward in memory. If you try to move data into some parts of memory, such as that occupied by the TUTOR monitor or certain DOS addresses, the computer will *crash* and you will have to reload the TUTOR monitor.

/Q   Quit to DOS

In response to the prompt

```
QUIT: D R
```

pressing *D* will switch to DOS and display the DOS prompt. The memory occupied by TUTOR will be released by DOS. Pressing */QR* will also return to DOS but will keep TUTOR resident in memory. This means that a new .EXE file will be loaded by DOS above TUTOR. Such a program could call TUTOR for the purpose of debugging by executing an *INT 60H* instruction.

/X   Toggles data or stack segment on and off

In response to the prompt

```
SEGMENT ON/OFF: D S
```

pressing *D* will toggle the data segment display on and off. Pressing *S* will toggle the stack segment display on and off.

/Z   Displays the copyright message

```
(c) 1992 by Richard E. Haskell, Inc. v4
```

on the command line. Pressing any key will return to the TUTOR monitor.

8086 TUTOR MONITOR SUMMARY

TABLE B.1   CURSOR KEYS TO SCROLL
THROUGH MEMORY

Key	Function
Right cursor	Advance 1 byte
Left cursor	Back up 1 byte
Down cursor	Advance 1 row
Up cursor	Back up 1 row
PgDn	Advance 7 rows
PgUp	Back up 7 rows
Home	Go to offset address 0000H
> - Go to: Offset or Seg Address	

TABLE B.2   FUNCTION KEYS

F1	Single step
F2	Single step over CALL or INT
F3	Execute breakpoint in loop
Ctrl F6	Execute TUTOR
F7	Help
F9	Reset DS and SP after F10
F10	Do relocation operation on EXE file

TABLE B.3   TUTOR COMMANDS

Command	Function
/A	Turn ASCII on/off
/B	Set breakpoints BREAKPOINT: S N F C S: Set breakpoint at cursor location N: Set breakpoint with no automatic removal F: Find breakpoint C: Clear breakpoint
/D	Delete bytes DELETE: NO. OF BYTES DELETE: ENDING OFFSET ADDRESS + 1
/E	Execute code EXECUTE: A G A: Enter starting address G: Go with address at cursor
/F	Find byte string FIND: ENTER HEX VALUES
/G	Change data segment display DATA SEGMENT: S O D S: ENTER SEGMENT ADDRESS O: ENTER OFFSET ADDRESS D: Display segment DS
/I	Insert bytes INSERT: ENDING OFFSET ADDRESS + 1 ENTER HEX VALUES
/J	Calculate jump displacement JUMP DISPLACEMENT: L S L: Long S: Short Enter destination and offset addresses
/L	Disassemble code LIST: P B S P: Page --> Next page Enter B: Block: Ending offset address + 1 S: Scroll --> Advance Enter
/M	Change memory CHANGE MEMORY: H A H: Hex values A: ASCII values

TABLE B.3   (*cont.*)

Command	Function

/P	Disassemble to printer
	PRINTER: P B S
	    P: Page
	        --> Next page
	        Enter
	    B: Block: Ending offset address + 1
	    S: Scroll
	        --> Advance
	        Enter

/R	Change register value
	REGISTER CHANGE: G P I S F
	    G: Change general register: A B C D
	    P: Change pointer register: S B I
	    I: Change index register: S D
	    S: Change segment register: S D C E
	    F: Change status flags (HEX)

/S	Save or load disk file
	STORAGE: L S
	    L: Load: <pathname>
	    S: Save – No. of hex bytes to save
	        Enter <pathname>

/T	Transfer block of data TRANSFER: DESTINATION SEGMENT ADDRESS TRANSFER: DESTINATION OFFSET ADDRESS TRANSFER: NO. OF BYTES

/U	Unassemble on right of screen
	UNASSEMBLE: P B C
	    P: Page
	    B: Block: Enter ending address + 1
	    C: Clear right half of screen

/Q	Quit to DOS
	QUIT: D R
	    D: Return to DOS
	    R: Terminate and stay resident

/X	Turn data/stack segment on/off
	SEGMENT ON/OFF: D S
	    D: Toggle data segment on/off
	    S: Toggle stack segment on/off

/Z	Copyright (c) 1992 by Richard E. Haskell, Inc. v4 Press any key to return

Appendix C

SUBROUTINE LISTINGS

Listing C.1 - Screen Display Subroutines File: *screen.asm*

```
          title   Screen display subroutines

;         useful key ascii codes
_esc      equ   27
_enter    equ   13
_bksp     equ   8


data      segment       public
kbuf      db    80 dup(?)
bufend    db    ?
vidseg    dw    0b800h                ;video RAM segment
span      dw    ?
sisave    dw    ?
svseg     dw    0
pageno    db    0
data      ends

          public vidseg,stvseg
          public savescr,restscr
          public svinit,relssb,resize
          public delay,tone,beep
          public chrout,mess,chrout1,getatt
          public setcur,rdcurs,inccur,deccur
```

Listing C.1 - *(cont.)*

```
                public clrscn,home,tab,chgatt
                public invatt,blank,clrwin,curoff
                public chrprt,hexasc,pbyte
                public togatt,crlf,mess2,fmess
                public getkey,dokey,invline
                public query,kbuf,bufend,span
                public enterq,sisave,pageno

code            segment public
                assume cs:code,ds:data

;               set video RAM segment address
stvseg          proc    near
                push    ax
                mov     ah,15
                int     10h                 ;get video state
                cmp     al,7                ;if monochrome
                jne     svg1
                mov     vidseg,0b000h       ; vidseg=b000
                jmp     svg2                ;else
svg1:           mov     vidseg,0b800h       ; vidseg=b800
svg2:           pop     ax
                ret
stvseg          endp

;               display char with current attribute
chrout1         proc    near
                push    ax
                push    bx
                push    ax                  ;save char
                mov     bh,pageno           ;page 0
                mov     ah,8
                int     10h                 ;read attribute
                mov     bl,ah
                pop     ax                  ;get char
                call    chrout              ;& display
                pop     bx
                pop     ax
                ret
chrout1         endp

                page
;               character output
chrout          proc    near
                push    ax
                push    bx                  ;save regs
                push    cx
                push    dx
                push    ax
                mov     bh,pageno
                mov     ah,3
                int     10h                 ;read cursor
```

Listing   C.1 - *(cont.)*

```
                mov     cx,1
                pop     ax              ;get char
                cmp     al,0dh          ;check for CR
                je      chr1
                cmp     al,20h          ;ignore ctrl
                jb      chr3            ; characters
                mov     ah,9
                int     10h             ;write char/att
                inc     dl              ;inc cursor
                cmp     dl,80           ;if end of line
                jb      chr2
chr1:           mov     dl,0            ;do CR
                inc     dh              ; LF
                cmp     dh,25           ;if end of
                jb      chr2            ; screen
                mov     cx,0            ;scroll
                mov     dx,184fh        ; entire
                mov     bh,07h          ; screen
                mov     ax,0601h        ; up
                int     10h             ; 1 line
                mov     dx,1800h        ;CR
                mov     bh,pageno       ;reset page no.
chr2:           mov     ah,2
                int     10h             ;set new cursor
chr3:           pop     dx              ;restore regs
                pop     cx
                pop     bx
                pop     ax
                ret
chrout          endp

                page
;               message display
;               si -> message in data segment
;               dh = row, dl = col
;               bl = attribute of message
mess            proc    near
                push    ax
                push    bx
                push    cx
                push    si
                mov     bh,pageno       ;page 0
                mov     ah,2            ;set cursor
                int     10h             ; at dh,dl
                mov     cx,1            ;1 character
                cld                     ;si increases
ms1:            lodsb                   ;[si]-->al
                cmp     al,0            ;message done?
                je      ms2             ;if so, return
                call    chrout          ;display char
                jmp     ms1             ;and continue
```

Listing   C.1 - *(cont.)*

```
ms2:            pop     si
                pop     cx
                pop     bx
                pop     ax
                ret
mess            endp

;               message display with current attribute
;               at current cursor positon
;               si -> message in data segment
mess2           proc    near
                push    ax
                push    bx
                push    dx
                call    rdcurs          ;read cursor
                mov     bh,pageno       ;page 0
                mov     ah,8
                int     10h             ;read attribute
                mov     bl,ah
                call    mess            ;display mess
                pop     dx
                pop     bx
                pop     ax
                ret
mess2           endp

;               fast message routine
;               si -> message in data segment
;               dh = row, dl = col
;               bl = attribute of message
fmess           proc    near
                push    ax
                push    di
                call    setdi           ;set di->vidRAM offset
                mov     ah,bl           ;ah=attribute
                mov     es,vidseg       ;es->video RAM
                cld
fms1:           lodsb
                cmp     al,0
                je      fms2
                stosw
                jmp     fms1
fms2:           pop     di
                pop     ax
                ret
fmess           endp

;               set di to video RAM offset address
;               di = row * 160 + col
setdi           proc    near
                push    cx
                mov     ah,0
```

Listing   C.1 - *(cont.)*

```
                mov     al,dh           ;dx=row
                mov     cl,5
                shl     ax,cl           ;ax=32*row
                mov     di,ax           ;di=32*row
                shl     ax,1
                shl     ax,1            ;dx=128*row
                add     di,ax           ;di=160*row
                mov     ah,0
                mov     al,dl           ;dx=col
                shl     ax,1            ;ax=2*col
                add     di,ax           ;di=video offset
                pop     cx
                ret
setdi           endp

                page
;               set cursor at dx=row:col
setcur          proc    near
                push    ax
                push    bx
                mov     bh,pageno       ;page 0
                mov     ah,2
                int     10h             ;set cursor
                pop     bx
                pop     ax
                ret
setcur          endp

;               read cursor
;               output:  dh=row   dl=col
rdcurs          proc    near
                push    ax
                push    bx
                push    cx
                mov     bh,pageno       ;page 0
                mov     ah,3
                int     10h             ;read cursor
                pop     cx
                pop     bx
                pop     ax
                ret
rdcurs          endp

;               inc cursor
inccur          proc    near
                push    dx
                call    rdcurs          ;read cursor
                inc     dl              ;inc dl
                call    setcur          ;set cursor
                pop     dx
                ret
inccur          endp
```

Listing   C.1 - *(cont.)*

```
;            dec cursor
deccur       proc    near
             push    dx
             call    rdcurs          ;read cursor
             dec     dl              ;inc dl
             call    setcur          ;set cursor
             pop     dx
             ret
deccur       endp


             page
;            clear screen
clrscn       proc    near
             push    ax
             mov     ah,15           ;read vid mode
             int     10h
             mov     ah,0            ;and set again
             int     10h
             pop     ax
             ret
clrscn       endp


;            home cursor
home         proc    near
             push    dx
             mov     dx,0            ;row=0 col=0
             call    setcur
             pop     dx
             ret
home         endp


;            carriage return line feed
crlf         proc    near
             push    ax
             push    bx
             push    cx
             push    dx
             call    rdcurs          ;read cursor
             mov     dl,0            ;do CR
             inc     dh              ; LF
             cmp     dh,25           ;if end of
             jb      cr1             ; screen
             mov     cx,0            ;scroll
             mov     dx,184fh        ; entire
             mov     bh,07h          ; screen
             mov     ax,0601h        ; up
             int     10h             ; 1 line
             mov     dx,1800h        ;CR
             mov     bh,pageno       ;page 0
cr1:         call    setcur          ;set cursor
             pop     dx
             pop     cx
```

Listing   C.1 - *(cont.)*

```
                pop     bx
                pop     ax
                ret
crlf            endp

                page
;               tab
tab             proc    near
                push    ax
                push    bx
                push    dx
                mov     bh,pageno
                mov     ah,3            ;read cursor
                int     10h
                add     dl,5            ;mov cursor +5
                mov     ah,2
                int     10h             ;set cursor
                pop     dx
                pop     bx
                pop     ax
                ret
tab             endp

;               get attribute of character at
;                dx = row:col and store in bl
getatt          proc    near
                push    ax
                call    setcur          ;set cursor
                mov     bh,pageno       ;page 0
                mov     ah,8            ;read char/attr
                int     10h
                mov     bl,ah           ;bl = attrib
                pop     ax
                ret
getatt          endp

;               change attribute of character at
;                current cursor position to bl
chgatt          proc    near
                push    ax
                push    bx
                push    cx
                mov     bh,pageno       ;page 0
                mov     ah,8            ;read char/attr
                int     10h
                mov     cx,1
                mov     ah,9
                int     10h             ;write char/att
                pop     cx
                pop     bx
                pop     ax
                ret
chgatt          endp
```

Listing   C.1 - *(cont.)*

```
            page
;           invert attribute of word at current
;            cursor position
invatt      proc    near
            push    ax
            push    bx
            push    cx
            mov     bh,pageno       ;page 0
ia1:        mov     ah,8            ;read char/attr
            int     10h
            cmp     al,20h          ;if blank
            je      ia4             ; quit
            cmp     ah,07h          ;if normal
            jne     ia2
            mov     bl,70h          ;make inverse
            jmp     ia3             ;else
ia2:        mov     bl,07h          ;make normal
ia3:        mov     cx,1
            mov     ah,9
            int     10h             ;write char/att
            call    inccur          ;adv cursor
            jmp     ia1             ;repeat
ia4:        pop     cx
            pop     bx
            pop     ax
            ret
invatt      endp


;           toggle attribute of character
;           at current cursor position
togatt      proc    near
            push    ax
            push    bx
            push    cx
            mov     bh,pageno       ;page 0
            mov     ah,8            ;read char/attr
            int     10h
            cmp     ah,07h          ;if normal
            jne     ta1
            mov     bl,70h          ;make inverse
            jmp     ta2             ;else
ta1:        mov     bl,07h          ;make normal
ta2:        mov     cx,1
            mov     ah,9
            int     10h             ;write char/att
            pop     cx
            pop     bx
            pop     ax
            ret
togatt      endp
```

Listing   C.1 - (*cont.*)

```
            page
;           invert line of text at
;           current cursor position
invline     proc    near
            push    ax
ivl1:       call    invatt          ;invert word
            call    togatt          ;invert blank
            call    inccur          ;inc cursor
            mov     ah,8            ;read chr/attr
            int     10h
            cmp     al,20h          ;repeat until
            jne     ivl1            ;blank
            pop     ax
            ret
invline     endp


;           blank line dh
blank       proc    near
            push    ax
            push    bx
            push    cx
            push    dx
            mov     dl,0            ;col 0
            call    setcur          ;set cursor
            mov     cx,80           ;80 blanks
            mov     al,20h          ;ascii blank
            mov     bl,07h          ;normal video
            mov     ah,9
            int     10h             ;print all 80
            pop     dx
            pop     cx
            pop     bx
            pop     ax
            ret
blank       endp


;           clear window
;           ch:cl = row:col of upper left corner
;           dh:dl = row:col of lower right corner
clrwin      proc    near
            push    ax
            push    bx
            mov     bh,7            ;normal attr
            mov     ah,6            ;scroll func
            mov     al,0            ;blank window
            int     10h
            pop     bx
            pop     ax
            ret
clrwin      endp
```

Listing C.1 - *(cont.)*

```
            page
;           hide cursor
curoff      proc    near
            push    ax
            push    bx
            push    dx
            mov     bh,pageno       ;page 0
            mov     dh,25           ;row 25
            mov     dl,0            ;col 0
            mov     ah,2            ;set cursor
            int     10h             ; off screen
            pop     dx
            pop     bx
            pop     ax
            ret
curoff      endp

;           print a char using teletype mode
chrprt      proc    near
            push    ax
            push    bx
            mov     bh,pageno       ;page 0
            mov     ah,0eh          ;write char in
            int     10h             ; al on screen
            pop     bx
            pop     ax
            ret
chrprt      endp

;           hex to ascii conversion
hexasc      proc    near
            cmp     al,0ah          ;if >= 0ah
            jb      ha1
            add     al,37h          ;add 37h
            jmp     ha2
ha1:        add     al,30h          ;else add 30h
ha2:        ret
hexasc      endp

            page
;           print a byte
pbyte       proc    near
            push    ax
            push    cx
            push    ax              ;save byte
            mov     cl,4
            shr     al,cl           ;hi nibble
            call    hexasc          ;conv to ascii
            call    chrprt          ;print char
            pop     ax              ;get byte
            and     al,0fh          ;lo nibble
```

Listing C.1 - (*cont.*)

```
                call    hexasc          ;con to ascii
                call    chrprt          ;print char
                mov     al,20h          ;print blank
                call    chrprt
                pop     cx
                pop     ax
                ret
pbyte           endp

;               delay
;               input: ax = no. of ticks to delay
;                      18.2 ticks per second
delay           proc    near
                push    ax              ;save regs
                push    cx
                push    dx
                push    ax              ;push #ticks
                mov     ah,0            ;time of day
                int     1Ah             ;  interrupt
                push    cx              ;push hi count
                push    dx              ;push lo count
                mov     bp,sp           ;bp -> lo count
dly1:           mov     ah,0
                int     1Ah             ;get new count
                sub     dx,[bp]
                sbb     cx,2[bp]        ;calc diff
                cmp     dx,4[bp]        ;repeat until
                jb      dly1            ;diff > #ticks
                add     sp,6            ;fix stack
                pop     dx              ;restore regs
                pop     cx
                pop     ax
                ret
delay           endp

                page
;               make a tone
;               dx = pitch of tone
;               bx = length of tone
tone            proc    near
                push    ax              ;save regs
                push    bx
                push    cx
                push    dx
                mov     al,0b6h
                out     43h,al          ;B6 in ctrl reg
                mov     al,dl           ;LSB pitch ->
                out     42h,al          ; counter reg
                mov     al,dh           ;MSB pitch ->
                out     42h,al          ; counter reg
                in      al,61h          ;PPI port B
```

Listing   C.1 - *(cont.)*

```
                mov     ah,al                   ; -> AH
                or      al,03h                  ;speaker on
                out     61h,al                  ;set bits 0,1
                push    ax
                mov     ax,bx                   ;delay bx ticks
                call    delay
                pop     ax
                mov     al,ah                   ;speaker off
                out     61h,al
                pop     dx                      ;restore regs
                pop     cx
                pop     bx
                pop     ax
                ret
tone            endp

;               beep a tone
beep            proc    near
                push    bx
                push    dx
                mov     dx,0300h                ;set pitch
                mov     bx,4                    ;delay .22 s
                call    tone
                pop     dx
                pop     bx
                ret
beep            endp

                page
;               wait for key and get key value
;               output:     al = ascii code of key
;                           function & cursor keys have
;                           al = scan code OR 80H
getkey          proc    near
gk1:            mov     ah,0
                int     16h                     ;wait for key
                cmp     ah,0                    ;ignore ^break
                je      gk1                     ;and Alt-keypd
                cmp     al,0
                jne     gk2                     ;if ascii = 0
                mov     al,ah                   ;use scan code
                or      al,80h                  ; OR 80h
gk2:            ret
getkey          endp

;               process a key
;               input: al = ascii code of key
;                      di -> jump table
;                      dx -> default subroutine
dokey           proc    near
```

Listing   C.1 - (*cont.*)

```
dk1:        cmp     al,cs:[di]          ;chk next code
            jne     dk2                 ;if a match
            call    word ptr cs:1[di]   ;call sub
            ret                         ;and quit
dk2:        cmp     byte ptr cs:[di],0  ;if not
            je      dk3                 ;end of table
            add     di,3                ;chk next entry
            jmp     dk1                 ; in table
dk3:        call    dx                  ;else call
            ret                         ;default sub
dokey       endp


            page
;           buffered keyboard input
;           at current cursor position
;           input asciiz string is at kbuf
;           # of character entered at span
;           output: none
query       proc    near
            mov     sisave,si
            mov     si,offset kbuf      ;si->kbuf
qy1:        call    getkey              ;get key
            mov     di,offset jmptbq
            mov     dx,offset tobuff    ;default
            call    dokey               ;process key
            jmp     qy1
query       endp


;           query jump table
jmptbq      db      _bksp               ;backspace
            dw      backsp
            db      _enter              ;enter
            dw      enterq
            db      _esc                ;esc
            dw      quit
            db      0


;           display & store char in kbuf
tobuff      proc    near
            cmp     si,offset bufend
            jb      tb1                 ;if end.of.buf
            call    beep                ; beep &
            ret                         ; quit
tb1:        mov     [si],al             ;store char
            inc     si                  ;inc ptr
            call    chrout1             ;display char
            ret
tobuff      endp

            page
;           backspace
```

Listing   C.1 - *(cont.)*

```
backsp     proc    near
           cmp     si,offset kbuf
           ja      bk1                     ;if 1st char
           call    beep                    ; beep & ret
           ret
bk1:       dec si                          ;back up & put
           mov     byte ptr [si],20h       ;20h in kbuf
           call    deccur                  ;back up & put
           mov     al,20h                  ;blank on
           call    chrout1                 ;screen
           call    deccur
           ret
backsp     endp

;          enter from query
;          exits from query
enterq     proc    near
           mov     byte ptr [si],0         ;make asciiz
           sub     si,offset kbuf          ;store #char
           mov     span,si                 ;in span
           mov     si,sisave               ;restore si
           pop     ax                      ;>enterq
           pop     ax                      ;>dokey
           ret                             ;>query
enterq     endp

           page
;          resize memory
resize     proc    near
           mov     ax,es                   ;ax=psp seg
           mov     bx,ss                   ;bx=stack seg
           sub     bx,ax                   ;reserve psp-ss
           add     bx,10                   ; + stack size
           mov     ah,4Ah
           int     21h                     ;resize mem
           ret
resize     endp

;          allocate save screen buffer
svinit     proc    near
           mov     svseg,0                 ;svseg = 0
           mov     bx,1000                 ;request 16000
           mov     ah,48h                  ; bytes
           int     21h
           jc      sv1                     ;if no error
           mov     svseg,ax                ;svseg = seg
sv1:       ret
svinit     endp

;          release save screen buffer
```

Listing   C.1 - (*cont.*)

```
relssb       proc    near
             cmp     svseg,0                  ;if allocated
             je      rel1
             mov     ax,svseg                 ;deallocate
             mov     es,ax                    ;es = svseg
             mov     ah,49h
             int     21h                      ;release mem
rel1:        ret
relssb       endp


             page
 ;           save screen
 savescr     proc    near
             push    ax                       ;save regs
             push    cx
             push    si
             push    di
             push    ds
             push    es
             cmp     svseg,0                  ;if buff exists
             je      svsc3
             std                              ;move 12000
             mov     ax,svseg                 ; bytes up
             mov     ds,ax                    ; 4000 bytes
             mov     es,ax                    ; to make hole
             mov     cx,6000                  ; in buffer
             mov     si,11998
             mov     di,15998
             rep movsw
             mov     ah,15
             int     10h                      ;get video state
             cmp     al,7
             je      svsc1                    ;set ax =
             mov     ax,0b800h                ; video ram
             jmp     svsc2                    ; segment
svsc1:       mov     ax,0b000h
svsc2:       mov     ds,ax                    ; to svseg
             mov     si,0                     ; buffer
             mov     di,0
             mov     cx,2000
             cld
             rep movsw
svsc3:       pop     es                       ;restore regs
             pop     ds
             pop     di
             pop     si
             pop     cx
             pop     ax
             ret
savescr      endp
```

Listing C.1 - *(cont.)*

```
            page
;           restore screen
restscr     proc    near
            push    ax                          ;save regs
            push    cx
            push    si
            push    di
            push    ds
            push    es
            cmp     svseg,0                     ;if buff exists
            je      rsts3
            mov     ah,15
            int     10h                         ;get video state
            cmp     al,7
            je      rsts1                       ;set ax =
            mov     ax,0b800h                   ; video ram
            jmp     rsts2                       ; segment
rsts1:      mov     ax,0b000h                   ;move 1st 4000
rsts2:      mov     es,ax                       ; bytes from
            mov     ax,svseg                    ; svseg buffer
            mov     ds,ax                       ; to tv ram
            mov     si,0
            mov     di,0
            mov     cx,2000
            cld
            rep movsw
            mov     ax,data
            mov     ds,ax                       ;ds = data
            mov     ax,svseg                    ;move last
            mov     es,ax                       ; 12000 bytes
            mov     ds,ax                       ; in buffer
            mov     si,4000                     ; down 4000
            mov     di,0                        ; bytes
            mov     cx,6000
            rep movsw
rsts3:      pop     es                          ;restore regs
            pop     ds
            pop     di
            pop     si
            pop     cx
            pop     ax
            ret
restscr     endp

;           quit to dos
quit        proc    near
            mov     ax,4C00h
            int     21h
quit        endp

code        ends
            end
```

Listing   C.2 - Disk Subroutines   File: *disk.asm*

```
title       DOS subroutines

data        segment        public
handle      dw     ?
bytbuf      db     ?
fnmsg       db     'Enter filename: ',0
em1         db     'Disk open error: ',0
em2         db     'Disk close error: ',0
em3         db     'Disk read error: ',0
em4         db     'Disk write error: ',0
em5         db     'Disk file error: ',0
data        ends


            extrn   mess:near,chrout:near,beep:near
            extrn   mess2:near,setcur:near
            extrn   curoff:near,pbyte:near
            extrn   clrscn:near,tab:near,query:near
            extrn   kbuf:byte,bufend:byte
            extrn   span:word,chrprt:near
            public open,close,read,write,rewind
            public gtbyte
            public sndbyte,openfn,movptr
            public getlen,sndcrlf,create,handle


            code    segment public
            assume cs:code,ds:data


;           open or create file
;           input:  dx -> asciiz string
;           output: bx = handle
open        proc    near
            push    cx
            mov     al,2                ;read & write
            mov     ah,3dh
            int     21h                 ;open file
            jnc     op2
            cmp     ax,2                ;if file
            jne     op1                 ; not found
            mov     ah,3ch              ;create
            mov     cx,0                ; normal attr
            int     21h                 ; file
            jnc     op2
op1:        call    open_err            ;error mess
            stc
            jmp     op3
op2:        mov     bx,ax               ;bx=handle
```

Listing   C.2 - *(cont.)*

```
op3:        pop     cx
            ret
open        endp

;           enter filename and open
;           input:    none
;           output:   handle is in 'handle'
;                     carry = 1 if not opened
openfn      proc    near
            push    bx
            push    dx
            push    si
            mov     si,offset fnmsg
            call    mess1                   ;display mess
            call    query                   ;enter filename
            cmp     span,0                  ;if no chars
            jne     of0                     ; set carry
            stc                             ; and quit
            jmp     of1
of0:        mov     dx,offset kbuf
            call    open                    ;open it
            jc      of1                     ;if error,quit
            mov     handle,bx               ;store handle
of1:        pop     si
            pop     dx
            pop     bx
            ret
openfn      endp

;           close file
;           input:  bx = handle
close       proc    near
            mov     ah,3eh
            int     21h                     ;close file
            jnc     cl1                     ;if error
            call    close_err               ; print it
            stc
cl1:        ret
close       endp

;           create file
;           (set length to zero to write over)
;           input:    dx -> asciiz string
;           output:   bx = handle
create      proc    near
            push    cx
```

Listing C.2 - *(cont.)*

```
            mov     ah,3ch                  ;create
            mov     cx,0                    ; normal attr
            int     21h                     ; file
            jnc     ct2
ct1:        call    open_err                ;error mess
            stc
            jmp     ct3
ct2:        mov     bx,ax                   ;bx=handle
ct3:        pop     cx
            ret
create      endp

;           read file
;           input:    bx = handle
;                     cx = # of bytes to read
;                     dx -> buffer address
;           output:   ax = # of bytes read
;                     ax = 0 if EOF
read        proc    near
            mov     ah,3fh
            int     21h                     ;read file
            jnc     rd1                     ;if error
            call    read_err                ; print it
            stc
rd1:        ret
read        endp

;           write file
;           input:    bx = handle
;                     cx = # of bytes to write
;                     dx -> buffer address
write       proc    near
            mov     ah,40h
            int     21h                     ;write file
            jnc     wt1                     ;if error
            call    write_err               ; print it
            stc
wt1:        ret
write       endp

;           get next byte
;           input:    bx = handle
;           output:   al = byte
;                     carry = 1 if EOF
gtbyte      proc    near
            push    cx
```

Listing C.2 - *(cont.)*

```
                push    dx
                mov     cx,1                    ;read 1 byte
                mov     dx,offset bytbuf
                call    read
                cmp     ax,0                    ;if EOF
                jne     gb1
                stc                             ; set carry
                jmp     gb2                     ;else
gb1:            mov     al,bytbuf               ;al=byte
                clc                             ;clear carry
gb2:            pop     dx
                pop     cx
                ret
gtbyte          endp

;               send byte
;               input:    bx = handle
;                         al = byte
sndbyte         proc    near
                push    cx
                push    dx
                mov     bytbuf,al               ;bytbuf=byte
                mov     dx,offset bytbuf
                mov     cx,1                    ;1 byte
                call    write                   ;send it
                pop     dx
                pop     cx
                ret
sndbyte         endp


;               send crlf
sndcrlf         proc    near
                mov     al,13                   ;send cr
                call    sndbyte
                mov     al,10                   ;send lf
                call    sndbyte
                ret
sndcrlf         endp


;               move pointer
;               input:    bx = handle
;                         cx:dx = offset value
;                         al = 0 - start of file + offset
;                              1 - inc ptr by offset
;               output:   dx:ax = new value of ptr
```

Listing C.2 - *(cont.)*

```
movptr      proc    near
            mov     ah,42h                ;move ptr
            int     21h
            jnc     mpt1
            call    ptr_err
            stc
mpt1:       ret
movptr      endp


;           rewind file
;           input:    bx = handle
rewind      proc    near
            push    cx
            push    dx
            mov     cx,0
            mov     dx,0                  ;offset=0
            mov     al,0                  ;mov ptr from
            mov     ah,42h                ; start of file
            int     21h
            jnc     rw1                   ;if error
            call    ptr_err               ; print it
            stc
rw1:        pop     dx
            pop     cx
            ret
rewind      endp


;           get length of file
;           input:    bx = handle
;           output:   dx:ax = length of file
getlen      proc    near
            push    cx
            mov     cx,0
            mov     dx,0                  ;offset=0
            mov     al,2                  ;mov ptr from
            mov     ah,42h                ; end of file
            int     21h
            jnc     gl1                   ;if error
            call    ptr_err               ; print it
            stc
gl1:        pop     cx
            ret
getlen      endp


;           disk errors
open_err proc       near
```

Listing   C.2 - *(cont.)*

```
                push    bx
                push    dx
                push    si
                call    beep
                mov     bx,ax                   ;bx=err code
                mov     dx,1801h                ;bottom line
                mov     si,offset em1           ;print
                call    mess2                   ; error message
                mov     al,bl
                call    pbyte                   ;print error code
                mov     al,'H'
                call    chrprt
                pop     si
                pop     dx
                pop     bx
                ret
open_err endp

close_err proc  near
                push    bx
                push    dx
                push    si
                call    beep
                mov     bx,ax                   ;bx=err code
                mov     dx,1801h                ;bottom line
                mov     si,offset em2           ;print
                call    mess2                   ; error message
                mov     al,bl
                call    pbyte                   ;print error code
                mov     al,'H'
                call    chrprt
                pop     si
                pop     dx
                pop     bx
                ret
close_err endp

read_err  proc  near
                push    bx
                push    dx
                push    si
                call    beep
                mov     bx,ax                   ;bx=err code
                mov     dx,1801h                ;bottom line
                mov     si,offset em3           ;print
                call    mess2                   ; error message
                mov     al,bl
                call    pbyte                   ;print error code
```

Listing   C.2 - *(cont.)*

```
            mov     al,'H'
            call    chrprt
            pop     si
            pop     dx
            pop     bx
            ret
read_err endp

write_err proc    near
            push    bx
            push    dx
            push    si
            call    beep
            mov     bx,ax               ;bx=err code
            mov     dx,1801h            ;bottom line
            mov     si,offset em4       ;print
            call    mess2               ; error message
            mov     al,bl
            call    pbyte               ;print error code
            mov     al,'H'
            call    chrprt
            pop     si
            pop     dx
            pop     bx
            ret
write_err endp

ptr_err    proc    near
            push    bx
            push    dx
            push    si
            call    beep
            mov     bx,ax               ;bx=err code
            mov     dx,1801h            ;bottom line
            mov     si,offset em5       ;print
            call    mess2               ; error message
            mov     al,bl
            call    pbyte               ;print error code
            mov     al,'H'
            call    chrprt
            pop     si
            pop     dx
            pop     bx
            ret
ptr_err    endp

code       ends
           end
```

Listing C.3 - Hercules Graphics Subroutines   File: *graph.asm*

```
        title   hercules graphics subroutines

        public line,plot,stherc,erase
        public messg,charwt,sinax,cosax
        public cpconv

data            segment     public
bit9flg         db      ?
video_seg       dw      0b000h                  ;video ram seg
vidtbl          db      53,45,46,7,91,2,87,87
                db      2,3,0,0,0,0,0,0


row_table       label word                      ;define row add
        line_num = 0
        rept 87                                 ;348/4
                dw      line_num * 90
                dw      2000h + line_num * 90
                dw      4000h + line_num * 90
                dw      6000h + line_num * 90
                line_num = line_num + 1     ;next row
        endm


sintbl  dw      00000,00175,00349,00524,00698       ;00 - 04
        dw      00872,01045,01219,01392,01571       ;05 - 09
        dw      01736,01908,02079,02250,02419       ;10 - 14
        dw      02588,02756,02924,03090,03256       ;15 - 19
        dw      03420,03584,03746,03907,04076       ;20 - 24
        dw      04226,04384,04540,04695,04848       ;25 - 29
        dw      05000,05150,05299,05446,05592       ;30 - 34
        dw      05736,05878,06018,06157,06293       ;35 - 39
        dw      06428,06561,06691,06820,06947       ;40 - 44
        dw      07071,07193,07314,07431,07547       ;45 - 49
        dw      07660,07771,07880,07986,08090       ;50 - 54
        dw      08192,08290,08387,08480,08572       ;55 - 59
        dw      08660,08746,08829,08910,08988       ;60 - 64
        dw      09063,09135,09205,09272,09336       ;65 - 69
        dw      09397,09455,09511,09563,09613       ;70 - 74
        dw      09659,09703,09744,09781,09816       ;75 - 79
        dw      09848,09877,09903,09925,09945       ;80 - 84
        dw      09962,09976,09986,09994,09998       ;85 - 89
        dw      10000                               ;90
axisv   dw      0,10000,0,-10000
signs   db      -1,-1,0,0
```

Listing C.3 - *(cont.)*

```
;        Monochrome display character set
;        16 bytes per character
;        ascii 00h - 0Fh
charset  db     000H,000H,000H,000H,000H,000H,000H,000H
         db     000H,000H,000H,000H,000H,000H,000H,000H
         db     000H,000H,07EH,081H,0A5H,081H,081H,0BDH
         db     099H,081H,07EH,000H,000H,000H,000H,000H
         db     000H,000H,07EH,0FFH,0DBH,0FFH,0FFH,0C3H
         db     0E7H,0FFH,07EH,000H,000H,000H,000H,000H
         db     000H,000H,000H,036H,07FH,07FH,07FH,07FH
         db     03EH,01CH,008H,000H,000H,000H,000H,000H
         db     000H,000H,000H,008H,01CH,03EH,07FH,03EH
         db     01CH,008H,000H,000H,000H,000H,000H,000H
         db     000H,000H,018H,03CH,03CH,0E7H,0E7H,0E7H
         db     018H,018H,03CH,000H,000H,000H,000H,000H
         db     000H,000H,018H,03CH,07EH,0FFH,0FFH,07EH
         db     018H,018H,03CH,000H,000H,000H,000H,000H
         db     000H,000H,000H,000H,000H,018H,03CH,03CH
         db     018H,000H,000H,000H,000H,000H,000H,000H
         db     0FFH,0FFH,0FFH,0FFH,0FFH,0E7H,0C3H,0C3H
         db     0E7H,0FFH,0FFH,0FFH,0FFH,0FFH,000H,000H
         db     000H,000H,000H,000H,03CH,066H,042H,042H
         db     066H,03CH,000H,000H,000H,000H,000H,000H
         db     0FFH,0FFH,0FFH,0FFH,0C3H,099H,0BDH,0BDH
         db     099H,0C3H,0FFH,0FFH,0FFH,0FFH,000H,000H
         db     000H,000H,00FH,007H,00DH,019H,03CH,066H
         db     066H,066H,03CH,000H,000H,000H,000H,000H
         db     000H,000H,03CH,066H,066H,066H,03CH,018H
         db     07EH,018H,018H,000H,000H,000H,000H,000H
         db     000H,000H,03FH,033H,03FH,030H,030H,030H
         db     070H,0F0H,0E0H,000H,000H,000H,000H,000H
         db     000H,000H,07FH,063H,07FH,063H,063H,063H
         db     067H,0E7H,0E6H,0C0H,000H,000H,000H,000H
         db     000H,000H,018H,018H,0DBH,03CH,0E7H,03CH
         db     0DBH,018H,018H,000H,000H,000H,000H,000H
;        ascii 10h - 1Fh
         db     000H,000H,040H,060H,070H,07CH,07FH,07CH
         db     070H,060H,040H,000H,000H,000H,000H,000H
         db     000H,000H,001H,003H,007H,01FH,07FH,01FH
         db     007H,003H,001H,000H,000H,000H,000H,000H
         db     000H,000H,018H,03CH,07EH,018H,018H,018H
         db     07EH,03CH,018H,000H,000H,000H,000H,000H
         db     000H,000H,033H,033H,033H,033H,033H,033H
         db     000H,033H,033H,000H,000H,000H,000H,000H
         db     000H,000H,07FH,0DBH,0DBH,0DBH,07BH,01BH
         db     01BH,01BH,01BH,000H,000H,000H,000H,000H
```

Listing C.3 - (*cont.*)

```
        db      000H,03EH,063H,030H,01CH,036H,063H,063H
        db      036H,01CH,006H,063H,03EH,000H,000H,000H
        db      000H,000H,000H,000H,000H,000H,000H,000H
        db      07FH,07FH,07FH,000H,000H,000H,000H,000H
        db      000H,000H,018H,03CH,07EH,018H,018H,018H
        db      07EH,03CH,018H,07EH,000H,000H,000H,000H
        db      000H,000H,018H,03CH,07EH,018H,018H,018H
        db      018H,018H,018H,000H,000H,000H,000H,000H
        db      000H,000H,018H,018H,018H,018H,018H,018H
        db      07EH,03CH,018H,000H,000H,000H,000H,000H
        db      000H,000H,000H,000H,00CH,006H,07FH,006H
        db      00CH,000H,000H,000H,000H,000H,000H,000H
        db      000H,000H,000H,000H,018H,030H,07FH,030H
        db      018H,000H,000H,000H,000H,000H,000H,000H
        db      000H,000H,000H,000H,000H,060H,060H,060H
        db      07FH,000H,000H,000H,000H,000H,000H,000H
        db      000H,000H,000H,000H,024H,066H,0FFH,066H
        db      024H,000H,000H,000H,000H,000H,000H,000H
        db      000H,000H,000H,008H,01CH,01CH,03EH,03EH
        db      07FH,07FH,000H,000H,000H,000H,000H,000H
        db      000H,000H,000H,07FH,07FH,03EH,03EH,01CH
        db      01CH,008H,000H,000H,000H,000H,000H,000H
;       ascii 20h - 2Fh  blank - '/'
        db      000H,000H,000H,000H,000H,000H,000H,000H
        db      000H,000H,000H,000H,000H,000H,000H,000H
        db      000H,000H,018H,03CH,03CH,03CH,018H,018H
        db      000H,018H,018H,000H,000H,000H,000H,000H
        db      000H,063H,063H,063H,022H,000H,000H,000H
        db      000H,000H,000H,000H,000H,000H,000H,000H
        db      000H,000H,036H,036H,07FH,036H,036H,036H
        db      07FH,036H,036H,000H,000H,000H,000H,000H
        db      00CH,00CH,03EH,063H,061H,060H,03EH,003H
        db      043H,063H,03EH,00CH,00CH,000H,000H,000H
        db      000H,000H,000H,000H,061H,063H,006H,00CH
        db      018H,033H,063H,000H,000H,000H,000H,000H
        db      000H,000H,01CH,036H,036H,01CH,03BH,06EH
        db      066H,066H,03BH,000H,000H,000H,000H,000H
        db      000H,030H,030H,030H,060H,000H,000H,000H
        db      000H,000H,000H,000H,000H,000H,000H,000H
        db      000H,000H,00CH,018H,030H,030H,030H,030H
        db      030H,018H,00CH,000H,000H,000H,000H,000H
        db      000H,000H,018H,00CH,006H,006H,006H,006H
        db      006H,00CH,018H,000H,000H,000H,000H,000H
        db      000H,000H,000H,000H,066H,03CH,0FFH,03CH
        db      066H,000H,000H,000H,000H,000H,000H,000H
        db      000H,000H,000H,018H,018H,018H,0FFH,018H
```

Listing C.3 - *(cont.)*

```
        db      018H,018H,000H,000H,000H,000H,000H,000H
        db      000H,000H,000H,000H,000H,000H,000H,000H
        db      018H,018H,018H,030H,000H,000H,000H,000H
        db      000H,000H,000H,000H,000H,000H,0FFH,000H
        db      000H,000H,000H,000H,000H,000H,000H,000H
        db      000H,000H,000H,000H,000H,000H,000H,000H
        db      000H,018H,018H,000H,000H,000H,000H,000H
        db      000H,000H,001H,003H,006H,00CH,018H,030H
        db      060H,040H,000H,000H,000H,000H,000H,000H
;       ascii  30h - 3Fh   '0' - '?'
        db      000H,000H,03EH,063H,067H,06FH,07BH,073H
        db      063H,063H,03EH,000H,000H,000H,000H,000H
        db      000H,000H,00CH,01CH,03CH,00CH,00CH,00CH
        db      00CH,00CH,03FH,000H,000H,000H,000H,000H
        db      000H,000H,03EH,063H,003H,006H,00CH,018H
        db      030H,063H,07FH,000H,000H,000H,000H,000H
        db      000H,000H,03EH,063H,003H,003H,01EH,003H
        db      003H,063H,03EH,000H,000H,000H,000H,000H
        db      000H,000H,006H,00EH,01EH,036H,066H,07FH
        db      006H,006H,00FH,000H,000H,000H,000H,000H
        db      000H,000H,07FH,060H,060H,060H,07EH,003H
        db      003H,063H,03EH,000H,000H,000H,000H,000H
        db      000H,000H,01CH,030H,060H,060H,07EH,063H
        db      063H,063H,03EH,000H,000H,000H,000H,000H
        db      000H,000H,07FH,063H,003H,006H,00CH,018H
        db      018H,018H,018H,000H,000H,000H,000H,000H
        db      000H,000H,03EH,063H,063H,063H,03EH,063H
        db      063H,063H,03EH,000H,000H,000H,000H,000H
        db      000H,000H,03EH,063H,063H,063H,03FH,003H
        db      003H,006H,03CH,000H,000H,000H,000H,000H
        db      000H,000H,000H,018H,018H,000H,000H,000H
        db      018H,018H,000H,000H,000H,000H,000H,000H
        db      000H,000H,000H,018H,018H,000H,000H,000H
        db      018H,018H,030H,000H,000H,000H,000H,000H
        db      000H,000H,006H,00CH,018H,030H,060H,030H
        db      018H,00CH,006H,000H,000H,000H,000H,000H
        db      000H,000H,000H,000H,000H,07EH,000H,000H
        db      07EH,000H,000H,000H,000H,000H,000H,000H
        db      000H,000H,060H,030H,018H,00CH,006H,00CH
        db      018H,030H,060H,000H,000H,000H,000H,000H
        db      000H,000H,03EH,063H,063H,006H,00CH,00CH
        db      000H,00CH,00CH,000H,000H,000H,000H,000H
;       ascii  40h - 4Fh   '@' - 'O'
        db      000H,000H,03EH,063H,063H,06FH,06FH,06FH
        db      06EH,060H,03EH,000H,000H,000H,000H,000H
        db      000H,000H,008H,01CH,036H,063H,063H,07FH
```

Listing C.3 - (*cont.*)

```
        db      063H,063H,063H,000H,000H,000H,000H,000H
        db      000H,000H,07EH,033H,033H,033H,03EH,033H
        db      033H,033H,07EH,000H,000H,000H,000H,000H
        db      000H,000H,01EH,033H,061H,060H,060H,060H
        db      061H,033H,01EH,000H,000H,000H,000H,000H
        db      000H,000H,07CH,036H,033H,033H,033H,033H
        db      033H,036H,07CH,000H,000H,000H,000H,000H
        db      000H,000H,07FH,033H,031H,034H,03CH,034H
        db      031H,033H,07FH,000H,000H,000H,000H,000H
        db      000H,000H,07FH,033H,031H,034H,03CH,034H
        db      030H,030H,078H,000H,000H,000H,000H,000H
        db      000H,000H,01EH,033H,061H,060H,060H,06FH
        db      063H,033H,01DH,000H,000H,000H,000H,000H
        db      000H,000H,063H,063H,063H,063H,07FH,063H
        db      063H,063H,063H,000H,000H,000H,000H,000H
        db      000H,000H,03CH,018H,018H,018H,018H,018H
        db      018H,018H,03CH,000H,000H,000H,000H,000H
        db      000H,000H,00FH,006H,006H,006H,006H,006H
        db      066H,066H,03CH,000H,000H,000H,000H,000H
        db      000H,000H,073H,033H,036H,036H,03CH,036H
        db      036H,033H,073H,000H,000H,000H,000H,000H
        db      000H,000H,078H,030H,030H,030H,030H,030H
        db      031H,033H,07FH,000H,000H,000H,000H,000H
        db      000H,000H,0C3H,0E7H,0FFH,0DBH,0C3H,0C3H
        db      0C3H,0C3H,0C3H,000H,000H,000H,000H,000H
        db      000H,000H,063H,073H,07BH,07FH,06FH,067H
        db      063H,063H,063H,000H,000H,000H,000H,000H
        db      000H,000H,01CH,036H,063H,063H,063H,063H
        db      063H,036H,01CH,000H,000H,000H,000H,000H
;       ascii 50h - 5Fh   'P' - '_'
        db      000H,000H,07EH,033H,033H,033H,03EH,030H
        db      030H,030H,078H,000H,000H,000H,000H,000H
        db      000H,000H,03EH,063H,063H,063H,063H,06BH
        db      06FH,03EH,006H,007H,000H,000H,000H,000H
        db      000H,000H,07EH,033H,033H,033H,03EH,036H
        db      033H,033H,073H,000H,000H,000H,000H,000H
        db      000H,000H,03EH,063H,063H,030H,01CH,006H
        db      063H,063H,03EH,000H,000H,000H,000H,000H
        db      000H,000H,0FFH,0DBH,099H,018H,018H,018H
        db      018H,018H,03CH,000H,000H,000H,000H,000H
        db      000H,000H,063H,063H,063H,063H,063H,063H
        db      063H,063H,03EH,000H,000H,000H,000H,000H
        db      000H,000H,0C3H,0C3H,0C3H,0C3H,0C3H,0C3H
        db      066H,03CH,018H,000H,000H,000H,000H,000H
        db      000H,000H,0C3H,0C3H,0C3H,0C3H,0DBH,0DBH
        db      0FFH,066H,066H,000H,000H,000H,000H,000H
```

Listing C.3 - *(cont.)*

```
        db      000H,000H,0C3H,0C3H,066H,03CH,018H,03CH
        db      066H,0C3H,0C3H,000H,000H,000H,000H,000H
        db      000H,000H,0C3H,0C3H,0C3H,066H,03CH,018H
        db      018H,018H,03CH,000H,000H,000H,000H,000H
        db      000H,000H,0FFH,0C3H,086H,00CH,018H,030H
        db      061H,0C3H,0FFH,000H,000H,000H,000H,000H
        db      000H,000H,03CH,030H,030H,030H,030H,030H
        db      030H,030H,03CH,000H,000H,000H,000H,000H
        db      000H,000H,040H,060H,070H,038H,01CH,00EH
        db      007H,003H,001H,000H,000H,000H,000H,000H
        db      000H,000H,03CH,00CH,00CH,00CH,00CH,00CH
        db      00CH,00CH,03CH,000H,000H,000H,000H,000H
        db      008H,01CH,036H,063H,000H,000H,000H,000H
        db      000H,000H,000H,000H,000H,000H,000H,000H
        db      000H,000H,000H,000H,000H,000H,000H,000H
        db      000H,000H,000H,000H,0FFH,000H,000H,000H
;       ascii 60h -6Fh    ''' - 'o'
        db      018H,018H,00CH,000H,000H,000H,000H,000H
        db      000H,000H,000H,000H,000H,000H,000H,000H
        db      000H,000H,000H,000H,000H,03CH,006H,03EH
        db      066H,066H,03BH,000H,000H,000H,000H,000H
        db      000H,000H,070H,030H,030H,03CH,036H,033H
        db      033H,033H,06EH,000H,000H,000H,000H,000H
        db      000H,000H,000H,000H,000H,03EH,063H,060H
        db      060H,063H,03EH,000H,000H,000H,000H,000H
        db      000H,000H,00EH,006H,006H,01EH,036H,066H
        db      066H,066H,03BH,000H,000H,000H,000H,000H
        db      000H,000H,000H,000H,000H,03EH,063H,07FH
        db      060H,063H,03EH,000H,000H,000H,000H,000H
        db      000H,000H,01CH,036H,032H,030H,07CH,030H
        db      030H,030H,078H,000H,000H,000H,000H,000H
        db      000H,000H,000H,000H,000H,03BH,066H,066H
        db      066H,03EH,006H,066H,03CH,000H,000H,000H
        db      000H,000H,070H,030H,030H,036H,03BH,033H
        db      033H,033H,073H,000H,000H,000H,000H,000H
        db      000H,000H,00CH,00CH,000H,01CH,00CH,00CH
        db      00CH,00CH,01EH,000H,000H,000H,000H,000H
        db      000H,000H,006H,006H,000H,00EH,006H,006H
        db      006H,006H,066H,066H,03CH,000H,000H,000H
        db      000H,000H,070H,030H,030H,033H,036H,03CH
        db      036H,033H,073H,000H,000H,000H,000H,000H
        db      000H,000H,01CH,00CH,00CH,00CH,00CH,00CH
        db      00CH,00CH,01EH,000H,000H,000H,000H,000H
        db      000H,000H,000H,000H,000H,0E6H,0FFH,0DBH
        db      0DBH,0DBH,0DBH,000H,000H,000H,000H,000H
        db      000H,000H,000H,000H,000H,06EH,033H,033H
```

Listing C.3 - (*cont.*)

```
        db      033H,033H,033H,000H,000H,000H,000H,000H
        db      000H,000H,000H,000H,000H,03EH,063H,063H
        db      063H,063H,03EH,000H,000H,000H,000H,000H
;       ascii   70h - 7Fh   'p'   -
        db      000H,000H,000H,000H,000H,06EH,033H,033H
        db      033H,03EH,030H,030H,078H,000H,000H,000H
        db      000H,000H,000H,000H,000H,03BH,066H,066H
        db      066H,03EH,006H,006H,00FH,000H,000H,000H
        db      000H,000H,000H,000H,000H,06EH,03BH,033H
        db      030H,030H,078H,000H,000H,000H,000H,000H
        db      000H,000H,000H,000H,000H,03EH,063H,038H
        db      00EH,063H,03EH,000H,000H,000H,000H,000H
        db      000H,000H,008H,018H,018H,07EH,018H,018H
        db      018H,01BH,00EH,000H,000H,000H,000H,000H
        db      000H,000H,000H,000H,000H,066H,066H,066H
        db      066H,066H,03BH,000H,000H,000H,000H,000H
        db      000H,000H,000H,000H,000H,0C3H,0C3H,0C3H
        db      066H,03CH,018H,000H,000H,000H,000H,000H
        db      000H,000H,000H,000H,000H,0C3H,0C3H,0DBH
        db      0DBH,0FFH,066H,000H,000H,000H,000H,000H
        db      000H,000H,000H,000H,000H,063H,036H,01CH
        db      01CH,036H,063H,000H,000H,000H,000H,000H
        db      000H,000H,000H,000H,000H,063H,063H,063H
        db      063H,03FH,003H,006H,03CH,000H,000H,000H
        db      000H,000H,000H,000H,000H,07FH,066H,00CH
        db      018H,033H,07FH,000H,000H,000H,000H,000H
        db      000H,000H,00EH,018H,018H,018H,070H,018H
        db      018H,018H,00EH,000H,000H,000H,000H,000H
        db      000H,000H,018H,018H,018H,018H,000H,018H
        db      018H,018H,018H,000H,000H,000H,000H,000H
        db      000H,000H,070H,018H,018H,018H,00EH,018H
        db      018H,018H,070H,000H,000H,000H,000H,000H
        db      000H,000H,03BH,06EH,000H,000H,000H,000H
        db      000H,000H,000H,000H,000H,000H,000H,000H
        db      000H,000H,000H,000H,008H,01CH,036H,063H
        db      063H,07FH,000H,000H,000H,000H,000H,000H
;       ascii   80h - 8Fh
        db      000H,000H,01EH,033H,061H,060H,060H,061H
        db      033H,01EH,006H,003H,03EH,000H,000H,000H
        db      000H,000H,066H,066H,000H,066H,066H,066H
        db      066H,066H,03BH,000H,000H,000H,000H,000H
        db      000H,006H,00CH,018H,000H,03EH,063H,07FH
        db      060H,063H,03EH,000H,000H,000H,000H,000H
        db      000H,008H,01CH,036H,000H,03CH,006H,03EH
        db      066H,066H,03BH,000H,000H,000H,000H,000H
        db      000H,000H,066H,066H,000H,03CH,006H,03EH
```

Listing C.3 - *(cont.)*

```
        db      066H,066H,03BH,000H,000H,000H,000H,000H
        db      000H,030H,018H,00CH,000H,03CH,006H,03EH
        db      066H,066H,03BH,000H,000H,000H,000H,000H
        db      000H,01CH,036H,01CH,000H,03CH,006H,03EH
        db      066H,066H,03BH,000H,000H,000H,000H,000H
        db      000H,000H,000H,000H,03CH,066H,060H,066H
        db      03CH,00CH,006H,03CH,000H,000H,000H,000H
        db      000H,008H,01CH,036H,000H,03EH,063H,07FH
        db      060H,063H,03EH,000H,000H,000H,000H,000H
        db      000H,000H,066H,066H,000H,03EH,063H,07FH
        db      060H,063H,03EH,000H,000H,000H,000H,000H
        db      000H,030H,018H,00CH,000H,03EH,063H,07FH
        db      060H,063H,03EH,000H,000H,000H,000H,000H
        db      000H,000H,066H,066H,000H,038H,018H,018H
        db      018H,018H,03CH,000H,000H,000H,000H,000H
        db      000H,018H,03CH,066H,000H,038H,018H,018H
        db      018H,018H,03CH,000H,000H,000H,000H,000H
        db      000H,060H,030H,018H,000H,038H,018H,018H
        db      018H,018H,03CH,000H,000H,000H,000H,000H
        db      000H,063H,063H,008H,01CH,036H,063H,063H
        db      07FH,063H,063H,000H,000H,000H,000H,000H
        db      01CH,036H,01CH,000H,01CH,036H,063H,063H
        db      07FH,063H,063H,000H,000H,000H,000H,000H
;       ascii 90h - 9Fh
        db      00CH,018H,030H,000H,07FH,033H,030H,03EH
        db      030H,033H,07FH,000H,000H,000H,000H,000H
        db      000H,000H,000H,000H,06EH,03BH,01BH,07EH
        db      0D8H,0DCH,077H,000H,000H,000H,000H,000H
        db      000H,000H,01FH,036H,066H,066H,07FH,066H
        db      066H,066H,067H,000H,000H,000H,000H,000H
        db      000H,008H,01CH,036H,000H,03EH,063H,063H
        db      063H,063H,03EH,000H,000H,000H,000H,000H
        db      000H,000H,063H,063H,000H,03EH,063H,063H
        db      063H,063H,03EH,000H,000H,000H,000H,000H
        db      000H,030H,018H,00CH,000H,03EH,063H,063H
        db      063H,063H,03EH,000H,000H,000H,000H,000H
        db      000H,018H,03CH,066H,000H,066H,066H,066H
        db      066H,066H,03BH,000H,000H,000H,000H,000H
        db      000H,030H,018H,00CH,000H,066H,066H,066H
        db      066H,066H,03BH,000H,000H,000H,000H,000H
        db      000H,000H,063H,063H,000H,063H,063H,063H
        db      063H,03FH,003H,006H,03CH,000H,000H,000H
        db      000H,063H,063H,01CH,036H,063H,063H,063H
        db      063H,036H,01CH,000H,000H,000H,000H,000H
        db      000H,063H,063H,000H,063H,063H,063H,063H
        db      063H,063H,03EH,000H,000H,000H,000H,000H
```

Listing C.3 - (*cont.*)

```
        db      000H,018H,018H,07EH,0C3H,0C0H,0C0H,0C3H
        db      07EH,018H,018H,000H,000H,000H,000H,000H
        db      000H,01CH,036H,032H,030H,078H,030H,030H
        db      030H,073H,07EH,000H,000H,000H,000H,000H
        db      000H,000H,0C3H,066H,03CH,018H,0FFH,018H
        db      0FFH,018H,018H,000H,000H,000H,000H,000H
        db      000H,0FCH,066H,066H,07CH,062H,066H,06FH
        db      066H,066H,0F3H,000H,000H,000H,000H,000H
        db      000H,00EH,01BH,018H,018H,018H,07EH,018H
        db      018H,018H,018H,0D8H,070H,000H,000H,000H
;       ascii A0h - AFh
        db      000H,00CH,018H,030H,000H,03CH,006H,03EH
        db      066H,066H,03BH,000H,000H,000H,000H,000H
        db      000H,00CH,018H,030H,000H,038H,018H,018H
        db      018H,018H,03CH,000H,000H,000H,000H,000H
        db      000H,00CH,018H,030H,000H,03EH,063H,063H
        db      063H,063H,03EH,000H,000H,000H,000H,000H
        db      000H,00CH,018H,030H,000H,066H,066H,066H
        db      066H,066H,03BH,000H,000H,000H,000H,000H
        db      000H,000H,03BH,06EH,000H,06EH,033H,033H
        db      033H,033H,033H,000H,000H,000H,000H,000H
        db      03BH,06EH,000H,063H,073H,07BH,07FH,06FH
        db      067H,063H,063H,000H,000H,000H,000H,000H
        db      000H,03CH,06CH,06CH,03EH,000H,07EH,000H
        db      000H,000H,000H,000H,000H,000H,000H,000H
        db      000H,038H,06CH,06CH,038H,000H,07CH,000H
        db      000H,000H,000H,000H,000H,000H,000H,000H
        db      000H,000H,018H,018H,000H,018H,018H,030H
        db      063H,063H,03EH,000H,000H,000H,000H,000H
        db      000H,000H,000H,000H,000H,000H,07FH,060H
        db      060H,060H,000H,000H,000H,000H,000H,000H
        db      000H,000H,000H,000H,000H,000H,07FH,003H
        db      003H,003H,000H,000H,000H,000H,000H,000H
        db      000H,060H,0E0H,063H,066H,06CH,018H,030H
        db      06EH,0C3H,006H,00CH,01FH,000H,000H,000H
        db      000H,060H,0E0H,063H,066H,06CH,018H,033H
        db      067H,0CFH,01FH,003H,003H,000H,000H,000H
        db      000H,000H,018H,018H,000H,018H,018H,03CH
        db      03CH,03CH,018H,000H,000H,000H,000H,000H
        db      000H,000H,000H,000H,01BH,036H,06CH,036H
        db      01BH,000H,000H,000H,000H,000H,000H,000H
        db      000H,000H,000H,000H,06CH,036H,01BH,036H
        db      06CH,000H,000H,000H,000H,000H,000H,000H
;       ascii B0h - BFh   character graphics
        db      011H,044H,011H,044H,011H,044H,011H,044H
        db      011H,044H,011H,044H,011H,044H,000H,000H
```

Listing C.3 - *(cont.)*

```
        db      055H,0AAH,055H,0AAH,055H,0AAH,055H,0AAH
        db      055H,0AAH,055H,0AAH,055H,0AAH,000H,000H
        db      0DDH,077H,0DDH,077H,0DDH,077H,0DDH,077H
        db      0DDH,077H,0DDH,077H,0DDH,077H,000H,000H
        db      018H,018H,018H,018H,018H,018H,018H,018H
        db      018H,018H,018H,018H,018H,018H,000H,000H
        db      018H,018H,018H,018H,018H,018H,018H,0F8H
        db      018H,018H,018H,018H,018H,018H,000H,000H
        db      018H,018H,018H,018H,018H,0F8H,018H,0F8H
        db      018H,018H,018H,018H,018H,018H,000H,000H
        db      036H,036H,036H,036H,036H,036H,036H,0F6H
        db      036H,036H,036H,036H,036H,036H,000H,000H
        db      000H,000H,000H,000H,000H,000H,000H,0FEH
        db      036H,036H,036H,036H,036H,036H,000H,000H
        db      000H,000H,000H,000H,000H,0F8H,018H,0F8H
        db      018H,018H,018H,018H,018H,018H,000H,000H
        db      036H,036H,036H,036H,036H,0F6H,006H,0F6H
        db      036H,036H,036H,036H,036H,036H,000H,000H
        db      036H,036H,036H,036H,036H,036H,036H,036H
        db      036H,036H,036H,036H,036H,036H,000H,000H
        db      000H,000H,000H,000H,000H,0FEH,006H,0F6H
        db      036H,036H,036H,036H,036H,036H,000H,000H
        db      036H,036H,036H,036H,036H,0F6H,006H,0FEH
        db      000H,000H,000H,000H,000H,000H,000H,000H
        db      036H,036H,036H,036H,036H,036H,036H,0FEH
        db      000H,000H,000H,000H,000H,000H,000H,000H
        db      018H,018H,018H,018H,018H,0F8H,018H,0F8H
        db      000H,000H,000H,000H,000H,000H,000H,000H
        db      000H,000H,000H,000H,000H,000H,000H,0F8H
        db      018H,018H,018H,018H,018H,018H,000H,000H
;       ascii   C0h - CFh   character graphics
        db      018H,018H,018H,018H,018H,018H,018H,01FH
        db      000H,000H,000H,000H,000H,000H,000H,000H
        db      018H,018H,018H,018H,018H,018H,018H,0FFH
        db      000H,000H,000H,000H,000H,000H,000H,000H
        db      000H,000H,000H,000H,000H,000H,000H,0FFH
        db      018H,018H,018H,018H,018H,018H,000H,000H
        db      018H,018H,018H,018H,018H,018H,018H,01FH
        db      018H,018H,018H,018H,018H,018H,000H,000H
        db      000H,000H,000H,000H,000H,000H,000H,0FFH
        db      000H,000H,000H,000H,000H,000H,000H,000H
        db      018H,018H,018H,018H,018H,018H,018H,0FFH
        db      018H,018H,018H,018H,018H,018H,000H,000H
        db      018H,018H,018H,018H,018H,01FH,018H,01FH
        db      018H,018H,018H,018H,018H,018H,000H,000H
        db      036H,036H,036H,036H,036H,036H,036H,037H
```

Listing C.3 - (*cont.*)

```
        db      036H,036H,036H,036H,036H,036H,000H,000H
        db      036H,036H,036H,036H,036H,037H,030H,03FH
        db      000H,000H,000H,000H,000H,000H,000H,000H
        db      000H,000H,000H,000H,000H,03FH,030H,037H
        db      036H,036H,036H,036H,036H,036H,000H,000H
        db      036H,036H,036H,036H,036H,0F7H,000H,0FFH
        db      000H,000H,000H,000H,000H,000H,000H,000H
        db      000H,000H,000H,000H,000H,0FFH,000H,0F7H
        db      036H,036H,036H,036H,036H,036H,000H,000H
        db      036H,036H,036H,036H,036H,037H,030H,037H
        db      036H,036H,036H,036H,036H,036H,000H,000H
        db      000H,000H,000H,000H,000H,0FFH,000H,0FFH
        db      000H,000H,000H,000H,000H,000H,000H,000H
        db      036H,036H,036H,036H,036H,0F7H,000H,0F7H
        db      036H,036H,036H,036H,036H,036H,000H,000H
        db      018H,018H,018H,018H,018H,0FFH,000H,0FFH
        db      000H,000H,000H,000H,000H,000H,000H,000H
;       ascii D0h - DFh  character graphics
        db      036H,036H,036H,036H,036H,036H,036H,0FFH
        db      000H,000H,000H,000H,000H,000H,000H,000H
        db      000H,000H,000H,000H,000H,0FFH,000H,0FFH
        db      018H,018H,018H,018H,018H,018H,000H,000H
        db      000H,000H,000H,000H,000H,000H,000H,0FFH
        db      036H,036H,036H,036H,036H,036H,000H,000H
        db      036H,036H,036H,036H,036H,036H,036H,03FH
        db      000H,000H,000H,000H,000H,000H,000H,000H
        db      018H,018H,018H,018H,018H,01FH,018H,01FH
        db      000H,000H,000H,000H,000H,000H,000H,000H
        db      000H,000H,000H,000H,000H,01FH,018H,01FH
        db      018H,018H,018H,018H,018H,018H,000H,000H
        db      000H,000H,000H,000H,000H,000H,000H,03FH
        db      036H,036H,036H,036H,036H,036H,000H,000H
        db      036H,036H,036H,036H,036H,036H,036H,0FFH
        db      036H,036H,036H,036H,036H,036H,000H,000H
        db      018H,018H,018H,018H,018H,0FFH,018H,0FFH
        db      018H,018H,018H,018H,018H,018H,000H,000H
        db      018H,018H,018H,018H,018H,018H,018H,0F8H
        db      000H,000H,000H,000H,000H,000H,000H,000H
        db      000H,000H,000H,000H,000H,000H,000H,01FH
        db      018H,018H,018H,018H,018H,018H,000H,000H
        db      0FFH,0FFH,0FFH,0FFH,0FFH,0FFH,0FFH,0FFH
        db      0FFH,0FFH,0FFH,0FFH,0FFH,0FFH,000H,000H
        db      000H,000H,000H,000H,000H,000H,000H,0FFH
        db      0FFH,0FFH,0FFH,0FFH,0FFH,0FFH,000H,000H
        db      0F0H,0F0H,0F0H,0F0H,0F0H,0F0H,0F0H,0F0H
        db      0F0H,0F0H,0F0H,0F0H,0F0H,0F0H,000H,000H
```

Listing C.3 - *(cont.)*

```
            db      00FH,00FH,00FH,00FH,00FH,00FH,00FH,00FH
            db      00FH,00FH,00FH,00FH,00FH,00FH,000H,000H
            db      0FFH,0FFH,0FFH,0FFH,0FFH,0FFH,0FFH,000H
            db      000H,000H,000H,000H,000H,000H,000H,000H
;           ascii   E0h - EFh
            db      000H,000H,000H,000H,000H,03BH,06EH,06CH
            db      06CH,06EH,03BH,000H,000H,000H,000H,000H
            db      000H,000H,000H,000H,03EH,063H,07EH,063H
            db      063H,07EH,060H,060H,020H,000H,000H,000H
            db      000H,000H,07FH,063H,063H,060H,060H,060H
            db      060H,060H,060H,000H,000H,000H,000H,000H
            db      000H,000H,000H,000H,07FH,036H,036H,036H
            db      036H,036H,036H,000H,000H,000H,000H,000H
            db      000H,000H,07FH,063H,030H,018H,00CH,018H
            db      030H,063H,07FH,000H,000H,000H,000H,000H
            db      000H,000H,000H,000H,000H,03FH,06CH,06CH
            db      06CH,06CH,038H,000H,000H,000H,000H,000H
            db      000H,000H,000H,000H,033H,033H,033H,033H
            db      03EH,030H,030H,060H,000H,000H,000H,000H
            db      000H,000H,000H,000H,03BH,06EH,00CH,00CH
            db      00CH,00CH,00CH,000H,000H,000H,000H,000H
            db      000H,000H,07EH,018H,03CH,066H,066H,066H
            db      03CH,018H,07EH,000H,000H,000H,000H,000H
            db      000H,000H,01CH,036H,063H,063H,07FH,063H
            db      063H,036H,01CH,000H,000H,000H,000H,000H
            db      000H,000H,01CH,036H,063H,063H,063H,036H
            db      036H,036H,077H,000H,000H,000H,000H,000H
            db      000H,000H,01EH,030H,018H,00CH,03EH,066H
            db      066H,066H,03CH,000H,000H,000H,000H,000H
            db      000H,000H,000H,000H,000H,07EH,0DBH,0DBH
            db      07EH,000H,000H,000H,000H,000H,000H,000H
            db      000H,000H,003H,006H,07EH,0DBH,0DBH,0F3H
            db      07EH,060H,0C0H,000H,000H,000H,000H,000H
            db      000H,000H,01CH,030H,060H,060H,07CH,060H
            db      060H,030H,01CH,000H,000H,000H,000H,000H
            db      000H,000H,000H,03EH,063H,063H,063H,063H
            db      063H,063H,063H,000H,000H,000H,000H,000H
;           ascii   F0 - FFh
            db      000H,000H,000H,07FH,000H,000H,07FH,000H
            db      000H,07FH,000H,000H,000H,000H,000H,000H
            db      000H,000H,018H,018H,018H,0FFH,018H,018H
            db      018H,000H,0FFH,000H,000H,000H,000H,000H
            db      000H,000H,030H,018H,00CH,006H,00CH,018H
            db      030H,000H,07EH,000H,000H,000H,000H,000H
            db      000H,000H,00CH,018H,030H,060H,030H,018H
            db      00CH,000H,07EH,000H,000H,000H,000H,000H
```

Listing C.3 - (*cont.*)

```
        db      000H,000H,00EH,01BH,01BH,018H,018H,018H
        db      018H,018H,018H,018H,018H,018H,000H,000H
        db      018H,018H,018H,018H,018H,018H,018H,018H
        db      0D8H,0D8H,070H,000H,000H,000H,000H,000H
        db      000H,000H,018H,018H,000H,000H,0FFH,000H
        db      000H,018H,018H,000H,000H,000H,000H,000H
        db      000H,000H,000H,000H,03BH,06EH,000H,03BH
        db      06EH,000H,000H,000H,000H,000H,000H,000H
        db      000H,038H,06CH,06CH,038H,000H,000H,000H
        db      000H,000H,000H,000H,000H,000H,000H,000H
        db      000H,000H,000H,000H,000H,000H,018H,018H
        db      000H,000H,000H,000H,000H,000H,000H,000H
        db      000H,000H,000H,000H,000H,000H,000H,018H
        db      000H,000H,000H,000H,000H,000H,000H,000H
        db      000H,00FH,00CH,00CH,00CH,00CH,00CH,0ECH
        db      06CH,03CH,01CH,000H,000H,000H,000H,000H
        db      000H,0D8H,06CH,06CH,06CH,06CH,06CH,000H
        db      000H,000H,000H,000H,000H,000H,000H,000H
        db      000H,070H,0D8H,030H,060H,0C8H,0F8H,000H
        db      000H,000H,000H,000H,000H,000H,000H,000H
        db      000H,000H,000H,000H,03EH,03EH,03EH,03EH
        db      03EH,03EH,000H,000H,000H,000H,000H,000H
        db      000H,000H,000H,000H,000H,000H,000H,000H
        db      000H,000H,000H,000H,000H,000H,000H,000H

data    ends

code    segment public
        assume cs:code,ds:data

;       set up hercules graphics
stherc  proc    near
        push    ax                          ;save regs
        push    cx
        push    dx
        push    di
        mov     dx,03bfh                    ;config switch
        mov     al,1
        out     dx,al                       ;allow graphics
        mov     ax,0b000h                   ;seg b000h
        mov     es,ax
        mov     cx,8000h                    ;word count
        mov     di,0
        cld
        xor     ax,ax                       ;ax=0
        rep stosw                           ;clear tv ram
```

Listing C.3 - *(cont.)*

```
                mov     dx,03b4h              ;6845 port
                mov     si,offset vidtbl      ;si->values
                mov     cx,16                 ;16 regs
                xor     ax,ax                 ;ah=0
sg1:            mov     al,ah                 ;reg no.
                out     dx,al                 ;select reg
                inc     dx                    ;dx=03b5h
                lodsb                         ;get value
                out     dx,al                 ;store it
                dec     dx                    ;dx=03b4h
                inc     ah                    ;next reg
                loop    sg1                   ;do all 16
                mov     dx,03b8h              ;control port
                mov     al,0ah                ;enable video
                out     dx,al                 ; & graphics
                pop     di                    ;restore regs
                pop     dx
                pop     cx
                pop     ax
                ret
stherc          endp

;               plot line
line            proc near
                push    ax                    ;save registers
                push    bx
                push    cx
                push    dx
                push    si
                push    di
                push    bp
                push    ax                    ;make space for yflg
                mov     bp,sp                 ;bp=initial sp
                mov     byte ptr 1[bp],0      ;yflg=0
                cmp     cx,ax                 ;if orig.x1>orig.x2
                jb      la                    ;then interchange
                xchg    cx,ax                 ;orig and endp
                xchg    dx,bx
la:             cmp     bx,dx                 ;if bx<dx then set
                ja      lb                    ; yflg=80h
                mov     byte ptr 1[bp],80h
lb:             push    ax                    ;push endp:x
                push    bx                    ;push endp:y
                push    ax                    ;push endp:x
                push    bx                    ;push endp:y
ln1:            mov     si,cx                 ;compute midp.x
```

Listing C.3 - *(cont.)*

```
              add     si,ax
              shr     si,1                  ;si=(x1+x2)/2
              mov     di,dx                 ;compute midp.y
              add     di,bx
              shr     di,1                  ;di=(y1+y2)/2
              jnb     ln2                   ;if carry set
              cmp     byte ptr 1[bp],0
              je      ln2                   ;then if yflg set
              inc     di                    ;round midp.y
ln2:          cmp     si,cx                 ;if midp=orig
              jne     ln3
              cmp     di,dx
              jne     ln3                   ;then
              call    plot                  ;plot orig
              pop     dx                    ;pop orig.y
              pop     cx                    ;          .x
              pop     bx                    ;pop endp.y
              pop     ax                    ;          .x
              jmp     ln4
ln3:          push    ax                    ;push endp.x
              push    bx                    ;            .y
              push    si                    ;push midp.x
              push    di                    ;            .y
              mov     ax,si
              mov     bx,di
ln4:          cmp     bp,sp
              jne     ln1
              call    plot                  ;plot orig
ln5:          pop     ax                    ;restore yflg
              pop     bp                    ;restore regs
              pop     di
              pop     si
              pop     dx
              pop     cx
              pop     bx
              pop     ax
              ret
line          endp

;             plot point at x=cx, y=dx
plot          proc    near
              push    bx
              push    di
              push    es
              call    plotad                ;calc addr
```

Listing C.3 - (*cont.*)

```
            or      es:[di],bl              ;or in 1
            pop     es
            pop     di
            pop     bx
            ret
plot        endp

;           erase point at x=cx, y=dx
erase       proc    near
            push    bx
            push    di
            push    es
            call    plotad                  ;calc addr
            not     bl                      ;not mask
            and     es:[di],bl              ;and in 0
            pop     es
            pop     di
            pop     bx
            ret
erase       endp

;           calculate plot addr at x=cx, y=dx
;           di --> addr   bl=mask   es=B000
plotad      proc    near
            push    ax
            push    cx
            push    dx
            mov     di,dx                   ;y-table
            shl     di,1                    ; index
            mov     di,row_table[di]        ;di->y-table
            mov     ax,cx                   ;ax = x
            shr     ax,1
            shr     ax,1
            shr     ax,1                    ;int(x/8)
            add     di,ax                   ;byte addr
            mov     bl,80h                  ;mask
            and     cx,7                    ;x mod 8
            shr     bl,cl                   ;get mask
            mov     ax,0b000h
            mov     es,ax                   ;seg b000h
            pop     dx
            pop     cx
            pop     ax
            ret
plotad      endp
```

Listing C.3 - (*cont.*)

```
            page
;           message display
;           input:si -> message
;                         cx = x
;                         dx = y
messg       proc    near
            push    ax                              ;save regs
            push    si
            cld                                     ;si increases
ms1:        lodsb                                   ;[si]-->al
            cmp     al,0                            ;message done?
            je      ms2                             ;if so, return
            call    charwt                          ;display char
            jmp     ms1                             ;and continue
ms2:        pop     si                              ;restore regs
            pop     ax
            ret
messg       endp


            page
;           character write
;           input:  al = ascii code of char
;                   cx = x-coord. upper-left
;                   dx = y-coord. upper-left
;           output: cx = cx(input)+9 = x-coord+9
;                   dx = dx(input) = y-coord

charwt      proc    near
            push    ax
            push    bx
            push    si                              ;save regs
            push    di
            push    bp
            mov     bx,cx                           ;bx = x
            mov     es,video_seg                    ;es->tv ram
            cld
            mov     bit9flg,0                       ;default no
            cmp     al,0c0h                         ; line draw
            jb      cw1                             ;check for
            cmp     al,0dfh                         ; line draw
            ja      cw1                             ; characters
            not     bit9flg                         ;yes, set flag
cw1:        xor     ah,ah                           ;ah = 0
            shl     ax,1                            ;mult by 16
            shl     ax,1                            ;16 bytes per
            shl     ax,1                            ; char in table
```

Listing C.3 - *(cont.)*

```
            shl     ax,1
            mov     si,offset charset       ;si->char set
            add     si,ax                   ;offset in tbl
            mov     bp,14                   ;char height=14
cw2:        mov     cx,bx                   ;cx = x
            mov     di,dx                   ;di = y
            shl     di,1                    ;2 bytes/entry
            mov     di,row_table[di]        ;row offset
            mov     ax,cx                   ;ax = col
            shr     ax,1
            shr     ax,1
            shr     ax,1                    ;int(x/8)
            add     di,ax                   ;char pos byte
            and     cl,7                    ;x mod 8
            mov     ax,es:[di]              ;get 2 bytes
            xchg    ah,al                   ;ah = [di]
            rol     ax,cl                   ;mov char to ah
            mov     ah,byte ptr [si]        ;ah= char line
            cmp     bit9flg,0
            je      cw3
            test    ah,1                    ;if 8th pixel
            je      cw3                     ; on, duplicate
            or      al,80h                  ; 8th bit
            jmp     cw4
cw3:        and     al,07fh                 ;erase pixel 9
cw4:        ror     ax,cl                   ;restore word
            xchg    ah,al                   ;restore order
            stosw                           ;write word
            inc     dx                      ;next row
            inc     si                      ;next tbl byte
            dec     bp                      ;do all 14 rows
            jne     cw2
            sub     dx,14                   ;restore orig y
            add     bx,9                    ;inc col by 9
            mov     cx,bx
            pop     bp
            pop     di                      ;restore regs
            pop     si
            pop     bx
            pop     ax
            ret
charwt      endp

            page
;           cursor position conversion
;           input:  dl = col
```

Listing C.3 - *(cont.)*

```
;                       dh = row
;           output: cx = x = 9*col
;                   dx = y = 14*row
cpconv      proc    near
            push    ax
            mov     cl,dl
            mov     ch,0                    ;cx = col
            mov     dl,dh
            mov     dh,0                    ;dx = row
            mov     ax,cx                   ;ax = col
            shl     ax,1
            shl     ax,1
            shl     ax,1                    ;col*8
            add     cx,ax                   ;cx = 9*col
            shl     dx,1                    ;row*2
            mov     ax,dx                   ;ax = 2*row
            shl     dx,1                    ;row*4
            add     ax,dx                   ;ax = 6*row
            shl     dx,1                    ;row*8
            add     dx,ax                   ;dx = 14*row
            pop     ax
            ret
cpconv      endp

;           sin ax
;           input:  ax = degrees
;           output: ax = sine value x 10000
sinax       proc    near
            push    bx                      ;save regs
            push    dx
            push    si
            or      ax,ax                   ;if negative
            jns     sn2
sn1:        add     ax,360                  ; add 360
            js      sn1                     ; until pos
            jmp     sn3
sn2:        mov     bx,360
            mov     dx,0
            div     bx
            mov     ax,dx                   ;ax=mod 360
sn3:        mov     bx,90                   ;find quad
            mov     dx,0
            div     bx                      ;ax = quad
            or      dx,dx                   ;if deg=0
            jne     sn4
            mov     si,ax                   ;find axis val
```

Listing C.3 - *(cont.)*

```
                shl     si,1                            ; ix*2
                mov     ax,axisv[si]
                jmp     sn7
sn4:            test    al,1                            ;in quad 1,3
                je      sn5
                sub     dx,90                           ;deg=90-deg
                neg     dx                              ;dx=deg
sn5:            mov     si,dx
                shl     si,1                            ;find sine
                mov     bx,sintbl[si]                   ; from table
                mov     si,ax                           ;find sign
                mov     dl,signs[si]                    ; from table
                or      dl,dl                           ;if negative
                jne     sn6
                neg     bx                              ;negate
sn6:            mov     ax,bx                           ;ax=sine
sn7:            pop     si                              ;restore regs
                pop     dx
                pop     bx
                ret
sinax           endp

;               cos ax
;               input:  ax = degrees
;               output: ax = cosine value x 10000
cosax           proc    near
                add     ax,90                           ;cos ax =
                call    sinax                           ;sin(ax+90)
                ret
cosax           endp

code            ends
                end
```

Appendix D

DOS FUNCTION CALLS

TABLE D.1   DOS INT 21H FUNCTION CALLS

AH = 00H	*Program terminate* Input: CS = segment address of PSP Output: none
AH = 01H	*Character input with echo* Input: none Output: AL = 8-bit character data
AH = 02H	*Character output* Input: DL = 8-bit character data Output: none
AH = 03H	*Auxiliary input from COM1* Input: none Output: AL = 8-bit input data
AH = 04H	*Auxiliary output from COM1* Input: DL = 8-bit output data Output: none
AH = 05H	*Printer output* Input: DL = 8-bit output data Output: none

AH = 06H	*Direct console I/O*
	Input: DL = character for output
	        = 0FFH for input
	Output: for output: none
	        for input: Z = 1 if no char ready
	                   Z = 0 if char ready
	                   AL = character data

AH = 07H	*Unfiltered character input without echo* Input: none Output: AL = 8-bit character data
AH = 08H	*Character input without echo* Input: none Output: AL = 8-bit character data
AH = 09H	*Output character string* Input: DS:DX → string (end with $) Output: none
AH = 0AH	*Buffered keyboard input* Input: DS:DX → input buffer Output: none
AH = 0BH	*Get input (keyboard) status* Input: none Output: AL = 00 if no character ready = 0FFH if character available

AH = 0CH	*Reset input buffer and then input*
	Input: AL = input function invoked
	        (01H, 06H, 07H, 08H or 0AH)
	        if AL = 0AH
	        DS:DX → input buffer
	Output: AL = 8-bit character data
	        except for function 0AH

AH = 0DH	*Disk reset* Input: none Output: none

TABLE D.1   (*cont.*)

AH = 0EH	*Set default disk drive* Input: DL = drive code (0 = A, etc.) Output: AL = no. of drives in system
AH = 0FH	*Open file* (uses file control block, FCB)
AH = 10H	*Close file* (uses file control block, FCB)
AH = 11H	*Search for first match* (uses file control block, FCB)
AH = 12H	*Search for next match* (uses file control block, FCB)
AH = 13H	*Delete file* (uses file control block, FCB)
AH = 14H	*Sequential read* (uses file control block, FCB)
AH = 15H	*Sequential write* (uses file control block, FCB)
AH = 16H	*Create or truncate file* (uses file control block, FCB)
AH = 17H	*Rename file* (uses file control block, FCB)
AH = 18H	*Reserved*
AH = 19H	*Get default disk drive* Input: none Output: drive code (0 = A, etc.)
AH = 1AH	*Set disk transfer area address* Input: DS:DX points to disk transfer area (DTA) Output: none

AH = 1BH	*Get allocation info for default drive*
	Input: none
	Output: AL = no. of sectors/cluster
	            DS:BX → FAT ID byte
	            CX = size of sector in bytes
	            DX = no. of clusters

AH = 1CH	*Get allocation info for specified drive*
	Input: DL = drive code (1 = A, etc.)
	Output: AL = no. of sectors/cluster
	            DS:BX → FAT ID byte
	            CX = size of sector in bytes
	            DX = no. of clusters

AH = 1DH	*Reserved*
AH = 1EH	*Reserved*

AH = 1FH	*Reserved*
AH = 20H	*Reserved*
AH = 21H	*Random read* (uses file control block, FCB)
AH = 22H	*Random write* (uses file control block, FCB)
AH = 23H	*Get file size in records* (uses file control block, FCB)
AH = 24H	*Set random record number* (uses file control block, FCB)
AH = 25H	*Set interrupt vector* Input: AL = interrupt type number DS:DX → interrupt routine Output: none
AH = 26H	*Create program segment prefix (PSP)* Input: DX = segment of new PSP Output: none
AH = 27H	*Random block read* (uses file control block, FCB)
AH = 28H	*Random block write* (uses file control block, FCB)
AH = 29H	*Parse filename* (uses file control block, FCB)

AH = 2AH	*Get system date*
	Input: none
	Output: CX = year (1980–2099)
	            DH = month (1–12)
	            DL = day (1–31)
	            AL = day of week (0 =
	                   Sunday)

AH = 2BH	*Set system date*
	Input: CX = year (1980–2099)
	            DH = month (1–12)
	            DL = day (1–31)
	Output: AL = 0 if successful
	            AL = 0FFH if date invalid

AH = 2CH	*Get system time*
	Input: none
	Output: CH = hour (0–23)
	            CL = minutes (0–59)
	            DH = seconds (0–59)
	            DL = hundredths of secs. (0–
	                   99)

AH = 2DH	*Set system time* Input: CH = hour (0–23) CL = minutes (0–59)

(cont.)

TABLE D.1 *(cont.)*

DH = seconds (0–59)
DL = hundredths of secs. (0–99)
Output: AL = 0 if successful
AL = 0FFH if time invalid

AH = 2EH   *Set verify flag*
Input: AL = 00 if turning verify flag off
AL = 01 if turning verify flag on
DL = 00
Output: none

AH = 2FH   *Get disk transfer area (DTA) address*
Input: none
Output: ES:BX → disk transfer area

AH = 30H   *Get MS-DOS version function*
Input: none
Output: AL = major version number
AH = minor version number

AH = 31H   *Terminate and stay resident*
Input: AL = return code
DX = memory size to save (in paragraphs)
Output: none

AH = 32H   *Reserved*

AH = 33H   *Get or set CTRL-Break flag*
Input: If getting status
AL = 00
If setting status
AL = 01
DL = 00 to turn checking off
DH = 01 to turn checking on
Output: DL = 00 if Ctrl-Brk checking off
DL = 01 if Ctrl-Brk checking on

AH = 34H   *Reserved*

AH = 35H   *Get interrupt vector*
Input: AL = interrupt number
Output: ES:BX → interrupt handler

AH = 36H   *Get free disk space*
Input: DL = drive code (1 = A, etc.)
Output: If drive valid
AX = sectors/cluster
BX = no. of available clusters
CX = bytes/sector

DX = clusters/drive
If drive invalid,
AX = FFFFH

AH = 37H   *Reserved*

AH = 38H   *Get or set country*
Input: get country

AH = 39H   *Make directory*
Input: DS:DX points to ASCIIZ string
Output: If carry = 1, then
AX = error codes (3 or 5)

AH = 3AH   *Remove directory*
Input: DS:DX points to ASCIIZ string
Output: AX = error codes (3 or 5)

AH = 3BH   *Change current directory*
Input: DS:DX points to ASCIIZ string
Output: AX = error code (3)

AH = 3CH   *Open/Create file*
Input: DS:DX points to ASCIIZ string
CX = file attribute:
01H = read only
02H = hidden
04H = system
08H = volume label
10H = subdirectory
20H = archive
Output: AX = file handle
If carry = 1, then
AX = error codes (3, 4 or 5)

AH = 3DH   *Open file*
Input: DS:DX points to ASCIIZ string
AL = access code:
0 = open for reading
1 = open for writing
2 = open for reading and writing
Output: AX = file handle
If carry = 1, then
AX = error codes (2, 4, 5 or C)

AH = 3EH   *Close file handle*
Input: BX = file handle
Output: If carry = 1, then
AX = error code (6)

AH = 3FH   *Read from file or device*
Input: BX = file handle
CX = count of bytes to read
DS:DX points to buffer to receive data

TABLE D.1   *(cont.)*

Output: AX = actual number of bytes
read
(AX = 0 means end of file
read)
If carry = 1, then
AX = error codes (5 or 6)

AH =   *Write to file or device*
40H   Input: BX = file handle
CX = count of bytes to write
DS:DX points to buffer
containing data
Output: AX = actual number of bytes
written
(must equal CX for no error)
If carry = 1, then
AX = error codes (5 or 6)

AH =   *Delete file*
41H   Input: DS:DX points to ASCIIZ string
Output: If carry = 1, then
AX = error codes (2 or 5)

AH =   *Move file pointer*
42H   Input: BX = file handle
CX:DX = offset value (CX is
high-order word)
AL = method code:
0 = move pointer to start
of file + offset
1 = increase pointer by
offset
2 = move pointer to end of
file + offset
Output: DX:AX = new value of file
pointer
If carry = 1, then
AX = error codes (1 or 6)

AH =   *Get or set file attributes*
43H   Input: AL = 0 − get file attribute
AL = 1 − set file attribute
CX = new attribute (AL = 1)
DS:DX points to ASCIIZ string
Output: If carry = 0, successful
CX = attribute (AL = 0)
If carry = 1, then
AX = error code (1, 2, 3, or 5)

AH =   *Device-driver control (IOCTL)*
44H   Input: AL = subfunction
BX = handle
(subfunction = 0, 1, 2,
3, 6, 7, A)

BL = drive code
(subfunction = 4, 5,
8, 9)
CX = # of bytes to read or
write
DS:DX points to buffer area
(subfunction =2 − 5)
DX = device information
(subfunction = 1)
Output: If carry = 0, successful
AX = # of bytes transferred
(subfunction = 2 − 5)
AX = value (subfunction = 8)
AL = status (subfunction
= 6, 7)
DX = device info (subfunction
= 0)
If carry = 1, then
AX = err code (1, 4, 5, 6, D
or F)

AH =   *Duplicate handle*
45H   Input: BX = file handle
Output: If carry = 0, successful
AX = new file handle
If carry = 1, then
AX = error code (4 or 6)

AH =   *Force duplicate of handle*
46H   Input: BX = first file handle
CX = second file handle
Output: If carry = 1, then
AX = error code (4 or 6)

AH =   *Get current directory*
47H   Input: DL = drive code (1 = A, etc)
DS:SI points to 64-byte buffer
Output: If carry = 0, successful buffer
filled with complete
pathname
If carry = 1, then
AX = error code (0FH)

AH =   *Allocate memory*
48H   Input: BX = number of paragraphs of
memory needed
Output: If carry = 0, successful
AX = initial segment of
allocated block
If carry = 1, then
AX = error codes
7 memory control
blocks destroyed
8 insufficient memory

(cont.)

TABLE D.1   *(cont.)*

	BX = size of largest available block
AH = 49H	*Release memory*
	Input: ES = segment of block to be released
	Output: If carry = 0, successful
	If carry = 1, then
	AX = error codes
	7 memory control blocks destroyed
	9 invalid seg. in ES

AH =   *Release memory*
49H   Input: ES = segment of block to be
                             released
            Output: If carry = 0, successful
                      If carry = 1, then
                         AX = error codes
                             7 memory control
                                 blocks destroyed
                             9 invalid seg. in ES

AH =   *Modify memory allocation*
4AH   Input: BX = new requested block
                             size in paragraphs
                     ES = segment of block to be
                             modified
            Output: If carry = 0, successful
                      If carry = 1, then
                         AX = error codes
                             7 memory control
                                 blocks destroyed
                             8 insufficient memory
                             9 invalid seg in ES
                     BX = maximum block size
                             available

AH =   *Execute program*
4BH   Input: AL = 00 if loading &
                                 executing program
                     AL = 03 if loading overlay
                     ES:BX → parameter block
                     DS:DX → ASCIIZ string
            Output: If carry = 0, successful all
                                 registers except CS
                                 & IP destroyed
                      If carry = 1, then
                         AX = error code (1, 2, 5, 8, A
                                 or F)

AH =   *Terminate with return code*
4CH   Input: AL = return code
            Output: none

AH =   *Get return code*
4DH   Input: none
            Output: AH = exit type
                     AL = return code

AH =   *Search directory for first match*
4EH   Input: CX = attribute to use in
                                 search
                     DS:DX points of ASCIIZ file
                                 specification

Output: If carry = 0
                     DTA contains data in Fig.
                     15.23
                      If carry = 1, then
                         AX = error codes (2 or 12H)

AH =   *Search directory for next match*
4FH   Input: none
            Output: If carry = 0
                     DTA contains data in Fig.
                     15.23
                      If carry = 1, then
                         AX = error codes (12H)

AH =   *Reserved*
50H

AH =   *Reserved*
51H

AH =   *Reserved*
52H

AH =   *Reserved*
53H

AH =   *Get verify flag*
54H   Input: none
            Output: AL = 00 if verify flag off
                     AL = 01 if verify flag on

AH =   *Reserved*
55H

AH =   *Rename file*
56H   Input: DS:DX → current ASCIIZ
                                 filename
                     ES:DI → new ASCIIZ filename
            Output: If carry = 0, successful
                      If carry = 1, then
                         AX = error code (2, 3, 5 or
                                 11H)

AH =   *Get or set file date and time*
57H   Input: BX = handle
                     If getting date/time
                     AL = 00
                     If setting date/time
                     AL = 01
                     CX = time
                        Bits 0BH–0FH = hours
                        (0–23)
                        Bits 05–0AH = minutes
                        (0–59)
                        Bits 00–04 = # 2 sec inc
                        (0–29)
                     DX = date

TABLE D.1 *(cont.)*

	Bits 09–0FH = year (+ 1980)	AH = 5BH	*Create new file*
	Bits 05–08 = month (1–12)		Input: CX = file attribute
	Bits 00–04 = day of mos. (0–31)		DS:DX → ASCIIZ path string
	Output: If carry = 0, successful		Output: If carry = 0, successful
	If getting date/time		AX = handle
	CX = time (see above format)		If carry = 1, then
	DX = date (see above format)		AX = error code (3, 4, 5 or 50H)
	If carry = 1, then		error 50H = file already exists
	AX = error code (1 or 6)	AH = 5CH	*Control record access*
AH = 58H	*Get or set allocation strategy*		Input: AL = function code
	Input: If getting strategy		00 if locking
	AL = 00		01 if unlocking
	If setting strategy		BX = file handle
	AL = 01		CX = region offset high
	BX = strategy code		DX = region offset low
	= 00 if first fit		SI = region length high
	= 01 if best fit		DI = region length low
	= 02 if last fit		Output: If carry = 0, successful
	Output: If carry = 0, successful		If carry = 1, then
	If getting strategy code		AX = error code (1, 6 or 21H)
	AX = strategy code		error 21H = lock violation
	If carry = 1, then	AH = 5DH	*Reserved*
	AX = error code (1)		
AH = 59H	*Get extended error information*	AH = 5EH	*Network machine name/printer setup*
	Input: BX = 0	AH = 5FH	Get/make assign-list entry
	Output: AX = extended error code		
AH = 5AH	*Create temporary file*	AH = 60H	*Reserved*
	Input: CX = file attribute		
	DS:DX → ASCIIZ path string	AH = 61H	*Reserved*
	Output: If carry = 0, successful		
	AX = handle	AH = 62H	*Get program segment prefix address*
	DS:DX → ASCIIZ file spec.		Input: none
	If carry = 1, then		Output: BX = segment address of PSP
	AX = error code (3 or 5)		

TABLE D.2 STANDARD ERROR CODES

Error code	Meaning
1	Invalid function number
2	File not found
3	Path not found
4	No handle available: all in use
5	Access denied
6	Invalid handle
7	Memory control blocks destroyed
8	Insufficient memory
9	Invalid memory block address
A	Invalid environment
B	Invalid format
C	Invalid access code
D	Invalid data
E	Not used
F	Invalid drive specification
10	Attempt to remove current directory
11	Not same device
12	No more files to be found

Appendix E

LOGIC ANALYZER HARDWARE

The logic analyzer program described in Experiment 1 at the end of Chapter 3 is used to test logic circuits that are built on a prototype breadboard and interfaced to the PC through a parallel printer port. We have mounted a prototype breadboard on a plexiglass base, as shown in Fig. E.1. A ribbon cable is connected to the parallel printer port, and the eight output data lines (pins 2–9 in Fig. 3.27) are connected directly to the eight banana jacks labeled Out0–Out7 shown in Fig. E.1 (see Table 3.1). The five banana jacks labeled In0–In4 in Fig. E.1 are connected to the input pins of the printer port (see Fig. 3.27 and Table 3.1) using a 330 Ω pull-down resistor as shown in Fig. E.2(a).

Three optional banana jacks representing test points (TST1–TST3) with adjacent LEDs can be used to test a point in the circuit for +5 V (LED on) or ground (LED off). The circuit for these test points is shown in Fig. E.2(b). These test points are useful for students to debug their circuits.

A 9-volt wall plug transformer is used to provide 5-volt power to the board using the circuit shown in Fig. E.3. The +5 volts and ground signals are connected to the two banana jacks labeled +5 V and GND in Fig. E.1. The student will connect +5 volts and ground to their prototype breadboard using No. AWG 22 solid wire with a banana plug on one end and the insulation stripped on the other end so that it can be plugged into the breadboard. This same type of wire is used to connect all of the banana jack signals to the breadboard.

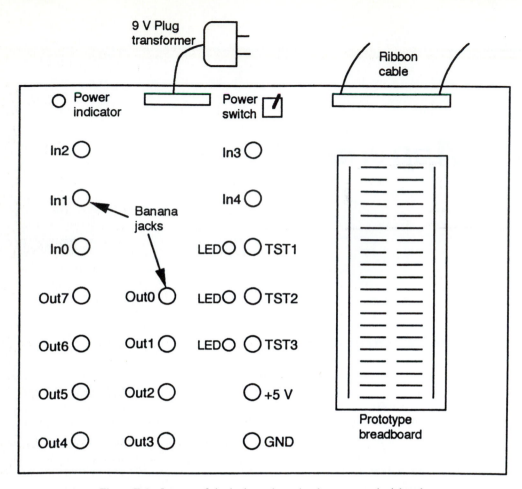

Figure E.1   Layout of the logic analyzer hardware on a plexiglass base.

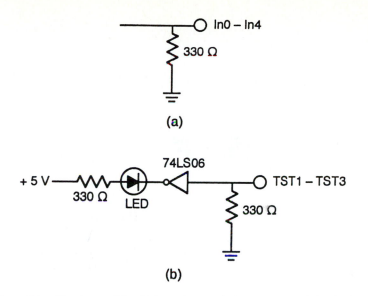

(a)

(b)

Figure E.2   Circuits used for (a) input banana jacks In0–In4, and (b) the 3 test points TST1–TST3.

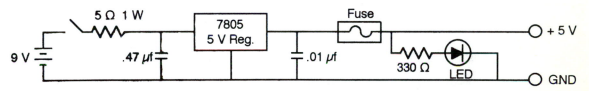

Figure E.3   Circuit used to produce the 5 volts on the logic analyzer board.

Appendix F

DATA SHEETS

GAL 16V8A/B High Performance E²CMOS PLD
Motorola MC6845 CRT Controller
National INS8250 Universal Asynchronous Receiver/Transmitter (UART)

GAL16V8B
GAL16V8A

High Performance E²CMOS PLD

LATTICE SEMICONDUCTOR CORP., 5555 N.E. Moore Ct., Hillsboro, Oregon 97124, U.S.A.
Tel. (503) 681-0118; 1-800-FASTGAL; FAX (503) 681-3037

FEATURES

- **HIGH PERFORMANCE E²CMOS® TECHNOLOGY**
  - 7.5 ns Maximum Propagation Delay
  - Fmax = 100 MHz
  - 5 ns Maximum from Clock Input to Data Output
  - TTL Compatible 24 mA Outputs
  - UltraMOS® Advanced CMOS Technology

- **50% to 75% REDUCTION IN POWER FROM BIPOLAR**
  - 75mA Typ Icc on Low Power Device
  - 45mA Typ Icc on Quarter Power Device

- **ACTIVE PULL-UPS ON ALL PINS (GAL16V8B)**

- **E² CELL TECHNOLOGY**
  - Reconfigurable Logic
  - Reprogrammable Cells
  - 100% Tested/Guaranteed 100% Yields
  - High Speed Electrical Erasure (<100ms)
  - 20 Year Data Retention

- **EIGHT OUTPUT LOGIC MACROCELLS**
  - Maximum Flexibility for Complex Logic Designs
  - Programmable Output Polarity
  - Also Emulates 20-pin PAL® Devices with Full Function/Fuse Map/Parametric Compatibility

- **PRELOAD AND POWER-ON RESET OF ALL REGISTERS**
  - 100% Functional Testability

- **APPLICATIONS INCLUDE:**
  - DMA Control
  - State Machine Control
  - High Speed Graphics Processing
  - Standard Logic Speed Upgrade

- **ELECTRONIC SIGNATURE FOR IDENTIFICATION**

FUNCTIONAL BLOCK DIAGRAM

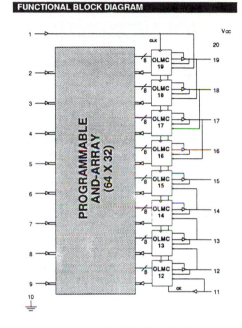

DESCRIPTION

The GAL16V8B, at 7.5 ns maximum propagation delay time, combines a high performance CMOS process with Electrically Erasable (E²) floating gate technology to provide the highest speed performance available in the PLD market. High speed erase times (<100ms) allow the devices to be reprogrammed quickly and efficiently.

The generic architecture provides maximum design flexibility by allowing the Output Logic Macrocell (OLMC) to be configured by the user. An important subset of the many architecture configurations possible with the GAL16V8A/B are the PAL architectures listed in the table of the macrocell description section. GAL16V8A/B devices are capable of emulating any of these PAL architectures with full function/fuse map/parametric compatibility.

Unique test circuitry and reprogrammable cells allow complete AC, DC, and functional testing during manufacture. As a result, LATTICE is able to guarantee 100% field programmability and functionality of all GAL® products. LATTICE also guarantees 100 erase/rewrite cycles and data retention in excess of 20 years.

PIN CONFIGURATION

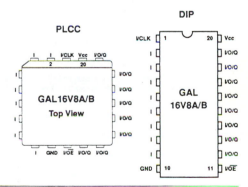

April 1991.Rev.A

Specifications *GAL16V8B*
GAL16V8A

GAL16V8A/B ORDERING INFORMATION

Commercial Grade Specifications

Tpd (ns)	Tsu (ns)	Tco (ns)	Icc (mA)	Ordering #	Package
7.5	7	5	115	GAL16V8B-7LP	20-Pin Plastic DIP
			115	GAL16V8B-7LJ	20-Lead PLCC
10	10	7	115	GAL16V8B-10LP	20-Pin Plastic DIP
			115	GAL16V8B-10LJ	20-Lead PLCC
			115	GAL16V8A-10LP	20-Pin Plastic DIP
			115	GAL16V8A-10LJ	20-Lead PLCC
15	12	10	55	GAL16V8A-15QP	20-Pin Plastic DIP
			55	GAL16V8A-15QJ	20-Lead PLCC
			115	GAL16V8A-15LP	20-Pin Plastic DIP
			115	GAL16V8A-15LJ	20-Lead PLCC
25	15	12	55	GAL16V8A-25QP	20-Pin Plastic DIP
			55	GAL16V8A-25QJ	20-Lead PLCC
			90	GAL16V8A-25LP	20-Pin Plastic DIP
			90	GAL16V8A-25LJ	20-Lead PLCC

Industrial Grade Specifications

Tpd (ns)	Tsu (ns)	Tco (ns)	Icc (mA)	Ordering #	Package
10	10	7	130	GAL16V8B-10LPI	20-Pin Plastic DIP
			130	GAL16V8B-10LJI	20-Lead PLCC
15	12	10	130	GAL16V8B-15LPI	20-Pin Plastic DIP
			130	GAL16V8B-15LJI	20-Lead PLCC
			130	GAL16V8A-15LPI	20-Pin Plastic DIP
			130	GAL16V8A-15LJI	20-Lead PLCC
20	13	11	65	GAL16V8A-20QPI	20-Pin Plastic DIP
			65	GAL16V8A-20QJI	20-Lead PLCC
25	15	12	65	GAL16V8A-25QPI	20-Pin Plastic DIP
			65	GAL16V8A-25QJI	20-Lead PLCC
			130	GAL16V8A-25LPI	20-Pin Plastic DIP
			130	GAL16V8A-25LJI	20-Lead PLCC

PART NUMBER DESCRIPTION

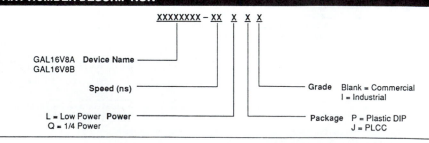

Specifications *GAL16V8B*
GAL16V8A

OUTPUT LOGIC MACROCELL (OLMC)

The following discussion pertains to configuring the output logic macrocell. It should be noted that actual implementation is accomplished by development software/hardware and is completely transparent to the user.

There are three global OLMC configuration modes possible: **simple**, **complex**, and **registered**. Details of each of these modes is illustrated in the following pages. Two global bits, SYN and AC0, control the mode configuration for all macrocells. The XOR bit of each macrocell controls the polarity of the output in any of the three modes, while the AC1 bit of each of the macrocells controls the input/output configuration. These two global and 16 individual architecture bits define all possible configurations in a GAL16V8A/B. The information given on these architecture bits is only to give a better understanding of the device. Compiler software will transparently set these architecture bits from the pin definitions, so the user should not need to directly manipulate these architecture bits.

The following is a list of the PAL architectures that the GAL16V8A and GAL16V8B can emulate. It also shows the OLMC mode under which the GAL16V8A/B emulates the PAL architecture.

PAL Architectures Emulated by GAL16V8A/B	GAL16V8A/B Global OLMC Mode
16R8	Registered
16R6	Registered
16R4	Registered
16RP8	Registered
16RP6	Registered
16RP4	Registered
16L8	Complex
16H8	Complex
16P8	Complex
10L8	Simple
12L6	Simple
14L4	Simple
16L2	Simple
10H8	Simple
12H6	Simple
14H4	Simple
16H2	Simple
10P8	Simple
12P6	Simple
14P4	Simple
16P2	Simple

COMPILER SUPPORT FOR OLMC

Software compilers support the three different global OLMC modes as different device types. These device types are listed in the table below. Most compilers have the ability to automatically select the device type, generally based on the register usage and output enable (OE) usage. Register usage on the device forces the software to choose the registered mode. All combinatorial outputs with OE controlled by the product term will force the software to choose the complex mode. The software will choose the simple mode only when all outputs are dedicated combinatorial without OE control. The different device types listed in the table can be used to override the automatic device selection by the software. For further details, refer to the compiler software manuals.

When using compiler software to configure the device, the user must pay special attention to the following restrictions in each mode.

In **registered mode** pin 1 and pin 11 are permanently configured as clock and output enable, respectively. These pins cannot be configured as dedicated inputs in the registered mode.

In **complex mode** pin 1 and pin 11 become dedicated inputs and use the feedback paths of pin 19 and pin 12 respectively. Because of this feedback path usage, pin 19 and pin 12 do not have the feedback option in this mode.

In **simple mode** all feedback paths of the output pins are routed via the adjacent pins. In doing so, the two inner most pins (pins 15 and 16) will not have the feedback option as these pins are always configured as dedicated combinatorial output.

	Registered	Complex	Simple	Auto Mode Select
ABEL	P16V8R	P16V8C	P16V8AS	P16V8
CUPL	G16V8MS	G16V8MA	G16V8AS	G16V8
LOG/IC	GAL16V8_R	GAL16V8_C7	GAL16V8_C8	GAL16V8
OrCAD-PLD	"Registered"[1]	"Complex"[1]	"Simple"[1]	GAL16V8A
PLDesigner	P16V8R[2]	P16V8C[2]	P16V8C[2]	P16V8A
TANGO-PLD	G16V8R	G16V8C	G16V8AS[3]	G16V8

1) Used with **Configuration** keyword.
2) Prior to Version 2.0 support.
3) Supported on Version 1.20 or later.

Specifications *GAL16V8B*
GAL16V8A

REGISTERED MODE

In the Registered mode, macrocells are configured as dedicated registered outputs or as I/O functions.

Architecture configurations available in this mode are similar to the common 16R8 and 16RP4 devices with various permutations of polarity, I/O and register placement.

All registered macrocells share common clock and output enable control pins. Any macrocell can be configured as registered or I/O. Up to eight registers or up to eight I/O's are possible in this mode. Dedicated input or output functions can be implemented as subsets of the I/O function.

Registered outputs have eight product terms per output. I/O's have seven product terms per output.

The JEDEC fuse numbers, including the User Electronic Signature (UES) fuses and the Product Term Disable (PTD) fuses, are shown on the logic diagram on the following page.

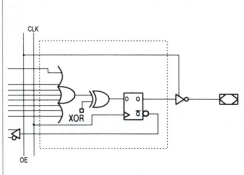

Registered Configuration for Registered Mode

- SYN=0.
- AC0=1.
- XOR=0 defines Active Low Output.
- XOR=1 defines Active High Output.
- AC1=0 defines this output configuration.
- Pin 1 controls common CLK for the registered outputs.
- Pin 11 controls common $\overline{OE}$ for the registered outputs.
- Pin 1 & Pin 11 are permanently configured as CLK & $\overline{OE}$.

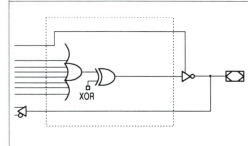

Combinatorial Configuration for Registered Mode

- SYN=0.
- AC0=1.
- XOR=0 defines Active Low Output.
- XOR=1 defines Active High Output.
- AC1=1 defines this output configuration.
- Pin 1 & Pin 11 are permanently configured as CLK & $\overline{OE}$.

Note: The development software configures all of the architecture control bits and checks for proper pin usage automatically.

Specifications *GAL16V8B* *GAL16V8A*

REGISTERED MODE LOGIC DIAGRAM

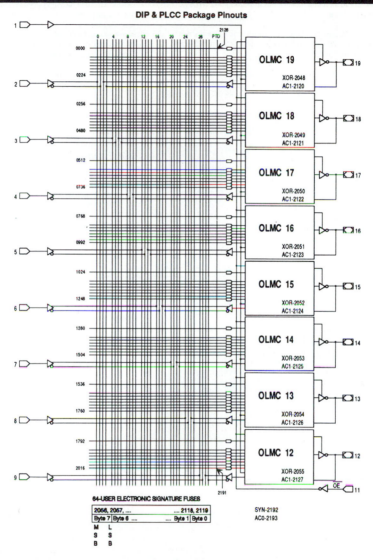

DIP & PLCC Package Pinouts

Specifications *GAL16V8B*
GAL16V8A

COMPLEX MODE

In the Complex mode, macrocells are configured as output only or I/O functions.

Architecture configurations available in this mode are similar to the common 16L8 and 16P8 devices with programmable polarity in each macrocell.

Up to six I/O's are possible in this mode. Dedicated inputs or outputs can be implemented as subsets of the I/O function. The two outer most macrocells (pins 12 & 19) do not have input ca-

pability. Designs requiring eight I/O's can be implemented in the Registered mode.

All macrocells have seven product terms per output. One product term is used for programmable output enable control. Pins 1 and 11 are always available as data inputs into the AND array.

The JEDEC fuse numbers including the UES fuses and PTD fuses are shown on the logic diagram on the following page.

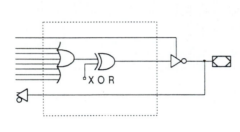

Combinatorial I/O Configuration for Complex Mode

- SYN=1.
- AC0=1.
- XOR=0 defines Active Low Output.
- XOR=1 defines Active High Output.
- AC1=1.
- Pin 13 through Pin 18 are configured to this function.

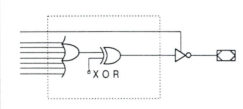

Combinatorial Output Configuration for Complex Mode

- SYN=1.
- AC0=1.
- XOR=0 defines Active Low Output.
- XOR=1 defines Active High Output.
- AC1=1.
- Pin 12 and Pin 19 are configured to this function.

Note: The development software configures all of the architecture control bits and checks for proper pin usage automatically.

COMPLEX MODE LOGIC DIAGRAM

DIP & PLCC Package Pinouts

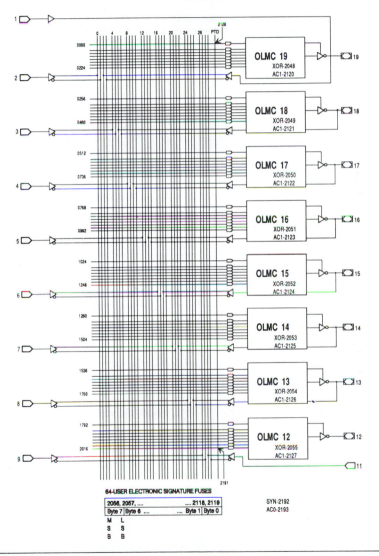

Lattice®
Semiconductor
Corporation

Specifications *GAL16V8B*
GAL16V8A

SIMPLE MODE

In the Simple mode, macrocells are configured as dedicated inputs or as dedicated, always active, combinatorial outputs.

Architecture configurations available in this mode are similar to the common 10L8 and 12P6 devices with many permutations of generic output polarity or input choices.

All outputs in the simple mode have a maximum of eight product terms that can control the logic. In addition, each output has programmable polarity.

Pins 1 and 11 are always available as data inputs into the AND array. The center two macrocells (pins 15 & 16) cannot be used as input or I/O pins, and are only available as dedicated outputs.

The JEDEC fuse numbers including the UES fuses and PTD fuses are shown on the logic diagram.

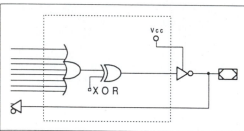

Combinatorial Output with Feedback Configuration for Simple Mode

- SYN=1.
- AC0=0.
- XOR=0 defines Active Low Output.
- XOR=1 defines Active High Output.
- AC1=0 defines this configuration.
- All OLMC **except** pins 15 & 16 can be configured to this function.

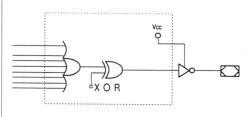

Combinatorial Output Configuration for Simple Mode

- SYN=1.
- AC0=0.
- XOR=0 defines Active Low Output.
- XOR=1 defines Active High Output.
- AC1=0 defines this configuration.
- Pins 15 & 16 are permanently configured to this function.

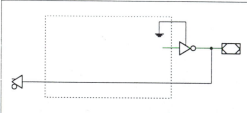

Dedicated Input Configuration for Simple Mode

- SYN=1.
- AC0=0.
- XOR=0 defines Active Low Output.
- XOR=1 defines Active High Output.
- AC1=1 defines this configuration.
- All OLMC **except** pins 15 & 16 can be configured to this function.

Note: The development software configures all of the architecture control bits and checks for proper pin usage automatically.

Specifications *GAL16V8B*
GAL16V8A

SIMPLE MODE LOGIC DIAGRAM

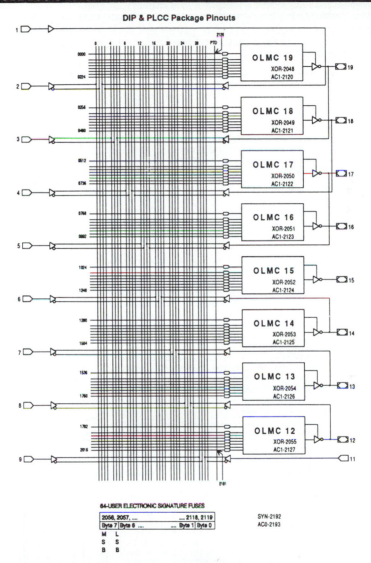

DIP & PLCC Package Pinouts

64-USER ELECTRONIC SIGNATURE FUSES

2056, 2057, ...	.... 2118, 2119
Byte 7	Byte 6	.... Byte 1	Byte 0

M   L
S   S
B   B

SYN-2192
AC0-2193

MOTOROLA

SEMICONDUCTORS

3501 ED BLUESTEIN BLVD., AUSTIN, TEXAS 78721

MC6845

CRT CONTROLLER (CRTC)

The MC6845 CRT controller performs the interface between an MPU and a raster-scan CRT display. It is intended for use in MPU-based controllers for CRT terminals in stand-alone or cluster configurations.

The CRTC is optimized for the hardware/software balance required for maximum flexibility. All keyboard functions, reads, writes, cursor movements, and editing are under processor control. The CRTC provides video timing and refresh memory addressing.

- Useful in Monochrome or Color CRT Applications
- Applications Include "Glass-Teletype," Smart, Programmable, Intelligent CRT Terminals; Video Games; Information Displays
- Alphanumeric, Semi-Graphic, and Full-Graphic Capability
- Fully Programmable Via Processor Data Bus. Timing May Be Generated for Almost Any Alphanumeric Screen Format, e.g., 80 × 24, 72 × 64, 132 × 20
- Single +5 V Supply
- M6800 Compatible Bus Interface
- TTL-Compatible Inputs and Outputs
- Start Address Register Provides Hardware Scroll (by Page or Character)
- Programmable Cursor Register Allows Control of Cursor Format and Blink Rate
- Light Pen Register
- Refresh (Screen) Memory May be Multiplexed Between the CRTC and the MPU Thus Removing the Requirements for Line Buffers or External DMA Devices
- Programmable Interlace or Non-Interlace Scan Modes
- 14-Bit Refresh Address Allows Up to 16K of Refresh Memory for Use in Character or Semi-Graphic Displays
- 5-Bit Row Address Allows Up to 32 Scan-Line Character Blocks
- By Utilizing Both the Refresh Addresses and the Row Addresses, a 512K Address Space is Available for Use in Graphics Systems
- Refresh Addresses are Provided During Retrace, Allowing the CRTC to Provide Row Addresses to Refresh Dynamic RAMs
- Pin Compatible with the MC6835

MOS
(N-CHANNEL, SILICON-GATE)

CRT CONTROLLER
(CRTC)

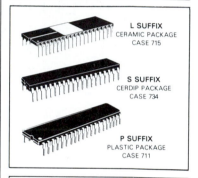

L SUFFIX
CERAMIC PACKAGE
CASE 715

S SUFFIX
CERDIP PACKAGE
CASE 734

P SUFFIX
PLASTIC PACKAGE
CASE 711

PIN ASSIGNMENT

GND	1	40	VS
RESET	2	39	HS
LPSTB	3	38	RA0
MA0	4	37	RA1
MA1	5	36	RA2
MA2	6	35	RA3
MA3	7	34	RA4
MA4	8	33	D0
MA5	9	32	D1
MA6	10	31	D2
MA7	11	30	D3
MA8	12	29	D4
MA9	13	28	D5
MA10	14	27	D6
MA11	15	26	D7
MA12	16	25	$\overline{CS}$
MA13	17	24	RS
DE	18	23	E
CURSOR	19	22	R/$\overline{W}$
V_{CC}	20	21	CLK

ORDERING INFORMATION

Package Type	Frequency (MHz)	Temperature	Order Number
Ceramic L Suffix	1.0	0°C to 70°C	MC6845L
	1.0	−40°C to 85°C	MC6845CL
	1.5	0°C to 70°C	MC68A45L
	1.5	−40°C to 85°C	MC68A45CL
	2.0	0°C to 70°C	MC68B45L
Cerdip S Suffix	1.0	0°C to 70°C	MC6845S
	1.0	−40°C to 85°C	MC6845CS
	1.5	0°C to 70°C	MC68A45S
	1.5	−40°C to 85°C	MC68A45CS
	2.0	0°C to 70°C	MC68B45S
Plastic P Suffix	1.0	0°C to 70°C	MC6845P
	1.0	−40°C to 85°C	MC6845CP
	1.5	0°C to 70°C	MC68A45P
	1.5	−40°C to 85°C	MC68A45CP
	2.0	0°C to 70°C	MC68B45P

MC6845

FIGURE 1 — TYPICAL CRT CONTROLLER APPLICATION

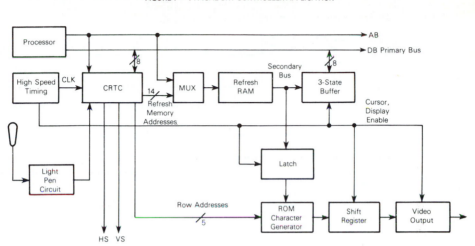

MAXIMUM RATINGS

Rating	Symbol	Value	Unit
Supply Voltage	V_{CC}	-0.3 to $+7.0$	V
Input Voltage	V_{in}	-0.3 to $+7.0$	V
Operating Temperature Range MC6845, MC68A45, MC68B45 MC6845C, MC68A45C	T_A	T_L to T_H 0 to 70 -40 to $+85$	°C
Storage Temperature Range	T_{stg}	-55 to $+150$	°C

THERMAL CHARACTERISTICS

Characteristic	Symbol	Value	Rating
Thermal Resistance Plastic Package Cerdip Package Ceramic Package	θ_{JA}	100 60 50	°C/W

The device contains circuitry to protect the inputs against damage due to high static voltages or electric fields; however, it is advised that normal precautions be taken to avoid application of any voltage higher than maximum rated voltages to this high-impedance circuit. For proper operation it is recommended that V_{in} and V_{out} be constrained to the range $V_{SS} \le (V_{in}$ or $V_{out}) \le V_{CC}$.

RECOMMENDED OPERATING CONDITIONS

Characteristics	Symbol	Min	Typ	Max	Unit
Supply Voltage	V_{CC}	4.75	5.0	5.25	V
Input Low Voltage	V_{IL}	-0.3	—	0.8	V
Input High Voltage	V_{IH}	2.0	—	V_{CC}	V

MOTOROLA *Semiconductor Products Inc.*

MC6845

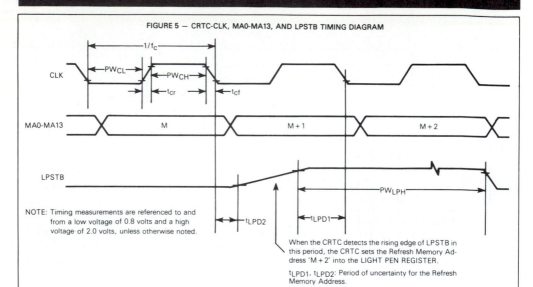

FIGURE 5 — CRTC-CLK, MA0-MA13, AND LPSTB TIMING DIAGRAM

NOTE: Timing measurements are referenced to and from a low voltage of 0.8 volts and a high voltage of 2.0 volts, unless otherwise noted.

When the CRTC detects the rising edge of LPSTB in this period, the CRTC sets the Refresh Memory Address 'M + 2' into the LIGHT PEN REGISTER.

t_{LPD1}, t_{LPD2}: Period of uncertainty for the Refresh Memory Address.

CRTC INTERFACE SYSTEM DESCRIPTION

The CRT controller generates the signals necessary to interface a digital system to a raster scan CRT display. In this type of display, an electron beam starts in the upper left hand corner, moves quickly across the screen and returns. This action is called a horizontal scan. After each horizontal scan the beam is incrementally moved down in the vertical direction until it has reached the bottom. At this point one frame has been displayed, as the beam has made many horizontal scans and one vertical scan.

Two types of raster scanning are used in CRTs, interlace and non-interlace, shown in Figures 6 and 7. Non-interlace scanning consists of one field per frame. The scan lines in Figure 6 are shown as solid lines and the retrace patterns are indicated by the dotted lines. Increasing the number of frames per second will decrease the flicker. Ordinarily, either a 50 or 60 frame per second refresh rate is used to minimize beating between the CRT and the power line frequency. This prevents the displayed data from weaving.

Interlace scanning is used in broadcast TV and on data monitors where high density or high resolution data must be displayed. Two fields, or vertical scans are made down the screen for each single picture or frame. The first field (even field) starts in the upper left hand corner; the second (odd field) in the upper center. Both fields overlap as shown in Figure 7, thus interlacing the two fields into a single frame.

In order to display the characters on the CRT screen the frames must be continually repeated. The data to be displayed is stored in the refresh (screen) memory by the MPU controlling the data processing system. The data is usually written in ASCII code, so it cannot be directly displayed as characters. A character generator ROM is typically used to convert the ASCII codes into the "dot" pattern for every character.

The most common method of generating characters is to create a matrix of dots "x" dots (columns) wide and "y" dots (rows) high. Each character is created by selectively filling in

FIGURE 6 — RASTER SCAN SYSTEM (NON-INTERLACE)

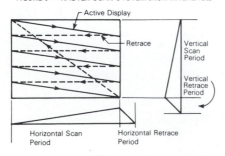

FIGURE 7 — RASTER SCAN SYSTEM (INTERLACE)

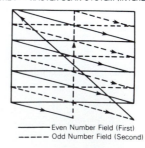

 MOTOROLA *Semiconductor Products Inc.*

MC6845

the dots. As "x" and "y" get larger a more detailed character may be created. Two common dot matrices are 5 × 7 and 7 × 9. Many variations of these standards will allow Chinese, Japanese, or Arabic letters instead of English. Since characters require some space between them, a character block larger than the character is typically used, as shown in Figure 8. The figure also shows the corresponding timing and levels for a video signal that would generate the characters.

Referring to Figure 1, the CRT controller generates the refresh addresses (MA0-MA13), row addresses (RA0-RA4), and the video timing (vertical sync — VS, horizontal sync — HS, and display enable — DE). Other functions include an internal cursor register which generates a cursor output when its contents compare to the current refresh address. A light pen strobe input signal allows capture of the refresh address in an internal light pen register.

All timing in the CRTC is derived from the CLK input. In alphanumeric terminals, this signal is the character rate. The video rate or "dot" clock is externally divided by high-speed logic (TTL) to generate the CLK input. The high-speed logic must also generate the timing and control signals necessary for the shift register, latch, and MUX control.

The processor communicates with the CRTC through an 8-bit data bus by reading or writing into the 19 registers.

The refresh memory address is multiplexed between the processor and the CRTC. Data appears on a secondary bus separate from the processor's bus. The secondary data bus concept in no way precludes using the refresh RAM for other purposes. It looks like any other RAM to the processor. A number of approaches are possible for solving contentions for the refresh memory:

1. Processor always gets priority. (Generally, "hash" occurs as MPU and CRTC clocks are not synchronized.)

2. Processor gets priority access anytime, but can be synchronized by an interrupt to perform accesses only during horizontal and vertical retrace times.

3. Synchronize the processor with memory wait cycles (states).

4. Synchronize the processor to the character rate as shown in Figure 9. The M6800 processor family works works very well in this configuration as constant cycle lengths are present. This method provides no overhead for the processor as there is never a contention for a memory access. All accesses are transparent.

FIGURE 8 — CHARACTER DISPLAY ON THE SCREEN AND VIDEO SIGNAL

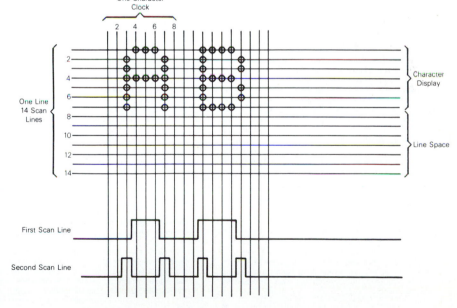

MOTOROLA *Semiconductor Products Inc.*

FIGURE 9 — TRANSPARENT REFRESH MEMORY
CONFIGURATION TIMING USING M6800 FAMILY MPU

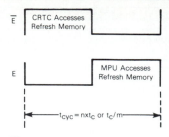

FIGURE 9 — TRANSPARENT REFRESH MEMORY
CONFIGURATION TIMING USING M6800 FAMILY MPU

Where: m, n are integers; t_C is character period

PIN DESCRIPTION

PROCESSOR INTERFACE

The CRTC interfaces to a processor bus on the bidirectional data bus (D0-D7) using $\overline{CS}$, RS, E, and R/$\overline{W}$ for control signals.

Data Bus (D0-D7) — The bidirectional data lines (D0-D7) allow data transfers between the internal CRTC register file and the processor. Data bus output drivers are in the high-impedance state until the processor performs a CRTC read operation.

Enable (E) — The enable signal is a high-impedance TTL/MOS compatible input which enables the data bus input/output buffers and clocks data to and from the CRTC. This signal is usually derived from the processor clock. The high-to-low transition is the active edge.

Chip Select ($\overline{CS}$) — The $\overline{CS}$ line is a high-impedance TTL/MOS compatible input which selects the CRTC, when low, to read or write to the internal register file. This signal should only be active when there is a valid stable address being decoded from the processor.

Register Select (RS) — The RS line is a high-impedance TTL/MOS compatible input which selects either the address register (RS = 0) or one of the data register (RS = 1) or the internal register file.

Read/Write (R/$\overline{W}$) — The R/$\overline{W}$ line is a high-impedance TTL/MOS compatible input which determines whether the internal register file gets written or read. A write is defined as a low level.

CRT CONTROL

The CRTC provides horizontal sync (HS), vertical sync (VS), and display enable (DE) signals.

NOTE

Care should be exercised when interfacing to CRT monitors, as many monitors claiming to be "TTL compatible" have transistor input circuits which require the CRTC or TTL devices buffering signals from the CRTC/video circuits to exceed the maximum-rated drive currents.

Vertical Sync (VS) and Horizontal Sync (HS) — These TTL-compatible outputs are active high signals which drive the monitor directly or are fed to the video processing circuitry to generate a composite video signal. The VS signal determines the vertical position of the displayed text while the HS signal determines the horizontal position of the displayed text.

Display Enable (DE) — This TTL-compatible output is an active high signal which indicates the CRTC is providing addressing in the active display area.

REFRESH MEMORY/CHARACTER GENERATOR ADDRESSING

The CRTC provides memory addresses (MA0-MA13) to scan the refresh RAM. Row addresses (RA0-RA4) are also provided for use with character generator ROMs. In a graphics system, both the memory addresses and the row addresses would be used to scan the refresh RAM. Both the memory addresses and the row addresses continue to run during vertical retrace thus allowing the CRTC to provide the refresh addresses required to refresh dynamic RAMs.

Refresh Memory Addresses (MA0-MA13) — These 14 outputs are used to refresh the CRT screen with pages of data located within a 16K block of refresh memory. These outputs are capable of driving one standard TTL load and 30 pF.

Row Addresses (RA0-RA4) — These five outputs from the internal row address counter are used to address the character generator ROM. These outputs are capable of driving one standard TTL load and 30 pF.

OTHER PINS

Cursor — This TTL-compatible output indicates a valid cursor address to external video processing logic. It is an active high signal.

Clock (CLK) — The CLK is a TTL/MOS-compatible input used to synchronize all CRT functions except for the processor interface. An external dot counter is used to derive this signal which is usually the character rate in an alphanumeric CRT. The active transition is high-to-low.

 MOTOROLA *Semiconductor Products Inc.*

Light Pen Strobe (LPSTB) — A low-to-high transition on this high-impedance TTL/MOS-compatible input latches the current Refresh Address in the light pen register. The latching of the refresh address is internally synchronized to the character clock (CLK).

V_{CC} and V_{SS} — These inputs supply +5 Vdc ±5% to the CRTC.

$\overline{RESET}$ — The $\overline{RESET}$ input is used to reset the CRTC. A low level on the $\overline{RESET}$ input forces the CRTC into the following state:

(a) All counters in the CRTC are cleared and the device stops the display operation.

(b) All the outputs are driven low.

NOTE

The horizontal sync output is not defined until after R2 is programmed.

(c) The control registers of the CRTC are not affected and remain unchanged.

Functionality of $\overline{RESET}$ differs from that of other M6800 parts in the following functions:

(a) The $\overline{RESET}$ input and the LPSTB input are encoded as shown in Table 1.

TABLE 1 — CRTC OPERATING MODE

$\overline{RESET}$	LPSTB	Operating Mode
0	0	Reset
0	1	Test Mode
1	0	Normal Mode
1	1	Normal Mode

The test mode configures the memory addresses as two independent 7-bit counters to minimize test time.

(b) After $\overline{RESET}$ has gone low and (LPSTB = 0), MA0-MA13 and RA0-RA4 will be driven low on the falling edge of CLK. $\overline{RESET}$ must remain low for at least one cycle of the character clock (CLK).

(c) The CRTC resumes the display operation immediately after the release of $\overline{RESET}$. DE and the CURSOR are not active until after the first frame has been displayed.

CRTC DESCRIPTION

The CRTC consists of programmable horizontal and vertical timing generators, programmable linear address register, programmable cursor logic, light pen capture register, and control circuitry for interface to a processor bus. A block diagram of the CRTC is shown in Figure 10.

All CRTC timing is derived from the CLK, usually the output of an external dot rate counter. Coincidence (CO) circuits continuously compare counter contents to the contents of the programmable register file, R0-R17. For horizontal timing generation, comparisons result in: 1) horizontal sync pulse (HS) of a frequency, position, and width determined by the registers; 2) horizontal display signal of a frequency, position, and duration determined by the registers.

The horizontal counter produces H clock which drives the scan line counter and vertical control. The contents of the raster counter are continuously compared to the maximum scan line address register. A coincidence resets the raster counter and clocks the vertical counter.

Comparisons of vertical counter contents and vertical registers result in: 1) vertical sync pulse (VS) of a frequency and position determined by the registers; 2) vertical display of a frequency and position determined by the registers.

The vertical control logic has other functions.

1. Generate row selects, RA0-RA4, from the raster count for the corresponding interlace or non-interlace modes.

2. Extend the number of scan lines in the vertical total by the amount programmed in the vertical total adjust register.

The linear address generator is driven by the CLK and locates the relative positions of characters in memory with their positions on the screen. Fourteen lines, MA0-MA13, are available for addressing up to four pages of 4K characters, eight pages of 2K characters, etc. Using the start address register, hardware scrolling through 16K characters is possible. The linear address generator repeats the same sequence of addresses for each scan line of a character row.

The cursor logic determines the cursor location, size, and blink rate on the screen. All are programmable.

The light pen strobe going high causes the current contents of the address counter to be latched in the light pen register. The contents of the light pen register are subsequently read by the processor.

Internal CRTC registers are programmed by the processor through the data bus, D0-D7, and the control signals — R/$\overline{W}$, $\overline{CS}$, RS, and E.

REGISTER FILE DESCRIPTIONS

The nineteen registers of the CRTC may be accessed through the data bus. Only two memory locations are required as one location is used as a pointer to address one of the remaining eighteen registers. These eighteen registers control horizontal timing, vertical timing, interlace operation, row address operation, and define the cursor, cursor address, start address, and light pen register. The register addresses and sizes are shown in Table 2.

ADDRESS REGISTER

The address register is a 5-bit write-only register used as an "indirect" or "pointer" register. It contains the address of one of the other eighteen registers. When both RS and $\overline{CS}$ are low, the address register is selected. When $\overline{CS}$ is low and RS is high, the register pointed to by the address register is selected.

TIMING REGISTERS R0-R9

Figure 11 shows the visible display area of a typical CRT monitor giving the point of reference for horizontal registers as the left-most displayed character position. Horizontal registers are programmed in character clock time units with respect to the reference as shown in Figure 12. The point of reference for the vertical registers is the top character position displayed. Vertical registers are programmed in scan line times with respect to the reference as shown in Figure 13.

Horizontal Total Register (R0) — This 8-bit write-only register determines the horizontal sync (HS) frequency by defining the HS period in character times. It is the total of the displayed characters plus the non-displayed character times (retrace) minus one.

 MOTOROLA *Semiconductor Products Inc.*

MC6845

FIGURE 10 — CRTC BLOCK DIAGRAM

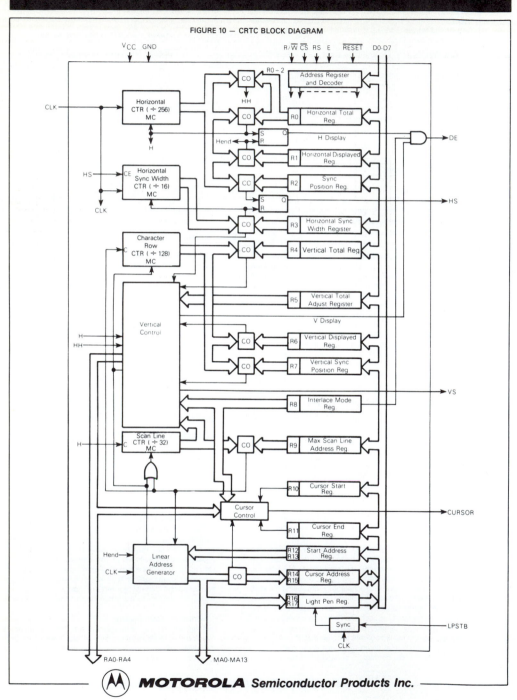

MOTOROLA *Semiconductor Products Inc.*

MC6845

TABLE 2 — CRTC INTERNAL REGISTER ASSIGNMENT

CS	RS	Address Register					Register #	Register File	Program Unit	Read	Write	Number of Bits							
		4	3	2	1	0						7	6	5	4	3	2	1	0
1	X	X	X	X	X	X	X	—	—	—	—								
0	0	X	X	X	X	X	AR	Address Register	—	No	Yes								
0	1	0	0	0	0	0	R0	Horizontal Total	Char.	No	Yes								
0	1	0	0	0	0	1	R1	Horizontal Displayed	Char.	No	Yes								
0	1	0	0	0	1	0	R2	H. Sync Position	Char.	No	Yes								
0	1	0	0	0	1	1	R3	Sync Width	—	No	Yes					H	H	H	H
0	1	0	0	1	0	0	R4	Vertical Total	Char. Row	No	Yes								
0	1	0	0	1	0	1	R5	V. Total Adjust	Scan Line	No	Yes								
0	1	0	0	1	1	0	R6	Vertical Displayed	Char. Row	No	Yes								
0	1	0	0	1	1	1	R7	V. Sync Position	Char. Row	No	Yes								
0	1	0	1	0	0	0	R8	Interlace Mode and Skew	Note 1	No	Yes							I	I
0	1	0	1	0	0	1	R9	Max Scan Line Address	Scan Line	No	Yes								
0	1	0	1	0	1	0	R10	Cursor Start	Scan Line	No	Yes		B	P		(Note 2)			
0	1	0	1	0	1	1	R11	Cursor End	Scan Line	No	Yes								
0	1	0	1	1	0	0	R12	Start Address (H)	—	No	Yes	0	0						
0	1	0	1	1	0	1	R13	Start Address (L)	—	No	Yes								
0	1	0	1	1	1	0	R14	Cursor (H)	—	Yes	Yes	0	0						
0	1	0	1	1	1	1	R15	Cursor (L)	—	Yes	Yes								
0	1	1	0	0	0	0	R16	Light Pen (H)	—	Yes	No	0	0						
0	1	1	0	0	0	1	R17	Light Pen (L)	—	Yes	No								

NOTES:
1. The interlace is shown in Table 3.
2. Bit 5 of the cursor start raster register is used for blink period control, and bit 6 is used to select blink or no-blink.

FIGURE 11 — ILLUSTRATION OF THE CRT SCREEN FORMAT

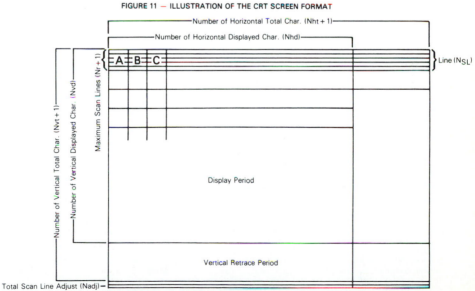

NOTE 1: Timing values are described in Table 5.

 MOTOROLA *Semiconductor Products Inc.*

Horizontal Displayed Register (R1) — This 8-bit write-only register determines the number of displayed characters per line. Any 8-bit number may be programmed as long as the contents of R0 are greater than the contents of R1.

Horizontal Sync Position Register (R2) — This 8-bit write-only register controls the HS position. The horizontal sync position defines the horizontal sync delay (front porch) and the horizontal scan delay (back porch). When the programmed value of this register is increased, the display on the CRT screen is shifted to the left. When the programmed value is decreased the display is shifted to the right. Any 8-bit number may be programmed as long as the sum of the contents of R2 and R3 are less than the contents of R0. R2 must be greater than R1.

Sync Width Register (R3) — This 8-bit write-only register determines the width of the horizontal sync (HS) pulse. The vertical sync pulse width is fixed at 16 scan-line times.

The HS pulse width may be programmed from 1-to-15 character clock periods thus allowing compatibility with the HS pulse width specifications of many different monitors. If zero is written into this register then no HS is provided.

Horizontal Timing Summary (Figure 12) — The difference between R0 and R1 is the horizontal blanking interval. This interval in the horizontal scan period allows the beam to return (retrace) to the left side of the screen. The retrace time is determined by the monitor's horizontal scan components. Retrace time is less than the horizontal blanking interval. A good rule of thumb is to make the horizontal blanking about 20% of the total horizontal scanning period for a CRT. In inexpensive TV receivers, the beam overscans the display screen so that aging of parts does not result in underscanning. Because of this, the retrace time should be about one third the horizontal scanning period. The horizontal sync delay, HS pulse width, and horizontal scan delay are typically programmed with a 1:2:2 ratio.

Vertical Total Register (R4) and Vertical Total Adjust Register (R5) — The frequency of VS is determined by both R4 and R5. The calculated number of character row times is usually an integer plus a fraction to get exactly a 50 or 60 Hz vertical refresh rate. The integer number of character row times minus one is programmed in the 7-bit write-only vertical total register (R4). The fraction of character line times is programmed in the 5-bit write-only vertical total adjust register (R5) as the number of scan lines required.

Vertical Displayed Register (R6) — This 7-bit write-only register specifies the number of displayed character rows on the CRT screen, and is programmed in character row times. Any number smaller than the contents of R4 may be programmed into R6.

Vertical Sync Position (R7) — This 7-bit write-only register controls the position of vertical sync with respect to the reference. It is programmed in character row times. When the programmed value of this register is increased, the display position of the CRT screen is shifted up. When the programmed value is decreased the display position is shifted down. Any number equal to or less than the vertical total (R4) and greater than or equal to the vertical displayed (R6) may be used.

Interlace Mode and Skew Register (R8) — The MC6845 only allows control of the interlace modes as programmed by the low order two bits of this write-only register. Table 3 shows the interlace modes available to the user. These modes are selected using the two low order bits of this 6-bit write-only register.

TABLE 3 — INTERLACE MODE REGISTER

Bit 1	Bit 0	Mode
0	0	Normal Sync Mode (Non-Interlace)
1	0	
0	1	Interlace Sync Mode
1	1	Interlace Sync and Video Mode

In the normal sync mode (non-interlace) only one field is available as shown in Figures 6 and 14a. Each scan line is refreshed at the VS frequency (e.g., 50 or 60 Hz).

Two interlace modes are available as shown in Figures 7, 14b, and 14c. The frame time is divided between even and odd alternating fields. The horizontal and vertical timing relationship (VS delayed by one half scan line time) results in the displacement of scan lines in the odd field with respect to the even field.

In the interlace sync mode the same information is painted in both fields as shown in Figure 14b. This is a useful mode for filling in a character to enhance readability.

In the interlace sync and video mode, shown in Figure 14c, alternating lines of the character are displayed in the even field and the odd field. This effectively doubles the given bandwidth of the CRT monitor.

Care must be taken when using either interlace mode to avoid an apparent flicker effect. This flicker effect is due to the doubling of the refresh time for all scan lines since each field is displayed alternately and may be minimized with proper monitor design (e.g., longer persistence phosphors).

In addition, there are restrictions on the programming of the CRTC registers for interlace operation:

1. The horizontal total register value, R0, must be odd (i.e., an even number of character times).
2. For interlace sync and video mode only, the maximum scan-line address, R9, must be odd (i.e., an even number of scan lines).
3. For interlace sync and video mode only, the number (Nvd) programmed into the vertical display register (R6) must be one half the actual number required. The even numbered scan lines are displayed in the even field and the odd numbered scan lines are displayed in the odd field.
4. For interlace sync and video mode only, the cursor start register (R10) and cursor end register (R11) must both be even or both odd depending on which field the cursor is to be displayed in. A full block cursor will be displayed in both the even and the odd field when the cursor end register (R11) is programmed to a value greater than the value in the maximum scan line address register (R9).

MOTOROLA *Semiconductor Products Inc.*

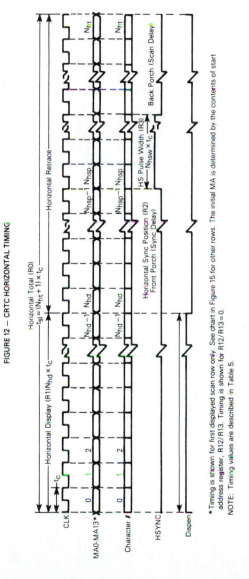

FIGURE 12 — CRTC HORIZONTAL TIMING

*Timing is shown for first displayed scan row only. See chart in Figure 15 for other rows. The initial MA is determined by the contents of start address register, R12/R13. Timing is shown for R12/R13=0.

NOTE: Timing values are described in Table 5.

MOTOROLA *Semiconductor Products Inc.*

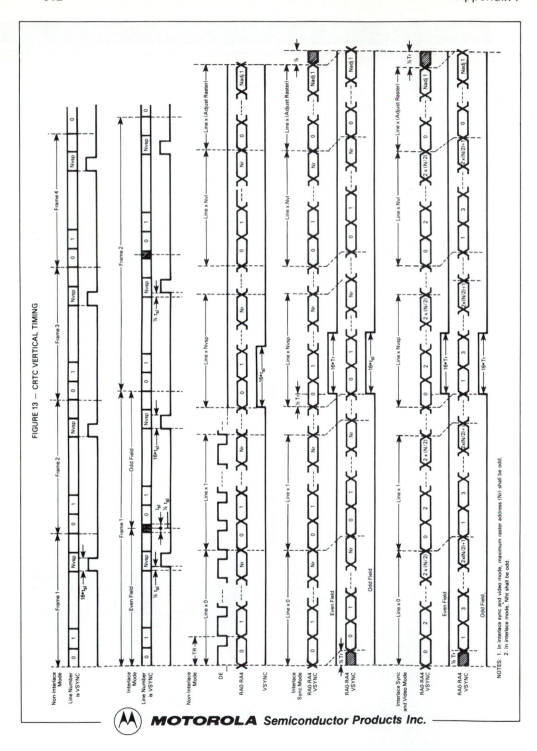

FIGURE 13 — CRTC VERTICAL TIMING

NOTES: 1. In interlace sync and video mode, maximum raster address (Nr) shall be odd.
2. In interlace mode, Nht shall be odd.

MC6845

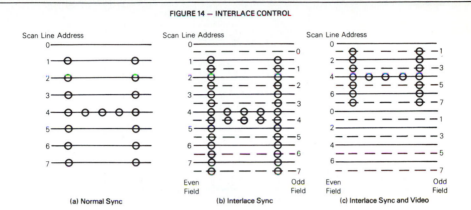

FIGURE 14 — INTERLACE CONTROL

(a) Normal Sync

(b) Interlace Sync

(c) Interlace Sync and Video

Maximum Scan Line Address Register (R9) — This 5-bit write-only register determines the number of scan lines per character row including the spacing; thus, controlling operation of the row address counter. The programmed value is a maximum address and is one less than the number of scan lines.

CURSOR CONTROL

Cursor Start Register (R10) and Cursor End Reigster (R11) — These registers allow a cursor of up to 32 scan lines in height to be placed on any scan line of the character block as shown in Figure 15. R10 is a 7-bit write-only register used to define the start scan line and the cursor blink rate. Bits 5 and 6 of the cursor start address register control the cursor operation as shown in Table 4. Non-display, display, and two blink modes (16 times or 32 times the field period) are available. R11 is a 5-bit write-only register which defines the last scan line of the cursor.

TABLE 4 — CURSOR START REGISTER

Bit 6	Bit 5	Cursor Display Mode
0	0	Non-Blink
0	1	Cursor Non-Display
1	0	Blink, 1/16 Field Rate
1	1	Blink, 1/32 Field Rate

Example of cursor display mode

When an external blink feature on characters is required, it may be necessary to perform cursor blink externally so that both blink rates are synchronized. Note that an invert/non-invert cursor is easily implemented by programming the CRTC for a blinking cursor and externally inverting the video signal with an exclusive-OR gate.

Cursor Register (R14-H, R15-L) — This 14-bit read/write register pair is programmed to position the cursor anywhere in the refresh RAM area; thus, allowing hardware paging and scrolling through memory without loss of the original cursor position. It consists of an 8-bit low order (MA0-MA7) register and a 6-bit high order (MA8-MA13) register.

OTHER REGISTERS

Start Address Register (R12-H, R13-L) — This 14-bit write-only register pair controls the first address output by the CRTC after vertical blanking. It consists of an 8-bit low order (MA0-MA7) register and a 6-bit high order (MA8-MA13) register. The start address register determines which portion of the refresh RAM is displayed on the CRT screen. Hardware scrolling by character or page may be accomplished by modifying the contents of this register.

Light Pen Register (R16-H, R17-L) — This 14-bit read-only register pair captures the refresh address output by the CRTC on the positive edge of a pulse input to the LPSTB pin. It consists of an 8-bit low order (MA0-MA7) register and a 6-bit high order (MA8-MA13) register. Since the light pen pulse is asynchronous with respect to refresh address timing an internal synchronizer is designed into the CRTC. Due to delays (Figure 5) in this circuit, the value of R16 and R17 will need to be corrected in software. Figure 16 shows an interrupt driven approach although a polling routine could be used.

MOTOROLA *Semiconductor Products Inc.*

FIGURE 15 — CURSOR CONTROL

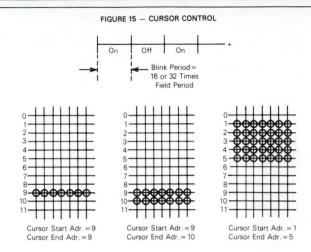

Cursor Start Adr. = 9
Cursor End Adr. = 9

Cursor Start Adr. = 9
Cursor End Adr. = 10

Cursor Start Adr. = 1
Cursor End Adr. = 5

FIGURE 16 — INTERFACING OF LIGHT PEN

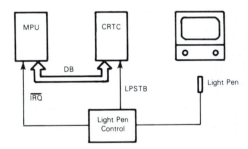

OPERATION OF THE CRTC

TIMING CHART OF THE CRT INTERFACE SIGNALS

Timing charts of CRT interface signals are illustrated in this section. When values listed in Table 5 are programmed into CRTC control registers, the device provides the outputs as shown in the timing diagrams (Figures 12, 13, 17, and 18). The screen format is shown in Figure 11 which illustrates the relation between refresh memory address (MA0-MA13), raster address (RA0-RA4), and the position on the screen. In this example, the start address is assumed to be zero.

TABLE 5 — VALUES PROGRAMMED INTO CRTC REGISTERS

Reg. #	Register Name	Value	Programmed Value
R0	H. Total	$N_{ht} + 1$	N_{ht}
R1	H. Displayed	N_{hd}	N_{hd}
R2	H. Sync Position	N_{hsp}	N_{hsp}
R3	H. Sync Width	N_{hsw}	N_{hsw}
R4	V. Total	$N_{vt} + 1$	N_{vt}
R5	V. Scan Line Adjust	N_{adj}	N_{adj}
R6	V. Displayed	N_{vd}	N_{vd}
R7	V. Sync Position	N_{vsp}	N_{vsp}
R8	Interlace Mode		
R9	Max. Scan Line Address	N_{sl}	N_{sl}

 MOTOROLA *Semiconductor Products Inc.*

July 1990

PC16450C/NS16450, PC8250A/INS8250A
Universal Asynchronous Receiver/Transmitter

General Description

This part functions as a serial data input/output interface in a microcomputer system. The system software determines the functional configuration of the UART via a TRI-STATE® 8-bit bidirectional data bus.

The UART performs serial-to-parallel conversion on data characters received from a peripheral device or a MODEM, and parallel-to-serial conversion on data characters received from the CPU. The CPU can read the complete status of the UART at any time during the functional operation. Status information reported includes the type and condition of the transfer operations being performed by the UART, as well as any error conditions (parity, overrun, framing, or break interrupt).

The UART includes a programmable baud rate generator that is capable of dividing the timing reference clock input by divisors of 1 to ($2^{16} - 1$), and producing a 16 × clock for driving the internal transmitter logic. Provisions are also included to use this 16 × clock to drive the receiver logic. The UART includes a complete MODEM-control capability and a processor-interrupt system. Interrupts can be programmed to the user's requirements, minimizing the computing required to handle the communications link.

The PC16450C/NS16450 is an improved specification version of the PC8250C/INS8250-B Universal Asynchronous Receiver/Transmitter (UART). The UART is fabricated using National Semiconductor's advanced 1.25 μ CMOS process.

The PC16450C/NS16450 is functionally equivalent to the original NS16450, INS8250A, NS16C450 and INS82C50A, except that it has improved AC timing specifications and it is CMOS.

Features

- Easily interfaces to most popular microprocessors.
- Adds or deletes standard asynchronous communication bits (start, stop, and parity) to or from serial data stream.
- Holding and shift registers eliminate the need for precise synchronization between the CPU and the serial data.
- Independently controlled transmit, receive, line status, and data set interrupts.
- Programmable baud generator allows division of any input clock by 1 to ($2^{16} - 1$) and generates the internal 16 × clock.
- Independent receiver clock input.
- MODEM control functions (CTS, RTS, DSR, DTR, RI, and DCD).
- Fully programmable serial-interface characteristics:
  - 5-, 6-, 7-, or 8-bit characters
  - Even, odd, or no-parity bit generation and detection
  - 1-, 1½-, or 2-stop bit generation
  - Baud generation (DC to 256 kbaud)
- False start bit detection.
- Complete status reporting capabilities.
- TRI-STATE TTL drive capabilities for bidirectional data bus and control bus.
- Line break generation and detection.
- Internal diagnostic capabilities:
  - Loopback controls for communications link fault isolation
  - Break, parity, overrun, framing error simulation.
- Fully prioritized interrupt system controls.

Connection Diagram

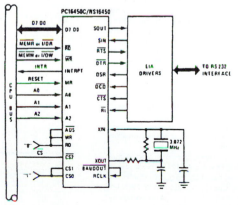

TL/C/8401–1

TRI-STATE® is a registered trademark of National Semiconductor Corporation

5.0 Block Diagram

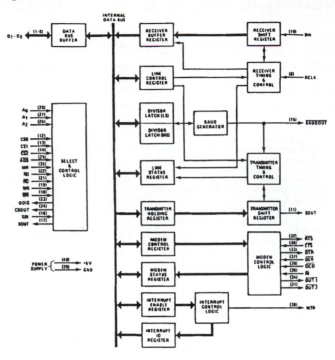

TL/C/8401–10

Note: Applicable pinout numbers are included within parenthesis.

6.0 Pin Descriptions

The following describes the function of all UART pins. Some of these descriptions reference internal circuits.

In the following descriptions, a low represents a logic 0 (0V nominal) and a high represents a logic 1 (+2.4V nominal).

A0, A1, A2: Register Select Pins 26–28: Address signals connected to these 3 inputs select a UART register for the CPU to read from or write to during data transfer. The Register Addresses table associates these address inputs with the register they select. Note that the state of the Divisor Latch Access Bit (DLAB), which is the most significant bit of the Line Control Register, affects the selection of certain UART registers. The DLAB must be set high by the system software to access the Baud Generator Divisor Latches.

ADS: Address Strobe Pin 25: The positive edge of an active Address Strobe (ADS) signal latches the Register Select (A0, A1, A2) and Chip Select (CS0, CS1, CS2) signals.

Note: An active ADS input is required when the Register Select (A0, A1, A2) signals are not stable for the duration of a read or write operation. If not required, tie the ADS input permanently low.

BAUDOUT: Baud Out Pin 15: This is the 16 × clock signal from the transmitter section of the UART. The clock rate is equal to the main reference oscillator frequency divided by the specified divisor in the Baud Generator Divisor Latches. The BAUDOUT may also be used for the receiver section by tying this output to the RCLK input of the chip.

Register Addresses

DLAB	A_2	A_1	A_0	Register
0	0	0	0	Receiver Buffer (read), Transmitter Holding Register (write)
0	0	0	1	Interrupt Enable
X	0	1	0	Interrupt Identification (read only)
X	0	1	1	Line Control
X	1	0	0	MODEM Control
X	1	0	1	Line Status
X	1	1	0	MODEM Status
X	1	1	1	Scratch
1	0	0	0	Divisor Latch (least significant byte)
1	0	0	1	Divisor Latch (most significant byte)

6.0 Pin Descriptions (Continued)

CS0, CS1, CS2: Chip Select Pins 12–14: When CS0 and CS1 are high and CS2 is low, the chip is selected. This enables communication between the UART and the CPU. The positive edge of an active Address Strobe signal latches the decoded chip select signals, completing chip selection. If ADS is always low, valid chip selects should stabilize according to the t_{CSW} parameter.

CSOUT: Chip Select Out Pin 24: When high, it indicates that the chip has been selected by active, CS0, CS1, and CS2 inputs. No data transfer can be initiated until the CSOUT signal is a logic 1. CSOUT goes low when the UART is deselected.

CTS: Clear to Send Pin 36: When low, this indicates that the MODEM or data set is ready to exchange data. The CTS signal is a MODEM status input whose conditions can be tested by the CPU reading bit 4 (CTS) of the MODEM Status Register. Bit 4 is the complement of the CTS signal. Bit 0 (DCTS) of the MODEM Status Register indicates whether the CTS input has changed state since the previous reading of the MODEM Status Register. CTS has no effect on the Transmitter.

Note: Whenever the CTS bit of the MODEM Status Register changes state, an interrupt is generated if the MODEM Status Interrupt is enabled.

D7–D0: Data Bus, Pins 1–8: This bus is comprised of eight TRI-STATE input/output lines. The bus provides bidirectional communications between the UART and the CPU. Data, control words, and status information are transferred via the D7–D0 Data Bus.

DCD: Data Carrier Detect Pin 38: When low, indicates that the data carrier has been detected by the MODEM or data set. The DCD signal is a MODEM status input whose condition can be tested by the CPU reading bit 7 (DCD) of the MODEM Status Register. Bit 7 is the complement of the DCD signal. Bit 3 (DDCD) of the MODEM Status Register indicates whether the DCD input has changed state since the previous reading of the MODEM Status Register. DCD has no effect on the receiver.

Note: Whenever the DCD bit of the MODEM Status Register changes state, an interrupt is generated if the MODEM Status Interrupt is enabled.

DDIS: Driver Disable Pin 23: This goes low whenever the CPU is reading data from the UART. It can disable or control the direction of a data bus transceiver between the CPU and the UART (see Typical Interface for a High Capacity Data Bus).

DSR: Data Set Ready Pin 37: When low, this indicates that the MODEM or data set is ready to establish the communications link with the UART. The DSR signal is a MODEM status input whose condition can be tested by the CPU reading bit 5 (DSR) of the MODEM Status Register. Bit 5 is the complement of the DSR signal. Bit 1 (DDSR) of the MODEM Status Register indicates whether the DSR input has changed state since the previous reading of the MODEM Status Register.

Note: Whenever the DSR bit of the MODEM Status Register changes state, an interrupt is generated if the MODEM Status Interrupt is enabled.

DTR: Data Terminal Ready Pin 33: When low, this informs the MODEM or data set that the UART is ready to establish a communications link. The DTR output signal can be set to an active low by programming bit 0 (DTR) of the MODEM Control Register to a high level. A Master Reset operation sets this signal to its inactive (high) state. Loop mode operation holds this signal in its inactive state.

INTR: Interrupt Pin 30: This goes high whenever any one of the following interrupt types has an active high condition and is enabled via the IER: Receiver Line Status; Received Data Available; Transmitter Holding Register Empty; and MODEM Status. The INTR signal is reset low upon the appropriate interrupt service or a Master Reset operation.

MR: Master Reset Pin 35: When this input is high, it clears all the registers (except the Receiver Buffer, Transmitter Holding, and Divisor Latches), and the control logic of the UART. The states of various output signals (SOUT, INTR, OUT 1, OUT 2, RTS, DTR) are affected by an active MR input. (Refer to Table I.) This input is buffered with a TTL-compatible Schmitt Trigger with 0.5V typical hysteresis.

OUT 1: Output 1 Pin 34: This user-designated output can be set to an active low by programming bit 2 (OUT 1) of the MODEM Control Register to a high level. A Master Reset operation sets this signal to its inactive (high) state. Loop mode operation holds this signal in its inactive state. In the XMOS parts this will achieve TTL levels.

OUT 2: Output 2 Pin 31: This user-designated output can be set to an active low, by programming bit 3 (OUT 2) of the MODEM Control Register to a high level. A Master Reset operation sets this signal to its inactive (high) state. Loop mode operation holds this signal in its inactive state. In the XMOS parts this will achieve TTL levels.

RCLK: Receiver Clock Pin 9: This input is the 16 × baud rate clock for the receiver section of the chip.

RD, RD, Read Pins 22 and 21: When RD is high or RD is low while the chip is selected, the CPU can read status information or data from the selected UART register.

Note: Only an active RD or RD input is required to transfer data from the UART during a read operation. Therefore, tie either the RD input permanently low or the RD input permanently high, when it is not used.

RI: Ring Indicator Pin 39: When low, this indicates that a telephone ringing signal has been received by the MODEM or data set. The RI signal is a MODEM status input whose condition can be tested by the CPU reading bit 6 (RI) of the MODEM Status Register. Bit 6 is the complement of the RI signal. Bit 2 (TERI) of the MODEM Status Register indicates whether the RI input signal has changed from a low to a high state since the previous reading of the MODEM Status Register.

Note: Whenever the RI bit of the MODEM Status Register changes from a high to a low state, an interrupt is generated if the MODEM Status interrupt is enabled.

RTS: Request to Send Pin 32: When low, this informs the MODEM or data set that the UART is ready to exchange data. The RTS output signal can be set to an active low by programming bit 1 (RTS) of the MODEM Control Register. A Master Reset operation sets this signal to its inactive (high) state. Loop mode operation holds this signal in its inactive state.

SIN: Serial Input Pin 10: Serial data input from the communications link (peripheral device, MODEM, or data set).

SOUT: Serial Output Pin 11: This is the composite serial data output to the communications link (peripheral, MODEM or data set). The SOUT signal is set to the Marking (logic 1) state upon a Master Reset operation or when the transmitter is idle.

V$_{DD}$, Pin 40: +5V supply.

V$_{SS}$, Pin 20: Ground (0V) reference.

6.0 Pin Descriptions (Continued)

WR, WR: Write Pins 19 and 18: When WR is high or WR is low while the chip is selected, the CPU can write control words or data into the selected UART register.

Note: Only an active WR or WR input is required to transfer data to the UART during a write operation. Therefore, tie either the WR input permanently low or the WR input permanently high, when it is not used.

XIN: (External Crystal Input), Pin 16: This signal input is used in conjunction with XOUT to form a feedback circuit for the baud rate generator's oscillator. If a clock signal will be generated off-chip, then it should drive the baud rate generator through this pin.

XOUT: (External Crystal Output), Pin 17: This signal output is used in conjunction with XIN to form a feedback circuit for the baud rate generator's oscillator. If the clock signal will be generated off-chip, then this pin is unused.

7.0 Connection Diagrams

Dual-In-Line Package

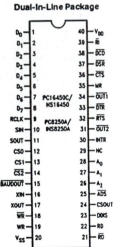

TL/C/8401–11

Top View

Order Number PC16450N/NS16450N
or PC8250AN/INS8250AN
See NS Package Number N40A

PLCC Package

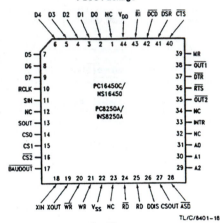

TL/C/8401–18

Top View

Order Number PC16450V/NS16450V
or PC8250AV/INS8250AV
See NS Package Number V44A

TABLE I. UART Reset Functions

Register/Signal	Reset Control	Reset State
Interrupt Enable Register	Master Reset	0000 0000 (Note 1)
Interrupt Identification Register	Master Reset	0000 0001
Line Control Register	Master Reset	0000 0000
MODEM Control Register	Master Reset	0000 0000
Line Status Register	Master Reset	0110 0000
MODEM Status Register	Master Reset	XXXX 0000 (Note 2)
SOUT	Master Reset	High
INTR (RCVR Errs)	Read LSR/MR	Low
INTR (RCVR Data Ready)	Read RBR/MR	Low
INTR (THRE)	Read IIR/Write THR/MR	Low
INTR (Modem Status Changes)	Read MSR/MR	Low
OUT 2	Master Reset	High
RTS	Master Reset	High
DTR	Master Reset	High
OUT 1	Master Reset	High

Note 1: Boldface bits are permanently low.

Note 2: Bits 7–4 are driven by the input signals.

8.0 Registers

The system programmer may access any of the UART registers summarized in Table II via the CPU. These registers control UART operations including transmission and reception of data. Each register bit in Table II has its name and reset state shown.

8.1 LINE CONTROL REGISTER

The system programmer specifies the format of the asynchronous data communications exchange and sets the Divisor Latch Access bit via the Line Control Register (LCR). The programmer can also read the contents of the Line Control Register. The read capability simplifies system programming and eliminates the need for separate storage in system memory of the line characteristics. Table II shows the contents of the LCR. Details on each bit follow:

Bits 0 and 1: These two bits specify the number of bits in each transmitted or received serial character. The encoding of bits 0 and 1 is as follows:

Bit 1	Bit 0	Character Length
0	0	5 Bits
0	1	6 Bits
1	0	7 Bits
1	1	8 Bits

Bit 2: This bit specifies the number of Stop bits transmitted and received in each serial character. If bit 2 is a logic 0, one Stop bit is generated or checked in the transmitted data. If bit 2 is a logic 1 when a 5-bit word length is selected via bits 0 and 1, one and a half Stop bits are generated. If

TABLE II. Summary of Registers

Bit No.	Register Address										
	0 DLAB = 0	0 DLAB = 0	1 DLAB = 0	2	3	4	5	6	7	0 DLAB = 1	1 DLAB = 1
	Receiver Buffer Register (Read Only)	Transmitter Holding Register (Write Only)	Interrupt Enable Register	Interrupt Ident. Register (Read Only)	Line Control Register	MODEM Control Register	Line Status Register	MODEM Status Register	Scratch Register	Divisor Latch (LS)	Divisor Latch (MS)
	RBR	THR	IER	IIR	LCR	MCR	LSR	MSR	SCR	DLL	DLM
0	Data Bit 0 (Note 1)	Data Bit 0	Received Data Available	"0" if Interrupt Pending	Word Length Select Bit 0 (WLS0)	Data Terminal Ready (DTR)	Data Ready (DR)	Delta Clear to Send (DCTS)	Bit 0	Bit 0	Bit 8
1	Data Bit 1	Data Bit 1	Transmitter Holding Register Empty	Interrupt ID Bit (0)	Word Length Select Bit 1 (WLS1)	Request to Send (RTS)	Overrun Error (OE)	Delta Data Set Ready (DDSR)	Bit 1	Bit 1	Bit 9
2	Data Bit 2	Data Bit 2	Receiver Line Status	Interrupt ID Bit (1)	Number of Stop Bits (STB)	Out 1	Parity Error (PE)	Trailing Edge Ring Indicator (TERI)	Bit 2	Bit 2	Bit 10
3	Data Bit 3	Data Bit 3	MODEM Status	0	Parity Enable (PEN)	Out 2	Framing Error (FE)	Delta Data Carrier Detect (DDCD)	Bit 3	Bit 3	Bit 11
4	Data Bit 4	Data Bit 4	0	0	Even Parity Select (EPS)	Loop	Break Interrupt (BI)	Clear to Send (CTS)	Bit 4	Bit 4	Bit 12
5	Data Bit 5	Data Bit 5	0	0	Stick Parity	0	Transmitter Holding Register (THRE)	Data Set Ready (DSR)	Bit 5	Bit 5	Bit 13
6	Data Bit 6	Data Bit 6	0	0	Set Break	0	Transmitter Empty (TEMT)	Ring Indicator (RI)	Bit 6	Bit 6	Bit 14
7	Data Bit 7	Data Bit 7	0	0	Divisor Latch Access Bit (DLAB)	0	0	Data Carrier Detect (DCD)	Bit 7	Bit 7	Bit 15

Note 1: Bit 0 is the least significant bit. It is the first bit serially transmitted or received.

8.0 Registers (Continued)

bit 2 is a logic 1 when either a 6-, 7-, or 8-bit word length is selected, two Stop bits are generated. The Receiver checks the first Stop-bit only, regardless of the number of Stop bits selected.

Bit 3: This bit is the Parity Enable bit. When bit 3 is a logic 1, a Parity bit is generated (transmit data) or checked (receive data) between the last data word bit and Stop bit of the serial data. (The Parity bit is used to produce an even or odd number of 1s when the data word bits and the Parity bit are summed.)

Bit 4: This bit is the Even Parity Select bit. When bit 3 is a logic 1 and bit 4 is a logic 0, an odd number of logic 1s is transmitted or checked in the data word bits and Parity bit. When bit 3 is a logic 1 and bit 4 is a logic 1, an even number of logic 1s is transmitted or checked.

Bit 5: This bit is the Stick Parity bit. When bits 3, 4 and 5 are logic 1 the Parity bit is transmitted and checked as a logic 0. If bits 3 and 5 are 1 and bit 4 is a logic 0 then the Parity bit is transmitted and checked as a logic 1. If bit 5 is a logic 0 Stick Parity is disabled.

Bit 6: This bit is the Break Control bit. It causes a break condition to be transmitted by the UART. When it is set to a logic 1, the serial output (SOUT) is forced to the Spacing (logic 0) state. The break is disabled by clearing bit 6 to a logic 0. The Break Control bit acts only on SOUT and has no effect on the transmitter logic.

Note: This feature enables the CPU to alert a terminal in a computer communications system. If the following sequence is used, no erroneous or extraneous characters will be transmitted because of the break.

1. Load an all 0s, pad character, in response to THRE.

2. Set break after the next THRE.

3. Wait for the transmitter to be idle, (TEMT = 1), and clear break when normal transmission has to be restored.

During the break, the Transmitter can be used as a character timer to accurately establish the break duration.

Bit 7: This bit is the Divisor Latch Access Bit (DLAB). It must be set high (logic 1) to access the Divisor Latches of the Baud Generator during a Read or Write operation. It must be set low (logic 0) to access the Receiver Buffer, the Transmitter Holding Register, or the Interrupt Enable Register.

8.2 TYPICAL CLOCK CIRCUITS

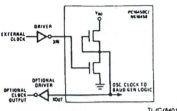

TL/C/8401–12

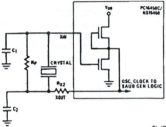

TL/C/8401–13

Typical Oscillator Networks

Crystal	R_P	R_{X2}	C_1	C_2
1.8–8 MHz	1 MΩ	1.5k	10–30 pF	40–60 pF

Note: These R and C values are approximate and may vary 2X depending on the crystal characteristics. All crystal circuits should be designed specifically for the system.

TABLE III. Baud Rates, Divisors and Crystals

Baud Rate	1.8432 MHz Crystal		3.072 MHz Crystal		8.0 MHz Crystal	
	Decimal Divisor for 16 × Clock	Percent Error	Decimal Divisor for 16 × Clock	Percent Error	Decimal Divisor for 16 × Clock	Percent Error
50	2304	—	3840	—	10000	—
75	1536	—	2560	—	6667	0.005
110	1047	0.026	1745	0.026	4545	0.010
134.5	857	0.058	1428	0.034	3717	0.013
150	768	—	1280	—	3333	0.010
300	384	—	640	—	1667	0.020
600	192	—	320	—	833	0.040
1200	96	—	160	—	417	0.080
1800	64	—	107	0.312	277	0.080
2000	58	0.69	96	—	250	—
2400	48	—	80	—	208	0.160
3600	32	—	53	0.628	139	0.080
4800	24	—	40	—	104	0.160
7200	16	—	27	1.23	69	0.644
9600	12	—	20	—	52	0.160
19200	6	—	10	—	26	0.160
38400	3	—	5	—	13	0.160
56000	2	2.86	—	—	9	0.790
128000	—	—	—	—	4	2.344
					2	2.344

8.0 Registers (Continued)

8.3 PROGRAMMABLE BAUD GENERATOR

The UART contains a programmable Baud Generator that is capable of taking any clock input from DC to 8 MHz and dividing it by any divisor from 1 to $2^{16}-1$. The output frequency of the Baud Generator is 16 × the Baud [divisor # = (frequency input) ÷ (baud rate × 16)]. Two 8-bit latches store the divisor in a 16-bit binary format. These Divisor Latches must be loaded during initialization in order to ensure proper operation of the Baud Generator. Upon loading either of the Divisor Latches, a 16-bit Baud counter is immediately loaded.

Table III provides decimal divisors to use with crystal frequencies of 1.8432 MHz, 3.072 MHz and 8 MHz for common baud rates. For baud rates of 38400 and below, the error obtained is minimal. The accuracy of the desired baud rate is dependent on the crystal frequency chosen. Using a division of 0 is not recommended.

8.4 LINE STATUS REGISTER

This 8-bit register provides status information to the CPU concerning the data transfer. Table II shows the contents of the Line Status Register. Details on each bit follow:

Bit 0: This bit is the receiver Data Ready (DR) indicator. Bit 0 is set to a logic 1 whenever a complete incoming character has been received and transferred into the Receiver Buffer Register. Bit 0 is reset to a logic 0 by reading the data in the Receiver Buffer Register.

Bit 1: This bit is the Overrun Error (OE) indicator. Bit 1 indicates that data in the Receiver Buffer Register was not read by the CPU before the next character was transferred into the Receiver Buffer Register, thereby destroying the previous character. The OE indicator is set to a logic 1 upon detection of an overrun condition and reset whenever the CPU reads the contents of the Line Status Register.

Bit 2: This bit is the Parity Error (PE) indicator. Bit 2 indicates that the received data character does not have the correct even or odd parity, as selected by the even-parity-

select bit. The PE bit is set to a logic 1 upon detection of a parity error and is reset to a logic 0 whenever the CPU reads the contents of the Line Status Register.

Bit 3: This bit is the Framing Error (FE) indicator. Bit 3 indicates that the received character did not have a valid Stop bit. Bit 3 is set to a logic 1 whenever the Stop bit following the last data bit or parity bit is a logic 0 (Spacing level). The FE indicator is reset whenever the CPU reads the contents of the Line Status Register. The UART will try to resynchronize after a framing error. To do this it assumes that the framing error was due to the next start bit, so it samples this "start" bit twice and then takes in the "data".

Bit 4: This bit is the Break Interrupt (BI) indicator. Bit 4 is set to a logic 1 whenever the received data input is held in the Spacing (logic 0) state for longer than a full word transmission time (that is, the total time of Start bit + data bits + Parity + Stop bits). The BI indicator is reset whenever the CPU reads the contents of the Line Status Register. Restarting after a break is received, requires the SIN pin to be logical 1 for at least ½ bit time.

Note: Bits 1 through 4 are the error conditions that produce a Receiver Line Status interrupt whenever any of the corresponding conditions are detected and the interrupt is enabled.

Bit 5: This bit is the Transmitter Holding Register Empty (THRE) indicator. Bit 5 indicates that the UART is ready to accept a new character for transmission. In addition, this bit causes the UART to issue an interrupt to the CPU when the Transmit Holding Register Empty Interrupt enable is set high. The THRE bit is set to a logic 1 when a character is transferred from the Transmitter Holding Register into the Transmitter Shift Register. The bit is reset to logic 0 whenever the CPU loads the Transmitter Holding Register.

Bit 6: This bit is the Transmitter Empty (TEMT) indicator. Bit 6 is set to a logic 1 whenever the Transmitter Holding Register (THR) and the Transmitter Shift Register (TSR) are both empty. It is reset to a logic 0 whenever either the THR or TSR contains a data character.

Bit 7: This bit is permanently set to logic 0.

Note: The Line Status Register is intended for read operations only. Writing to this register is not recommended as this operation is only used for factory testing.

TABLE IV. Interrupt Control Functions

Interrupt Identification Register				Interrupt Set and Reset Functions		
Bit 2	Bit 1	Bit 0	Priority Level	Interrupt Type	Interrupt Source	Interrupt Reset Control
0	0	1	—	None	None	—
1	1	0	Highest	Receiver Line Status	Overrun Error or Parity Error or Framing Error or Break Interrupt	Reading the Line Status Register
1	0	0	Second	Received Data Available	Receiver Data Available	Reading the Receiver Buffer Register
0	1	0	Third	Transmitter Holding Register Empty	Transmitter Holding Register Empty	Reading the IIR Register (if source of interrupt) or Writing into the Transmitter Holding Register
0	0	0	Fourth	MODEM Status	Clear to Send or Data Set Ready or Ring Indicator or Data Carrier Detect	Reading the MODEM Status Register

8.0 Registers (Continued)

8.5 INTERRUPT IDENTIFICATION REGISTER

In order to provide minimum software overhead during data character transfers, the UART prioritizes interrupts into four levels and records these in the Interrupt Identification Register. The four levels of interrupt conditions in order of priority are Receiver Line Status; Received Data Ready; Transmitter Holding Register Empty; and MODEM Status.

When the CPU accesses the IIR, the UART freezes all interrupts and indicates the highest priority pending interrupt to the CPU. While this CPU access is occurring, the UART records new interrupts, but does not change its current indication until the access is complete. Table II shows the contents of the IIR. Details on each bit follow:

Bit 0: This bit can be used in an interrupt environment to indicate whether an interrupt condition is pending. When bit 0 is a logic 0, an interrupt is pending and the IIR contents may be used as a pointer to the appropriate interrupt service routine. When bit 0 is a logic 1, no interrupt is pending.

Bits 1 and 2: These two bits of the IIR are used to identify the highest priority interrupt pending as indicated in Table IV.

Bits 3 through 7: These five bits of the IIR are always logic 0.

8.6 INTERRUPT ENABLE REGISTER

This register enables the four types of UART interrupts. Each interrupt can individually activate the interrupt (INTR) output signal. It is possible to totally disable the interrupt system by resetting bits 0 through 3 of the Interrupt Enable Register (IER). Similarly, setting bits of this register to a logic 1, enables the selected interrupt(s). Disabling an interrupt prevents it from being indicated as active in the IIR and from activating the INTR output signal. All other system functions operate in their normal manner, including the setting of the Line Status and MODEM Status Registers. Table II shows the contents of the IER. Details on each bit follow.

Bit 0: This bit enables the Received Data Available Interrupt when set to logic 1.

Bit 1: This bit enables the Transmitter Holding Register Empty Interrupt when set to logic 1.

Bit 2: This bit enables the Receiver Line Status Interrupt when set to logic 1.

Bit 3: This bit enables the MODEM Status Interrupt when set to logic 1.

Bits 4 through 7: These four bits are always logic 0.

8.7 MODEM CONTROL REGISTER

This register controls the interface with the MODEM or data set (or a peripheral device emulating a MODEM). The contents of the MODEM Control Register (MCR) are indicated in Table II and are described below. Table II shows the contents of the MCR. Details on each bit follow.

Bit 0: This bit controls the Data Terminal Ready (DTR) output. When bit 0 is set to a logic 1, the DTR output is forced to a logic 0. When bit 0 is reset to a logic 0, the DTR output is forced to a logic 1.

Note: The DTR output of the UART may be applied to an EIA inverting line driver (such as the DS1488) to obtain the proper polarity input at the succeeding MODEM or data set.

Bit 1: This bit controls the Request to Send (RTS) output. Bit 1 affects the RTS output in a manner identical to that described above for bit 0.

Bit 2: This bit controls the Output 1 (OUT 1) signal, which is an auxiliary user-designated output. Bit 2 affects the OUT 1 output in a manner identical to that described above for bit 0.

Bit 3: This bit controls the Output 2 (OUT 2) signal, which is an auxiliary user-designated output. Bit 3 affects the OUT 2 output in a manner identical to that described above for bit 0.

Bit 4: This bit provides a local loopback feature for diagnostic testing of the UART. When bit 4 is set to logic 1, the following occur: the transmitter Serial Output (SOUT) is set to the Marking (logic 1) state; the receiver Serial Input (SIN) is disconnected; the output of the Transmitter Shift Register is "looped back" into the Receiver Shift Register input; the four MODEM Control inputs (DSR, CTS, RI, and DCD) are disconnected; and the four MODEM Control outputs (DTR, RTS, OUT 1, and OUT 2) are internally connected to the four MODEM Control inputs. The MODEM Control output pins are forced to their inactive state (high). In the loopback mode, data that is transmitted is immediately received. This feature allows the processor to verify the transmit-and received-data paths of the UART.

In the loopback mode, the receiver and transmitter interrupts are fully operational. The MODEM Control Interrupts are also operational, but the interrupts' sources are now the lower four bits of the MODEM Control Register instead of the four MODEM Control inputs. The interrupts are still controlled by the Interrupt Enable Register.

Bits 5 through 7: These bits are permanently set to logic 0.

8.8 MODEM STATUS REGISTER

This register provides the current state of the control lines from the MODEM (or peripheral device) to the CPU. In addition to this current-state information, four bits of the MODEM Status Register provide change information. These bits are set to a logic 1 whenever a control input from the MODEM changes state. They are reset to logic 0 whenever the CPU reads the MODEM Status Register.

8.0 Registers (Continued)

Table II shows the contents of the MSR. Details on each bit follow.

Bit 0: This bit is the Delta Clear to Send (DCTS) indicator. Bit 0 indicates that the CTS input to the chip has changed state since the last time it was read by the CPU.

Bit 1: This bit is the Delta Data Set Ready (DDSR) indicator. Bit 1 indicates that the DSR input to the chip has changed state since the last time it was read by the CPU.

Bit 2: This bit is the Trailing Edge of Ring Indicator (TERI) detector. Bit 2 indicates that the RI input to the chip has changed from a low to a high state.

Bit 3: This bit is the Delta Data Carrier Detect (DDCD) indicator. Bit 3 indicates that the DCD input to the chip has changed state.

Note: Whenever bit 0, 1, 2, or 3 is set to logic 1, a MODEM Status Interrupt is generated.

Bit 4: This bit is the complement of the Clear to Send (CTS) input. If bit 4 (loop) of the MCR is set to a 1, this bit is equivalent to RTS in the MCR.

Bit 5: This bit is the complement of the Data Set Ready (DSR) input. If bit 4 of the MCR is set to a 1, this bit is equivalent to DTR in the MCR.

Bit 6: This bit is the complement of the Ring Indicator (RI) input. If bit 4 of the MCR is set to a 1, this bit is equivalent to OUT 1 in the MCR.

Bit 7: This bit is the complement of the Data Carrier Detect (DCD) input. If bit 4 of the MCR is set to a 1, this bit is equivalent to OUT 2 in the MCR.

8.9 SCRATCHPAD REGISTER

This 8-bit Read/Write Register does not control the UART in any way. It is intended as a scratchpad register to be used by the programmer to hold data temporarily.

9.0 Typical Applications

Typical shows the basic connections of an PC16450C/NS16450 to an 8088 CPU

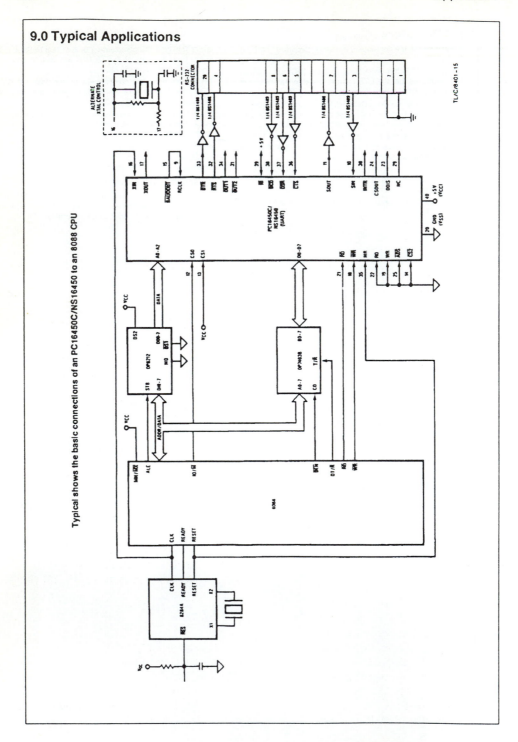

Index

INTRODUCTION TO COMPUTER ENGINEERING
By Richard E. Haskell

Prentice-Hall

YOU SHOULD CAREFULLY READ THE FOLLOWING TERMS AND CONDITIONS BEFORE OPENING THIS DISKETTE PACKAGE. OPENING THIS DISKETTE PACKAGE INDICATES YOUR ACCEPTANCE OF THESE TERMS AND CONDITIONS. IF YOU DO NOT AGREE WITH THEM, YOU SHOULD PROMPTLY RETURN THE PACKAGE UNOPENED, AND YOUR MONEY WILL BE REFUNDED.

IT IS A VIOLATION OF COPYRIGHT LAW TO MAKE A COPY OF THE ACCOMPANYING SOFTWARE EXCEPT FOR BACKUP PURPOSES TO GUARD AGAINST ACCIDENTAL LOSS OR DAMAGE.

Prentice-Hall, Inc. provides this program and licenses its use. You assume responsibility for the selection of the program to achieve your intended results, and for the installation, use, and results obtained from the program. This license extends only to use of the program in the United States or countries in which the program is marketed by duly authorized distributors.

LICENSE

You may:

a. use the program;

b. copy the program into any machine-readable form without limit.

LIMITED WARRANTY

THE PROGRAM IS PROVIDED "AS IS" WITHOUT WARRANTY OF ANY KIND, EITHER EXPRESSED OR IMPLIED, INCLUDING, BUT NOT LIMITED TO, THE IMPLIED WARRANTIES OF MERCHANTABILITY AND FITNESS FOR A PARTICULAR PURPOSE. THE ENTIRE RISK TO THE QUALITY AND PERFORMANCE OF THE PROGRAM IS WITH YOU. SHOULD THE PROGRAM PROVE DEFECTIVE, YOU (AND NOT PRENTICE-HALL, INC. OR ANY AUTHORIZED DISTRIBUTOR) ASSUME THE ENTIRE COST OF ALL NECESSARY SERVICING, REPAIR, OR CORRECTION.

SOME STATES DO NOT ALLOW THE EXCLUSION OF IMPLIED WARRANTIES, SO THE ABOVE EXCLUSION MAY NOT APPLY TO YOU. THIS WARRANTY GIVES YOU SPECIFIC LEGAL RIGHTS AND YOU MAY ALSO HAVE OTHER RIGHTS THAT VARY FROM STATE TO STATE.

Prentice-Hall, Inc. does not warrant that the functions contained in the program will meet your requirements or that the operation of the program will be uninterrupted or error free.

However, Prentice-Hall, Inc., warrants the diskette(s) on which the program is furnished to be free from defects in materials and workmanship under normal use for a period of ninety (90) days from the date of delivery to you as evidenced by a copy of your receipt.

LIMITATIONS OF REMEDIES

Prentice-Hall's entire liability and your exclusive remedy shall be:

1. the replacement of any diskette not meeting Prentice-Hall's "Limited Warranty" and that is returned to Prentice-Hall with a copy of your purchase order, or

2. if Prentice-Hall is unable to deliver a replacement diskette or cassette that is free of defects in materials or workmanship, you may terminate this Agreement by returning the program, and your money will be refunded.

IN NO EVENT WILL PRENTICE-HALL BE LIABLE TO YOU FOR ANY DAMAGES, INCLUDING ANY LOST PROFITS, LOST SAVINGS OR OTHER INCIDENTAL OR CONSEQUENTIAL DAMAGES ARISING OUT OF THE USE OR INABILITY TO USE SUCH PROGRAM EVEN IF PRENTICE-HALL OR AN AUTHORIZED DISTRIBUTOR HAS BEEN ADVISED OF THE POSSIBILITY OF SUCH DAMAGES, OR FOR ANY CLAIM BY AN OTHER PARTY.

SOME STATES DO NOT ALLOW THE LIMITATION OR EXCLUSION OF LIABILITY FOR INCIDENTAL OR CONSEQUENTIAL DAMAGES, SO THE ABOVE LIMITATION OR EXCLUSION MAY NOT APPLY TO YOU.

GENERAL

You may not sublicense, assign, or transfer the license or the program except as expressly provided in this Agreement. Any attempt otherwise to sublicense, assign, or transfer any of the rights, duties, or obligations hereunder is void.

This Agreement will be governed by the laws of the State of New York.

Should you have any questions concerning this Agreement, you may contact Prentice-Hall, Inc., by writing to:

Prentice Hall
College Division
Englewood Cliffs, N.J. 07632

YOU ACKNOWLEDGE THAT YOU HAVE READ THIS AGREEMENT, UNDERSTAND IT, AND AGREE TO BE BOUND BY ITS TERMS AND CONDITIONS. YOU FURTHER AGREE THAT IT IS THE COMPLETE AND EXCLUSIVE STATEMENT OF THE AGREEMENT BETWEEN US THAT SUPERCEDES ANY PROPOSAL OR PRIOR AGREEMENT, ORAL OR WRITTEN, AND ANY OTHER COMMUNICATIONS BETWEEN US RELATING TO THE SUBJECT MATTER OF THIS AGREEMENT.

ISBN 0-13-489436-7